ALSO BY CHARLES B. STROZIER

Lincoln's Quest for Union: A Psychological Portrait

Apocalypse: On the Psychology of Fundamentalism in America

EDITED BY CHARLES B. STROZIER

The Year 2000: Essays on the End

(with Michael Flynn)

Genocide, War, and Human Survival

(with Michael Flynn)

Trauma and Self

(with Michael Flynn)

Self Psychology and The Humanities:

Reflections on a New Psychoanalytic Approach

(writings of Heinz Kohut on the humanities)

The Leader: Psychohistorical Studies

(with Daniel Offer)

The Public and Private Lincoln: Contemporary Perspectives

(with Cullom Davis, Rebecca Veach, and Geoffrey Ward)

Heinz Kohut (1913–1981) stood at the center of the twentieth-century psychoanalytic movement. After fleeing his native Vienna when the Nazis took power, he arrived in Chicago, where he spent the rest of his life. He became the most creative figure in the Chicago Institute for Psychoanalysis, and is now remembered as the founder of "self psychology," whose emphasis on empathy sought to make Freudian psychoanalysis less neutral.

Charles B. Strozier brings to his telling of Kohut's life all the tools of a skillful analyst: intelligence, erudition, empathy, contrary insight, and a willingness to look far below the surface. In the new introduction by the author included in this softcover edition, Strozier explores his experience in the role of biographer, particularly his commitment to psychological biography, with frankness and intimacy, as he provides readers with a sharp and perceptive survey of the art of recording lives.

Praise for *Heinz Kohut: The Making of a Psychoanalyst*

"Strozier faced a truly daunting task in probing the life of a man who was as complex and duplicitous as he was gifted. Yet he succeeds brilliantly in conveying Kohut's intellectual power, and in making clear how and why he became the most influential clinical psychoanalyst of the last half-century. Strozier brings an extraordinary combination of empathy and breadth to this masterful biography."
—Robert Jay Lifton, coauthor of *Who Owns Death?: Capital Punishment, the American Conscience, and the End of Executions*

"This striking story of a single man is also a history of psychoanalysis in the twentieth century. Strozier has turned a light on post-Freudian psychoanalysis as he has illuminated the life of its most distinguished member."
—Arnold Goldberg, M.D., author of *Being of Two Minds* and editor of the series *Progress in Self Psychology*

"Strozier leaves no stone unturned in this exhaustive study of Kohut's character, life, and ideas, offering a detailed look at the theoretical differences that separate him from Freud. Compelling and masterfully written, it is a balanced and affecting story of a courageous yet flawed man's struggle to break free from orthodox constraints and a painful childhood to find his own voice."
—Lee Scheier, *Chicago Tribune*

"Charles Strozier has produced a landmark book on Kohut [that] explores the path, personal and political and conceptual of 'the making of a psychoanalyst.' . . . The book is very detailed and meticulous as well as arrestingly written, holding the attention of the reader in the twists and turns of Kohut's developments within the contexts of life and politics in Vienna and the U.S., and of course psychoanalytic politics. It is an impressive work of scholarship that reveals both Kohut's flaws and genius."
—Douglas Kirsner, *The Australian Journal of Psychotherapy*

"It is rare in the growing library of biographies of psychoanalysts to have a work that is characterized, as is this volume, by thorough research, psychological insight into the person's inner life, and an appreciation of the relevance of the person's thinking for clinical work. . . . Strozier did an exhaustive job of interviewing people who had known Kohut. He not only tracked down many of Kohut's patients and supervisees but also found Kohut's closest friend from his childhood in Vienna. As a historian, Strozier did not overlook archival research, locating, for example, the Nazis' inventory of the Kohut family's assets in the Viennese State Archives and Kohut's candidate file from his period as a student at the Chicago Institute. . . . Strozier's biography accomplishes everything that I could expect of it. Strozier tells Kohut's life story, explicates his work and its relationship to classical psychoanalysis, and gives the reader a sense of what Kohut was like as a person. Strozier does all this while providing a readable, energetic narrative."

—James William Anderson, *Contemporary Psychology*

"Strozier gives us a vivid picture of Kohut the man and allows us to see the many areas of overlap between his theory and his personality."

—Robert May, *Journal of the History of the Behavioral Sciences*

"On the twentieth anniversary of Kohut's death, and after seventeen years of painstaking work investigating Kohut the man, through both his own subjective lens as a historian of ideas and the memories of those who knew, loved, and/or hated Kohut, Dr. Strozier has produced a monumental work that succeeds in powerfully conveying the emergence of self psychology as a new and influential analytic paradigm. Furthermore, he has done so without sacrificing the reality of the complex man who gave birth to the movement, a man whom he admired partly for personal reasons. . . . A major contribution."

—Linda A. Chernus, *Clinical Social Work Journal*

"Charles Strozier has crafted a significant psychoanalytic study of Heinz Kohut. He comes to his task well equipped. . . . Given the complex, dramatic, and controversial aspects of Kohut's life and work, Strozier has come up with a well-balanced dynamic picture."

—Robert J. Marshall, *Modern Psychology*

"The biography of Heinz Kohut is a story that should be required reading for anyone entering the practice of psychiatry, especially those beginning in psychoanalysis."

—Jo Rogers, *MyShelf.com*

"The author recounts the gripping, moving, and instructive story of this driven, creative, cultured intellectual, who was much respected as a teacher and therapist but disliked for his arrogance. . . . Too important to leave to professionals, this accessible work is highly recommended for all libraries."

—*Library Journal*

"I had never heard of Heinz Kohut until I read Charles B. Strozier's biography of him. Glancing beforehand at the some 500 pages of text, I expected a long, boring treatise about an obscure academic figure. I was wrong. Strozier's *Heinz Kohut: The Making of a Psychoanalyst* turned out to be interesting, unpretentious, and entertaining. . . . I found Strozier's tolerance for complexity wonderful. . . . A wide audience would do well to read [the book], not only to learn about an intellectually and sexually complex man, but to think about how that complexity may apply to their own lives."

—Angela Watkins, *Roanoke Times*

"Strozier has written a fine biography . . ."

—R. H. Balsam, *Choice*

"The richly probing results of a profound immersion in the Kohutian psychoanalytic universe, one that tried to put a human face on Freudian positivism."

—*Kirkus Reviews*

"For an adherent of self psychology to write an unflinchingly critical biography of the admired founder of the movement is a major creative feat of empathy and scholarship, a feat that Charles B. Strozier has accomplished. While he valorizes Heinz Kohut, Strozier does not hesitate to relate his selfishness and narcissism, his lies and deceptions, his 'protean sexuality' and 'apparently fluid sexual boundaries.' The book explains the concepts of self psychology, including the 'self,' the selfobject, and the idealizing and mirroring transferences, in clear English."

—Peter Loewenberg, *The Journal of American History*

Heinz Kohut

Heinz Kohut

The Making of a Psychoanalyst

CHARLES B. STROZIER

OTHER

Other Press
New York

Frontispiece: A page of Heinz Kohut's shorthand—an idiosyncratic amalgam of German and English—in which he composed the first drafts of all his scientific writings and important letters (Courtesy of Chicago Institute for Psychoanalysis)

A different version of the Introduction appeared as "Autobiographical Reflections on Writing the Biography of Heinz Kohut" in *The Annual of Psychoanalysis* 31 (2003). Reprinted with permission.

First softcover edition 2004

10 9 8 7 6 5 4 3 2 1

Library of Congress Cataloging-in-Publication Data

Strozier, Charles B.
    Heinz Kohut : the making of a psychoanalyst / by Charles Strozier.–
1st pbk. ed.
        p. cm.
Includes bibliographical references and index.
    ISBN 1-59051-102-6 (pbk. : alk. paper)
    1. Kohut, Heinz.   2. Psychoanalysts–United States–Biography.   I. Title.
    BF109.K6 S77 2004
    150.19'5'092–dc21

                                                        2003022682

For Cathryn

CONTENTS

INTRODUCTION TO THE

SOFTCOVER EDITION

There are few figures in the history of psychoanalysis as interesting and important as Heinz Kohut. He had a way of imposing himself on others. He was brilliant, lively, outgoing, interesting, and always compelling. He was truly charismatic and at the center of any conversation or meeting, whether of three people or 900. For the most part, you felt better after an encounter with him, and you certainly learned something. At the same time, he could be impossibly self-centered, at times almost with a certain innocence, and grandiose to a fault. To say he was a man of contradictions understates the case.

Born in Vienna in 1913, Kohut was raised in an assimilated Jewish family, imbued with European high culture. He trained in medicine at the University of Vienna before being forced to emigrate in 1939 after the Nazis took over. Kohut settled in Chicago where he made his life for the next four decades. A cautious man, in the 1940s he only gradually shifted from neurology, to psychiatry, to psychoanalysis. But once ensconced in the Chicago institute, he embraced analysis with the fervor of a convert. He spent the 1950s and the first part of the 1960s as "Mr. Psychoanalysis," he later joked, widely noted for his orthodoxy, admired by all the right people.

But something was happening to Kohut on the inside that coincided with a half-conscious crisis in the field. Time had eroded much of the humanism in the Freudian legacy. Psychoanalytic theory and practice, for various historical reasons, was fast becoming anachronistic, committed to values of autonomy despite a yearning for connection; focused on grim ideas about insight despite a pervasive interest in empathy after war and holocaust; and obsessed with the intricate workings of guilt despite the culture's embrace of the tragic.

In a burst of creativity that began in the mid-1960s and lasting for the remaining 15 years of his life, Kohut found his voice and explored narcissism in new ways that led to what he called in the end a "psychology of the self." He began his real work in the second half of his sixth decade, when most people are preparing for retirement. Kohut's reformulation of mainstream psychoanalytic thinking was the pivotal event in the transformation of the field into what is generally termed "relational psychoanalysis."[1] Many had flailed at the stout walls of classical psychoanalysis and ego psychology. It took someone from the inside to think things through from the ground up, discard the debris but recover what remained valuable in its clinical insights for the next century. Kohut may well have saved psychoanalysis from itself.

This book explores the complex tale of Kohut's life in the old and new worlds, together with the way his story got woven into the fabric of his ideas. Kohut's own protean sexuality and identity confusions fitted him uneasily into the world of psychoanalysis as Freud constructed it. His project became that of changing the theory to finding a place for himself in it. And there are larger meanings. Kohut lived out in his life and formulated in his work the core issues of contemporary America. He touched the pulse.

II

This book was first published in April, 2001. In early June, around the time I learned it had been nominated for a Pulitzer Prize, the book was reviewed in the Sunday *New York Times*. I had a dream. In it I was flying through the air, soaring really, and feeling wonderful. In front of me was a man in a gray suit with lovely and intricate wings like those of a fly greatly magnified. It was Kohut. We flew along joyfully until we came to a bridge. To avoid hitting it, he went into a dive and passed just underneath the structure itself. I followed him but somehow got off course and crashed into the water. He came to my rescue—it got vague, and ended. I would say the dream suggests I am flying, if a bit precariously, in Kohut's wake. I am a mighty bird, buoyed but behind him, Icarus unmasked. The dream raises the question: Who are we psychologically who write biographies of really creative people?

It is not always the case that biographers personally know their subjects. I did know Heinz Kohut. I am a scion of an old University of Chicago family, and Kohut knew my family rather well. He was friendly with my French professor father, Robert M. Strozier, but was especially close with the man who later became my stepfather, Howell Wright, chairman of pediatrics at the University in the 1940s when Kohut was a rising young neurologist. He knew my mother, Margaret Wright, herself something of a University of Chicago institution. Until the day he died and for a number years, both lived in the same apartment building in Hyde Park. When I first met Kohut at his 60th birthday party in 1973 (I was 29), he was cordial and very warm in his greeting. Later, when I was a candidate in the Chicago Institute for Psychoanalysis after 1976 and at the start of my academic career as a history professor at a branch of the University of Illinois, he heard me present some papers and seemed impressed enough to draw me into the outer edges of his circle. Neither then nor later was I at the heart of things, but I did experience firsthand the workings of his charisma. I organized some events with Kohut and edited and published a short article of his in a journal I had started. He and I (and two others) were on a panel about self psychology and the humanities at the first self conference in 1978, and I worked with him and Arnold Goldberg in hosting a major conference on history and psychoanalysis in 1980. We even collaborated on a book together, which involved some interviews I did with him in the winter and spring of 1980–1981.[2]

It can be challenging to immerse oneself in the life of someone else for a prolonged period. Kohut died in 1981; I began the book in 1982, and published in the spring of 2001. For most of my 40s and 50s (that is, I conceived of the book when I was 38 and published when I was 57), Heinz Kohut occupied my imagination. I lived with the details of his life in Vienna and Chicago, his relationships, his dreams and hopes, his confusions and contradictions, and all the complicated ideas that tumbled out of his head in paper after paper and book after book. I read and reread his letters until I knew his style so well that I myself could have ghostwritten an imaginary epistle to Anna Freud or Kurt Eissler. I poured over his papers and books, which I also talked about endlessly in seminars and presentations and wrote elaborate notes that in time became themselves small essays and essentially drafts of sections of the book itself. I gathered pictures from various phases of his life and looked at them often to keep the image of

the man alive in my mind. I am a visual person, and I found that to conceive of the life I had to see the man from the robust young medical student to the exceedingly thin and ill man on his last stage at Berkeley, as well
as early pictures of his mother, his friends such as Jacques Palaci and Robert Wadsworth, and members of the group (John Gedo, Arnold Goldberg,
Paul and Marian Tolpin, Ernest Wolf, Michael Franz Basch, and Paul and
Anna Ornstein), as they looked when he knew them, and others who entered his life. Finally and importantly, I talked about Kohut with those who
knew him. I conducted every kind of interview, from the formal and taped
variety to fleeting comments in social settings. The woman who I believe
to be Miss F (though it was never acknowledged) told me an important
story in a crowded elevator between the 24th floor of 180 North Michigan
Avenue and the lobby. As she rushed off into the cold I quickly took out
pen and paper and wrote up what she had just said.

It was startling how Kohut changed in my mind in the course of my
research. A book like this biography is a moving target, and perhaps as
with a painting it was never really finished but eventually abandoned in
exhaustion. In the first few years of my work, as skeletons came tumbling
out of the closet, many in Chicago turned on me as the messenger in ways
that I thought was unfair. I would say, in fact, that I was the target of
much malicious gossip. I was quite alone with my project, though thankfully after 1986 I was in New York and far from what I experienced as the
toxic air along Lake Michigan (though Arnold and Constance Goldberg
and David Terman remained steadfast in their support and conviction that
my work would pay off in a valuable book). I am also stubborn, frankly,
and I found that the opposition steeled my own resolve. Slowly, very slowly,
things settled, and I was accepted as the biographer and as serious in my
purpose. By 1994, even the Kohut family softened its opposition. The full
set of the correspondence became available in the Kohut Archives of the
Institute and I had an invaluable interview over two days with Thomas
A. Kohut in 1996. I was able to interview the other surviving family members as well, especially Hans Lampl, Kohut's cousin from Vienna. Members of the group all granted interviews, more patients came forward, and
I established a very close tie with the invaluable Siegmund Levarie, the
last and best link to Kohut's childhood. (Siegmund is actually an emeri-
tus colleague at CUNY and lives two blocks from me in Brooklyn.)

Over those many years, Kohut became a different man for me. If at
first—between about 1982 and 1986—he was a genial if somewhat remote
and idealized figure, he became in time intensely imbedded in my soul,

remote, to be sure, but also complex, close, immediate, palpable, present. A man I knew personally as "Heinz" became "Kohut" in my imagination. He moved beyond the two-dimensional and in my experience became a nuanced and decidedly three-dimensional man. As the most thoughtful reviewers have noted, the book presents Kohut's many contradictions but in a way that never loses respect for the man himself. For some that is baffling, but it is exactly my point.

But I changed as well over the years as I researched and wrote the book. I would mention five important factors. First, my personal life stabilized. From the late 1970s until the mid-1980s, I was in a deteriorating marriage and sometimes in despair, dealing with single-parenting three children. Kohut once asked me with a twinkle in his eye if I knew his definition of a good marriage. It is, he said, when only one person is crazy at a time. But my life gradually settled as I became happy with a new wife after 1985. Probably more than anything, that allowed me to focus more energy on this complex scholarly project to which I had committed myself. Second, after 1986 I was a professor at The City University of New York and working on a daily basis with Robert Jay Lifton, who was always interested in Kohut and mentored me in countless ways that helped me grow and mature. Lifton and I ran a research center together, taught together, wrote articles and books together, and talked and talked and talked. Lifton was, of course, remote from Kohut but interested in his ideas and as my friend was keenly eager to see me complete my work. Third, I signed a publishing contract with Farrar, Straus & Giroux in 1994. That gave me much needed confidence and brought to my side two top editors, Jonathan Galassi and Paul Elie. Fourth, during the calendar year 1997 when I was on sabbatical and wrote the first draft of about 800 pages, I was in frequent contact by e-mail with a good friend, Tessa Philips, a psychoanalyst in Sydney, who proved an invaluable friend and helped me fight through my doubts as the first formulations took shape. Finally, I was changed psychologically and spiritually in some basic ways when I began my practice in 1992. (I used to say in the twenty years before that that I had a thriving practice but my patients were all dead.) I had long thought I could teach and write in my professional life but that there were not enough hours in the day to see patients as well. I was wrong. I found a half-time practice was wonderful. I loved the stories, the expanded empathy in me and my patients, and the challenges of taking on such responsibility for others' lives. To my astonishment, my patients even got better. Along the way, my wife said I became a better person. I also learned in new ways what the theory is all about. I actually doubt I could have written this biography except as a historian *and* a psychoanalyst. Doing self psychology gave me an understanding of the theory that I had never possessed before then. It is different up close and in the clinic.

III

The most basic of assignments—to remain honest in the work—seems hard for many contemporary writers. One can even say honesty is under siege in modern biography. A decade ago, Stephen Oates, in what was the first major plagiarism scandal of recent years, was unmasked for having copied much of his biography of Abraham Lincoln from Benjamin Thomas. Oates was even formally chastised by the American Historical Association for plagiarism sins in the second degree and required to acknowledge his indebtedness to Thomas in future editions. Stephen Ambrose, with his army of researchers producing middle-brow histories, turns out to have cribbed much of it in shameful and outrageous ways. Doris Kearns Goodwin, a former Harvard professor, no less, was caught with forged quill in hand. She got kicked off the PBS News Hour and was forced to resign from the Pulitzer Prize Committee but has now begun a comeback on CNBC. The more complex case is that of Joseph Ellis, author of a fine study of Thomas Jefferson and another of what he calls the "founding brothers." Ellis, a campus star at Mt. Holyoke, it turns out, spun out over the years in his lectures some rather extraordinary tales of himself in Vietnam, including being a witness to atrocities, even though he never served there. A bright student checked it out and a scandal ensued. Interestingly enough, no one (yet) has impugned Ellis's historical scholarship. Perhaps he figured he could reasonably lie about the twentieth century. It is merely present, contemporary, only a step away from journalism. What matters and must remain sacrosanct is the real past, the eighteenth century.

I am thankful I wrote the *first* biography of Kohut. My book may be criticized but it can't be said to have been cribbed from someone else. But this issue of honesty in biography has an intriguing analogue in Kohut's own life. It is difficult to imagine a more original thinker in psychoanalysis after Freud than Heinz Kohut. In a field of endless self-reference and pretentious derivation, where old ideas get renamed and repackaged ad nauseum, Kohut surely was one of four or five thinkers actually to have moved things along. And yet the cloud of plagiarism hangs over his work. It is all in Donald Winnicott, they say, or Sandor Ferenczi, or Paul Federn, or, of course, in Sigmund Freud. Most such criticism is facile and reflects the observer's lack of real understanding of Kohut or the intellectual history of psychoanalysis. At the same time, one has to confront the fact that this hugely creative and original man had a complex relationship to honesty. In his arrogance, at least once (with David Terman) Kohut failed to acknowledge some very specific ideas that were communicated to him in conversation and in writing. Nor is the question of honesty only in relation to his ideas. Kohut as a man was full of secrets, ambiguities, contradictions, and sometimes outright lies.

The areas of Kohut's obfuscation were significant. All his life he remained confused about his identity as a Jew. At best one can say he negotiated opposing elements concerning his identity within which he constructed personal myths that moved toward self re-creation. A year before his death Kohut told Susan Quinn, who interviewed him for an article in the Magazine section of the *New York Times* (Quinn generously shared the transcript of her interview with me[3]), that his mother was Catholic and dragged him to mass on Sundays as a child. That preposterous statement follows many others in a lifetime of ruses about his origins. In other areas as well, Kohut could be maddeningly obtuse. He wove an elaborate tapestry of lies around his illness during his last decade. His sexual identity is unclear. (My descriptor is "protean," which is a word that attempts to capture seeming multiplicity while being honest to my lack of definitive information on the subject.) And in his final years he wrote an entire case history, "The Two Analyses of Mr. Z," that is a disguised autobiography but is at the same time as complete and honest a self-portrait as we have of any major figure in the history of psychoanalysis.

There is a long, if not quite distinguished, tradition beginning with Sigmund and Anna Freud of hiding oneself in the story of one's patient, though it can be fairly said that few have been quite as radical in such ventures as Kohut. But there is an even more interesting angle to take on Mr. Z. Why write it in the first place? Why go to such lengths to present one's own story in such exquisite detail and in such psychological depth and then build such an elaborate disguise around it? In part, the answer is obvious. He was very famous and enormously controversial at that point (1978) and would have been mercilessly criticized and had his revelations used grievously against him. It makes a lot of sense that, having decided to write an autobiography, he was then forced by the circumstances of his life to build a disguise around the form of presentation. In the end, however, I am more impressed by the decision to write the autobiography than the

lie required to make it public. In Mr. Z Kohut told the deepest of all possible truths about himself wrapped in the enigma of a faked case. And, of
course, to bring it home, I cannot believe that anyone of Kohut's profundity and ambition, a man set on creating a whole new general psychology,
did not want his ruse to be uncovered in time by some clever researcher.
He wrote the case, in other words, for people like me to untangle it.[4]

Chasing it all down, however, was quite a task. Given his masks, he
made for an elusive target. He kept his papers but had his son, Thomas
A. Kohut, destroy his patient notes. His most interesting comments were
off-the-cuff, and, as with Clinton, one might say Kohut was at his best
winging it before an audience. Certainly, his widow and son were absolutely convinced he never would have wanted a cradle-to-grave biography written about him (they told me this repeatedly) and certainly not a
psychologically informed one. They then reacted with rage when I didn't
listen to them and proceeded on my own course.

Can we be so sure what Kohut wanted? I have naturally wondered often
why, at the height of his fame in the mid-1970s, he would draw into his
circle a young psychologically minded historian, except to cultivate him
as his biographer. It is important to stress that he never said anything to
me or anyone else along these lines. He gave no hint, subtle or otherwise, no knowing wink, in any of our interactions, to suggest that he
wanted me to write his biography, nor did he ever make a comment to a
colleague that was later shared with me to that effect. I was not only not
designated, I was entirely self-appointed. I took on the project only after
his death. It was in the spring of 1982 that I "suddenly" decided to write
the book. That coincided with the publication of my Lincoln book and I
think I then had the psychic space to imagine something new.[5] In the
years I knew and worked with Kohut, I never once had the thought or
the fantasy that I would write his biography. But why wouldn't he want
it? Kohut knew he was a major thinker in psychoanalysis and, he felt,
second only to Freud. He was also an extraordinarily interesting man,
in part because of his idiosyncrasies. That is the kind of story people
like me like to tell. I hardly think he felt I was the only person qualified
to write about him. I would suspect that if he had any fantasies along these
lines it would have been that he hoped there would be fifty biographies
on groaning shelves written over many decades. But I was at hand, and
timing is everything.

Kohut, it seemed to me, was keenly aware of my own idealizing needs
without knowing anything about their specifics. (He was not, after all,

my therapist.) As a child, I was strongly attached to my dynamic father, and the trauma of my youth came when he died suddenly at 53 in 1960 after giving a speech in Chicago. We were living in Florida then—my father was president of Florida State University—and was under consideration for the presidency of the University of Chicago. I had just turned 16, and his death left an aching hole. I think in my own despair I sought a number of surrogates, who probably inevitably failed to measure up, and against whom I reacted rather strenuously. I suspect that is why I found my professors in graduate school so foppish and ignorant. I experienced Kohut, however, in very different ways. He never failed me. He was always kind, generous, respectful—worthy, one might say, of my idealization. I know well from my research how difficult Kohut could be to those in closer and more regular contact with him than I ever was. I was also hardly blind to his obviously charismatic and self-centered ways. But somehow he structured the parameters of our relationship so that I never had to suffer to get the gift of what he had to offer.

I came to feel in the course of my work that my goals intersected rather intimately with Kohut's dreams for his own symbolic immortality and the future of self psychology. I have large ambitions in this book—and, for better or worse, it is a very ambitious book—namely, to fulfill the unrealized project he undertook. I try to make coherent Kohut's often tentative and sometimes awkwardly phrased but highly original formulations *and* show the very great evolution of his thought. Since Kohut was always in dialogue with Freud and constantly changing his mind about things between 1966 and 1981, and since many of his best ideas were in taped lectures and the actuality of his clinical work in the memory of a thousand patients, which I tapped into, one has to see the flow in one place to appreciate fully its richness. My goal was to bring Heinz Kohut back into focus in the psychological world and remind people where contemporary psychoanalysis comes from. That world, of course, itself has changed from the one in which Kohut was situated. In the world of clinical psychoanalysis, Freud is fast fading from view, while in the academy one can say we have lost the department of psychiatry but won the department of English. Such "victories" are mixed blessings.

IV

As a 15-year-old boy in the Döblinger Gymnasium, Kohut read the *Iliad* and the *Odyssey* in their original Greek. In his literature classes, he memorized

huge sections of the poetry of Goethe. It might be said Kohut as an adolescent lived intellectually and spiritually in the ancient world and in the
classics of German (and Christian) Europe. The one important contemporary writer he read and reread as an adolescent was Thomas Mann,
especially *The Magic Mountain*, that miraculous tale of Hans Castorp's
coming of age. Later (in his 30s), as Kohut moved into psychiatry and
psychoanalysis, he absorbed Freud with the same intensity he had earlier
read Mann; by the 1950s one can say there were those who knew Freud as
well as Kohut but no one knew the master better. To some extent Kohut's
interests in Homer, Goethe, Mann, and Freud continued. His letters to
Siegmund Levarie in the 1970s still contained references to Goethe. He
never stopped quoting and writing about Freud. And by his bedside just
prior to his death were two books, Moses Haddad's *History of Roman
and Greek Literature* and Victor Hugo's, *Les Misérables*. Perhaps one never
fully loses interest in what one really knows.

But equally striking are the changes in Kohut's reading as he moved
into his more creative exploration of self psychology. From the mid-1960s
on he intentionally stopped reading all journals and scientific writings in
the field, and consulted Freud only when he had to quote something or
be sure he was right about a disagreement. (It was all in his head anyway.) Kohut passed idle time with mysteries but what engaged his soul in
those last fifteen years or so were Franz Kafka, Marcel Proust, and Eugene
O'Neill. There was seldom a seminar presentation, or lecture, or a dinner party for that matter at which he failed to quote something about
Gregor Samsa feeling like a cockroach and listening to his parents talk
about him in the third person; or being tried without knowing the charges;
or the visitor to the village trying to call the count for an entire novel and
never connecting; or some aspect of that *recherche du temps perdu* that
defines the self's enduring meanings; or his favorite quote of all in these
years from *The Great God Brown*, "Man is born broken. He lives by mending. The grace of God is glue."

This sequence in Kohut's reading represents a personal deepening
of great significance while simultaneously connecting with a historical
move from the old Europe to the new, from the modern to the postmodern, and from the confidences before Cubism to the ambiguities of
meaning after the Holocaust. I am also intrigued with the ways Kohut's
new reading recapitulates the story of the transformation of biographical
and autobiographical genres of the last 200 years as they have progressed
from rational, political, and male modes of discourse to their introspec-

tive, psychological, fluid, contradictory, confusing, and open-ended contemporary forms.

To elaborate that point, I would suggest there are four principle streams of influence on biography as we know it.

(1) The oldest is the political, public, mostly male form. The prototype is Plutarch's *Lives*. In these exquisitely written pieces, Plutarch traces the stories of public figures from emperors and statesmen to generals and other great men. He evokes the relevant aspects of their lives in order to understand their role as public figures. The canvas is always very large indeed. The best writers today within this tradition are David McCullough (Teddy Roosevelt, Truman, John Adams), Garry Wills (Nixon, Lincoln, Reagan, John Wayne), and Robert Caro (Robert Moses and Lyndon Johnson), with many others writing valuable contributions.

(2) In the middle ages there arose the moral and instructive form. The prototype was the Christian *Lives of the Saints* in which the point of the telling is exemplary, didactic, hortatory, and the goal is to elucidate principles of love, compassion, sacrifice, transcendence, and humility. In the contemporary scene, Oprah perhaps best represents the apotheosis of this form. In its cousin, autobiography, one sees it often in books like Billy Graham's *Just As I Am*, though the tradition can also lead to noble work indeed, as with Gandhi's *My Experiments With Truth*.

(3) In the eighteenth century Enlightenment, the personal portrait emerged. The great new work that defined the personal portrait was James Boswell's hagiographical *Life of Samuel Johnson*. The worshipful tone of Boswell's *Life* is actually ironic, for we now see Johnson as a minor figure in intellectual history, whereas Boswell himself has been the subject of numerous biographies and his papers (at Yale) are regarded as one of the most valuable collections in the world. That Boswell would, in the end, become much more important than the subject of his biography inevitably stirs the fantasies of a scribbler like me. In any event, the biographical form Boswell defines is characterized, it seems to me, by three things: endless detail, a focus on the intimate facts of a subject's life, and the systematic bringing into the story of the experience, even the subjectivity, of the biographer himself or herself. One finds this form of biography everywhere today. It is most accessible in publications such as *Ladies Home Journal* or

People Magazine. An entire television channel broadcasts stories in this mode 24 hours a day (The Biography Channel). A notch up the intellectual ladder built by Boswell leads you to the new journalism of Norman Mailer, Truman Capote, and Maureen Dowd, while a humorous, mocking version would be the Gonzo journalism of Hunter Thompson.

(4) Finally, there is an emerging tradition in biography that is still young and fragile, not really nameable quite yet, with echoes in Plutarch and hints in Boswell; tentative beginnings in the nineteenth century with someone like William Herndon's biography of Lincoln, obviously grounded in Freud but first articulated in a coherent biographical form in Lytton Strachey's *Eminent Victorians* (1918), and most magnificently realized in Erik Erikson's studies of Luther (1958) and Gandhi a decade later (1969). Such is psychological biography, which as a scholarly mode of writing most closely approximates for subjects we deem worthy of scrutiny what we actually do with patients. Psychological biography looks into early experience and is concerned as much with quirks and neuroses as achievements. The point is to find the true self. There is no theoretical or moral limit in determining relevance, and as Steven Marcus has put it rules out "no secret embarrassment, no shameful memory or episode," *as long as* it is "pertinent to the central project of understanding how a significant life came about." The larger, more visible, story of the life in politics, science, or art remains the central task to explain. But the imperative of psychoanalysis forces the biographer to include the public *and* the private, the work *and* the life. It can be a daunting task and requires its own form of careful selection. The best one can do, along with Lytton Strachey, is to row out into the vast sea of facts and drop a bucket or two.[6]

There is no question I would like to see my biography of Kohut in this last tradition. It is one that connects the richness of psychological inquiry with a determined respect for historical truth. Psychologically informed biography makes historical figures fully human, complex, and endlessly interesting. An abiding empathy with one's subject is the goal, a psychological position that deepens and yet simultaneously complicates the biographer's task.

Kohut was fond of the Latin aphorism, *Habent sua fata libelli*, or "Writings have their own destiny." And so I have written a biography that has taken a life out of the inchoate past and shaped it into a narrative for others to experience in their own way and to determine its destiny.

NOTES

1, 2. See Notes, pp. 389–390.
   3. That transcript and all my notes and research materials have been deposited in the Kohut Archives of the Chicago Institute for Psychoanalysis.
   4. Geoffrey Cocks first revealed the secret of Mr. Z in his Introduction to *The Curve of Life* (1994), quoting Thomas A. Kohut as his source. Cocks, however, failed to do additional research to back up his assertion, which left many still unconvinced.
5, 6. See Notes, pp. 389–390.

Part One

VIENNA

1913–1939

One

PREHISTORY

On May 3, 1913, Heinz Kohut was born to Felix and Else Kohut in old Austria's great city of Vienna. Both parents were talented and financially comfortable members of the city's assimilated Jewish elite and lived in the Ninth District at Liechtensteinstrasse 121. Felix, dashing at twenty-four, was a brilliant pianist in active training for a concert career. The First World War, however, was to shatter such dreams and force him into business, while leukemia would end his life prematurely at forty-nine in 1937. Else, twenty-two at the birth of her only son, was a beautiful, very dramatic, and determined young woman who sang well and later ran her own business. In 1940 she would follow her son into immigration to escape the Nazis and live several decades in Chicago before dying in 1972 at eighty-two years of age.[1]

The prehistory of the family exists more in myth than fact. Take the patrimonial name itself. "Kohut" is a fairly common Jewish name that is probably derived from the Hebrew name קוהת (Kohath), the son of Levi (one of the sons of Jacob) mentioned in Genesis 46:11. There was, furthermore, a distinguished line of Rabbi Kohuts from Hungary in the nineteenth century, including Alexander Kohut (1842–1894), a great philologist who came to America in 1885 and wrote a prodigious eight-volume study of the Talmud; his son, George Alexander Kohut, who became a learned rabbi and, like his father, was an important figure at the Jewish Theological Seminary of New York City; another Hungarian writer, Adolf Kohut (1848–1917); and several other Hungarian Kohuts who were leaders of the Jewish community.[2]

Kohut himself, however, never said his name came from the biblical son of Levi and certainly never mentioned any rabbinic forebears. On the contrary, his story, as woven in the family, was that "Kohut" means "rooster" in Czech and that most Bohemian Kohuts were Christian. In fact, the Czech word for rooster (*kohout*) is similar, though the likelihood that any of Heinz Kohut's ancestors were Christian Kohuts in Bohemia is slim indeed. His maternal family, furthermore, the Lampls, was descended from Jews in Slovakia, a fact about which Heinz Kohut, as best one can tell, never once commented in his adult life. Both sides of Kohut's family were almost certainly, then, part of the vast migration of Jews to Vienna from the provinces of the Austrian Empire after mid-century; Kohut once told an interviewer that both the Kohuts and the Lampls had been in Vienna for several generations, which would put both families in that first wave of Jewish immigrants in the 1850s and 1860s.[3] Some Jews had been in Vienna for nearly a millennium, but after the revolution of 1848 the government lifted the traditional restrictions on Jewish residence. Jews flocked to Vienna from the shtetls and towns of the Austro-Hungarian Empire. They helped transform the arts, commerce, and banking in the old capital. From a population of 2,000 in 1847, by the First World War there were about 200,000 Jews in Vienna, or 10 percent of the total population of two million, and by the mid-1930s the number of Jews in Vienna had risen to nearly 300,000, with the population of the city rising accordingly.[4] Jews helped transform the culture of Vienna within a generation. Things had never been better, as the Viennese say, and they had never been worse.[5]

Kohut's paternal grandfather, Bernhard (or, in the Jewish records, Bernat) Kohut, born in 1842 to Ignaz Kohut and Ester Hupka Kohut, was an English teacher in a gymnasium, having worked his way up from elementary-school teaching.[6] A gymnasium teacher was accorded a greater degree of status in society than we would associate with a high school instructor. They were called "professor" and bore themselves with some dignity and stiffness, as Heinrich Mann captured in his novel *Professor Unrat*, made famous in the movie *The Blue Angel* with Emil Jannings and Marlene Dietrich. Bernhard, who politically yearned for the ideal of a united Germany that included Austria,[7] was true to his professorial stereotype. Two stories about him became part of family lore. One concerned a ritual he had on Sundays. The family, including Bernhard and his wife, Sophie Fischl Kohut, and the children, Felix, Anna (born 1879), Richard (born 1883), and Friedrich (born 1891), all of whom, except for

Felix, died in the Holocaust, would gather for their main meal of the day. There would be talk and chatter as the children tried to contain themselves as they waited for the climactic end of dinner. Then, with much pomp and circumstance, the father would call the child to his side who had behaved the best. He would give a key to that child, who would go to a designated box, put the key in, and open it. Inside would be an apple. The child would take the apple to the father, who would ceremoniously peel it according to his mood. In a good mood, he would peel the apple thickly, in a bad mood he would peel it thinly. In any event, the favored child got the peel and the father ate the apple. The wife got the core. The other story about this ornery patriarch is that when he was dying he made his children stand and slam the door to his bedroom as loud as they could to keep him from slipping away. That haunting sound of the door slamming stayed with Felix the rest of his life as a metaphor for death.[8]

The Lampl family, partly because of the longevity of Else, reached more deeply into Heinz's experience. Her parents were Sigmund Lampl and Franziska Ullmann Lampl. They had four children, of whom the eldest, Rudolf, died at two (1884–1886). Else was born in 1890. She had two younger brothers. The older, Wilhelm (born in 1892), called Willy, served in the First World War and was something of a hero. When the Second World War started, Willy never left Vienna and died with his child in the Holocaust. He probably assumed that he was safe because of his heroic record in the first war. The next boy, Hans Lampl, was a cosmopolitan young man. Only nineteen when Heinz Kohut was born, Hans had wide-ranging interests in music and culture that he was to share with his talented nephew. As a young man, Hans started several small business partnerships; after the first war he became an executive of a large company that produced pulp and fine paper. He survived the second war by moving to London. The last Lampl child was Else's younger sister, Mitzi, who was an invalid, probably retarded, and perhaps disturbed in other ways. She lived all her life at home with her aging parents, who cared for her. Walter Lampl, Hans's son, remembers visiting his grandparents as a child and seeing this mysterious aunt in the back, darkened room of the apartment. One suspects the Lampls were ashamed of letting her out. Mitzi died sometime in the 1920s.[9]

For the rest the names and stories fade into obscurity. The only real curiosity about Heinz Kohut's genealogy is his personal myth about the Christian Kohuts from Bohemia. It is not the kind of issue about which it was possible for there to be confusion. Jews in Vienna had no doubt about their ethnicity. They were required by law to be members of the "Israelite community," as it was designated. Because of its autonomy, Jews had to pay taxes collectively as a unit through their elected representatives.[10] In schools Jews were segregated for separate religious instruction. Felix and Else also had a Jewish wedding ("Eingetragen in dem Trauungs-Protokole der Israelitischen Kultusgemeinde in Wien," says their wedding certificate). The only curiosity is that there and on her birth certificate Else's name is spelled "Elsa" (her middle name was Sara), which is the more common German, as opposed to Austrian, version of her name.

It was certainly true, however, that Heinz's parents had different religious identities. His father was conventionally Jewish. Felix came out of a Jewish family, was raised religiously and bar mitzvahed, and never questioned his personal or spiritual relationship to the faith of his fathers. Felix was not Orthodox but he was observant. He and Else reserved seats in the temple in the Ninth District near the Liechtenstein Park. He attended temple on most holy days, often with his nephew, Walter Lampl, because his son, Heinz, was not interested. On Yom Kippur, Felix honored tradition by walking from his house to the temple. Felix moved in upper-middle-class circles that sharply separated him from the teeming Jewish community of mostly poorer immigrants settled in Leopoldstadt. But Felix was a religious man, and when he died young of leukemia in 1937 it was natural that his wife and son gave him a full Jewish funeral, though it does not seem that they sat shiva.

Else Lampl, on the other hand, had a much more complex relationship with religion. She was born Jewish in a family that mostly remained committed to its faith and observant of its rituals. Both her parents and all her ancestors were Jewish, and her family may have included some noted rabbis. She was thus "racially" Jewish, as the Nazis defined such things, and was forced to flee Vienna after the Anschluss; undoubtedly she would have otherwise perished in the Holocaust. She was also formally part of the Jewish community in Vienna (the Kultusgemeinde). When Siegmund Levarie's father, Josef Löwenherz, was gathering votes for the Progressive Party in their bid to take control of the Kultusgemeinde in the mid-1930s (when they won, he was appointed vice-president), Löwenherz personally called Else to ask for her vote. Else furthermore "looked Jewish" (according to her grandson, Thomas, and others who knew her), though she was, of course, privileged, educated, and assimilated. She married a Jew,

Felix Kohut, and attended temple with her husband on the major Jewish holidays. She did cut corners. While Felix would walk to temple on Yom Kippur, Else would drive her car to the vicinity of the temple, park it, and walk the rest of the way.[11]

As a girl, however, Else also seems to have established some kind of relationship to the Catholic Church. She may even have been confirmed. One of the items she took with her out of Vienna into emigration was a confirmation bracelet. The bracelet has remained in the family.[12] Furthermore, the slight variation in the spelling of her name may reflect her dual identities. On all legal, that is, Jewish, documents she is "Elsa" (birth and wedding certificates and the Inventory of Jewish Wealth, which the Nazis forced her to complete in 1938), while she was otherwise "Else." Thomas Kohut, her grandson, always understood that Else was Catholic in her childhood and "would have described herself probably as a Christian." She grew up with Christmas trees during the holidays, and the Lampls— and later the Kohuts—celebrated Christmas (Weihnachten) by exchanging presents on December 24, as was customary.[13] Else clearly had a layered religious identity that embodied contradictions about both ethnicity and belief. As Thomas Kohut sees it, her Jewish origins and life and involvements seemed not to fulfill her spiritual yearnings, and in some way she connected with Catholicism as a girl. That made her, in the eyes of her grandson, a Catholic by belief in a world that came to insist she had to stand up and be counted ethnically as a Jew, which became, of course, the great crisis of identity for all converted Jews throughout Germany after 1933 and Austria after 1938. Faith for Else seemed to take precedence over birth as she sought to define her identity in an individual way that allowed for a crossing of lines in many directions.

But this official "family" version of her story may itself embody contradictions that reflect the pain of forced emigration and the residues of her own early struggles. Siegmund Levarie, Heinz's best childhood friend, was often around the Kohut home and was to know Else well in America. He says it is preposterous to think of her as anything but completely Jewish. He scorns the idea that she was confirmed a Catholic in Vienna. "One can pick up a junk bracelet in any jewelry store," he said.[14] Walter Lampl (born 1921), furthermore, Else's nephew, who was close to the Kohuts, went to synagogue with Felix, and kept up contact with Else in emigration, doubts seriously that there was ever any kind of conversion on her part. Certainly he never heard anything about it. His own father and Else's brother, Hans Lampl, had renounced his Judaism in the 1920s purely as a business decision. He was an utterly agnostic man. All one did was to change one's religious affiliation from Jewish to Roman Catholic on the appropriate forms. He never was confirmed or went to church. There was no shame about the way Hans handled his religious identity, nor was there anything secret about it. But it was naturally known in the family. Walter Lampl also points out that it was common for Viennese Jews, even quite religious ones like himself, to have Christmas trees and celebrate Weihnachten. It was a fun holiday for children and was, in a sense, Judaized.[15]

Else remained officially—which meant legally—a Jew. She did not become a convert to Catholicism; to begin with, to have done so would have made her marriage illegal, for intermarriage in Vienna required prior conversion of the non-Catholic partner.[16] Had she gone to church as an adult, someone in the family would have noticed, which is what makes Walter Lampl's testimony so significant. Else's confirmation, if it occurred at all, was thus probably part of a passing adolescent experimentation, long before she met Felix and started her family. The existence of the bracelet and the story of the confirmation—which even if part of a personal myth constitute something real historically—suggest that Else had a profound religious confusion in her core self. Psychologically, she seemed to think of herself as some kind of complex mixture of Judaism and Christianity, though she retained into adulthood the identity and self-presentation of a Jew. It was a kind of spirituality that defied religious convention and certainly mocked the categories the Nazis established.

Else's personal struggles with her Jewish religion and identity were not in isolation. Assimilation in all its forms, including its end product, conversion, touched the experience of many affluent and educated Jews in Vienna at the turn of the century. There were, to be sure, broad cultural associations of Jews with dirt and evil that prompted both anti-Semitism and self-hate.[17] But the move away from Judaism and toward Christianity was equally, if not primarily, based in the affirmation of a shared culture. It was common for Jews to shed their Judaism once exposed to the culture and humanism of Vienna. Freud, for example, could not read the Hebrew that his father inscribed in the family Bible and considered himself a determined atheist who felt that organized religion was at best foolish.[18] He was well educated, successful, bourgeois, and an integral part of Viennese cultural life in the early decades of the century. At the same time and however assimilated, Freud was clear about his Jewishness. He joined B'nai B'rith in 1897, collected Jewish jokes, and associated mostly with Jews; Carl Jung was important to Freud at first precisely because he was not Jewish and broke the stereotype of psychoanalysis as a Jewish science.[19]

Other Jews more eagerly sought to shed their Jewish ethnicity along with their religion. That attempted transformation usually began with conversion to Christianity. Sometimes, "conversion" was purely pragmatic and perfunctory, as with Else's brother, Hans Lampl. More commonly, however, conversion was a prelude to intermarriage. There were quite a few such conversions in Vienna: some 9,000 between 1868 and 1903.[20] Many converts or their children became quite famous, including Alfred Adler, Hugo Bettauer, Hermann Broch, Karl Kraus, Gustav Mahler, Arnold Schoenberg, and Ludwig Wittgenstein. And yet even with conversion and intermarriage the subjective sense of being Jewish remained, if subtly. For one thing, the world at large, especially after 1890 and with mounting intensity after 1933, kept alive the sharp distinction between Catholics and anyone ethnically Jewish. Hugo von Hofmannsthal, for example, was not Jewish by religion and only one-quarter by descent, but he was a clear product of assimilation, as was Wittgenstein. In this sense, far from producing a complete merger with the surrounding populace, "assimilation was in itself a Jewish phenomenon."[21]

The story of the assimilation of Viennese Jews, however, taking place as it did on the cusp of the Anschluss and the Holocaust, has not been a neutral historical problem. Its history has gotten encrusted with clichés, especially that of Vienna "waltzing toward the abyss." Many Zionists and others who read history backward now mock the self-absorbed pretensions of cultured Jews aspiring to forget their origins and merge with the larger Christian world. Among such observers, a few clairvoyants are exempt from the charge of naive complacency. The rest are in a "freefall that prefigures the collapse of western culture itself."[22] Written this way, history mocks those who believed in assimilation into a society that was so brutally to expel them. Few, for example, possessed the insight and commitment of Schoenberg, who reembraced Judaism after Hitler came to power in 1933. Perhaps only the lemmings as metaphor captures the past in this historicist perspective.

But from within the contemporary world of Viennese Jewish experience, assimilation looked very different. The future seemed boundlessly hopeful. There had been only rapid economic, social, and cultural progress for the Jews who escaped the shtetl and towns of eastern Europe for the wonders of Vienna. They were hardly blind to the politics of Karl

Lueger, the openly anti-Semitic mayor of Vienna in the 1890s, or the rantings of people like Georg von Schönerer, or the vile propaganda of the rising Nazi party in the late 1920s and early 1930s.[23] Virulent anti-Semitism, after all, was hardly new in the historical experience of central and eastern European Jews. They had suffered centuries of pogroms and other abuses. But late-nineteenth- and early-twentieth-century Vienna, for all the dangers that lurked at the margins, seemed different. At least until 1933 in Vienna, and to some extent until 1938, one could reasonably hope for the emergence of more tolerant political alternatives and refuse to abandon the contours of an assimilated life. Even the image of decadence one associates with fin de siècle Vienna is wrongheaded, especially its Jewish face. It is an art not of decline but of uplift. The work of Gustav Mahler and Arthur Schnitzler, for example, is "defiant and liberating," challenging the staid art of the nineteenth century. In science, Freud's work, in particular, challenged the contemporary formalistic approaches to mental illness and opened up new pathways to the soul with his work on dreams. Finally, in politics, Jews, and Viennese Jews most of all, really believed in the idea of a transnational cultural identity. Mocked by anti-Semites, this vision of something beyond fascist nationalisms has a deep appeal after Auschwitz and Hiroshima.

Two

BEGINNINGS

Felix and Else Kohut fit snugly into the cultural and assimilated world of Viennese Jewry. Married in 1911, the Kohuts had two years together before Heinz was born. This must have been a heady time in their lives. Much of Felix's life was absorbed in piano playing as he moved toward his career goal as a concert pianist. Else warmed to his performances, and there is some evidence she actively participated at times with him as a singer at soirees.[1] It is quite an image: young Felix, the brilliant pianist, accompanying his lovely and dramatic wife, Else, in songs before a group of cultured Viennese decked out in their fashionable best in some mansion on the Ring. Stefan Zweig, part of that same world, put it well: "It was only in regard to art that all felt an equal right, because love of art was a communal duty in Vienna."[2]

But in time came parenthood with its new commitments. As young Jews, Felix and Else naturally gave their new baby boy, eight days after his birth, the bris milah, or ritualistic circumcision, in their temple, the Müllnergasse synagogue, located in the Ninth District. Heinz's religious name was Wolf Hersh, formally recorded in the records of the Kultusgemeinde. This legal registration of the boy as a member of the "Israelite community" was extremely important from the point of view of the Austrian government. Heinz's Yiddish name linked him to countless generations of Jews. Until the eighteenth-century Enlightenment, Jews in Europe made no distinction between their secular and religious names. But by the early twentieth century, and especially among assimilated Viennese Jews, it was the custom to have a secular name that differed entirely from one's religious name given at the bris. In Vienna at the time, one's religious name was customarily, though not necessarily, Yiddish. The religious name was usually drawn from the religious names of dead relatives (in the Ashkenazic tradition) as a way of fostering families and spiritual continuity. The secular name of Heinz's father was Felix, his grandfather was Bernhard or Bernat, and his great-grandfather Ignaz, but their religious names are not known.[3]

In all respects, that critical first year or so of Heinz's life seemed happy. The parents were close and the future seemed bright. Felix moved in heady circles with his music. Else was also probably as happy as she ever was in her life. She was in the flush of her beauty and in love with her husband. Her joy with life, it seems, carried over to her early relationship with Heinz, at least to the extent that he is accurately describing himself in his later autobiographical case, "The Two Analyses of Mr. Z" (hereafter "Mr. Z").[4] There Kohut says that however "severely distorted" the mother's personality would turn out to be, at twenty-two she was young and full of vitality when Heinz was born. She had an "intense relationship" with her little boy. As long as he remained a baby, the "interweaving of her with him" seemed to bring out her "healthiest attitudes." He was the "apple of her eye." This is quite clear from photographs of the period, as Kohut says in "Mr. Z." When in her arms, the "facial expression and general demeanor" of the boy is that of a healthy and happy baby. Equally significant, Z's adult personality reflected those solid beginnings. "There was a core of vitality, playful vigor, and enterprisingness in Mr. Z's personality that had survived from earliest times, despite the distortions it underwent later."[5]

More indirectly, it is hard to believe that anyone with the zest and enthusiasm for life that Heinz Kohut displayed had not been warmly embraced and mirrored by his mother in his earliest experience. Enthusiasm was at the core of Heinz Kohut's personality. He often enraged people or hurt them badly with his intense narcissism, but the rest he charmed as if by magic with his zest for everything. He racheted up a few notches the intensity of everything in which he participated.[6] Enthusiasm, furthermore, lies at the heart of what Kohut was to call the cohesive self. His notion was that a vital self has the capacity for enthusiasm—that reaching out to others and the world to take the risks so necessary if one is to find intimacy, fulfillment, and creativity. Enthusiasm in these terms is both maker and measure of the cohesive self.

The joys of Heinz's first year, his intimacy with his mother, the closeness of the family, and the hopes for an unbounded future all came crashing down before Heinz could even talk. It was truly a paradise lost. In the summer of 1914 war engulfed central Europe. Looming on the horizon for the last decade, war had come to seem almost inevitable for most Europeans. The Germans, aggressively expansionist for the last half century, were particularly eager in their embrace of war as a way of claiming their place in the sun. To oppose them the French, British, and Russians had built a sturdy alliance. The fragile Austro-Hungarian Empire was Germany's weak cousin, and it was the empire's meddling in the Balkans that led to the assassination of Archduke Franz Ferdinand in Sarajevo that summer, which set in motion war itself. The old proud empire, with its conglomerate of peoples and languages, mobilized an army to fight Russia along a front that was to stretch from Silesia in the west to the Caucasus in the east. In most big battles the Germans had to prop up the Austrians, yet they moved relentlessly forward because the Russian army was even more badly served than they by the collapse of autocracy. The Austrians won their small part of the war, it might be said, and completely lost the peace because of the more significant and memorable overriding German defeat.[7]

Among the soldiers who fought for the empire on that constantly shifting Russian front was Felix Kohut.[8] It is impossible to know what mix of personal pride and civic duty prompted Felix to join up, though we do know he rose to become a corporal and won the Silver Cross and the bronze medal of honor.[9] Felix also moved around a lot. When Italy declared war against Germany and Austria in 1915, he shifted to that front, where he fought until he was captured. It was from the Italian prisoner of war camp that Felix returned home to Vienna in 1918.[10]

Heinz was just sixteen months old when the war came. From his point of view, Felix's enlistment had to be something approaching a disaster. All of a sudden, for no reason that he could possibly understand, Heinz irrevocably lost his father for his entire infancy, through toilet training and walking and talking and exploration and discovery of self. Occasionally, Felix would return on furlough, but never for long, and once he and his mother traveled to see Felix briefly in Italy.[11] For young Heinz his father must have seemed a mystical figure in his heavy uniform and enormous rifle, stopping by for a few weeks to disrupt the equanimity of his mother and the family, disappearing just as suddenly into the mist.

At least the war years for Heinz were physically safe and even comfortable. As soon as the war started, Else and her one-year-old child went to live with her parents, who had moved to a house outside of Vienna. It was more secure, and she surely benefited from the financial and emotional support of her family in those years. It was hard living in Vienna during the war, but life in the countryside, with gardens of fresh vegetables and animals that produced eggs and milk and other dairy products, made things at least bearable. The surrounding forest, as well, famed in Viennese legend, yielded its treasure of mushrooms, which Heinz learned to pick at his mother's side. Kohut also once described himself as an infant fat from eating farina. This wheat-based meal was prepared in a distinctively Viennese way. Heated, it was served with a great glob of chocolate in the middle. Children then typically created rivulets in the farina with their forks to let the chocolate run through.[12]

Heinz's inner life during these years from one to five is more difficult to reconstruct. Most of what Kohut says in his autobiographical case of Mr. Z, if read carefully, refers to the period after he was five (and had continuous memory). One could read those memories backward in time and assume, for example, that the pathology of Else in relation to her son began to express itself in those war years. To a degree, of course, some of her idiosyncrasies must have been present all along. But that is not how Kohut wrote up the case, and this form probably follows the psychological reality as the infant Heinz experienced it. Besides, as the theory would have it—and in contrast with Freud in this regard—potentials within the self are only realized in the unfolding context of history. All we know with reasonable certainty (from "Mr. Z") is that during the war Heinz slept in Felix's bed, which was placed next to Else's. Such proximity brought Heinz into intimate contact with his mother as they jointly braved the very real dangers of the world. Perhaps those dangers aroused the early expressions of the paranoia that lurked below the surface in Else. In "Mr. Z," for example, the mother is highly intrusive about his toilet training and took unusual interest in the inspection of his feces up to the time he was six. Perhaps she was also consumed with fears about her husband's life and loyalty. In "Mr. Z," as disguise, it is not the war that takes Felix away during Heinz's infancy but an illness. The father then falls in love with his nurse and decides to leave his wife, though he returns home when Heinz is five. Maybe, in fact, Felix took on mistresses, especially toward the end of the war in Italy or even in the prisoner of war camp.[13]

In any event, the coming home of Felix was a jolt for everyone in the family. Certainly, it was never the same again between husband and wife. At first they tried to maintain something of a relationship, and at least slept in the same bed and continued their sexual connection. When Felix returned and the family moved into its own apartment, and somewhat later a house, a couch was moved into the parental bedroom and placed crosswise at the foot of the bed. The couch was low enough and the bed high enough to prevent Heinz from seeing anything. But he could feel the vibrations of his parents' sexual activities. Later, in his "Freudian" analysis, Kohut reconstructed that he had confused these primal scene memories with the serious quarrels between his parents. As he puts it in "Mr. Z": "He had experienced the intercourse not as lovemaking but as a fight." By the time Heinz was eight, however, he was moved into his own room and the parents took to separate beds. From there they went their separate ways, filling their lives with mistresses and lovers. We meet one of Felix's girlfriends in "Mr. Z"; Else, for her part, chose as one of her lovers a man named Kohut (though he was not a relative). This liaison began when Heinz was about ten and Felix "apparently did not object."[14]

In "Mr. Z" Kohut reports a dream of his father's return. The father is loaded with packages of gifts. As he tries to enter, the boy desperately struggles to shut the door against the father's pressure. The Freudian interpretation of the dream to which Z/Heinz came in his first analysis was the ambivalence of the child toward his oedipal rival, who, he feared, would end his exclusive possession of the mother and destroy him by castration after all the years away. Surely, in somewhat different terms, at some level Heinz felt bedeviled by anger at his father's return. His deeper understanding of the dream, however, toward the end of the second analysis, was "of a boy who had been all-too-long without a father; of a boy deprived of the psychological substance from which, via innumerable observations of the father's assets and defects, he would build up, little by little, the core of an independent masculine self." The fright in the dream spoke to the traumatic state that threatened the boy's psychological survival.[15] One could say, somewhat epigrammatically, that Heinz's first understanding of his dream in response to his father's sudden return was that he wanted to keep his father out, but that its truer meaning was that he wanted to let him in. The terror was the suddenness of it all.

Nor was Felix the same. One can only imagine the horrors of war that he had seen and experienced in his four years away. As early as 1915 Freud remarked on the way the war had created a newly destructive self. "We cannot but feel that no event has ever destroyed so much that is precious in the common possessions of humanity," he wrote. The war was "more bloody and more destructive" than anything that came before; was "cruel," "embittered," and "implacable"; ignored the "prerogatives of the wounded"; and "tramples in blind fury on all that comes in its way." Civilized nations in regular intercourse had suddenly turned on each other with "hate and loathing."[16] Felix was in the thick of it all, especially during his three years on the Russian front, where men died by the millions. In the big battles, there were hundreds of thousands of casualties. And though in Italy the battles were not as big, he was captured there and had to endure being a prisoner. Surely, such experiences affected something basic in the soul of this sensitive musician. He did not touch a piano for five years and his concert career was finished. He went into business, Kohut said himself in an interview not long before his own death, "or something like that." Felix resumed playing the piano but not seriously. He would accompany Else while she sang Schubert lieder, and they would sometimes together play four-hand piano. There was music everywhere in his life. But "his heart wasn't in it." The war had aged Felix prematurely. "I was deprived of a young, vigorous father," Kohut said of Felix. "He was replaced by an old man, a grandfather, and that was not the same."[17]

This Felix, who dreamed of concert halls filled with cultured Viennese cheering his piano playing, found himself forced to enter the paper business and play the piano as a hobby.[18] At thirty his best years were behind him. Everything tasted of anticlimax. He was stuck in trauma. He turned into himself, became withdrawn, unavailable. Perhaps he felt some shame about being on the losing side in the war, feelings that contributed to his secretiveness. Siegmund Levarie remembers him as a "colorless" person who "wasn't very much in evidence. He didn't talk much to us." "He didn't project," Levarie said at another time. Felix seemed touched with sadness as his key relationships fell apart. Certainly he was never to be close with Else again. But something also broke down in his relation to his son. Kohut recalled toward the end of his own life how he first became interested in medicine and in asking questions in general about how things in the body fit together, especially the way the brain works, as a result of playing a doctor in a grade school play. His father, he said, was annoyed by all of his questions. Felix the artist had little sympathy for or understanding of science. He asked his son, "Why can't you be like the other boys?" It hurt Heinz immensely and led the boy to feel that there was "some kind of distance that existed between my father and me." Heinz felt that "I bothered him and it bothered me that he was not proud of my interests."[19]

And yet there were some deeper sources of identification of Heinz Kohut with his father. For one thing, the two were strikingly similar in appearance, which gave a physical grounding to the many ways in which Heinz identified with Felix. Though Felix was remote, Heinz "idealized him greatly." Kohut later said: "As a child I remember that every night before going to sleep I had to say a little bedtime prayer with an improvised ending, which asked that my father (who at the time was away at war) return safely." The earliest surviving letter of Kohut's is to his father from the ten-year-old Heinz, written while on vacation with Else in the mountains. It was July and they were hiking and swimming. The day was hot, Heinz writes, and he went for a dip, "because in this heat it is no pleasure to walk for three-quarters of an hour." Heinz notes that a "big twenty-fourth jubilee celebration" was being held for the local pastor. The previous evening there had been a torchlight procession. There were Chinese lanterns hanging in the windows of the homes and the whole village was decorated. That morning he had been awakened by cannon fire. It was all very exciting for him. "We are taking a lot of walks and picking strawberries," he adds. He asks how his father is, asks him to write, and signs off "Many kisses, Heinz."[20]

There was much talent and goodness in this artistic man with which a boy could identify. Father and son also grew closer as Heinz matured. Both father and son shared an intimate relationship with a difficult woman. Felix escaped from her (which is how Kohut explained his father's pervasive absence in "Mr. Z"), while Heinz struggled for his whole life to disentangle himself from his mother. Else was the pivot of a deep connection between father and son. One time, Heinz and Felix went skiing together and the boy discovered that there was a wonderful, lively side to his father. "He had a way with the waiters and chambermaids"—Kohut says in "Mr. Z"—"and was soon surrounded by a circle of followers who were fascinated by his stories and appeared to look up to him." The father was the life of the party, where he sang and laughed and joked. Heinz reveled in the closeness of the trip and the happy, competent father he witnessed away from his mother. It was the first time he saw this side of his father. Later, in medical school, Heinz wrote several scientific papers that greatly impressed his father. One day Felix said to him, "You know, Heinz, you have done things that I could never do. I'm *very* proud of you." It made Heinz extremely pleased.[21]

Even in the house with Else it is not entirely clear that Felix was that remote or depressed. Walter Lampl, Felix's nephew, describes Felix as "jovial, always joking, very personable, and friendly." Certainly Heinz's fascination with music came largely from Felix. Everyone who knew Heinz as an adult remarked on his extraordinary musical talent. He could listen to a concert and then intelligently critique its most subtle moments for hours. His knowledge of music and musicology was prodigious; two of his early articles deal with the psychology of music. His tastes centered on the European classics, but he came to like jazz and other popular American styles. In 1940 one of the first things Kohut did after getting settled in Chicago was to go see Duke Ellington perform. Kohut only stayed away from playing an instrument. He did take piano lessons as a child but gave it up at about thirteen, just as he was becoming proficient. He seemed to feel he could never play as well as his father, so it was better not to try.[22]

Kohut's style of creativity also seems to have reflected an identification with Felix. Most thinkers in psychoanalysis, indeed in the sciences in general, present their work, whether orally or on the written page, in a straightforward way that moves teleologically from a discussion of the literature on the subject, to some kind of data presentation, to conclusions. In a rhetorical sense, the form has the subtlety of a third-grade composition. Kohut, on the other hand, is polythematic and improvisational in his writings (this was even more striking in his oral presentations). He keeps several ideas on the page at one time. He hints up front at what lies ahead, rather like a leitmotiv in a Wagnerian overture. He circles his subject, repeating the theme but in a new key, reversed, or up a third. It has the feel of Bach or Mozart or Louis Armstrong. At its best there is a kind of controlled passion in Kohut's writing that reaches the core of an issue with profound understanding; at its worst, a rambling that never finds an effective end. But the rhetorical style is a musical one.[23]

Felix, in other words, was not as completely silent in the psychological life of Heinz Kohut as it might seem. But there is also no question that the most powerful and enduring influence in his life was Else. Kohut struggled his entire life to disengage himself from the enmeshing influence of his mother. She was a corrosive presence in his own sense of self. It took a huge effort for him to establish his separateness from her, to escape from the long shadow his mother cast, to find his own true center of authenticity. The father, in turn, was first absent and then no substitute in the crucial years; just when Heinz truly connected with him as a young man, he died. It is all there in "Mr. Z," just as it was in his life. The struggle is imbedded.

From an early age, though probably beginning with new intensity after

Felix's return from the war, Else refused to allow a separation between herself and her adored son. As we learn in "Mr. Z," she regularly searched for any blemish on his skin. By Heinz's adolescence that became a hunt for blackheads to pop. It was a Saturday afternoon ritual he had to endure. She had no genuine interest in him, he felt, only in his blackheads. "Her control over them fascinated her," and she approached these inspections "with an intensity, a self-righteous certainty, and adamant commitment that allowed no protest and created almost total submission." The actual ritual had two stages. At first she would describe in great detail the results of her examination. Then Else, who prided herself on her "long and hard fingernails," would squeeze the blackhead and proudly show an "extracted plug of sebum" to her son. It brought her great satisfaction, and Z/Heinz too felt at least some temporary relief. The worst days were when there was nothing to be found, or she was unable to get any pus out.[24]

His mother was everywhere in his life. Perhaps not surprisingly she entered his fantasy life, especially that surrounding his masturbation, which began, as best he could remember, at the time of Felix's return, and continued, "with increased intensity," after he got his own bedroom at eight. From the ages of five to eleven, Kohut says of Z, his masturbatory fantasies were nearly always elaborations of themes from *Uncle Tom's Cabin*, which his mother had read aloud to him when he was young. In his fantasies he was a slave bought and sold by other women for the use of women. He was like cattle, an object, without a will of his own. It got quite graphic: "He was ordered about, treated with great strictness, had to take care of his mistress' excrements and urine—indeed, in one specific, often repeated fantasy, the woman urinated into his mouth, i.e., she forced him to serve her as an inanimate vessel such as a toilet bowl."[25]

In his first (Freudian) analysis, Kohut came to understand this masturbatory activity as part of his early attachment to his mother, rather than a defensive retreat from competition with the newly present father in late infancy. In Freudian terms, in other words, Kohut was saying that his libidinal fixations with his mother lay deeply imbedded in his psyche and were more archaic than the more normal sexual yearnings and confusions associated with the Oedipus complex. From his second analysis, Kohut's self-psychological understanding of his fantasies and his masturbation in relationship to his mother put the stress instead on the depression and hopelessness that his mother's intrusiveness evoked in him. He felt annihilated. At a moment of great anxiety toward the end of his second analysis,

Heinz (as he says in "Mr. Z") had a dream of his mother. She is seen from behind and is starkly outlined. Part of the meaning was the way it evoked her icy withdrawal from him whenever he attempted something independent, especially in the direction of maleness. But in associating to the dream image, Heinz's greatest anxiety came in trying to think about the invisible, unseen, frontal view of his mother. The interpretation of the dream that he came to in his first analysis, namely that he feared seeing her castrated genitals, worked at the surface of his feelings. His later and, he felt, deeper interpretation of the dream was that, at his most primitive, preverbal level of consciousness, he feared that she had lost not her penis but her face.[26]

Kohut's parental imagoes, to conclude, worked at many levels in his consciousness. His father was a distant source of idealization whose abrupt departure was a kind of death for the baby Heinz. The mysterious return of Felix when Heinz was five stirred in the young boy vast hopes for the recovery of a father. Instead, Heinz encountered a man he mostly experienced as a grandfather, depressed, remote, and unavailable. There were times of closeness, and Felix in general provided an important, if silent, source of identification for Heinz. He always yearned for closeness with Felix, and at times found it, especially in his late teens and early twenties when he connected with his prematurely aged father. Then it was too late. Else, on the other hand, was so present in Heinz's early life that she allowed little room for maneuver outside of her orbit. At first her own happiness with life muted the harsher edges of her personality and made it possible for her to suffuse Heinz in his first year with love, devotion, peace, and happiness. When that world died in the fires of war, Else became desperate to hold life together for Heinz—and herself. Through the war years and his infancy, she mostly succeeded. But the return of Felix brought new challenges and the unraveling of her marriage. Heinz became her emotional pawn as her private world imploded.

Three

THE TUTOR

Else's extraordinary involvement with her son's body carried over to his mind and soul. She took Heinz everywhere and seldom let him out of her sight. She vacationed with him often and was particularly fond of taking him to Italy to visit art museums. She could not even stand to let him go to school, probably fearing in part that it would not be good enough. For four years, when Heinz was six to ten, through the equivalent of most of what we know as elementary education, Else kept Heinz at home and hired as principal tutor for him the man who would have been his teacher at school. For his last year in elementary school, Heinz then entered school with this same teacher. But many others contributed to his education. A French lady came to the apartment to speak French with him; as he said vaguely toward the end of his life, there were other "Fräuleins and Mademoiselles."[1] Else was clearly thorough in her selection of teachers, and Heinz got the best possible instruction in elementary reading, writing, literature, mathematics, and science.

In Vienna at the time, it was not unheard of, though it was unusual, to skip the first year of grade school. Heinz's friend, Siegmund Levarie, was kept home for his first year, though he now has no idea why. All Levarie recalls is getting instruction from a tutor and having to take an exam to pass into the second grade. Education was not bureaucratized and surrounded by the kind of legal pressures to which Americans are accustomed. It did not matter if some of your earliest education included a mix of home instruction and classroom learning. But even in its contemporary Viennese context Heinz's four years of home instruction and only one year in the classroom was a radical departure from the norm. Else's grip on her adored son was tight. Heinz only left his mother during the day to attend school at a time when American children would normally be going into fifth grade.[2]

The prospect of this first separation from his mother at ten may have also touched off something in her. Kohut's discussion of the mother's liaison in "Mr. Z," when she was "intensely involved with another man, a married friend of the family," dates the affair from the time when Heinz was approximately ten and Else was clearly in the wake of the deterioration of her relationship with Felix. After the war, Else and Felix fought all the time and the tension in the household was palpable. At eight Heinz got his own bedroom and his parents moved into separate rooms of their own. Either implicitly, or very likely explicitly—in a way that was quite common then in Vienna—Felix and Else agreed that their relationship had ended and that they would stay together as a family but find intimacy with others. Through these crises with Felix, Else kept Heinz by her side all day, every day, out of school, in sight and separated at most by a room when he would be with the tutor. But as the end of his first decade approached she knew she had to relent and send her son off into the world. She had to recognize that his developing needs required at least a measure of independence from her. At just that point, she in turn got "intensely involved with another man."[3]

Heinz, as a result, lost the one firm anchor for his self—his overly intrusive mother—just as he finally was dispatched from his tutors to begin his formal education. Things became highly atomized in the family. From "Mr. Z," we know that Felix was off making money, traveling, and having affairs. Else, while much more present (and still popping blackheads on Saturday, for example), began to develop her own life and interests. She was soon to open her own store in Vienna, something then rarely done by a woman of her class and regarded as quite progressive.[4] These complex changes in the emotional fabric of the family took their final shape in the years just before and after Heinz began school. As Else sent him from her side to school she turned from him to take on a lover, which may or may not have been her motivation but is probably how he experienced it. Things were never the same from sometime toward the end of Heinz's first decade. Everybody in the family started moving in separate directions, a process that only accelerated with time. Within a few years, for example, everybody in the family was taking separate vacations throughout Europe, including Heinz when he got a little older; the adult Kohut was to recall how he often received postcards from his parents from different ends of Europe. It all left him with a great sense of loneliness, which is the one term he always used to characterize his childhood. His adult friend, Ernest Wolf, reported that Kohut "did not talk very much about his childhood, hardly at all." Even celebratory events in his childhood were lonely. The adult Kohut once referred to "the *emptiness* of *my* birthday parties as a child," for which "the reason lies deep." "It was very sad," his widow said of Kohut's childhood. "When he talked of it I would cry."[5]

And yet Heinz survived the fragmentation of the family remarkably well, in no small part due to the lucky presence of a warmhearted tutor named Ernst Morawetz, who entered his life just as his mother left it. There had, of course, been many tutors in Heinz's life up to that point. He was quite familiar with adults coming into the house to instruct him in everything from math, to art, to French, to history. For the most part, as best one can tell, those tutors were terminated when he started school. But Else, it seemed, wanted Heinz to do exceptionally well. He was special. Perhaps she also empathized with his loneliness, not to mention feeling a good dose of guilt, as she moved outward for love and meaning and the family disintegrated. Her solution was to hire yet another tutor, only this one was mainly to be a companion. It was the spring or summer of 1924 and Heinz at the time was ten or eleven, while Morawetz, a university student, was somewhere between nineteen and twenty-three.[6]

Morawetz apparently had no formal educational tasks to accomplish with Heinz; that, after all, was being taken care of in school, where he was doing well. Morawetz's "job," it seems, was simply to provide extra intellectual stimulation for his young charge. Most afternoons after school, which finished at 1:00 p.m. in Vienna at the time, Morawetz would show up and take Heinz to a museum, an art gallery, or the opera, or they would read together or simply talk about interesting subjects. They developed a deep rapport. They communicated as much nonverbally as with words. One intellectual game they played was to think through how things might have happened differently if some important historical event were altered. The game required extensive knowledge and creative leaps of imagination. One person would wonder, for example, how the architecture of Vienna would have been altered if Socrates had not died. The one could follow the other through two millennia of cultural history with but an occasional question.

Morawetz seemed at the most important level to have been a savior for his intensely lonely charge. As Kohut later put it:

> I had this private tutor, who was a very important person in my life. He would take me to museums and swimming and concerts and we had endless intellectual conversations and played complicated intellectual games and played chess together. I was an only child. So it was in some ways psychologically life-saving for me. I was very fond of the fellow.

Morawetz was Heinz's first real friend. The boy's entire life up to then had consisted of older tutors, the ever-present Else, and a distant Felix. In Morawetz Heinz found companionship, connection, and deep empathy. Heinz learned a huge amount about the world from his older friend. In "Mr. Z," Kohut describes those years with the camp counselor/Morawetz as "extremely happy ones," maybe "the happiest years of his life, except perhaps for his early years when he possessed his mother seemingly without conflict." The boy idealized the older man, who was a "spiritual leader," able to share his "almost religious" love for nature, as well as teach him about literature, art, and music.[7]

The relationship between Morawetz and Heinz was also sexualized. As Kohut puts it in "Mr. Z" in a long dependent clause: "overt sexual contact between them occurred occasionally—at first mainly kissing and hugging, later also naked closeness with a degree of tenderly undertaken manual and labial mutual caressing of the genitalia. . . ." If we take that out of its Latinate armor, what happened is that they began by kissing and hugging each other and moved to lying naked, tenderly fondling each other and sucking on each other's penises, apparently without ejaculation. Kohut also reports that the relationship ended when Z/Heinz reached sexual maturity and the counselor/tutor once tried unsuccessfully to enter him anally and another time came when Z was caressing him.[8] Besides the discussion in "Mr. Z," Kohut once also told his colleague, Ernest Wolf, of "some sexual acting out as an adolescent" in which he had engaged.[9] There seems little doubt that the relationship with Morawetz was sexualized. The question is what does it mean?

Heinz probably put his experience with Morawetz into the context of the ancient Greeks, about whom he was beginning to read in depth. For the Greeks, it was normative for grown men to have sex with prepubertal boys in ways that did not interfere with their adult heterosexuality, or the future sexual orientation of the boy. Such sexual experiences were an extension of the self, not a limiting of it. Vase paintings of homosexuality, for example, are celebrations of maleness, not depictions of something corrosive or subversive. The Greeks expected and welcomed homosexuality. It realized something between men and did not close off possibilities in other areas.[10] Ancient Greece, however, was not the same as contemporary Vienna. As elsewhere in Europe, a sense of evil pervaded notions of homosexuality. It was not a form of sexual activity tolerated as normal, though Freud's theories were beginning to alter attitudes. A sexualized relationship with another male carried with it elements of shame. At the very least, Heinz had to have been ambivalent in his feelings about what he and Morawetz were doing, feelings that probably became clearer as he matured.

At the same time, Heinz's relationship with Morawetz was vital, loving, intimate, and deeply empathic. In his eyes the tie to the tutor was a wonderful and helpful one that sustained him through the second worst crisis (the first being when his father left for war) of his intensely lonely childhood. As he seems to have experienced it at the time, and certainly conceptualized it later, Heinz felt that the sexualization of his relationship with Morawetz was incidental and meant little to his own sexual identity. This understanding of the meaning of emotional connection and the devaluing of sex per se was to play a huge role in Kohut's later theories about the self. His position has often been misunderstood. He never questioned, for example, that there are drives. He once pointedly stressed in a taped interview intended for publication that "man wants to fuck and kill."[11] But the point of his disagreement with Freud is that our need for connection precedes and transcends our sexual or aggressive drives. The way we love sexually symbolizes and concretizes our deepest needs. The self is not, as Freud would have it, an accidental by-product of the vagaries in the development of the sexual instinct. Kohut sought to reverse that sequence and in the process create a psychology of the self.

Kohut's understanding of his relationship with Morawetz, in other words, yielded quite significant theoretical gain. And yet, at the same time, by current standards what went on sexually between Heinz and Morawetz can only be defined legally as childhood sexual abuse. Their sexual play was *not* the kind of casual and occasional homosexual activity that is often part of the experience of prepubertal boys. It was far more important and prolonged. Heinz's first love, one can say, was Ernst Morawetz. If such a seduction of a prepubertal boy by a man around twenty or older were to occur in contemporary America and become known, the man would most likely be punished and possibly incarcerated. It is called pedophilia. It may be that Kohut was deluded about the nature of his own victimization and confused about the way tender feelings are often an integral part of exploitation. But we also need to take seriously Kohut's own interpretation: "He [Mr. Z] insisted that sexuality had not been prominent: it was an affectionate relationship."[12] Heinz Kohut, the lonely preadolescent, idealized Ernst Morawetz, the university student who filled a huge hole in his life at just the right moment. The two merged to a remarkable extent, as Heinz clearly met as well some powerful self needs in Morawetz. What mattered in their relationship was the empathy and affection. It seems a reasonable argument. This is not to defend child abuse, which is abhorrent. But it may well be that our sense of the exploitation of children has become too ideological and leads us to miss the subtlety of love and connection that can arise even in deeply unequal relationships.

Four

YOUNG MAN KOHUT

For most of Heinz's adolescence the Kohuts lived in an apartment in the Ninth District, where they had moved after Felix returned from the war. Sigmund Freud lived not far off. Sigmund Lampl, Else's father, ran a dry goods store in the neighborhood that sold tools and other items. Else also opened her paper store, called Galanterie & Papierwaren, at Währingerstrasse 48 in the Ninth District around the time Heinz went off to gymnasium.[1] It was a small retail store offering paper goods for writing and school. Walter Lampl remembers her giving him free pencils and pads of paper when he went off to first grade in 1927, and it was probably established a few years earlier. Everyone in the family, and many in Vienna, remarked on the fact of a woman owning and running a store. It was not a project she handed over to others. She opened and closed the store, handled inventory, and hired and fired the help. Presumably, Felix staked her for the capital needed to set up the store, though it is not impossible that her father, with his own store nearby, helped as well. For Else it was clearly a move of great independence that brought her a sense of responsibility and accomplishment. For Heinz, however, it was yet another huge change that marked the transformative moment at the end of his first decade.

Felix Kohut, meanwhile, who had responsibility for marketing in Bellak & Kohut,[2] traveled frequently, which also met his emotional need to get distance from his difficult wife and maintain his relationships with his mistresses. He was very good at his business and by the mid-1920s was doing well financially. As a mark of the family's improved status, Felix and Else decided to build a house on the outskirts of Vienna, in Grinzing in the Nineteenth District, near the end of the trolley car line. It was a big investment and a decided move up the social scale, both in terms of class and ethnicity: the Ninth was a mixed urban community with many Jewish residents of modest means, whereas the population of the Nineteenth District was decidedly upper-middle-class and less than 1 percent Jewish. The move, largely because of the expense, proceeded in stages. At first the Kohuts just purchased the lot at Paradiesgasse 47. The family would visit the site to admire the trees and the setting and to prepare for their future lives. Some years later the Kohuts actually built the house, which they moved into in 1932. The house was comfortable but not splendid or pretentious. The furnishings were typically bourgeois, with soft couches and chairs in abundance. In the living room was a grand piano, which Felix and Heinz played at different times. A maid helped clean and serve meals, and a cook bought groceries and prepared the food, for what was, after all, a professional family with both parents working. In the driveway Else parked her 1928 Citroën C, which she had come to enjoy driving about town and from which she ferociously cursed at any male driver who dared to get in her way. Felix, it seems, did not drive.[3]

Felix and Else were involved in all kinds of cultural activities, separately and together. Heinz said he grew up in an "atmosphere of art and music." His parents read books all the time, and went to the theater, concerts, opera, and museums. They always had subscription tickets to the theater. As Siegmund Levarie put it, "that kind of thing was taken for granted." Kohut later joked that one of his images of the primal scene was of chamber music from the next room. Until he was fifteen or sixteen, Heinz was usually taken to the opera or the theater by his mother or Morawetz, as often as three times a week, though it was Felix who took him to see his first, and highly memorable opera: "When I was a boy in Vienna my father introduced me to the opera by taking me to *Die Meistersinger*. I have never forgotten that evening and, although my tastes have changed, the magic of opera has never ceased to affect me deeply." Levarie, who attended the opera just as often, recalls meeting Heinz accidentally at their first hearing of Beethoven's Ninth Symphony. They were both terribly excited and talked about it for years. Later, the two boys also went together to the opera and theater; it was cheap (two schillings), and standing room in the fourth gallery was sometimes free. When they were accompanied by their parents, however, they sat in reserved seats.[4]

In the fall of 1924, some four months after turning eleven years old, Heinz entered the Döblinger Gymnasium, located at Gymnasiumstrasse 183 in the Nineteenth District, where the Kohuts planned to build their house. It was a well-regarded school in the humanistic tradition of education. The eight-year program of study combined what Americans know as middle and high school; as well as at least the first year of college.

The Döblinger Gymnasium was undoubtedly the formative educational experience of Heinz's life. In this school he became completely immersed in the classical and humanistic traditions of Europe, which he ever after intensely idealized. The culture of the ancient world became as familiar to Heinz Kohut as that of the Europe in which he actually lived. The focus was on classical languages, which were studied at a very high level of sophistication; at fifteen years of age, for example, Heinz could read the *Iliad* and the *Odyssey* in the original Greek.[5]

Several teachers left their mark on Heinz. One was Rabbi Benjamin Murmelstein, his religion instructor.[6] Murmelstein was a kind and learned man who knew the classics well. There was nothing specifically religious in the instruction. The students did not study Hebrew with him, but they did learn about the Torah and the tradition of the Talmud. Another teacher, Ignaz Purkarthofer, taught history and became one of Heinz's "great idols." Purkarthofer was a large man who walked around with a great bundle of keys that gave him the air of a janitor. Heinz's friend, Siegmund Levarie, was surprised when he discovered Heinz had dedicated his last book in part to Purkarthofer (though he noted there were three misspellings in the name). "Heinz was sentimental," Levarie said.[7] But Heinz adored this teacher, who never quizzed the students about names and dates and was generally the "low man on the totem pole" because he was so easygoing. When he lectured a whole new world opened up for Heinz.

> I remember him talking about the French absolutarian rulers and the type of parks they built, how the trees had to be exactly in line, and how this corresponded with the economic system and the hierarchy of power distribution, and how this contrasted with the English garden and English society and the organization of the aristocracy vis-a-vis the king and the democratization that led them to handle their

landscapes differently. Ideas like that were tailor-made for
me to listen to.

An equally important influence on Heinz was his Greek teacher, Oskar
Weidinger, who took a great interest in his pupils. Heinz was deeply devoted to him (and looked him up when he first revisited Vienna in 1957).[8]
It happened that Heinz had Weidinger all six years that he studied Greek.
At the outset there were two classes in his Untergymnasium. Weidinger
was the Greek instructor for Heinz's group, which began its studies in
the third year. By the last two years enough of his classmates had flunked
out that the school combined the classes into one.[9] Weidinger was assigned to be the Greek teacher for these last two years. Such extended
contact six days a week for six years in one of his two favorite subjects
cemented the bond that Heinz felt for his devoted teacher. Weidinger also
was more relaxed with his students than many of the other instructors.
On Saturdays, when classes ended at noon, he invited as many as wanted
to stay and read the Greek tragedies.[10]

Weidinger's relaxed approach to his students was the exception to the
rule of strictness that prevailed in the Döblinger Gymnasium. Students
sat in desks in long rows from 8:00 a.m. to 1:00 p.m. Monday through
Friday and from 8:00 a.m. to noon on Saturday. The classes ran fifty minutes, with ten minutes in between. Besides Latin, Greek, and history, Heinz
studied German language and literature, mathematics with a man named
Scharf, physics, chemistry, some gymnastics, regular instruction in religion, and some work in singing and penmanship.[11] The overall atmosphere
was one of intense but high-level education that at times could be violent
and sadistic. Heinz told one story of a boy who became the scapegoat for
a teacher. Whenever the teacher got chalk on his hands he would walk
over and wipe them on the boy's hair. As Levarie put it, however, the
teachers ranged from "miserable sadists" to "loving, concerned, and warm
persons."[12]

The students survived because many teachers were in the latter category, for example Purkarthofer and Weidinger, because they had the
second half of the day to themselves, and undoubtedly because the extraordinary education they were receiving was itself empowering. They
also got back at the sadistic teachers in well-planned pranks that Heinz
talked about all his life. Once they all moved their desks forward imperceptibly, in unison, until they had the teacher pressed up against the wall.
Another prank was to hum quietly or twang some rubber bands on one

side of the room. As soon as the teacher went to that side of the room to investigate, the noise would stop there and begin on the other side. In perhaps their most colorful escapade, the class hired a trumpeter to play outside the window. The teacher yelled for someone to close the window, but before it could be done a student threw more money out so that the trumpeter would keep playing. Just as they reached graduation, Heinz and his peers published a traditional satirical newspaper that mocked the foibles of their teachers.[13] Playing pranks and being a trickster became part of Heinz Kohut's self style.

Heinz's actual academic performance at the gymnasium was quite good, though not brilliant, and at times and in some subjects decidedly mediocre. He consistently received a *sehr gut*, or A, in religion, German, and the minor subjects like writing and physical education. For the most part, he received a *gut*, or B, in the rest, including Latin, history, math, and science. There were, however, quite a few *genugend*, or C, grades. In 1924–1925, for example, he received C's in three major subjects—history, mathematics, and science. The next year he pulled up his grades in history (to A) but kept his C in math. In year IV (1927–1928) he received C's in Latin, Greek, history, and math, all of which he pulled up the following year—except for Greek. By year VI (1929–1930) Greek was up to a B but Latin had slipped back to a C. And so it went until his final marks for the last two years, which determined his class standing for his *Matura*, or diploma. Heinz received five A's, three B's, and two C's (Latin and mathematics).[14]

Education, however, continued for Heinz after school ended each day. For the first two years or so, he spent the afternoon with his tutor, Ernst Morawetz, in museums, at concerts, or in close conversation. There were other activities as well. Heinz often played chess, at which he was quite accomplished. Until he was thirteen he took piano lessons. He was just at the point of becoming very good. His friend Siegmund Levarie, who actually became a musician and one of the leading musicologists in the United States, recommended an outstanding teacher. But Heinz stopped at that point, though he would occasionally return to play the piano for pleasure. Heinz also played soccer quite often (he was the goalie), ran track, cycled, played tennis, and boxed well; some of these latter activities were taught in the gymnastics part of the school curriculum. He liked to ski and told a friend later how he would often ski alone for most of a day with his guitar strapped to his back, stopping occasionally to rest and play. Heinz began to smoke cigarettes at sixteen or seventeen. Levarie did not smoke, and it became a standing joke between them that if Levarie ever were to smoke he would take his first cigarette from Heinz. In the evenings there were opera and theater.[15]

He also read all the time. In school, of course, it was mostly the classics, from Homer to Goethe, that he absorbed. "I was a great reader when I was a child," he said late in life. He liked philosophy, including Schopenhauer, Nietzsche, and "even" Kant. Sometimes, he said, he and Siegmund Levarie would skip school to have more time to read, which is an image, if there was one, of truancy in the life of young intellectuals. "I used to sit in parks," Kohut said, "and read for hours on end." Heinz first read Freud's *Introductory Lectures* as an adolescent but was not particularly moved. Sometimes, they walked by Freud's house, but he was only important to them as one of many great Viennese thinkers whom they admired. The writer who stirred Heinz's imagination, however, was Thomas Mann, and the book that had the single greatest impact on the adolescent Kohut was *The Magic Mountain*. Heinz was on vacation in the mountains of Yugoslavia when he first read it; he then reread it twice in a short period. "I used to go rowing out on the lake, alone," Kohut said later, "and read *The Magic Mountain*."[16]

This philosophical novel is a kind of coming-of-age story for a young intellectual. Like Heinz himself, Hans Castorp is a lonely, inquisitive, talented young man. He is just out of university as the novel opens but rather indolent with his inheritance. He decides to visit his cousin Joachim at the tuberculosis sanatorium Bergdof in Davos, perched in the mountains. Hans enters the rarified, otherworldly atmosphere of death in the sanatorium with a mix of awe and fascination. A woman has just died in the bed to which he is assigned, filling his first night with confused dreams. Hans tries to ground himself but constantly gets confused, even lost, in the death imagery that surrounds him. A kaleidoscope of characters march through the pages of the novel, from Hans's dying cousin to Herr Settembrini, who discourses breezily on literature and philosophy as a counterpoint to the darker musings of Naphta, to Clavdia Chauchat, after whom Hans lusts. Settembrini senses there is something wrong from the outset with Hans's remaining at Bergdof. He is too young and too morbid, likely to get sucked into the vortex of suffering. He advises the young man to leave, to escape. The warning is not heeded. And indeed halfway through the novel, after extending his "visit," Hans is diagnosed by the chatty doctor, Behrens, with his own case of TB.

Hans Castorp finds an odd vitality in the dying world of Davos. It brims with the music of life in the thin air of the mountains. Music can always be heard between the lines of a Thomas Mann novel. Davos also breathes the life of the mind. Hans gains a new kind of education, as he takes in the ideas of Settembrini and forebodings of Naphta. He even encounters psychoanalysis from the assistant doctor, Krokowski, who is constantly foisting it off on the patients. Hans connects with his cousin in ways he never could before Bergdof, when they had not used each other's names in conversation because it seemed too intimate. And Hans mines a rich lode of relationships in the elaborate dining room where he takes his five meals a day. Bergdof is a world alive though filled with "Horizontals," as Settembrini calls the patients. The sharp contrast is to the seemingly alive world "below," the civilization of nineteenth-century Europe on the brink of its own demise in the slaughter of the First World War. In the final pages in a kind of dream sequence, Hans leaves Davos and joins the army to die in the war with his "face in the cool mire, legs sprawled out, face twisted, heels turned down." Farewell, says the narrator, "Farewell, Life's delicate child!" Self-discovery and death become one in the journey of Hans Castorp.

Art, as well, fascinated the young Heinz Kohut, and he became quite visually literate from his frequent visits to museums, at first with Morawetz and later with Levarie. Heinz liked classic paintings and came to know Italian art extremely well; later he compared his discovery of self, which he said was, in a sense, obvious, with the discovery of the equally self-evident but long-ignored concept of perspective in painting, which had been developed out of the work of the Florentine architect of the early fifteenth century, Filippo Brunelleschi.[17] Heinz also kept up with contemporary artists. In fact, Levarie reports being introduced to the subtleties of contemporary art by his friend. Heinz knew the work of the Secession (Gustav Klimt, Oskar Kokoschka, and others) and once, with great excitement, brought Levarie to see the recent work of Egon Schiele—an eye-opener for Levarie. Heinz read the most current critical writings about art and other aspects of culture. He knew the work of Karl Kraus, for example, who defined the moral standards for contemporary cultural developments in Vienna and even throughout Europe.

Heinz was also devoted to Robert Musil, who was widely regarded as the Austrian Proust. His masterpiece, *The Man Without Qualities*, was not to be published until later, but even in the 1920s he was respected by a small circle of intellectuals. Once, in an act of effrontery, self-confidence, and surprising assertiveness, at least as Levarie saw it at the time, Heinz phoned Musil upon the publication of his latest book and asked if he could come talk with him. Musil was probably so astonished that he agreed; in that age of hierarchy and status it was not the Austrian norm for famous writers to entertain eager adolescents in afternoon chats. Heinz was different. At all of sixteen or so, he showed up to visit with flowers of respect and had tea and a talk with Robert Musil.[18]

An important part of Heinz's cultural universe was his knowledge of all things French. Else made sure that he began to learn the language during those years of early home instruction. Later, his tutoring in French almost certainly continued. In the summer of 1929 he and Levarie also went to stay for two months with a Madame Vénacourt and her husband in St. Quai-Portrieux near St. Malo, along with thirteen or fourteen other lodgers from around Europe. Heinz and the others had French instruction in the mornings but were free to wander after that. All of this exposure made Heinz fluent in the French language and decidedly Gallic in his sentiments. "I spoke French well and I read French writers, knew the French Gothic cathedrals," he said late in life.[19]

The maturing of Heinz's friendship with Siegmund Levarie reached the point that their minds moved in a common track. At the end of their study at the gymnasium students had the option in the Greek class of taking a comprehensive exam or writing a thesis. Both friends decided to write theses. Levarie chose the ambitious task of comparing Xenophon and Plato on Socrates *and* translating a major portion of Plato's *Apology*. Levarie did well with the task until the end, when he simply could not find a way to conclude. Heinz, who of course had been discussing the subject with Levarie, offered to write the last couple of pages for him. The offer was accepted, and Heinz, without any difficulty, concluded Levarie's honors thesis for him.[20]

Heinz's own thesis proved more problematic, not for intellectual but political reasons. The thesis itself is a detailed, informative, and well-written analysis of Euridipes' play *The Cyclops*.[21] It is a substantial effort, forty pages long in German. He divides the essay into five parts. First, he mentions his three basic sources, though this "bibliography" is actually quite misleading, for the essay is very learned and in the course of it he draws on many other sources, including Aristotle, Herodotus, the Homeric stories in particular, and the Greek myths in general. In the second section, Heinz discusses the origin of *The Cyclops* in the satyr play tradition and how it shaped Greek tragedy. In the third section, "The Action and Its Effect on the Spectator," Heinz provides a detailed summary and analysis of the movement of the play. He notes the key turning points of the plot, the narrative structure in general, and how Euridipes keeps the rapt attention of the "spectator." In the fourth section, "The Character of the Personages as Motive Forces for the Action," Heinz analyzes the key characters and their symbolic meanings: Odysseus, Cyclops, and Silenus. In a final section, Heinz turns to what he regarded as an anomalous second ending to the play, which he guesses comes from the influence of the satyr play tradition.

Heinz's essay on Euripides, which was the triumph of his gymnasium education, got him into trouble with his detested Latin teacher, Franz Hartel. Although the thesis was written for Heinz's Greek teacher, Weidinger, Hartel, a fascist and member of the Nazi party, was on the committee that had to approve the thesis. Hartel charged that the thesis was too good and must have been plagiarized. It was a vicious blow for Heinz, who fought back for all he was worth. Harsh words were exchanged. Hartel openly mocked the thesis in class for its pretensions. "He said something about driving the nail into the coffin," said Levarie. The subtext of 1932 Viennese anti-Semitism hung in the air. Heinz's only recourse was to call in his father. Felix then had a shouting match with Hartel, who finally backed down. The thesis was accepted and Heinz graduated. But the furor was not without consequence. Hartel gave Heinz a C for his final grade in Latin. That C, together with another in math, kept Heinz from graduating with honors.[22]

Throughout his life, Kohut reveled in describing his adolescent activities in the German Youth Movement. This distinctively Germanic phenomenon, the Wandervogel, founded by Karl Fischer, took shape in the early years of the century and spread rapidly among educated middle-class youth. It was an intensely idealistic movement that was both a rebellion against modern, materialistic society and an attempt to connect with nature and earlier, imagined historical forms. The Wandervogel stressed the simple life. Its members rediscovered peasant songs and folklore. The medieval days of yore with its manly virtues and poetic love were its ideal; some groups even adopted medieval names and customs. But most of all they walked, or rambled, throughout the countryside and had "encampments" with huge fires, around which they would sit and sing their favorite songs. In time the Wandervogel became more ideological and authoritarian and was an important precursor to Nazism. But its origins and perhaps its essence were idealistic and romantic, and it sought to revitalize German youth at a time of alienation and utter deadness. Erik

Erikson, like Kohut, not to mention most middle-class boys (and girls in auxiliary groups) born between 1890 and 1920, was profoundly influenced by the Wandervogel. As Walter Laqueur, a historian of the movement, puts it: "Very deep emotional chords were struck; the genuineness of this experience cannot be doubted."[23]

As an adult, Kohut taught the Wandervogel songs to his son, Thomas, who can still sing them. Kohut always called them "Boy Scout songs," though this was simply to make them comprehensible in an American context. In fact, Kohut was also a Boy Scout, or Pfadfinder, as well as a member of the Wandervogel.[24] The Pfadfinder, though profoundly influenced by the Wandervogel, had a different history, were more specifically Christian in ideology, much more hierarchical, and less idealistic.[25] But it was the Wandervogel that seemed to have had the greatest impact on Kohut, and from which he once suggested "certain features" of his adult personality were drawn. "I am thinking here of a characteristic idealism I have," he said, which had the downside of making him a "bit of a pollyanna." But far more important benefits were derived from the experience: "I have not only the capacity to be enthusiastic myself, but also the ability to inspire enthusiasm in others for the causes in which I believe." That enthusiasm and idealism, he said, were part of his "nuclear self." They clearly had childhood precursors that got "firmed" during adolescence. With aging he saw in himself a shift away from his adolescent enthusiasms, less of the Pollyanna, and more of an emphasis on the continuity and survival "of the values for which I have lived."[26]

The idea of adolescence as a normative time of storm and stress in development is a relatively new one historically. Except for a thin layer of the elite in most cultures historically, children experienced sexual maturity late (at seventeen or eighteen) and then almost immediately married and started their own families. Neither families nor society allowed an extended search for a personal and sexual identity. In the last few hundred years, however, with improved diet and better housing and sanitation, not to mention other benefits of modern life like increased wealth, opportunities for travel, and more and better education, the time for the onset of puberty began to drop dramatically and the age at marriage moved forward in the life cycle. Adolescence filled the developmental gap.[27]

Psychoanalysis in the twentieth century has sought to provide a theory of what this relatively new stage of life is all about. Sigmund Freud was all but oblivious to it, but in 1936 his daughter, Anna Freud, wrote about puberty as the time for the return of the oedipal drama but now in a wholly new physical and sexual context. This radically new emotional setting allowed for symbolic enactments with substitute and appropriate objects—adolescents fall in love. She also was the first to stress many of the psychological confusions of adolescents, especially their totalistic approach to things, which is the psychological response to the experience of an overwhelming onrush of the drives. Anna Freud later extended these ideas in other essays that reflected her own tumultuous adolescence.[28]

The great theorist of identity, however, was Anna Freud's analysand, Erik Erikson, who stressed three principles about identity that are worth considering: the unconscious principle, or the ways in which we make the crucial decisions about love and work before we become fully aware of them; the epigenetic principle, or the grounding of identity in earlier developmental stages with their own crises; and the psychosocial principle, or the links between what happens inside the individual and the broader culture.[29] Erikson was undoubtedly overly schematic and somewhat parochial in his Western bias, not to mention the serious problem pointed out by feminists that he generalized a male model of development.[30] Still, Erikson helped isolate the key questions to ask about this stage of life. In his historical studies of Martin Luther and Mahatma Gandhi, he also suggested how to pursue the meanings of identity in life history.

Heinz Kohut's own self experience as it took shape in adolescence was grounded in an identification with European high culture. At this time he also formulated for himself the goal of becoming a doctor. Early on, it seems, he decided he could not be the creative artist his father had been. He liked to figure things out. Art was his love, science his work. He had a clear image of himself as an intellectual in touch with the great traditions of Western culture and the most current of Viennese developments. He was as *au courant* as anyone in the cafes along the Ringstrasse. He could be difficult and was what one might now call "spoiled." Walter Lampl remembers visiting often in the Kohut home. Heinz seemed distinctly bothered by this much younger rival—the only other child in the extended clan—and put Walter down in ways that he now considers in retrospect "mild abuse." In his relations with the world, Heinz showed a certain brashness and self-confidence but as well an overweening enthusiasm and exuberance for everything he read and encountered. He seemed at ease with the choices that were propelling him in a defined direction. He embraced the emergent consequences of his commitments.

There was, however, turbulence below the surface that was grounded in his profound alienation from his family and early experience, especially with his mother. He drew a veil over whole areas of his early life and youth and only allowed glimpses into it in an occasional anecdote. It was all too painful and sad, too filled with loneliness, even despair. This turning against his family seemed to involve for Heinz a rejection of his Jewishness, at least in part or at some level. He once told a colleague that he was not allowed to play with Jewish children when young.[31] Even more suspect was his claim (made in an interview published in the *New York Times*) that "my mother was a devout Catholic and dragged me to mass as a kid, and my father disapproved of that." Siegmund Levarie's reaction to this statement when he read it was one of utter befuddlement. Why would his old friend cover up being Jewish, he thought? Levarie added ironically that he did not check up every Sunday to see if Heinz and his mother were going to church, for the absurdity of the notion was self-evident to him. Walter Lampl echoed Levarie on this issue, as did Jacques Palaci, who knew Kohut well in Vienna during the 1930s.[32] It defies all the evidence to believe that Heinz Kohut was dragged to church by his mother on Sundays.

In fact, besides the bris as a child, Heinz was almost certainly bar mitzvahed on April 20, 1926 (the Sabbath most immediately preceding his thirteenth birthday), in the Müllnergasse synagogue.[33] The uncertainty about the bar mitzvah comes from the destruction of the actual synagogue records during Kristallnacht in 1938; it was not the practice to note the bar mitzvah in the records of the Kultusgemeinde. Heinz's father, his cousin, Walter (who was the only other child in the family), and his friend Siegmund were all bar mitzvahed, as was common among Orthodox *and* assimilated Viennese Jews. As Walter Lampl put it, he cannot imagine Heinz *not* being bar mitzvahed, though Walter himself was too young at the time (three) to remember the event. The family always went to the same temple, and it would have been most unlikely not to have brought the thirteen-year-old Heinz into the community with this ritual. Finally, Heinz probably performed the crucial religious ceremonies some years later at his father's funeral, including the recitation of kaddish in Hebrew, something he would not have been allowed to carry out if he had not been bar mitzvahed. Memories here are unfortunately dim. Walter Lampl can only vaguely recall the funeral but guesses that Heinz must have said kaddish. Levarie, who was also there, cannot recall the service itself but does remember the ceremony at the Jewish cemetery where Felix was buried.[34]

The bar mitzvah, which was a big public event in the synagogue, was no small matter for Heinz Kohut. In his contemporary Vienna it made the young man a member of the autonomous religious community. The bar mitzvah was also highly symbolic, marking his entry into adulthood and celebrating his commitment to the faith of the fathers. With the bar mitzvah Heinz was now subject to the commandments. Furthermore, the bar mitzvah is chosen rather than imposed, active rather than passive. As a rite of passage, it has great personal, religious, and ethnic significance. In preparation one must learn a fair amount of Hebrew and be able to read an extended passage from the Torah, as well as say the blessing. The service itself is in Hebrew, and the father plays a special role along with the rabbi. All wear yarmulkas, of course, as well as the tallis, or prayer shawl. To be bar mitzvahed does not preclude drifting from the faith in later years, but it makes one forever a member of the larger cultural world of Judaism.

The argument has been made with some passion that, as a thoroughly assimilated Jew, Heinz never incorporated Jewishness into his core self during his early childhood. "Jewish culture, Jewish food, Jewish jokes were alien to him," says Ernest Wolf. Kohut, he says, did not think of himself as a Jew because his family had been "totally assimilated." He therefore could not have later denied his Jewishness or have been conflicted about it in his youth, since in his depths he never thought of himself as anything but part of the larger Christian culture. Any other view fails, according to this argument, to empathize with the way Kohut experienced himself.[35]

Though plausible, such a blinkered interpretation seems to accept too easily the deeply conflicted and split-off attitudes toward his own identity as a Jew that in fact characterized Heinz Kohut. His psychological style, one might say, was highly dissociated. It is probably the case that Heinz at some level identified with the complex spiritual yearnings of his mother. Maybe in that psychological and spiritual sense he saw himself as having a special relationship to the Catholic Church, though it seems unlikely. Perhaps, as well, he was taken to mass once or twice by his mother as a child. Such experiences, however, did not make him Christian, any more than they made his mother a Catholic. Furthermore, there is no reason to believe that just because he grew up as an assimilated Viennese Jew he failed to consolidate a core sense of self as a member of the larger Jewish community of which he was an integral and formally initiated member. Kohut was not a believing or observant Jew, but that begs the question. It would seem that Heinz Kohut negotiated a number of contradictory elements concerning his religious and ethnic identity within which he constructed a personal myth that even in adolescence was moving toward self re-creation.

Five

IN THE UNIVERSITY

The University of Vienna, and especially its medical faculty, had long been regarded as one of Europe's most venerable institutions of higher learning. Founded by Duke Rudolph IV in 1365, it was a crucial part of the historical process of creating what became Austria. The university underwent a reformation under Empress Maria Theresa in the latter part of the eighteenth century. She placed particular emphasis on the faculty of medicine, which soon acquired a reputation for having one of the most advanced schools of its time. In the early nineteenth century the university was further modernized under the reign of Emperor Francis Joseph I, who stressed values of academic freedom and scientific research. Students and faculty were at the center of the uprising in 1848, which led to an occupation by the military and closer ties to the monarchy and church. After that the university negotiated a precarious position between learning and politics, but managed to become by the early twentieth century a "citadel of secular rationalism," in the words of Carl Schorske. Its imposing building on the Ringstrasse evoked the Italian Renaissance and symbolized liberal culture. More than any institution in Vienna, the university had traditionally resisted the ideological onslaught of the old right. In the 1930s, however, the university became a Nazi stronghold.[1]

Kohut left the cosy world of the gymnasium and entered the University of Vienna in the fall of 1932. He was nineteen years old. The university, as was generally true throughout Europe, had four faculties from among which students had to choose at the outset: philosophy (which covered everything from chemistry to music and literature), theology, law, and medicine. Kohut joined the medical faculty, as had long been his intention. It was a six-year program with labs but only minor tests along the way until the very end, when there was a series of difficult examinations. The assumption was that university students were young adults and could responsibly handle the challenge of professional study and training. There were no deans of students watching their behavior or any rules of conduct governing their life outside the classroom. There were also no dorms, which meant that Kohut lived at home throughout his studies at the University of Vienna. To enter the university was a developmental milestone, to be sure, but it lacked the transformative character of the rite of passage Americans call "going to college."[2]

Partly because Kohut lived at home during the six years he attended the University of Vienna (except for a half-year stay in Paris), he remained enmeshed in his relationship with his mother. Now he could tease and provoke her more freely; he took pleasure, for example, in her shock when he described at the dinner table his first dissection of a human cadaver. Kohut described himself in his early twenties (in "Mr. Z") as having a "pale and sensitive face, the face of a dreamer and thinker," though he adds that the face "stood in noticeable contrast to his athletic appearance." Physically he was quite healthy; his only medical episode was a tonsillectomy at the age of twenty. But Kohut was an isolated and lonely young man in his early years at the university. He read a lot and went to concerts and the theater with his mother and a friend with whom he had been close since school. It was a "pathological and unsatisfactory" mode of existence for an "intelligent and handsome young man." What kept it in a kind of delicate balance and spared Z/Kohut "the full impact of a confrontation with his inhibitions" was the continued presence of the friend. When that friend withdrew into another relationship, Z/Kohut was thrown into a kind of panic.[3]

Apparently, however, he did not turn to further homosexual activity after the relationship with Morawetz. At least that is how Kohut tells his story in "Mr. Z." We do learn there of his frequent, indeed addictive, masturbation, accompanied by masochistic fantasies. He says there were no explicitly homosexual elements of fantasy that accompanied the masturbation. Kohut, in fact, goes so far as to say of himself via "Mr. Z" that homosexual desire was not part of his adult self. He claims, speaking objectively about himself as the analyst of Z: "Indeed, although I was of course alert to the possibility of homosexual propensities, I could not, with the exception of an anxiety dream toward the end of analysis, discern any unusual homosexual tendencies in Mr. Z, or any unusual defensive attitudes concerning homosexual stimulation, either in the first or in the second analysis."[4] One has to wonder, in reading such an unlikely global statement, whether Kohut is denying his own homoerotic feelings in the form of a self-serving analytic stance.

In any event, what Kohut calls in "Mr. Z" his panic at his friend's "withdrawal into a relationship" may have been a disguise for the actual departure of Siegmund Levarie, who went to the United States in 1932–1933 at the invitation of his uncle. That year determined Levarie's desire to become a musicologist and live in America. He returned to Vienna in 1933 to finish his Ph.D. at the university, however, because a meaningful doctorate in musicology was not yet offered in America. For the remaining years of their study at the University of Vienna, Kohut and Levarie met often after their classes late in the evening in some coffeehouse to talk. Their conversation drifted from current reading to exhibits and performances and to what they had learned that day. Levarie can still recall the time Kohut explained to him with great enthusiasm why the stomach does not digest itself. Levarie thought it was a little disgusting.[5]

Kohut and Levarie continued as well to share their deep interest in Goethe, whose work they knew so well from their time in the gymnasium. Once when Kohut was in Paris, Levarie sent a complicated message in code that directed Kohut to a specific page of an early work of Goethe, the *Noten und Abhandlungen zu besserem Verständnis des West-östlichen Divans*. Kohut read Levarie's perplexing note while eating breakfast at a bistro, recognized the handwriting, and felt suddenly transported back to Vienna. He also felt he had to solve the mystery of the cipher immediately. Since he was in the Latin Quarter, Kohut wandered over to the library of the Sorbonne, where he searched out the relevant volume in a German edition of Goethe's work from 1840. With a "studious expression," Kohut says of himself ironically, he found the passage Levarie's cipher referred to and figured out that the message meant he was supposed to write his friend.[6]

Levarie was not the only friend Kohut spent time with in the famed coffeehouses of Vienna. He was in a social group that met and talked about ideas. It was inclusive and apolitical; even after the Anschluss some Nazis remained in it. Kohut was also close in these years to Peter Roth. Late in life Kohut wrote to Roth and recalled the many hours they had spent sipping coffee and talking about various authors and books, about

Rainer Maria Rilke and the meaning of the angel in his 1923 book, *Duineser Elegien*, and "a million and one things." Such conversations were the stock-in-trade of the coffeehouses, which, as Stefan Zweig pointed out, were a peculiar Viennese invention. They were a democratic club to which you were invited for the price of a cup of coffee. People would sit for hours, nursing one or two cups. All kinds of newspapers and magazines from around Europe would be available to peruse. But most of all you talked and talked and talked. Kohut himself said he often talked in the coffee-houses until 3:00 a.m. With Peter Roth, Kohut was in fact close enough to have their coffeehouse conversations spill over to Roth's apartment: "One evening we sat together in your apartment, talking for hours, drinking Cognac as we talked. When we wanted to get up we couldn't, either of us. But you could reach over to the coffee-maker & brew us a strong cup of coffee or two, and that got us going again."[7]

Kohut's reading and interests, as all this suggests, continued to be focused on literature and the arts. He wrote poetry and at least one libretto for a friend, Franz Krämer, who was a student of the great modernist composer Alban Berg. Kohut enjoyed his work in medicine, but that was professional and did not engage his soul. One friend who knew Kohut in the 1930s says he never remembers him once saying anything about Freud or psychoanalysis. But that may reflect the vagaries of memory. In fact, it seems, Kohut was reading Freud, but without the fascination of later years. "[Reading Freud] seemed interesting," he said later, "but not deeply stirring." Kohut moved toward depth psychology slowly. Levarie can recall his friend beginning to develop a more serious interest in Freud in the 1930s, though hardly with the passion of his next decade. "We were very catholic in our reading," as Levarie put it. "Everyone in Vienna was interested in Freud and psychoanalysis." It was, he said, "in the air." One of Kohut's best friends in medical school was the president of the Association for Medical Psychology. He invited various speakers who interested Kohut, but he found the group itself odd. They were intrigued by mysticism and had special concerns with astrology and homeopathy. "I had never been taken by mystical persuasions," Kohut said of himself. And he found Freud "guilty by association."[8]

Along with literature, music continued to absorb Kohut's attention. He continued to attend opera and concerts regularly. After one concert, he followed Wilhelm Furtwängler to a restaurant to watch him eat. Kohut positioned himself near enough to the famous conductor to carry on a conversation with him. He felt no compunction or shyness. He asked Furtwängler politely if the Camembert cheese was runny enough and if the rest of the food was to his liking. On other occasions, Kohut (together with Levarie) sneaked into the university concert hall to listen to rehearsals of Arturo Toscanini conducting. It was a glorious experience.[9]

Kohut's interests were also broadening, and one of his discoveries of the early 1930s was American jazz. In his usual way, Kohut learned all that he possibly could about this distinctive form of music from his remote location in central Europe. Improvisation, the essence of jazz, seemed to appeal to his sense of creativity. In Vienna before 1938—that is, before the takeover by the Nazis, who found jazz abhorrent—there were regular jazz concerts on Sunday mornings at ten o'clock in a park. The performers were mostly visiting musicians from America. Hans Lampl, Else's brother, a cultured man himself, used to go with Kohut to these concerts. Afterward they would talk for hours. The two grew quite close, and Hans once took his nephew on a vacation with him to Italy. Kohut also took to playing jazz records on his phonograph while he studied. Walter Lampl remembers once seeing Kohut standing with his open textbook while he waved his arms conducting an imaginary group blaring forth a jazz composition.[10]

In 1936 Kohut decided to do some internships—or, perhaps more accurately, externships—in two Paris hospitals. He was in his fourth year of medical school when he embarked on this study abroad, which lasted from late February through the end of August.[11] It is not clear how the arrangements came to be made, but Kohut probably used some contacts at the university. It was not an uncommon practice to leave the university for a while for special training, though the length of time Kohut was gone was extraordinary. In an institutional sense, it was easy. There was no formal permission required. You asked a friend to register you in the enrollment book for the courses missed during your absence. There was nothing illegal or immoral about it. The professors did not care at all. Your only obligation was to complete exams at the end of your studies, not in individual courses along the way. Of course, you wanted to be a familiar face when exam time came, and there was some advantage in knowing your professors and their idiosyncrasies. But you certainly had no obligation to be in class every day.[12] The courses Kohut missed that semester included surgery, internal medicine, infectious diseases, anatomy, pharmacology, and psychiatry. He picked up the knowledge for these courses on his own.

In Paris Kohut worked first in an internal medicine ward at the Hôtel-

Dieu, one of the largest hospitals in Paris at the time, right next to the Cathedral of Notre Dame. After that he transferred to the Hôpital St. Louis, which specialized in cases of syphilis. The Hôpital St. Louis was a particularly powerful experience. What one sees, he said in a letter to Levarie, is "truly dreadful. You have no idea (and I had none as well) how hideous this syphilis is." He had seen a Negro that day with a "sorrowful expression" who showed him his sores. Kohut was aghast. For the rest of his life Kohut remained intrigued—and horrified—at the devastating effects of tertiary syphilis. And yet Kohut sought to place its horror in some kind of philosophical context as he wrote Levarie, looking out the window at the soft colors of early spring in Paris. "Life is downright strange—what with the green of trees and syphilitic sores—but sometimes on the whole rather beautiful, is it not?"[13]

Despite these important involvements and experiences, it is pretty clear that the medical student did relatively little serious work during his stay in Paris and spent most of his time in the museums and concert halls. It was a time to enjoy life for him and soak up the culture of Paris. He also "discovered girls" in Paris, as Kohut later told Jerome Beigler, though it is curious he says nothing about this in a disguised way in "Mr. Z." Did he have a relationship with a woman, or did he go to prostitutes? Certainly neither his friend Jacques Palaci (who was in Vienna *and* Paris with Kohut) nor Levarie nor Walter Lampl—the key witnesses to young Kohut—ever mentioned an affair in these years, and Kohut says of young Z that he was "unable to form any relationships with girls."[14] That leaves only prostitutes, who were readily available and a convenient means of satisfying the sexual needs of a shy young man. It does make some sense. Kohut was at last away from the stifling grip of his mother, alone in romantic Paris. It may have been the time and place to take that decisive step toward maleness and lose his virginity.

Perhaps Kohut's academic half year abroad at some level was also a modeling of himself after the young Freud, who left Vienna in the 1880s for Paris, where he attended some of Charcot's lectures on hysteria. Kohut seems never to have mentioned such an idea to anyone and it shows up in none of his writings (or taped interviews). But who knows what goes on at the deepest levels of consciousness (and unconsciousness)? The later sequence of Kohut's professional life, from the study of medicine to a specialization in neurology, later psychiatry, and finally psychoanalysis, bears a striking resemblance to the steps in Freud's own. In the mid-1930s this identification with Freud, to the extent that it existed, was not at all consciously clear to Kohut; indeed, he studied syphilis rather than psychiatry in Paris. Still, Kohut certainly knew well of Freud's life and was already then moving toward psychoanalysis. Perhaps what one can say with reasonable conviction is that, as Kohut later moved toward a closer identification with Freud, he may well have retrieved for subsequent psychological use his experiences in Paris as the first step in that process.

One of Kohut's good friends in Paris was Jacques Palaci, a warm, cultured, and outgoing man. Palaci, who was also studying medicine at the Sorbonne, suggested that one reason he connected with Kohut was that Palaci spoke perfect German and Kohut, while fluent in French, felt more comfortable speaking German. Palaci was two years younger than his Viennese friend, but because of how their birthdays fell they were only a year apart in school.[15] Palaci knew twelve languages, many fluently, and played the violin. At the time he had no intention of studying psychiatry and was in medical school mainly because he wanted to find something useful to do with his life. He was a member of a distinguished and wealthy Sephardic Jewish family from Turkey. Palaci had relatives who had served the sultan and had distinguished themselves in various ways over the years in the Turkish government. Palaci's father, however, was a businessman who worked in steel. He had offices all over Europe, including Paris and Vienna. Once when Palaci was a child the family took a trip to Paris. There were so many relatives and children and governesses that his father had to take over the whole floor of a fancy hotel.[16]

Once in an interview I asked the voluble Palaci what Kohut was like in Paris when he was twenty-three. Palaci paused and smiled as he conjured up the image of his old and dear friend from the distant era. Kohut, he said, was enormously ebullient and exuded warmth. He had a captivating smile and great charm. He was athletic-looking, though stocky, and had abundant "blond locks." "He was very seductive," Palaci said. He was somewhat out of sync with his peers and generally seen as eccentric but by no means weird. He was certainly not regarded as a genius or anything more than a very interesting young man in a circle of equally talented students. Kohut also had a peculiar "narcissistic walk," which with some humor Palaci stood up and imitated in the middle of the busy restaurant where the interview was being conducted. With an extremely erect posture, his shoulders thrown back, his head held high, and his chin jutting in the air, Palaci swung his arms in an exaggerated way and kicked out his legs with each step. After the demonstration, Palaci added that there was a certain haughtiness to Kohut's walk, a large degree of self-absorption, and not a little "prissiness" to it.

After the academic year was over, Palaci invited Kohut to visit him in Istanbul that summer of 1936. Kohut agreed, but the two friends differed over the best time for the visit. At last Kohut arrived in Istanbul and stayed for two and a half weeks. He came with a gift of a complete set of Goethe. Kohut also proceeded to have a strong flirtation with Palaci's sister, Laura. For her part, Laura seemed to have fallen in love with Kohut. Laura, a good pianist, would play for Kohut, and then they would talk by the hour. Unfortunately, Laura Palaci later developed severe psychia-tric problems and was hospitalized. Her treatment during the 1940s prompted Palaci himself to become a psychoanalyst.

In one respect, Kohut's self-presentation baffled the Palaci family. He seemed to be Jewish, had a Jewish name, and had Jewish sensibilities. But in all the discussions of politics and culture he acted as a non-Jew and put himself outside of the frame of reference of Jewish concerns. When talk turned to the complicated ways in which minorities were discriminated against in the Ottoman Empire after 1919, for example, Kohut showed no sympathy for or understanding of the status of Jews within the empire. At the time, jurisdiction over Turkey itself was divided among Britain, France, and Italy, and the many different minorities, including the Jews, suffered various indignities. It was very complex, and the family often discussed these legal, social, and political issues. It was in these kinds of discussions that Kohut's distance and apparent non-Jewishness manifested themselves. Kohut expressed a tolerant and accepting attitude toward Jews, as though their concerns did not affect him personally. Palaci at the time felt something was false, and he and his entire family talked about it after Kohut left.[17]

Yet the two friends became very close. Largely influenced by Kohut, Palaci transferred from the Sorbonne to the University of Vienna in the fall of 1936. As before, he and Kohut saw each other in the coffee houses and at concerts, though their studies, now that they were further along, took more attention. Palaci was surprised, however, that Kohut failed to include him in his family, especially after the warm hospitality Palaci's family had extended to Kohut in Istanbul. During the two years that Palaci knew Kohut in Vienna, he was in Kohut's home only three times. Palaci described the house as having an atmosphere of "solitude." He said there was "no feeling of life there." Neither parent was ever visible. The occasional lunch to which Palaci was invited was formally served by a maid in a black outfit with a dainty white napkin around her waist. Kohut in general had a strange reluctance to share information about his family, as though he felt a deep shame. Palaci, for example, was never told about the death of Felix in 1937.[18]

That death was in fact traumatic for Kohut. Felix, it seems, developed an acute form of leukemia—for which there was no real treatment then— and died within six months, on November 30, 1937. His son was "devastated," as his cousin Walter Lampl put it. Lampl recalls dropping by the house to offer his condolences. Kohut was sitting at the piano, his hands gripping his arms, crying uncontrollably. The funeral three days later was held in the Müllnergasse synagogue, where all important family rituals had been conducted. Felix was then buried in the Jewish cemetery with an appropriately marked gravestone. It is not clear whether the family sat shiva.[19]

That loss of his father, it seems, and the emptiness it left in his life, prompted Kohut to seek psychotherapeutic treatment with a man named Walter Marseilles. The treatment was brief, but it is significant that Kohut's decisive move toward the world of psychotherapy was impelled by the death of his father. In some ways Walter Marseilles was an odd choice. He was actually not a psychoanalyst but a psychologist who was interested in the Rorschach test. Esther Menaker, an American who was analyzed by Anna Freud and who studied at the Vienna Psychoanalytic Institute during the 1930s, knew Marseilles then (and during the war in America) and found him "arrogant, pushy, and very difficult."[20] After Marseilles left Vienna, he first failed as a therapist in New York, presenting himself, it seems, as an analyst, and then moved to Chicago, where he persuaded Sears, Roebuck & Co. to hire him as a graphologist to evaluate credit applications based on handwriting. He had some passing contact with Kohut at the time. Much later, in the mid-1970s, after Marseilles had returned to Germany, he looked up Kohut, who was giving a lecture in Munich at the university. He asked, "Did I damage you much?" Kohut replied politely, "No, you just took things much too fast." Marseilles followed that up some months later with a strange transatlantic phone call, saying he was being persecuted by the U.S. State Department and seeking Kohut's help. He died shortly after that.[21]

At least Marseilles was available as a non-Jew in the steadily fragmenting world of Viennese psychoanalysis.[22] Of the fifty-six members of the

Psychoanalytic Institute in 1932, only fifteen remained by 1936. Recent graduates, like Erik Erikson, left as soon as they completed their work at the Institute. Freud's books were burned. Anti-Semitism was becoming increasingly open and virulent.[23] When Esther Menaker arrived in Vienna in 1930 with her husband, William, both of whom were agnostic American Jews, they stumbled on a *Fackelzug*, or torchlight parade of the Nazis around the Ring. Thousands of angry brown-shirted men were involved. The family the Menakers were staying with told them such *Fackelzüge* went on all the time. The Menakers were enraged, and that parade and the general atmosphere of anti-Semitism caused something of a crisis of consciousness for them; William Menaker said that Hitler made him a Jew (*"Hitler hat mich geheilt"*).[24] The great crisis for the Viennese, of course, was not to come until the spring of 1938, but a sense of creeping danger was seriously undermining the psychoanalytic community well before that. Freud and his colleagues (those who remained) mostly downplayed the extent of the threat and in retrospect clearly placed much too much emphasis on the apparent differences between Austria and Germany. There was to be no bulwark against Nazism.

Kohut's treatment with Marseilles was brief because it was so ineffective. Once Kohut had a dream in which he was looking into an enormous deep hole, which he was afraid he was going to fall into. There was, in fact, a deep hole in Kohut's life at the time, and the world itself was something of an opening chasm. Marseilles's interpretation, however, was that Kohut felt the therapist was going to push him into it.[25] Kohut, though hardly expert in these matters as yet, had little patience with such premature transference interpretations and left Marseilles within a few months. He did retain, however, one apparently enduring connection to Marseilles: a knowledge of shorthand, which became his preferred mode of writing for the rest of his life. Even as an accomplished author, Kohut always wrote his first drafts in these weird Austrian German shorthand squiggles, dictated from them in English into a recording machine, had that typed up and then endlessly revised. Kohut's knowledge of shorthand seemed related to Marseilles, who had interested him in attending a lecture by a graphologist, Ludwig Klages. Kohut recalled his initial interest in graphology much later in writing to his old friend, Peter Roth, who had also been in treatment with Marseilles in the 1930s.[26]

After he left Marseilles in early 1938, Kohut seems to have immediately sought out August Aichhorn for an analysis. Aichhorn was a talented, affable figure in Viennese psychoanalysis, a close friend of Freud (with whom he often played cards), and warmly regarded for his work with delinquents. He was a nonmedical analyst and a Christian, which is why he could remain relatively unharmed, even through the war. One of his sons, however, a conservative Austrian nationalist, was interred in Dachau for a while before the war. Aichhorn was born in 1878 after his father's career in banking had collapsed in the crash of 1873. The impoverished young man turned to education and began his career as a schoolmaster in Vienna in the late nineteenth century. From there he moved on to work with delinquents and in time ran two reform schools after the First World War. Anna Freud met him through her work with children and encouraged him to go into psychoanalytic training. After some hesitation he undertook his analysis and training courses in 1922 at forty-four years of age. His first and only book, *Wayward Youth*, was published in 1925; it included an approving introduction by Freud himself.[27] Aichhorn was much beloved: "A favorite photograph of Aichhorn," says one biographical account, "reveals a smiling *bon vivant* with a cavalier beard and hat tilted at a rakish angle. This was no thin-lipped pedagogue but a lover of life. . . ."[28]

Why Aichhorn? First and most important, Aichhorn had a reputation as a master clinician, which, after Marseilles, was a blessing. Having been burned once, Kohut probably decided to go right to the top. Second, Aichhorn's Christianity was probably a modest assurance of continuity in the unstable world of Viennese politics in early 1938, as well as reflecting Kohut's own complex identifications. For the second time, Kohut sought out a non-Jew as a therapist in a professional world that was almost entirely Jewish. Finally, Aichhorn was one of the closest living links in Vienna to Freud. That connection legitimized Aichhorn, but Kohut was also moving along a path toward psychoanalysis more than even he may have consciously recognized.[29]

Actual analysis with Aichhorn vastly deepened Kohut's interest in the field. Kohut most of all liked the kind of integrity Aichhorn brought to the clinical encounter. Kohut found Aichhorn "classical" in his practice— which meant using the couch, remaining mostly silent, and interpreting material in terms of oedipal themes—but there was a kind of "human freedom" in the man that gave Kohut a "basis of freedom" in himself. Aichhorn was not "stodgy, strait-laced, or overly reserved." If anything, the straitlaced one was Kohut himself. Aichhorn used to tell him with a gentle humor: "If only I could inject into you some of the blood of my delinquents!"[30]

Aichhorn, it seems, was also loose with what are often called "parameters" in psychoanalysis, which basically means breaking the rules. In a
wonderful exchange between Kohut and Aichhorn after the war, Kohut
asked about Schnidi, the dachshund that was always jumping on his stomach and interrupting his associations. Aichhorn replied that poor Schnidi
had long ago left for the "eternal hunting grounds" and described his
gruesome death in 1940 after eating something on a walk. Kohut in turn
replied: "Poor Schnidi, he was very close to me—he must have often had
to fulfill the role of brother to your patients and felt some ambivalent
feelings directed on to him, but I, an only child, had more of a feeling of
identification with him." Kohut, it seems, never lost his fondness for the
humanity that Aichhorn allowed himself to reveal to his patient. Kohut
once gave a photograph of Aichhorn to his colleague, Ernest Wolf, who
had just published an article titled "Ambience and Abstinence." On the
back of the photograph Kohut inscribed: "Lots of ambience and little
abstinence."[31]

There was, as well, a connection with Aichhorn through Elizabeth
Meyer, whom Kohut later married. Meyer, born in 1912, was from a Protestant German-American family in Wisconsin. After attending Wheaton
College in Massachusetts for two years, she transferred to the University
of Wisconsin to finish her B.A. in 1934, majoring in social work. As a teen-
ager she had gotten to know the powerful Chicago psychoanalyst Helen
Ross at Camp Kechuwa, which Ross ran on the Upper Peninsula of Michi-
gan. Ross continued to mentor Meyer after the camp in a variety of ways.
It was she who encouraged Meyer to study social work. Ross also con-
vinced Meyer that the best training for her after college would be in
Vienna, at the source, after which she could make a mark for herself in
America. Ross even made the arrangements for Meyer to be analyzed by
Jenny Waelder in Vienna.[32]

Elizabeth Meyer came to Vienna to study psychoanalysis in 1936. She
rented a room from a friendly and supportive family and from her window could look out at the spires of St. Stephen's Cathedral. She made
many friends, went skiing often, and got deeply into her analysis. Meyer
also enrolled in various courses at the Institute, including one taught for
social workers by August Aichhorn. She never met or heard of Heinz Kohut,
but their mutual connection to Aichhorn (and, of course, to Vienna) helped
cement their relationship later on. Meyer stayed in Vienna until 1939
and left with Jenny Waelder, her psychoanalyst husband, Robert, and
their two daughters; it was in fact only because of Meyer's protection

that the Waelders were allowed to leave. Together they sailed back across the ocean. On the boat, however, Robert Waelder made a pass at her, which she and Kohut laughed much about later, though one wonders how she felt about it at the time.[33]

For all this good feeling and the important role Aichhorn played in Kohut's life, there was a shadow side to August Aichhorn. Jerome Beigler, who was later analyzed by Kohut and entered the field himself, was a young psychiatrist with the U.S. Army in 1945. He was stationed near Vienna and went to visit Aichhorn on the encouragement of Lionel Blitzsten from Chicago. As a gift, Beigler took the famous analyst a carton of cigarettes. Beigler ended up staying with Aichhorn for two days and talking at great length. He was not impressed. He found Aichhorn to be fiercely conservative and anti-Russian, with hints of anti-Semitism. Beigler asked Aichhorn about his two former analysands, Paul Kramer and Kurt Eissler, who were then rising stars in Chicago. Aichhorn was particularly high on Eissler, whom he saw as his successor and the future leader of psychoanalysis in America. Aichhorn never once even mentioned the name of Heinz Kohut in any context, though of course he might have been maintaining professional confidentiality.[34]

Six

A CRUMBLING UNIVERSE

A politically divided and militarily puny Austria proved defenseless against the German colossus that emerged after 1933. Anschluss, or union, between Austria and Germany, which had long been the dream of many on the right *and* the left in both nations, came increasingly to mean in the real world of politics the forceful takeover of Austria by Hitler. A state of continual crisis filled the air in relations between the two countries. In 1933 Hitler tried to destabilize the Austrian economy. The next year he surreptitiously prodded the Nazi party in Austria to attempt a putsch, which failed but led to the death of the fiery Chancellor Engelbert Dollfuss and the appointment of the more docile and lawyerly Kurt von Schuschnigg. Much independence was traded away in the next few years. The end of Austria seemed imminent.

By early 1938 the situation in Austria had become extremely tense. In February Hitler summoned Schuschnigg to Berchtesgaden, where he put on a tantrum and forced the Austrian chancellor to sign a protocol that virtually sealed his country's future. By the agreement, the openly pro-German Arthur Seyss-Inquart was made minister of the interior with powers over the police, the Nazi party was given new political status, and those still jailed from the 1934 putsch were freed. Once Schuschnigg returned to Vienna, however, and was freed of Hitler's demonic presence, he began to waffle. Feeling he could afford to resist, Schuschnigg defiantly decided to hold a plebiscite on March 13 asking the Austrian people in essence whether they wanted to remain a free, proud, and independent country. The wording would have assured the outcome. Hitler, needless to say, was enraged, for he knew such a vote would humiliate him as well as the Austrian Nazi party, which was nowhere near majority status in the country. On Friday, March 11, he therefore ordered an invasion of Austria under the command of Hermann Göring. That afternoon Schuschnigg called off the plebiscite and ordered the army not to resist, then resigned himself. Later in the day, from his corner office in the Ballhausplatz, he spoke to the nation in a radio transmission. He explained that he was yielding to force in order to prevent bloodshed. He had surrendered Austria to Germany, whose troops were at that moment marching across the border. Schuschnigg ended with a tearful *"Gott schuetze Oesterreich"* ("May God protect Austria"). There was an audible scuffle as the Nazis in the room forcibly pulled Schuschnigg away from the microphone.[1]

The Nazi takeover of Austria left Kohut with the feeling, as he put it, of a "crumbling universe." It caught him completely off guard. "I was passionately involved with German and Austrian culture," he recalled. "This was the peak of humanity to me—Goethe and the great German philosophers and writers and the German musicians and the whole refined Viennese culture." He loved that culture and completely identified with it. Then, all of a sudden "these bullies" came along and said they were the real Germans and he was nothing, a foreigner who didn't belong. Overnight he became radically devalued and a persona non grata. It profoundly affected his self-esteem. "It was the end of a world, it was the end of an era," he said. He felt annihilated. "I had the feeling it was the end of my life," not in the biological sense but in terms of the continuity of "my cultural existence." Vienna after the first war, he said, had been impoverished but enormously rich culturally. He had been at the center of all that—and quite separated from politics. He suddenly had it all taken away; his life lost meaning. Heinz Kohut was traumatized for the second time by war.[2]

The Anschluss confronted Kohut and all Jews in Vienna with a radical new reality. It no longer mattered whether you were educated or illiterate, assimilated or orthodox, rich or poor. Hermann Göring, stating official policy, declared that Vienna must be *Judenfrei* (free of Jews) in four years. Beginning on Saturday, March 12, 1938, Austrian mobs, boiling over with rage, began to mistreat all Jews and loot stores. The initial targets were the more visibly identifiable Jews from the shtetl who were concentrated in the Leopoldstadt district of the city. The mobs forced these Jews in their traditional black robes to get on their knees and wash the sidewalks

with the fringes of their religious undergarments, and sometimes, as an
even more malicious joke, they made the men use their beards. Riots and
marches were staged everywhere. Siegmund Levarie remembers running
into an angry group returning from a rally that Saturday. Among the
screaming men was Franz Hartel, the Latin teacher from the gymnasium
who had charged Kohut with plagiarizing his honors thesis.[3]

A few days later Jacques Palaci encountered Kohut in front of a famous cafe on Währingerstrasse, across from the Anatomical Institute,
which was a part of the medical school. The cafe already had a sign posted
in front of it that read "No Dogs or Jews Allowed." Both bemoaned the
terrible state of things. Palaci said that at least Kohut didn't have to worry,
to which Kohut replied: "What do you mean, of course I do, I'm Jewish." "Oh," said Palaci, "it must be some grandfather who was Jewish."
"No, I am Jewish on both sides," said Kohut. Palaci accepted the news
gravely but still found it so astonishing that he fretted for the next half
century over whether what Kohut told him really could be true.[4]

That summer a series of anti-Semitic laws were passed. Jews were not
allowed to go into the parks. The benches were marked *Nur für Arier*
("For Aryans only"). Jews could no longer go to the theaters, the cine-
mas, or the opera. Jewish students were forced out of gymnasiums and
the university. Jewish businesses were handed over to Aryan "comptrol-
lers." All Jewish bank accounts were frozen. The assault on Jews was as
total as it was offensive.[5]

A continual crisis gripped Kohut's life from the moment of the Anschluss.
There were assaults on his emotional well-being at every turn. He was also
confronted with one immediate and another symbolic loss. Most immediately, Kohut's best friend, Siegmund Levarie, left for Chicago that July.
Because Levarie had already planned to go to the United States, he had
a visa lined up and thus had no trouble getting out.[6] Levarie's departure left Kohut, once again in his life, alone with only his mother in a
hostile world. At the same time, however, Levarie remained Kohut's best
hope for salvation from the ravages of a mad, anti-Semitic Vienna.
Levarie had promised to get Kohut out of Vienna as soon as he could
make the arrangements with his uncle in Chicago to provide the affida-
vit. One concrete problem Kohut faced was that he was apparently to
be denied his M.D. after six years of hard work at the university medical
school. He was finished with his course work, so there was nothing technically to disqualify him (unlike the younger Palaci, who never actually
finished medical school). New Nazi regulations, however, prevented Kohut

from taking his exams at the normally appointed time that spring. For the entire spring and summer of 1938, he thought he would not get his degree. Kohut was haunted by where he could finish his studies. Switzerland was apparently "as good as shut off" to Jews, he wrote Levarie, and it would take two and a half years of study to complete his degree in Prague. Chicago seemed more hopeful, and clearly Levarie was urging it; besides, Aichhorn had "many friends" there (especially his two former analysands, Kurt Eissler and Paul Kramer) "who certainly will be able to help me on in their field." Kohut, however, fretted about a stipend and how he would live, as well as whether his degree, if he should get it, would be sufficient for him to get a position. His life was all filled with doubts and anxieties. But at least Levarie was not letting him down. "Your letter arrived today," Kohut wrote at the end of August. "You can imagine how anxiously I was waiting for it. The best: the wonderful matter-of-factness with which you undertake the great efforts connected with all of this and which has allowed me and you to grow together into a common 'we.' You know: Gratitude is a state of being!"[7]

The symbolic loss Kohut faced was Freud's departure from Vienna on June 3, 1938. It was virtually the final blow to psychoanalysis in Vienna.[8] Sigmund Freud represented one of the greatest minds that Vienna had produced and epitomized the culture Kohut idealized. Freud as well was newly significant to Heinz Kohut as the founder of the field Kohut was much more actively a part of since his analysis with Aichhorn had begun at the beginning of 1938. Few actually knew when Freud was leaving Vienna. His exit visa had been arranged at very high levels and no one wanted to confound his departure by offending the Nazis with a demonstration. Aichhorn, however, learned from Freud himself which train he would be taking and told Kohut that this was his one chance in a lifetime to see this icon (the well-known Aichhorn could not be present because of the secrecy surrounding Freud's departure).

In later years, Kohut never tired of telling the story of Freud's departure from Vienna. With a friend, Franz Krämer, Kohut strolled onto the otherwise empty platform with feigned indifference that sunny June day, just prior to the departure of the Orient Express for Paris. Freud, in a wheelchair, had already been boarded onto the train by the time Kohut arrived, though he spotted the bustle on the platform where Freud's wife, Martha, was milling about with Anna Freud, Dorothy Burlingham, some servants, a Doctor Josephine Stross (who was there in place of Freud's personal physician, Max Schur, who had had an emergency appendectomy

that morning, and Freud's chow, Lun. Kohut spotted a woman, whom
he presumed to be a maid, sobbing on the platform next to the window
of the compartment where Freud was sitting. Anna Freud was trying to
console the maid. Freud's face was calm, and, as though embarrassed by
the show of emotion, he was trying to pay no attention to the crying
woman. Soon, however, whistles blew, all were boarded, and the train
slowly began to move out of the station. Kohut, who had held himself
back up to that point, walked up toward Freud's compartment, caught
his eye, and tipped his hat. Freud graciously took off his traveling cap
and waved back at Kohut.[9]

That event became for Kohut what he called a "personal myth," though
the only evidence we have that the scene actually occurred and in the way
he described it is from Kohut himself. No one who knew Kohut, however, failed to hear some version of the story at least once. The scene evoked
enduring Viennese continuities in a fragmenting world. It also helped
consolidate Kohut's emerging, if still-fragile, commitment to psychoanalysis. As Kohut put it nostalgically at his grand sixtieth birthday celebration, seeing Freud off came at a moment that was a "low point of my
life" and "yet also in its compelling power the wellspring of the most
important commitments of my future." "I was a young man," he continued. "The world that I had known, the culture in which I had grown up
had crumbled. There was nothing to which to hold on." Suddenly, he
found himself tipping his hat to the great founder of psychoanalysis, almost alone on the platform, as the train carried Freud away. That moment in the train station became the "germinal point for my professional
and scientific future."[10]

It was fortunate that Kohut was in analysis. If anything, treatment at
that crucial point in his life helped him work through some of the pain he
was experiencing. As Kohut put it at the time, analysis helped him "clear
away the rubble of the past" and deal with the way he repeated things in
the present. And yet it is an interesting, if somewhat baffling, image: young
Kohut trudging off five times a week for his fifty minutes with August
Aichhorn, lying on the couch clearing away the rubble of the past, relating his dreams and feelings, waiting eagerly for the analyst's words, and
all as the Nazis systematically dismantled, brick by brick, the edifice of
Viennese life and culture as Kohut knew it. If Kohut was not quite ready
to confront such contradictions, at least the external crisis and the solace
he found in treatment during it had a profound effect on him by deepening his commitment to psychoanalysis itself: "I will also try sometime

to help others to heal their own suffering and live life more clearly," Kohut wrote Levarie.[11]

The Nazis in the meanwhile were ruthless in their determination to make Vienna *Judenfrei* after the Anschluss. In the spring of 1938 they promulgated a decree that all Jews had to file a complete inventory of their wealth and possessions or face "heavy penalties," including imprisonment and/or outright confiscation. Kohut went right to work. The original form he completed on July 12 listed basically no wealth, though he claimed an inheritance of 13,798 reichsmarks from Felix that was being held by Else during her lifetime; from that sum he deducted the cost of his father's funeral, which was probably some kind of accounting trick he and Else had been advised to use. He also listed some jewelry and art objects valued at 931 reichsmarks, including a ring with three gems, a gold chain, three other rings with two gems, a gold fountain pen, two pairs of gold blazer buttons, two old coins, a silver cigarette case, and a gold neck chain. Later, the form was twice revised—on November 12, 1938, and February 2, 1939—with the value of his inheritance cut more than in half (to 5,903 reichsmarks), while the value of his meager possessions remained about the same. Below his signature was the requisite "Heil Hitler."

There was also the matter of selling the house, as required by the Nazi edicts that summer. By the end of August, some buyers, the Kraulics, had presented themselves, and Kohut hoped that everything would go "quickly and painlessly."[12] In fact, it took until the following spring for the sale— really, the steal—to be finalized, and that not without the threat of violence. Once Herr Kraulic called Else in the middle of the night in the summer of 1938 to threaten that if she did not agree soon to "sell" him the house he would have her son sent to a concentration camp.[13] Needless to say, they eventually got the house, which they registered in the name of Mrs. Kraulic, and paid only 23,000 reichsmarks for it, or 40 percent below the value estimated by Nazi authorities themselves the previous year. Of that sale price the emigration tax office took 20,000 reichsmarks and the finance office another 1,200 reichsmarks. The house was essentially confiscated.[14]

Kohut's tenuous situation with his education clouded the summer of 1938 even further. He had no idea whether the Nazis would let him take his exams. "I don't know . . . whether we shall be given a date at all," he wrote Levarie, "and what this span of time, in which I am to take 8 exams [if it were to work out], will look like." It all made him feel "tired and

depressed."[15] But without warning—which is how these things worked—
in September the Nazis ruled suddenly that Jewish students who had been
in their final year at the time of the Anschluss could take their exams, but
that it must be done immediately and the Jewish professors must be replaced with Aryan ones. Kohut had four weeks to complete everything—
and then he had to take the exams with mostly new professors sporting
large Nazi buttons on the lapels of their suits. One Tuesday Kohut took
his pediatrics exam, followed a week later by psychiatry, ophthalmology
the next day, and dermatology the following Saturday, and so on for four
grueling weeks. He described himself as "shattered" by the whole experience and not at all sure whether he had passed. But he did pass, perhaps
focused as never before by the pressure. Heinz Kohut was awarded his
M.D. from the University of Vienna on November 3, 1938.[16]

Within days his world was again turned upside down. On November 7 a young Jew, Herschel Grynszpan, murdered a German diplomat,
Ernst vom Rath, in Paris. This portentous event, which Kohut noted in a
letter coincided with an earthquake and a lunar eclipse in Vienna, was followed by Kristallnacht, or the Night of Broken Glass, November 8–9. In
this carefully orchestrated destruction, the Nazis used the vom Rath murder as the pretext for turning loose the mobs to burn down the synagogues
and Jewish businesses throughout Germany and Austria. Else's store was
looted and destroyed that night, with documentation of its "confiscation"
duly noted on November 12 in Else's official file with all the pompous sadism of the Nazi bureaucratic style. In Vienna itself, eighty-eight synagogues
were burned to the ground; only one, next to the Kultusgemeinde, was
spared. The mobs also threatened individual Jews and homes known to
be owned by Jews. Kohut and his mother were extremely vulnerable in
the otherwise mostly Christian Nineteenth District. They were offered
and took refuge in the apartment of Joseph and Sophie Löwenherz
(Levarie's parents) during the actual Kristallnacht, but the next day they
moved in with other friends until the general terror ended because
Löwenherz was not at all sure his apartment was safe.[17]

Gradually the city returned to a tense state of equilibrium. One result
of the chaos was that the Nazis froze all Jewish bank accounts. Kohut
found himself without sufficient funds to live. As a result, he got some
clerical work in the Rothschildspital, the hospital of the Jewish community in Währing, through his old religion teacher at the gymnasium,
Rabbi Benjamin Murmelstein, and a Quaker, Frank van Gheel Gildermeester (who was assisting Jews through the Kultusgemeinde). Kohut

also began to study English seriously and took lessons from a Mrs. Kaan for a while, though the lessons ended abruptly when the Nazis decreed at the end of November that there could be no further contact between Aryans and Jews. Kohut was sad, because "she was an excellent teacher and a nice human being." Yet the depression seems to have lifted from Kohut's life after he received his M.D. Some joking entered into his letters. He had finished his studies and gotten his degree and was now completely focused on emigration. He was now firmly committed to going to Chicago, where Else would also go somewhat later via Italy. He began to inquire whether he needed to bring any documents with him other than his medical degree. He also secured the services of an attorney and a tax advisor to help prepare for his emigration. It was only a matter of time.[18]

It was also time to wind up his psychoanalytic work with Aichhorn. There is no record of exactly when Kohut finished his treatment. Kohut did later say that his analysis ended prematurely and at a "decisive moment." It must have been incredibly frustrating to have the vagaries of world politics force a premature termination of his analysis. Aichhorn, in his generosity and volubility, tried to ease the transition. Toward the end he told Kohut one day: "I have seen you lying on this couch for a long time; it is time you saw me lying on it." With that he called in one of his sons to take his picture lying on the couch, and later he gave it to Kohut as a souvenir.[19]

The wait for all the papers and visas and stamps that would make emigration possible was agonizing. In February a letter came from a refugee friend of Levarie's uncle, a man who was a young doctor in America, urging Kohut to work hard at his studies. Kohut told Levarie he found the letter "unbelievably blunt, and astounding in its lack of personal comprehension of the present situation," for it naively urged Kohut to "work hard at your studies and grind it out!" That simply won't do, Kohut cried out. "I can't conceive of anyone here who in the middle of all the daily agitations could muster the peace and quiet to sit for hours with a book." Despite his anxiety, Kohut did report he was finding it restful to work on his and Levarie's projected index for the sixty volumes of Goethe's collected works, *Letzter Hand*, published between 1827 and 1832. Kohut was pleased with himself and planned to have the document bound. "*Tempora mutantur* [times change]," he wrote philosophically. "How different it [the world] was when we began it [the index]." Other tasks as well were moving toward completion. Kohut managed to have the major taxes paid, including the 20,000 reichsmarks to the Reich Emigration Tax Office, and a special Jewish business tax "in the interests of eliminating Jews" (*Entjudungsauflage*) of 975 reichsmarks.[20]

By the middle of March 1939, Kohut's emigration seemed "imminent." Rabbi Murmelstein, working through the Kultusgemeinde, arranged for a transport of Jews to leave Vienna for a camp in England. He secured passports for 125 people and designated Kohut as the leader of the group. As Kohut now faced a future far from the devastation and threats that surrounded him in Vienna, his optimism and some of his insouciance returned. Practicing his English, he called Levarie "Mister" in a letter and referred enthusiastically to a Chicago concert of Levarie's attended by the famous composer Paul Hindemith. He concluded hopefully and ironically: "Cross your fingers for me once again that everything will go well and that not too long from now you will receive, even if not me in full life-size, a short letter in my handwriting with an English stamp glued on it."[21]

Before the end of March, the transport of Jews led by Kohut left Vienna on the Orient Express bound for Paris. By other trains and ships it safely reached England. Some five months later Germany invaded Poland, precipitating the war in which tens of millions died on the battlefields and in the ovens of the extermination camps.

Part Two

IN THE FOOTSTEPS
OF FREUD

1939–1965

Seven

A NEW AMERICAN SELF

In England, Kohut and his 125 companions were shipped immediately to Kitchener Camp for refugees at Richborough near Sandwich, Kent, as arranged by Rabbi Murmelstein and Pastor Gildermeester. This camp was to be a temporary staging ground for Kohut while he waited to be processed for his trip to America. The wait, however, lasted a full year. In April he learned he would certainly not leave before the fall, and in May he heard even worse news: the American government had changed its emigration policies to favor German Jews still in Germany. Those Jews safely in England were given a lower priority for visas. That meant waiting close to a year before even beginning the normal processing, which could take as long as several months.

Camp life was quite distressing for Kohut. He complained that it made him "abundantly nervous."[1] He was hardly being mistreated, though one has to wonder at the implicit English bureaucratic anti-Semitism that determined the segregation of these middle-class Jewish immigrants in a relatively rural camp. Movement was restricted and the camp inmates could not leave without permission. They were not exactly prisoners, but neither were they recognized as foreign aliens granted rights as citizens during their temporary wait for visas. There was plenty of food and decent housing, some good conversation with other Viennese intellectuals, and even some moments of levity, as when the camp would challenge the locals to chess (at which the Jews always won handily).[2] In time the camp was expanded to make room for additional refugees, and the English did all they could to make life comfortable. From the outset, Kohut himself was also "well regarded" as the "founder, director, and cashier" of the camp bank. He even managed to keep all his accounts balanced. Within a month, however, he assumed the more familiar and rewarding job of medical assistant in the camp hospital.[3]

But it all weighed heavily on Kohut. In May 1939 he wrote Levarie that "it will be rather difficult to get out of here," and complained: "I am quite worn out by the unbelievable uniformity of my days, which with all their fullness are fully fruitless."[4] There were continual problems with details of visas and the turmoil of emigration as the "civilized" world collapsed into war. He seemed to have trouble with some money that was supposed to be sent to Levarie for safekeeping and could only hope that the boxes with his possessions that he had shipped from Vienna to Chicago would arrive safely; he was mainly concerned with his volumes of Goethe, which he urged Levarie to open so that he would know they were safe and in "human hands."[5]

Kohut's keener concern was his mother. "She is very desperate," he reported shortly after his own arrival in England, but also very "brave," which he probably heard directly or indirectly from Murmelstein or Gildermeester.[6] What is not clear is why she stayed in Vienna. It is unlikely she believed that her supposed Christianity would save her.[7] Perhaps it was just her stubborn refusal to face the depth of the threat to her life. There was no doubt Else's life in Vienna was in turmoil. Since the Anschluss she had faced the state robbery of much of her not insubstantial wealth. In her official file the forms proliferated, tracking, however imprecisely, the steady depletion of her funds. Her net wealth was variously listed as 96,000 reichsmarks, 91,000 reichsmarks, and 170,000 reichsmarks. The only certainty was that with each assessment she ended up with less. The house had been basically stolen by the Kraulics for 60 percent of its value and much of the rest taken by the government in bogus taxes. Else's store was looted during Kristallnacht and then officially appropriated, as dutifully reported on another form. Her other source of wealth was her share of Felix's ownership in his business with Paul Bellak, which she valued in one form at approximately 55,000 reichsmarks. It is unclear from the records whether the Nazis intended to expropriate the business. It may be that Else was able to liquidate her inheritance, for at some point before she left Vienna she managed to hide on her person a rather large, if indeterminate, amount of money. It seems she continued to live at Paradiesgasse 47 until shortly after Heinz left for England. At that point the sale of the house seems to have been finalized, and she moved to Währingerstrasse 50/12, which was next door to her old store in the Ninth District and perhaps connected to it.[8]

She held on, though life itself became increasingly precarious after the war began on September 1, 1939. Siegmund Levarie, having saved her son, proved equally loyal to her. He managed to get her an American visa through the same wealthy uncle who had helped Heinz a year earlier. Else packed up her possessions in early February 1940 and shipped them to Chicago. She got out a surprising amount, including china, silverware, pictures, and small rugs. Even more remarkably, she smuggled out the money she had been carrying with her. Jews were strictly forbidden to take out money, but if anybody in Vienna could fool the Nazis, it was Else Kohut.[9] On February 26, 1940, at last she left Vienna by train for Italy, where she boarded an American ship and ended up in Chicago in mid-March.[10]

Kohut, meanwhile, felt "charred in the purgatory of camp life," overcome by intense anxiety for his mother and the frustration of enforced idleness that took from him any control over his fate.[11] He may also have been overcome with survivor guilt. Why was he alive and his mother still caught in the grip of Nazi terror? He had been so filled with hope when he first left Vienna in March 1939. A new future awaited him eventually in America, far from the violence of his beloved but now-crazed Vienna. He had assumed, reasonably, that Else would be right behind him and they would rejoin each other in Chicago. Instead, he got stuck in a remote English refugee camp, safe if helpless, while his mother faced mounting dangers in Nazified Vienna that must have raised questions in his mind whether she would ever escape. The worst for him seemed to have been the start of actual war in September 1939. He knew from his earliest memories how war separates loved ones and can destroy the body and the soul, scarring one for life. As he was as a child, he was again utterly passive as the German army marched into Poland and threatened to expand its dominance from Paris to Moscow. For the second time in his life, Heinz Kohut was traumatized by a major war.

His immediate response was to get sick; by October 1939 he had pneumonia.[12] He realized that camp life would only prolong and perhaps worsen his illness, so he petitioned to recover in the care of his uncle Hans Lampl. Hans had left Vienna before the war to assume an executive position as a foreign agent of the Austrian paper firm, Leykam-Josefsthal A.G.[13] Hans had an apartment in London, from which he worked and where he established his sick nephew in October 1939. There Kohut lay in bed in complete solitude, reading, sleeping, waking, and sleeping again.[14] In time Kohut recovered from his pneumonia. Perhaps because of his illness he also secured permission to leave England for America somewhat sooner than he had originally thought would be the case. On February 22, 1940, he got passage on a British convoy sailing to America. Kohut left from Liverpool in what turned out to be a twelve-day trip across the ocean, full of its own terrors, the convoy zigzagging to avoid German submarines, passing by Newfoundland and Nova Scotia before arriving at its destination in Boston on March 4. He had $25 in his pocket, just enough for the bus to Chicago, which would become his home for the rest of his life. Kohut arrived on March 5, completely broke, and phoned Levarie from the downtown bus station.[15]

It happened that Kohut's call came on the day of the second performance of Bach's *St. John Passion* in Bond Chapel at the University of Chicago. Levarie, jointly with Robert Wadsworth, had newly translated the text into English and conducted. Frederick Stock, of the Chicago Symphony, attended. After the performance there was to be a large reception in the evening. Levarie fetched Kohut from the bus station in the late morning. Kohut bathed and rested, then went immediately with Levarie to the performance of the *Passion* and to the reception, as he was quite eager to meet Stock. Kohut's new life in America began with a ritual that re-created his happiest moments in Vienna: going to a good concert with Siegmund Levarie.

The reception after the *Passion* that March 5, 1940, proved momentous in other ways as well, for it was there he met his best lifelong friend, Robert Wadsworth. Kohut and Wadsworth instantly warmed to each other. They discovered they had been born on the same day (May 3, 1913) and quickly dubbed themselves "birthday brothers."[16] No one was more significant in Heinz Kohut's adult life than Robert Wadsworth. Born to a well-to-do family in Norwood Park on the North Side of Chicago, Wadsworth was a brilliant and highly literate librarian and musician, very Anglo-Saxon in self-presentation.[17] He was one of the few Americans Kohut ever met whose education, learning, and general culture approached his own. In the late 1930s Wadsworth was finishing his dissertation for his Ph.D. in library science at Columbia, while serving on the staff of the *Oxford English Dictionary*, located at the University of Chicago. In 1939, when Levarie needed help with his translation of Bach's *St. John Passion*, the chair of the department of music, Cecil Smith, recommended his friend, Wadsworth, as someone with an exquisite knowledge of both English and music. Levarie became a good friend of Wadsworth and he was eager to introduce him to Kohut.

Wadsworth had a delicate charm and an ironic sense of humor. He looked at the world with the eyes of a Henry James, noting the subtlest of feelings in himself and those around him. His letters mine nuance from a life barely lived beyond his work at the University of Chicago Library and the four walls of his Hyde Park apartment, where he lived alone with his cats (which he would take pictures of and send to friends). His great passion was music. He played the organ well and went to concerts several times a week. He also played the organ at a Lutheran church on Sundays. He was especially fond of Wagner's *Ring* cycle and would travel to New York, Seattle, and other places to hear performances of it. He was also intrigued by anything associated with travel by train. He had memorized an incredible number of train schedules from around the country. He and Cecil Smith, for example, used to compete with each other to see who could devise the most complicated way to get to New York, and when he took vacations it was always by train by himself on the most obscure of routes; along the way he wrote detailed and wonderfully literate letters about what he was seeing and experiencing to a selected number of close friends. He also did quirky things like memorize the serial numbers of every trolley car in the Chicago system, which was then rather extensive.[18]

Wadsworth and Kohut completely immersed themselves in each other's lives. Few days went by when they were not in contact either over lunch, on the phone, at a symphony, or, if separated, by frequent letters. The connection also extended to the Wadsworth family. Robert's aunt Alice, his mother's sister, lived alone in Hyde Park, and Kohut got to know her well. Robert's parents first invited Levarie to Thanksgiving dinner in 1939, then added Kohut and his mother in 1940, and by the late 1940s the meals included Kohut's and Levarie's wives and then their children. Eventually, the Kohuts came to be Thanksgiving hosts for Wadsworth, who also joined them on all the other celebratory family days (especially Christmas and Easter). Wadsworth himself was utterly self-effacing; he once wrote to Levarie: "I have very little confidence in my ability, or my fitness, to play a part in any other life, but I hope you will try to keep a place for me in yours."[19] Wadsworth adored Kohut. He turned over his soul to his Viennese "birthday brother" and allowed him to dominate him with a kind of childlike innocence. In 1944, for example, Wadsworth got tuberculosis. Kohut immediately took charge of his illness and his life, deciding where he would go to recuperate, how long he would stay, and making all the arrangements concerning his personal affairs (including the care of his cats). Wadsworth wrote Levarie, then in the army: "The presence of Heinz in the hospital has been a tremendous boon. He made all arrangements for me and I rely upon him for advice and guidance. He is someone in whom my parents and I unite in placing our confidence and I can't be grateful enough for my 'birthday brother.' "

Tall and exceedingly thin, effeminate, shy, full of strange movements and mannerisms, odd and yet captivating, Wadsworth baffled most observers. To some he looked like what today would be called a "queen," though he also seemed decidedly asexual, innocent, naive. "He certainly wasn't heterosexual," as Thomas Kohut put it. "Whether he was actively gay, I don't know. My guess is that he was probably not actively gay." And, he continued, Wadsworth was "very weak and happy to have my father dominate him. . . . [He] ceded the stage . . . and was part of the audience."[20] There are those who assumed later that Wadsworth and Kohut were lovers in the early 1940s, and certainly such ideas, if not generally uttered, came to be widely whispered in the tight and gossipy world of Chicago psychoanalysis.[21] The more protective and not to be discounted view is that of Paul Ornstein. "If you had ever seen him," Ornstein said, "you could not imagine anybody being attracted to him sexually. I cannot imagine a homosexual who would want Wadsworth as his partner." For Ornstein it was only Wadsworth's charm and brilliance that attracted Kohut. "Once you sat down with him and heard him talk," Ornstein said, "you would forget about the constant movements, because he had so much to say." Kohut felt Wadsworth had an encyclopedic mind and was one of his few equals in terms of talking about literature, music, and culture. "For me to imagine that there was anything [between them] other than an intellectual resonance is just inconceivable." Besides, Ornstein added, Kohut had tremendous loyalty to friends, especially those he met early on when he felt lost in America.[22]

Else's safe arrival in Chicago in March 1940 was a great relief for Kohut. Levarie arranged for her to stay with a family in Hyde Park, on the South Side of Chicago near the university, though he kept her trunks stored in the basement of the Sylvan Arms apartment building at the corner of 56th Street and Kenwood Avenue, where he lived and where Kohut stayed at first. Else surprised everyone who met her with her fierce resolve, intelligence, and resourcefulness. She immediately made friends and used the money she had smuggled past the Nazis to open a shop she called "De Elsie's" on 47th Street near Drexel Avenue, selling women's clothing and accessories. Within a fairly short period of time she got her own apartment and was settled in her adopted country. Somewhat later, she bought a car that she loved to drive around Chicago. If any driver dared cross her, she would curse at him angrily and loudly in German.[23]

One task facing Kohut was to learn English better. He began his studies by memorizing much of *Alice in Wonderland*, from which he was fond of quoting for the rest of his life. To learn about American history and also work on his English he read some high school textbooks.[24] Kohut was, of course, experienced in learning languages and must have possessed as well a native gift for learning grammar, vocabulary, and idiomatic expressions. He learned very quickly, for example, how to pronounce the *th* sound and not mix up his *v*'s and *w*'s. But around language there was also a degree of myth-making in Kohut. When he was courting Elizabeth Meyer later, he told her he arrived in Chicago knowing almost no English at all, whereas in fact Levarie had been quite struck with how much English Kohut knew when he first arrived. Kohut had, after all, just lived a year in England, even though he was mostly surrounded by Viennese Jews speaking German and was then secluded in his uncle's London apartment. He also came to feel shame that he had learned American history by reading high school textbooks. Within a few years he began denying it and by the end of his life would expand rather pedantically about how he had become acquainted with American history in the 1940s by reading The Federalist Papers. One cannot exclude the possibility that later on he read the Papers, but his roommate in the early 1940s was there with him while he read those high school textbooks. Something of a self-refashioning was in process. America allows that, this land of second chances. It left him, however, between worlds. For the rest of his life he was never sure whether he dreamed in English or German.[25]

Once settled, Kohut needed to serve an internship in some hospital. It had become an established rule by then, with all the European Jewish doctors flocking into the country, that anyone with a foreign medical degree had to serve a year as an intern before getting licensed in this country. In Kohut's case, of course, such an internship was by no means redundant. It was the logical next step after the awarding of his medical degree from the University of Vienna. Kohut managed to get hired by Chicago South Shore Hospital, south of Hyde Park in a Swedish neighborhood.[26] He earned $30 per month plus room and board and free laundry. It gave him independence and put his career back on track, though he was not happy there and worked hard to get out. Kohut later reported the humorous difficulties he had examining patients who mostly spoke Swedish, which he did not further complicate his life by trying to learn. He was also a little rusty medically. On his first night as an intern a patient on the ward got restless. Kohut offhandedly instructed the nurse to give him a sedative. The patient promptly died, because the restlessness was not discomfort from his illness but the physical state that is often the immediate precursor to death; the sedative unnecessarily hastened the end.

Kohut managed not to kill too many more patients after that and successfully completed his internship by the end of March 1941.[27] On April 1, 1941, he then began a coveted residency in neurology at the University of Chicago's Billings Hospital. Kohut had been lobbying actively for this position and had been selected by the world-renowned neurologist Richard B. Richter.[28] At first his salary was only marginally better than during his internship, but it improved each year as he moved from an assistant resident to an assistant in neurology to an instructor. By 1945 he was making $3,000 a year. Richter, furthermore, treated Kohut as a very special young doctor and mentored him in various ways, co-authoring one article with him and making it clearly known that he intended for Kohut to be the head of the neurology section of the Department of Neurology and Psychiatry, of which he himself was chair, as soon as Kohut finished his residency.[29]

Kohut loved playing the role of a doctor in his starched white coat with a stethoscope around his neck. He was stocky then, even slightly plump, but handsome, and he wore his wavy, blondish hair brushed back, European style. Charles Kligerman, then a fourth-year medical student, described the first time he met Kohut in June 1941. Kligerman had worked up a case and was to present it to the new resident in neurology. It was a hot day and Kohut was sweating and nervous in his new role. But "his keen, intelligent blue eyes and firm chin gave him an air of quiet authority that progressively increased along with his zest, as he discussed the case." In retrospect, Kligerman—who would become a lifelong friend—felt the scene evoked the essential Kohut: "No matter what the stress at the surface, personal or creative, one always felt the calm, unruffled solidity at the core. And he could always rise to the occasion. Any intellectual challenge was an instant inspiration."[30]

There was, however, a shadow on Kohut's self. Much was at stake that summer of 1941 and in the few years afterward. His whole future lay on the line. At least for a time he seemed to impose some severe controls over his interests. Such focus fought against Kohut's free and wide-ranging immersion in cultural experience and human knowledge in all fields, which was so essential to his creativity. This moment of great potential professional advancement in his life required a reining in of his talents. He was now truly the doctor he had played in the school drama, but it was a very new role. There were many lines to learn before he would become competent in his newly chosen field of neurology. Such are the normal struggles of any talented young man locating himself in a universe of satisfying and productive work. For Kohut, however, there was an edge to his struggles that grew out of his early experience but that surely reflected as well the more recent traumas of war and emigration. He sought control and boundaries. The rhythms of his life became exceedingly, and somewhat artificially, ordered in ways that could become compulsive. When he studied his textbooks he sat at his desk, always in a straight chair, and marked the pages of his text with different-colored pencils. He leaned forward oblivious to the world, completely absorbed in what he was reading. At times, his roommate said, it looked as though he would eat the book.[31]

A great crisis came and passed when Japan attacked Pearl Harbor on December 7, 1941. That night Kohut, his mother, and Robert Wadsworth listened attentively and with dread to the radio. It was not just that war had reached them all the way in Chicago but that Kohut was liable for the draft. Barely a week after Pearl Harbor he received his questionnaire, which was part of the registration process. The news particularly shook Wadsworth, who wrote Levarie (already in the army): "Heinz has been perfectly wonderful, and I have come so to depend on him that the news of his questionnaire struck me an ugly blow. . . . Certainly it will be hard on his mother, but she appears to be a person of tremendous vitality and courage." Levarie himself served five years, mostly in the Pacific but with occasional trips to bases in the United States. During one of those assignments in the middle of the war, Kohut visited and marveled at his cultured friend in fatigues, which made him look identical to the thousands of other young men then in uniform. Kohut remarked sardonically, dangling a cigarette from his mouth, that it was a "radical way to become an American."[32]

Somehow, Kohut missed the draft and the war, for which he later gave at least two mutually exclusive explanations. He told Aichhorn that he was never drafted because of his appointment in the hospital.[33] The problem with this explanation is that many young physicians were drafted, for example Kohut's friend Charles Kligerman. In a completely different context—Kohut's application for admission to the Chicago Institute for Psychoanalysis—he said that he had applied for a commission in the army but was rejected in October 1942 because he was not a citizen. Levarie, however, had been drafted and sent to war without yet completing the necessary waiting time for citizenship. The best one can guess as to why he never served in the military is that he was probably simply lucky and his number never came up.[34] But the lies are telling. On certain issues, Kohut, it seemed, needed to deceive.

Kohut lived at Billings Hospital for seven years, from 1941 to 1948, the first three with Jay McCormick in the residents' quarters of the "Home for Destitute and Crippled Children" at the corner of 59th Street and Ellis Avenue. Thomas Szasz, himself an immigrant and later a famous psychiatrist, lived down the hall. Both Kohut and Szasz were noted by the other Americans as quite distinctive for their European habit of wearing hair nets to bed; it was for them the customary way of keeping the wave in their hair. Kohut's first real girlfriend was astonished to learn he slept and showered with a hair net. Once she saw him dressing after a shower. He was buttoning his shirt and still wore the net so that his hair would not be mussed when he pulled on his sweater.[35] Besides being different, Kohut could also be rather mysterious. He would often disappear without warning or notice. Jay McCormick, for example, knew that Kohut spent a lot of time with Robert Wadsworth but never met him, nor was he invited to join them in any activity, just as he never met Kohut's mother, who of course lived in the neighborhood. Kohut also had some mysterious source of income (undoubtedly from his mother). Residents only made $30 a month at the beginning, a salary that rose in the third year to $155 a month. Analysis alone could cost as much as $20 a month. Kohut also dressed better and ate out more often. McCormick could barely see an occasional movie on his income (which was the same as Kohut's).[36]

There is no doubt Kohut was extremely good at neurology and in time would have become famous in it and made a lot of money. He was wonderful with patients and a noted teacher. Medical students particularly enjoyed his ability to mimic perfectly the motoric tics that one encounters so often in neurology. Such an ability would seem to be a precursor, on a physical level, of Kohut's later emphasis in psychoanalysis on empathy, where one thinks oneself into the imagination of another. Kohut's immediate success in teaching and clinical work was doubly rewarded by his superiors, because the hospital was so short-staffed during the war. Emotionally, as well, the world of the hospital met Kohut's needs. It was contained, predictable, hierarchical, limited, bound up in its own rules, secure, and separate from the diverse and sometimes confusing pressures of society. The hospital had abundant external structure to contain his internal turmoil. In terms of research, the hospital world of neurology lacked entirely the open-endedness of psychoanalysis. Kohut's research was done mostly in the laboratory, and was empirical and highly scientific; he spent countless hours, for example, staining slide samples and examining the results under the microscope. He published articles on neuro-optic myelitis, lymphoblastoma, and encephalitis, gave some speeches, and wrote at least one book review. It was the beginning of a solid career in neurology, and after he left it, a part of him always longed to return to it.[37]

Neurology was appealing as well in terms of Kohut's new American identity. At the University of Chicago it was a very Anglo-Saxon specialty (unlike psychiatry), and most neurologists were people like Richter, who was a man of great elegance and distinction. It made Kohut feel he was not a lowly Jewish refugee. His friend Paul Ornstein once asked him why he had entered neurology at first, rather than psychiatry. Kohut said it gave him "status after having arrived here a nobody." Neurology was more prestigious, more elitist.[38] Professional ambitions merged, in other words, with Kohut's long-standing ambivalence about his Judaism. It was around this time, as best one can tell from the evidence, that Kohut began presenting himself ethnically as half-Jewish at most (and not Jewish at all if he thought he could get away with it). He told Jay McCormick, for example, that he used to go to church in Vienna, and both McCormick and his wife, Peggy (whom McCormick married in 1944), remained confused then and later about Kohut's identity. It was also in these years, it seems, that Kohut decided he was a Christian by belief. He hardly had a conversion experience, as he always had great disdain for displays of religious enthusiasm.[39] He did join the Unitarian Church at 57th Street and Woodlawn Avenue, near the university. Unitarianism was the perfect compromise for a spiritual man torn by his Jewish and Christian identities who had come to embrace Jesus as the religious figure of paramount significance in his life. The highly educated and sophisticated community of this

Unitarian Church with its succession of intellectual pastors easily allowed Kohut to "become Christian" without any display or embarrassing rituals, and to accept Jesus as a great teacher without concern for the great mystery of the Trinity, or indeed of the Resurrection. At the same time, Kohut's Unitarianism appeared to some, even at least one dear friend, as a "cover."[40]

Finally, the path from neurology to psychiatry and psychoanalysis replicated the professional career of Freud, who was a very accomplished neurologist with an extensive bibliography long before he wrote his first paper in what he started calling "psycho-analysis." Certainly, Kohut was keenly aware later of the way his training repeated that of Freud. "Until about 15 years ago," he said in an interview in 1964, "it was very common for men to enter psychoanalysis from neurology—Freud himself, for instance, was a neurologist and neuropathologist before becoming an analyst."[41] And yet it hardly seems likely that Kohut identified with Freud in 1941 sufficiently to model his training on that of the master. His analysis with Aichhorn had been instrumental but not decisive in moving Kohut toward psychoanalysis.

Much changed in Kohut's life after March 1939. He was, among other things, lucky to be alive and certainly had to be grateful for the opportunity to begin a real career in neurology at a great university. Kohut also threw himself into his work with the commitment of a man destined for success, even fame, in his chosen specialty. He quickly won acclaim from his chair and mentor. He published some important articles in the field. Medical students loved him and he had a sterling reputation with patients. But something gnawed at Kohut. Neurology seemed to bore him. He grew tired of staining tissue samples and sitting long hours peering into a microscope. The work was too much in and of the laboratory and not sufficiently in touch with real human feelings and suffering. Neurology failed to excite Kohut's creativity.

As time passed, Kohut seemed to feel more grounded and secure. His actions were less motivated by the sense of urgency that had surrounded him since the Anschluss. The trauma of emigration, if not yet over, was beginning to ebb. He knew English well now and was only waiting for his citizenship (which came, after the customary five-year wait, in 1945).[42] He had nothing directly to fear from the war. The only nagging problem he faced was his severe allergies, which had never bothered him in Vienna but became a source of constant misery in the hot and humid late summers of Chicago.[43] Otherwise, his health was robust.

He had a good career on track with a decent income, and though Levarie was away in the army until 1946 he had a soul mate in Wadsworth. Else hovered perilously close but at least lived a neighborhood away. Gradually, Kohut allowed himself to take more risks in both his work and his relationships.

Eight

PSYCHOANALYSIS, AT LAST

In November 1942 Kohut applied for admission to the Chicago Institute for Psychoanalysis. This highly regarded center of training was at that point only in its second decade. Psychoanalysis generally was still on the margins in the United States, though poised to take over American psychiatry; in 1939 all formally constituted psychoanalytic organizations in the country included only 79 members and 213 students. But among those psychoanalytic organizations the Chicago Institute was preeminent. It began, really, when Robert Maynard Hutchins, the dynamic young president of the University of Chicago, brought Franz Alexander to the university as a visiting professor for the academic year 1930–1931 as a way of transforming the Department of Psychiatry. Alexander spent the year bitterly fighting the old guard, until he finally gave up and went to Boston. He was persuaded the next year, however, to establish an institute separate from the university.[1] Alexander took as his model Freud's establishment of the Vienna institute as a freestanding training center apart from the university, though the actual model for the form of the Chicago Institute for Psychoanalysis was the Berlin institute. Alexander, who was a good fund-raiser, secured major support from some prominent members of the Chicago community, especially Alfred K. Stern, who became chairman of the new institute's board and Alexander's patient; he received a $500,000 start-up grant from the Rockefeller Foundation and more modest but important support from the Rosenwald and Macy Foundations. Alexander tapped into a lot of money in the middle of depression-ridden

Chicago, which was the result of both his charisma and the excitement in the air about psychoanalysis. His initial staff consisted of associate director Karen Horney (hired at $15,000), whom Alexander knew as a fellow analysand of Hanns Sachs, and Thomas French, Helen McLean, Catherine Bacon, Lionel Blitzsten, and Karl Menninger. In time Horney and Menninger left, and Theresa Benedek, Helen Ross, and others joined the staff.[2]

The key idea of the Institute was to create a separate and freestanding unit where psychoanalysts could work together and train candidates who wished themselves to become psychoanalysts. The Chicago Institute from the outset also had serious research goals of transforming the world of psychiatry (and influencing the way we think about the human soul, one might say). It held regular scientific meetings, and over the years members of the staff produced hundreds of publications. The universitylike structure of the Institute included offices, classrooms, a library, a kitchen and dining area, and a lay board that assumed legal and fiscal responsibility for the Institute—and gave Alexander dictatorial control over affairs. Close relationships were established with the medical schools and universities in the area, and in time most members of the staff held academic appointments in various departments of psychiatry in the Chicago area.[3]

Psychoanalytic training in Chicago, which was modeled on that in Berlin in the 1920s, occurred in a freestanding institute (that is, entirely separate from a university). The first step in the process was to be accepted into a "didactic" or training analysis, or a complete psychoanalysis with a fully certified training and supervising analyst at the Institute. Several staff members interviewed the candidate, and then there was a group interview. If accepted, the candidate was assigned a training analyst for his or her didactic analysis. At some point after a year or two into the didactic analysis—which began for most medical doctors (who completely dominated the field) during their residencies in psychiatry at a hospital—the candidate began course work in the Institute and was assigned several generally low-fee analysands from the Institute clinic. These "control" cases were closely supervised by senior training analysts, and at least one patient had to be taken through termination before graduation. It was an arduous process, which meant few were fully certified until they were about forty years old.[4]

Kohut had his interviews at the Institute in November and December 1942. He was rejected. It will probably never be known why, as his Institute file contains no specific information on the issue and all the players are dead. It is clear, however, that the rejection was decisive. Kohut was not even allowed to begin his didactic analysis. As Thomas French wrote him on behalf of the training committee: "In accordance with our usual policy, the [Training] Committee would suggest that you undertake a therapeutic analysis and that the final decision as to your candidacy for training be postponed until after a period of analysis." The decision of the committee was not, in fact, "usual policy." If everything had gone well in the interviews, the training committee would surely have given him credit for his work with Aichhorn (not to mention Marseilles) and let him begin his training analysis. Certainly, Kohut himself understood that he had been rejected. He wrote Aichhorn later, "A couple of years ago when I sought a training analysis at the Institute here I was turned down. . . ." The message from the training committee was that he needed to have additional psychoanalytic treatment to get healthy enough to be allowed to begin his training analysis. This arcane distinction between a therapeutic and a didactic analysis has great meaning in the world of psychoanalysis. To be refused to be allowed even to begin a didactic analysis meant Kohut was kept off the track that could lead to becoming a psycho-analyst. The clear suggestion is that those who interviewed him felt he had some major flaw(s) in his character that needed to be addressed be-fore he could assume the position of treating others, even as a beginning candidate. It is hardly likely that those who interviewed Kohut found him not up to the task intellectually. Paul Ornstein, always protective, argues that what got in the way for Kohut was his narcissism, and he added that if Freud were to apply to most institutes today he probably would be re-jected. Perhaps. But there were plenty of narcissistic psychoanalysts in the 1940s, and even a few in later years. What there was not was an accepting attitude toward anyone who deviated from the strictest of heterosexual standards. Joan Fleming, in this regard, apparently set the conservative tone at the Institute in the 1940s. But she found a receptive audience. The value system that dominated American psychoanalysis in the post-heroic period after Freud had no way of comprehending, and therefore admit-ting someone with Kohut's apparently fluid sexual boundaries. Later, when he was more secure personally and professionally, he would say that he had always been dismayed that psychoanalysis was so rigid and doctri-naire about issues of sexuality.[5]

Kohut, however, was not to be undone by such impediments. He found a clever way of handling the impasse in his psychoanalytic career: he selected Ruth Eissler, with whom he began treatment in March 1943,[6] as his therapeutic analyst (though the selection of Eissler came after some tentative exploration of the possibility of being analyzed by Helen Ross).[7] Eissler just happened to be as well a training and supervising analyst at the Institute. In his 1946 letter to Aichhorn, Kohut says that Lionel Blitzsten suggested he seek treatment with Ruth Eissler.[8] But he hardly needed Blitzsten to tell him how well connected Ruth Eissler was. Kohut knew that Ruth Eissler was the wife of Kurt Eissler, the former analysand of August Aichhorn, who felt Kurt Eissler represented the most promising future leader in American psychoanalysis. Kohut's strategy, clearly, was to begin his therapeutic analysis, which, if successful, would be converted into a training analysis, and in due course he would be accepted into the Institute. On a personal level, the analysis linked him to Vienna and his beloved Aichhorn, while professionally it connected him, however tentatively at this point, with the future leadership in psychoanalysis.

One December day late in 1943 just before the holidays, Kohut spotted a tall, beautiful young woman walking about the hospital in the brightly starched uniform of a volunteer. She was slender and shapely, with dark hair, a warm smile, a gentle modesty, and the high cheekbones of an Anglo-Saxon.[9] Kohut noted where her office was and later that day appeared at her door to ask her to dinner. She was instantly attracted to this fascinating young doctor who was interested in everything. He was quite handsome, she felt. He was neatly dressed, extremely well mannered, and courteous in an Old World way. He exuded charm.

Barbara Bryant, then twenty, had just arrived from New York to run and expand the volunteer program at the hospital under the supervision of a Dr. Whitecotton. Bryant was bright and familiar with music, though, as she herself put it, she was unformed, generally naive about cultural matters, and much less well educated than Kohut. She was also linked to Levarie, as her stepfather was a musicologist at the university.[10] The roles Kohut and Bryant quickly assumed in their relationship were that she became the student and lover of her adored teacher. That first Christmas he gave her a copy of Thomas Mann's *The Magic Mountain*, which she began to read immediately and discussed with him in great detail. As they decorated the tree, he talked of the holidays he had spent as a child in Vienna, his homes and coffee shops, the Ring, the palaces, the gymnasium and university. He wanted her to know it all in ways he had not talked to anyone about (except perhaps Wadsworth) since arriving in America. He even drew her an elaborate map of Vienna, marked with the personal sites of his life.

Soon Bryant and Kohut were inseparable. At first they dined together in the hospital, but they moved to restaurants after she was reprimanded by Dr. Whitecotton; it was deemed disreputable for a single woman to be spending so much time with a man. She had been living with her mother but soon found a room for rent with a Miss Halliday on 57th Street between Blackstone and Dorchester Avenues. When Miss Halliday traveled, which was often, she let Bryant use the kitchen: "Heinz and I would cook in, so to speak," she said. They generally had some contact almost every day and went out somewhere together at least three times a week for the next year and a half. They were implicitly but not formally engaged. He seemed able to open up with her and to trust her as no one else; he told her, for example, that both his mother and his father were Jewish. Sometimes Kohut and Bryant simply walked on the Midway for hours, which Kohut jokingly compared to the Ring. They also went often to the Museum of Science and Industry, which was near Lake Michigan and within walking distance of Hyde Park—and it was free. Kohut loved this celebration of American capitalism, which so epitomized the culture of his new country. At other times, they spent whole days in the Art Institute, and she gained, she said, the equivalent of a complete university education in art from Kohut. They went to all kinds of concerts, free and paid, amateur and professional, jazz and classical. He read the newspaper carefully each day and made notes on places he wanted to go and things to do; he then set their itinerary. Usually it included some kind of ethnic restaurant, for Kohut loved to experiment with different places to eat. For the opera, however, which was not then performed in Chicago more than a few weeks a year, first he took her in style to an upscale French restaurant and then to good seats near the center of the theater. Nothing was to be spared for the opera.[11]

In the spring of 1944 Kohut made an important decision. He decided to switch his appointment (he had by then been made an instructor) from neurology to neurology and psychiatry. Kohut's new appointment in the hospital might seem to be a modest adjustment in title. The two specialties were, after all, combined then into one department, which Richter chaired. But the change was fundamental and reflected the new direction in which he was moving. He entered the world of psychiatry, which for him was naturally and inevitably connected with psychoanalysis. Kohut moved out of the laboratory and into the clinic. It was a conscious and avowed decision that reflected maturity, self-confidence, and a deeper awareness of his strengths and interests. Richter, his former mentor, was painfully aware of what the new title signified. Kohut would certainly never head the neurology section, nor follow in the great man's footsteps. Richter was furious and never really forgave Kohut. He saw Kohut's move into psychiatry as a loss to real science, and to himself.[12]

Perhaps to soothe Richter, though surely as well to demonstrate to himself and the world his unusual talents, Kohut decided as late as May 1946 to take his board exams in neurology, followed in October 1949 by his boards in psychiatry. It was partly a matter of status for Kohut. He became a specialist in neurology, certified at the highest level with an academic appointment in a major research hospital, some two years after deciding to leave the field. He was, of course, still reeling from the trauma of emigration, and certification in neurology provided a secure fallback from any risks associated with psychiatry and psychoanalysis. He worked hard for these gains. The day in the hospital began at 8:00 a.m. and continued until dinner. Others might relax then with light reading, but if he was not out with Bryant, Kohut was poring over his scientific journals. Others interested in psychoanalysis often skipped the psychiatry boards as tiresome and unnecessary. Kohut took two boards and excelled in both.[13]

There is no question about it: for all his tentativeness, initial difficulties, and lingering attachments to the hospital world of neurology, after the winter of 1944 Kohut had decisively moved into psychoanalysis and was determined, one way or another, to make it his life's vocation. Typically, he threw himself into his new activity with great enthusiasm. He began reading Freud as never before and found sources of identification with him that in fact had never existed during his Vienna years, when he frequently walked by Bergasse 19 on the way to a coffee house to talk about Robert Musil or Egon Schiele. Kohut became very active in two journal clubs that met twice a week in the Department of Psychiatry under the leadership of its chair, Henry Brosin.[14] Charles Kligerman, for example, returned from the war in 1945 to live down the hall from Kohut in the residency quarters of the "Home for Crippled and Destitute Children" in Billings Hospital. The two became close friends, in part based on Kligerman's broad cultural interests and his musical abilities (he played the violin) but also because he became a psychiatry resident. Kohut greeted him: "Now you are one of us." Forty years later (at Kohut's memorial service) Kligerman described their walks on the Midway, when their talk "inevitably turned to Freud and psychoanalysis, a subject which poured out of Heinz with irresistible enthusiasm. His idealization of Freud was complete."[15] Kohut also talked often of Freud to Barbara Bryant, whom he persuaded to enter her own psychoanalysis. She was much more tepid in her enthusiasm for the field, however, and came to resent having to get up every day an hour earlier to go to her appointment. She may have been too normal for psychoanalysis. In any event, she got almost nothing out of it.[16]

There is some irony about Kohut's enthusiasm for psychoanalysis at this point in his life, as his actual work with Ruth Eissler was a burdensome chore, depicted in "Mr. Z" as an extended failure of understanding and empathy on her part. Everything, it seems, was by the book—and entirely wrong. In the first year, she insisted, Kohut fell into a "regressive mother transference" associated with his deluded and grandiose attempt to re-create in the psychoanalytic situation his early experience of a loving, doting mother without any competition from siblings or a rivalrous father. She insisted that his demands and sense of entitlement, especially his anger at any irregularity in the schedule, proved her interpretation of the transference. He resisted all such ideas with rage, insisting she did not understand him. Indeed, he seemed filled with rage for much of this early period, along with some depression and even some suicidal ideation. He became calm—and the transferential situation changed dramatically—only after about a year and a half, when she introduced one of her interpretations with the phrase, "Of course, it hurts when one is not given what one assumes to be one's due." As Kohut would later understand, such empathic communications constitute the essence of healing in psychoanalysis and are the precondition for a patient's being able to take in the meaning of any interpretations. The significance of that turning point, however, was not apparent to Kohut or Eissler at the time.

In the next and prolonged middle phase of the analysis, Eissler saw Kohut as dealing with oedipal issues, his castration anxiety, the childhood masturbation, his fantasy of the phallic woman, his preoccupation with the primal scene, and his relationship with Morawetz. Kohut was preoccupied then with his own narcissism and denial, which she said he fell into to protect himself against the feelings of anger toward his father for wishing to possess his mother sexually and his intense castration anxiety over his feelings of rivalry toward the father. That anxiety, she argued, was the main reason for his retreat as a child to an earlier developmental phase and why he clung to pregenital drive aims (the masturbation and homosexuality, most of all).

Things proceeded along these impeccably classical lines through the dissolution of the transference neurosis and into the termination phase. In this latter stage of the analysis, Eissler seems to have put a good deal of emphasis on his emerging heterosexuality and increasing separation from his mother. Such behavioral benchmarks betray, as always, the subtle but pervasive value system in psychoanalysis. What was wrong with this crucial final stage of termination, Kohut says, was its flatness and lack of affect. He was not characterologically obsessive, one who kept separate his thoughts and feelings. He had, in fact, always been quite expressive, which made the absence of passion from this stage particularly revealing of some deeper, troubling issues with the analysis itself. Writing with the advantage of hindsight, of course, and for the didactic purpose of juxtaposing Freudian understanding versus the theories he came to later, Kohut suggests he nevertheless saw even at the time that something was deeply wrong with what he had experienced in analysis with Ruth Eissler. He readily acknowledged that he was a little better for the experience and that she had helped him somewhat. At the same time, he was not healed.

Kohut's relationship with Barbara Bryant, meanwhile, was proceeding well. "They had a serious thing going," as Jay McCormick put it. Kohut seemed to change somewhat in the relationship. He became less intense and more fun to be around. He did not dominate social gatherings—a trait for which he was to become infamous later—laughed a lot, joked (especially after a couple of martinis), and told funny stories about himself, like his delightful account of wandering around in a dense London fog, or his story about a patient who told him he was in the hospital because he painted his ear. Kohut asked him why that got him into the hospital. Because he painted it polka dot, the patient replied.[17]

Kohut and Bryant spent most Saturday evenings with Jay and Peggy McCormick, who had just married, in the McCormicks' new apartment at 56th Street and Everett Avenue in Hyde Park. By that point, of course, Kohut and Jay McCormick had known each other for several years and were the best of friends. It was, nevertheless, a complicated relationship for McCormick. Smart and self-effacing, very warm, and exceedingly friendly, McCormick had never encountered anyone in his life like Kohut.

The Viennese doctor was from a different cultural universe, which
McCormick found enormously appealing and was central to his intense
idealization of Kohut. McCormick could not believe how much Kohut
knew about things, nor how hard he worked, nor how well he did. It both
inspired McCormick toward greater efforts and made him feel like an idiot,
especially when Kohut told McCormick he was the only illiterate psychoanalyst. When he was moody Kohut could be mean and insulting, but
even at best he was exceedingly arrogant. In the McCormicks' new apartment were two tall, delicate, and quite expensive vases they had received
as wedding gifts. Kohut never directly told them the vases were in bad
taste. He simply threw his hat on one every time he walked into the apartment. It was a minor miracle one never broke.

Kohut could also sharply contradict McCormick when he thought his
friend was wrong about something. Kohut once asked McCormick why
he was so interested in boats. McCormick replied that he was not sure
but that he had been interested in them since boyhood and had chosen
to have his internship and residency near a lake just so that he could sail.
Kohut said no, he must have been interested in them because his analyst
liked to sail. McCormick heatedly replied that was not the case, but Kohut
refused to relent. It made McCormick feel helpless: He had so much invested in the power of Kohut's word, even though he knew his friend in
this case was dead wrong, that he came to doubt his own feelings. Once,
however, McCormick got the upper hand on Kohut without knowing why,
even in retrospect. He told Kohut a Jewish joke. A father tells his son to
jump from a ladder. Twice he catches him but the third time he lets him
fall to the floor. "That's so you learn never to trust anyone, even your
father," McCormick said as the punch line. Kohut was enraged at the joke
and made it clear he found it deeply offensive. McCormick innocently
thought it had to do with Kohut's complicated feelings about his father.

Kohut also *never* apologized for his rage, for his arrogance, or for
hurting his friend. It was not his style. Kohut would, however, after hurting McCormick's feelings, change quickly in mood and later do something kind and generous to win McCormick back. Once McCormick told
Kohut how he had wanted to be a millionaire when he graduated from
high school and asked his father not to give him the customary watch but
ten shares of stock. His small investment portfolio went belly up in
no time, and McCormick learned quickly about the market. Shortly after
that Kohut gave him a nice Swiss watch he had taken with him out of
Vienna. It was as though he was doing what McCormick's father had

not. Another time (after his analysis) Kohut went out of his way to take McCormick with him to dinner at the luxurious apartment of Kurt and Ruth Eissler, to include him in an auspicious event. Jay McCormick always felt Kohut liked him but did not respect him. McCormick, for example, felt when they both began doing analytic work in the late 1940s that Kohut would never have approved of what he was actually doing with his patients. In 1948 Jay and Peggy McCormick moved to the far North Side of Chicago. To find his own voice as a psychoanalyst, McCormick felt that he had to make a life in Chicago far from Heinz Kohut.

Sometime in the spring of 1945 things also began to fray with Barbara Bryant. Part of the problem, no doubt, was the convergence of his love relationship with the early, stormy period of his analysis, which called forth all of his most disturbing images of Else. But the real woman was also very much in the picture. "His relationship with his mother was always in our way," Bryant put it. Kohut kept Else completely hidden during his entire relationship with Bryant. He never introduced them, nor told her about his mother's shop. He never even told Bryant exactly where his mother lived, even though it was within walking distance of where she lived and particularly close to the McCormicks' apartment. He did tell Bryant that Sunday was his mother's day, and dutifully each Sunday afternoon he disappeared to be with Else. Only once did Bryant see her, and that was quite by accident. Bryant was having Sunday dinner with a friend at the Windermere Hotel in East Hyde Park. It happened that Kohut was there as well with Else. Kohut blanched when Bryant walked over to say hello. He got himself together enough to introduce her to his mother but said nothing to indicate anything about their relationship. Bryant was quite sure Else had no idea who she was.[18]

One night as they were saying good night on Miss Halliday's porch, Kohut told Bryant that "there was this working out" of his feelings he had to do and that she "would not be a part of it." She was shattered. He said that it had something to do with his analysis and his feelings about his mother. "We had meant so much to each other," she said, "that I couldn't believe that he really meant what he was saying." It felt to her as though he had worked through some things and that she was on the "discard pile." Later, as she thought about it, she realized how issues between them had been building gradually. "You get a feeling about these things." He was a complete puzzle in some ways and in others easy to read. But the business about his mother—which was the central issue—she could never figure out. "He was a particular puzzle with this thing about his mother."

Kohut was equally vague with the McCormicks about his mother. Peggy taught him how to drive a car in the Bryant period. On weekends they usually went down to Soldier Field by the lake, where he could drive around the parking lot without bothering anybody or encountering traffic. It was difficult for him to learn, as he was not mechanically minded and had waited until he was an adult to begin. Once, returning from Soldier Field, they turned off the Outer Drive at 47th Street. As they drove down the street Kohut remarked offhandedly that the clothing shop they had just passed was his mother's. Flabbergasted, Peggy almost did not believe her ears. Nor could she get him then, or later, to say more about it. It was off base. You were not to intrude. He clearly gave off signals hinting that "I'd just rather not talk about it."[19]

Else was, in fact, going through her own personal struggles and crises. The shop was successful, and she had plenty of friends in her life, including some suitors. She had begun to paint small landscapes and would in time have some modest exhibitions. She was always active in things. She also had a good measure of financial independence from her business and whatever money she had smuggled out of Vienna. Certainly she seemed to have sufficient resources to help finance her son's minor extravagances, like the opera with Bryant, and perhaps other important items, like his four-year psychoanalysis. But something was happening to her spiritually. A customer, Eleanor Roth, became Else's closest friend. Roth, a Catholic, talked to her of God and faith and introduced her to her own church in Huntley, Illinois, near Woodstock, northwest of Chicago. Sometime in the late 1940s Else decided to convert and was sponsored by Roth in her church.[20] Kohut, needless to say, had nothing to do with his mother's latest religious experiment, and apparently talked with no one about her conversion then or later. Of course, it has to be asked: After all her forays in Vienna, was this a definitive conversion?

Nine

CANDIDATE AT
THE CHICAGO INSTITUTE

At times in the second half of the 1940s a deep melancholy swept over Kohut. He wrote to August Aichhorn after the war that he lived with "something like a chronic homesickness" while at the same time he noted with astonishment that it was no longer "second nature" for him to write in German. He was tugged in two directions. English was taking over his tongue and America his soul. And yet he continued to long for the city of his youth, the lost universe of the past. His dreams still all took place in Vienna, he said, though at times "it seems like a foreign city to me." Vienna was suffused in images of death and destruction. "Almost all of my relatives," he writes, "died in various concentration camps." And he mentions some family members lost in the Holocaust: Else's brother, Uncle Willy Lampl, with his daughter; one of Felix's brothers with his wife and son and Felix's sister, Anna; someone he calls another sister of Felix who must, however, have been a sister-in-law; "etc., etc."[1]

Aichhorn, for his part, kept Kohut up to date on the doings of the Kraulics, the couple who had appropriated Paradiesgasse 47 for a fraction of its value. In 1946 Aichhorn had taken a vacation in Gastein and Mr. Kraulic was staying in the same hotel. Somehow, Kraulic knew of Aichhorn's connection with Kohut and took the opportunity to tell Aichhorn that he had remodeled the house and was still living there. Aichhorn noted with a bit of irony that Kraulic clearly "does not feel quite well in his skin" about what he did and seemed worried whether he would be able to hold onto the property. It might not be sufficiently "aryanized,"

Aichhorn added ironically. In a letter the next year Aichhorn wrote to express his pleasure that Kohut's uncle Hans Lampl was back in Vienna. Maybe Hans would be able to dislodge Kraulic, whom Aichhorn described with disdain as a "typical Nazi." Kohut, in turn, replied that Kraulic was in fact yielding nothing, maintaining that he had not been a Nazi, and seemed to have entirely forgotten that he called Else in the middle of the night to tell her if she didn't sell the house immediately he would make sure her son ended up in a concentration camp.[2]

Aichhorn, in general, became an important figure in Kohut's life between 1946, when they resumed contact, and 1949, when Aichhorn died. One of the few remaining figures from Freud's inner circle and the only one to last out the war in Austria, Aichhorn represented a direct link to Kohut's beloved Vienna, as well as a potent symbol of many meanings in Kohut's newly affirmed profession of psychoanalysis. Kohut first learned that Aichhorn had survived the war from his analyst, Ruth Eissler. He immediately wrote (in June 1946) and filled him in on the details of his life since his emigration. It is a long, chatty, and very frank letter, filled with emotion at this reconnection with the analyst whom he most admired and with whom he undoubtedly wished he could have completed his didactic analysis. For the next three years Aichhorn and Kohut exchanged letters every few months. Much mutual respect developed between them. Aichhorn expressed genuine amazement at the way Kohut (and Else, whom he had met in Vienna) were able to rebuild their lives. He was fascinated in the details of Kohut's life at the hospital, how much money he made, what his training was like at the Institute, how he interpreted dreams in his cases. He also kept up with the gossip, like the latest on the struggle over Franz Alexander's attempt to shorten psychoanalysis, which was creating major divisions in the staff of the Institute. Aichhorn urged caution on his protégé: Listen to what people say but hold onto the rock-solid truth of what Freud taught. Beware of deviance. "As long as I am the head of the Vienna Psychoanalytic Society here in Vienna," he wrote, "Freud's theory will be preserved pure and undiluted. The rock Freud blasted contains so many valuable fragments that there is plenty of work still to do for future generations. Let us be modest stonemasons after the giant."[3]

Kohut, for his part, seemed eager to take the advice. He saw himself as a Freudian in the making. Aichhorn was the perfect model. But there was also something of a reversal of roles between the two men. In their earlier analytic work, Kohut was the young, confused patient healed and molded in the caring hands of the older master therapist who stood at the right hand of the creator. After the war Kohut was clearly a rising star in training in an affluent land of hope with a good job and decent income. Aichhorn was old and tired now, near death, and very poor in postwar Vienna. Kohut knew that and in his first letter asked Aichhorn what he could send him. Aichhorn replied that the Eisslers provided for him in such a generous way that anything Kohut sent would be a luxury. Perhaps not to be outdone by the Eisslers but also surely out of a genuine sense of compassion, Kohut proceeded to send Aichhorn occasional "care packages" of food and books like Otto Fenichel's *The Psychoanalytic Theory of Neurosis* and Theodore Reik's *Listening with the Third Ear*, as well as to order regular shipments of coal so that his mentor would keep warm in the winter. Aichhorn was grateful. "You always do know what is most necessary at the moment," he wrote. The aging analyst was too proud to ask for anything directly, but he dropped hints. His reticence once elicited some harsh words from Kohut: "That you don't want to tell me what you need most urgently makes me a little bit angry. Do it and without the feeling that you are forcing me to send what you desire without fail. If it should be too difficult for me, financially speaking, I will not do it— that I promise you."[4]

In general, Kohut let his guard down with Aichhorn as with no other colleague, then or later. He talked of very personal matters. He seemed to want to stay in Aichhorn's consciousness. He went out of his way to specify things like his exact title as it changed and he moved up the academic ladder, along with his income. He even tolerated a question about why he was not married yet; then when he did marry, he wrote a description of his honeymoon trip and his new apartment in loving detail. He let Aichhorn know of his initial failure to be accepted at the Institute. He also described for him his rather serious automobile accident of December 18, 1946. Kohut was driving Else's car and had the bad luck, as he put it, to get in the way of a bus. He was unconscious for an hour, may have cracked his skull, and did break his collarbone. A passerby put his coat over him to keep him warm until the ambulance arrived; Kohut later tried but was unable to find the man to thank him. Kohut did, however, spend three weeks in the hospital. At least, he reports, the car will soon be made "healthy" again, and the costs of the accident were all covered by insurance.[5]

Aichhorn as well kept Vienna alive in Kohut's imaginative world, which helped him retain Vienna as the objective correlative of his life, the

point of reference for everything else, the symbol of who he was *and* all
that was lost and dead. This was true of psychoanalysis itself and especially Aichhorn's symbolic link to the person of Freud. But it was equally
true of the actual city itself. Initially in America during the early 1940s,
Kohut talked to everyone he got at all close to about Vienna (though he
avoided more general discussions of Hitler and Germany and certainly
the Holocaust; the city itself, as a concrete symbol, was safer). He also
joked with both Bryant and Charles Kligerman about how the Midway,
lined with the neo-Gothic buildings of the university, reminded him of
the Ring. After the war, however, the images of Vienna retreated into his
dreams, occasional conversations, and letters to Aichhorn. Kohut once
complained to Aichhorn of how hot it was in Chicago, hotter than Vienna
ever got. He always seemed to compare the cities he visited to the Austrian capital. For example, he traveled to Washington, D.C., in early summer, 1948, for the meetings of the American Psychoanalytic Association.
He enjoyed his visit but was mostly "untouched" by the city, for it so lacked
the splendor of Vienna. All the buildings were alike and the style was an
uncomfortable mix of the Viennese Parliament and the Neue Hofburg,
"if you can imagine something like that."[6]

Kohut decided—undoubtedly with the approval of Ruth Eissler—to re-
apply to the Institute in the fall of 1946. He formally submitted his application on September 29, 1946. He listed as his references Henry Brosin
(the head of psychiatry at the University of Chicago); his analyst, Ruth
Eissler; and Joan Fleming, who was on the staff of the Institute. This time
Kohut was interviewed by a committee that included Helen Ross and
Theresa Benedek. Even after nearly four years of his training analysis and
all his careful preparation, once again the training committee found cause
for concern. As before, nothing was put in writing in his file, so one has
to infer the deliberations of the committee. It seems they clearly accepted
his work with Eissler as a training analysis, for they admitted him to the
Institute and allowed him to begin taking courses. But they held off giving him permission to take on his first control case until, as Kohut reported to Aichhorn, "they get to know me better."[7] In all his dealings
with the Institute, Kohut was kept on a short leash.
    That fall of 1946 he began his course work.[8] He quickly established him-
self as an earnest Freudian, applauding the orthodox teaching of Eduardo
Weiss and quietly questioning Theresa Benedek's significant departures

from classical technique. She recommended, for example (following Franz Alexander), several ways to shorten analysis, from scheduling irregular hours to seeing the patient less often. She urged candidates not to analyze every single resistance and symptom but rather to go for the underlying conflicts and "principal dynamisms." This clinical approach to psychosomatic disease was the heart of Alexander's work. It was basically foreign to Kohut, but at this point, as a vulnerable new candidate not yet even approved for his first control case, Kohut was cautious in his criticisms. He played both sides of what was then a deeply divided Institute—and was actively courted by the key players. It was in his interest to remain neutral.

Kohut took a huge step forward in his career when he was made assistant professor of psychiatry on July 1, 1947. In the European tradition it is, of course, a more momentous event to become a professor than it ever has been in America, with its far greater number of colleges and universities. For Kohut the appointment meant he had reached the pinnacle of academic achievement and had crossed the magical threshold separating ordinary mortals from great figures of learning. For a Viennese intellectual to become a professor was an accomplishment of the highest order. Kohut's friend, Charles Kligerman, told how Kohut, on learning of his appointment, produced a box of photos from his childhood. He took each photo out ceremoniously. Of a shot of his parents on their honeymoon feeding the pigeons in the Piazza San Marco, he said: "Here are the parents of the future Assistant Professor." Of himself in short pants by a lake: "Here is the future Assistant Professor at camp in France." And so on through the entire box. Both men laughed uproariously, though Kligerman also sensed the incredible joy of the moment and wondered later whether receiving any of the many other awards Kohut received could have matched the pleasure he felt at that moment.[9]

For the next three years Professor Kohut continued his course work at the Institute. At one time or another he studied with all the analysts on staff and became conversant with every nuance of Freud's thought and that of his immediate successors.[10] Kohut's scientific reading in these years was also highly focused. "I'm reading quite a bit, mostly Freud," he wrote Aichhorn. He slogged through the early papers, then *The Interpretation of Dreams*, "Mourning and Melancholia," the case histories, the introductory and new lectures, *Beyond the Pleasure Principle, Group Psychology and the Analysis of the Ego, The Ego and the Id, Inhibitions, Symptoms and Anxiety, The Future of an Illusion*, and other books and papers.

He struggled with Otto Fenichel's *The Psychoanalytic Theory of Neurosis*, which he found so much like an encyclopedia that "the minute I open it I lose all desire."[11] He also went back to Aichhorn's *Wayward Youth*, "diligently studied" Anna Freud's *The Ego and the Mechanisms of Defense*, and got through Theodore Reik's *Masochism in Modern Man*, which he found full of "brilliant observations and deliberations." He took special care to search out Wilhelm Reich's *Character Analysis*, the writings of Karl Abraham, and Sándor Ferenczi's collected works. For all this apparent breadth, it is perhaps worth noting that during his training he never seems to have read Carl Jung, Otto Rank, nor any of the lesser figures around Freud. The only "deviant" whose work he seemed to know and care about was Sándor Ferenczi. He did once make what a participant later called a "very good" three-hour presentation on Melanie Klein around 1948 to a reading group at the University of Chicago Department of Psychiatry of which he was a part.[12] Otherwise, he was reading very much in the mainstream.

The other crucial part of psychoanalytic training that he had been held back from at first was his "control" cases. A candidate had to see four such psychoanalytic cases, usually provided by the clinic and seen at a reduced fee, under supervision with a senior analyst on staff. To be approved for one's first control case was the decisive step for a candidate into clinical psychoanalysis. By the end of Kohut's first year's work, in the summer of 1947, he was finally deemed ready for baptism by fire and given his first two control cases. He was now, at last, a full-fledged candidate. His first case was a man whom he began seeing five times a week and diagnosed as "masochistic character, psychosexual impotence."[13] In a letter to Aichhorn, Kohut allowed himself to emphasize that such frequency was quite rare at the Institute, for most of the cases were seen only two or three times a week (given the impact of Alexander). "It does seem to me that such treatments [that is, the shorter ones] have very little to do with proper analysis," he wrote, asserting his real feelings. Kohut also complained to Aichhorn that his supervisor, Fritz Moellenhoff from Berlin, never made himself available to meet with him. The analytic material had piled up. But in less than six months Kohut was feeling better about the case, though he remained somewhat baffled about its deeper meanings. It seems his patient was an intelligent professional man without any particular symptom but a general unease with life. He complained loudly and got aggressive if Kohut tried to "lead him toward more fruitful considerations." Kohut suspected that behind all these defenses lay deep feelings of guilt because of his prematurely deceased father. Such an interpretation of the central pathology in the case remained faithful to Freud's ideas about mourning and guilt. One cannot help feeling, however, from his brief description of the patient to Aichhorn, that Kohut's very first case in psychoanalysis had what he would later call a "narcissistic personality disorder."[14]

Kohut's second control case was a depressed woman with severe abdominal cramps who spent weeks at a time in bed, neglected her children, and had become dependent on sleeping pills. She developed a strong transference to him and faithfully attended analytic sessions. Kohut sought unofficial supervision on the case from Paul Kramer, who was also a Viennese Jew analyzed by Aichhorn. When Aichhorn learned that Kohut was in supervision with Kramer he was delighted. Aichhorn described Kramer as his "dear friend" and hoped Kohut was learning from him. Indeed he was. Kohut wrote, "I have the impression that I learn a lot from him, considerably more than from the others." Kohut complained, however, that Kramer was rather harsh on him and spent supervisory sessions analyzing Kohut's attitude toward a difficult patient, which sometimes elicited Kohut's own protests and guilt. Still, Kramer was generally satisfied with him and expressed the sole criticism that Kohut was hiding his hostility behind a facade of neutrality. Aichhorn replied, urging Kohut to take his work with Kramer very seriously, as he was one of the best. "I know him very well." Furthermore, he tried to encourage Kohut by noting that he himself with supervisees was also often "responsive to the transference relation of the analysand towards the analyst and his countertransference," though he added he was never harsh.[15]

In the early winter of 1948 Kohut was approved for his third and fourth control cases.[16] This assignment represented a significant step, for under the rules that then prevailed at the Chicago Institute, to be cleared for a third control was a kind of minigraduation. At this point the candidate could begin to take on analytic patients in private practice. Furthermore, Kohut completed his training analysis that March. He was now on the cusp of full legitimacy in psychoanalysis. As it turned out, Kohut's third control was a rather easy case; at least it seemed to present none of the daunting challenges of his first two cases. The patient was a student at the University of Chicago who complained of premature ejaculation, or as Kohut explained to Aichhorn (in English), he was "quick on the trigger." Kohut noted that the patient had some other troubles, especially a problem with submitting to authority, as well as exhibiting various passive homosexual tendencies. Still, Kohut had the impression things were going rather well with this case.[17] His final control seemed as well to present no special problems in treatment.

Kohut was gaining increased confidence in his clinical abilities. He felt better about his control cases as his patients seemed to be improving under his care. He was able to make up his own mind about the debate swirling around the Institute over the best form of psychoanalytic treatment. He was able to discuss clinical issues, like his approach to dream interpretation, with a new authority. Aichhorn asked him once how he interpreted his patients' dreams. Kohut responded that he first listened to the dream, along with immediate and subsequent associations, trying to place it in the context of that treatment hour. If he felt he understood the dream he would give an interpretation, which was less of the dream per se and more "an intervention that concerns the whole mood of the patient." For example, he described for Aichhorn a patient who recently reported a series of dreams that suggested the analytic situation. There was a classroom and a student who was behaving insincerely toward the professor and keeping secrets. Kohut said he gave no immediate interpretation but waited for further associations. But before the end of the hour he asked the patient what he was keeping secret. With another patient, one with very strong resistances, he noted that in general she only told him small fragments of her dreams. If he was successful in overcoming some of her resistances, she "suddenly" remembered other parts of a dream that were in turn transparent, like an image of tearing out Kohut's wife's hair that expressed her jealousy.[18]

By the spring of 1950 Kohut felt ready to take his exams and move toward full certification as a psychoanalyst. He wrote Helen Ross on June 9 in her official capacity as head of the training committee informing her of his intention to take the exams. He reported that he had finished all the necessary course work and that his four control cases were "quite far along in therapy." The committee evidently agreed, for he took his exams on October 17, 1950, and easily passed. Kohut was now a psychoanalyst.[19]

Siegmund Levarie returned from the war in 1946 and resumed his professorship at the University of Chicago in the Department of Music. In the same year he also took on responsibility to direct a concert series in Mandel Hall, the performance theater of the University of Chicago at the corner of 57th Street and University Avenue. He decided to try a sophisticated series of concerts that would focus on chamber music, as there was then no other such series anywhere in Chicago. Kohut attended all the concerts arranged by his friend. It became a tradition between them as well to return to Levarie's apartment after the performance to talk about it, often with other assembled guests. At one concert in 1947 Levarie programmed a Bartók string quartet. The audience of mostly students giggled repeatedly throughout the performance. The sounds were simply too new and strange; it was only the cultural upheavals of the 1960s in America that made Bartók a musical hero. Kohut and Levarie talked long into the night about the meaning of those giggles from otherwise smart and relatively informed people. It reminded them of the way the Viennese first responded to the work of Arnold Schoenberg. They agreed on some general principles about the psychology of music and decided a paper was definitely in order. It was to be Kohut's first publication in psychoanalysis. Kohut became the senior author of the paper, which he clearly felt contained mainly his ideas. Levarie helped him with "some of the formulations and especially with the detailed knowledge [of music]." The actual writing, however, was completely shared. "On the Enjoyment of Listening to Music" was finished in the spring of 1948, and would appear in the *Psychoanalytic Quarterly* in 1950.[20]

The basic thesis of the paper is that much of our earliest experience with noise is threatening to the self, but that we are protected by certain biological mechanisms (we are born deaf, for example) and by the soothing care of the mother. Musical pleasure itself perpetuates that sequence on a symbolic and very abstract level. The silence before the beginning of a concert, for example, increases the threat that sudden sound will intrude, while at the same time enhancing the enjoyment of the subsequent harmony. Bartók was experienced by those students as disruptive sound, for they had no musical familiarity with the chords and harmonies. The process of adjustment to the new sounds is a subtle one. The "curve of tension" cannot be too great or sudden, or too easily experienced, as in much popular music. To be enjoyed, music must evoke a "primitive ego state" of mastery through "incorporation and identification." An "ecstatic listener" to one of Beethoven's great symphonies does not clearly differentiate between himself and the outside world. "He experiences the sounds as being produced by himself, or even as being himself, because emotionally they are what he feels." There are, of course, a nearly infinite number of ways musically to control the tensions of sound on the way to their solution. But true enjoyment comes when the listener can enlarge his or her identity "to embrace a whole primitive, nonverbal universe of sounds after the original threat is overcome." Such a move to the primitive Kohut and Levarie call an "ability to regress," which must go along with the full range of one's complicated principles of self organization that allow one to recognize, understand, and master.

In the fall of 1947 Kohut was also thinking about Thomas Mann's novella *Death in Venice*. He took the opportunity of Helen McLean's seminar at the Institute that fall on "Psychoanalysis and Literature" to present an early version of his thoughts on the work. He later revised the essay in the spring of 1950 and made it his Institute graduation paper.[21] At the time Thomas Mann was still alive. Kohut never met the writer, but apparently felt—surprisingly, one must say—that his interpretation of the novella might be harmful to Mann's reputation, since it dealt with the underlying homosexual themes in the story. These themes are obvious to the contemporary reader—one observer has said the novella constitutes "a virtual Baedeker's guide to homosexual love." Kohut's hesitations indicate both the force of his conflicts and the strength of the taboo against homosexuality within his cultural milieu. In any event, he decided to withhold publication of the essay until after Mann's death (in 1955), whereupon he returned to the paper and prepared it for publication in the *Psychoanalytic Quarterly* in 1957.[22]

Kohut begins his paper with a brief account of the life of Thomas Mann, noting two important points: Mann's homosexual crush on a friend as an adolescent and his dark fears about suicide and death. Mann, Kohut says, wrote *Death in Venice* during a period of great personal stress that accentuated his conflicts around sex and death. What he managed, however, was to "sublimate" these issues into the "creation of an artistic masterpiece." An analogous psychological transformation, it would seem, from conflict to creativity, is exactly the step Kohut himself took in the course of the 1940s as he moved out of his own trauma of escape from death-immersed Europe to find professional and personal meaning in his life.

The hero of the story is the troubled writer and artist Gustav Aschenbach. At the beginning of the story, he can barely work and has to take frequent naps and walks to restore himself. On one such walk he finds himself in a cemetery and encounters a weird red-haired man with a prominent Adam's apple. That image then leads into a chapter on Aschenbach's life that borrows some important aspects of Mann's own experience, including even the detail of his mother's foreign background. Aschenbach then decides to take a trip and ends, as if by fate, in plague-infested Venice. Along the way he encounters another apparition, a man with gruesome yellow teeth. A third encounter with yet another aspect of death—this with an evil-looking gondolier—further heightens the tension of the story. But at this point the decisive moment of the story arrives, as Aschenbach first spies on the beach the gorgeous figure of a fourteen-year-old Polish boy, Tadzio, with his mother, governesses, and two sisters. Tadzio, the charmed favorite, is a boy of perfect beauty, godlike, pale, and sweet, of "chaste perfection." Aschenbach is engulfed with a consuming passion for Tadzio, whom he follows about Venice and begins to watch on the beach with abandon (to the concern of the boy's mother). Tadzio inspires Aschenbach's reflections on the nature of beauty. His whole creative self has come alive. He is transfixed when he can gain a glimpse of Tadzio and especially when he can catch his attention. A sudden smile from the boy at one such encounter leaves Aschenbach breathless, and the words "I love you" form on his lips. But death is everywhere in Venice. Aschenbach knows he should flee but cannot leave Tadzio. At this point Aschenbach has a fourth symbolic encounter, with a street musician whose swollen facial veins, tongue, and Adam's apple suggest the final agonies of death. And soon the inevitable happens. Aschenbach eats some infected strawberries. He learns Tadzio is about to leave Venice. He watches from the beach, dying, as the boy moves toward the sea and waves, as if inviting him "into an immensity of richest expectation."

The story, Kohut notes, centers on Aschenbach's "breakdown of sublimated tenderness and the nearly unchecked onrush of unsublimated homosexual desire in the aging writer." Aschenbach's disintegration unleashes the power of his previously sublimated sexual desires, which now find their truest expression in his passion for Tadzio. But his love transgresses the "cultural structure of a lifetime." Aschenbach's creativity, which seemed "related to the feminine principle," waxed and waned according to the power of his homosexual strivings. Kohut further suggests that such a relationship between creativity and homosexuality may have more general significance, as the idea is "fully compatible" with an "old and well-substantiated psychoanalytic thesis."[23] He argues that Aschenbach's archaic and powerful yearnings for the mother express themselves in the story in a number of diffuse but highly significant symbols. As with Hans Castorp in *The Magic Mountain*, the longing for death is itself mother-related. In *Death in Venice* Ashenbach cannot extricate himself from the warm embrace of the sick and dying city. And finally he is beckoned by the mother sea into which the beautiful Tadzio merges at the end.[24]

One day in the early spring of 1948, Kohut discussed material from one of his patients in the continuing case seminar for first-year candidates led by Thomas French. Such seminars are the heart of the curriculum in all psychoanalytic training institutes. For the most part they are deadly dull, for candidates read verbatim from their careful notes. The seminar goes on for hours because of the enormous amount of material to get through. Sometimes the teacher makes a comment or criticism, and the class asks questions that may lead to an interesting discussion. But in time the student always returns to the text and plows on. Kohut, on the other hand, as was his wont, spoke entirely extemporaneously. He had memorized the relevant clinical exchanges, the dreams and his interpretations, the course of the transference. He was articulate, clear, detailed, and charming, especially for the Institute's clinic social worker, Elizabeth Meyer, who had sat in on the class. She fell instantly in love.[25]

Kohut responded in kind. He had not been in a serious relationship since Barbara Bryant (though there was someone named Doris after Bryant whom Levarie said "wasn't very memorable"). When Aichhorn had asked him on November 19, 1946, when he planned to marry, Kohut replied the following February 2 that he could only answer the question "with difficulty." He was still in analysis and had many other (unspecified) problems as well. It just would have to wait. But when Meyer came along a year later he was in a very different place emotionally. He was ready to fall in love with a woman. He was out of analysis and his career was firmly on track. He felt secure, ready to take new risks. There was also much about her that fit his needs. She was not only in a field closely related to psychoanalysis, but actually present at the Institute working in the clinic. She could be strong-willed, but at thirty-six was also definitely available for marriage. The key thing, however, was the Vienna connection. That is what Kohut stressed in a letter to Aichhorn. He said Meyer was of German descent (though not Jewish) and had spent time in Vienna in analysis with Jenny Waelder, neglecting to add that she also had been one of Aichhorn's own students. It was as though they had always known each other, or at least been joined at some deeper level. "What was for me so decisive was that she knew Vienna," Kohut said late in life, "and she knew a little bit what the essential self of mine was."[26]

He was so ready, in fact, that the courtship barely lasted into the fall. Kohut reported to Aichhorn that when he told a good friend (probably Levarie) that he was getting married, the friend said drily, "It's about time." There is no evidence of what Kohut and Meyer did together, but one has to guess they spent a lot of time talking about Vienna. And this time he introduced his fiancée to his mother. He and Meyer decided to move quickly, and on October 9, 1948, they were married at her parents' home in Milwaukee. It was a simple ceremony, with only Meyer's parents, her sister Gretchen, and Else attending. A judge who was a friend of the family performed the ceremony. For their honeymoon they borrowed Else's car and went for a week or so to the Great Smoky Mountains of Tennessee. "It was indescribably beautiful," Kohut gushed rather uncharacteristically to Aichhorn. The mountains, he noted, are somewhat higher than the Wienerwald, and "the colors of the fall and the peculiar landscape were truly unforgettable."[27]

The trip was cut short because just before the wedding Kohut succeeded in finding an apartment—he took over the flat where the McCormicks had lived at 56th Street and Everett Avenue when they moved to the North Side of Chicago. To get the apartment was a stroke of "unbelievable luck" because of the housing shortage in Chicago, and he and his new wife were eager to return from their honeymoon and get moved in. They were located within easy walking distance of the university and the Illinois Central commuter train to downtown Chicago, where the Institute was located. The rent was $90 a month, affordable on his salary of $7,500, which represented a substantial increase in just one year, plus Elizabeth's of $4,700 from the Institute. The couple immediately splurged on a couch and rug that each cost $300, an armchair for $270, a dining room table and six chairs for $450, and other smaller items. "You can imagine the pleasure it brings me to have my own home," Kohut wrote Aichhorn. He now had a household.

And he had someone he could love. In the full flush of his courtship, Kohut wrote "My dearest, sweetest Betty" after she left for a trip to New Hampshire. "You see," he wrote, "there is no more caution and, boy!, it's wonderful." He recalled how once she started with pleasure at seeing him from a car window and another time how they met and talked in a fish market with its smells and crowds. As he rambled on, he said it made him think he was writing like James Joyce in *Ulysses*. And he told of his life since he had last seen her, of moving the furniture around in his office, of dining with Wadsworth, of his mother (of course in a "tragic mood"), who commented on how much he clearly loved Betty, of his work, and of his various activities the next day. Then he tired and needed to sleep. "Well, darling," he ended, "my eyes won't stay open any longer. I send you all the love I have and a million and one kisses. Heinz."[28]

Ten

DOMESTICITY

"The marriage," Charles Kligerman said later, "stabilized Heinz."[1] All the years of drift and lonely exile, of searching for sexual identity and a partner, of uncertainty, even, at times, of confusion, ended now at thirty-five in marriage to Elizabeth Meyer. He was not unready for the tasks that lay ahead, the promising career in psychiatry and psychoanalysis, the scholarship he planned, the dreams he harbored. But Kohut seemed clearly to feel that he could not make the journey without a wife. Partly it was convention. He could hardly hope to be accepted as a serious psychoanalyst in the 1950s without a wife. Alone, his career would have gotten quickly off track. He would have been seen as odd. It also seems clear he had fallen in love with Elizabeth Meyer and probably sensed he needed the controls and limitations of a relationship. Marriage brought a focus to Kohut's sometimes wildly disparate interests. He seemed to sense that he needed someone more grounded than himself, someone who was sensible, nonthreatening, endlessly accepting of his quirks, and definitely willing to cede center stage. No one could be close to Heinz Kohut who was unwilling to relinquish the limelight.

The transformative event of the marriage was the birth of the Kohuts' only child, Thomas August Kohut, on March 11, 1950. The given name honored Kohut's fondness for Thomas Mann, while the middle name celebrated the Aichhorn connection. Furthermore, Kohut's nickname for his son was Gustl—the German diminutive of August—and the dedication of his second book was "To G., and to his generation." For the first two years of the marriage, Elizabeth Kohut continued in her job as social worker in the clinic of the Institute. But once Thomas was born she decided to devote herself to homemaking, returning to work half days in 1961 as a psychotherapist in the student mental health clinic of the University of Chicago.[2] The 1950s were the days, of course, when few women continued their careers while their children were young. Elizabeth defined herself within the home and of the home. It was Heinz Kohut's career that would be made and their child whom she would principally raise.

Kohut maintained an idealized image of Thomas, this only son of an only son. One of Kohut's favorite artists was the sixteenth-century Italian Melozzo da Forli, who painted children with cherubic faces who he said looked just like Thomas. Whenever he mentioned this painter, it would be with great enthusiasm. Kohut, it seems, was determined to be present in his son's life the way his own father had not been. He knew it mattered what happened between father and son and that you could not ever make up for time lost in early years into mid-adolescence. So Kohut did a lot of things with Thomas, from games to trips to museums, and talked with him about his life and concerns. Kohut would take Thomas fishing, for example, when they visited Wisconsin, and tell him stories for hours of the ancient Greeks, of Herodotus and Thucydides, of the Spartans, of the battles of Thermopylae and Marathon. In general, Kohut took charge of Thomas's education, constantly exhorting him to do better. Until Thomas was an adolescent, Kohut's dream was that his son would become a doctor. Once Kohut took him on a complete tour of Cook County Hospital. He also bought a calf's heart and other organs and they dissected them together and built a slide collection. He was mentoring Thomas, preparing him for larger tasks.[3]

This intense nuclear unit defined Kohut's existence. "Family," however, included not just Elizabeth and Thomas but several other relatives who joined in many family functions and rituals. The most important relative not in the house was, of course, Else, who lived just a neighborhood away. She continued to be successful with her business and gathered around her a circle of friends. She took to painting small landscapes and even took lessons at the Art Institute. At one point in the early 1960s (then in her late seventies) she found a man, a Mr. Fantus, whom she met in her art classes at the Art Institute. She told Kohut she was willing to have sex with him but he could not manage it. His children were terrified that she was going to marry their father and take his money. All she wanted, however, was the companionship. In general in the 1950s and early 1960s, Else was around all the time, every holiday and regularly for dinner. Her presence never stopped making Kohut nervous. "She was the only person who could really get to my father," as Thomas puts it. Part of the problem as well was that no one else in the family liked Else, so that when she was present the temperature rose. Elizabeth's sister, Gretchen Meyer, found her "pushy and aggressive," and was repulsed by the way she would speak directly into your face and poke you with her finger. "She was seductive," says Thomas; "she used to paw at me." Elizabeth herself despised her mother-in-law and always had to grit her teeth in her presence. As Thomas says, no one liked Else who knew her up close, though she could be admired from afar for her talents and assertiveness and simply for how she had survived the twentieth-century horrors.

Gretchen Meyer was a much gentler presence in the family. Gretchen, an unmarried high school English teacher at Francis Parker School on the North Side of Chicago, had an uncanny physical resemblance to Elizabeth; indeed, they looked like twins. An important series of events in 1957 brought Gretchen more closely into the Kohut family. In 1953 the Kohuts had moved from their relatively small apartment at 56th Street and Everett to a more elegant place at 5433 East View Park along Lake Michigan near the Museum of Science and Industry. By 1957 the Kohuts decided on a further move up to the distinctive Cloisters, a large and stately apartment building on the corner of 58th Street and Dorchester Avenue, near the university and across the street from the Lab School, where Thomas was enrolled. Their apartment, 12C, faced west over Jackman Field and, farther in the distance, the spires of the neo-Gothic buildings of the university. The Kohuts' move to the Cloisters coincided with the death of the father of Elizabeth and Gretchen Meyer. It was decided that Gretchen would then take over the East View apartment with her aged and increasingly senile mother, Dora, and a devoted African-American woman named Eddie, who was the mother's caretaker. In the summer of 1957 Dora had been hit by a car in an accident perhaps brought on by her senility (she seemed to walk into it), and required extensive nursing. All this family caretaking was only possible, however, because Kohut himself helped pay the rent (he contributed $75 of the $115). Gretchen wrote Kohut that she felt bad about taking the money, and offered to knit sweaters that she said she could sell at Francis Parker High School, among other rigorous ways of budgeting. Kohut replied with generosity that it was only natural that he should be providing support for her and her mother.

That is what family is all about. Kohut's only concern was that Gretchen was worried about bothering him. He said they would start with the $75 per month and see if the amount needed to be raised later. "For the rest, we will see and handle things as they come along." In any event, he certainly wanted to assure her that she did not have to turn to knitting sweaters.[4]

The subtext of this communication was Kohut's genuine fondness for Gretchen and his deep love for his mother-in-law, Dora Meyer. For to the degree to which he disliked his own mother, Kohut adored his mother-in-law. In the family, Else was "Granny" and Dora "Grandma." Kohut doted on "Grandma," talked to her, and supported her for years after she became senile. At her funeral he gave a touching memorial that Thomas still treasures as one of the most moving speeches his father ever gave.[5]

Other people hovered at the margins, the most important of whom by far was Robert Wadsworth. He was something of a beloved fixture in the family. Wadsworth came over for dinner often and spent every important holiday with the Kohuts. One can only guess how often Wadsworth and Kohut himself talked or met just as friends, but Thomas and his aunt Gretchen, for example, could not imagine a family event of any significance without Kohut's oldest and dearest American friend. He became an essential part of the family landscape.

The Kohuts were very close to the Levaries, but that ended in 1954 when Siegmund left Chicago to assume the chairmanship of the music department at Brooklyn College (he later joined the Graduate Center of the City University of New York). After that, Kohut and Levarie wrote periodically and got together whenever the opportunity arose. There was always the tone of prewar Viennese coffee house banter in their correspondence. Levarie once joked that Kohut must be a sadist for referring to an opera he had seen in Frankfurt without telling him which one and writing about a person named Stedel he did not know. Kohut dutifully replied without missing a beat from their school days that he had seen *The Coronation of Poppaea*, sung in Italian with Irmgard Seefried as Poppaea. Stedel, he added, was the founder and benefactor of Frankfurt's Art Institute and owned Rembrandt's *The Blinding of Samson*, as well as "a marvelous Van Eyck Madonna and Child, splendid Cranach, Memlings, etc., and—it really does exist!—Goethe by Tischbein."[6]

When Levarie's sister's husband contracted an incurable disease in the mid-1950s, he consulted Kohut about what to tell his sister, Ada. Kohut replied that, in general, those who really want to know about death will ask and find out for themselves. The others prefer to live in denial, which he felt should be honored (though one important exception is if there is a need to make a will). One should not force the knowledge of death on the dying, Kohut advised. He recommended that Levarie and his wife, Norma, Levarie's parents, and anyone else responsible who was involved should make detailed plans to deal with the children and to make plans for Ada's future to the extent possible. Such preparations, Kohut felt, would be very reassuring for her when death came. On second thought, however, he added a P.S. stressing that the plans for Ada's future not be presented to her as a fait accompli but as suggestions over which she had complete control. "Activity, too," Kohut concluded, "can be very helpful to a person in crisis."[7]

Kohut also had a quasi-familial relationship with Peter Vander Veer, the son of a deceased colleague whose wife committed suicide around the same time. Peter, then an early adolescent, suddenly became an orphan, though he had an older brother in college. The Kohuts informally adopted Peter. He never actually moved into the apartment, but Thomas remembers that he was with them a great deal in the 1960s, took some vacations with them, and was there for all the holidays. For the rest of his life Kohut continued to help Peter whenever he could, as when he wrote a number of letters in the 1970s strongly supporting Peter's application for various residency programs.[8]

Kohut's deepest emotional attachments, however, lay within the tight confines of his nuclear family. He was a man of ritual and regularity, of predictable order, of routines that could in moments of stress get tinged with compulsiveness. He got home from work around 5:30 and dinner was at 6:00. In the 1950s, when he was still pudgy and weighed between 150 and 160 pounds, he ate full meals at dinner. In the early 1960s, however, when he was approaching the age of fifty (his father died at forty-nine), he stopped smoking cigarettes, began jogging—he did the mile in under seven minutes, mostly in Jackman Field across the street from the Cloisters—and lost a good deal of weight, getting down eventually to his ideal of 128 pounds. To lose weight and then to maintain it, he ate very lightly during the week, including a lunch of lettuce and cottage cheese doused in ketchup, but he indulged himself with a good wine and normal meals on the weekend. He never varied from his diet once he had established the pattern and remained thin for the rest of his life.[9]

After dinner Kohut would disappear into his study to work. There were always letters to write and things to attend to. Gretchen Meyer always thought of him as a workaholic in this regard. When Thomas was young there was homework and other activities in the early evening in which he might participate occasionally, but generally he tended to his correspondence in the two hours or so right after dinner. At around 8:30 Kohut would emerge from his study to listen to records for an hour or so. It was a very important part of his day. No disturbances were allowed, and he listened intently. Elizabeth, who was not particularly musical, would sit with him and knit but often fell asleep. After that Kohut might work for a while more, but then around ten o'clock he would undertake the final rituals of the day. First he would walk Tovey, which was a production, especially once they moved to the Cloisters, for it meant taking the elevator down and walking out through the courtyard to the street. When he returned from the walk the family would have what they called a "tea party," or in their private language, a TP. Everyone would eat something light, such as yogurt, and then go to bed around eleven (in the 1950s Thomas obviously went to bed earlier). Kohut, who seemed not to need more than about five hours of sleep a night, would continue to read and work until sometime between 1:00 and 2:00 a.m., only what he read at this point of the day was mostly literature, perhaps Goethe, Thomas Mann, Boris Pasternak, Proust, Eugene O'Neill, a Greek play, or some worthwhile study of literature or history.[10]

The day began at 6:30 for Kohut. Once he had lost weight and started running, he would begin with a series of exercises to get warmed up. Then he would cross the street to Jackman Field and run his mile or so for the day. He would come back, shower, dress, and have breakfast. By 8:00 he was off to work, which was itself highly ordered. Patients came by the hour, and for most of the 1950s and 1960s he saw patients almost entirely in traditional psychoanalyses of four or five sessions a week, which meant there was not even much variety from day to day in the patients he saw in his clinical practice. He sat in exactly the same chair all day, doing pretty much the same thing with the same people.

Kohut's self-presentation was elegant and formal. He was never without a suit and tie, and he had his shoes custom-made. He was not a dandy, but he could be arch. Once in the late 1950s, Ernest Wolf was with some other candidates at the Institute when it was still located at 664 North Michigan Avenue. They were waiting for the elevator at the top floor. A "youngish man, well dressed, of very serious mien" with a Germanic accent, whom he did not then know, came up to the group and told them that if they were traveling to the ground level it was all right to use the elevator. If, however, they were simply going to the floor below where there were additional classrooms, they should not tie up the elevator but rather walk. The man was Kohut. Wolf, himself a Jewish refugee from Nazi Germany, was enraged at such authoritarianism. He felt Kohut was "ascetic and disciplined, Teutonic and commanding," and vowed to take the elevator whenever he damn well pleased. Wolf had heard about Kohut as the star of the Institute but had not yet met him. It was not an auspicious beginning.[11]

Kohut was also capable of prodigious amounts of work. One has only to read the thousands of published and unpublished letters he wrote and carefully copied to appreciate how much time he spent in correspondence. At this stage of his life, from the early 1950s until the mid-1960s, he carried a huge burden with his organizational work in psychoanalysis and with reading and commenting on manuscripts for the *Journal of the American Psychoanalytic Association*, for which he served on the editorial board for many years. He was always conscientious about such tasks. Anyone who knew him in these years was struck with how seriously he took everything and how hard he worked. He told Charles Kligerman that he only managed by compromising his social life. When he traveled he carried three or four folders with him and would work in transit, waiting for a connection, and on the plane. Kohut's old friend, Jay McCormick, once happened to be in the seat next to him on a plane ride to New York and was "appalled at his capacity for work." Kohut only briefly chatted with McCormick as the plane took off and then turned to a manuscript he was working on. He also told McCormick that he usually worked at night after Elizabeth went to bed, even after a social event on the weekends.[12]

Kohut was self-absorbed but he was not dour. He always had subscription tickets for the symphony, which he regularly attended during the season. He had acquired the habit of wearing an old coat that he would throw under the seat rather than a good one that had to be checked. That way he did not have to waste time waiting to get his coat after the performance. He was knowledgeable about music but not ostentatiously so. His interests continued to be wide-ranging; he kept up, for example, with contemporary developments in jazz. But he generally preferred classical music. He continued to love opera (his favorite was still Wagner's *Die Meistersinger*) and thrilled to all the great music of the church (Bach was probably his favorite composer). Somewhat later he wrote his old friend in Paris, Jacques Palaci, whom he and Elizabeth planned to visit, asking that Palaci buy tickets for a concert while they were there. Kohut was very clear about his tastes. For opera, he requested Beethoven's *Fidelio*, Wagner's *Die Meistersinger*, or almost anything by Verdi (though he would prefer *Falstaff* and *Otello*). He also said he liked French operas, such as those on the Faust theme. But, he said, no *Butterfly, Bohème, Tosca*, or other "popular favorites." Stick with the "heavier fare," he said: Beethoven, Bach, Brahms, Bruckner, and "some of the better moderns."[13]

Eating with small groups of friends was an important social experience for Kohut, to which he brought his customary intensity. With another couple or two he liked going to ethnic restaurants in Chicago; his favorite was a Greek restaurant on Halsted Street. He also loved to have dinner parties on the weekends. Charles Kligerman, perhaps gilding the lily a bit, described the way Kohut sparkled at such dinner parties, which were his favorite form of entertainment, as opposed to larger gatherings where he felt more ill at ease (probably because he could not dominate or control them). But at home around his own table, said Kligerman, "his Viennese wit bubbled over." He would go on about a rare Trockenauslese wine, expound on Verdi's *Falstaff* or Schubert or Hugo Wolf as sung by Dietrich Fischer-Dieskau, or describe in detail a hike in California or in the Grisons in Switzerland. Thomas has vivid memories of such parties from his childhood. Most of the guests were also immigrants, European Jews educated like Kohut in the high culture of the West, people like Bernard Kramer, Martin Grotjahn, Hurgnon Witzleben, Paul Kramer, Richard Sterba, and (the non-Jewish) Fritz Moellenhof, whom Kohut admired greatly for his elegant German dueling scars. Thomas recalls listening in amazement as a child while his father and his friends sat around talking German, which he did not then understand but enjoyed hearing. In those days Kohut's friends were his equals, roughly his age, and his colleagues in psychoanalysis.[14]

Kohut relished vacations in Europe, which were sometimes associated with psychoanalytic meetings in Paris, Rome, Berlin, wherever. If he had a chance, for example, of going to a place like Siena, with its great art, Kohut would buy books and read in advance to prepare himself for the experience. The family's regular vacation spot, however, was in Carmel, California. Kohut had always suffered in Chicago from severe allergies during the late summer months. August, the traditional vacation month for psychoanalysts anyway, was torture. And so, beginning in 1951, Kohut began what became a long tradition of spending his vacation in California. That first year the Kohuts found a small house in Carmel with an

open fireplace and a lovely garden. During the vacation both Else and
Dora paid visits, though not at the same time. They all took car trips up
and down the beautiful California coast, lay on the beach, and swam in
the swimming pools. Everyone got a "wonderful bronze California tan
on our bodies."[15]

After that Kohut both extended the vacation to two months, from mid-
July to mid-September, and was able to find an arrangement with an
English couple that gave them a more permanent place in Carmel. The
English couple owned the house but wanted to return home in the late
summer and so were willing to rent to the Kohuts for the months they
wished to be there. There was a main house, where the family stayed. In
front was a large lawn where the family and whatever friends or guests
were visiting regularly played croquet in the evening. But in the back, quite
separated from the house, was a two-car garage with a small apartment
above it. Kohut took this apartment as his study. He could sit there all
morning and watch Thomas play in the yard but otherwise be completely
isolated. There was no phone. All he did was write.[16]

Kohut usually added the descriptor "beloved" when he wrote about
Carmel.[17] His routine was to work in the morning until early afternoon
and then swim and walk and play in the later afternoon and early evening.
But work was protected. Until the end, it was during these two summer
months in Carmel that Kohut did most of his writing. As Thomas remembers, Kohut "would sit there with his yellow legal pads and write in his
unintelligible Austrian shorthand and then rewrite his first draft and then
dictate it and get it typed and sent to him. No notes. He would just start
to write." There was much mailing of material back and forth to his secretary, which he would go over, dictate again, get retyped, and repeat as
many times as it took until he felt he had it right. Thomas remembers
that his father wrote "draft after draft after draft after draft." But there
were never notes. He told Thomas that he had to be sure every word was
exactly what he wanted to say. Kohut kept a thesaurus nearby and would
spend a lot of time getting things precise.

Several points are worth making about this process of writing. One
is that he seems to have let his ideas build up during the rest of the year
so that he was primed for an intense period of writing the minute he
arrived in Carmel. Ideas tumbled out of him. Second, in form Kohut
wrote the way he talked, with a kind of planned chaos, an associative style
that circled and deepened rather than moved along any simple narrative
line. Finally, it is quite striking that the crucial first draft of anything that

mattered was written in his obscure Austrian shorthand. In what language
was he thinking, English or German? Shorthand, of course, is symbolic.
It also becomes necessarily individual, as one changes languages and adapts
the symbols to a new grammar and set of words. In Kohut's case, there
are many identifiable German characters in his shorthand, but they spell
out, as best one can tell, English words. His shorthand was so idiosyncratic as to suggest that the "language" in which he most creatively
thought was a peculiar mix of German and English. At the very least, it
was English spelled with German shorthand characters. At his creative
core Kohut remained attached to aspects of his German roots for his initial formulations. From that version his first dictated draft then had to be
in the best English he could muster in order for his secretary to type it.
Thereafter, increasingly more complete drafts forced him into purely
English formulations. But it would seem quite possible he composed in a
language that combined English with German symbols and perhaps German phrases or even grammar at times. It may be that his oeuvre is at
some level a translation.[18]

Besides Carmel in the summers, Kohut began taking regular weekend trips to a house in Wisconsin that Gretchen bought in 1957 (and for
which Kohut put up the down payment). Part of the purpose in buying
the retreat was to ease Gretchen's burden of caring for her mother. She
often went to the Wisconsin house on weekends while Eddie would be
off, and Kohut, Elizabeth, and Thomas would stay in the apartment on
East View Park to care for Elizabeth's and Gretchen's mother. At other
times, the Kohuts went to Wisconsin. Because of Kohut's allergies, it was
an impossible place for him to visit in the summer, but they loved it in
the winter. Both he and Elizabeth liked cross-country skiing, though
sometimes coming out of the pine plantations there would be some pretty
steep downhills. Kohut also liked bird-watching. As always with an activity in which he engaged, he studied it carefully, bought books, and learned
a great deal about the birds he saw.[19]

Kohut, no doubt, was as adjusted to being American by the 1950s as
any immigrant possibly could be. And yet at times he still felt a vague
homesickness for Europe, and especially his native Vienna, for the feel of
the place, "its houses, mountains, streets." It kept slipping away. He
staunchly resisted assignments to speak in Vienna, yet longed for it. He
could hardly imagine what a real Viennese street would look like, he told
Levarie in 1951. Such memories evoked longings for his childhood. "The
cliché that America is a land with little past, and Europe with a lot of it

has emotional significance," he once wrote. America lacks even fairy tales and a mythology. Such things may mean more than we even realize. Maybe for those old New England families with a sense of the past there is not the same absence of tradition, he continued. But then again, what about Henry Adams, who found himself only "at home" in Europe? Well, Kohut said in his letter, changing paragraphs and moving on, "enough tears shed."[20]

Kohut was unable to visit Vienna until 1957. Even then it was forbidden fruit that stirred up confused feelings. "I will never forget my first return to Vienna after the war," he wrote some years later. "Without the presence of Betty and Tom my playing with psychological fire might well have led to chaos." During the trip Kohut took Thomas (then seven) to see all the key sites from his childhood, including the house on Paradiesgasse and the Döblinger Gymnasium. He showed his son the actual rooms in which he studied and the desks where he sat, which of course prompted a retelling of the many anecdotes from his school days. He also visited with Hans Lampl, who then held a "high governmental position" and was a man of "considerable influence." On the day before they were to leave, probably in anticipation of his death, which was to occur not much later, Hans wanted to give Thomas a special gift. He first took the family out to dinner and afterward to Muehlhausen, a toy store that was the FAO Schwarz of Vienna. They arrived after nine o'clock, long past closing time, but Hans had arranged to have the store opened specially for them. The lights were turned on, and they had the entire store to themselves. Hans turned to Thomas and said, "You may have anything here you like." Thomas was speechless and nearly paralyzed. But with some prodding he began to choose first this and then that in a mounting frenzy. They went upstairs to look at the electric trains and all the other toys. Thomas asked, "Can I really have anything I want?" "Yes, you may," said Hans. Everything began going into boxes—engines, cars, various stop signs, bridges, houses, and mountains from the train set, and other toys from around the store. Thomas began picking up various items. "This?" he asked. "Yes, you may," said Hans. "And this?" "Yes." And on it went. Kohut watched Thomas's face get flushed with excitement. Hans and the store manager and the clerk were watching the spectacle with glee. But Kohut was becoming uncomfortable. It was a dream come true but too much of a dream. Finally, Kohut told Thomas softly but firmly, "I think now that we have enough."[21]

Perhaps Kohut himself could not stand the stimulation. He was already taut from being in Vienna. The toy store scene symbolized overpower-ing stimulation, which was also his point in telling the story when he did, at his sixtieth birthday celebration in 1973.[22] He seemed in these middle years always striving to contain himself, to hold in his bursting enthusiasms, to keep himself focused and directed in order to make it in the world and in his profession and not let himself be thrown off guard by his erupting passions. He had to be conventional in these years. He had to be accepted. It was not a time to take risks. Rejection or failure would have been too devastating, given how hard it had been to estab-lish himself. He seemed to feel precarious, even though the actual con-ditions of his life were quite secure.

Kohut's politics as well reflected his caution. As a young man Kohut had stood above the fray as an aesthete in the Viennese coffee houses, generally apolitical and only moderately involved, and certainly well to the right of the socialism that swept many European campuses in the 1930s. He hardly noticed the world of politics until his universe crumbled around him. In the 1940s Kohut completely identified with his country of adop-tion and became a loyal American. In the late 1940s he apparently became concerned about the disruptions to academic life caused by the surge of anti-Communism; it probably brought back terrifying images from his youth. Kohut kept in his personal file University of Chicago president Robert Hutchins's 1949 report to the faculty about what he character-ized as absurd charges of Communism at the university from the state legislature in Springfield. In the report, Hutchins was sarcastic (and quite funny) about the bumbling provincials downstate, though within a year or so much more extensive and serious charges of Communism were leveled at the university by U.S. Senator Joseph McCarthy, and many careers were destroyed. Kohut in general was a moderately liberal Demo-crat. He was definitely less radical than Elizabeth, who was more in-clined toward socialism. Kohut idealized John F. Kennedy, for example, and gave a touching eulogy for the slain president after the assassina-tion.[23] On the social discontent of the 1960s, Kohut spoke with the voice of numbed reason. In 1964, for example, he wrote Mayor Richard J. Daley after some racial riots in Chicago. He pointed out gratuitously that such disturbances mostly occur in the hot summers months. Why not build swimming pools in poor neighborhoods with loudspeakers to broadcast music? It would be a cheap investment with a large payoff.[24] There is, of course, nothing wrong with building swimming pools for young people, but such a proposal as a way of warding off urban discontent smacked in

1964 of condescension, elitism, and great distance—or lack of empathy, in his own terms, for the real issues that drove the politics of the civil rights movement.

In other ways, as well, Kohut moved with caution and sought at all costs to be accepted. He became more assertive about his Christianity. He had always celebrated Christmas with a tree and presents, and Christmas rituals now became central in his own family; besides, his wife was Christian. He could also now justifiably say his mother was Catholic, since she had converted in 1948, though such a statement hardly captured his authentic experience, given the secrecy with which he handled that event. He read *Christian Century* and increasingly began acting as though he were not Jewish. He felt it was important for Thomas to have a Christian upbringing and become familiar with the Bible. He became good friends with the pastor of the Unitarian Church, John (Jack) F. Hayward, and occasionally even gave a sermon.[25] For many people who knew Kohut, one of the most amazing things about first reading the selected edition of his letters that was published in 1994 was the matter-of-fact way his Jewishness comes out in letters to old friends. He never actively hid being Jewish from those who cared to know, or did know, or were out of his past in some way, though even then he could obfuscate; he told Charles Kligerman, for example, that his mother was Jewish but not his father. But anyone new in his life, like a patient or younger colleague or new friend, was almost always in doubt whether he was Jewish. Gretchen Meyer said, "We, I guess, knew that Heinz had a Jewish background but it never came up, you know. It was no issue." It was only after Kohut died that she learned from Walter Lampl about Felix's taking Walter to synagogue. Kohut had never told *that* family story. Gretchen felt the issue of being Jewish must not have mattered to Kohut at all, because "he certainly never talked about it." She does remember him talking about how Else in his childhood had "not yet" turned Catholic.

It also seems he obscured his religious and ethnic identity from his own son. Thomas's sense of his father was that he was not only militantly non-Jewish but that he was Christian in a basic and authentic way. "He didn't experience himself as Jewish," Thomas says now with certainty. It was important to him, and he was "quite open about this: He was not Jewish." "He was a Christian." Thomas once came home from school and used the word "schmuck." Kohut said, astonishingly: "I think that's a Jewish word, or a Yiddish word." Kohut also told Thomas that the hardest thing about what he called his "time of troubles" in the refugee camp

in England was that all the other inmates had an identity. They were Jewish. He was not. He was Viennese, and that was lost. "The others had
this identity they could carry with them. But he didn't have that."

As a mature man and already one of the leading psychoanalysts in the
country, Kohut seemed to feel the need to reconfigure his past to bring it
into line with his new ambitions.[26] In what might be called his core self,
he appeared to struggle with profound issues of confusion over who he
was and where he came from.

Eleven

THE COUCH

Kohut began seeing patients in psychoanalysis on a full-time basis in 1949. That was how he spent his days and how he supported himself and his family. He was highly invested in his practice. He once said one reason people became psychoanalysts was that they were searching for missing aspects of their own personality. "We immerse ourselves in others. We need to understand. There is a need/urge that makes us do that."[1] There were, of course, outside activities—speeches, meetings, Institute classes, and University of Chicago seminars—but they were fitted into and around his clinical practice. He did nothing academic or professional that supplanted or even eroded his primary life as a clinician. He never had a "sabbatical," no stint at a think tank, nor even a really extended break from his work. His only relief from full-time practice was his vacation in Carmel each summer. In these early years, Kohut also hardly varied the externals of his clinical routine. He restricted his practice to seeing patients only in actual analysis, which meant four or sometimes five sessions a week. He was sufficiently well known and respected to be able to make that choice. As part of his responsibilities to the Institute, Kohut did supervise candidates, but with that exception, the form of his actual clinical practice in the 1950s and early 1960s never changed much. He saw his patients as often as possible each week. He never exhorted them, said gratuitous things about himself to them or sought to educate them. He was, first and foremost, a psychoanalyst.

The "pure gold" of psychoanalysis had some specific markers for Kohut that distinguished it from the "base alloy" of other kinds of psychotherapy.[2] The patient lay on the proverbial couch while Kohut sat behind him or her and out of sight on a straight-backed wooden chair. The only real rule was that the patient was to say whatever came to mind, with as little self-censorship as was humanly possible. The agenda belonged to the patient. Treatment stretched out almost indefinitely and was certainly open-ended. If Alexander tried to shorten psychoanalysis in the 1940s, Kohut became noted for his eight- and ten-year analyses in the 1950s. Kohut's case histories are full of descriptors such as "prolonged," "unhurried," "gradually unfolding," "enduring," and "patient." Kohut felt it was important to give things time to express themselves in treatment. Change otherwise was superficial. Nor did he think the analyst should be too eager to offer interpretations. When a patient acted out or made repeated slips (like coming late or leaving early), for example, unlike most analysts who interpreted such behavior, he preferred to wait and not confront the patient with the meaning of such unconsciously motivated behavior, at least for a while. To act too soon reflected the therapist's impatience and his or her own frustrated need to know. It was the result, in other words, of the therapist's own needs. The problem with frequent confrontations was that the patient comes to experience intrusions from his unconscious as misdemeanors. Kohut's goal, on the contrary, was to create an "atmosphere in which the patient might, non-defensively, discover the self-assertive, positive meaning of an act that he was formerly able to undertake only outside of his awareness."[3]

Kohut's offices were quite modest. In his very early years of practice he shared an office with Lester McLean at 30 North Michigan Avenue. After that he moved to the Chicago Institute for Psychoanalysis, then located at 664 North Michigan Avenue, where he spent most of the 1950s and early 1960s in his own office, which was part of a two-person suite. In 1966 he moved, along with the Institute, to 180 North Michigan Avenue, at the northern edge of the Loop, or downtown area, where he remained until his death. Kohut's office, number 2308, was rectangular, with the entrance at the right end. On the wall to the right of the entrance were bookcases with a desk and chair in front of them. In the right corner of the room behind the door was a sink. Along the facing wall were three windows looking east. To the left of the door was an easy chair with a stand next to it with a box of Kleenex. Along the left wall was the couch and next to it in the back left corner Kohut's rather uncomfortable-looking chair. Above Kohut's chair were pictures of Freud and August Aichhorn.[4]

Kohut, it seems, was regarded from the beginning as a superb therapist who took on the most difficult cases. Arnold Goldberg says, "I never
met anyone who was in analysis with him who didn't adore him," though
he added there was a case toward the beginning of Kohut's career that
"failed badly." Goldberg says Kohut "truly loved all of his patients."
Goldberg once watched as Kohut listened to a paper being given by a
patient who was then a resident. Kohut had a look of pure joy on his face
at the accomplishment represented by the paper. Ernest Wolf, who worked
with Kohut for years, heard only praise for Kohut's clinical skills. At the
same time, the greatest clinician in Chicago was generally regarded as Louis
Shapiro. He was the one you went to if all else failed. Like anyone, Kohut
occasionally lost his focus. Arnold Goldberg once taught a seminar from
notes Kohut took during an analysis in the mid-1960s when Kohut was
president of the American Psychoanalytic Association. On one page Kohut
had written, "I am so upset today I can't even listen." Kohut himself could
also be quite modest. He once noted a case in which there was much
improvement, but in the end he and the patient were stumped in certain
areas. And he added: "I could give you literally hundreds of examples of
feeling stumped in trying to understand psychological configurations."
He once told some candidates: "I made my mistakes."[5]

But Kohut was a fine therapist. For him empathy was the key. He
seemed to have a remarkable ability to follow the flow of a patient's associations. He was in the experience. It was not dissimilar from the way he
listened to music; in fact, the carryover may have been quite specific. He
could detect the subtlest changes of beat and rhythm, hear the harmonies, follow the development of themes, and always sense as things moved
toward resolution. With a patient he seldom took notes during a session
(though he often did after the hour) but could recall the minutest of
details. At the same time, Kohut always knew where a patient was in the
transference. He kept the big picture in his mind as he completely immersed himself in the specifics. He got invested in people. For patients
this was generally a thrilling experience, making them feel listened to as
never before.[6]

A strange thing happened when George Klumpner began his analysis
with Kohut in September 1963.[7] Klumpner made what he himself now
calls a "nutty" request to delay paying anything for the rest of the year
in order to derive a tax benefit. There was, in fact, such a benefit to be

derived—but it came at the expense of Kohut's receiving no payment for treatment until January 1964. Kohut agreed to the request with remarkable equanimity, though with some misgivings that he honestly acknowledged when he wrote the case up. Kohut told Klumpner, however, that besides the tax advantage to be gained, he wondered what else might be involved. "It might well be," Kohut wrote in his last book, "that we would later discover that his request and my compliance with it had a significance for him that went beyond what we could know at this point." And in fact as both Kohut and Klumpner came to see it, his agreeing to the odd request proved to be decisive. Klumpner had done his training analysis with Helen McLean, with whom he stayed for eight years, though he never felt understood by her. He thought she was rigid, judgmental, and "knew all the answers." As Kohut sensed, Klumpner was not acting out something from childhood so much as expressing the need, at the outset of the analysis, for some positive evidence that this experience, as opposed to his work with McLean, would be for him alone. Kohut also may have sensed the need for special care with Klumpner, whom he described in a private letter to a colleague as having a "very mild thought disorder" and even after analysis still showing some "mildly unusual thinking processes."[8]

The analysis lasted eight years and ended on June 30, 1970. A stiff and uptight Klumpner gradually got attached to Kohut. As the first summer break approached, Kohut gave him his phone number and address in Carmel. Klumpner reacted with surprise. He thought: "Why would I need this? Why would I need him? As if he was important to me." In fact, however, "he became very important." One way Kohut found of gently but decisively cutting through Klumpner's thick wall was the way he handled dreams with him. Klumpner reported dreams in part to avoid spontaneity and regression in session. In his compulsive way, he would report the dream and go through all the details of the elaborate process of interpretation and association according to the Freudian book. Kohut let that happen but found a way of extracting the meanings in the dream that related it to what was happening between the two of them. He did not let Klumpner get too abstract. He always found where Klumpner was psychologically at the moment in the transference. It was very reassuring for the patient and made him feel understood.

Kohut told Klumpner at the outset of treatment, "I will do what I can to help you try and understand yourself." It was, in a sense, the basic goal of the therapy. And Klumpner felt he lived up to that promise. There were aspects of Klumpner's childhood experience, for example, that were actually quite foreign to Kohut. Klumpner's father was a doctor who had been born in South Dakota before it was a state. He was a Protestant and a Midwesterner. Life on the frontier was rugged. There was not much room for those who went around feeling sorry for themselves or falling apart. The elegant Viennese Kohut tried to understand that, but he never really could. Deep down, Klumpner thought Kohut felt it was something out of Zane Grey. But what mattered to Klumpner was the effort Kohut put into trying to understand his past. "He always listened to the analytic material and tried to understand it with his full attention." Kohut was also entirely nonjudgmental. He *never* (Klumpner emphasized) came up with the kind of formulaic nonsense so prevalent in much of psychoanalysis. Kohut always wanted to wait and see and never judge. Once, while traveling, Klumpner went to an "adult" bookstore. He felt very guilty about it and only reluctantly confessed it. Kohut's reaction was not only not to shame Klumpner, which Klumpner was sure McLean would have done, but to acknowledge that this probably had more to do with his frustrated curiosity as a child than any acting out of needs.

There were some points of quiet disagreement. Kohut insisted that Klumpner had an idealizing transference. Klumpner never felt it, however, and was convinced it was the wrong diagnosis. He did not object, because the diagnosis seemed to matter to Kohut. At the end of his analysis, Klumpner also expressed some regret at not recapturing more repressed childhood memories. Kohut said he had recovered a lot. Klumpner said that that simply was not true. There were many of Kohut's reconstructions he recalled, but that was not the same as Klumpner's own memories. Kohut refused to agree.

Another issue was more problematic. Klumpner's father was a general practitioner who used to get lots of pharmaceutical samples. His mother saved them all. There was a closet off the bathroom with deep shelves where she stored them. It looked like a drugstore. After Klumpner's father died, his mother, who lived for many years after that, slowly used up the drugs for her own illnesses. One day she proudly announced that she had finally used up all the medicine samples in the closet. When Klumpner reported that in session, Kohut's quick judgment was that she was psychotic. Klumpner says he knew his mother was nutty but she was not at all psychotic (Klumpner was, after all, a psychiatrist). Kohut did not argue with him but clearly disagreed. Klumpner thought this was part of Kohut's own psychology. "He was being nice to me and I would be nice in turn," Klumpner put it rather innocently.

Once Klumpner saw a classmate coming out of Kohut's office as he was going in for his hour. He asked if that person was also in analysis with him. Kohut answered that he thought if Klumpner wanted that information he should really ask the classmate. It was handled well and in just the right tone. Kohut did not put him down for asking an inappropriate question. He did not rebuff Klumpner, but at the same time he protected the woman's confidentiality. Another time Kohut told Klumpner, in connection with dealing with his own patients, that when he had to make a choice between doing what he felt was right as a matter of principle and what he thought would be a more human response, making the more human response would rarely be an error.

In general, Kohut did a reasonable amount of talking in the last third of the hour. He was not one of those analysts, Klumpner said, who listen, say nothing, and send you on. He worked hard at listening. But in the last third he wanted to try and make sense of things. Sometimes what Kohut said was merely summative, sometimes it was more interpretive. But he was always accepting of Klumpner's limitations and needs. Even if he did not really understand things, Kohut would let him know he had been listening and cared. As the analysis finally wound down, Kohut left it entirely up to Klumpner to decide when he wanted to stop and only joined the discussion about an ending date once one had been set. Klumpner never returned to analysis, as he did not feel he needed it, and became, as Kohut put it in a letter, "quite creative in a highly specialized field."[9] Klumpner's own sense is that Kohut helped him discover the "pleasures of loving, working, learning, playing, and the American Psychoanalytic Association."

Another early case that Kohut wrote and talked about all his life was a woman he saw in the late 1950s or early 1960s and called Miss F. She was twenty-five and had labile mood changes. She was incapable of intimacy and lived a lonely, isolated life. Her mother had been cut off from her feelings and unable to provide any emotional sustenance for her daughter. Whenever the child tried to speak about herself the mother subtly deflected the focus of attention onto her own depressive self-preoccupations. In treatment, F. demanded that Kohut listen quietly to her whining complaints, and if he gave an interpretation it could do no more than repeat what she had already said. If Kohut made an interpretation that went beyond her understanding of things in any way, F. would get enraged and accuse him in a "tense, high-pitched voice" of undermining her, of destroying all she had so carefully gained, and of "ruining her analysis." She told him to shut up, in other words, and he had enough sense to obey.[10] What was perhaps most impressive therapeutically about this episode is that Kohut spontaneously created an empathic environment in which F., and perhaps many others, could express her rage at him before he had developed a theory for comprehending the meaning of such outbursts.[11]

The success of Kohut's treatment in the early period, however, was mixed. Peter Barglow was written up as Mr. W. in Kohut's second book, *The Restoration of the Self* (1977), though he was treated between 1966 and 1972.[12] Some experiences subsequent to analysis have made Barglow less enthusiastic about self psychology and Heinz Kohut than he probably was closer to the time of his analysis. It clearly enhanced his self-esteem to be a Kohut case history. But Barglow left treatment with distinct ambivalence and less of an upbeat feeling of having been cured than Kohut conveys or seemed to understand in what he wrote in *The Restoration of the Self*. "In some ways I was helped," Barglow said cautiously, though he quickly noted Kohut made some major mistakes, and there were some severe shortcomings in the analysis.

Barglow was a young psychoanalyst when he was in treatment with Kohut. He had had a previous training analysis and, like Klumpner, sought this one for himself. As a therapist, Barglow felt that Kohut had a "tremendous ability to listen and pay attention." He was "focused." But he did not seem particularly warm to Barglow, though he was always very supportive. Barglow acknowledges that he was a difficult patient, for he often would fall half asleep on the couch as he associated to a dream. Kohut stayed with him patiently.

One curious note of distance between Barglow and Kohut, something that is clearer in retrospect than it was at the time, is that Barglow, who was a European Jewish immigrant, thought Kohut was Christian.[13] Barglow was quite aware at the time that Kohut never mentioned Jews or made Jewish jokes (or seemed to quite get them when somebody else made them), though Barglow just assumed it was because Kohut was Christian. Everything about Kohut's self-presentation was Christian. Once Kohut commented in rather self-mocking tones of an exhibit about himself that had been set up in the Institute Library: "It looks like a shrine for Saint Heinz." For Barglow Kohut spoke in a clearly Christian rhetoric. It was startling, though not an issue that matters much to him, when he learned later of Kohut's Jewishness and the actual affinity in their ethnic and cultural backgrounds; they even both married non-Jews.

In his treatment of Barglow, as with other patients, Kohut was always keenly aware of the current state of the transference and with any and all of Barglow's transference ideas. To get at that he was attentive to the smallest of details. On that he could be scrupulous. Once Barglow arrived for session and commented that in the parking lot he had bought a paper and the machine gave him the paper and returned his dime. He reported the story as a joke but Kohut insisted on analyzing it; ironically, Barglow had to acknowledge that the analysis of the returned dime led to a very useful insight. Another time he mentioned something about his supervision with Theresa Benedek, whom he referred to as sexy. Kohut laughed and said that was perhaps an objectively true observation but that he also detected a transference.

In other ways, Kohut took quite an active and, by the standards of many, an unanalytic role in Barglow's life in terms of some moral and personal issues. Once, for example, Barglow was planning to buy a new and rather fancy apartment. Kohut told him not to, as he thought it was pretentious and too grand. Another time Kohut insisted he return a small check that Barglow had reason to accept. Barglow had done some work for the McGovern presidential campaign. He had put on a fund-raiser and had fronted much of the expense for the event. He was later sent a check (for $100) by someone who had attended, as a contribution to the campaign. Barglow was going to keep the money because he was still owed much more than that. Kohut insisted he send it back, on the general grounds that you should not fool yourself. Barglow obeyed. In a third example, Barglow got married during his analysis, which Kohut did not oppose, though he expressed some surprise at Barglow's sentimentality and romanticism about his relationship with his new wife. Kohut seemed unable to comprehend such an attitude. He did advise Barglow to stay away from someone with whom he had had an earlier relationship. "That's a bad idea," Kohut said categorically.

Barglow felt there were several major areas in which Kohut failed him. First, Kohut never fully appreciated the pathology of his mother and her significance in shaping his life. Kohut dealt with her in general ways that were basically formulaic.[14] Barglow was also convinced that Kohut minimized the effect of his separation from his parents as a child. Part of the problem is that in disguising the case for publication, Kohut covered over some important details. Kohut says Mr. W. was separated from his parents for "the span of more than a year" when at three and a half he was sent to live with grandparents in central Illinois.[15] The actual separation lasted a full two and a half years, while the father was being treated for tuberculosis at Bergdof, the famous sanitorium depicted in *The Magic Mountain*. For most of the father's treatment the mother stayed with him. It was awful for Barglow; he came to feel it was the turning point of his childhood. Kohut never seemed to understood that, nor did he grasp the probable impact of the father's TB on Barglow's varied hypochondriacal symptoms.

Kohut made a major mistake with at least one of Barglow's physical symptoms. The patient entered analysis complaining of two specific chronic problems. One was that his eyes often drooped in exhaustion at inopportune times. He would get sleepy in sessions (as analyst and analysand). Barglow also had itchiness, irritations, and other problems with his anus. Kohut insisted both symptoms were hypochondriacal, and through six long years of analysis Barglow dealt with every conceivable aspect of the symptoms. It turned out, Barglow said, that Kohut was right about his eyes. At one point he had even thought of surgery, but was talked out of it by Kohut, something for which Barglow is now quite grateful. But with his anus it was quite a different story. Kohut is adamant in the case history that the itching was hypochondriacal. In fact, as it turned out, Barglow had an anal fissure. After the analysis was over and perhaps out of reach somewhat from the transference, Barglow had surgery—without telling Kohut. It was completely successful and relieved all his symptoms.

Others, as well, came through Kohut's hands in these years and are willing to talk about their experience. Paul Tolpin as a young psychiatrist was analyzed by Kohut in the early 1950s. He found Kohut helpful and certainly his doctor of choice from among several possibilities he considered. He cannot now remember much about the analysis, except that it followed the classical rules strictly. For the most part, Kohut remained empathic despite those rules, but in one very important respect they worked against what would have been the most effective way of responding to Tolpin's needs. The termination of an analysis for the orthodox is a formal stage in treatment that emerges within a defined conceptual framework. It is when the "transference neurosis" (or the artificial illness created in the experience of the therapy) gets "resolved" or "worked through." Termination, it is felt, takes six months to a year and is marked by all kinds of *very* concrete criteria (which few would now hold to, partly influenced by Kohut's own later work). According to the script, when the analysis is over, the patient says good-bye and ventures out into the world. When Tolpin seemed to have successfully completed the termination phase of his analysis, Kohut sent him off. What Tolpin realized later is that he did not want to leave treatment so abruptly and would have been much better off (and not later in need of additional treatment from another analyst) if he could have tapered off and perhaps kept seeing Kohut in psychotherapy, even for years. Such a model, however, was not yet imaginable for Kohut in his classical period.[16]

Similarly, Michael Franz Basch was analyzed by Kohut in the 1950s. Born in 1929 in Germany to a Jewish medical family, Basch came to America at ten to escape the Nazis. His father never managed to reestablish his distinguished career as an internist and had to accept a struggling general practice without much prestige, while his mother soon got Parkinson's disease. Meanwhile, Basch went to medical school and entered psychiatry. He began analysis with Kohut in 1956. Analysis was, on the one hand, a liberating experience, and Basch always felt enormously grateful to Kohut for "unlocking his creativity." At the same time he deeply regretted he had not been analyzed after Kohut's work on the self, for he saw how much more open and easy and intimate his former therapist became in his later years.[17]

Kohut, it would seem, in the first decade and a half of his career, was as good an analyst as his theory allowed him to be. He was to change.

Twelve

MR. PSYCHOANALYSIS

In the 1950s and early 1960s, Kohut came to play a prominent role in mainstream psychoanalysis. In Chicago he was quickly recognized as the brightest and most creative analyst in the Institute at a time when psychoanalysis in America was undoubtedly the psychotherapeutic treatment of choice. Kohut was the rising star. As early as 1956 he was offered (and turned down) the prestigious chairmanship of psychiatry at the University of Chicago.[1] He rewrote the curriculum at the Institute, then taught its legendary two-year theory course for a decade. He dazzled colleagues. Nationally, he became active in the American Psychoanalytic Association ("the American," as psychoanalysts called it). He served on the editorial board of its journal, on numerous committees, and, in time, as president of the organization. He also got close to all the major figures in the field, especially Heinz Hartmann, Kurt Eissler, and Anna Freud, and was acquainted with anyone else who mattered. His publications were few but highly regarded, ranging from two papers on the psychology of music to studies of literature, biography, and history; in terms of the theory, he published an early and hugely significant paper on empathy that would in time define the core of his new psychology. For now, however, Kohut was the respectable, cautious man of the future, assiduously cultivating his reputation as the chosen one to provide leadership for the next generation of psychoanalysts. That became his professional identity. It is not surprising that after his apostasy Kohut later (half) joked that in the 1950s and early 1960s he was "Mr. Psychoanalysis."

Kohut graduated from the Institute in the fall of 1950 and became a training and supervising analyst in early 1953.[2] The triumph of his ambitions, however, was that he was simultaneously appointed to the staff of the Institute, joining ten or twelve other analysts who completely controlled its clinical and training operations. That appointment remained Kohut's primary commitment for the rest of his life.[3] Once on staff Kohut quickly occupied a special place in a group of talented and very competitive psychoanalysts. He served on many standing committees in the Institute, including the progression committee, which decided whether a student was ready to go from one supervised case to the next, as well as the admissions and graduation committees. Louis Shapiro recalled that Kohut was "impressive" from the outset. "He always had something very thoughtful and very profound to say." He was never open about himself, and was generally remote. But he had an air about him. Everyone noticed Heinz Kohut. Some, of course, like Theresa Benedek, were envious and came to dislike Kohut. But he barely noticed, locked as he was within himself. At the Wednesday afternoon scientific meetings of the Institute, Kohut almost always commented at length on the presentation. He would become withdrawn and intense as he prepared to speak. Then he would hold forth in ways that would always be elegant and usually much more interesting than the presentation itself. Everyone waited for him to speak at the meetings. "We knew he was a little different," says Jerome Beigler. His letters to colleagues on scientific matters were often passed around, treated as authoritative statements on an issue.[4]

Kohut's idealization of the analytic project at that point in his life was very great; indeed, he brought to it the enthusiasms of a convert. He saw psychoanalysis, among other things, as the best means known to the psychological sciences for searching after truth. He knew, of course, that many actual analysts failed to live up to their potential or to the possibilities that the profession offered. But what must not happen, he felt, was to compromise in any way the noble goals of the profession. Psychoanalysis would be "doomed" if it became simply a profession of therapists. Not everyone, of course, could discover new truths. But "every analyst" must be more a practitioner than a technician, just as institutes must be more like universities than trade schools. He was adamant that institutes must not become vocational training schools. If analysts stopped searching for "significant discoveries about the human mind with the aid of their unique investigative instrument," the profession would simply get absorbed into dynamic psychiatry and disappear forever.[5]

Of all Kohut's activities in the Institute in these years, none interested him more than his work on the curriculum. The departure of Alexander in the early 1950s gave the new director, Gerhart Piers, the opportunity to rethink the basic purpose of the Institute, indeed of psychoanalysis itself. The curriculum had always been somewhat haphazard and basically a reflection of the idiosyncrasies of Alexander, whose ideas on the "corrective emotional experience" and whose willingness, even eagerness, to shorten analytic treatment had increasingly stirred opposition. Kohut, who had managed to negotiate a middle ground in these fights during his years of training, could now express his real feelings that any tampering with the traditional model threatened the integrity of the enterprise. Given the impact of Alexander, Kohut's desire to reestablish orthodoxy at the Institute represented something of a new vision in the early 1950s. Piers, who was an institutional but not an intellectual leader, recognized the value of Kohut. Piers therefore decided in 1953 to appoint him, along with Louis Shapiro and Joan Fleming, to design an entirely new curriculum for the Institute.[6]

Kohut's contribution to the committee's work was decisive. It was his idea to approach the teaching of psychoanalytic theory from a historical perspective. That became the organizing principle of the new curriculum. Candidates began with various courses on Freud's books and papers and from there moved into a three-year sequence on psychoanalytic theory. There were courses on dreams, technique, current literature, and special topics like Freud's five major case histories. By the time the committee finished its work the curriculum had stretched to five years and ended with a lengthy written exam. In one sense the curriculum both broadened and deepened what had been in place previously. One should keep in mind, however, that within it there was no room for Carl Jung, Sándor Ferenczi, or Otto Rank, except in the most cursory of ways; there was nothing systematic of the then-emerging English school associated with Donald Winnicott and his colleagues; and it would seem there was no mention made at all of Melanie Klein. The committee also decided that candidates should get their first control case very early, some six months into the first year of training, a decision that put them at odds with other leading institutes in the country.[7]

The most important experience for candidates in the new curriculum, however, became Kohut's two-year theory course. Teaching that course was for him a "passionate affair" and highly "cathected." The course was not, as Kohut once explained, a history of psychoanalytic psychology but a study of "psychoanalytic psychology presented according to historical principles." The first part, which went up to about 1920, overlapped the second in many ways, though the "essential continuity" was honored. In the first year of the course, Kohut dealt with key concepts from the principal points of view in psychoanalysis (dynamic, topographic, economic, and genetic). He made some specific historical observations, as in describing Freud's development from hypnosis to free association. But mostly there was no attempt "to follow Freud's own summaries of the basic discoveries." Instead, he focused on concepts like trauma, the traumatic neurosis, the actual neurosis, play, mourning, and working through. In the second year of the course, dealing with the development of psychoanalytic psychology from 1920 to 1937, Kohut addressed the major additions to the theory, especially the structural concept of the psyche. As he put it: "The course [that is, the second year] begins with a survey of those factors which led to the shift in emphasis from the id to an equal stressing of id, ego and super-ego; and from the emphasis on the sexual drives to an acknowledgment of the role of aggression." The stress was on narcissism, aggression, and the superego. Breaking chronology, in the second year of the course Kohut combined a thorough study of Chapter 7 of *The Interpretation of Dreams* with Freud's 1926 *Inhibitions, Symptoms, and Anxiety*.[8]

In terms of what Kohut later became, what is most astonishing about the course is how completely "Freudian" it was. From two different typed and bound sets of student notes from the course that have survived, one can get quite a good feel for the flow of the material. There is not a hint in these lectures of where Kohut would move later. He was in and of classical psychoanalytic theory. He moved logically and coherently from Freud's early papers on hysteria to the papers in the 1920s, though as he explained in his theory of the course, he developed his ideas not so much chronologically as thematically. The lectures show Kohut working as the consummate "metapsychologist," or theoretician on a grand scale. To speak about Freud in these terms was then his voice, the language he felt most comfortable speaking.[9]

Kohut's teaching style was unique to him. He was well organized, though deceptively so, giving the impression he taught entirely off the cuff and was different each time he lectured. That was the myth he liked to perpetuate. In fact, the sequence of his lectures followed a very well-thought-out plan that repeated itself. Kohut knew where he was going on any given day. He left none of his own notes for the course, though he may well have actually written out his lectures and then memorized them, as was Freud's style (which was clearly Kohut's model).[10] At the outset of each class, Kohut would ask for questions from the assigned reading for that day in the course. He might take two or three questions, pause reflectively, and then start talking, ostensibly in response to the questions but in fact according to his own plan. Sometimes he would elaborate on a single point for half an hour. But once he started talking he did not want to be interrupted. It was a monologue, though as Ernest Wolf has said, "an amazing one."[11]

The evaluations of Kohut's teaching—such evaluations have always been an important tradition at the Chicago Institute—were outstanding, though there has since developed an off-putting tendency to mythologize the "simple and lyric" quality of Kohut's lecture style.[12] Paul Ornstein, a devoted follower with a more critical view, says of Kohut's teaching style that it was brilliant but so good and articulate that it "made every one of us feel so small that it was actually pedagogically . . . a failure." It intimidated everyone. Ornstein himself did not realize how powerful these feelings were until many years after he took the course. At the time the students simply idealized Kohut and those sessions because "nobody but nobody could put together analytic theory as clearly" as Kohut. If he had allowed someone to record the sessions, Ornstein believes, they could have been published almost as is. Ornstein too notes that Kohut always seemed to speak off the "top of his head" and that his style was unique. He never allowed anyone to speak during the class, except for the few questions he took at the beginning. Kohut's apparent rationale for such a format, Ornstein believes, was that you cannot ask any meaningful questions until you digest the material.

Such a European approach to teaching fitted Kohut's character, as well. As John Gedo has put it, Kohut had "an absolute command of his material." But he was aloof and had an air of mystery about him. Despite his mastery of English, he came across as a Viennese intellectual "to a remarkable degree." Gedo believes it was Kohut's Old World background that led him to insist in his theory course that everyone take notes while he lectured (which is why such complete candidate notes from the course have survived). Gedo, however, typically rebelled and felt it was demeaning to be forced to take elaborate notes on a lecture. So he decided at the outset he would encapsulate the entire two-year course on a single sheet of paper, which he carried around, folded, in his pocket. At least that is how Gedo tells the story in his 1997 memoirs, long after a messy break with Kohut. In an earlier version of the story, when he was still very much a close friend and colleague of Kohut's, Gedo gently mocked his own adolescent rebellion against taking the notes and added the charming detail that the single sheet of paper became for him a kind of talisman filled with microscopic and in the end completely incomprehensible writing on both sides of the paper. He carried it around with him to magically ward off evil.[13]

Not everyone, however, was so impressed with Kohut's teaching style, especially those outside the circle of candidates in training, whose future careers in large part depended on the goodwill of the senior figures in the Institute (who double, or triple, as their analysts, supervisors, and teachers). Morris I. Stein, who was then an associate professor of psychology at the University of Chicago, and thus hardly a neophyte himself, took a course Kohut taught at the Institute in 1954 on psychoanalytic literature. Stein was a research candidate in the Institute that year and again in 1958. In the course, candidates selected a paper and made some comments on it, and Kohut concluded with his observations. Stein selected for his commentary Freud's 1905 "Three Contributions to a Theory of Sexuality." Even before he presented, Stein was appalled at the passivity of the candidates, their fawning obeisance to Freud, and Kohut's role in fostering their spirit of infantilism. Partly out of rebellion, he therefore skipped the obligatory introductory phrases about the brilliance of Freud and moved right into the material with something like "Freud was a nineteenth-century rationalist . . ." That, however, was all he could get out of his mouth before Kohut attacked him viciously ("wiped the floor with me" was Stein's phrase), saying he was disrespectful. Kohut went on for an hour about the need to honor Freud's genius. Stein was shocked, in fact so much so that he "didn't even have time to be embarrassed." He did not open his mouth again in that class, though at the request of a couple of the classmates at the end of the hour he was able to present his ideas at the next meeting. For Kohut it was a passing moment that he seemed to forget.

Some months later, Kohut heard Stein give a paper on creativity and suggested afterward that Stein get in touch because he had some material that was relevant to Stein's work. Stein nodded politely but ignored the request, still furious with Kohut. Some months after that, Stein's analyst, Irene Josselyn, asked him in session why he had not gotten in touch with Kohut and added that his name had come up to be given a patient for supervised therapy. Stein, offended again at this intrusion into his analysis, reiterated to her his feelings about what had happened in the course and added that as a research candidate he was not interested in getting a referral. But she insisted that he would understand the theory better if he saw the psychoanalytic process from the point of view of an analyst. Somewhat against his better judgment, Stein decided to try and be friendly. He wrote Kohut and said something about how his unconscious had intervened and he had "forgotten to get in touch with him." Stein was surprised by and impressed with Kohut's friendly reply, which included a line he has always remembered: "As Freud said, 'The unconscious should only be used to excuse the person and not to accuse the person.' "[14]

Kohut also reached beyond Chicago. He served the American Psychoanalytic Association diligently throughout the 1950s, but the culmination of his activities with the American was his four-year stint as, first, president-elect (1962–1963), and then president (1964–1965). He wanted that honor dearly and saw his election as an important milestone in his career. He was delighted to garner messages of congratulation from far and wide. The triumphant moment came at the meetings in St. Louis in May 1963 when he was actually elected president. He had just turned fifty and was "on the top of our organizational hierarchy." There were flowers and gifts everywhere. Among the letters was an unsigned telegram from Else in Chicago: "To me it seems like yesterday." He was very moved. As "crazy" as he felt her to be, he said, that simple expression of her authentic pleasure in his success "was one of the best things she ever did. It was not a make-up."[15]

The presidency of the American turned out to be a huge job. The minutes of a single meeting of the Executive Council alone (say, that of December 3, 1964) could run to fifteen single-spaced typed pages and include all kinds of large and small items. The president had to coordinate and supervise the work of numerous committees and maintain a vast network of relationships. This executive meeting was then followed by an even larger meeting of the members of the American at the Commodore Hotel in New York City on December 6. Kohut must have gotten a lot out of such work, but the task was absorbing. For example, he wrote a seven-page, single-spaced letter to all members of the American in November prior to the meetings in New York. In it he describes what he sees as his role as the new president. He also outlines the procedures he followed for staffing the various committees of the organization. It is chillingly bureaucratic.

Kohut was the complete master of the intricate world of administrative leadership. When his old friend, Jay McCormick, was elected as an alternate to the board of special standards of the American, he asked Kohut how to steer through the murky waters of the organization politically. He was impressed with the thoroughness of Kohut's explanation. All of Kohut's time was focused on his duties. He once told Kurt Eissler that he was spending "a number of weekends" in New York in connection with his work on the American. Before the (1963) December meetings, he added, he planned to spend a whole week there, at the end of which Betty would join him. For the rest, "there are all the obligations which I will take conscientiously for the next year and a half, and I do not know how much time there will be left for seeing friends." At the least, he hopes "there will be a chance to get together even if only for part of an evening."[16]

There were endless brushfires to put out. Once a fight erupted among French analysts over which of two rival groups was to be represented on an International Psycho-Analytical Association symposium about fantasy that Kohut was to chair. He wrote to Rudolph M. Loewenstein, who resided in France, to learn more about the details of the psychoanalytic scene in that country. Kohut told Loewenstein that he was not unduly worried about the situation and understood that such situations "have a way of developing," yet he hoped to learn from Loewenstein more about the French situation so that he might defuse some of the tension. He also, sensibly, made clear to Loewenstein that he was not after gossip—"a detailed exposé"—but just a few highlights about the situation of psychoanalysis in France so that he could deal with the problems surrounding the symposium better.[17]

A more serious problem concerned the man who served as president-elect during Kohut's term as president, Victor Rosen, who fell in love with a former patient and planned to marry her. The affair became widely known. Kohut put heavy pressure on Rosen either not to marry or to postpone the wedding until he could have some further analytic work and come to understand the possible irrational motivations in his decision. On this Kohut was decisive: "Yet, when the unusual step of marriage to a former patient hinges on the answer to the question whether the transferences and counter-transferences had been sufficiently resolved, one would not expect an analyst to come to a decision until he has undertaken a renewed psychoanalytic investigation of his motivations." Kohut was quite direct about his larger concern for the effect of Rosen's action on the organization he headed and on "our students and patients." When you become president, Kohut lectured him, you will be "an example for and a representative of our science." Perhaps, he granted, Rosen as an individual was acting courageously in opposing the rigid and outworn conventions of society. But given his official position there was more at stake here than his personal life. Many would believe that, if condoned, Rosen's actions would suggest a loosening of the ethical insistence that analysts not make use of "their patients' emotional attachment for any purpose other than to enlarge their mastery over themselves through insight." Kohut ended with an earnest plea that Rosen at least postpone his apparent decision to marry and stressed that he felt no rancor toward him. His only concern was for the future of psychoanalysis itself.[18]

It was also during his presidency that the storm broke over the statements of some psychiatrists and psychoanalysts regarding the mental health of Barry Goldwater during the U.S. presidential campaign of 1964. Along with two other officers of the American, Kohut issued a strongly worded statement condemning such "unverified impressions." Any professional judgment regarding the "mental stability" of a person could only be the result of "carefully evaluated psychological data," which was of necessity confidential and could only be obtained "in a therapeutic relationship." None of these conditions was present in the heat of a political campaign, Kohut and his colleagues wrote. A severe mental illness would obviously be a disqualifying precondition for a candidate, but such a condition would not escape the attention of the public in a democracy. The psychiatrist or psychoanalyst, like any citizen, was entitled to his or her views on public issues. But such private opinions "must not be regarded as scientific inferences that are derived from valid and secure observations." To confuse the two "serves no constructive purpose in the political life of the nation," and, besides, harms science in general and psychiatry and psychoanalysis in particular.[19]

So Kohut was busy. A large part of the appeal of his power and position with the American was the recognition it brought him from leading figures in his field. His exalted position in that community became an important part of his personal mythology. "I was at the center [of psychoanalysis]," he said, "and beloved by everybody and on the right kind of handshaking terms. In every room I entered there were smiles." Of all those important people who now recognized Kohut, none mattered more to him than Anna Freud. His first direct contact with her came at a 1964 meeting in Princeton at which he presented his ideas on the selection of candidates. Right after the meeting he wrote her: "It is a good feeling for me that I can write to you now without having to introduce myself and to know that my name calls up an image in you." He noted the significance of her meeting with "younger" analysts (which he put in quotes because most were even then "bald and/or greying") and that "a sense of the continuity of our science was significantly furthered." He dealt with a technical issue, very gently expressed some doubt about a distinction she made, and enclosed several of his papers for her to read. Anna Freud wrote back a friendly reply, expressing her admiration for his comments during the Princeton meetings and dismay, with him, that so many in psychoanalysis were trying to woo academic psychology with its alien methods. "Why is the majority so blind?" she asked in a way that clearly cemented her relationship with Kohut.[20]

In the next couple of months Kohut and Freud exchanged more letters. Kohut talked of his hopes for leadership of the American. She expressed her hopes that he would provide leadership for "revolutionary moves" in the organization. That prompted an exceedingly long and complex reply from Kohut on August 4, 1964, which must have occupied many days in the early part of his Carmel vacation. The letter was produced in the laborious style otherwise reserved only for his essays (from shorthand to dictation). Kohut focused on his commitment to psychoanalysis as a "broadly based human psychology with its own body of knowledge and methodology." He expressed caution about what could be accomplished. He was certainly not a revolutionary, he said, though the idea led him into an ethnic history of the two groups that contributed to the growth of American psychoanalysis. On the one hand, he said, were the Jews barely out of the ghetto, for whom participation in American psychiatry was a hugely liberating experience. These Jews were mostly doctors and deeply committed to medicine. Alongside the Jewish doctors as healers and helpers were the mostly Anglo-Saxon, Protestant Christians who were deeply committed to progressive social action and social reform. The best-known such Protestant groups were the "mystical Quakers" and the "rationalistic Universalists and Unitarians," who received their "baptism of fire" during the Abolitionist period. Kohut felt the goal for revitalizing psychoanalysis was to get the Jews and the Protestants to work together. The Jewish medical dominance of psychoanalysis in contemporary America was unfortunate, but if institutes were dominated by the Protestants alone it would probably move psychoanalysis toward nonscientific "healing through love" and other cures by identification. The result would be a rise in existential psychiatry and analysis, as it existed in Europe, which he clearly saw as unfortunate. The best hope therefore was "a realistic acceptance of this strongly established balance of preferences," which would gradually be improved upon, not upset by revolutionary means.[21]

For Kohut his relationship with Anna Freud was now on a new footing of intimacy that linked him directly to the founder, and he was determined to keep it that way. From then on Kohut attended very carefully to anything having to do with her. Among other things, he participated in an effort in the first half of 1965 to raise some money to honor her seventieth birthday.[22] That fund-raising effort in fact had been initiated by Kurt Eissler, who was another extremely important figure for Kohut. Eissler, of course, went further back than Anna Freud. Both Kohut and Eissler had been analyzed by August Aichhorn. Occasionally, Kohut went to dinner at the Eisslers' in the late 1940s. But they remained on formal terms, and the Eisslers' departure for New York in the late 1940s further separated their worlds. They were still "Dr. Eissler" and "Dr. Kohut" until the mid-1950s.[23]

Kohut's prominence in the American in the first half of the 1960s, however, brought the two men closer together. One, the leading figure from the Chicago Institute, and the other, one of the leading figures from the New York Institute, forged a powerful psychoanalytic friendship. They wrote each other several times a year and got together, often with their wives, whenever Kohut was in New York. Kohut occasionally wrote separately to Ruth (his former analyst) and she to him, but Kohut's real affection and respect was for Kurt. "What a welcome surprise," he wrote in a letter in 1961 when he opened a package containing Eissler's book on Leonardo da Vinci. He found the book "impossible to put down" and "not only a fascinating scientific treatise but also a work of art in its own right." Two years later, Kohut wrote Eissler that he was "truly overwhelmed" by Eissler's kindness in sending him his two-volume study of Goethe and that he was eagerly looking forward to reading it. "You have given me—and all of us!—so much that I would despair of trying to express my gratification," though he knew the real joy was in the act of creation itself. Kohut's praise could only be an "echo" to someone "whose position in the very forefront of creative contributors to our science is assured without any doubt."[24]

Kohut, however, was also very careful with Eissler, who occupied a position of such power and respect within the psychoanalytic community. Once he apologized profusely for having used a personal argument in trying to persuade Eissler about something during a business meeting of the American, even though it seemed to have been a very minor thing and he was not even sure Eissler took his comment amiss; such sensitivity Kohut showed very few people in the world. Kohut also carefully worked over drafts of his letters to Eissler; one sample, undated though probably from sometime in 1962, has so many parts crossed out and corrections written between the lines it is almost illegible. At other times, he would write out the first draft of his letters to him in shorthand, granting his letters a rare significance.[25] It mattered to Kohut what he said to Eissler and exactly how he phrased it. Contact extended to families as well, and both Eisslers gave gifts to Thomas; Ruth once gave him a subscription to *Opera News* and Kurt once sent him some Austrian stamps.[26] Ruth wrote warmly to both Heinz and Elizabeth in 1966 after a visit, thanking them for their hospitality (the Eisslers presumably had stayed in the Kohuts' apartment) and praising Thomas for his "charm and intelligence."[27] In fact, one would never know from the correspondence that Kohut had been analyzed by Ruth Eissler. They were completely at ease with each other, involved professionally and personally in all aspects of the world of psychoanalysis.

The other professional relationship of great significance to Kohut was with Heinz Hartmann, whom he intensely idealized as the major theoretician in psychoanalysis. Hartmann seemed to be someone Kohut could relate to without conflict or envy; Hartmann also died early enough (in 1970) so that he never had to react to Kohut's move away from classical theory. The two men began corresponding in the 1950s, but their friendship was really the product of the early 1960s and Kohut's greater prominence in psychoanalysis. Kohut dutifully sent Hartmann his addresses, papers, and books as they were published. It elevated Kohut's self-esteem to feel connected to Hartmann, which could lead to some surreptitious self-enhancement. In 1964 Hartmann sent Kohut an inscribed copy of his newly published *Essays on Ego Psychology*. Kohut wrote back immediately and described a recent meeting of the Chicago Psychoanalytic Society that had discussed Hartmann's 1939 book *Ego Psychology and the Problem of Adaptation*. Kohut reported that even the "least sophisticated" seemed to appreciate Hartmann's contributions to psychoanalysis. It was just such arrogance that led to Kohut's estrangement from old friends. Paul Kramer, for example, Kohut's supervisor in the 1940s, came to regard Kohut as "arrogant and peculiar." Kohut could never understand why Kramer had turned on him; even years later he continued to talk about how Kramer was the analyst who had had the greatest impact on him in his training.[28]

But it was Hartmann whom Kohut probably wanted to impress more than any man alive. On April 30, 1962, Charles Brenner wrote Kohut asking him to be on a panel at the upcoming meetings of the American on the methodology of psychoanalysis. Hartmann was to be the chair. Kohut immediately and enthusiastically agreed. In the fall it turned out that the panel was canceled because one member got sick, but from the moment Kohut accepted the invitation he began to think about what his contribution would be. He clearly spent a great deal of time writing out his thoughts on the subject while in Carmel that summer, filling nearly fifty pages of a yellow pad with cramped writing in pencil and producing another thirty or so pages of notes on scraps of paper, sometimes in his shorthand and at other times in regular English. All this writing was to be the basis for a major statement on the subject, even though he would have had but ten to fifteen minutes to talk on the panel itself.[29]

From a later perspective, Kohut came to feel that his administrative duties with the American and its related network of relationships forced him to live a life for which he was "not really made." It left him drained and stopped the flow of his creative juices, something he only fully realized after he had broken free. The costs were huge for him to remain on the "right kind of handshaking terms" with the psychoanalytic elite. Even at the time, Kohut's ambivalence was apparent. It was the tradition for the outgoing president to address the organization at the meetings at the end of his term of office. Kohut had his paper written, but at the last minute developed a severe case of laryngitis, a psychosomatic symptom if there ever was one. Kohut himself was decidedly embarrassed, and knew what his colleagues were thinking. He quickly asked his old friend, Martin Stein, to read the essay. In his introduction to the talk, Stein expressed his warm enthusiasm for Kohut's work for the American, which Kohut greatly appreciated, "since I value you and your opinions very highly." In this follow-up letter of thanks, Kohut added, by way of trying to further justify his laryngitis, that he was still bothered by it and that it turned out to be part of a "much more general infection." He got a "rather severe purulent tracheitis" as well as some "gastrointestinal disturbances" and muscle and eye aches so typical of the flu. Furthermore, whatever it was went through the whole family, as both Elizabeth and Thomas fell sick; Elizabeth even fainted and was "nearly pulseless for a few endlessly long seconds."[30]

And yet there were clearly great rewards for Kohut in his service with the American. It brought him national prominence, was a huge boost to his career, and broadened the stage for the presentation of his emerging ideas. He had worked hard to achieve the presidency, and he never really regretted it. He felt he had served the "great science which has filled our lives." Ironically, as well, Kohut's very ambivalence about his work and ultimate dissatisfaction with the way his colleagues behaved within the organization may have taught him some instructive lessons about narcissism. He wrote once that there was nothing wrong with the field itself; it was the people in it "who are carrying on their work on the basis of these ideas." They were self-centered and self-absorbed, narcissistic in the worst sense of the word. It was stressful for him to have to deal with the "emotional demands" of his colleagues and all the "emotionally charged issues in our profession." But he learned from the experience. In what was perhaps more than a throwaway line, Kohut often later said that he had learned all he knew about narcissism from his service as president of the American.[31]

Thirteen

ON EMPATHY

The jewel of Kohut's early writing is his paper on empathy. It is startling in its originality, even if its implications were exceedingly murky at the time. Somehow, Kohut's life experience led him to grasp from the outset the essential contradiction of classical psychoanalysis: it was a science of empathy disguised in the garb of positivism. Freud discovered new ways of knowing and healing but passed on a confusing legacy that too easily scientized the project. One might say there was an epistemological wound in the heart of psychoanalysis.

Freud had never been entirely clear about empathy. He came to the idea late, and then never elaborated it. He noted in a stray footnote in his 1921 essay on group psychology that empathy is "the means of which we are enabled to take up any attitude at all towards another mental life";[1] in the text he writes, "A path leads from identification by way of imitation to empathy, that is, to the comprehension of the mechanism by means of which we are enabled to take up any attitude at all towards another mental life." It is easy to get lost walking on Freud's path from identification to imitation to empathy. From this cursory reference, it would seem Freud took for granted that empathy is an essential part of grasping another person's psychological experience. The German word Freud used, *einfühlen*, means, as Michael Franz Basch has pointed out, to feel or find one's way into another's state of mind.[2] Freud left it at that. He never considered where empathy comes from or how it develops, how it works in the experience of the therapist or the patient, whether it can be instilled in a candidate training to become an analyst, whether it heals, or indeed anything further about empathy than just that it is there in the therapeutic process and that it is essential. Freud's concern was with interpretation and insight, which he considered the key elements in psychoanalytic healing.[3]

Among the followers of Freud, the only figure who thought about issues relating to the therapeutic use of empathy was Sándor Ferenczi. A brilliant clinician, Ferenczi experimented creatively with the practice of psychoanalysis, especially with more disturbed patients, something one can trace in his *Clinical Diaries.*[4] He is most noted for his practice of "mutual analysis" with his patient RN. He went quite far in reaching the most disturbed people. He made no secret, for example, of often kissing patients, for which Freud chastised him in 1931. The break with Freud, however, did not appear to result from his clinical experiments but from Ferenczi's bold assertion in 1932 that actual childhood sexual abuse was, after all, at the heart of most trauma that he treated. For that sin Ferenczi was banished, and when he died on May 26, 1933, a "hushed silence fell" on the Vienna institute.[5]

We know Kohut was interested in Ferenczi in the 1940s and reading his works, though most of what Ferenczi published in his lifetime was tangential at best to a theory of empathy or even its clinical uses. Nor does it seem Ferenczi's ideas reached Kohut indirectly through the filter of Franz Alexander (who was analyzed by Ferenczi). If anything, as discussed in earlier chapters, Alexander's experimentation with treatment turned Kohut against any departure from the strictest of classical approaches to psychoanalysis. Besides, Kohut had a theoretical dispute with Alexander. He felt Alexander's near-obsession with psychosomatic medicine biologized psychoanalysis. For that Kohut could forgive no one.[6]

Ferenczi and Alexander, however, represented a mere collateral stream to the main psychoanalytic river after Freud. The problem was that neither Ferenczi nor any of his followers were systematic thinkers who developed a coherent theory of empathy, or even the beginnings of a theory, in which to ground their creative clinical experiments.[7] The Freudian mainstream overwhelmed everybody in the postwar years. Ego psychology, which was so coherent it became rigid and scholastic, reigned triumphant in psychoanalysis. In the process, the theory narrowed and lost much of the supple grace that its founder lent it in the widespread effort to make it scientific and empirical. Freud's "blank screen," the mostly metaphoric image of what the analyst presents to the patient, became the

Heinz Kohut, age eighteen months, October 1914.
Courtesy Thomas A. Kohut

With Felix and Else, 1917. Courtesy Thomas A. Kohut

A 1923 advertisement for the paper store Feliz Kohut ran with Paul Bellak in Vienna.

On October 12, 1939, shortly after the outbreak of the Second World War, Else, still in
Vienna, had her picture taken in a studio on
Kärntnerstrasse 43. She was forty-six years
old. Courtesy Siegmund Levarie

Jacques Palaci, Kohut's close friend from
medical school in Vienna, lived in New
York after the war but eventually settled
in Paris. Courtesy Diana Palaci

A contemporary photograph of Paradiesgasse 47, the Kohut home after 1932. In August
1938, Else was forced to sell the house to the Kraulics for much less than its value after a
late-night call in which she was threatened that if she delayed, her son would be sent to a
concentration camp. Courtesy Walter Lampl

Kohut with his analyst, August Aichhorn, in early 1939. Much later Kohut gave a copy of this photo to Ernest Wolf with an inscription on the back describing his analysis: "Lots of ambience and not much abstinence." Courtesy Ernest Wolf

Kohut in medical school in the 1930s, looking robust with wavy hair. Courtesy Jacques Palaki

August Aichhorn, early 1939. "I have seen you lying on this couch for a long time," Aichhorn told the young Kohut at one of their last sessions. "It is time you saw me lying on it." He then asked one of his sons to take the picture and later gave it to Kohut as a souvenir. Kohut had to terminate his analysis with Aichhorn prematurely to escape the Nazis in Vienna. Courtesy Ernest Wolf

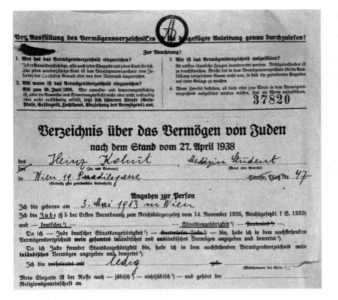

A page from the Inventory of Jewish Wealth, a form the Nazis required Kohut to complete in 1938.

Kohut, sixth from left, with coworkers at the First Aid Station in the refugee camp in England. He stayed there from March 1939 until October of that year, when he got pneumonia and was allowed to move into his uncle Hans Lampl's London apartment. Courtesy Thomas A. Kohut

Kohut (left) and his "birthday brother," Robert Wadsworth (right), striking matching poses in Chicago, while their friend Siegmund Levarie clicked the shutter on May 30, 1942. Courtesy Siegmund Levarie

Robert Wadsworth, May 8, 1943. Courtesy Siegmund Levarie

Siegmund Levarie at the University of Chicago in 1939. Courtesy Siegmund Levarie

Kohut, Wadsworth, and Levarie, November 1941. Returning from a Wadsworth family Thanksgiving in Norwood Park, they stopped at a photo booth to take an impromptu picture.

Courtesy Siegmund Levarie

Kohut, spring 1941, as he embarked on his internship at Chicago South Shore Hospital on the far South Side of the city. His first night on duty he prescribed the wrong medicine to a dying patient, who promptly expired. Courtesy Siegmund Levarie

Kohut walking with his mother on a Chicago sidewalk in July 1942. Courtesy Siegmund Levarie

The Cloisters, an apartment complex at 58th Street and Dorchester Avenue, where the Kohuts lived in Apartment 12C from 1957 until Heinz Kohut's death. After the early 1960s, he ran his daily mile, usually under seven minutes, in Jackman Field across the street.

Kohut at a dinner party in 1951 with his wife, Elizabeth, his mother, Else, and baby Thomas. The future was very bright. Courtesy Siegmund Levarie

Robert Wadsworth in the 1950s. Courtesy Frank Wadsworth

actual stance that a good therapist sought to present to a patient. Theories of transference and countertransference proliferated. Elaborations of the "Oedipus complex" became a growth industry by itself. But most of all, commentary on the psychoanalytic theory of drives became a variation of talmudic exegesis; even someone as smart and sensitive as Erik Erikson never abandoned Freud's theories of instinct and drive and merely elaborated them in his own terms. Drive theory was ubiquitous in the 1950s and 1960s. Most felt that it defined psychoanalysis. Kurt Eissler, no less, toyed with the idea that it might be possible to measure psychic energy.[8]

In such a context, Kohut's early work on empathy was a radical departure that challenged the assumptions of psychoanalysis as it was then understood. It changed the questions and restated the problems in the field without abandoning the project itself. It was not uncommon for American psychologists to move away from Freud out of frustration with drive theory. But there was no one like Kohut who so intensely idealized psychoanalysis itself, who lived off it, who was so central to its institutional structures, and who then challenged it at such a fundamental level. His goal was quite simply to remake the theory, and by extension the practice, in his own eyes. The irony is that Kohut himself was not fully aware, or was not yet prepared to face fully, how at odds he was with the existing "metapsychology" of psychoanalysis. It took many years after he wrote his empathy paper for Kohut himself to grasp its implications.[9]

Kohut must have been thinking about the ideas in his empathy paper from the early 1950s, and probably began sharing them more widely in his courses and informal discussions after he joined the staff of the Institute in 1953. Sometime in 1955 or 1956 he was asked to present his ideas on empathy as the main paper at the upcoming twenty-fifth anniversary of the founding of the Chicago Institute in November 1957. He actually wrote the first draft of the paper in 1956, probably in Carmel. Besides at the anniversary of the Institute, he also delivered the empathy paper at the Psychoanalytic Congress in Paris in 1957. The reception at the Institute anniversary was warm and enthusiastic. Franz Alexander, who returned for the ceremonies, recognized the importance of Kohut's work immediately and said the paper would have a "dramatic impact on the future of psychoanalysis." The next year Kohut submitted the final version to the *Journal of the American Psychoanalytic Association* (at a time when he was on the editorial board). It was at first rejected. The readers seemed to feel that it posed too basic a challenge to the theory and therefore was not appropriately psychoanalytic. Maxwell Gitelson, however, intervened and insisted the *Journal* not engage in ideological censorship. The paper was reconsidered, accepted, and finally appeared in 1959 under the title "Introspection, Empathy, and Psychoanalysis: An Examination of the Relationship Between Mode of Observation and Theory."[10]

Kohut's basic point about empathy is epistemological. He wants to clarify the way of knowing in psychoanalysis. And so he begins with a dualism that governed his thinking for the rest of his life: We can investigate our physical surroundings with our senses and mechanical elaborations of those senses with instruments like the telescope and microscope, but we can only know our inner world through introspection and its vicarious form, empathy. "Our thoughts, wishes, feelings, and fantasies cannot be seen, smelled, heard, or touched." They have no existence in the physical world, and yet to say they are not real is absurd. He grants that bodily processes we experience as feelings can be studied and recorded by sophisticated means, something that has progressed much further in brain research since Kohut wrote his paper. But such investigations do not actually measure or describe feelings, only the underlying physiological processes that are the biological substrate of feelings. Kohut's essential "operational" point remains valid: "We speak of physical phenomena when the essential ingredient of our observational methods includes our senses, we speak of psychological phenomena when the essential ingredient of our observation is introspection and empathy."[11]

Observations, of course, in any science are ordered into increasingly abstract concepts and generalizations that are quite far from the data of observation. It is, in fact, the nature of scientific inquiry, which Kohut esteems, to search for such ordering principles. In zoology the concept of a "mammal" is very far from the multitude of actual animals we can observe in nature. Similarly, the psychoanalytic concept of drives is empirically based in innumerable psychological experiences, though one cannot directly observe a drive. Repression, in turn, describes the conditions of the disappearance and emergence of thoughts and fantasies.

But, he asks, are introspection and its vicarious expression, empathy, the only constituents of a psychological observation? Are there not some psychological facts that derive from a sensory, or nonintrospective, observation of the world? His answer to this key point rests largely on his claim for the hermeneutics of observation. What makes something psychological is the meaning we attach to it, not its formal external character. We can measure a man of unusual size but only appreciate his tallness through introspection. We can describe precisely the upward rise of the skin above the eye but only know through introspection what the raising of an eye-brow means. A stone may fall and kill a man, but that action only be-comes psychological to the extent we can empathize with the experience of the victim. We can measure the sound waves of certain uttered words but only know through introspection and empathy that they were spo-ken in anger. Kohut is categorical: "Only a phenomenon that we can attempt to observe by introspection or by empathy with another's in-trospection may be called psychological." But because of the complicated ways in which measurement and introspection mix, Kohut amends his first defi-nition to say that introspection and empathy must be present "as an essential constituent" for an observation to be considered psychological. In self analysis it is there alone; in scrutinizing the free associations of an analysand, empathy is the essence of the skilled analyst's ability to com-prehend the patient.[12]

Kohut then turns to six themes in his effort to comprehend the place of empathy in psychoanalysis. He notes, first, that there are strong im-pediments to the free associative exploration of introspection that derive from the "defense function of the mind." Put simply, the patient fears the "unconscious contents and their derivatives." But such resistance at the individual level has much broader points of reference in the culture, which explains why psychoanalysis has so strongly resisted acknowledg-ing wholeheartedly that introspection and empathy constitute its unique epistemology, that is, its very own mode of observation. "It seems we are ashamed of it and do not want to mention it directly," for it evokes the mystical and the non-Western, Kohut says. Introspection may also arouse a fear of helplessness and passivity in the face of repressed ideas that we uncover from the unconscious. There is much dread at facing prolonged analytic treatment. Some, however, will embrace treatment for just such reasons, as an escape from reality, analogous to mystical cults and "pseudo-scientific mystical psychology."[13]

Second, besides irrational resistances to introspection, there are also realistic limitations to its application. "There can be little doubt about the fact that the reliability of empathy declines, the more dissimilar the observed is from the observer." Early experience, or deep regressions dur-ing sleep, neurosis, or fatigue, for example, are far removed from our im-mediate introspective experience. It is important to express that difference in the immediacy of experience with the language we use. Too often we ascribe concreteness when we are much less certain of what we feel. Kohut advises talking of "tension instead of wish, of tension decrease instead of

wish fulfillment, and of condensations and compromise formations instead of problem solving." At other times the problem is more operational. It is extremely difficult to introspect the meanings of the earliest
of interactions between mother and child, but it is no substitute to call
on the observations of social psychology. That muddies the methodologi-
cal waters considerably.[14]

Third, Kohut addresses the relation of introspection and empathy to
the meanings of transference. He notes that Freud's great discoveries were
of the unconscious and of transference. Freud felt that the analyst, to the
extent he becomes a transference figure, is not experienced as a real person but as the carrier of unconscious memories. Freud, however, was
basically limited in his clinical work to neurotics, or those for whom oedipal issues were in the forefront of their consciousness. Since then psychoanalysis has begun to deal with more disturbed patients, Kohut says.
Empathy with these patients leads to very different psychic states in which
the analyst becomes the primitive figure: "While it is true that all transferences are repetitions, not all repetitions are transferences." The logic
of Kohut's distinction—which he was not yet ready to face—is that empathy with disturbed patients leads to earlier and more archaic states of
consciousness that may be completely unrelated to, or precursors of,
oedipal issues.

Fourth, Kohut addresses a variety of issues relating to empathy and
dependence. His challenge is to the psychoanalytic assumption that emotional states of dependence one uncovers in therapy correspond roughly
to childhood experience, as, for example, in the idea that the regressed
patient evokes the normal baby at the breast. Kohut finds such a notion
foolish at best, based as it is on faulty introspection and empathy. The
pathology that emerges in therapy, he says, is the return of childhood
pathology, not the evocation of what is normal. Empathy with ordinary
children proves that in a moment. The normal baby at the breast is not
a helpless, regressed entity; it should rather be compared with the sprinter
at the end of a hundred-yard dash, or the violinist at the height of the
cadenza, or a lover at the peak of sexual union. Kohut also objects to
the psychoanalytic tendency to ascribe dependence to orality, or a par-
tial drive experience. It is the "insistent clinging" rather than the "association with a particular drive" that characterizes dependence in most
situations. To illustrate this point he relates the tale of a patient who
had been one of thirty survivors in a concentration camp at which over
100,000 were killed during his stay.[15] When the Nazi guards fled before

the Russian advance, the survivors could not make themselves leave for four long days.[16]

Fifth, Kohut considers the drives, which he defines as abstractions from "innumerable inner experiences." A drive "connotes a psychological quality that cannot be further analyzed by introspection." What we can know through introspection is the experience of feeling driven, of wanting, or wishing, or striving. Freud often conflated this distinction, which is why he could move so easily and uncritically from primary narcissism and primary masochism to Eros and Thanatos. That progression stands biology on its head. Such confusion also led Freud to some extraordinary nonsense about female sexuality, which, Kohut says, is quite obviously not a mere retreat from disappointed maleness. "The female must have primary female tendencies," Kohut says categorically. But in a qualification that he probably added for political reasons, he says that it is unlikely Freud failed to understand this because he had a "blindspot that limited his powers of observation." Freud, Kohut says, simply lacked the clinical evidence that might have deepened his understanding in this area.[17]

Kohut concludes his essay with some philosophical reflections on free will and determinism. His point is to enlarge the realm of free will. Most of Freud's work, especially his early writings, Kohut says, allow for only a strict psychic determinism. In 1923 (*The Ego and the Id*) Freud at least puts in a footnote that the goal of psychoanalytic psychotherapy is "to give the patient's ego *freedom* to choose one way or the other." But Freud never elaborated. Basically he left the issue of psychic autonomy confused. In fact, Kohut feels that free will is an extensive, vital, necessary dimension of experience. It can also be investigated. Through introspection, Kohut argues, we can observe "the experience of an active 'I.' " That "I-experience" cannot be further broken down, made the by-product of a theory of instinct. It is, on the contrary, "beyond the law of motivation, i.e., beyond the law of psychic determinism."[18]

The rest of Kohut's early work was safer and less creative. As one surveys his scattered observations on theory, it is astonishing to see how completely Freudian he was. His goal was to advance Freud's insights. He was a worker in the vineyard, modest if not altogether humble. The point of reference was always Freud. He taught Freud, he talked about Freud, he wrote about Freud, he thought about Freud. Freud is the exemplar. Kohut's sentences seem to begin and end with Freud. His discourse is

Freudian. No one, literally no one, knew Freud better than Kohut, though the major figures in ego psychology knew him as well. Part of what is interesting in the early Kohut is therefore not his reliance on Freud but the subtle ways he reinterprets Freud as he attempts to explain him. The most interesting and original moments occur when that tension moves toward contradiction.[19]

But for the most part in these early years, besides his work on empathy, Kohut became known for his work on applied analysis. Music became his specialty. After his first paper with Levarie, Kohut wrote a second in 1957 that extended his investigations without breaking new theoretical ground.[20] He also pondered problems of method in applied analysis, while he continued to read and study Goethe.[21] This work, in turn, led him to the Nazis and attempts to understand the period of history that had shaped his youth. In one of his more extended commentaries, he wrote to his friends Alexander and Margarete Mitscherlich about German guilt. The guilt of the many in a historical event like that of Nazi Germany, he said, was not simply that of the individual but was widely, indeed universally, shared. Even the victims shared some guilt, he said. Kohut's goal, however, was not to blame the victims but to tease out the most general of human lessons from the historical experience of the Holocaust.[22] Any kind of meaningful opposition to Nazism, he asserts, would have required truly heroic actions and brought on instant retribution. It was a world of total evil. Almost no one made such gestures. "Yet it is just this choice between heroism and guilt that must be brought home to people if humanity is to survive." Kohut's point was to outline the psychological possibilities for such heroism. It wouldn't do alone to confront Germans (and all humanity) with their past sins as passive onlookers and make them feel guilty. Guilt alone does not make heroes. People need to see that they themselves were victims, too, "that the highest, most differentiated, most precious part of their own personalities had been killed" in the experience of not heroically resisting Nazism. To arrive at that kind of understanding might prompt Germans and others to want to recover their old ideals, to heal the past, and inspire at least in some "the will to survive in a sense that is more meaningful than biological survival."[23]

Kohut also had a view of Hitler, reached sometime in the late 1950s, that he never really changed but repeated with slight variations for the rest of his life. In what seems to have been his first formulation in 1960, he felt Hitler had a kind of "healed-over psychosis" in which the "reality testing remains broadly intact so long as it is in the service of the psychosis, of the central idée fixe." Hitler, he felt, had come out of his intensely lonely, hypochondriacal phase of late adolescence "with the fixed idea that the Jews had invaded the body of Germany and had to be eradicated." In another context, Kohut contrasted Hitler with Joseph Goebbels in ways that he thought might suggest a larger generalization about prejudice. Psychologically, Hitler's walled-off psychosis can be contrasted with Goebbels's more benign phobias, which translated into the malevolent hatreds of Hitler in comparison to the "much less fixed prejudice" of Goebbels.[24]

In 1964 Kohut responded to an Austrian journalist who was writing a piece about him for a magazine. Given the venue, he took the request seriously, and besides enclosing a copy of his vita he wrote a letter summarizing his scholarly work of the previous twenty years. Like his specialty, psychoanalysis, he says, "I have been standing with one foot in biology and with the other in the humanities." He had done research in everything from neurology to music and the humanities. He had also been drawn to "basic theoretical questions concerning the nature of the methodology of psychoanalytic explanations." Kohut's concise conceptual survey of where he stood on the cusp of creativity illustrates how orthodox and mainstream he saw himself as Mr. Psychoanalysis. Given his personality, it may have been that he could never have reached beyond convention without first grounding himself as a husband and father, a respected leader in his field, and a cautious modern interpreter of Freud. He was about to step out of the shadows.

Part Three

BREAKING FREE

1965–1970

Fourteen

NEW FORMS

The summer of 1965 was something of a turning point for Kohut. Then fifty-two years old, he had just finished his stint as president of the American Psychoanalytic Association, which had capped a half decade of intense involvement in administrative matters. He was exhausted and driving himself "at a pace which is not quite appropriate for my age."[1] It had been years since he had written anything of substance. And yet ideas on narcissism were brewing inside his head as though in a pressure cooker. That summer in Carmel, as least as Kohut saw it later, was transformative. He was "bursting at the seams." He sat there in his study over the garage, completely isolated, watching his family outside on the lawn, and wrote furiously for four weeks. He was in a peak state of "absolute abandon." Ideas poured out of him. "Essentially everything I've written since then," he said in 1980, "I wrote in those weeks in that one summer."[2] There is no doubt that the notion he wrote down all his key ideas in those four weeks is an absurd exaggeration. He was a long way from bringing coherence to his ideas in ways that would later lead him to talk of a "self psychology." But something happened to Kohut that was of importance that summer of 1965.

Anyone in contact with Kohut noticed the change. Candidates who took his courses in these years (or were supervised by him), for example, knew that they were being exposed to some startling new concepts. David Terman was a candidate who happened to catch Kohut just at the moment of transition. It happened that Terman in the beginning of his training attended Kohut's last psychoanalytic theory course in the Old Freudian frame, taught while he was president of the American. It was interesting but not remarkable. But Terman then took all of Kohut's courses after 1965, when he taught only seminars and clinical case conferences that dealt directly with narcissism. Terman said it was the most exciting thing he has ever experienced. He was keenly aware of being present at the discovery of something. Kohut, however, was not always easy to understand. Arnold Goldberg recalls being hopelessly confused in the mid-1960s when Kohut would talk about the "idealization of the superego." Years later he asked Kohut why he did not explain the idea better. Kohut replied: "I didn't understand it myself."[3]

The one specific paper that Kohut drafted in the summer of 1965 in Carmel in the flush of his new insights was what he later called "Forms and Transformations of Narcissism." He knew he had to deliver it as the plenary address of the past president of the American at the meetings in New York on December 5, 1965.[4] His ideas in this paper were clearly brewing the previous winter and spring. In February, he wrote his friend Alexander Mitscherlich that "what belongs most privately to the individual, namely the (repressed?) narcissistic fantasy, might be one of the crucial specific factors in the social pathology of our age."[5] The next month he had an exchange with Anna Freud about death and some disagreements he had with her father's views on transience.[6] Kohut felt Freud's ideas were "metapsychologically incompletely worked out," which was a rather assertive thing to say to Anna Freud, though he quickly added that what Freud was getting at was "of great significance" and gives us a "clue to the understanding of the metapsychology of the quality we call wisdom that he hoped soon to describe in greater detail."[7] In ways that were typical for Kohut at this stage, he could only describe a new idea of his own as an interpretation of something that lay hidden in Freud.[8] Certainly, "Forms and Transformations" has an aura of legitimacy. The first sentence quotes Heinz Hartmann's definition of narcissism as the "libidinal cathexis of the self";[9] there are frequent allusions to Freud's 1914 essay on narcissism; and the very idea of "transformations of narcissism" is presented as an extension of Freud's basic insights. Perhaps Kohut gave away too much.

Kohut deeply objected to the idea that narcissism, or any form of self-absorption, is necessarily bad. That conventional view dominated psychoanalysis in general after Freud and was particularly strong in Chicago, where there was quite a lot of interest in the subject on the part of a number of analysts around Lionel Blitzsten. The Blitzsten group gave lip service to the idea of "healthy narcissism," but they really took Freud's stance that any form of intense self-involvement was an interference with the development of higher forms of love for others. The favored way of dealing with expressions of such attitudes in the patient was to adopt a joking, ironic stance that was supposed to kindle the patient's humor but often slid into "sarcasm, ridicule, even mockery." At the start of his career, it seems Kohut tried to adopt this party line, but something in him rebelled against treating people that way and in seeing some of the greatest creations of human culture as merely defensive.[10]

The notion that narcissism was bad, Kohut argued, was also the product of a cultural bias, "the intrusion of the altruistic value system of Western civilization."[11] He would prefer to look at the problem "more dispassionately." A focus on the self is thus simply one of two possible ways of loving (or "libido distribution"). The investments we have in other people are more prized in the culture and seem much less primitive and more adaptive than investments in the self. But one should seriously question such a judgment, based, as it is, on psychological prejudice. Analysts all too often make a concerted effort to replace a patient's self-centeredness with almost any kind of move toward someone of the opposite sex. It would be much more appropriate with such patients, Kohut argues, to try to foster in them some kind of transformation of their primitive self-involvement into one of its higher forms.

The term Freud used to describe the original state of being of the infant was "primary narcissism." This is not a state that can be observed by extrospection, Kohut notes. Primary narcissism is rather an extrapolation through empathy into the state in which the distinction between self and other has not yet been established. Kohut's analogy for explaining primary narcissism is to the way an adult experiences his or her own body and mind and one's ability to control them. They are owned by and part of the self. In the same way the baby feels joined to the mother psychologically. She is the mind and body of the baby's self. Kohut then postulates that this primary self state gives way to two interrelated but differentiated forms centered on one's own sense of self wonder and on an idealized image of the other.[12] In one aspect of self experience we cling to our original feeling of omnipotence, and in another to our sense of the "original bliss, power, perfection, and goodness" of the parent figure."[13] As he puts it epigrammatically: "Man is *led* by his ideals but *pushed* by his ambitions." Such a neat formulation can, of course, be misleading. For one thing, it can often be difficult to distinguish one's ideals from one's ambitions. Ambitions are often disguised as ideals, as in adolescence, and sometimes there are "lucky moments in our lives" or "lucky periods in the lives of the very fortunate" when the two converge. But ambitions and ideals remain discrete psychological processes. Our ideals are our internal leaders. We love them and long to reach them. If we fail miserably to reach them we wallow in humiliation, though more normally our experience is "an emotion akin to longing." Ambitions, in turn, can be-come autonomous and peremptory, resulting in a deep sense of shame. Grandiosity then gets repressed and the consequence in the adult self is wild vacillation between irrational overestimation and feelings of inferiority.

The interplay of grandiosity and ideals in the self—what he felt is superficially called identity[14]—determines the distinctive nature of personality. To illustrate this point, Kohut turned to the historical example of Winston Churchill, whom he greatly admired. Many such "outstanding personalities" who become political leaders have an inner balance that is dominated by grandiose ambitions. As he was to argue later, in fact, grandiosity is the essential component of creativity.[15] The key to employing one's sense of greatness effectively, however, is to find ways to channel and direct it into the mediating structures of the self. For Churchill this was not an easy task. As a young man, he often placed himself in situations that required daring escapes, as in the Boer War. Kohut wonders whether at some level Churchill felt he could fly, which is probably the most typical of all grandiose fantasies. Kohut notes in this regard Churchill's account in his autobiography of a brush with death as a child. He was being chased by some relatives in a game. He came to a ravine and decided to jump onto some trees below to escape capture. He only woke up three days later and remained in bed for three months with various injuries. Kohut comments ironically: "Luckily, for him and for the forces of civilization, when he reached the peak of his responsibilities the inner balance had shifted."[16]

Grandiosity and idealization exist as forms of narcissism that are complemented in turn by several kinds of transformations. The notion of transformation is a developmental one, of course, and Anna Freud and others quickly understood what Kohut was talking about as a "developmental line" of narcissism, similar to what she felt her father had defined for libido, or sexual development.[17] The meaning of such "lines" had been one of Anna Freud's most important contributions to psychoanalytic thought. Kohut himself, however, while content for the moment to be understood in those terms, never mentions it in the paper.[18] To be seen as the formulator of a new line gave him legitimacy, for it put his ideas in a familiar landscape. Nevertheless, at some level he almost certainly sensed it was conceptually limiting to restrict the huge field he was opening up merely to another developmental line paralleling the course of sexuality.

The first such transformation Kohut considers is creativity. It is not just that many creative people are grandiose, or that scientific activity is often prompted by the great performances of others that stir one to action. It is that creativity itself is a form of transformed narcissism. The mere fact that creative people alternate between periods of intense productivity when they think highly of their work and other times when they completely devalue it suggests, as much as anything, this connection between high and low. One can also see the residues of the earlier forms in the most advanced expressions of scientific work partly in the often child-like ways of the creative individual. The major task of life, Kohut said elsewhere, is to remain actively creative, and that can only come from "the ability to be in touch with the playful child deep in the personality," to hold onto the "freshness of the child's encounter with the world."[19] The creative individual is less psychologically separated from the world. As he says, "the I-you barrier is not as clearly defined." Like the air we breathe the creative individual invests those aspects of the surround that support the work. Inner and outer merge, as in what Kohut calls the "prototypical description of creativity": "and the Lord God formed man of the dust of the ground, and breathed into his nostrils the breath of life; and man became a living soul." Creativity grows from this soil.

Empathy is Kohut's second example of transformed narcissism. Empathy is the way we gather psychological data about other people. That capacity, which can become highly refined and is of special significance for the psychoanalyst, is analogous to the capacity to "identify a face in a single act of apperception" without adding up all the details. And, indeed, such recognition emerges out of the same context as empathy. "The small child's perceptual merging with the mother's face constitutes simultaneously its most important access to the mother's identity and to her emotional state."[20] The capacity for empathy originates in our earliest merger with the mother, whose feelings, actions, and behavior are included in the self. "This *primary empathy* with the mother," Kohut says, "prepares us for the recognition that to a large extent the basic inner experiences of other people remain similar to our own." Primary empathy defines our first perception of reality. Such perceptions give way in time to "nonempathic forms of cognition" that allow for discrimination of the object in relation to the self. Such forms are later highly prized and can become overly idealized. The analyst, on the other hand, seeks a sustained use of empathy to understand the inner states of patients.

The consideration of empathy leads Kohut as well into a discussion of transience and death. The primary empathy with the mother is connected, he says, to a primary identity with her that becomes the "precursor of an expansion of the self, late in life, when the finiteness of individual existence is acknowledged." The beginnings of the self in primary identity form the basis for what Freud called the "oceanic feeling" that is so important for spiritual people. But the significance of the primary identity with the mother goes beyond the powerful evocations of spirituality that can be evoked in the self. Kohut's clear suggestion in this difficult passage, which he fails to make explicit, is that primary identity also gives way to a merger with a God concept in the face of death. The issue is not denial but one of cosmic narcissism. It is thus a "great psychological achievement" and a "rare feat" to acknowledge the finiteness of existence. The result is not hopelessness "but a quiet pride which is often coupled with mild disdain of the rabble which, without being able to delight in the variety of experiences life has to offer, is yet afraid of death and trembles at its approach."[21]

The third example of transformed narcissism Kohut discusses is that of humor, which may seem like a poor cousin next to God. But there are important points of contact between the "quasi-religious solemnity of a cosmic narcissism" and the human capacity for humor.[22] Both connect at their deepest level with death. Excessive joking and all forms of sarcasm, of course, can be highly defensive, just as one has to distrust a too easy acceptance of finiteness. Neither the clown nor the saint is quite genuine. Yet one has to be impressed with those who can contemplate death philosophically. Humor and cosmic narcissism, which emerge out of the same narcissistic matrix, are crucial ways in which we face death without denial or in a kind of "frenzied mental condition" that one often sees in the early stages of war. On the contrary, death can allow for a withdrawal of feelings for the self and, accompanied with some sadness, a transference of those feelings onto "the supraindividual ideals and to the world with which one identifies." Kohut adds: "The profoundest forms of humor and cosmic narcissism therefore do not present a picture of grandiosity and elation but that of a quiet inner triumph with an admixture of undenied melancholy."[23]

Kohut concludes his paper with the "ultimate challenge" of explaining wisdom, which he says rests largely on the transcendence of narcissism and may be defined as an "amalgamation of the higher processes of cognition with the psychological attitude that accompanies the renouncement of these narcissistic demands." Wisdom partly results from the possession of ideals, the capacity for humor, and the acceptance of transience, but is also much more. Certainly, the wise must have broadly based knowledge, which is why wisdom cannot be an attribute of youth. There must also be in wisdom a "maximal relinquishment of narcissistic delusions" without abandoning thought. The ultimate act of cognition, after all, is the recognition of death. Things are in perspective for the wise, including the ironic sense of their own wisdom. The ego's mastery over the narcissistic self, Freud's rider on the horse, is perhaps helped by the fact that the horse has also gotten older.

Fifteen

THE DEATH OF ELSE

There is never a simple relationship between experience and creativity. The synergy, almost by definition, cannot be disentangled. At times, however, there are moments in a life when events occur that are so essential they force a radical realignment of self structure. For Heinz Kohut such an event seemed to be the confirmation of his mother's paranoia just as he plunged into the depths of trying to understand narcissism. There was no sudden day when Else went mad, nor did she ever appear to become openly psychotic in a sustained way. But in the years after 1965, when Kohut was in his mid-to-late fifties, Else began to demonstrate, as he says in "Mr. Z," "a set of circumscribed paranoid delusions" (her neighbors were out to get her, for example) that, together with her declining health, led to her commitment in a nursing home in the summer of 1970.[1]

The patterns of Else's life between 1965 and 1970 for the most part continued earlier rhythms. She took her art courses, painted, traveled, spent time with her friends. She visited the Kohut family regularly (at least once a week) and probably talked much more frequently with Kohut himself. But she was becoming a special burden; her mental state raised questions whether she could in fact continue to live alone. Since Else was by no means completely mad, however, it does not seem she readily assented to her son's new diagnosis of her; in the end, it was only her failing health and a stroke that allowed Kohut to have her committed to the nursing home. Even then he went to see her every single Sunday he was not himself out of town.

The gradual validation of Else's paranoia had a remarkable and counter-intuitive impact on Kohut's emotional state. He felt liberated. Kohut spoke frequently in the family in these years of how important it was to him to have it confirmed that Else was crazy, though it was both freeing and terrifying at the same time.[2] As Kohut says of himself in his autobiographical "Mr. Z," his reaction to the confirmation of his mother's paranoia was that he was constantly losing his grip on his new understanding of Else and what that meant for himself. The "emotional toll" was great and his insights were repeatedly interrupted by doubts and a kind of "nameless fear." What was real? Whose reality could he trust? His or his mother's? It was only the constant return to the fact of his mother's craziness that made him sane.[3]

Kohut now saw, and wrote in "Mr. Z," that his childhood had consisted of a continual struggle to escape the throes of Else's crypto-psychotic entrapments. At last he understood that her "intense, unshakable convictions" had been translated into "attitudes and actions which emotionally enslaved those around her and stifled their independent existence." Else gave him huge "emotional gifts" but they were only bestowed "under the unalterable and uncompromising condition that he submit to total domination by her, that he must not allow himself any independence, particularly as concerned significant relationships with others." The external confirmation of Else's paranoia also clarified the disappearance of Felix from the family. He had to escape from her grasp to save himself. In the process Felix sacrificed his son.[4]

Kohut could now begin to appreciate, as he puts it in "Mr. Z," the "depression and hopelessness" that Else's attitudes evoked in him. Looking back, he could see that she had had no interest in him, only in his feces and pimples, which had fascinated her "with an intensity, a self-righteous certainty, and adamant commitment that allowed no protest and created almost total submission." Her absorption later on in the objects of her life (furniture, art, and bric-a-brac) carried over from the way she had treated him. He now could fully appreciate the significance of the way she insisted he keep his door open when he finally got his own room. There could be no separation. The masturbation themes, as well, came into much sharper focus. There was little here having to do with drive demand and gratification. It was rather "the depression of a self" seeking meaningful assertion but caught in the suffocating and enmeshing tendrils of an oppressive mother. Only through masturbation could the young Heinz feel that he was alive.

The meaning of familiar dreams changed as well. As he struggled with his new grasp of his experience, Kohut sometimes felt himself disintegrating and beset by hypochondriacal concerns. Then he dreamed of "desolate landscapes, burned-out cities, and, most deeply upsetting, of heaps of piled-up human bodies." Kohut, one might say, revisited the Holocaust in his struggle to realign the elements of his self. Only once in these dreams did his mother appear. He saw her from the back, naked, turned from him. The image filled him with "the deepest anxiety he had ever experienced." It reminded him of her "icy withdrawal" when he made any moves toward independence, especially toward "independent maleness." But the deepest meaning of the dream was the unseen part of her frontal view. As he reflected and associated to the dream image, it filled him with terror. He lacked words for his anxiety. And his dread had nothing to do with a missing penis. What he feared was that the unseen frontal view of his mother showed she had no face.[5]

The most puzzling and yet important consequence of the confirmation of Else's craziness was that it seemed to play a vital role in unlocking Kohut's creativity. He was now freed to explore in his own original ways the deeper meanings of highly regressed states. The psychological death of Else, one might say, made possible *The Analysis of the Self*. Kohut could now emerge from his mother's oppressive shadow. He visited her most Sundays, though he complained often of the burden it put on him. Else would try to coax him to stay longer by saying, just as he was about to leave, "Heinz, I had the most wonderful dream last night." Any contact unraveled him. He once took a call from Else during a supervisory session with a candidate and got surprisingly angry afterward. But at least Kohut could now manage the problems of her care mostly from a distance. He kept in close touch with her doctor, James M. Goldringer, and expressed his warm thanks for the care his mother was receiving as he prepared for a trip to Germany in early October 1970. Kohut gently urged Goldringer to make Else's life as comfortable as possible without disturbing the hospital routine too much. "I know that her complaints have often not much to do with reality," he wrote.[6]

Else died peacefully on October 14, 1972, though she stirred things up to the very end. She went through some kind of deathbed conversion with a Catholic priest who attended to her in the nursing home. One can say of this conversion, if nothing else, that it was her last. In one of her final conversations with Kohut she gave him a clock she had gotten out of Vienna with the words "Don't let them [her long-deceased brothers] take it away from you." Else's death left Kohut numb with hurt, incapable even of mourning. A patient of Kohut's at the time heard about Else's death and expressed his condolences. Kohut responded matter-of-factly, "Well, you know, she was old, it was time." Else, a Catholic, was buried in St. Mary's Cemetery next to the nursing home. Kohut moved on with his life, though always with Else at some level of consciousness. Jerome Beigler recalls that once in a seminar in the 1970s Kohut commented as an absurd aside that "crypto-psychotic mothers end up dying in nursing homes."[7]

Sixteen

FAMILY AND OTHER STRUGGLES

Few people are more intensely focused on their own creative work than the mature Kohut was, beginning in 1965, when he was fifty-three years old. He recognized the personal cost. Kohut says of himself in "Mr. Z" that interpersonal relationships never played the "dominant role in his life" that they do for the majority of people and never provided him with his "most fulfilling experiences." Kohut's relationship with Elizabeth continued in its quiet way. She was his partner on the journey but seemed to relinquish her identity in some fundamental way. She was reticent to the point of shyness and seemed clearly to have accepted her role as a silent, supportive presence in the tumultuous, creative world of her husband. If she was ambivalent—how could she not have been?—it was not apparent and does not appear in the record. Kohut himself never talked about her in his correspondence or with friends except in the most cursory of ways, which contrasts sharply with his frequent, extended comments on his son. Elizabeth clearly occupied an important, if not vital, niche in Kohut's emotional life, though she herself remained in the shadows. She had gone back to work half-time in the early 1960s as a therapist at the University of Chicago Mental Health Clinic.[1] That carved out for Elizabeth something of a separate identity from her husband and created for her a work space with its own set of friendships, obligations, and commitments. Her job, however, remained half-time. Her other half she gave to Heinz Kohut.

With his son, things were forced, however earnestly he tried. Kohut continued to take Thomas places, talk about his studies, and always care about what he was thinking. Kohut would not be distant like Felix. In 1968 Kohut wrote a long letter to the Metropolitan Opera in New York, asking for tickets to an upcoming performance of *Die Meistersinger* and explaining how his own father had taken him to that opera when he was a boy and he wanted to repeat the experience with his son. His concern was that, though he would mail his envelope just past midnight on the date when the letters were to be postmarked, he stood at a disadvantage because "hordes of semi-professional and professional ticket getters" in New York would have their envelopes delivered before his could arrive. The Met must have responded to Kohut's unusual request, for over that Christmas holiday Thomas joined his father for a special weekend together in New York, where they saw *The Play of Daniel* in a church and *Die Meistersinger* at the Met. Kohut and his son also had a "cherished tradition" of stag dinners once or twice a year that often found them in the Quadrangle Club (for faculty) of the University of Chicago, after which they often played a "leisurely father-son game of billiards."[2]

Kohut's involvement in his son's life, however, could become oppressive. Once when Thomas, as an adolescent in the mid-1960s, was off at Camp Kechua in Michigan, Kohut wrote him a chatty letter, describing the events on that July Fourth, the flags and fireworks, and how he and Elizabeth had played tennis in the morning and gone off in the afternoon to a dreadful soccer game in Soldier Field between the Poles and Hungarians. Kohut wonders if Thomas still remembered the German children's songs he taught him, and his concern that Thomas might have forgotten them prompts him to write out one of them, with a translation, on a separate sheet of paper. The thought that his son might forget the words to the songs prompts Kohut to shift his tone from chatty reportage to exhortation. He hopes that his son will be a "good camper and a good sport." He strongly urges self-denial and discipline: "Don't show it too much if you are out of sorts or a little homesick but keep your chin up and your spirits high." Keep focused and never give up. Play your best even if you are losing in the game. What matters is hard work. In anything that you cannot do well, keep at it and never give up. "Time, effort, and repetition can do a great deal." Kohut even throws in two banal clichés: " 'Rome was not built in a day,' " he says, and "masters don't fall from heaven." The only relief from such overbearing advice to his adolescent son comes in the last sentence: "And remember that I am very proud of you even though I seem to do a lot of nagging sometimes."[3]

Behind the prodding was a note of fear that Thomas would not live up to his promise. With reluctance Kohut gave up fairly early on his fantasy of his son's becoming a doctor. As he told an old friend once, Thomas was weak in math and science and, besides, "lacks the self-discipline to pass his boards."[4] But the issue, in a sense, lay deeper and more within Kohut himself than anything to do with the weaknesses (or strengths) of his son. Kohut developed a special voice in which he spoke to Thomas. He became The Father, consciously supreme and prodding, stiff, a little rigid, loving and encouraging but overly earnest and involved, not quite intrusive but definitely too eager in ways that bordered on the oppressive. Kohut, for example, wrote Thomas in 1964 from New York, where he and Elizabeth were at the annual meetings of the American Psychoanalytic Association. Thomas, then fourteen, had just written his parents a letter in which he commented on some of Else's paintings. Kohut replied how interested he was in the boy's reactions. He agreed with the observation that the paintings were bright but wondered "whether they express happiness." But it did not really matter, Kohut said, for the key idea was that Else was busy and remained happy (and perhaps out of his hair?). Kohut also described the opera he had seen the night before, commented on the weather, and expressed his concern about the health of Tovey, the dog. Then Kohut fell into his typical Polonius ending: "Glad to know you are working hard." Keep at it and don't get discouraged, "even if your grades won't stay up or move up. It always takes quite a long time until one sees results in things of this kind."

"He was too close," Thomas says now. "At least he was too close to me." To survive, Thomas became combative in struggles with his father, often in alliance with his mother. There was a lot of tension and fighting at dinner, for example, often over mundane matters like table manners, though as Thomas got older and more caught up in the issues of the 1960s the disputes became more political. Thomas would often storm off. Early on, however, Thomas picked up that Kohut was not really angry at him for making such scenes. He actually respected the independence it showed and subtly encouraged it. As Thomas came to understand it, his father welcomed his rebelliousness. "I knew he liked it," Thomas says. "He fought me. But I was also getting positive signals. He did not want me to be a goody-goody." The family was a very "passionate, fighting family," as Thomas puts it. "It was not a family where everybody kept things inside and sort of simmered." Elizabeth, too, joined in the battles. Typical arguments pitted Thomas and his mother against Kohut. He was much too powerful a figure to take on alone. "You needed your allies. It was an intense experience, that family. I never had any doubt as a child that my parents loved me. That was never a question. I never worried about them getting divorced. But it was very hard to share the stage with him. For unless it was critical, he had to be number one and the center of everybody's attention."

Thomas's experience of his father, in fact, alternated between profound respect and a kind of embarrassment he felt at Kohut's narcissism, especially in public. "It was always, 'Well, let's talk about me' kind of thing. 'And then I did this.' It was embarrassing and painful." In alliance with his mother, Thomas would make valiant efforts to rein in his father. Thomas and Elizabeth would jointly tell him that he simply had to stop being so narcissistic. When Kohut was feeling good, he could acknowledge the criticism and be able to take it in, saying, "I can't help myself." On the other hand, when things really counted, "he was fabulous. Just fabulous. He would be there, he would be empathic." But for Thomas the hard times came when things were not at a critical stage. Then Kohut was utterly self-absorbed, unempathic, distant, removed. Thomas also wonders whether part of what he experienced at home was a function of his father's work as a therapist. All day he had to tune into other people's feelings. When he came home the last thing he wanted to do was give some more. It was as though he was saying, "It's my turn. Let me take take take."

The Vietnam War, however, caused the most serious disruption in Kohut's relationship with his son. Never particularly political in general—he had hardly noticed the Nazis until they took over Vienna—Kohut spent 1966 and 1967 focusing on his new theories of narcissism. He knew about the war and surely kept up with it, but it was hardly at the forefront of his consciousness. For example, he never once mentioned Vietnam in any letter that has survived from those years, which were a period of mounting concern in the country. His son, however, was already becoming opposed to the war as a junior and senior at the University of Chicago Laboratory School between 1966 and 1968; Thomas also got caught up in the cultural movements of the 1960s in high school (and attended the Woodstock music festival in the summer of 1969). Dinnertime arguments intensified. The crisis came, however, when Thomas entered Oberlin College in the fall of 1968 and immediately got involved in radical protests against the war. That fall he and some twenty other students expressed their opposition to Navy recruiters on campus by going on a hunger strike. Thomas also planned to fight his draft classification and apply for status as a conscientious objector.[5]

Kohut was appalled. He was liberal, to be sure, favoring things like gun control, but events were fast outpacing him.[6] He found the actions of the police *and* the demonstrators outrageous at the Democratic National Convention in Chicago in August 1968. On October 1 he sent Thomas two issues of the radical *I. F. Stone's Weekly* with the wry comment that they would undoubtedly "pour fuel on the fire of your alarmed pessimism about the state of the nation."[7] But he could not comprehend Thomas's radical antiwar position. "You are beginning to think of yourself," he wrote his son in November, "as belonging . . . to a small group of activist protestors on your campus who feel that the social and political system of our society is intolerable and that one must take personal risks even for the small chance of changing it." The war, Kohut continued, was both immoral and foolish. But "the complexity of social events is staggering" and there was hardly a better alternative political and cultural system than the American. Both the Soviet system and the Communist regime in China had brought "gruesome side effects in suffering and loss of freedom." One sees here the fervent love for America of an immigrant and the sentiments of a man traumatized by the upheavals of his own youth. Perhaps he also worried about his own reputation.

Their struggles intensified until once, in April 1969, Thomas hung up the phone on his father during an argument about a proposed demonstration against Robert K. Carr, the president of Oberlin. Kohut was beside himself. He had disputed Thomas's reasoning during their conversation, which had resulted in the impasse. "Things have certainly come to a fine pass," Kohut wrote. "You believe that you have the right to indulge in this type of impulsive, disrespectful, offensive behavior which completely disregards our feelings because we did not back you up, as you called it, when you tell us that you want to participate in a sit-in or a strike, as an immediate action against a dictatorial move by Carr." Kohut characterized Thomas's actions against the Oberlin president as "nothing short of a declaration of war" which is how bigger wars begin. In such situations, each side convinces itself that it is right, neither backs down, "and the process of escalation starts and goes on until a point of no return is reached."[8] Kohut, shall we say, engaged in his own escalation. Thomas's opposition to his father during that first year in college was probably the first—and last—time anyone really stood up to Heinz Kohut. It left Kohut incoherent with anger.

And then, suddenly, it was over. Thomas managed to express his convictions at Oberlin that spring and not get expelled. The college itself, after a crisis, moved more in unison against the war along the lines of its historic opposition to injustice (in the period before the Civil War Oberlin was a hotbed of opposition to slavery and an important stop on the underground railroad). Equally important in terms of the relationship, Kohut came around to his son's view of the war. In May 1970 Kohut wrote Alexander Mitscherlich about the "complicated" political conditions in America that had inspired some wonderful reactions. At Oberlin, students and faculty had suspended all academic activity, including exams, when Nixon invaded Cambodia and students were shot by National Guardsmen at Kent State University. Instead of classes, there were extended discussion groups, Kohut reported with pride. Thomas also had recently gone to Washington to demonstrate against the war. In the letter Kohut describes Nixon as a "sly politician" who heads a "reactionary regime," which was a far cry from where Kohut had been politically as recently as a year earlier. Thomas himself, his father wrote proudly, was at the forefront of the idealistic antiwar activity going on throughout the country. "In spite of our concern about Tom we are also very proud of him and his involvement with issues of peace and social justice."[9]

The other significant personal relationship in Kohut's life—with Robert Wadsworth—continued as before. Wadsworth was often present for dinner and a fixture at major family holiday events. It seems the two talked on the phone on a regular basis, perhaps almost daily. There was a scare, however, in the late 1960s when Wadsworth developed a problem in his pancreas. Kohut became extremely worried that it might be cancer; he talked with Wadsworth a lot about it, advised him on what he should tell his mother and how to deal with his family, and generally helped him think about how to get his affairs in order. The fears, however, were groundless. Wadsworth made a complete recovery.[10]

In his professional relationships, Kohut continued to cultivate important figures in the field. Perhaps more than ever, as he explored ideas that would eventually take him away from orthodoxy, he needed to stay tied to tradition. He and Kurt Eissler remained close, as he did with Ruth, which was as much a stamp of approval from the establishment as could exist. It was also in these years that Kohut's relationship with Heinz Hartmann deepened. Hartmann reviewed the manuscript of *The Analysis of the Self* and, in Kohut's words, "gave his approval." In the last letter in the correspondence, Hartmann, in the scratchy handwriting of a very old man, thanks Kohut with great feeling for remembering his birthday and

sending flowers. After Hartmann died in early 1970, Kohut wrote glow-
ingly to Mitscherlich that Hartmann's death meant the end of an epoch,
that he was a magnificent man, a real aristocrat of the spirit (*"ein wahrer
Aristokrat des Geistes"*). The night he heard of Hartmann's death, Kohut
also called John Gedo (waking him up) with the news. Gedo felt he was
supposed to say, "The Heinz is dead, long live the Heinz"—that, in other
words, the psychoanalytic torch had passed from one Heinz to the next.[11]

Kohut also continued to cultivate Anna Freud, who dominated British psychoanalysis and was the immensely important connection to the
founder. She was iconic in her symbolic significance, and Kohut courted
her favor assiduously in the 1960s, especially after his term as president of
the American ended in late 1965. Early that year, Kohut sent Anna Freud
a copy of his eulogy for Maxwell Gitelson. In her reply, Anna Freud wrote
of her great fondness for Gitelson and how she had "pinned very many
hopes for the future of analysis on him." She asks, "Who will take his role
now? Will you be the one?" In the fall of 1965 she was notified that the
University of Chicago planned to give her an honorary degree, which
Kohut might have initiated with the administration. Kohut immediately
wrote her a note of congratulation and pointed out what a great thing it
was also for psychoanalysis. She in turn responded with genuine warmth
to his "Forms and Transformations of Narcissism," which she had read
over the holidays. She was "very excited" about the paper and found his
argument "very convincing." "I feel it to be one of the most beautiful
analytic papers which I have read in recent years." The treatment of the
forms of narcissism was excellent, and the discussion of the transformations was "in the very best analytic tradition. There has been no analytic
writing like this, really, for a very long time."[12]

Sometime in the spring or early summer of 1966, Kohut asked Freud
to stay with him while she was in Chicago to get her honorary degree
from the university that fall. She accepted his offer, though she was concerned that she would be a burden because she would be staying a week
or so for various other obligations she had agreed to. Kohut wrote back
immediately, assuring her there was no problem. He then attended to the
details of her trip and corresponded with and talked to numerous people
in Chicago who wanted Freud to do something with them. He fended
most off and kept himself at the center of the planning. He (and Elizabeth) also dealt with other out-of-towners, like Freud's friend Dorothy
Burlingham, who came to the ceremony and dinner at the Kohuts afterward, as well as Oliver and Henry Freud, whom he invited to the dinner

and put up at the Windermere Hotel in Hyde Park (and paid their bill out of his own pocket).[13]

The visit was a stunning success for Kohut. Anna Freud was gracious at the university and the Institute, went to the requisite receptions, and gave some well-received seminars. Either Kohut himself or Elizabeth was always at her side. Kohut also took her around Chicago in some off time. One store they visited was the famous department store Marshall Field's, in the Loop. Anna Freud was very impressed at the opulence and said she liked material things. "It's the Jewish in me," she joked. Kohut responded without humor that most people like material possessions and it is not necessarily a Jewish thing. She said wryly, "No, it's the Jewish in me." In the spacious Kohut apartment things went extremely well, and Anna Freud bonded at a personal level with Kohut and his family. At one point during the visit Elizabeth had expressed admiration for the amber necklace that Anna Freud was wearing. On the last day as she was leaving, Anna Freud took it off and put the necklace around Elizabeth's neck as a gift.[14]

After that visit the letters were more frequent. Anna Freud was petulant about some photographs that were taken of her in a seminar she conducted at the Institute, and Kohut quickly agreed that the publicity seeking of the Institute administration was loathsome. But there were no bad feelings, and Kohut worked hard to keep relations between him and Anna Freud at a high level of theory *and* on a very personal basis. Once Tovey, the Kohut dog, wrote Coco, the Freud/Burlingame dog, a letter that noted he was being very American about using a first name so quickly—but then he had no other name. Tovey observed that his three people had been talking about all the nice presents they had been getting, including the collar Elizabeth got, which he thought was rather flimsy to make such a fuss about. And so on with a playful silliness that kept things intimate.[15]

In 1969 Kohut exchanged a series of letters with Anna Freud about John Gedo, whom Kohut had recommended for a brief visit to Hampstead Clinic. She had reluctantly agreed to the visit, for she questioned the value of only a four-to-six-week stay at an institution as complex as the Hampstead Clinic. Gedo, however, complained that the clinic was boring and completely useless for his training. On June 4, 1969, Anna Freud wrote to Kohut that "I am not at all sure that Dr. Gedo is happy here although I do my best to look after him or have him looked after. . . . Also, I think he misses home." Kohut replied immediately: "I wish I could say anything helpful with regard to John Gedo. As you know I think highly of him and I do hope that he will loosen up a bit. He has a splendid mind and he is undoubtedly taking in more than one would believe from watching him. Whether anything else is going on in him I don't know." That was a very shrewd observation, and was followed a month later by a letter thanking her for her help with Gedo: "He is undoubtedly a sensitive and in some respects difficult person. But so are many gifted people, and I hope that you did not mind it."[16]

Anna Freud was so high on Kohut that in 1968 she began to encourage him to run for the presidency of the International Psycho-Analytic Association (IPA). In fact, despite his withdrawal from top leadership positions in psychoanalysis after 1965, Kohut had not completely absented himself from administrative responsibilities after his term ended as president of the American. Between 1965 and 1968 he was a vice-president of the International, having lobbied for the position through Kurt Eissler in 1964. The next year, Kohut noted, also in a letter to Eissler, that he had just served on the program committee for the upcoming meetings in Amsterdam of the International (and read "innumerable horrible papers for it"); that he hoped to be chair of the program committee for the next meetings of the International; that he was currently a member of the program committee of the American for its meetings; and that he had just been reelected to another three-year term on the editorial board of the *Journal of the American Psychoanalytic Association*. He also served as the chairman of the Committee to Organize a Pre-Congress Conference on Training in Copenhagen in July 1967, in preparation for the meetings of the International the following year.[17]

So while he was free from the most extensive of his commitments after 1965, Kohut remained close to psychoanalytic politics. Part of the reason was his intense idealization of the enterprise. He genuinely believed that psychoanalysis was a "science which constitutes a significant step forward in Man's cultural development. . . ."[18] To have the world's leaders in his field urging him to run for the presidency of the International made it difficult for him to resist the tug. It was a huge commitment, he knew, one that lasted four years and would surely interrupt his creative work. The presidency of the International alternated between an American and a European (or at least a non-American), and in 1968 it was the turn for an American to be president. The Eisslers, it seems, were the first to begin pressuring Kohut to run, perhaps in collaboration with Anna Freud. The other two candidates—Leo Rangell and Jacob Arlow—lacked Kohut's intellectual weight, and Rangell especially enjoyed the unwelcome (to Freud and the Eisslers) support of the Kleinians in California, England, and Latin America. There was no greater anathema to Anna Freud than the Kleinians. She and Melanie Klein had struggled for decades over the meaning of how to treat children psychoanalytically, and she hated to see Klein's followers take over the IPA.

As Kohut pondered the issue he wrote Anna Freud in July to be sure she wanted him to run, since many in New York were already trying to outmaneuver Rangell and Arlow on his behalf. It was a circumspect letter that made no commitment about a decision until after his summer vacation, when he would be better able to judge whether he had finished his book. Kohut was clear that he felt no drive at this time to be president and was only considering making a run for it out of duty. But he did suggest he was strongly leaning in that direction. He also presented his qualifications to Anna Freud as if to secure her support. He said that once into a leadership position he enjoyed his activities, was conscientious and responsible, and most of all was "able to translate my ideals into suitable form which strengthens those who support analysis in our increasingly broad and diffuse ranks."[19]

The next month Kohut wrote Anna Freud from Carmel further exploring the prospects of a bid for the presidency of the International. Her reply strongly urged him on. She shrewdly spoke both to his vanity and his idealism, assuring him of her warm support and of how important it was at this juncture to save psychoanalysis from complete fragmentation ("when you have to watch psychiatry, psychology, existentialism and Kleinianism all pulling away from analysis, you begin to wonder where all this is leading to"). Kohut replied on December 3 that he was willing to be nominated for the presidency. He had made good progress with his book and expected to finish it by the following summer. Some other projects as well were nearly completed and he seemed to see himself at a crossroads ("My other work will be wound up, too"). Kohut expressed his thanks for her support ("Your letter moved me deeply") and then launched into some quite elaborate politicking for two long paragraphs. Once into it, Kohut was not going to take the task of getting elected lightly. A month later he wrote Freud expressing great optimism for the future of psychoanalysis: "Barring a war or a political holocaust which would do away with Western civilization as we know it, I believe that analysis will not only survive but become ever more strong and influential, notwithstanding the attacks and the defections."[20]

Then came the bombshell. Anna Freud wrote Kohut on February 10 (for the first time switching her salutation from "Dear Dr. Kohut" to "Dear Heinz Kohut") that it did not look as though he had the votes to be elected. The Europeans, for unfathomable reasons, were moving toward support of Rangell. Anna Freud was quite surprised by these developments and felt terrible for her part in encouraging him to run, but also believed it was not a "good thing to offer oneself for defeat." Kohut was in fact devastated. He had already begun a very active campaign to be elected and had "written more than a hundred personal notes to people in all parts of the world who would, as I had reason to believe, support my candidacy in Rome." He felt "waves of hurt pride and anger" at the certainty of his defeat and some despair at having to abandon plans for the IPA "that had begun to form in my mind." He spent one very "disturbed night" that was presumably sleepless. He did feel that Rangell was the lesser of two evils (compared with Arlow) "for the simple reason that he is a weaker person—more guided by needs for personal success and without strong convictions." At least Kohut could now get on with his work, though even in ending his letter on that note he was frank about his hurt. "My major efforts can now be devoted to my scientific goals, and—after I will have been done with my reaction to the present disappointment— I will now have a chance for a fruitful period of work." Furthermore, his hurt endured. The following fall he wrote Anna Freud, urging her not to feel guilty but explaining cryptically that "my reaction is based on a complex background that I do not feel up to explaining in writing." As much as a year later he made an oblique reference in some lectures about how hurt he had been by the whole IPA fiasco.[21]

In retrospect there is little doubt that it would have been a bad mistake for Kohut to become president of the International Psycho-Analytic Association in 1969. It would have short-circuited most of his creative work in the 1970s, which is the basis of his legacy. His only lasting contribution would have been *The Analysis of the Self*, the implications of which took him a decade of dedicated work without any administrative involvements to untangle. But Kohut himself, apparently as a way of handling the disappointment at his defeat, was not quite ready to acknowledge what really had happened in the fateful months leading up to February 1969. A myth took shape in his mind—and therefore in the minds of many others—that he had considered a run for the presidency but withdrew because of his commitment to his work. Certainly, junior colleagues such as John Gedo were persuaded that the IPA presidency was something

Kohut could take or leave and his defeat was not much of a disappointment. But others (who at some level must have known better) also bought into Kohut's lie. Charles Kligerman, oddly, one has to say, strenuously argues in a paper he wrote well after Kohut died that Kohut withdrew his name from the IPA candidacy in early 1969 because of his commitment to his writing. It was a very painful decision, Kligerman says, given all of Kohut's interest in the work of the IPA. The withdrawal of his name was "one of the most painful decisions of his life," but it was a "manly decision" (whatever that means) that was necessary to deploy his energies toward his work, "to the fulfillment of his true self, if you will." Even Kohut's widow fiercely maintained that her husband had not been forced to withdraw from the running for the IPA presidency in 1969, and battled tenaciously to maintain that position despite all the evidence to the contrary.[22]

Seventeen

ON COURAGE

In October 1970 Kohut was scheduled to go to Germany to give some important lectures. His first book was in production (and would appear in the spring of 1971), so he was able to spend his time in Carmel that summer reading and preparing his talks. He wrote John Gedo that he had gone to Berkeley for a week to work in the library and be alone to think. His powers of concentration were high. He slept easily "right through the riots" of that year, which were no more than two blocks away.[1]

The first lecture, on October 7 at the Free University of Berlin, was in honor of the fiftieth anniversary of the Berlin Psychoanalytic Institute.[2] The occasion prompted Kohut to reflect on the most general place of psychoanalysis in the world. Needless to say, as was his wont, he was decidedly optimistic for the future of his idealized enterprise. Psychoanalysis, he noted, was under attack from both the left and the right. Though much of the criticism was either pedantic or biased, he acknowledged there was a real question whether the "intensive investigation of the inner life of man" could be justified in a world with so many troubles and burning issues. Was such work not an "immoral luxury"? What, if anything, was the contribution of psychoanalysis to civilization and human existence, not just to the life of a few privileged individuals?

Certainly, Freud influenced the moral fashions of the twentieth century, but that was not at all Kohut's main concern. The fashions might well have changed anyway, and, besides, did that really matter? His concern was with the much more ambitious, indeed pretentious, notion that psychoanalysis exerts a "profound influence on the actions and thoughts of mankind" and thus affects the flow of history. Great consequences could flow from tiny beginnings, and his examples of this were the work of Jesus and the Gospels in shaping the morality of the West for two thousand years and the impact of Darwin's theory. Kohut's point was that ideas often prevail over the bigger battalions. In certain key areas he felt psychoanalysis was in a position to make a substantial contribution to society. The minutest of inquiries in the therapeutic realm offer insight into human aggression and violence, that scourge of history. Psychoanalysis also helps us understand leadership, especially the charismatic kind so destructive in twentieth-century European history, and the more virulent forms of prejudice that have been the basis of recent genocide. These issues were now newly urgent since we live in an age with "the means for self-annihilation" at our disposal. Surely psychoanalysis was not alone in its potential to contribute to such understanding. But its efforts to "expand the realm of man's consciousness and thereby that of his self-control and creative responsiveness" gave psychoanalysis a special and valued place in the struggle of human society not to succumb to the invidious forces of history.

Later that week, on October 12, Kohut extended these ideas when he delivered the Peace Prize Laudation in honor of his friend Alexander Mitscherlich in the Paulskirche in Frankfurt am Main.[3] The event was Kohut's most public presentation of his life. The president of the Federal Republic was in attendance and Kohut's speech was broadcast to a European audience of 20–30 million people. He was very impressed with himself.[4]

Alexander Mitscherlich, a medical doctor and psychoanalyst, had first studied the way doctors had perverted their oaths in working for the Nazis, especially in the death camps of the Holocaust. After that he had played a key role in reestablishing psychoanalysis to a position of respect in Germany. He wrote several well-received books on the nature of Germany's collective guilt and offered some suggestions on the origins of the country's retreat into barbarism under Hitler.[5] Kohut met Mitscherlich sometime in the 1950s, but as was true of so many of his other national and international friendships, it was during his tenure as president-elect and then president of the American in the first half of the 1960s that he became truly close to him. On a personal level, there is no question Kohut had tremendous respect for Mitscherlich. At the lecture, he gave a good summary of Mitscherlich's life's work, making much of it clearer than Mitscherlich had in the original. Kohut dwelled on his friend's deep humanity and efforts to undertake "direct and active steps toward a national therapy" after the tragedies of war and Holocaust. Kohut was especially good in describing what had not been mourned in Mitscherlich's notion of Germany's "inability to mourn," and how important it was to gain "release from the past" in order to move forward as individuals and as societies. To reach "a dignified communal existence," Kohut concluded, we must follow the road of "courageous determination" that Mitscherlich defined.[6]

Kohut's triumphant return to Germany in 1970 and his emotional speeches on the past and his hopes for the future connected with his own yearnings to understand how the violence of movements like that of the Nazis could be resisted. In fact, it was around this time that he drafted the most personal of all his essays (except for "Mr. Z"), "On Courage," though it was only published posthumously.[7] The essay reflects a quest to examine the sources of heroic opposition to the Nazi behemoth (even if small and entirely squashed). At the same time, one has to suspect he saw his own work on the brink of publication as a book he knew would cause a sensation as a heroic challenge to the received wisdom of psychoanalysis. A historical essay, "On Courage" works at several levels of subjective meanings.

The paper takes as its topic the exploration of what sources of psychological strength allowed a handful of ordinary people in Austria and Germany—his examples are the Austrian peasant Franz Jaegerstaetter and the German university students Hans and Sophie Scholl—to oppose the Nazis, even at the cost of their lives. Kohut was not interested in the "rational resisters," like Claus von Stauffenberg, who attempted to assassinate Hitler in 1944, as their motivations were obvious. It was, instead, the very hopelessness of the actions of ordinary people that intrigued him. Franz Jaegerstaetter simply refused to obey Nazi edicts and was sent to prison and then killed. The Scholls were students in Munich who tried to organize a resistance movement against the Nazis. Both were easily caught and killed. Were they crazy to take on the Nazis without weapons, organization, or support? Or did they display a kind of simple courage that has deep meaning in the modern age? The question Kohut confronts directly is that of the sanity of these humble resisters. If simply mad, they can be admired but offer no larger human example. What he explores, on the contrary, is the proposition that they represented a higher and certainly deeper psychological truth that they reached in their actions.

The argument of the essay is that certain core ideals in the nuclear self of such martyrs allow them to hold firm to human values, even in the face of the greatest threat to themselves and their society. They simply refuse to participate in the collective violence. They resist because they have no other choice. Kohut's extended answer to whether they are mad basically applies the criteria he had developed in his 1966 paper about the measures of transformed narcissism. He finds great humor and wisdom in the peasant Jaegerstaetter. Hans Scholl acts out of a deep empathy for the suffering of Jews he encounters. And Sophie Scholl, on the night before her death, achieves a transcendence in her final dream that is truly uplifting.

The authentic martyrdom of Jaegerstaetter and the Scholls suggests to Kohut that there is a more general value to thinking about this idea of a nuclear self as the "continuum in time, that cohesive configuration in depth, which we experience as the 'I' of our perceptions, thoughts and actions." Self in general meant to Kohut (at this point) "an abstraction derived from psychoanalytic clinical experience" and was a "potentially observable content of the mind." He believed then (unlike his later thinking) that there was a multiplicity of selves, but was especially concerned in this essay with some core locus of meaning to experience. This "nuclear self" thus "contains the individual's most enduring values and ideals but also his most deeply anchored goals, purposes and ambitions." Kohut's martyrs acted from a heroic, and ultimately tragic, adherence to the dictates of their nuclear selves. There is always such a tension, he believed, between such core values in the self and the coarse demands for adaptation to a cruel and often violent world. Such a struggle for self-realization, he concludes, is the essence of the art we call "tragic," and the last section of the essay treats tragedy from the Greeks through Shakespeare. Such art is mostly lost in the contemporary world because we now need "greater dosing, more refinement, a larger admixture of neutralizing reflection." We can no longer face the tragic on stage because we cannot tolerate it in our lives.[8]

There are some confusions and contradictions in the courage paper and some undeveloped ideas. Kohut defines courage basically in terms of holding fast to one's ideals. But how does that relate to grandiosity and those central purposes and ambitions, which in theory have an equal place in the nuclear self? His attempt to address this question seems to lie in a digression about Winston Churchill, which is interesting in and of itself, but never clarified. Second, Kohut's concern with heroes, even simple ones, is somewhat anachronistic and recalls the nineteenth-century[9] (and twentieth-century psychoanalytic) fascination with great men. When

Kohut thought about history he tended toward such concerns. Third, the elaborate structure Kohut suggests for the self in this essay—many selves in all the structures of the psyche and some kind of nuclear configuration—is top-heavy and conceptually unmanageable. His thinking here and elsewhere reflects his deep yearning for structure in his idea of the self. He would be very uncomfortable with much of postmodern thinking. Finally, there is a certain unexplored tension in the essay between Kohut's emphasis on the multiplicity of selves and the idea of a nuclear self, which is holistic, unifying, grounding. At this point he can articulate but not confront this contradiction. His confusion is particularly apparent when he talks about the malleability of the nuclear self in adolescence. What are the limits—and potentials—of change?

Such caveats should be kept in perspective. Kohut never revised "On Courage." The essay had to be edited and structured into its present format after his death. But it remains a very good essay that takes some huge risks in Kohut's creative departures from his more conventional psychoanalytic writings. "On Courage" also looks forward to some central ideas of the self he only fully formulated at the end of the decade. The death of tragic man, he concludes, is not, as Freud would have it, opposed to life. Death, on the contrary, is an "integral part of the life curve of the self."[10]

Eighteen

THE GROUP TAKES SHAPE

By the spring of 1969 Kohut, then about to turn fifty-six, was deeply into the writing of the book he would eventually call *The Analysis of the Self*. He had gotten some preliminary responses from important peers, especially Anna Freud and Heinz Hartmann, but at this crucial juncture he seemed to feel he needed direct input from the immediate and younger colleagues in Chicago who had begun to cluster around him, who were former patients or had been or were currently in supervision with him, had taken his courses, knew his work, and were largely committed to his emerging paradigm, to the extent he and they understood it. And so in April 1969 Kohut formed a group.

There are, of course, many reasons why Kohut would gather together younger colleagues "in their first decade of independent work after graduation from institutes"[1] to read and comment on the final version of what he knew would be a controversial publication in the field. He surely wanted to eliminate as many errors as possible and make his formulations as clear as he could. The relative youth of that first group is, however, worth some comment. The force of Kohut's personality, together with the inevitable envy from colleagues cast in his shadow, had alienated many analysts in Chicago even by that point, with the exception of Louis Shapiro, Charles Kligerman, Jerome Kavka, and a few others. Besides, most of Kohut's peers had long since made up their own minds about the nature of psychoanalysis and the deeper meanings of narcissism. They were not receptive to Kohut's ideas in the same way younger people were.

It is also in the nature of the way psychoanalytic institutes are structured that a dynamic presence like Kohut most directly influences his patients, analysands, and candidates, who at first loosely gather around the charismatic figure and then later refer patients to each other, recruit other, more junior, members, and a movement is born. Such is the institutional basis for the sectarian nature of psychoanalysis. Without even much trying, such a nascent following was beginning to coalesce around Kohut in the late 1960s, though a self psychology *movement* was far in the future and probably not consciously in Kohut's mind, or at least not concretely formed as a specific goal (though that it never crossed his mind seems unlikely).

No group formed around an exciting figure in psychoanalysis, however, could fail to have echoes of Freud's own group that took shape in the first decade of the twentieth century. Beginning in 1902, Freud (at the urging of Wilhelm Stekel) asked a small number of colleagues to come to his home on Wednesday evenings. He agreed with Stekel that psychoanalysis needed such a forum to remain vital and to serve as the basis for recruiting new members. After his break with Wilhelm Fliess, Freud may also have needed a following for his own psychological sustenance. The format for Freud's evening seminars—designated the Wednesday Psychological Society—followed the old rabbinic traditions. After a presentation, the names of those present were drawn from an urn to determine the order of commentary. Many rabbis had used just such a procedure to insure that students were not overwhelmed by the comments of the most learned teachers. At Freud's home the discussions were lively, often heated, and no matter when he spoke still completely dominated by the presence of Freud. By 1908 the Wednesday group evolved into the Vienna Psychoanalytic Society, the model for countless such groups around the world, while Freud himself solidified his relationship with his most loyal followers after his break with Carl Jung in 1912–1913 by giving them a secret ring to wear in a special ceremony. A loosely formed group with seemingly only intellectual interests, in other words, was transformed within a decade by its charismatic leader into an enduring institution, on the one hand, and a secret band of disciples committed to spreading the word, on the other. Stekel himself wrote in his autobiography that from the outset he was "the apostle of Freud who was my Christ."[2]

And so it was with Kohut. "The group" were his disciples, or *die Jünger*, the German term that Kohut, not without some irony and even sarcasm, used for the group in the privacy of his family.[3] "I do have the tendency," he said once, "largely overcome—to elevate certain figures in my surroundings above their actual worth."[4] Kohut seemed intrigued with the parallels between his followers and those of Freud and discussed at least once the way Freud had given his disciples secret rings to bind them to him in a ritual of almost religious significance.[5] Even at this early period, Kohut's younger followers were keenly aware of the parallels with Freud. There was much joking about who was the Carl Jung, or the Otto Rank, or the Alfred Adler, or the Sándor Ferenczi of the group. But the jokes were not made in Kohut's presence.[6] The cultish undertow of the group was in turn apparent, if mostly disavowed, to its members as well; Ina Wolf, for example, would later dub the inner circle the "sacred seven" (Arnold Goldberg, Michael Franz Basch, Paul and Anna Ornstein, Paul and Marian Tolpin, Ernest Wolf).

There were distinct advantages that came with participation in the group, from building a movement of international significance to the friendship with and recognition by a man they regarded as a genius.[7] Without a doubt their lives were profoundly altered by knowing Heinz Kohut. They were never again the same. There were, however, costs. To remain close to Kohut meant relinquishing a measure of one's own self. He cast a huge shadow. Kohut used his followers mercilessly for his own purposes.[8] There were constant calls, and one could be beckoned at a moment's notice. He followed up such contacts, even brief encounters, with a note or another call to make an appointment for the next encounter. It kept the connection alive and helped regulate, as Kohut once noted in general about leaders, his own self-esteem.[9] He sent out *die Jünger* to speak for him and spread the word. They were no longer entirely separate from his person. For over a decade he defined their existence. Everything centered on him and his passionate efforts to create a new psychology. He and they were on a mission. It was intense and exhilarating but equally maddening and exhausting. For Kohut the group was both a constant force in his psychological universe and a shifting movement he could never fully control. Kohut, to a degree, thought of his followers in a collective sense, however much he nurtured the individuality of each significant relationship. At times he tended to objectify "the group" as he mocked their fawning loyalties.[10] But he also desperately needed them.

The key figure initially—destined to be its rebellious Carl Jung—was John Gedo; indeed it seems that the very idea of the group may have been his.[11] Gedo, a Hungarian refugee, had trained at the Institute in the late 1950s and later had become a kind of protégé of Kohut's. Immensely bright and learned in matters of culture, he could be abrasive and was forever alienating people and needing protection in the tight world of the Institute. Kohut followed Gedo's early publications closely and took a special interest in their relationship.[12] Since Gedo's later break from Kohut was so acrimonious and emotionally disruptive, one has to be cautious about his reports of what happened then. Gedo claims that he never actually liked Kohut but found him a useful ally and protector as he was getting established in psychoanalysis. He did, however, feel used. Kohut, for example, asked Gedo in early 1969 to do some research for a proposed book on the polemics of psychoanalysis. Kohut received Gedo's work but then dropped the project without bothering to inform Gedo.[13] Gedo also concluded that Kohut sent him to England to study at the Hampstead Clinic in 1969 merely to ascertain Anna Freud's real feelings about Kohut's early writings on narcissism and was overly and inappropriately insistent to talk with him the moment he returned to Chicago.[14]

The other central figure in the group, and in time its designated leader, was Arnold Goldberg. Goldberg was the rising star among the younger analysts in the Institute. Witty, brilliant, edgy, and a good leader, Goldberg was a close friend of Gedo's (with whom he was then writing a book)[15] and had done some supervision with Kohut. Goldberg was widely regarded as one of the best teachers on the staff, even though he had just begun, and was well read in psychoanalysis and philosophy. Many younger analysts looked up to him.

Goldberg was the Peter on whom the church would be built. Kohut came to trust him most of all. In recommending him for appointment as a training and supervising analyst, Kohut wrote of Goldberg in 1972:

> His intelligence is very high, . . . he is among the most creative (if not the most creative) of his generation, and . . . he is an attractive person. He is clearly a fine observer of psychological matters and has an unusual grasp of subtle nuances. Most importantly, he is introspective and able to put his insights to good use. I fully support his appointment as a training analyst.[16]

Goldberg's special status, however, brought with it huge expectations. In 1972 he published a long and adulatory review of *The Analysis of the Self* but said, as his one critical observation, that it was a difficult book. The day the review appeared Kohut was on the phone asking if Goldberg

really thought the book was so difficult. He also got involved in all aspects of Goldberg's personal affairs, including his divorce and remarriage
to Constance Obenhaus, as well as the joy of the birth of the Goldberg
daughter, Sarah, in 1978. Kohut turned to Goldberg for advice and support on a whole range of topics. He began to phone almost every day. As
Constance has reported, the family would sit down to eat dinner expecting that before long there would be "The Call." It was welcome in one
sense but equally dreaded and feared.[17] For Kohut there was much to talk
about, from drafts of papers, to preparations for panels, to gossip about
developments in the Institute, to the attacks. "The latest," Kohut once
exclaimed to Goldberg: "I am unmasked as a Sullivanian. That pleases
me, because I took care of that nicely already in a footnote in my old paper
on Introspection." And he concludes: "You are courageous, and you are
young."[18] In the summer of 1974, in preparation for their trip to Italy,
Kohut prepared for the Goldbergs (and the Wolfs, who were going with
them) a detailed list of all the restaurants they were to eat at, including
descriptions of each place and general instructions about calling ahead,
how to make reservations, and so forth. On the list was a favorite ice cream
parlor outside of Rome. "This is the best ice-cream we've ever had," he
wrote enthusiastically on the sheet of paper he gave them.[19]

The most original of *die Jünger* was Michael Franz Basch, who positioned
himself at the edge of the group as a decidedly ambivalent disciple. He
was notably absent from Kohut's machinations in dealing with the outside world, friendly or critical, and he appears never once to have been
chosen as a substitute for him or to write a reply to someone. Basch kept
his distance, perhaps for self-protection, and besides had intellectual interests that went beyond self psychology, however much he remained a
critical thinker in the movement. There was also in general a certain formality and aloofness about Basch. As late as the mid-1970s he still addressed
his former analyst as "Dr. Kohut," though he finally broke through to
"Heinz" in the middle of 1975. His style was formal and reserved. He
always wore three-piece suits with white shirts and cuff links. At a tribute
to him in 1996 after his death earlier that year, his daughter, Gail Basch,
began by saying that she wanted to report her father did not, in fact, sleep
in his three-piece suit.[20]

Kohut himself, it seems, recognized the rebel in Basch and both applauded it and tried to connect with it. Basch once sent Kohut a paper he

had written about narcissism. Basch described the paper in advance as "devastating" in its criticisms of Kohut's work. Kohut, however, was easy about the challenge—in fact welcomed it and praised the paper, expressing his admiration for what Basch wrote. Kohut only disagreed with a few relatively minor points. He did urge his former analysand to stay in closer touch with him and in his reply enclosed a copy of a current manuscript of his own as a preliminary to that discussion. Kohut ended by thanking Basch again for his efforts. "I know the deep protective concern which is the motivator of your critical admonitions," which has the message of accepting the criticism but at the same time keeping him in the fold. Basch responded that he was "relieved that you understand my motives in writing as I did. I knew you would, of course, you always have." That easy acceptance secured Basch within the movement. His interests in general psychology took Basch into an exploration of Piaget and learning theory, which was only of passing interest to Kohut. To Basch, however, such exploration was in the interest of connecting Kohut's work with broader developments in psychology. He once wrote Kohut, for example, about feedback loops. The cat, he said, has a future-oriented sense of where to jump to catch the mouse. By 1976 Basch was becoming almost over-enthusiastic in his responses to Kohut. The latest thing Kohut sent was a "jewel" and the basis for combining the sciences, another a "masterpiece." Another time he gushed about how the center had shifted in psychoanalysis and in a short while everyone would recognize that "your work will be acknowledged as focal by everyone of consequence. Not only are you not leaving psychoanalysis, you are psychoanalysis, now and in the foreseeable future."[21]

Basch yearned for recognition from Kohut, which he only partly received. He spoke at Kohut's memorial service of his former analyst's effusive charm when he first read some of Basch's early papers in the late 1960s. Kohut went over the material with great care and then spent several hours with him, talking about all details of his work.[22] It made Basch feel recognized and spurred him on to further creative work to live up to Kohut's enthusiastic expectations. Later, when they were closer colleagues, he regularly sent Basch his papers (and expected immediate responses, one should add, and was highly annoyed if he did not get them). There were, as well, many conversations, and Michael and Carol Basch were an integral part of the group's social activities in Kohut's home and elsewhere. And yet the disappointments could be monumental. In his self-absorption, Kohut inflicted some awful wounds on Michael Basch.

At dinner once, during a discussion of the Nazis, Kohut said with surprise to his former analysand forced to flee the Holocaust, "I didn't know you spoke German."

Paul and Anna Ornstein were the only members of the group living outside of Chicago.[23] Kohut wrote of Paul that he had an "open and friendly, yet forceful, personality which . . . will stand him in very good stead in his future administrative, organizational, and educational activities." Of Anna Ornstein, Kohut wrote that she was a skilled clinician and a "devoted, conscientious, resourceful researcher."[24] Paul, of course, had a much longer and deeper history with his mentor, but Anna had some extended supervision with Kohut in the early 1970s and herself got enmeshed with Kohut at the height of his fame in the late 1970s. Paul continued his monthly supervision until the end, became after 1975 the editor of Kohut's papers (the first two volumes of which came out in 1978), and talked with him on the phone every weekend, often for extended conversations. Anna and he spent a good deal of time socializing with the Kohuts whenever they were in Chicago; the couples also got together in Cincinnati for special events such as the honorary degree Kohut received in 1973 from the University of Cincinnati and his annual lectures there. One huge annual event that was a command performance was Kohut's birthday party in May. All the group came, and he acted with such infectious enthusiasm it was hard not to enter into the spirit of the event.[25]

Both the Ornsteins were from Hungary and felt a special connection to Jewish history and culture. Anna had been an inmate at Auschwitz after the roundup of the Hungarian Jews in June 1944. In the early years of the war, Paul had studied Jewish philosophy in a rabbinical school in Budapest. He then went to medical school only because the Nazis closed down his career in Judaica. The Ornsteins, in other words, were both European and the most Jewish of the group, something that seemed to elicit profound ambivalence on the part of Kohut. With Anna, for the most part he seemed to try to bracket that part of her experience so it could be bypassed, ignored. He kept from her the full extent of his own Jewish past, but she knew that the Nazis had forced him to flee Austria. His failure to talk about the Jewish part of himself, to put it forward in some meaningful sense, left Anna feeling "betrayed by him." Whenever something came up about Israel or the Holocaust, for example, she "could not really feel connected to him." The lines were very carefully drawn. Anna has never been shy in talking about her experience as a survivor. But she feels now that when she expressed her thoughts and feelings with Kohut about anything touching Jewish experience, she "paid for it."[26] Anna Ornstein lived in a kind of bubble of marginalization within the group.

Paul Ornstein, on the other hand, could more easily subsume his Jewishness in his relations with Kohut. He simply kept his strong commitments as a Jew separate from his idealization of Kohut. He did, however, have some strange experiences. In the early 1970s as Ornstein was getting to know him better and moving into a new status within the group, Kohut said to him once out of the blue, "Paul, you must often have wondered about my Jewishness." Ornstein was astonished but kept quiet. "I settled this issue for myself a long time ago. My father was Jewish. I am not. I made that choice, and that is that."[27] Ornstein, without even knowing Kohut's actual past, asked himself silently how one could make such a choice about one's identity. But he said nothing. Another time Ornstein's father was visiting from Hungary and was eager to ask Kohut whether he was related to the famous Hungarian rabbi of the same name. Ornstein begged his father not to bring up the subject. He knew "instinctively" it was the wrong thing to ask. Ornstein also learned to avoid conversation about Israel if at all possible. Kohut was driven to distraction by seeing Jews dress and act in what he seemed to feel was a kind of stereotypical Jewish way. After the 1967 war, for example, and the Israeli conquest of the West Bank and of East Jerusalem, he was appalled at the images on television of Jews wailing at the wall. It enraged, even shamed Kohut. "He wanted an Anglo-Saxon, non-demonstrative reaction to death," Ornstein said. Kohut was also assertively non-Jewish in his self-presentation. He once went to lunch at a kosher deli with Ornstein. He ordered a ham and cheese sandwich and a glass of milk, something so outrageous as to be deliberately offensive. The clerk said politely but firmly he could not serve such food in the deli, for it was kosher. Kohut proceeded to make a huge scene. Raising his voice, he said he would eat what he wanted where and when he wanted, that it was a public restaurant, and demanded to be served what he had ordered. Everyone noticed.[28]

Ernest Wolf has said that the purpose of the group was to give Kohut "positive, harmonious resonance."[29] Certainly no one did that better than Wolf himself. Born in Germany, he went through the Institute in the 1960s and was in supervision with Kohut between 1966 and 1968. During the 1970s he and Kohut got increasingly enmeshed. After Kohut's death, Elizabeth Kohut told Wolf her husband felt closest to him. Kohut always recommended Wolf as a substitute for himself in anything having to do with culture or history.[30] Wolf, it seems, was entirely accepting and unquestioning, completely caught up in his idealization, without conflict about his role, and respectful of the boundaries Kohut required. Wolf has since written of the way Kohut would expound on things and yet remained a "very private, even secretive, person, who hid his own past in a fog of generalities."[31] In the last couple of years of his life, when he felt most needy and vulnerable, Kohut often turned to the nonthreatening Ernest Wolf. In the morning he often asked Wolf to come talk before their first patients arrived at the Institute and would then call most evenings to chat. At one point in these years Wolf got a new phone system that allowed him to dial automatically by pushing the star button and then one of the numbers (though for some reason the system only included numbers two through nine). He was explaining how it all worked to Kohut during one evening phone conversation: Wolf's wife was number two, his office was three, and so on. They went on to other subjects, and after a while hung up. A few minutes later the phone rang. It was Kohut. "Who's number one?" he asked.[32]

Kohut (and probably Elizabeth as well) was also comfortable with Ina Wolf. The two couples became practically inseparable in the 1970s. Ina Wolf, who has always kept a detailed personal date book, has reconstructed that between December 4, 1971, and October 8, 1981, she and Ernest had dinner five or six times at the Kohuts' with just the two couples (she was uncertain about one date), 47 times with just them but in a restaurant, 18 times at the Kohuts' with others and 12 such times in restaurants, 2 times when just the Kohuts came to their house, another 11 times when the Kohuts and others had dinner at their house, and 8 times when they were together with the Kohuts but at someone else's house. In all, the Wolfs got together socially with the Kohuts in these years 103 or 104 times, or roughly once a month over a decade (not counting the six to eight weeks when the Kohuts were in Carmel).[33] Wolf loved the pomp and circumstance that Kohut brought to a meal, especially his fussing over the special Mosel he served before dinner, the vintage Burgundy or Bordeaux with the meat, and the sweet Sauterne or Spatlese Rhein with desert. Kohut took pains with all the details of a meal (as with anything in which he participated), which he loved to share. He taught Wolf, for example, how to fill a wineglass exactly halfway.[34]

Paul Tolpin tells of the late 1940s when he and his wife, Marian, were in medical school and heard of a psychiatrist from the University of Chicago who was apparently remarkable in teaching interviews he did with psychotic patients at Cook County Psychopathic Hospital. The Tolpins attended a couple of such clinical seminars and were amazed at the skill young Kohut demonstrated in connecting with the sickest of patients. Both, however, promptly forgot about him as their lives moved in other directions. Within a few years, however, Paul ended up in analysis with Kohut as part of his training. In later years, Kohut regularly exchanged messages with Paul at the Institute and talked with him often.[35] Kohut probably saw in Tolpin an earnest searcher after truth who could be a useful ally.

David Marcus was also invited into this first incarnation of the group. Marcus was a young analyst who was then in supervision with Kohut. He was painfully shy and awkward but was the analyst of an important case that Kohut used often in his theorizing. Kohut and others regarded him as a gifted clinician able to translate large ideas about the self into psychoanalytic practice. In the group, however, he was nearly mute and probably felt ill at ease. He would not last.

In the spring and early summer of 1969 this group met with Kohut in his apartment nine times.[36] Guests arrived at the Cloisters at eleven o'clock on Saturday morning and took the small, elegant elevator that opened on the twelfth floor into the apartment itself. Since guests were announced by the doorman at the outside gate, Kohut would be there to greet them as they walked out of the elevator into the foyer of his apartment. The view from the living room windows looked west over Jackman Field and the Lab School, while beyond were the neo-Gothic spires of the buildings of the University of Chicago. When all were assembled, the group moved into Kohut's study, which was just large enough to accommodate it. The meetings lasted about two hours. Around 1:00 p.m. they would break for lunch, which had been prepared by Elizabeth. She never joined the actual group discussions, but he would occasionally refer to her ("Betty doesn't like this diagram," for example). Lunch was cold cuts laid out in the Austrian style. There would be the inevitable stories and banter. Serious talk was now over and Kohut could hold forth in his usual way.[37]

For the participants the meetings were not particularly intellectually rewarding, but for Kohut himself the experience was immensely gratifying. He told Anna Freud at the time: "Some of their [the group's] responses moved me more deeply than anything that I have experienced in my professional life."[38] The comments were sometimes trivial and dealt with small issues of grammar; some found that part of the discussion exceedingly boring.[39] For the most part, however, discussion dealt with the substantive issues raised by the chapter Kohut had distributed. Gedo dominated and was in general the "guiding spirit" of the meetings. The members of the group tended to ask questions that sought greater clarification from the text. There was, without a doubt, a fawning respect for Kohut, but the group did express its confusion about certain topics, which had an important impact on the structure of the book. The way Kohut had begun the book they found very difficult to understand. They felt he had jumped into his subject matter too abruptly. Their comments convinced him that he had to write a new beginning, which is now Chapter 1, "Introductory Considerations." This chapter in many ways summarizes the themes of the entire book, providing the crucial definitions while setting the tone for his approach to narcissism.

The group, in other words, worked at several levels for Kohut. It brought him some valuable criticisms of his book and led to a basic restructuring of the manuscript. *The Analysis of the Self* is a better book for the feedback. But surely more importantly, the discussion looked forward from a book to a group, from ideas to a movement. The camaraderie of that first group carried forward into the next decade. The key figures got defined, though some would shuffle in and out in coming years. The group, one might say, concretized Kohut's charisma and launched what was then only a dimly perceived project in self psychology but what would become a movement eventually extending well beyond Kohut's own death.

Nineteen

THE ANALYSIS OF THE SELF

It is a curious fact of Kohut's creativity that his major theoretical work came in the second half of his sixth decade. Kohut was just beginning when many people are preparing for retirement. Perhaps he was delayed by all those years spent laboring in the vineyards as Mr. Psychoanalysis, storing up impressions, doing his clinical work, preparing for something original. But that is not how Kohut himself understood his own experience, at least from the vantage point of 1980. The best work in psychoanalysis, he said then, comes when you are fairly old. Physicists do their best work at twenty, mathematicians at nineteen. But in depth psychology, he said, you have to live long enough to "become detached from the intensity of the experience," to be able to remain close enough to it and yet detached. Besides, there are two kinds of psychologies. One kind remains immersed in experience—"mysticism and excitement, and cure through love and what have you"—and then the "totally detached ones." Neither is right absolutely. You have to do both at the same time, he says, but you cannot really do that until you get a little older.[1]

One wonders, as well, whether something in Kohut's location in Chicago nourished his insights into narcissism. As Napoleon came from Corsica, Genghis Khan from Siberia, or even Lincoln from Springfield, great nation builders are often from the periphery. The same principle may work in some analogous form in scientific fields. The distance from the center brings freedom and clarity, particularly for someone as insecure and needing of constant affirmation as Kohut. Had he been a part of the New York psychoanalytic scene he might well have been stifled. He could never have been the star he was in Chicago. Toward the end of his life Kohut was once asked whether there was something about the ambience in the Chicago Institute that encouraged his work on narcissism. His reply was curious. He said that he did not really "live in Chicago," for his commitments lay elsewhere and he was always part of "psychoanalysis as a whole." But his point was to impress his interviewer. For then he described in detail how Anna Freud stayed with him for ten days in 1966.[2] His name-dropping proves the point. Had he been any closer geographically to Anna Freud, Heinz Hartmann, or even Kurt Eissler, he might never have become Heinz Kohut.

But however one locates his life within his work, the culmination of Kohut's reflections on narcissism came with the publication of his first book, *The Analysis of the Self*, in the spring of 1971. He was just shy of his fifty-eighth birthday. Typically, he had embraced the project in fits and starts, but by 1967, if not sometime late in 1966, he had firmly committed himself to a book. Paul Ornstein recalls Kohut pulling out pages from a drawer to read to him in supervision as early as 1966, but that manuscript was surely the 1968 paper that he was then writing to Anna Freud about.[3] All this suggests the key moments of creation of *Analysis* were his months of vacation in Carmel during the summers of 1967 and 1968. He wrote in his study above the garage but also found it useful to take extended trips to the library at Berkeley. By April 1969 Kohut told Anna Freud his book was "nearing completion," and in June he reported to René Spitz that he was "putting on the finishing touches" to the manuscript. By that Christmas he was "more or less finished," though "there are always new thoughts to be added."[4] In the spring of 1970 he finally let go of the manuscript and submitted it to International Universities Press.

Analysis is a difficult book, with meanings that can seem contradictory. It employs the abstract and highly technical language of Freudian ego psychology but describes a landscape of the self that (if one really takes it in) allows the jettisoning of drive theory while retaining the idea of multiple perspectives; opens up a new approach to development that makes the Oedipus complex irrelevant; defines trauma without libido; and develops a new set of clinical ideas about dealing with a sicker class of patients from those usually treated by psychoanalysts. The book has three parts: an important introduction; a long discussion of idealization, followed by another of grandiosity; and a concluding section on special clinical issues of treating "narcissistic" patients. No one before Kohut had broken down the problem of the self in such terms. His theory is in equal parts phenomenological and developmental. The book is not what it appears to be. Kohut presents *Analysis* as a monograph for specialists on healing more disturbed patients and merely claims the modest goal of defining narcissism as a "line of development" (as opposed to relatedness, or "object love"). All that, however, was a mere cover to keep the orthodox off guard. Certainly, he succeeded. The major reviews of the book at the time, continuing through to more recent discussions, repeat with mind-numbing regularity Kohut's ostensible purpose, as though it makes a difference.[5]

In fact, *Analysis* is only superficially about narcissism as a line of development. It is a book about the self. Implicit in its framework is a new psychological paradigm freed from the fragmented model of the soul as broken up into an id, an ego, and a superego. *Analysis* furthermore is for the self what Freud's *The Interpretation of Dreams* is for the unconscious. *Analysis* creates an idea of the self as a separate, holistic concept for contemporary psychological thought. The instincts fade away as Kohut embraces human beings rather than victims of drives. A radically altered therapeutics as well emerges logically from *Analysis*, one that is engaged, flexible, open-ended, mutual, and empathic. *Analysis* makes possible the pure gold of psychotherapy.[6]

Narcissism, as the ostensible topic of *The Analysis of the Self*, presents many problems of definition. As an amorphous term in psychoanalysis, narcissism included ideas of self-love and selfishness (as Kohut discussed in his 1966 essay, "Forms and Transformations of Narcissism") but was also understood to be the key to explaining the more serious forms of mental illness, including the psychoses, which had always been at the outer edge of the theory.[7] Most commonly it was assumed that the "narcissistic illnesses" were simply more severe versions of what were more accessible for study in the neuroses. But that was a troubling and rather simple-minded assumption for anyone who thought seriously about these issues. Following Heinz Hartmann, Kohut defines narcissism in his book as the "cathexis of the self" and says that it occupies "half of the contents of the human mind—the other half being, of course, the object." But what is this matter of a "cathexis"? As the instinctual charge derived from the libido, narcissism for Kohut apparently only makes sense as the state one can describe when the cathexes are directed onto the self. The absurdity of such discursive acrobatics is readily apparent, and leads Kohut to say, for example (in italics), that "*narcissism . . . is defined not by the target of the instinctual investment . . . but by the nature or quality of the instinctual charge.*"[8] It is as though electricity can be good or bad, depending on whether it strikes a bridge or is harnessed for human service. But there is an important idea in Kohut's unfathomable prose if one can extract it from the drive theory in which it is buried. He is concerned with the quality of the way we relate to others, rather than the mere fact of otherness.

That distinction lies at the heart of Kohut's contribution to psychoanalytic thought. Freud spent much time describing the complicated ways in which we relate to others and retain representations of them and their symbolic substitutes within what he called the ego. But he always assumed that self and other were separate and that the goal of development was some marked degree of autonomy. These ideas, which embody an entire value system, directly influenced all later thinkers in psychoanalysis, including the "object relations" school that attempted to find ways of using Freud's language (and perspective) to describe early states of engagement with the world. Melanie Klein, for example, talks of "introjects" and very early states (or positions) of envy, depression, and paranoia.[9]

Kohut took a different approach and altogether shifted Freud's focus, even as he used his language. What matters, Kohut stresses, is the quality of how we relate to others, not the fact that to an outside observer our world may be peopled or even variously represented in the self. What matters is our experience of these others. Perhaps Kohut's key point is that there is no self except in that context. Others (and their symbolic equivalents) are used to form the fabric of our beings and at the same time are experienced as part of the self. These are the "self-objects." Furthermore, as Kohut would clarify later, the end point of development, that is, normality and happiness, is not autonomy and separation but a more profound engagement. We never lose our need to retain our self-objects, or our complex, often self-involved, relationships with them. It is, in fact, through those relationships that the self is formed and continues to exist.

The task of *Analysis*, however, is not to pursue in any *systematic* way such general psychological issues. Kohut's project in the book is the narrower and more clinical one of attempting to understand, and offer clinical recommendations on how to deal with, a new class of patients in psychoanalysis (or at least an older category seen very differently). The subtitle of the book is "A Systematic Approach to the Psychoanalytic Treatment of Narcissistic Personality Disorders." These "NPDs" are patients suffering from "specific disturbances in the realm of the self" stuck at early stages of development and weighted down by the "archaic configurations" of their selves, "though it is important to emphasize not only the deficiencies of the psychic organization of these patients but also the assets."[10] NPD symptoms tend to be ill-defined. These patients initially have trouble focusing on their essential problems and instead often describe secondary manifestations like work inhibitions or fantasied (or actual) perverse sexual activities. In their personalities they usually lack humor or proportion, as well as empathy for the needs of others. They brood about their bodies and are often filled with psychosomatic symptoms. What NPDs cannot see is the secondary quality of all such experience. "The eye, as it were, cannot observe itself," Kohut says. In treatment the NPD patient is able to articulate pervasive feelings of emptiness and depression that are relieved when the transference is established. When that tie is broken or interrupted, however, the patient often feels not fully real, loaded down by dulled emotions, lacking in zest, and generally depleted. In contrast with the psychoses or borderline states (which Kohut thought of as "covert psychoses"),[11] these symptoms are not rigidly established. A pervasive hypochondriacal brooding, for example, may alternate with a sudden period of feeling alive and happy, which in turn is followed by a period of chronic dullness and passivity. Any rebuff, even the absence of expected approval, quickly leads to a state of depletion.[12]

The central issue is always self-esteem. NPDs are highly vulnerable, prickly, and volatile. They cannot regulate their self-esteem and maintain it at normal levels. Any disturbance in their fragile equilibrium results in a range of experiences extending from anxious grandiosity and excitement, to mild embarrassment and self-consciousness, to severe shame, hypochondria, and depression. Much lies deeply imbedded with these patients. Their overt complaints are not a reliable guide to their real problems. Behind a vague description of a lack of zest, for example, may well lie a diffuse vulnerability and defects in self-esteem regulation, along with disturbances in the maintenance of a system of ideals. Screens and covers are pervasive. One can only get to the deeper knowledge of the real disturbance in the "spontaneously developing transference." The presenting symptomatology cannot, in itself, be fully trusted.[13]

The "self-object transferences," as Kohut describes them in *Analysis*, depart sharply from the conventional understanding of "transference" in psychoanalysis. Initially, as part of his work on dreams in 1900, Freud defined transference as the attachment of an unconscious thought to some preconscious idea with which it has a symbolic connection. Intensities get transferred and the unconscious thought is "covered." It is, he says, like an American dentist who wants to practice in Austria. He needs a medically qualified practitioner to serve as a stalking-horse for him. As a result of his (awful) treatment of Dora the next year, however, Freud came to understand a much broader meaning for transference: "They are new editions or facsimiles of the impulses and phantasies which are aroused and made conscious during the progress of the analysis; but they have this peculiarity, which is characteristic for their species, that they replace some earlier person by the person of the physician." It is a given in Freud's drive theory that those infantile "facsimiles" reproduced in treatment in relation to the analyst via the transference are libidinal in nature.[14]

In the realm of the self, on the other hand, transferences mobilize early experiences of the other in two basic forms: the grandiose self (as Kohut now calls it to avoid the "tautology" of the "narcissistic self") and the idealized parent imago. In the core of our beings we retain the tightly interwoven notions that "I am perfect" and "you are perfect, but I am part of you." These early "configurations," or "central mechanisms," coexist from the beginning in the stage of the cohesive self, but their mostly "independent lines are open to separate scrutiny."[15] Under "optimal developmental conditions," grandiosity is gradually tamed and integrated into the personality, grounding one's ambitions and purposes and the enjoyment of one's varied activities. As such, grandiosity comes to provide important aspects of self-esteem. Analogously, idealization becomes the basis of our deepest values, which we hold up to ourselves for guidance and direction and which also help maintain our self-esteem. Trauma disrupts the process of integration of both grandiosity and idealization into the more mature structures of the self. Instead, the earliest and most primitive aspects of the self continue to exist unaltered and unchanged. It is these damaged self structures that then get mobilized in the self-object transferences.[16]

The "self," in turn, that Kohut analyzes in his book lies close to the immediacy of experience. It is in a different realm from personality or identity, concepts that he feels lie in a "different theoretical framework more in harmony with the observations of social behavior." What Kohut is really saying (not very convincingly, one might note), of course, is that notions of "personality" and "identity" are superficial and the products of observation from the outside, rather than the result of the empathic investigations of psychoanalysis. The self, on the other hand, is a "low-level" abstraction that emerges within the psychoanalytic situation. It is a "content of the mental apparatus" but not one of the agencies of the mind. The self is, however, a "structure within the mind" because it has energies (it is "cathected") and has "continuity in time" or endures. This self Kohut imagines has a psychic location, while at the same time many, often inconsistent, self representations are present within the agencies of the mind (id, ego, superego).[17]

Such a definition of self, which was consistent with Kohut's thinking in the last half of the 1960s, contains within it a number of contradictions, including that of location together with dispersal, of structure and more elusive representations, and of differing levels of abstraction. Kohut goes well beyond talking about an amorphous "sense of self," but no sooner has he located a place for the self and suggested its formal structures than he returns immediately to the idea of self representations dispersed throughout the psyche. Kohut's definition of self, in fact (as opposed to his more nuanced use of the concept in context), is quite elusive and almost no definition at all, for the simple reason that he is trying to make the self subservient to Freud's model of the mind, which is in turn dependent on drive theory. The advantage of Kohut's definitional vagueness, on the other hand, is that it reflects honestly the ambiguities of the very idea of self in twentieth-century psychology up to that time. William James noted that the question of life is "Who am I?" But we cannot focus on "I." It is evanescent and slips away. We can only talk of self, which is necessarily the object of our subjectivity. The self is what I can conceive. "Whatever I may be thinking of," as James puts it, "I am always at the same time more or less aware of *myself*, of my *personal existence*.[18]

The first major theme Kohut discusses in his book is idealization. In the Freudian schema, idealization is suspect. It is said to mask envy, hatred, aggression. Interpretation in treatment consists of disclosing the reality that lies behind the patient's tendency to raise the analyst to exalted heights of wisdom and kindness. Shrouded in the noise of present feelings are always the "deeper" truths of the oedipal drama. Kohut argues against the very assumptions behind that approach to the meaning of idealization. He feels that the lost experience of perfection assigned to the other returns as the central experience of the self in relation to the analyst during treatment. One feels empty and powerless when separated from that other. Developmentally, Kohut argues, the baby initially merges into the dimly perceived "mother-breast" that becomes a connection to a person whose functions are taken on as one's own. The subsequent "taming, neutralization, and differentiation" of these first expressions of idealization occur because the real figure of the mother (for the most part) inevitably comes up short in her concrete emotional responses. In the best of circumstances, the child makes increasingly realistic assessments of that figure, which involves a measure of disappointment, and leads to an emotional redirection of feelings from the figure to an internalized imago that sustains the same functions in the self.[19]

This process of structure building in the self Kohut calls "transmuting internalization," which is an idea he adapts (with full credit given) from Freud's 1917 paper, "Mourning and Melancholia." Freud argued that the withdrawal of feelings from lost others occurs in a fractionated way, bit by bit, in order to carry out effective mourning, and that the crucial consequence of this process is the regressive identification with the lost object. Kohut argues analogously that first there must be a developmental readiness for the formation of structure in the self (or a "receptivity for specific introjects"). There is then an "optimal frustration" with the idealized other that prompts an emotional retreat from her or him and an internalization of some functions that had previously been performed by the idealized other. The reason the process is dosed (or "fractionated") is so that the child can relinquish aspects of the other in stages without having to be rendered helpless by a sudden, traumatic loss of the omnipotent other, which Kohut says is usually due to the early experience of the mother's unreliable empathy, or her depression, or physical illness, or absence or death. Such trauma interrupts the process of optimal internalization. As a result the child remains fixated on the primitive images of the other, and will be forever dependent on substitute figures in what can only be described as an "intense form of object hunger." The hunger is intense because such people are looking for "missing segments" in their psychic structure. The people and things sought after are not longed for but needed "in order to replace the functions of a segment of the mental apparatus which had not been established in childhood."[20]

Kohut argues that traumatic disruptions in the relationship with the idealizing other in general lead to three categories of disturbance, depending on when the original trauma occurred. In the earliest disturbances a diffuse vulnerability is the result. It is difficult for such people to establish any kind of permanent homeostasis in their personality. Somewhat later trauma—Kohut is intentionally vague about the exact timing here—results in a basic interference in the processing of sexual desire in the self and creates a readiness toward sexualization. In such patients one often encounters perverse fantasies or acts, which clearly suggests Kohut's ideas on the developmental self origins of the perversions. Finally, when the trauma occurs in later infancy, when there is a degree of cohesiveness established in the self, what results is a core defect in the capacity for idealization. Such people strive constantly for external leader figures to provide approval and soothing that their internal psychic structures cannot provide.[21]

These stages of possible failure in the structure of idealization in the self can be extremely difficult to ascertain retrospectively because of what Kohut calls the *"telescoping of genetically analogous experience* [his italics]." The tendency of the mind is to superimpose later, noncritical experiences over the earlier, pathological ones. For Freud, of course, such processes of substitution were entirely defensive and based on the ego's attempt to ward off unconscious thoughts and impulses. Kohut, while not disagreeing that symbolic substitution may serve important defensive functions in the psyche (at least at this point in his thinking he was willing to concede that), stresses instead that telescoping more importantly is a manifestation of the "synthesizing power of the mind" and expresses early trauma in analogous images that are less conflicted.[22]

Self-esteem, as always, is central. "Anything that deprives the patient of the idealized analyst creates a disturbance of his self-esteem: he begins to feel lethargic, powerless, and worthless." What precipitates such states may seem to the uninitiated (or the clinically obtuse) to be minute and unimportant. The sensitivity of the patient is exquisite and the nature of the response to minor failings on the part of the analyst so out of proportion that adult logic cannot be used to explain it. Only if one constantly remembers the extent to which the patient has grafted an archaic self onto the omnipotent figure of the analyst can one begin to understand (and empathize with) what is happening in the therapy.

Once mobilized, however, the idealizing transference may stabilize for prolonged periods, during which the patient feels "whole, safe, powerful, good, attractive, active so long as his self experience includes the idealized analyst whom he feels he controls and possesses with a self-evident certainty that is akin to the adult's experience of his control over his own body and mind." Sooner or later, however, this state of grace is bound to be disrupted by external events, whether from a major empathic breakdown in the treatment, or, more commonly, failures to appreciate the full impact on the patient of minor irregularities in schedule, weekend separations, slight tardiness, or vacations. The response on the part of the patient is usually one of rage and, most importantly for someone in an idealizing transference, despondency, followed immediately by temporary regression to various archaic forms.

The working-through process with the idealizing transference involves a gradual withdrawal of primitive attachments to the analyst and the establishment of "psychological structures and functions" that give the patient greater freedom of choice and action. The path, however, is customarily stormy. Over and over again there will be regressive swings in response to disappointments in the idealized analyst. For some, such swings will involve a retreat into perverse activities from which a rescue is only possible through "appropriate interpretation." Others might reexperience such activities in memory—as, for example, the recall of a voyeuristic search for the absent mother's underwear and putting it on in an attempt to reestablish a symbolic union with a depressed mother who had been hospitalized.[23] At other times, patients will recall (and be grateful for now understanding) childhood attempts to revive some feeling of being alive: putting one's face against the cold floor in the basement; staring in the mirror to assure oneself of being whole; smelling things, including oneself; various masturbatory activities; and any number of grand and sometimes dangerous athletic feats. Memory and understanding in therapy work together in a process of healing.

Mr. A. serves to illustrate Kohut's ideas about the idealizing transference.[24] A young man in his mid-twenties. A.'s initial complaint was that ever since adolescence he had felt sexually stimulated by and attracted to men. It quickly became apparent, however, that A.'s homosexuality was "not prominent" and "occupied a rather isolated position in his personality." What mattered were the indications of a "broad personality defect" that manifested itself in his depression and lack of zest, along with an extreme sensitivity to criticism that profoundly affected his self-esteem. A. was forever in search of guidance and approval from others in positions of authority over him. As long as he felt their approval, he was okay. But at the slightest sign of their discontent with him he would feel drained and depressed. Then he got enraged, became cold and haughty, and could no longer work effectively.

Mr. A.'s key childhood experience was his traumatic disappointment in the "power and efficacy" of his father. The family had fled Europe when A. was nine. The father, once prosperous, failed repeatedly at various business ventures in America, always seeming to sell out in panic at just the wrong moment. A. came to feel overwhelmed by the contrast between his father's ambitions and the desperate disappointment he felt when his father failed. Important precursors in this idealization–disappointment sequence stirred A.'s feelings. The father had owned a flourishing business in eastern Europe before the war and had been especially close to his son, whom he often took to his factory and playfully asked for advice on how to run things. This paradise was suddenly lost when A. was six. The family, which was Jewish, relocated from the eastern European country where they lived to another country to escape the invading German armies, then three years later fled Europe altogether, first for South America and later for the United States.

Mr. A., in other words, could be considered a kind of Holocaust survivor, a fact of his early experience virtually ignored in Kohut's account of the case. Some have criticized Kohut for what they consider an unconscious avoidance of this issue that may be related to his personal ambivalence about his own Jewish identity. Some years after the publication of *The Analysis of the Self*, psychoanalyst Martin Bergmann was leading a workshop in New York on second-generation Holocaust survivors.[25] Everyone in the group was keenly interested in talking with Kohut about the Holocaust-related themes in the case of Mr. A. Psychoanalyst Judith Kestenberg was designated to contact Kohut. His initial (written) reply to her request warned, "One might say that he [A.] belongs into the category that your group is investigating—but perhaps not quite." For his own reasons, he would "rather not write about the details of the case," though he was perfectly willing to talk with her, more than once if that would help. The only thing he could not do was come to New York. Shortly after that he and Kestenberg had a phone conversation in which he politely but adamantly refused to give a presentation at the workshop, because, he said, "the case had nothing to do with the Holocaust." She was left with the feeling that he was "totally oblivious to an important dimension of the case."[26]

Of course, Kohut had a point about Mr. A. not being really either a second-generation or a first-generation Holocaust survivor. At the same time, Kohut's distinction may have been splitting hairs. Certainly A. was a Jewish survivor of Nazi violence. His early experience was directly and profoundly affected by the invading German armies between 1939 and 1941, even though neither he nor his parents were touched directly by the tragedy of the Holocaust. A. experienced the full force of prejudice in his prewar eastern European country (from the context it seems to be Poland). There were two other issues for Kohut. First, he distrusted what he considered the ideological (that is, Freudian) orientation of the Bergmann workshop. He was also a very sick man in 1977 and refusing all presentations marginal to his creative life.[27]

In any event, Kohut's emphasis on the role of the father in Mr. A.'s psychology in no way slights the significant pathology of the mother that he felt lay buried, or telescoped, in the noisy issues around the father. A.'s mother was "deeply disturbed," someone who, despite her apparent calm, tended to "disintegrate with terrible anxiety and unintelligible (schizoid) excitement when she was exposed to pressure." She was shallow, unempathic, and unpredictable and "must have" contributed to A.'s broad insecurity and diffuse vulnerabilities. But Kohut's focus, and what he strongly argues was central to A., was his profound disappointment in his idealized father. In the transference, A. expressed that disappointment in two insatiable demands he placed on Kohut. One was that Kohut had to share A.'s values and goals and thus imbue them with significance. The other was that he had to confirm that he felt the patient had lived up to his values and goals. Otherwise, A. felt that all his successes were meaningless and he became depressed.

Three general theoretical issues of importance occupy Kohut's attention in the last few pages of his discussion of Mr. A. One is his stress on the significance of the actual personality of the parents, rather than gross external events, in shaping the self. Freud was ambivalent about the role of the parent in personality formation. He felt parents are the carrier of ideals and trauma, to be sure, but there is something flat and two-dimensional about the figures in the oedipal drama, who serve for the most part simply as a projective screen for the child's instinctual investments. In putting self at the center of experience, Kohut returns people to the developmental story. Events, of course, like war, Holocaust, and seduction, matter a great deal, especially when they coincide with a prolonged absence of empathy from caretakers. The external event, however, never, in and of itself, determines a specific, predictable psychological response. It is probably fair to say Kohut underestimated the potential traumatic impact of extreme situations, irrespective of psychological context. At the same time, he may have reestablished a more balanced relationship between self and society in his deep distrust of what he considered the fatuous language of much of social psychology.

Second, Kohut describes a general relationship between disappointed idealization and the eruption of grandiose feelings and behaviors (or technically what he calls in Mr. A. the "*propensity toward a reactive hypercathexis of the grandiose self*"). Whenever A. was disappointed in figures of authority in his life, or in Kohut himself in the transference, he became cold and haughty, adopted certain odd speech patterns, and combined a manifest sense of superiority with self-consciousness, shame, and hypochondria. These self expressions are what Kohut later describes in general as clinical examples of the "grandiose self." He mentions them briefly in this case because of A.'s tendency to fall back on such manifestations as a secondary response to his disappointment in his idealizations. A.'s grandiosity, in other words, is "reactive," something that is very common in cases like A.'s, especially in the early stages and much later when for prolonged periods he felt unreal in the newness of his self adjustments that came as a result of progress in his therapy.

Finally, Kohut deals with Mr. A.'s homosexual fantasies and their relation to his self disorders. Perversions, which without question include homosexuality for Kohut, are always tricky. They can so completely enslave the personality that they call forth widespread regressions that cover up the central pathology. Kohut's strong impression, however, is that in most cases "specific circumscribed disturbances" in the self form the nucleus of the perversions. In the case of A. his homosexuality had never proceeded beyond fantasy. He had engaged in some sexually tinged wrestling in adolescence and often purchased magazines of male body-builders. In his fantasies he would enslave a strong man and make him helpless. Sometimes he ejaculated at the fantasy of masturbating a physically strong man and thereby draining him of his power, and he probably nurtured a less conscious fantasy of swallowing the man's semen.[28] As the analysis progressed, the fantasies receded and eventually they disappeared altogether. Kohut's idea is that A.'s homosexual tendencies represent "sexualized statements about his narcissistic disturbance." Perversions, in other words, are sexualizations of self pathology. Kohut is not convinced the self issues can always be unraveled from the perversion, but he would seem to believe that in general homosexuality and other perversions are secondary elaborations of the self.

Kohut extends his clinical examples of the idealizing transference with the case of Mr. B., who was seen by a female analyst in regular consultation with Kohut.[29] The patient established a very deep idealizing connection to the analyst. For the most part, the analyst was able to stay attuned to the patient and prevent his fragmentation. But inevitable disruptions like vacations threatened the cohesiveness of his personality. He would then become extremely cold and imperious. During one extended vacation break from the analyst, B. was able with great difficulty to stabilize himself by withdrawing into lonely but reasonably satisfying intellectual activities. As he put it later, he "rowed out alone to the middle of the lake and looked at the moon." When the analyst returned, B. at first resisted reconnection. He was full of rage for a long time and remained, he said, "unplugged." The sequence of psychological reactions B. experienced around the separation from his analyst repeated crucial events from his childhood. His mother, who was highly involved in all aspects of his life, had supervised and controlled his every move. His feeding time was regulated by a timer. B. felt he had no mind of his own. As he got a little older he would withdraw to his room and close the door to create some private space. At that point his mother had a buzzer installed in his room to summon him to her side whenever she wanted. As Kohut says, it is not surprising B.'s first reaction to the return of his analyst was rage after he had managed to find some peace by rowing out to the center of the lake to look at the moon.

Such a case suggested to Kohut the power of the split-off fantasy. Mr. B.'s psychological sense of his mother simply could not be modified or integrated into his personality (without analysis). It lay behind a wall, entirely separate and split off. B. could only search for substitute external omnipotent powers from whom he hoped to gain strength and temporary support. In the case of Mr. A., his idealizing transference related more specifically to his father, though telescoped into those feelings was much to do preverbally with his mother and his early fixations to aspects of her pathology. It is also significant that such telescoping of early and highly regressed feelings in the idealized transference with later experiences may manifest itself in "vague and mystical religious preoccupations." The transference stirs feelings in the analysand that the idealized analyst is full of boundless power and knowledge and wise to the point of perfection. Once this state of equilibrium is reached in treatment with such patients, there is generally a decline in the vague depression, irritability, shame propensities, and hypochondria that had constituted the patient's original symptomatology.

Kohut also drew several conclusions about the characteristic ways in which patients reveal they are entering an idealizing transference. They may dream, for example, of climbing a soaring mountain while looking

for secure footing on some path. Details in such dreams can be quite telling. Is the mountain icy and cold, suggesting much about the early self-
objects? Another indication of the early stages in the activation of an
idealizing transference is that the patient may sink into philosophical and
religious preoccupations about the meaning of existence, and of life and
especially death, suggesting fear of extinction by one's own deep wish for
merger with the analyst. Later, on the cusp of a retreat into haughtiness
(a reactive grandiosity), there are often dreams of falling, which seem to
be an intentional contradiction of the most common narcissistic fantasy
of all, that of flying.

The best response of the analyst to a patient in the process of establishing
an idealizing transference, Kohut says, is to help define these resistances with
"friendly understanding," but otherwise simply to let the regressive processes
unfold without interruption and the transference establish itself spontaneously. In the early stages, one must avoid making premature transference
interpretations, which the analysand experiences mostly as "prohibitions or
expressions of disapproval." Nothing should be hurried. The patient moves
into the transference in response to an inner need, not because of some special activity of the therapist. As treatment proceeds, it is also wrong to be
unusually friendly in order to establish a good therapeutic alliance, or to nudge
along an idealizing transference, or, as Freud cautioned against, to play
prophet, savior, or redeemer.[30] For the most part patients experience such
behavior of the analyst as seductive or patronizing. On the other hand, a false
distance behind what Freud called the "mirror" blocking out the "opaque"
doctor is equally inappropriate, especially the ludicrous conventions of analytic coldness that were developed (mostly) by American psychoanalysts in
the decades following the Second World War.[31] As Kohut comments in a
footnote, "To remain silent when one is asked a question, for example, is not
neutral but rude."[32]

The idealizations of narcissistic patients, however, are not always easy
for analysts to accept. It can disrupt the analyst's own sense of self by falsely
stimulating his or her grandiosity. The analyst then rejects the patient's warm
praise, Kohut says, feeling embarrassment, self-consciousness, shame, and
in more extreme cases hypochondriacal preoccupations. The uneasiness of
the analyst is also most likely to occur early in treatment when the idealization erupts rapidly and the analyst is caught off guard and unable to prepare emotionally for what is often intense (and quite unrealistic) adulation.
The values of the culture furthermore reinforce the analyst's vulnerability.
We are taught to turn away from praise and not to listen to it.

Kohut, for example, was once consulted by a colleague about a prolonged stalemate that had developed in his analysis of a young woman, Miss L. For some time Kohut was perplexed about why treatment was going nowhere. When it became clear that the stalemate had been present from the beginning, Kohut went back with the analyst to the first few sessions of treatment. It then came out that L., a Catholic, had presented a series of dreams in the early hours of her analysis that contained the figure of an inspired, idealistic priest from her childhood. During her associations, the analyst remarked that *he* was *not* a Catholic, ostensibly to sharpen her hold on reality. The comment had halted any further progress in the analysis. His rebuff touched on a central issue in her psyche. She clung to some early idealizations, including that of the priest, that had been "an attempt to escape from the threat of bizarre tensions and fantasies caused by traumatic stimulations and frustrations from the side of her severely pathological parents." L.'s understanding of the analyst's comment was that he would not allow himself to be a good and idealized version of herself.[33]

It hardly matters how subtle the rejection is of the patient's idealization on the part of the analyst. One early comment stalemated Miss L.'s analysis for two years and would have killed it altogether but for the intervention of Kohut. Sometimes, the rejection may take the form of a "slight overobjectivity" or "coolness" in the analyst's voice. Perhaps the most common form of rebuff, however, and one easily rationalized, is when the analyst disparages the patient's idealization with humor and sarcasm. No patient misses the meaning of such communications. Kohut, in the end, while empathetic about the difficulties analysts often face with the idealizations of narcissistic patients, is categorical that the only proper stance to assume when one becomes the target of an idealization by a narcissistic patient is to "accept the admiration." At the same time, one has to recognize how difficult it can be in the later stages of treatment when a patient who once grandly admired the analyst now suddenly belittles him or her. Endless patience and a grasp of the underlying dynamics will carry the sensitive analyst through these trials and significantly enhance the working-through process.[34]

Miss F. is the archetypal case of a patient in what Kohut calls the second major "self-object transference," that of mirroring.[35] At twenty-five F. sought analysis because of "diffuse dissatisfactions" despite her professional success, social contacts, and series of love relationships. She felt she was different[36] and isolated, unable to be intimate with anyone. In treatment she suffered from sudden shifts of mood associated with "pervasive uncertainty about the reality of her feelings and thoughts." She easily alternated between states of anxious excitement about her "preciousness" with states of depletion and immobility. Her relations with people were empty and served primarily as an escape from her painful inner tensions.

Miss F.'s mother had been deeply depressed at critical periods in F.'s childhood. Nothing she did as a girl evoked pleasure or approval. On the contrary, the mother had an uncanny way of deflecting onto herself any attempt by F. to express her needs or seek attention. When F. came home from school as a girl she would joyfully anticipate telling her mother of her activities and play and successes. The mother would appear to listen but "imperceptibly the topic of the conversation shifted and the mother began to talk about herself, her headache and her tiredness and her other physical self-preoccupations." Because F. was deprived of that "optimal maternal acceptance," she had no way of transforming her own needs for affirmation into adaptably useful self-esteem. F.'s older brother compounded her trauma with his sadistic treatment and grabbing of the family limelight. The father, it seems, was an emotional cipher in the family and would vacillate between involvement with his daughter and emotional withdrawal over long stretches.

For an extended period in the early phase of the analysis, Kohut was completely baffled by Miss F.'s needs. She began each session with a friendly and calm manner, reporting on her life and dreams with appropriate affect. Things seemed on track, except that Kohut reluctantly had to admit to himself he was bored and had to struggle to remain attentive. He seemed outside of F.'s psychological universe—except, ironically, she could not tolerate his silence. Regularly, about halfway through the session, F. would suddenly get violently and inexplicably angry at him for being silent and not providing her with any support. At these moments, Kohut learned in time he could calm her by summarizing or repeating what she had already said, serving as a mirror reflecting back her communications. But if he went beyond that and added an interpretation, even if minor, she went into a rage and would "furiously accuse" Kohut in a "tense, high-pitched voice" that he was undermining her, destroying all she had built up, and was "wrecking the analysis."

Kohut is frank about his emotional difficulty at first with being reduced to a mere mirror in the primitive world of Miss F. He acknowledges that some "specific hindrances" in his personality kept him for a prolonged period from responding appropriately to the extreme demands of this very difficult patient. Besides, F. was the first, and breakthrough, case in his understanding of narcissism. She taught him the centrality of the need for empathy from the analyst and the relative insignificance of formal psychoanalytic interpretations. F. taught Kohut to listen. Furthermore, her insistent needs, her whining and noisy complaints, made no (good) sense in terms of the theory Kohut had been taught and in which he so completely believed. Freud's structural model could not explain F. Kohut had his own emotional difficulties with F.'s whining, it is fair to say, but he also lacked a conceptual framework within which to understand her.

And yet Kohut, without full awareness of what he was doing or what Miss F.'s tirades meant, created an empathic environment that allowed her to emote loudly and relentlessly manipulate him in the transference. Everything in a part of him must have rebelled against letting her continue analysis in such a disruptive way. He struggled personally with feelings of boredom that alternated with anger at her refusal to let him do what he did best—make interpretations. His Freudian side, furthermore, must have half-suspected F. was in a strong "defense transference" that could only be broken down by getting through to her about the oedipal meanings of her behavior. Failing that, she should have been shifted from analysis into psychotherapy, perhaps with someone else. A more conventional analyst, in other words, might well have banished F. for her refusal to listen to him. Kohut, on the other hand, drew on some deep resources to remain empathically connected to his difficult patient.

Ultimately, Kohut felt, what led him to understand F. was the needy and vulnerably fragile tone of her voice. It represented the insistence of the young child who has never been listened to. There was little of the adult in F., and certainly none of her preoccupations with Kohut seemed drive- or object-related. She began to make some sense to him, however, when he thought of her unusual needs in terms of primitive narcissistic states. Kohut's mirroring thus calmed her. But when he was quiet or most of all when he went beyond providing simple approval or confirmation, he instantly became her depressed mother, who deflected all of F.'s needs onto herself. Once he was clear about what he represented to her, Kohut was able to make interpretations that aided F. He explained how he felt she related to him as a replica of her depressed mother. The "correctness" of the interpretation led her to recall many episodes of the way her mother had treated her, as with her return from school. Then F. would feel "drained of energy" and "empty." After much analytic work, how-ever, F. managed to reinsert the transference rage against Kohut into those memories and feel and understand (and thus cure) her despair.

The most important theoretical question that F. raised for Kohut was the meaning of her primitive grandiosity, which got activated in a mir-roring transference. Freud understood grandiosity as a defensive ego process, a libidinal retreat from failure in love (or loss). This state of "secondary nar-cissism" sets up the ego in a condition of brittle self-assertion.[37] Kohut, on the contrary, came to believe that the primal state of the self is one that concentrates absolute perfection onto oneself and disdainfully assigns imperfections to the outside world. He calls this state, or process, the "grandiose self." Optimally, the completely self-centered child learns to accept realistic limitations and relinquishes crude expressions of exhibi-tionism, replacing them with "ego-syntonic goals and purposes." The actual early figures who empathically mirror the child's grandiosity lin-ger symbolically in the self's specific goals and purposes. But these same goals and purposes, as well as many crucial aspects of our self-esteem, bear the mark of our original grandiosity, however effectively integrated. Trau-matic interruptions, however, split it off, which makes the grandiosity no longer subject to realistic influence.[38]

It is a given that the gradual relinquishment of the most outrageous demands of the grandiose self is essential to the cure of people like Miss F. Such a process of therapeutic change for the place of grandiosity in the self is thus parallel to that of idealization. But not entirely. For someone with an "ego of average endowment," the grandiose delusional claims of the self can be highly disruptive and need taming in the analysis. For a gifted person, however, it is precisely their grandiosity that pushes them to the best use of their capacities and thus to a "realistically outstanding performance." In this context Kohut mentions Winston Churchill, Goethe, and Freud. Surely, at some level and probably one not far out of conscious-ness, Kohut would include himself in that list of gifted people for whom grandiosity stimulates their creativity. Kohut felt that idealizing needs support productivity, but that grandiosity is the essential engine of cre-ativity. It is therefore "adaptive" for certain people in ways that would be pathological for ordinary mortals.

Clinically, Kohut breaks down the transference expressions of the gran-diose self into three forms, depending on the severity of the regression. The most archaic form renders the analyst a mere extension of the pa-tient. This transference relationship with the analyst assumes a quality that might be called a kind of primary identity or a merger. In this form of the mirror transference, there is a regressive diffusion of boundaries in which the analyst is experienced as part of the patient's essential being, rather like an amoeba. Such incorporation of another self creates security for the disturbed patient, which allows therapy to proceed. But for the analyst as the target of these needs the work can present special problems. The analysand in the throes of this deepest form of the mirror transference comes to expect "unquestioned dominance" over the person of the therapist. Many analysts find such tyranny oppressive. There is no question that patients who fall into this first category of the mirror transference are the most difficult and challenging of all those with self disorders to work with in therapy, other than those who are actually psychotic.[39]

A somewhat less regressed form of the mirror transference occurs when the patient experiences the analyst as being very similar to himself or herself. In dreams and especially fantasies, such a patient will frequently imagine the therapist is a twin or some kind of alter ego. In time Kohut was to separate out "twinship" as an altogether separate self-object transference. At this point in his thinking, however, he argues that twinship is simply a kind of intermediate form of mirroring. What is most surprising about his discussion of twinship in this section of *The Analysis of the Self*, however, is how remarkably undeveloped it is, suggesting either that he had not had extensive clinical experience with its expressions or that he was not then particularly interested in the phenomenon of patients creating alter egos in the person of the analyst. It seems not to have been a subject he had thought much about in depth.[40]

The most frequently encountered form of the mirror transference—for which the term itself really should be reserved—is the relatively more mature mobilization of that early state of blissful self-centeredness. This "mirror transference proper" replays the normal phase of development in which the "gleam in the mother's eye" reflects back the child's exhibitionistic display, confirms it, and provides the grounding for a secure sense of self-esteem. As with the mother then, so with the analyst later, the self-object only matters to the extent that he or she is "invited to participate in the child's narcissistic pleasure and thus to confirm it." Kohut uses the image of the mirror to capture the ways in which patients experience analysts as extensions of themselves and therefore need to have their feelings reflected back to them. Only rarely is that reflection experienced literally. Few patients, for example, dream (or fantasize) of looking at the analyst as if seen in an actual mirror, and it would be foolish indeed to repeat back to a patient *exactly* what he or she said.[41]

There is, however, something very powerful about the image of the mirror. Visual contact represents some of the most significant interactions between a mother and child, and when disturbed the need to be looked at and to gaze at in return can be sexualized. Mr. E., for example, one of the preeminent cases in self psychology, had a mother who recoiled from her son because of her chronic malignant hypertension (from which she died when he was fifteen) and depression. It was only through looking intently at her face that E. could locate her within his constricted universe. E.'s father had long since withdrawn as a self-object substitute. In treatment with a candidate who was in supervision with Kohut, E. was afraid of looking at his analyst because of a fear that he would overburden him with his gaze. As Kohut notes, that gaze was the "carrier of the wish to be held" and probably suckled by the mother. Over weekend breaks E. began painting pictures of his analyst in which he would draw himself in the place of the eyes of the analyst. In moments of the greatest stress he had what might be called psychotic bodily delusions, as, for example, when he was a child and thought a goldfish was looking at him and another time during therapy when he felt he was taking on the bodily or facial features of his dead mother. Not surprisingly, E.'s visual investments were sexualized and his life was full of perverse fantasies and actions. He engaged in repeated and often dangerous voyeuristic activities in public toilets. He sought to take in the power of the male penis with his penetrating gaze. His perversion had begun one day at a carnival when he was eleven. He was on a swing and wanted his very sick mother to admire his skills. When she could not get interested, he turned away from her and for the first time went into a public toilet to stare at a man's penis. In time during therapy, E.'s perversion receded as he developed a keen interest in photography (disguised as painting in the published case), at which in time he truly excelled, winning prizes and becoming an artistic and commercial success. E.'s journey from despair to creativity is one of the most moving in all of self psychology.[42]

It is true in general that adult experiences in the transference are never the direct replicas of normal development phases. They are, instead, the "regressively altered editions" of early experience. For the most part, however, Kohut is struck by the relative absence of distortion in the ways early grandiosity needs enter the transference. The infantile, one might say, is insistently and noisily present in the therapy of a patient in a mirroring transference.[43] Mr. B., for example, ostensibly sought therapy because of sexual disturbances and problems in his marriage. In fact, he suffered from a much more diffuse personality disorder that included feelings of emptiness and frequent rage. Within weeks after adjusting to analysis, he reported experiencing treatment as soothing and "like a warm bath." During sessions and soon throughout the week his feelings of emptiness subsided, he felt whole, and he became more productive. On weekends, however, he would become so distraught and full of rage that he began to worry about his sanity. An epiphany came in his treatment when the analyst prefaced one of her interpretations with the phrase "As you told me about a week ago . . ." B. was intensely pleased that the therapist could remember something from that long before and experienced a new sense of cohesiveness. The remark by the analyst reconnected B. along a time axis, locating him meaningfully within his own narrative.[44]

In the normal course of therapeutic events, the mirror transference follows naturally from what is usually a brief period of idealization.[45] This typical expression of the mirror transference is an important and therapeutically useful phase of treatment. What seems to be occurring, Kohut says, is that the initial idealization of the analyst is a kind of "intermediate step on the backward path of the analysand's not yet completed therapeutic regression." In such cases, the period of idealization gives way quickly to the much longer and otherwise dominant phase of the mirror transference. Mr. K., for example, began his analysis with a brief period of idealizing his analyst's appearance, behavior, and capabilities, which re-created his attempt at about three and a half to establish his father as an admired figure after a rejection by the mother. The father, however, was unable to respond to his son's needs and turned away from him. The boy then sought some renewal of the solace he had once experienced with his mother. That activated the full force of his grandiosity in the mirror transference and occupied the attention of the analyst and patient for most of the treatment. The initial phase of idealization in such cases is actually a good prognostic sign, just as the mirror transference that follows it offers possibilities for healing.[46]

It can be a challenging experience, Kohut explains at some length in *Analysis*, treating patients deeply immersed in a mirror transference. It is easy, among other things, for the analyst to be bored by the patient's need to make him or her a mere reflection. The patient's "demands for attention, admiration, and a variety of other forms of mirroring and echoing responses" are not, in and of themselves, intellectually challenging. The total focus is on the minutiae of the patient's life and feelings and memories

without any real input from the analyst. For prolonged periods the analyst is there simply as an empathic echo. The analyst "as an independent
individual" tends to be blotted out. The process is one that does little to
gratify the analyst's own narcissistic needs. Such objectification can lead
the unwary analyst toward subtle forms of rejection and emotional numb-
ness. Close listening may stop and responses become canned. In some
cases, there may even be overt anger leading to exhortation that reflects
the analyst's impatience. It is only through understanding the therapeutic process in the mirroring transference that these dangerous responses
of the analyst can be mitigated. As Kohut himself came to feel in his own
work, it is, in fact, enormously stimulating and difficult to track the minute
swings of feeling and there is much to interpret—if the analyst grasps the
actual dynamics of what is going on. After *Analysis*, Kohut himself stopped
talking about the analyst's boredom while treating a patient in a mirroring transference, because he himself stopped feeling bored or upset any
more and came to believe his own earlier reactions were simply a by-
product of the discovery process.[47]

But even in the monograph Kohut shows that much of what one encounters in treating disorders of the self is fascinating and engrossing.
Many of the fantasies, for example, are only seemingly trivial. The most
commonly encountered such fantasy is that of being able to fly, but there
are many others. Mr. C. had a dream in which the question arose of finding his successor. He thought, "How about God?" His associations—
against much resistance—led to a childhood fantasy that he actually was
God. Mr. D. recalled with great difficulty his childhood fantasy that he
ran the streetcars through thought control emanating from his head, which
furthermore existed disconnected from his body above the clouds. Mr. H.
reported an early fantasy that everybody he encountered was his servant or
slave and though everyone knew it they never talked about it. Kohut stresses
that all such fantasies are surrounded by shame, and that it takes a great
deal of patient therapeutic labor to uncover them. The results may seem
unworthy of all the effort and quite disappointing for the analyst. *"Parturi-
ent montes,"* Kohut says, quoting Horace, *"nascitur ridiculus mus"* ("Mountains in labor give birth to a ridiculous mouse").[48]

Expressions of split-off grandiosity are exceedingly asocial. Acting out,
for example, can be dangerous and illegal. Mr. E., with his voyeuristic
activities in public toilets when he was separated from or disappointed in
his analyst, frequently risked arrest. Kohut's conceptualization of what
happens in such circumstances is that the patient temporarily regresses

from the mirror transference to the much more primitive level of a merger. Such regressions can also occur in fantasy. Mr. I. at one point during treatment brought in some of his childhood diaries and read them in their entirety. The analyst tried to remain interested but in fact betrayed, ever so slightly, his feelings of boredom and annoyance at being excluded from the active analytic process of direct communication. That night the patient dreamed, first, of catching a big fish and showing it proudly to his father, who was disappointed. In the second scene of the dream I. saw "Christ on the cross, suddenly slumping; the muscles suddenly relaxing, dying." I. had hoped for an approving acceptance of his childhood self in reading the diaries. Feeling rebuffed, he retreated to a fantasized merger with Christ, who in death reunites with God.[49]

Such dreams reflect, in general, in their totality the central psychological issues in focus at that moment within the self. Unlike Freud, who treated the "manifest content" of the dream as a mere symbolic carrier of the deeper and unconscious latent thoughts, Kohut focuses on the dream itself as enormously illuminating. The implicit distinction Kohut makes at this point in his thinking (that is, in 1971) is that the direct reflection of one's psychological state in the dream is most characteristic of narcissistic patients, while the more familiar neurotic has dreams with all the elaborate disguises Freud described. Kohut's idea is that the focal issues in the self at the moment find symbolic expression in the dream (or fantasy) in ways that are relatively undisguised and certainly free of the elaborate "dream work" processes familiar to Freud.[50] That does not mean such dreams are simple. Mr. J., for example, began treatment with frequent flying dreams. As he got better, J.'s flying dreams subsided, as did the disruptive expressions of his grandiosity in his life and work. Once, however, Kohut detected a slight regression on the part of J. and forcefully interpreted the continuing role of grandiosity in his work, despite his significant progress otherwise. In response J. had a dream of walking, but in an exaggerated way—and a tiny distance off the ground. Mr. K., when breaks occurred in the analysis, dreamed of spinning wheels to represent his "regression to bodily tensions." A patient in termination dreamed of swallowing a clarinet, which Kohut understands partly as representing the analyst's penis but more importantly his voice, for the clarinet kept playing music from the patient's stomach.[51]

Kohut also acquired new clinical perspectives on color in dreams from his work with narcissistic patients. Mr. A., toward the end of his analysis when he was in fact much better, even though his gains were recent and fragile, dreamed in color of people as toy soldiers. At the same time in his life A. was experiencing a mild sexual disorder (premature ejaculation) in his relationship with his wife. Kohut interpreted both the dream and the sexual disturbance—"always such a sensitive indicator of the equilibrium of the personality"—as temporary intrusions of A.'s old anxieties. His new self forms were not completely stable. He was still in the process of accepting the new image of himself. This interpretation led Mr. A. to recall that in fact the dream had not only been in color but in technicolor, exaggerated and artificially sharp and clear. Kohut concludes that *in general* color in dreams signifies the "intrusion of unmodified material," or a flooding of the self that is experienced as unbearable tension.[52]

The vulnerable self can easily be flooded, which is one way of stating Kohut's definition of trauma, a subject in which he was deeply interested and that he wrote about all his life. In this technical study, his focus is on clinical issues and the characteristic ways NPDs succumb to traumatic states. Sexualization, for example, of their "needs and conflicts" is one typical response. They are also easily hurt, they "become quickly over-stimulated," and their excessive fears spread and become "boundless." Much work in analysis is spent on interpreting traumatic states. A patient, for example, especially early on, will report feeling flooded with shame and humiliation at having told a joke in some social setting that fell flat, or having talked too much at a dinner party, or having been dressed inappropriately at some event. What makes the shame traumatic is that the patient experienced humiliation at exactly the point of expecting to shine and gain acclaim. The unraveling of such scenes in all their tortured detail can be "important moments in the analysis of narcissistic patients." For long periods the analyst must "participate empathically" in the patient's acute pain and anger that the humiliation cannot be undone. Then gradually the dynamics of shame and flooding, including their childhood origins, can be interpreted.[53]

Later in the treatment, in the middle and even final stages, traumatic states of the patient can be prompted paradoxically by correct and empathic interpretations.[54] Mr. B., for example, had gotten to the point of tolerating separations better and no longer needed to masturbate to induce sleep. In one session he reported that his mother seemed not to like her own body and recoiled from touching B. The analyst made the interpretation that as a result B. had never been able to experience himself as "lovable, loving, and touchable." B. was quiet, then said: "Crash! Bang! You hit it!" and recalled how his mother and former wife made him feel "like vermin and filth." Then he cried to the end of the session. For the next week B. slipped into a deeply regressed state. He was disheveled, had trouble sleeping, and felt overwhelmed by disturbing dreams of eating breasts. He no longer felt alive. He said he was like a broken radio with tangled wires. At first baffled at what was going on, the analyst came to understand that the patient's traumatic state resulted from his feeling overwhelmed with excitement at the very correctness of her interpretation. Once that became clear, the analyst could help B. minimize the extent and power of future reactions to her (correct) interpretations.

The voice of *The Analysis of the Self* is decidedly off-putting. *The Analysis* is filled with technical, clinical instructions for fellow analysts on the treatment of deeply troubled patients. It is written as a monograph, not a book, intentionally restricting his audience to "experts." Readers are not welcomed in but pushed away. Repetitions abound. Whole chapters are out of place. Gems of insight are buried in otherwise long, turgid paragraphs. Digressions proliferate. Anna Freud once advised Kohut to avoid his tendency toward *Einschachtelungen* (insertions) that "break the flow of thoughts."[55]

But the worst is the language. There is much talk in *Analysis* about "narcissistic cathexes" and of "libidinal cathexes passing through the object" on their way to an "idealization of the superego." There are "mergers with archaic objects" and "grandiose self-objects" that divide and subdivide. "Mirror transferences" can be found in their actuality and in a "narrower sense." And everything Kohut says about narcissism is compared with the classical Freudian view of the "transference neurosis" in which the "central psychopathology concerns structural conflicts over (incestuous) libidinal and aggressive strivings which emanate from a well-delimited, cohesive self and are directed toward childhood objects which have in essence become fully differentiated from the self." A common occurrence in the treatment of narcissistic patients, Kohut says, in italics, is the "*propensity toward a reactive hypercathexis of the grandiose self.*" Kohut's text is an unrelieved meditation in the grand and almost incomprehensible tradition of psychoanalytic metapsychology.[56]

The Analysis of the Self is in some ways the realization of that tradition. Early on Freud committed himself to an instinct theory. The crucial assumption of that theory, grounded in nineteenth-century psychology, is that it takes psychic energies, or cathexes, to run the self. Without this energy, so went the logic of the metaphor, the operations of the "psychic apparatus" made no sense. Without drives there appeared to be no explanation for motivation. For about two decades Freud's thinking about psychoanalysis and the nature of libidinal development remained relatively simple. The most interesting of his attempts to think further about drive theory came with his 1905 book on sexuality, in which he distinguished between the source of an instinct at the border of the body and self; the aim of the drive, whether outward or back onto oneself; and the object of the drive. In the theory there is a continuously flowing source of libidinal pressure (those cathexes) requiring satisfaction that can oscillate rapidly between seemingly contradictory aims (sadism and masochism) and easily substitute objects of gratification. Most importantly, sexuality has a history in its development through various "erotogenic zones" in the body. We are shaped psychologically and spiritually, one might say, in the wake of that early history.[57] Freud's theory brought together in original ways all kinds of loose strands in the air at the time, from fascination with the problem of bisexuality to various ideas on homosexuality. If he had written nothing else, Freud would have made a mark for his short book on sexuality in 1905.

In the teens Freud extended his drive theory in two directions that were to be of great consequence. First, he developed his ideas about narcissism in 1914 as an extension of libido theory, in part to clarify his disagreement with Carl Jung. Second, in his 1917 paper "Mourning and Melancholia," Freud notes the apparent similarity between the two states, which serves to heighten the significance of their subjective differences. "In mourning it is the world which has become poor and empty; in melancholia it is the ego itself." In melancholia, or depression as we would say now, there is no object to relinquish. The ego itself is impoverished. Self-esteem plummets. But it is the murky conclusion to the essay that is most important for Kohut's work. There Freud asks about the quality of the object choice that preceded the depression. Filled with (perhaps constitutional) ambivalence toward the object, the libido is detached and forced into the unconscious, "the region of the memory-traces of *things* (as contrasted with *word*-cathexes)." This unconscious position continually attracts libidinal cathexes to itself and forces "the regression of libido into the ego."[58] Narcissistic object choices, in other words (as Kohut would clarify), are the precondition for depression.

By the early 1920s Freud elaborated his structural theory of id, ego, and superego, which became the cornerstone of drive theory. He had worried for some time about an important contradiction in his earlier topographical model of the mind: Why cannot all preconscious memories become conscious if we shine on them the light of attention? Indeed, it seemed, the more he thought about it, most important memories and ego functions were dynamically unconscious without being repressed and a formal part of what he had always called the "system Unconscious." The unconscious was more complex than he had realized *and* ego functions were infinitely more varied in their operations than could be understood simply in terms of their relation to consciousness. So he devised his new model to address these basic concerns. His new id encompassed all of what was in the old "seething cauldron" of instinctual impulses, repressed material, and archaic states of relatedness. The new ego emerged out of this id and its elaborate system of defenses warded off the dangers of instinctual annihilation. The crucial developmental step in this model comes with the disintegration of the Oedipus complex when the superego is formed out of the regressive identifications he had first begun to think seriously about in "Mourning and Melancholia."[59]

The rest were glosses on this complex story of the fate of the drives. Essays such as "The Economic Problem of Masochism" (1924) address the peculiar issue of moral masochism. Two years later Freud's short book *Inhibitions, Symptoms, and Anxiety* returned to the central significance of castration dread and most of all stressed that the task of repression was to distort or displace the "instinctual representative" and to transform the "instinctual impulse" or libidinal charge into anxiety. This affective signal, which is the economic consequence of repression, becomes the motive force for the basic functioning of the psyche in the theory. Anxiety warns us of danger and prompts the ego to act in some way to protect the self. Freud's most important and interesting extension of these ideas was his attempt to explain the motive forces in civilization itself and what he calls its pervasive "discontents" in *Das Unbehagen in der Kultur* (1930). To become civilized means to deny our desires, which given the economic consequences of repression means excessive anxiety and unconscious guilt, which in turn only feeds more repression. Life in culture, he thought, was an unceasing round of despair and denial.[60]

There was very little of substance added to this theory in the years after Freud. Anna Freud described the ego's "mechanisms of defense" in clear terms in 1936 but really only reformulated her father's writings between 1924 and 1926.[61] Heinz Hartmann wrote about the important question of adaptation to one's environment in 1939; the early Erik Erikson deepened this work with historical and anthropological considerations.[62] But even Erikson clung to drive theory in his ideas about epigenesis and development. A long section in *Childhood and Society* (1950), for example, restates in fond terms the key ideas of Freud about infantile sexuality.[63] In general, in fact, most of what seemed like important advances at the time read now like minor quibbles. No one was questioning the assumptions of the theory. To glance at the pages of the leading journals in psychoanalysis during the 1950s and 1960s, for example, is a mind-numbing experience. It was a standard joke in those years among the most orthodox thinkers in psychoanalysis that no one had really done anything in the field except Freud. In retrospect, such views were not far off the mark.

But the one important area that had been left undeveloped by Freud was how drive theory could explain narcissism and, by extension, the self. Kohut had no pretensions that he was extending psychoanalytic understanding (and treatment) to the psychoses, but he did claim to be articulating a theory that made it possible to treat psychoanalytically a much more disturbed class of patients. He was also, he thought, rounding out Freud's theory, completing it. To carry out that project required a warm embrace of Freud's language of metapsychology. Kohut was certainly aware of the political issues involved. He was much more likely to have his ideas accepted by the mainstream if he expressed them in the language of drive theory. But surely the issues involved in his (often confused) form of expression in his 1971 book lay deeper. To speak in the language of metapsychology was, for Kohut, the most general, the purest level of theory in psychoanalysis. To clarify an important issue like narcissism at that level, he felt, was to contribute to the history of ideas in a fundamental way.

And yet Kohut so completely used drive theory as to hopelessly abuse it. He ran it into the ground and revealed its absurd character and false assumptions about human nature. The contradiction in Kohut's thinking here curiously parallels the early struggles of Freud himself. As Erikson has noted, Freud found himself in a kind of "desperate obedience to physiology" at the very moment of his early clinical insights into hysteria, which suggested a much more supple and complex model of the mind. Psychological truth for Freud at the time lay only in explanations about the physiological substrate of processes within the psyche. Such forms of conceptualization were what he knew after years of training, especially in the lab of his mentor, Ernst Brücke. Confronted with some challenging clinical material that he was actually beginning to understand in new ways, Freud retreated to the old and familiar as he attempted to formulate a general psychology in pure physiological terms. In his "Project for a Scientific Psychology," which he wrote as a long letter to his friend, Wilhelm Fliess, in 1895, Freud described "material particles" of the nervous system that were organized in ways to manage "qualities and quantities of excitation" in response to external stimuli. As Erikson puts it: "Physical concepts are combined [in Freud's "Project"] with histological concepts to create a kind of neuronic Golem, a robot, in which even consciousness and thought are mechanistically explainable on the basis of an over-all principle of inner constancy."[64] Within weeks Freud had recanted his theory to Fliess, then forgot about it altogether, and when presented with the discovered document late in his life tried to have it destroyed. But in fact Freud's physiological language in the "Project" was not so forgotten and carried over significantly to his early thinking in psychoanalysis. The more dense sections of Chapter 7 of *The Interpretation of Dreams* only make sense in terms of the "Project." Erikson's conclusion is that a creative thinker's complicated relationship to his early training illustrates "the pains to which a discoverer will go *not* to haphazardly ignore the paths of his tradition, but to follow them instead to their absurd limit, and to abandon them only when the crossroad of lone search is reached."[65]

So it was with Kohut. *The Analysis of the Self* stands ironically as a profound indictment of the very drive theory it attempts to bolster. Kohut was hardly the first to challenge drive theory. No one, however, had ever offered a clinical psychoanalytic alternative to the theory that clarified the actual data of observation within a new frame. That this new vision was partly disguised, even for Kohut himself, is one of the wonders of the discovery process. Kohut could not think about the new forms of transference he had named, for example, except in libidinal terms. The idealizing structures in the self as he first formulated them result from the peculiar consequences of the dissolution of the Oedipus complex. Narcissism in general is defined as one kind of libido distribution. The very term "self-object," so central to Kohut's theory, rests in its initial formulation in *Analysis* on the idea of libidinal incorporation of the object by the self. Kohut's theory, in fact, is so pervasively grounded in drive theory that it seems to require it. From the vantage of 1971, it appeared to Anna Freud, Heinz Hartmann before he died (as best we can tell), Kurt Eissler, and most other leaders in the field, and certainly to Kohut himself, that drive theory had reached a new level of sophistication. In fact, Kohut demonstrated how ridiculous the theory really was. *The Analysis of the Self* is an ending just as much as a beginning. By some kind of inner logic Kohut needed to write the book as a footnote to Freud. In the process, however, he discovered just how far that note came to supplant the text itself. Its language—which is, after all, the voice of the self—implodes with contradictions.

And yet *The Analysis of the Self* is a masterpiece that transformed psychoanalysis, proving what Erikson said in another context: "True insight survives its first formulation."[66]

In terms of intellectual influences, part of Kohut's framing of *Analysis* was to make clear his debt to those who had previously touched on questions of narcissism. His thirteen-page bibliography at the end of the book includes 273 references to everyone from August Aichhorn, to Sándor Ferenczi, to Freud and Hartmann (of course), to Phyllis Greenacre, to Otto Kernberg, to Melanie Klein, to Susanne Langer, to Joseph Sandler, and to D. W. Winnicott. It would be difficult to imagine a more complete list of relevant publications on the subject of narcissism in 1971 (though any bibliography can be artificially extended almost indefinitely), just as it is unlikely the widely read Kohut was not familiar with the sources he cites. The third paragraph of the "Preface" to *Analysis*, furthermore, summarizes the most important ideas leading up to his own work: Hartmann's separation of the self from the ego, Erikson's work on identity, Margaret Mahler's idea that a "separate psychobiological existence" emerges out of the union of the mother and child, and the theoretical formulations of Edith Jacobson and Annie Reich, both of whom he probably mentioned as nods to the orthodox, not as genuinely important sources of his ideas.[67]

Kohut's approach to the existing scholarship on narcissism in his monograph is not unreasonable. He clearly establishes the tradition within which he is writing, but then largely dispenses with an elaborate scholarly apparatus. There are few internal references and most footnotes are substantive, though Kohut hardly ignores any writer of significance. He writes his book not primarily in relation to what others have said but in response to his own clinical experience and what was inside of him, because he felt strongly that everything in psychoanalysis up to that point dealing with narcissism was in a conceptual jumble. One cannot read the monograph closely and claim its ideas are borrowed directly from any-one or from any specific school. One way to think of Kohut's contribu-tion is that he made the paradigm shift that gave new meaning to what had until then existed half-said in the margins.[68] In retrospect and in something of a reversal of chronology (though typical in intellectual his-tory), Ferenczi, Fairbairn, and many others now seem prescient and rele-vant in ways they never did before Kohut. After 1971 one could begin to understand what people were trying to say before that. In some cases, on the other hand, as with Erikson or some in the British "object relations school," it might well be said that Kohut needed to close himself off from influence, or he might have discovered just how common were their con-cerns. He might have lost his particular focus and compromised his own creativity. As a result, it can be fairly said that Kohut was probably less familiar with some relevant writings than he might have been. But it can-not be claimed that anyone had already written up everything Kohut said in *The Analysis of the Self.*[69]

It was therefore startling and enormously upsetting for Kohut when the charge of plagiarism emerged in a crucial review of his book in 1973. A young British analyst, Martin James, had been assigned *The Analysis of the Self* for the *International Journal of Psycho-Analysis.* James had actu-ally been in touch with Kohut during the previous year and expressed his great enthusiasm for the book. But his actual review was mostly negative, calling *Analysis* "less a scholarly work and more a work of populariza-tion" and objecting to Kohut's apparent attempt to keep the orthodox Freudians happy with his metapsychological language. But it was his con-cluding sentence that really threw Kohut: "It seems that, since unconscious plagiarism is an endemic force in psychoanalytic writing and theorizing, this is really a synthetic book much influenced, in fact but not in attribu-tion, by those preoccupied by the theory of development in the earliest mothering period."[70] James apparently sent Kohut a copy of the review prior to publication including that sentence but decided the next day to delete it from the version he actually submitted to the journal. Kohut, not knowing of James's decision to delete the offending passage, reacted with fury. He telegrammed both James and Joseph Sandler, the *IJPA* editor, that he was "deeply disturbed by allusion to plagiarism, especially in last paragraph." Kohut then wrote an angry and hurt letter to James and another to William H. Gillespie, a member of the editorial board of *IJPA,* imploring him for the sake of fairness to intervene. He copied both letters to Anna Freud.[71]

At this point Sandler called Kohut to explain the confusion about the drafts James had submitted and to report that all was settled. He assured Kohut that he need not worry. Kohut was relieved but immediately wrote Anna Freud to discover the real story (and surely, as subtext, to keep her lined up on his side in the dispute). He explained what had happened and noted that at least with the offensive sentence deleted, "I am not greatly disturbed about the rest even though I find that neither Dr. James's criticism nor his praise are hitting the mark." He did express some doubt about Sandler's account but was willing to exonerate him. What he could not figure out was why James had sent him the old version of his manuscript. Kohut remained full of doubts and questions. Anna Freud wrote back that she had also talked with Sandler and was glad the matter was settled. She added that the person James was probably trying to "defend" (her sarcastic quotation marks) was Winnicott, "to whom he was very devoted." She had also had a similar experience with Winnicott himself. He once wrote such a nasty review of one of her books that the journal actually refused to publish it. He later apologized, said he did not know why he had done it, and even claimed he liked the book. She concluded, "So that is how it is."[72]

The plagiarism charge, however, has hung in the air ever since the publication of *The Analysis of the Self*. It is commonly muttered that Kohut took his ideas from Winnicott, Ferenczi, Fairbairn, Mahler, or whoever, or that he never read them and should have, for they had long since formulated his essential ideas. These are different charges, of course. The first—actual plagiarism—is the easiest to dispense with. *Analysis* is an original and important work of scholarship in psychoanalysis. It consolidates a number of loose conceptual strands in the field and establishes the conceptual basis for what is now the main focus in psychoanalysis on relational issues, intersubjectivity, and the self. Before Kohut, psychoanalytic theory talked about patients in ways that objectified their experience. A theory of self is of necessity connected, mutual, interdependent. There are many contending views at present in what can be very generally called relational psychoanalysis, from the constructivists to the postmoderns to the intersubjectivists. What they share, however, is a basic sense of experience (which is to say, self) that first entered psychoanalytic thinking in a coherent way with Kohut.

Analysis is also the turning point in the history of drive theory. Before 1971 most respected analysts clung to the theory with some degree of respect, if with ambivalence. Few felt really comfortable with words like "cathexis" or concepts like libido, or could figure out the intricacies of superego formation as opposed to that of the ego ideal. They stumbled on, however, muttering their incoherent phrases, because the theory seemed to capture a larger human truth. After Kohut, on the other hand, and a psychoanalytic theory of the self, only the troglodytes would continue to speak of "cathexes" and "libido distribution."

It is a different issue whether others formulated certain of Kohut's essential ideas before him, even if vaguely and not as part of a coherent theory, and whether he failed adequately to acknowledge their work. He never questioned that there were many in psychoanalysis who were interested in some of the same problems he was. He learned from many people and knew the work of the key figures well. Paul Ornstein thought Kohut had insomnia and stayed up half the night reading, as he certainly seemed to know everything about anything.[73] Kohut's interest in Ferenczi, for example, dated back to the 1940s. Ferenczi was something of a clinical genius who carried through a number of radical therapeutic experiments with empathy. What he lacked was a theory. Kohut was particularly interested in two of Ferenczi's papers, "Four Stages in the Development of Reality" and "The Confusion of Tongues." Kohut did have scorn for Ferenczi's later therapeutic experiments and his "simplistic view" that one could belatedly compensate for early deprivations. No therapist, Kohut felt, can make up for love that is missing in a patient's childhood.[74]

Kohut was even more intimately familiar with the work of Melanie Klein and her followers in Britain and throughout the world. In the case of Klein, however, familiarity bred contempt. Kohut had first encountered Klein's early work when he was a young psychiatrist at the University of Chicago. In the 1950s and 1960s he followed her publications closely, as he did nearly everything in the field. In his administrative work with the American, especially during his term as president, he often had discussions, both theoretical and clinical, with Kleinian analysts. He came to understand their perspective from the inside. He was impressed with Klein's close clinical attention to early pathological states. He was appalled, however, with her explanations, which he found odd and essentially wrong. He felt, among other things, that Klein's theories imposed adult categories of development on young children, whom she imagined as calculating, driven, intentional. He also thought there was something perverse about the way Klein regarded the baby as evil. She argued, for example, that the nursing infant typically harbored violent fantasies toward the mother's breast. He wrote Anna Freud once how astonished he was to find how Kleinian everyone was in a visit he made to South America. And he was quite disdainful. "I have often predicted that they will finally die out because of the sheer boredom which their formulations must cause them." In another letter to Freud two weeks later, he called Klein herself "pathological," though he hoped her followers might become more normal with her death (in 1960). Kohut's views of the Kleinians remained unchanged during the rest of his life. In the late 1970s Bernard Brandchaft, himself trained as a Kleinian, remarked on how deep was Kohut's knowledge of their work, despite his disagreements with their conceptualizations.[75]

The mystery is Donald W. Winnicott, the English analyst who had written beautiful clinical vignettes about children and grasped the openness of their psychological boundaries. It was Winnicott who first talked of the "transitional object." Most of those close to Kohut have always assumed he simply did not read Winnicott and was unaware of any points of convergence between his work and that of Winnicott. Such, for example, is the strong view of Thomas Kohut.[76] Paul Ornstein is rather more cautious. He says Kohut surely knew about Winnicott but "ignored and bypassed him" as someone with interesting clinical ideas but not an important theoretician.[77] Ornstein's view is supported by Kohut's comments on Winnicott in his University of Chicago lectures to the Mental Health Clinic during the academic year 1969–1970, or just as he was putting the final touches on his manuscript. Someone (the names are not provided in the published text) in the seminar asked Kohut about the relationship between "primary narcissism" and the "transitional object." Kohut first examined his understanding of primary narcissism and then turned to its relationship with what Winnicott calls the transitional object. He noted that Winnicott came up with the term—and the crucial paper is in the bibliography of *Analysis*—but that the concept was really from Freud's "Beyond the Pleasure Principle" (1920). In that paper Freud gives the "first" account of a transitional object in the game of "fort-da" with the spool of thread that he played with his grandson.[78] In other words, Kohut reduced Winnicott's best-known concept to a footnote of an idea that began with Freud. It is not surprising Kohut never read much more widely in Winnicott's other writings. In other ways, as well, Kohut ignored Winnicott. He felt that Winnicott, like Ferenczi, was good on empathy at the clinical level but remained locked in drive theory. Winnicott's useful stray insights were not therefore part of a coherent *theory* of empathy.

Other, more tangential influences on Kohut's thinking in these years include the cognitive developmental theorist Jean Piaget (though Kohut specifically denied that Piaget had any impact on his thinking).[79] Kohut was also so oblivious to Carl Rogers that he never once mentions his name in anything written that has survived, or in the extant lectures that have been transcribed and published, even though Rogers was for a time in the 1960s at the University of Chicago.[80]

One has to wonder, however, about the influence of the most important of the early psychoanalytic thinkers on Kohut's work (with the exception of Freud himself), Carl Jung. By far the best and most balanced discussion of Jung and Kohut is by Mario Jacoby, who sees many areas of overlap between the two thinkers and much simultaneous discovery of similar things but expressed in quite different terms.[81] The evidence, as very intelligently laid out by Jacoby, is that Kohut and Jung were coming at some common problems from quite different traditions and that each spoke within his own, exclusive discourse. Jacoby, a respected Jungian, thinks that charging Kohut with a simple recycling of Jung's best ideas is neither fair nor accurate. Kohut's studied avoidance of Jung, however, may reflect the politics of psychoanalysis more than any real intellectual ignorance of what that wily Swiss analyst was up to. Jung was the first to talk systematically about the self in psychoanalysis, the first to object to drive theory, and he had many specific ideas of great relevance for a deeper understanding of narcissism. But Jung was always controversial after his noisy break from Freud, and much of his later behavior, especially his obliging stance toward the Nazis after 1934, has tainted him in other ways.[82] Kohut never talked about Jung in his lectures or conversations and Jung is conspicuously absent from the bibliographies of his books. Kohut was probably aware of some aspects of Jung's ideas about the archetypes, but in general he seems not to have read Jung's writings and was only interested in Jung's correspondence with Freud as a part of Kohut's deep fascination with the master.[83]

In some respects, the debate about attribution of *The Analysis of the Self* is tedious and entirely predictable. William James once commented on the "classic steps" in the life of a theory. First it is attacked as utterly absurd. Then it gets accepted as obvious and insignificant. Finally, it is understood as so important that its opponents claim that they had said it all before.[84]

Part Four

A THEORY AND

A MOVEMENT

1971–1977

Twenty

DEATH AND THE SELF

Kohut lived his last decade in the shadow of death. In the early summer of 1971, at fifty-eight years of age, just after the publication of *The Analysis of the Self*, his doctor discovered in a routine medical examination that he had an enlarged spleen. Kohut decided, somewhat fatalistically, to delay further diagnostic testing and instead travel to Vienna for the meetings of the International Psycho-Analytic Association, and then take his vacation as usual that summer in Carmel, though he talked morosely about it at times as his last. When he returned to Chicago in September he went in for tests and was diagnosed as having lymphoma (or lymphatic cancer), which is similar to but not the same disease as leukemia.[1] The cancer never really went into remission, but it spread slowly and seemed largely under control until the middle of 1977.[2] In those first six years of cancer Kohut's most serious complaint was that it affected his immune system and he often got colds and flus. The worsening of his disease from 1977 on, however, ground him down in general and made necessary more aggressive treatment. First, the doctors tried a round of chemotherapy in the summer of 1977, which gave him a sore throat, aching feelings, pain on the top of his eyeballs, and a mounting fever. The drugs were discontinued within two months.[3] A year later, in the fall of 1978, he received some radiation treatment, for which he had to prepare by having weekly blood tests.[4] Then came a series of shocks that will be described in greater detail later. By the summer of 1981, as a result of his cancer and other ailments, he was bone-thin and down from his customary 128 pounds to

100 pounds. He developed edema, or severe swelling throughout his body. When he died on October 8, 1981, a significant percentage of his weight was in the form of cancer tumors spread throughout his body.[5]

It would be difficult to overstate the impact that cancer had on Kohut. It shattered his personal myth of invincibility. In his moment of greatest glory Kohut was brought low by a disease that was completely outside of his control. His first reaction to the news of the enlarged spleen that summer of 1971 was to assume he was on the verge of death. In the hospital that fall he then raged at various people, including the internist who told him early on that his rock-hard spleen suggested a malignancy. Kohut felt that was an unempathic communication. He also spun out some rather wild fantasies under the stress of trying to adjust to his illness. He told John Gedo, who was one of only four friends whom he allowed to visit him in the hospital, that the cancer was caused by his exposure, thirty years earlier, to radiation leaks from Enrico Fermi's then-secret experiments on nuclear fission under the abandoned stands at Stagg Field. Nothing ordinary, it seems, could bring Kohut down. Gedo thought Kohut was acting paranoid, though he added that the thought of Kohut unraveling made him "dizzy with anxiety."[6]

In trying to understand Kohut's response to cancer, one should keep in mind its larger cultural associations. As Susan Sontag, who herself suffered from cancer, has so aptly argued, this disease, unlike any other, is our culture's metaphor for the ugliness of death.[7] Cancer is unseemly. You rot from within, your body awry in some fundamental disjunction. There is nothing elegant or even tragic about cancer. On the contrary, it is felt to be shameful. Not all diseases have such cultural associations. In the nineteenth century, for example, there was something romantic about tuberculosis, and novels and plays from that time feature beautiful maidens in white lounging on couches with bloodied handkerchiefs dangling from their delicate fingers as they tragically expire. Furthermore, sanatoriums, where privileged TB patients often spent years in good conditions with clean air, could be sites of deepened self-awareness, as Hans Castorp discovers in *The Magic Mountain*. Heart disease, to take another example, has cultural meanings of mechanical breakdown, of a body moving toward death but in a natural sequence that connects life processes with endings. Not so with cancer. People often cannot even say the word, and refer obliquely to "the big C" or use euphemisms to avoid direct confrontation with it. In our day AIDS has begun to assume some of the opprobrium that cancer carried in the early 1970s.[8]

Even from his hospital bed Kohut moved to contain the knowledge of his cancer. He insisted that no one in his family tell anyone. It was a "deep and dark secret," his son says. Miriam Elson, for example, who knew the Kohuts well, lived down the street from them on Dorchester Avenue, and had hired Elizabeth to work at the university's Student Health Center in the early 1960s and encountered her on a daily basis, was consistently lied to. Elson had asked whether Kohut had cancer, too.[9] Only within the bosom of the family for the next decade did Kohut allow himself to talk about the anxiety of the latest blood results or the terrors of an upcoming round of treatment. It brought them close but also created a "kind of hell" for the family, as his son puts it. As Kohut became more driven and obsessed with his health, he sucked them into the vortex of his anxiety. They all awaited the latest news, sure that it was for the worst. It did not help that his doctor, Oglesby Paul, was anxious himself and seems to have exaggerated the dangers, perhaps because he knew he was dealing with a distinguished patient. As Thomas Kohut says, "He and we would wait for the next blood test, and he was constantly having blood tests, checking the platelet counts, etc." The ostensible reason for all the secrecy, Kohut explained to his son, was to protect his patients. But Kohut was aware there was more to it than that and he would at times talk to his family about how there was "something a bit shameful about his disease, something unpleasant," and how injured he was by having his body attack itself in that way. "My father," says Thomas Kohut, "was very intolerant of weaknesses on his part."[10]

The family closeness, while at times suffocating under the weight of the cancer, intensified the mutual interdependencies around the hearth. Kohut had often read drafts of his papers out loud to his wife. Now it became a regular, indeed insistent, practice for Kohut to gather Elizabeth and Thomas to read them early versions of the papers he was writing at an alarmingly rapid rate, even as he lamented the "slowness with which I work."[11] Vacations with his family became highly prized moments. A trip to Europe in August 1973, which included some psychoanalytic meetings in Paris, was a precious opportunity to be together. When Kohut's young German friend, the journalist Tilmann Moser, intruded on the Kohuts in Switzerland, seeking to spend a day with him, Kohut felt obliged to push him aside. The journalist was hurt and later wrote an anguished letter to Kohut, which prompted a fatherly but firm reply on the nature of serious relationships with people as "largely wordless and without clear contents and conceptions."[12] Probably the most rewarding aspect of the family closeness for Kohut was the healing of his relationship with Thomas (at least as Kohut experienced it). Even as cancer was suspected but not yet confirmed in the early fall of 1971, Kohut reached out playfully to his son in a chatty letter about soccer.[13] Three years later Kohut accepted a rare invitation to speak at the University of Minnesota in order to visit Thomas (with Elizabeth), who was doing his graduate work in history there, and his girlfriend, Susan.[14] The next year, when Thomas and Susan got married, Kohut described the event to Jacques Palaci as a "very significant event in our life and we are very happy about it."[15] Later, Kohut paid for the analysis of both Thomas *and* Susan. Once in a family gathering, Gretchen Meyer (Elizabeth's sister) referred to the need to save for old age. Kohut disagreed: "Look, the best guarantee for your old age, or anyone's old age, is the good will of the next generation."[16]

At the boundary of family and community, on the other hand, the impact of his illness was to make Kohut increasingly needy, self-involved, and difficult to tolerate. Fear of death, in general, lurks underneath extreme narcissism.[17] For Kohut, as well, his newly intense, complete self-absorption served to ward off fragmentation. It became his only available means of psychological survival. In social situations, for example, "he would get narcissistically inflated and all blown up and in that state do injurious things to people." He was "impossible." It was amazing to other women, reports Constance Goldberg, that Elizabeth never did anything to stop the process, never brought him back to reality. Perhaps she felt helpless. If anyone, for example, revealed the slightest indication of not being adequately educated or culturally informed—most Americans, one might say—Kohut could be mercilessly dismissive. "To say he [Kohut] didn't suffer fools lightly is an understatement. Lunch with Heinz and guests could be brutal."[18] If he discovered at a dinner party that no one spoke German he would recite long passages from Goethe.[19] Thomas Kohut was constantly embarrassed by his father's fits of narcissism in social settings and later would berate him about the need to rein himself in. "I can't control myself," Kohut explained more than once to his son.[20] Tilmann Moser once visited Kohut in Chicago in 1972. Kohut held a dinner party to introduce him to his closest Chicago friends. The host dominated everything, argued with Thomas, and let nothing happen around the table that was not centered on him. On the way down the elevator, Moser asked Arnold Goldberg how he stood it. "Only because he is a living national treasure," Goldberg replied.[21]

The quasi-family relationship that seemed to intensify in the wake of cancer during Kohut's last decade—or at least became more public in Kohut's urgent state—was that with Robert Wadsworth. The two apparently talked all the time, though Wadsworth remained at the margins of Kohut's life. Sometimes he entered more centrally, but in curious ways. In 1973 Kohut got an honorary degree from the University of Cincinnati and gave a number of lectures and seminars there. One "clinical case" he discussed was in fact his friend, Robert Wadsworth. His only concern was whether he had been clever enough to disguise it from Wadsworth himself, who was in the audience.[22]

The almost complete absence of letters between Kohut and Wadsworth for most of the 1970s—indeed from the time they met in 1940—except for a few letters between 1977 and 1981, is difficult to account for. Kohut carefully preserved his correspondence with everyone in the world, except with the man who mattered most in his life. One can, however, peer into the window of their relationship from the few surviving letters.[23] As he had in the 1940s, Wadsworth after 1977 wrote long, chatty letters to Kohut whenever they were separated about his life, his travels, his music, and his cats. A friend named Paqui was starting chemotherapy. A female relative in Seattle was expecting a baby. He cooked boiled liver for his cats, Schatzi and Lucius. He lunched on the Marshall Field's veranda with "all the old ladies" because it was raining and he missed his bus. He talked of his nervousness about taking the train home to Hyde Park, rather than the local bus or the Jeffrey Express. And he talked of his relationships. In 1977 he had a "new dancer friend" and wrote Kohut of an elegant meal with him "feasting on brook trout." Another day some of the dancer's friends joined them for dinner, and Wadsworth reported, "I'm becoming a cradle snatcher in old age!" Two years later Wadsworth mentioned planning to go to an organ recital at which he would probably see a dreaded figure, "my first glimpse of N. since you-know-when." Intimacy and a shared history are assumed in the surviving letters.

It would seem that Kohut's relationship with Wadsworth was platonic by the 1970s (whatever it was earlier). John Gedo feels that Kohut had "overcome" his homosexual ties with Wadsworth in his analysis with Ruth Eissler and that his "creativity helped to keep it in abeyance."[24] Arnold Goldberg, who entered Kohut's world as a junior colleague in the mid-1960s, feels that the Kohut he knew had at best a "latently homosexual" relationship with Wadsworth. "It was homo-erotic but not homosexual." Kohut, Goldberg says, had many male friends—Charles Kligerman, Jacques Palaci, Siegmund Levarie—and Wadsworth was one of those men with whom Kohut was "closely bonded." Constance Goldberg, a shrewd observer, added that the Kohut she knew was overflowing with passion about his work but was "profoundly asexual" with women.

For all of Kohut's often desperate efforts to keep the knowledge of his cancer secret and lead his life as though he were well, the fact of his illness was fairly widely known. Besides Siegmund Levarie and Wadsworth, he told Anna Freud and may have revealed himself to other old friends. Even many of his junior colleagues knew of his illness. Paul Ornstein and John Gedo had both visited him in the hospital and Ornstein reports seeing his enlarged spleen, which was outlined on Kohut's belly by a colored pen. They knew what the diagnosis had been. Kohut himself later told Michael Franz Basch about his cancer. Others found out through the rumor mill, which began grinding out the story almost as soon as Kohut entered the hospital.[25] When he was taken sick in 1977, Kohut was, after all, the leading psychoanalyst in Chicago, with an international reputation. Roy Grinker, the dictatorial head of psychiatry at Michael Reese Hospital for many years, found out right away about the cancer and apparently stopped people in the halls to let them know. That is how Arnold Goldberg first found out. In time everyone close to Kohut knew he had something like leukemia. Even many patients knew. He was quite open and honest about his sickness with one female patient of whom he was particularly fond.[26] In the group, there were often discussions about Kohut's illness, and concern that he might be sicker than he let on.[27] There were, as well, many clues, like the times he had to stop his Institute classes early because he felt tired from illness.[28]

And yet, astonishingly, the knowledge of Kohut's cancer in his circle and within the psychoanalytic community in Chicago after 1971 was largely disavowed. John Gedo, out of friendship, kept his own counsel before his rupture with Kohut in 1974, and was out of the loop after that. Some did not want to confront this disagreeable fact; others, like his special patient, treasured the secret knowledge they possessed and would not even consider compromising him. But how so many dealt with the knowledge of Kohut's life-threatening illness, as well as the power of his charismatic presence in their lives, says much about the human capacity to dissociate when confronted with something decidedly unpleasant. When Paul Ornstein visited Kohut in the hospital, Kohut gently but matter-of-factly said that he would really prefer if he would not tell anyone about his cancer. Ornstein not only obliged but entirely forgot himself what he had seen with his own eyes in 1971. For an entire decade, Ornstein, himself a medical doctor, wondered about the "mystery" of Kohut's recurrent colds and flus that were clearly systemic and related to the spreading cancer. Kohut once fainted while visiting the Goldbergs, which seemed not to prompt any deep inquiry.[29] Others in the group as well kept their information about Kohut's illness as a kind of middle knowledge, which is how many deal with anything touching death.[30] They all knew at some level, and yet did not know. They continued to act with each other and, probably even more importantly, with themselves as if he were fine and would live forever.

Kohut, of course, fed this process in a variety of ways. He had specifically instructed Paul Ornstein to keep the knowledge of his illness to himself. To others he acted as though he were not sick at all. He kept running his speedy mile each morning in Jackman Field across the street from the Cloisters (at least until about 1977), writing books, and becoming more famous. He also fended off the occasional question[31] about the cancer by completely obscuring his answer. When Paul Tolpin once asked him about it directly, he said: "Who knows who has leukemia?" and "What's leukemia, anyway?" Another time Kohut told Ernest Wolf that he had had a splenectomy but said it had nothing to do with leukemia. Perhaps Kohut rationalized these answers on the grounds that he actually had lymphoma rather than leukemia.[32] Kohut was in general unapproachable about personal issues, especially after he got cancer. He might, for example, regale his dinner guests with a story from his childhood in Vienna but bristle at a question that hinted of self-revelation. He gave out clear signals he did not want anyone to ask about things he did not want to talk about. And in the 1970s his close colleagues in Chicago who knew at some level about his cancer were all decidedly younger, in structurally weak and dependent relationships to him; some were (or had been) in treatment, others were (or had been) in supervision, and all were in thrall in his presence.

Sometimes, however, Kohut's ruses failed. Then he simply lied. One analyst in treatment with Kohut at the time heard the rumor and at his next session directly asked Kohut whether he had cancer. Kohut asserted that the rumor was untrue, that his protracted illness resulted from an infection secondary to his cardiac problems, and that though it had proven difficult to treat effectively it was not a malignancy. The patient was puzzled, but convinced, by this answer. And he continued to think that those who maintained that Kohut had cancer were misinformed or malicious. When, after Kohut's death, he finally learned that Kohut had indeed had cancer—and had not told him the truth—he was surprised. He is quite certain he would not have been undone by the truth, does not think Kohut thought he would have been, and cannot believe that Kohut doubted he would have kept quiet about it in deference to those who did not know.[33]

The attempt to contain the knowledge of his illness created other problems as well for Kohut. He was notorious throughout the country, indeed in the world, for turning down invitations to speak in the 1970s with flimsy excuses, which gave him the reputation of someone unwilling to defend his controversial ideas. In part Kohut constitutionally resisted public events that honored him (which of course fought against his fierce desire for fame and recognition). He knew public praise overstimulated him, and, as he once told Alexander Mitscherlich, he got little real pleasure from such praise and most often it caused him "distinct displeasure." He only endured exposure if it in any way furthered the "scientific or humanitarian ideals which I have espoused."[34] What he failed to mention to Mitscherlich was the role of his cancer[35] in keeping him out of the limelight. In Janet Malcolm's book *Psychoanalysis: The Impossible Profession*, Aaron Green speaks with disdain of the way Kohut sent his "emissaries" out to defend his ideas but would not go himself.[36] Green was right about sending out emissaries but wrong about the reason. Because of the cancer almost nothing except vacations and a rare professional obligation or event drew Kohut away from Chicago. Three times in four years he fended off invitations from Harvard to be a visiting professor and give special lectures. He turned down giving the Freud lecture in Vienna in 1972. He gave up on long-standing meetings in Princeton, ostensibly because the participants were "rather inimical toward my work." And so it went on an almost weekly basis for a man who was fast becoming the most controversial and reclusive psychoanalyst in the world. The only important exception Kohut made was to give seminars twice a year (until the mid-1970s) at the University of Cincinnati, which made him a visiting professor and bestowed on him a much-valued honorary degree in November 1973. There were several reasons for making Cincinnati an exception. It was relatively close and the Cincinnati Institute was historically a "geographic" of the Chicago Institute. But the real reason was that Paul Ornstein was indefatigable in lobbying for his home institution. Ornstein realized, however, after several futile efforts to get Kohut to make the trip,

Kohut strikes a formal pose in the mid-1970s. He was at the height of his creative output, though he worked in the shadow of illness. Courtesy Chicago Institute for Psychoanalysis

Kohut at a meeting in the 1970s. Courtesy Ernest and Ina Wolf

John Gedo, about 1970. Kohut's first and most important designated follower, Gedo broke noisily from the group in 1974. Courtesy John Gedo

Arnold Goldberg, Kohut's most trusted lieutenant, at a reception in the 1970s. Kohut picked Goldberg to lead the self psychology movement after his death. Courtesy Arnold and Constance Goldberg

Constance Goldberg with Sarah, 1978. Kohut wrote Arnold Goldberg on some drawings made by the three-year-old Sarah: "You, like all of us, must sometimes wonder what life is all about, whether it is worth the pain and anxieties. But seeing Sarah's colors and focus wipes all questions away." Courtesy Arnold and Constance Goldberg

Kohut with Paul Ornstein in the late 1970s. Warm, voluble, and outgoing, Ornstein was at the center of the group and one of Kohut's close friends. Courtesy Paul and Anna Ornstein

Anna Ornstein in the 1970s. A survivor of Auschwitz, Ornstein was supervised on a case by Kohut, who described the patient at length as Mr. M. in his second book, The Restoration of the Self.
Courtesy Paul and Anna Ornstein

Ernest and Ina Wolf, around 1980. The Kohuts often socialized with the Wolfs; throughout the 1970s they met for dinner at least once a month.
Courtesy Ernest and Ina Wolf

Paul Tolpin at a seminar in the 1970s. Tolpin was analyzed by Kohut in the early 1950s and in 1969 became a core member of the group. Courtesy Paul and Marian Tolpin

Marian Tolpin in the 1970s. Throughout the decade, Tolpin saw Kohut three times a week, mostly for analysis (when she lay on the couch) but often for supervision (when she sat in a chair face-to-face). It was her choice. Courtesy Paul and Marian Tolpin

Michael Franz Basch in the 1970s. After his analysis with Kohut in the 1950s, Basch at first tentatively but then wholeheartedly joined the group. He was a formal man, noted for his three-piece suits and French-cuffed shirts. Courtesy Carol Basch

David Terman, about 1975. Terman was a talented young analyst who kept just beyond the boundaries of the group. Kohut, it seems, drew on some of Terman's ideas without credit. Courtesy David Terman

Arnold Goldberg with Morton Shane at a seminar, late 1970s. Courtesy Paul and Anna Ornstein

A seminar in the late 1970s. Left to right: Estelle Shane, Kohut, Evelyn Schwaber, and Ernest Wolf. Courtesy Paul and Anna Ornstein

Dinner at the Goldbergs', late 1970s. From left: Evelyn Schwaber, Michael Franz Basch, Arnold Goldberg, Paul Tolpin, Ina Wolf. Courtesy Paul and Anna Ornstein

Ernest Wolf with Kohut, May 12, 1977. Wolf was Kohut's best friend in the group. Courtesy Ernest and Ina Wolf

Jacques Palaci around the time of Kohut's death in 1981. After 1978, Palaci made a habit of attending the annual self psychology meetings. Courtesy Diana Palaci

Two colleagues from California, Arthur Malin (left) and Bernard Brandchaft, talk with Marian Tolpin at dinner around 1980. Courtesy Paul and Anna Ornstein

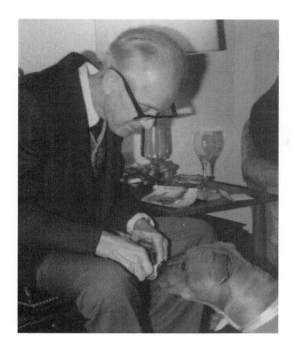

Kohut at a party, communing with a friendly dog, late 1970s.

Robert Stolorow with Kohut, August 20, 1981, in Carmel. After a talk, Kohut insisted on taking a picture of them together. He set up the tripod and camera, only to discover that he had ruined the film. Stolorow was sent to fetch film at a store. Half an hour later, with some humor, the picture was snapped. It is one of the last photographs of Kohut. Courtesy Robert Stolorow

Kohut at his desk in his beloved summer home in Carmel, California. Courtesy Ernest and Ina Wolf

Some of the members of the group assembled in 1989 for a going-away party for Elizabeth Kohut. She was leaving Chicago to enter a retirement home near her son, Thomas, and his family in Williamstown, Massachusetts. From left: David Terman, Mari Terman, Marian Tolpin, Paul Tolpin, Elizabeth Kohut, Arnold Goldberg, Michael Franz Basch, Constance Goldberg, and Carol Basch. Courtesy David and Mari Terman that he was reluctant to travel without Elizabeth at his side. Ornstein shrewdly got his chair to increase the travel budget for his project, and soon Kohut was a regular at the University of Cincinnati.[37]

But even closer to home, the stories grew exceedingly complex. In the fall of 1972 Ernest Wolf had the idea of organizing a sixtieth birthday celebration for Kohut the following spring. It happened that Wolf was then chair of the program committee for the Chicago Psychoanalytic Society. He thought it would be a good idea for the Society to sponsor such an event. Wolf brought up the idea rather innocently at a committee meeting and was immediately laughed out of the room. No one in Chicago, he was told, or indeed the world in psychoanalysis (including Freud), had had such a party on their sixtieth birthday—and now was not a good time to start. Wolf persisted, however, and brought up his proposal from the floor during a Society meeting. Again there was universal disdain for the idea, including most vigorously from some supposed friends of Kohut like Samuel Lipton. There was even some intrigue that followed the meeting. An anonymous threat was made to reveal some undisclosed incriminating information about Kohut (his illness, his sexuality?) if plans proceeded for the celebration. The rumor got back to Kohut as coming from the chair of the Society, Robert Kohrman. Kohut, in his usual indirect way, asked Charles Kligerman to confront Kohrman, who vigorously denied the charge in a letter to Kohut, who in turn accepted his explanation.[38]

Wolf, however, was not to be deterred. He asked a circle of friends each to donate $150 as seed money and to serve on a kind of informal program committee. He also secured the institutional and financial support of George Pollock, the director of the Institute, for what was emerging as a major conference. Most of the actual administrative and secretarial work was done by Ina Wolf, and Kohut himself played a role in writing to some of the more important people.[39] In one sense the event that eventually took place on June 2, 1973, in the Chicago-Sheraton Hotel was the first self psychology conference. Alexander Mitscherlich came from Frankfurt, Paul Parin from Zurich, and Jacques Palaci from Paris. Albert Solnit came from Yale, Robert LeVine from Harvard, René Spitz from Denver, Lawrence Friedman from New York, Joseph Lichtenberg from Washington, and a featured speaker was the urbane and distinguished historian of Vienna, Carl Schorske, from Princeton. People as diverse as Anna Freud, Ruth Eissler, Rudolph Loewenstein, and Marianne Kris let themselves be listed as members of the "Honorary Committee." Mary Gedo and Arnold

Goldberg were discussants on panels that were spaced throughout the day.[40]

The culminating event of the conference was an evening banquet with John Gedo as the speaker. Wolf naturally asked Kohut if he would participate sometime during the planned symposium, or at the banquet, or both. Kohut begged off with an absurd story about how he had developed a hysterical symptom that made him choke sometimes when he was talking. Whenever it happened, he said, he could not continue speaking. He was afraid he might be in the middle of a presentation and have to beg off in what would be very embarrassing circumstances. The lie, of course, contained within it a certain emotional truth and suggests Kohut's omnipotent sense that he could control the beliefs of others. In the end, Kohut agreed to be listed on the program after the banquet as giving "Some Thoughts in Response" to the main address by John Gedo. His supposedly modest comments became in fact a full-length presentation that he worked on quietly throughout the winter and spring and that turned out to be a blend of the personal and scientific perfectly suited for the occasion.[41] In retrospect, Wolf believes Kohut's initial hesitation about presenting had to do with his uncertainty about his health. He did not yet know what the course of his illness would be and how long he would last.[42]

Kohut's relationship to death, it is fair to say, was heavily split and disavowed. As with issues surrounding his identity, that is, his Jewishness, as well as his sexuality, there was a pattern of sustained contradiction. In a part of himself he acted psychologically as though he were in complete denial of death, while at the same time he lived in a self that he knew was dying. In such a world, his own personal myths took on oddly separate lives. Of course, he knew that he was sick, and at least until the end could talk about it quite rationally with the members of his family. But he also lived out a myth of health. He could lie about it convincingly because he had at some level convinced himself that he was an immortal genius struggling to complete his appointed task. In everything he became more focused and self-absorbed, alternately incredibly generous with friends, colleagues, and patients, and impossibly narcissistic.

That focus opened Kohut up to primal matters. In this perhaps his dissociation aided him. He reached new levels. It may well be that Kohut's great discoveries were all clinical in nature and made before he got cancer. These include, among other things, his recognition that analysts had been shaming their patients in the guise of offering interpretations;

that neurotic pathology is often a mere cover for narcissistic issues; that idealization is not a defense; that mirror transference needs are ubiquitous; and that rage is a by-product of self fragmentation.[43] But much can be said for Kohut's later work. In classical psychoanalytic terms, 1971 marked a turn for Kohut from clinical theorizing to his later, metapsychological phase, in which he built the outlines of a general theory of psychology. That was no mean feat. At the center of this latter phase in Kohut's thinking was a clear and explicit break from Freud and drive theory. He changed his understanding to an all-embracing definition of the self in the broad sense. The self found agency, one might say, in the Jamesian sense, as Kohut found his voice. Even something as seemingly small as taking the hyphen out of "self-object" in 1977 marked a rather large conceptual shift in his thinking. Death forced Kohut toward the more radical (and creative) implications of his thinking. It allowed him to come out from under the tyranny of Freud and the power of orthodox psychoanalysis. Death forced Kohut to think for himself.

Death also kept Kohut alive. He had a mission. Kohut's clear sense of his own immortality lay within self psychology. That was the arena in which he felt he could permanently leave his mark. His unusual talents and insights put him in touch with the pulse of the historical moment. Drive theory was dead, but no one before Kohut had found a way to question its basic assumptions while retaining the intellectual and spiritual core of psychoanalysis.[44] Kohut knew he had solved that problem but that his explanation was only half-clear by 1971. Illness threatened completion of that project. There is no question he talked about his illness and his work in these terms, at least to his family.[45] His fear, as death loomed, was of leading an incomplete life, of not finishing his work. Perhaps we all share such fears, but the dread of not finishing may well be that much more acute for the extremely talented. Kohut knew he was shaking up psychoanalysis in a profound way and that only he could carry through the revolution. His sense of himself required a fierce devotion to completing the task, which was now potentially compromised by premature closure.[46]

Authenticity became Kohut's obsession. He yearned at times with a kind of childlike innocence to be whole, complete, consistent, honest. And in his work he was. Yet in much of his personal life he harbored secrets and lies. Kohut himself at some level was acutely aware of these contradictions. In *The Analysis of the Self* there is a curious interlude of several pages about lying, which examines it from several points of view.[47] The passage is disconnected from the text, unintegrated into the argument. Kohut himself even seems to have been split off from this passage; after the book was published he once called Arnold Goldberg to ask *him* where he had written about lying.[48] The apparent point of the passage is Kohut's concern with the "unusually gifted person," which was part of his general concern with issues of integrity. Whenever that question came up later in other contexts, Kohut's favorite example was that of Beethoven. This great musical creator would not tolerate transposing a single musical note for any reason other than for purely artistic considerations. But once a piece was finished and had become a commercial product, Beethoven would often fraudulently sell it to several publishers at the same time to make more money. Kohut drew several conclusions from this story. One was that analysts must be absolutely scrupulous in their work with patients, but the rest of their lives was their own. Kohut, for example, always paid all his taxes but did not hold it against a candidate if he cut some corners in areas where discovery was almost impossible and where almost everybody else did the same thing. More importantly, however, Kohut pushed his theory about Beethoven in ways that showed his absolute sense of entitlement. "I would not be surprised," Kohut wrote Siegmund Levarie, "if a thorough investigation of such acts [Beethoven's lack of scruple about selling his manuscripts to several publishers simultaneously] would point up a higher morality, e.g. that, in order to protect and support his creative self, Beethoven considered the question of morality or immorality in the usual sense as irrelevant, just as a revolutionary might consider a murder in the service of his idealized cause as a moral act."[49] Genius, in other words, marches to its own unique ethical drumbeat.

For all his rationalizations, the reality of illness and death could not be ignored. It was with Kohut every moment of his life. His lifelong tendency toward compulsivity, for example, became exaggerated. He started tracking his weight every day to within a quarter of a pound around his ideal weight of 128, and kept meticulous records on small pieces of paper that he stapled together.[50] He became fussy in new ways; for example, he carried on a detailed correspondence with the Chicago Parks Department because the attendant at the underground lot where he parked his car failed to give him the right receipt, and he exploded at the Institute's administrator about the "Goddam radiator cover" in his office that he was unable to remove.[51] He also insulated himself against criticism, friendly or hostile. "You can say things 60 million times," he once told a seminar at

the Institute that was tape-recorded, "but people will still not hear you."
It reminded him of Laurence Sterne's Tristram Shandy, who has to pee
so badly that he does it out an open window. In the process, however,
Tristram has his penis injured by the falling window. He is okay, but a
rumor circulates around town that Tristram has lost it. There is a grave
family council about how to dispel the rumor. Uncle Toby suggests that
Tristram should publicly expose himself in the marketplace. But the father says morosely that even that will not work, because once people believe
a rumor, it won't go away.[52]

Kohut was not usually so light about the world's reactions to his work.
He wrote Jeanne Lampl-de-Groot in 1973, for example, praising her ability to absorb criticism and even learn from it. "I know I *should* feel the
same way," he says, but he can't. "It is only very rarely that I am able to
accept a direct, concrete emendation to the results which previous work
has led me." He once considered this attitude a flaw, a residue of his
grandiosity. But now he has worked it out differently. He grants that he
may be wrong about things, but the issue is simply that critics are not
generally "in tune with where I am working and struggling at the time."
To attend to noisy critics is to lose his concentration, which compromises "my ultimate results."[53]

In a related vein, Kohut closed out other thinkers to an extraordinary
degree after 1971. Basically, he stopped reading psychoanalytic literature,
something he made no attempt to hide. Before cancer Kohut was much
more scholarly than most realize and thoroughly versed in the literature
of psychoanalysis. But in his last decade he simply could not take in what
anyone else had to say. It broke his focus. He told his friend Jacques Palaci
that it had become too depressing to read what others had to say. "Either
you find they say it better or it's not good and you've wasted your time."
After you turn sixty, he said tellingly, you only have time to write and follow
your own thoughts and ideas. Reading is a "bottomless pit."[54] Kohut
hardly shut himself off from the world of ideas. He would glance at journals and occasionally refer to a paper by Freud. But when he read in his
last decade it was mostly outside of psychoanalysis. It was a decision that
freed him to create his own psychology, while opening up more time for
what he really loved anyway: listening to music and reading literature,
history, and the arts. His evening habit of putting aside an hour or so
after dinner to listen to music became now an unwavering ritual. He kept
careful lists of his favorite composers and once took the time to write
down his twenty-three most admired specific recordings of Beethoven,

Brahms, Prokofiev, Haydn, Ravel, Schubert, Bizet, Schoenberg, Bach, and Wagner for the International Repertory of Music Literature.[55] Kohut eagerly read a new translation of Marcel Proust's *A la recherche du temps perdu*. He returned to Thomas Mann, Kafka, Eugene O'Neill, Shakespeare, Goethe. He read new books coming out on Hitler and Nazi Germany. He returned to philosophy; one of his last book orders before he died was for Giambattista Vico's *Autobiography*. He even made time occasionally for a good mystery novel. But he kept away from science. He told Ernest Wolf that it would have to be up to others to fill in the references for his work. He was in too much of a rush.[56]

One important effect of Kohut's withdrawal into his own head was to sharpen, sometimes artificially, the differences between his emerging ideas and those of others. Certainly, the articulation of how his notions of the self departed from Freud's drive-based system became the obsession of his life. At least with Freud, Kohut acknowledged his debt. But with other thinkers he often talked and wrote as though there was no one ever who had written anything that remotely fitted into the tapestry of ideas he was weaving. All ego psychologists became epigones of Freud's flawed system. Erikson, whom he had never liked, was dismissed now with a wave of his hand. He stopped thinking altogether about people like Ferenczi, Abraham, and Rank. He hardly bothered with the Kleinians. Kohut's need to distance himself from all others was the only way he could protect his creativity. In the late 1960s, for example, Kohut had spoken generously (almost certainly more so than he really believed) about the way he and Margaret Mahler were "digging tunnels from different directions into the same area of the mountain," and about how the only real difference between his ideas and those of Otto Kernberg was that he thought narcissism was healthy while Kernberg thought it was pathological. By 1978 the differences between self psychology and these two figures now appeared to him to be "much more basic than they did a decade ago," especially around the outlook regarding the "scientific evaluation of the nature of man and the significance of his unrolling life." The effect especially of early selfobjects on development from the perspective of an adult differs dramatically from the direct observation of someone like Mahler and her limited conceptual categories. Kernberg, Kohut felt, was in another world altogether.[57]

Kohut's new focus had its downside. It led him at times, perhaps without full conscious awareness, to absorb the ideas of others as though they were his own. At least one grandiose encroachment led him perilously close to actual plagiarism, though most such charges were by innuendo and essentially frivolous.[58] John Gedo claims that Kohut intended to take his essential idea about the self ("Heinz swallowed my idea about self-as-structure") but then misunderstood it, so no actual plagiarism occurred.[59] As if that is not a complicated enough idea, Gedo also felt that Kohut "blackmailed" him into leaving the development of a psychology of the self exclusively to Kohut, not to mention failing to give him credit for suggesting the title of Kohut's first book. Kohut was, says Gedo, a "ruthless, egocentric person."[60] Such charges, of course, laced as they are with venom, are impossible either to refute or to confirm.

David Terman's experience with Kohut is quite a different matter.[61] No one was more loyal to the ideas of Heinz Kohut than Terman, a talented and creative psychiatrist who was a candidate at the Institute in the late 1960s. Somewhat younger in age and at an earlier point in his career than the people who made up the inner circle around Kohut, Terman staked out a position immediately outside the periphery of the group. His exposure to Kohut's ideas began early (when in 1966 he happened to take Kohut's first course at the Institute on his emerging ideas about narcissism). Two years later Terman began supervision with Kohut, which he paid for privately, because he was so eager to become more familiar with his work. Terman stayed in supervision with Kohut for nearly four years and in the end presented two different cases to him. In supervision Kohut was enormously helpful about the content of the patients' problems. He was always clinically perceptive and clarified all kinds of issues that helped Terman deal with some very difficult situations. Terman frequently had the experience, for example, that whenever he used Kohut's ideas in treating his patients, things invariably changed for the better and disturbances would be solved. Terman feels to this day that Kohut was far and away the best supervisor he ever had and that he learned more from him than from anyone else he ever dealt with.

But from the beginning of supervision, Terman had the distinct impression Kohut did not like him as a person. Kohut put him down for his failures with his patients, and even added occasional gratuitous insults, like telling him his French accent was bad when in fact Terman spoke the language fluently and took pride in the fact that French people had always complimented him on his accent. In supervision Kohut never provided support for him in his struggles with his patients. One case, in particular, was a very narcissistic woman who constantly berated Terman for being an idiot and failing her completely, which he was to learn is often the case with such patients. Kohut never once reassured him, or pointed out how common it was to go through what was happening to him. Kohut also never once told Terman he was doing as well with his patient as anyone could, or made him feel in any way that he was not as stupid as his patient thought he was. Kohut only commented on the patient and the patient's pathology.

As with many younger colleagues who were supervisees and often patients, Kohut easily socialized with Terman outside of the clinic. At the 1971 meetings of the International Psycho-Analytic Association in Vienna, Terman spent an afternoon with Kohut. These were the first meetings of the IPA in Vienna since the 1930s, and Anna Freud and everyone else in psychoanalysis attended. Terman at the time was head of the Candidates Association for the Western Hemisphere and made a presentation to a plenary session. Afterward, Kohut took Terman and his wife, Mari, to lunch and on a tour of Vienna. Kohut was expansive about how the restaurant where they ate was where Schubert had dined. Kohut talked lovingly of Schubert's songs, especially "Erlkönig," a haunting tale of a boy dying in his father's arms. Terman, a pianist himself, from then on began listening to and collecting various editions of Schubert's music. But that afternoon, Terman began to tire of Kohut, who talked nonstop about this and that site, its history and how it connected with his life, and what his experiences had been in relation to it. Well before the tour was over Terman began to feel almost nauseated at the complete self-absorption of Kohut and his utter lack of regard for Terman's needs and interests at that moment.

And yet Terman continued to be enthusiastic about Kohut's work. "I have no doubt that I witnessed an historic occasion this afternoon," Terman wrote Kohut in early 1974 after a seminar at the Institute. Kohut's thoughts, Terman added, "may do no less than mark the entrance into a cultural and human expansion of utterly unanticipated dimensions."[62] After Terman's graduation from the Institute (in 1972), he began teaching courses there[63] and doing research in areas that related to what has become self psychology. He got to know John Gedo fairly well (and Gedo still regards him as the most original of all Kohut's followers),[64] as well as Ernest Wolf. In 1972 the three published a paper jointly on adolescent process as a phase in self development.[65]

Terman also began to think ahead of where Kohut was at the time in relation to both the concept of lines of development and the general meaning of that central psychoanalytic myth, the Oedipus complex. Kohut himself was still ostensibly committed to the idea that there are two lines of development, a narcissistic or self line and another, object-related line, which was the way he stayed tied to drive theory as he was in fact soaring beyond it. The single most important consequence of this bifurcated theory was that Kohut insisted to himself and therefore to others that he retained the idea of the Oedipus complex as central to development. Terman, to his credit, recognized the intellectual artificiality of such a position before anyone else. In a paper that he wrote in the fall of 1974 and finished in early 1975, "The Self and the Oedipus Complex," Terman formulated the notion that it only made sense to think of one line of development, that of the self, and that the Oedipus complex, such as it is, can only reasonably be considered a phase in self development rather than some kind of supraordinate experience out of which self structures emerge.

Terman felt excited about his paper, which seemed to him a creative extension of the ideas in *The Analysis of the Self* and a formulation Kohut would welcome. Not so. Terman gave the paper in draft form to Kohut in February 1975. Assuming the stern voice of the mainstream psychoanalyst, Kohut replied in a long letter, pointing out all the oedipal material Terman had missed in his discussion of the case at the heart of the paper.[66] Terman then presented his paper at a meeting of the Chicago Psychoanalytic Society on May 27, 1975.[67] Philip Holtzman, one of two commentators, delivered a blistering attack full of vitriolic scorn. He was incensed at the very idea of one line of development of the self and the abandonment of the traditional understanding of the Oedipus complex. As best Terman can remember, Kohut was in the audience and added his own fuel to these fires.[68] But even if Kohut missed the Society meeting, Terman recalls several private conversations with Kohut about the paper. Terman was struck with his own complete inability to change Kohut's mind. In fact, Terman felt that Kohut seemed unable to get what he was talking about.[69]

Two other experiences that year further discouraged Terman in his quest to have his ideas recognized. First, his paper was turned down by the *Annual of Psychoanalysis* (which was published by the Chicago Institute) in a dismissive letter written by Michael Franz Basch on behalf of the editorial committee. It is impossible to say whether the ever-loyal Basch was acting as Kohut's delegate, consciously or unconsciously, but the rejection made Terman depressed and feel isolated.[70] Then, at a panel that December in New York at the meetings of the American Psychoanalytic

Association on oedipal issues, Terman was taken to task by Otto Kernberg and others for harboring such stupid ideas about the Oedipus complex.[71] Terman decided to put the paper away, and only published it a decade later.[72]

All this would be an insignificant and passing episode in the history of psychoanalysis, except that within five years Kohut came to precisely the position Terman had arrived at in the winter of 1974–1975. Terman essentially realized the logic of Kohut's own argument in *The Analysis of the Self* before Kohut himself. Kohut began to move in Terman's direction in his second book, *The Restoration of the Self* (1977), when he distinguished the Oedipus complex from an oedipal period. But by his last book, which he worked on through 1980 and 1981 and which was published posthumously in 1984 (*How Does Analysis Cure?*), Kohut goes on at great length about how there is one line of development and the so-called Oedipus complex is only one potential phase in self development.[73] Nowhere in either book is any credit given to Terman, nor did Kohut ever say anything to Terman, or to anyone else in the self psychology movement, as best one can tell, to indicate that Terman deserved to be recognized for his contribution. Undoubtedly Terman's formulations were tentative and incomplete and not expressed in the context of the general psychology toward which Kohut was moving. For that reason and because Terman's ideas were imbedded in Kohut's own work, the failure in attribution probably does not quite qualify as plagiarism (though the term means the appropriation without credit of the words *or* the ideas of someone else). Terman himself, generous perhaps to a fault, feels that Kohut almost certainly would have arrived at his final theoretical positions without having read the Oedipus paper, and he therefore believes that one cannot call Kohut's appropriation of his ideas plagiarism.[74] But then again, maybe Kohut would not have gotten to that point without the earlier work of Terman lodged in the more distant recesses of his memory. It is a rather basic rule of science that you must recognize someone else who has an idea that is communicated to you concretely in conversation *and* in writing before you yourself write it up in your own terms. Kohut seemed to disavow what Terman shared with him in 1975 and then convince himself it was his own discovery five years later. Kohut's treatment of David Terman was, at the very least, unconscionable and reveals his most unlovely side.

Twenty-one

ON RAGE

Perhaps the most common criticism of Kohut's work is that he fails to deal with aggression adequately. In his emphasis on empathy, so the argument goes, Kohut directed attention away from human evil and the violent potentials in the self that are essential to grasp and confront if we are to understand the astonishing capacity of humans to engage in war, persecution, torture, abuse, and ordinary, garden-variety cruelty. For Kohut, it is said, things are sugarcoated. One loses entirely the crucial insights Freud gained into the "seething cauldron" of id impulses. Even if one concedes, as most observers now would, that classical psychoanalysis as a form of treatment is only clinically relevant in radically modified form, Freud as a philosopher of the human soul properly understood and appreciated the varied forms of aggression. Kohut is uplifting, the critics say, but in the end superficial, naive, best fit for the surface, where Americans mostly dwell psychologically.

Such criticism drove Kohut to distraction. It was the kind of charge that led him to say his critics read *between* the lines of his work.[1] His views on aggression differed from those of Freud, to be sure, but he hardly ignored the topic; he was, in fact, deeply concerned with the issue of aggression, both at the level of the individual and in history, and he had some original things to say about it. His strategic mistake may have been partly that he separated out his thoughts on the subject from *The Analysis of the Self* and then did not return to them in any systematic way in his last two books, especially *The Restoration of the Self*, which remains his most widely read work.[2] Perhaps Kohut felt there was no need for reiteration, since he had absolute faith in the completeness of his one full-length discussion of the topic, "Thoughts on Narcissism and Narcissistic Rage," which he first delivered in New York as the A. A. Brill Lecture of the New York Psychoanalytic Society on November 30, 1971, and published the following year in the *Psychoanalytic Study of the Child*.[3] There was no question in Kohut's mind that this was the "best paper" he ever wrote.[4] It brought together years of reflection and articulated a nuanced position about aggression that has yet to be fully appreciated in psychoanalytic theory or psychology in general.

Kohut's concern with rage also had a powerful personal subtext. He began writing about rage during his 1971 summer vacation in Carmel as he awaited the dreaded diagnosis of cancer after postponing further tests to ascertain the cause of his hardened spleen; he then finished the paper that fall after the confirmation and initial treatment of the disease.[5] Kohut railed at the gods who sought to destroy him but took his misery to a higher level of human understanding.

Kohut's rage paper begins slowly, in the rhetorical style he used in teaching seminars—circling, associating, warming to his subject. He describes two works of the great German writer, Heinrich von Kleist, and their relation to narcissism and rage. He talks about Emil Ludwig's biography of Freud, which was unusually hateful and seemed to be a response to a critical comment about the author by Freud two decades earlier.[6] He talks about the irrelevance of Alfred Adler's idea of "organ inferiority" for any deep understanding of rage. And with a wave of his hand he dismisses as utterly "simplistic" the then-dominant psychoanalytic notions (derived from Freud) that war, intolerance, and persecution are due, ultimately, to a regression to the undisguised expression of a drive, that is, that aggression is part of our biological makeup and that the evils wrought by human aggression can be accounted for by the thinness of the "civilized layer of the human personality." Neither history nor the human soul can be contained in such reductionistic formulas, he felt. Too much of violence, for example, is ordinary and all too human, as with the Nazis. The most gruesome destructiveness, Kohut says, is not the result of wildly regressive and primitive behavior; it is "orderly and organized activities in which the perpetrators' destructiveness is alloyed with absolute conviction about their greatness and with their devotion to archaic omnipotent figures."

Rage, Kohut notes, comes with many faces, from the fleeting annoy-

ance of a minor criticism to the furor of the catatonic or the grudges of
the paranoic. But it is never "normal" and part of a developmental phase
to which one returns under stress. We do not regress to rage. There is no
such thing as primary and secondary rage, just as there is no developmental line of rage. Rage only exists in its raw, primitive, elemental form
when aggression is mobilized in the service of images from early childhood. Mature aggressions, on the other hand, are bounded. Their aim is
definite, such as defeating an enemy who stands in the way of a cherished
goal, or the aggressive pursuit of someone we love.[7] One's object in such
encounters is regarded as a separate center of initiative, someone who is
relatively autonomous and whom we relate to as a whole being. The enemy
that calls forth rage, on the other hand, is not a person but a flaw in a
world experienced as a mere extension of self, an infantile psychological
environment that precariously maintains self-esteem.

The phenomenology of rage is that it consists of a desperate need for
revenge, an unforgiving fury for righting the wrong of a minor irritant
and undoing a hurt by any means, along with a "deeply anchored, unre-
lenting compulsion" in the pursuit of one's aims. There can be no rest
for someone who has suffered a narcissistic injury, which suggests the
origin of rage in perceived psychological injuries like ridicule, contempt,
and conspicuous defeat. The sequence here is important. The narcissistically vulnerable person responds with heated imagination to an otherwise
minor slight, which in turn provokes a state of fragmentation that unravels the self. Rage is the by-product.[8] For Freud, it is worth noting, the
sequence is exactly the opposite. We are constantly stirred by aggressive
impulses that are ultimately of a biological origin and are only contained
by the thin defensive wall erected in the process of ego development. It is
only natural that things break through at times. In fact, the capacity to
"sublimate" aggressive drive urges is a rare gift. The human norm for
Freud is aggression and violence. His is a grim view of human nature and
his theory a grand elaboration of his dark pessimism.

In rage, as Kohut sees it, there is always a lack of proportion between
the perceived injury and the nature of the revenge that is pursued. There
is an utter disregard for reasonable limitations on the hurt one can cause
others. Rage involves a boundless wish to obtain revenge (as in some di-
vorces).[9] Empathy, most of all, is missing for those felt to be offenders.
At the same time, the pursuit of that goal sharpens one's reasoning capacities. Cognition is not compromised but enhanced. Rage, like death,
focuses the self. Captain Ahab calls forth his greatest skills to pursue the

tormenting white whale, Moby Dick. Michael Kohlhaas, in the story by Heinrich von Kleist of the same name, mobilizes a wide following and creates havoc and revolution in his determined effort to right the wrongs he has suffered. And a leader like Hitler, filled with inchoate rage, was able to subordinate a whole class of rational technicians to help him realize his grandiose and paranoid dreams. In this regard, Kohut was particularly interested in the relationship between Hitler and his architect, Albert Speer, who shared none of his Führer's personality characteristics but played an important historical role in actualizing his hatreds.[10]

The forms of rage can be acute or chronic. The explosion of wrath in the clinic is most familiar to analysts treating those with disturbances of the self who respond with fury at the analyst's minor failures to remember something, or at otherwise innocuous moments of inattention or small irregularities in schedule. There are, of course, times when a patient's anger at an analyst's laziness, stupidity, or inconsiderateness is appropriate. But even the best and most attentive therapist cannot forestall the occasional rage of the narcissistically needy patient, who is primed to respond with rage at any and all failures in empathy. Rage can also become chronic. In such a case a person gets organized psychologically around rage, which becomes the purpose of one's being. Nothing is more terrifying, or tragic. Chronic rage that might begin in a grudge and end in a vendetta is "the most pernicious" of all human afflictions, says Kohut. And like so much else in human psychology, such forms of rage can be perpetrated in the cycle of generations, whether in the hills of West Virginia or in the racial antagonisms of urban America.

The signs and symptoms of rage in patients and more generally in the self can be direct or quite subtly indirect. In its overt form, an analyst (or anyone at all psychologically sensitive, for that matter) can easily feel in others the archaic fury of rage, its lack of empathy, its disconnection from realistic goals, and its lack of proportion to the injury that was suffered. But for the most part rage lies hidden behind a wall, where it is carefully disguised to protect against the debilitating effects of its expressions. The most common such form of self protection is literally a wall, that is, people retreat into their homes, where they isolate themselves socially and become detached and cut off. Many people, of course, who are lonely and depressed seek solace in their apartments filled with the noise of television and perhaps the company of pets. But someone attempting to contain rage lives not only alone but with a fantasized sense of superiority.

One of the more dramatic forms of rage is the self-mutilation of psychotics. Such patients regularly cut themselves badly in often baffling ways. Kohut argues that what is happening prior to the cutting is a breakup of the body self during states of fragmentation. One is no longer whole. There is no cohesive image or symbol of the self. The fragments become unbearable to retain and a great burden that requires removal. The eye, for example, must be cut out ("If thine eye offend thee, pluck it out," Kohut quotes from Matthew 18:9). An offending body part, now experienced as no longer part of the self, must be removed. The part is dead, which he still awkwardly expresses as having lost its "narcissistic libidinal cathexis." The self-mutilation of psychotics, in this sense, is a desperate attempt to restore vitality and, however confused, recover life and hope.

Suicide, as well, may grow out of a rage response to the loss of self cohesion, at least in cases in which the suicide is preceded by feelings of unbearable emptiness and intense shame. The whole self no longer feels alive. There is a complete loss of self-object connection. An attenuated form of this response can emerge from the matrix of physical illness or disability. Sometimes children, for example, will have a "catastrophic reaction" to a brain injury that curtails one's ability to carry out simple tasks. In adults, there is often a great deal of rage following strokes, in cases of aphasia, or in the early stages of Alzheimer's. The disease or physical injury, in such cases, disrupts one's self organization, generating shame and fragmentation. The injury comes from outside the self and yet is experienced within it. We first feel through our bodies. That inchoate state of the body-self returns in illness or injury. One feels fragmented, full of shame, without words or meaningful forms of expression. Such is the breeding ground of rage.

An even more attenuated form of the same process—Kohut's version of the psychopathology of everyday life—has to do with simple forgetting. New patients, for example, not to mention most humans, often react to their own slips of the tongue with rage. Their reaction has nothing to do with the revelation of their unconscious motivations in the slip itself, as Freud argued. The issue is more the exposure and resulting shame from accidental self-revelation that is experienced as a narcissistic injury. There are many such fleeting moments of rage in daily life. It is not uncommon, for example, to find oneself excessively preoccupied with a situation where one has suffered a slight. Perhaps a joke fell flat at a party. A new outfit was criticized. A waiter was arrogant and surly about one's ignorance of fine wines. One stays with the scene, reworks it, remembers and replays it, far out of proportion to the significance of the event itself. The purpose of such preoccupation is to magically wipe out the incident, even to the point of doing away with oneself to eliminate the tormenting memory. In the most extreme cases, one fantasizes death to hold back being flooded with shame.

The treatment of rage in narcissistic patients can be quite difficult. One must be prepared for many assaults. The slightest failure in empathy evokes wrath. But sometimes, especially with the most strongly armored patients, an expression of rage is to be welcomed. Treatment gradually loosens the defensive walls with which such patients have protected themselves, releasing rage, either in the transference or in acted-out form outside of treatment. Such eruptions represent positive, forward movement, an opening up, however, and should be readily accepted by the analyst. At the same time, expressions of rage should never be confused with mature aggression. The difference is huge. An advanced and healthy self aggressively seeks out others or their symbolic equivalents. "Narcissistic rage," on the other hand, "enslaves the ego and allows it to function only as its tool and rationalizer."

The working-through process of therapy via the empathic responsiveness of the analyst expands the vulnerable self and allows it to grow and become more cohesive. Gradually, old hurts are relinquished. Mr. A., for example, found himself able to contain his biting sarcasm. Mr. P., whose pathology lay between a perversion and a paranoid psychosis, often transgressed sexually, after which he was particularly harsh on his young son. The result was that the child developed a stammer. The boy's tongue, Kohut says, became a battleground of preverbal rage. In such cases one can never expect treatment to radically alter the self. The relinquishment of narcissistic claims, which is the precondition of rage, can never be absolute. The therapeutic goal, in other words, is the gradual transformation of the troubled self out of which rage emerges. But one cannot make excessive demands for improvement in the patient, Kohut stresses. There will always be a "residual propensity to be temporarily under the sway of narcissistic rage" when such a patient's "archaic narcissistic expectations are frustrated."

Kohut concludes his essay by explicitly, though very tentatively, extending his ideas about rage to groups in history. His key point is that some of the most important crises in human experience (like the Nazi period) make sense only in terms of the workings of rage at collective levels. Kohut kept pondering these issues well into 1973 and was soon at work at what is probably his most complicated but interesting paper on rage, history, and charisma. The historian John Demos later remembered fondly when Kohut first presented this work. The paper was distributed ahead of time to a small group of invited participants. There was a "keen sense of anticipation and excitement—mixed with just a little bit of awkwardness" as Kohut arrived. He began by saying he would perhaps make a few preliminary comments about his paper to "break the ice" and proceeded to talk extemporaneously for most of the next hour. Demos was stunned. "Such an ice breaking I have never experienced," he said, "either before or since." In fact, "it was if some vast arctic sea had been completely and dazzlingly rearranged, by the time these so-called 'preliminary remarks' were finished." Demos felt he had observed a "truly creative intelligence at work from close up."[11]

In his charisma paper, Kohut takes as his point of reference how difficult it is for analysts to think calmly about Freud, given their deep immersion in his works and even his inner world through the close study of *The Interpretation of Dreams*, which is so central to the curriculum of all institutes (even though he makes some assumptions about the prevailing idealization of Freud that could no longer be taken for granted today). "The pull toward establishing a gross and uncontrolled identification with Freud is strong," he says, as is the equally intense and irrational debunking of the toppled father figure. But the powerful idealization of Freud for analysts "forestalls the development of certain exquisitely painful experiences of narcissistic imbalance in the analyst (such as pangs of jealousy and envy)," while for the movement as a whole it serves as a counterforce to the unfortunate tendency toward splinter groups. As Freud himself argued, psychoanalytic group cohesion is established in part and safeguarded by the imago of the leader, whom all members hold in common as their collective ego ideal. But more importantly: "A firm group self supports the productivity of the group just as a firm individual self supports the productivity of the individual."

Freud's self-analysis is Kohut's point of departure into this "group self." Many poets and artists, he notes, have been systematically introspective at least since the beginning of culture, and both Freud and Josef Breuer had experience with the analysis of others by the late 1890s. But what marked Freud's self-analysis as a first was the systematic, scientific way he went about introspection that made his method generally available to others. His analysis, furthermore, was for the first time one that aimed at the "depth-psychological comprehension of the total personality" as opposed to the more narrow focus on symptom relief. But he was not entirely alone in his endeavors. Freud managed his analysis only with the timely help of Wilhelm Fliess, whom he shrewdly kept at a good distance (Berlin) and only occasionally visited. What exactly did Fliess mean to Freud?

Fliess was clearly not the traditional analyst for a patient in the process of self-exploration. For one thing, he was removed from the scene. It is difficult to imagine real treatment from someone outside of the room. That separation between the two men is partly why Freud never came to understand transference through all the years of his relationship with Fliess. Freud was not in a familiar healing relationship with his friend and thus did not experience the feelings toward him that he would later understand are the heart of the analytic experience. What was going on for Freud, Kohut argues, was instead a "transference of creativity" of his narcissistic, or self, needs. Freud came to require the imagined presence of Fliess as a crucial participant in his own inner struggles as he gained his great insights. Freud sought out another person to join him in his universe whom he needed to idealize far beyond reality in the years of discovery. "Freud's self-analysis," Kohut says, "was a creative spell which was simultaneously worked through analytically," just as Mr. E. transformed his perverted gazing at genitals into original and creative work in photography.

Freud, too, in his creative struggles in the late 1890s and early 1900s, was enfeebled and at the mercy of powerful forces he could not fully control. Such in general is the process of any genius at work. Discovery leads into "lonely areas" and results in a "deep sense of isolation." Freud found some protection against annihilation at these moments by choosing a person in his environment whom he could see as all-powerful, a figure with whom he could "temporarily blend." Nor was Freud's experience unique. Picasso sought out Georges Braque during the discovery of cubism in much the same way, building him up in his mind as his alter ego. At the height of their mutual exploration of the new art form their paintings became virtually indistinguishable.[12] The reverse of this process, "the disintegration of artistic sublimation," can be seen in Mann's *Death in Venice*, in which Aschenbach unravels (and dies) because of his love for the boy Tadzio.

At this point Kohut asks a deceptively simple question: "What are the characteristic features of the person who is especially suitable to become the admired omnipotent self-object for the creative person during the period when he makes his decisive steps into new territory?" The answer is surprising. It seems the others in these relationships must possess "unshakable self-confidence" and express their opinions with an "absolute certainty" bordering on paranoia. What makes such people uniquely suited to play this role of omnipotent selfobject is the ease with which they judge others and point out their moral flaws. Most of us have internal restraints on such exuberant self-expression. But no restraint exists for those charismatic or messianic figures who have identified with their own grandiosity or their idealized image of themselves. Without shame or hesitation, these figures "set themselves up as the guides and leaders and gods of those who are in need of guidance, of leadership, and of a target for their reverence."

Charismatic figures have few feelings of guilt and seldom suffer any pangs of conscience for their behavior. They are unusually "sensitive to injustices" and quick to accuse others in very persuasive ways. That in turn evokes guilt and shame in their followers, who become submissive and allow themselves to be "treated tyrannically." Such behavior on the part of charismatic leaders appears to originate in a basic "stunting of their empathic capacity." They have little real understanding of other people's needs. In the childhoods of charismatic and messianic leaders, Kohut guesses that their initial experience of feeling bathed in mirroring and in the presence of idealized figures with which they can merge is followed by "abrupt and unpredictable frustrations." Their unique resolution of that trauma, perhaps drawing on some congenital abilities, is then to take over for themselves those selfobject functions that should have been performed for them. The cost, however, is that they continue to live in a decidedly archaic world filled with rage at the torment they suffered in first knowing the security and comfort of empathy and then having it abruptly withdrawn. In response they become "superempathic with themselves and their own needs" but furious with the world. They assert their perfection self-righteously and demand control over others to serve as vicarious regulators of their self-esteem. Their peculiar sensitivities put them in direct touch with the archaic needs of the group.

Such are the Fliesses of the world—or the Hitlers, or any number of cult leaders who have imposed themselves on the religious landscape over the millennia. There is thus an analogy between the self needs of the creative individual, particularly at confused moments of discovery or insight, and what Kohut calls the "group self" in the throes of historical crisis. Kohut is cautious about the practice of psychologically naming complex collective configurations in terms of individual psychology. He considers the term "group self" (wisely, one might add) only "potentially fruitful" and thinks it much too early to tell whether such efforts will be successful. But there are ways in which Germany, for example, after the First World War, showed at the level of the group the kind of self depletion Kohut writes about with Mr. E. or Freud in the midst of his creative crisis. Extreme vulnerability made Germans collectively yearn for the utter certainty of Hitler and his pronouncements and opened it to radical change in its history and institutions.[13]

The glue of the group self in such extreme situations is rage in its chronic, organized form. The worst abuses of Nazism were "decidedly human" and "an intrinsic part of the human condition." The most gruesome human destructiveness, he says, comes not in the form of "wild, regressive, and primitive behavior," but as highly focused and organized activities "in which the perpetrators' destructiveness is alloyed with absolute conviction about their greatness and with their devotion to archaic omnipotent figures." In part, such attitudes inspire violence because of the grandiosity that gets attached to one's group. The perfection of the "we" in turn requires the degradation of the "other" outside the group. But the more crucial factor is the way rage comes to structure basic motivations within the group. Injury and trauma create rage, which can then come to unify the self and make it coherent *and* deadly at the same time. As with the paranoic, the self, whether individual or at the level of the group, "has a firm, an impeccably firm, a frighteningly firm self, once his convictions are established. . . ."[14]

With an expanding sense of confidence, Kohut in his rage and charisma papers takes on the challenge of the philosopher and the historian. He felt comfortable in his wider disciplinary commitments. "I am not a historian," he said in a lecture late in 1973—"unfortunately." He believed the integration of self psychology into history—as a craft and as the expression of collective memory—was the challenge for the future, "the natural development that ought to follow the revolutionary step Freud took with regard to the psychology of the individual." Drive theory leads the unwary into the private and inaccessible realm of a figure's loves and hates, unconscious fantasies, and symbolic interactions with contemporaries. Self theory, on the other hand, encourages the investigator to avoid such pitfalls. It is the readily observable—the ideals and values, the grandiosity, the work, the fears, the rage, and the complex issues of self-esteem maintenance—that is of primary concern in self psychology. Such an approach hardly abandons what psychoanalysis calls the genetic per-spective and what historians regard as the central question of origins. But Kohut gives new psychoanalytic meaning to matters closer at hand in time and more comprehensible in form. Kohut manages to recover for histo-rians what is most usable in psychoanalysis. Knowledge in general, he felt, cannot be artificially separated from a human purpose: "The idea that his-tory is only a science of data collection and meant only for other histori-ans is utter nonsense." "The inquiring human mind," he once said in response to criticism from the literary critic Erich Heller, "will not be stifled by prohibitions."[15]

Twenty-two

SELF AND THEORY

Kohut, probably more than any other psychological theorist in recent decades, wrote in general about humans in ways that grew intimately out of his own experience (while never doubting his ideas were, in turn, historically conditioned). But his personalism per se hardly compromises the integrity of his ideas.[1] Perhaps any thinker, especially a psychological one, draws on his or her own conflicts as the basis of insight. The question, however, is not whether theories are subjective but whether such insight can be generalized. In this regard, it may be that the patterns of Kohut's life reflect the times and that his finger is unusually tight on the collective pulse. Kohut, it seems, creatively extends himself into his ideas, weaving a web that catches us up out of threads from his own past.

The extrapolation from Kohut's own experience, for example, led directly or indirectly to his insights about empathy, narcissism, the selfobject, grandiosity, idealization, sexualization, self-state dreams, and many other constructs. The more one learns of Kohut's life, in fact, the better one can appreciate the nuances of his ideas. To know the actual Else deepens one's understanding of Kohut's explanation for the development of splits in the self as a result of inadequate mirroring. To know Felix is to grasp how varied and fragile idealization can be. And mirroring and idealization, in turn, are the constituent elements in a self psychology that has important meanings in the realm of culture and history.

Sometimes, however, the self-referential quality of Kohut's writings limits the more general applicability of his psychology. Take, for example,

Kohut's view of what he considered the defining personality split of the
era, occurring so frequently that he was inclined "to assign to it the label
of a particular form of psychopathology." In this personality—as he said
in a 1973 seminar—the male child is strongly bonded with the mother
who "stimulates the child's grandiosity beyond its phase-appropriate
duration and favors the child above the father." The father is demeaned
while the child's self-esteem expands to unhealthy limits. The child senses
that he will retain his mother's adulation only if he remains a part of her
personality. But maturational pressures induce the boy to seek separateness from the mother. He wants his independence. He wants to roam the
world. He wants to be like his father, to be a chip off the old block, which
in turn touches the father's pride. That is how these patterns should unfold and normally do. But in the case of our representative boy the mother
interferes and refuses to allow him room to separate. The demeaned father in turn is unable to set himself up as an alternative figure of idealization, except in passing and in some "enclave" of the child's self. Out of
such a configuration comes a "vertical split" in which the boy becomes
boastful and overly exhibitionistic but without a real sense of independent initiative. He is only part of the mother's self and her psychological
organization. In the central part of the boy's self there is "a deeply sad
and deprived" core in which aspirations to become independent and successful as a man have never been encouraged.[2]

Kohut's abiding self-reference included, as well, the way he privileged
male stories in his clinical case material. There were exceptions. Miss F.
was the first to define the contours of grandiosity for him, and he often
mentioned her significance for him in the formation of his theory.[3]
Marian Tolpin spoke warmly of Kohut's empathy as a therapist, as have
many other female patients.[4] The distinction seems to be between Kohut
as therapist versus Kohut as a man of ideas. As a psychoanalyst, Kohut
seemed easily able to transcend the limits of gender and understand in
depth the experience of individual women he treated. But as a theoretician Kohut excluded, if not quite banished, women from his clinical
discourse. He acknowledged a definite imbalance in the proportion of
men to women in his practice, which he accounted for, inadequately one
might say, in terms of having a downtown practice.[5] In his papers and
books, mostly from his last decade (with the exception of Mr. H. from
the music paper in the 1950s), Kohut discusses twenty-four lettered cases,
omitting S and T. Of the lettered cases, fourteen are people he treated
(Mr. A., Mr. B., Mr. C., Miss F., Mr. G., Mr. H., Mr. J., Mr. N., Mr. O.,

Mr. P., Mr. Q., Mr. U., Miss V., and himself as Mr. Z). Three of the lettered cases he treated were women: Miss F. of *The Analysis of the Self*, Miss V. of *The Restoration of the Self*, and one unidentified male case in *Analysis* who is actually a woman in disguise.[6] One should add to this list three other unlettered cases of patients he discusses in his last book, *How Does Analysis Cure?*, including a middle-aged male lawyer (pp. 121–151), a woman (pp. 195–196), and a male scientist mentioned in a footnote (p. 218 n. 3). That makes the proportion thirteen men to four women whom Kohut actually treated and about whom he felt comfortable discussing in support of his ideas. The ratio remains pretty much the same if one includes the many instances in which Kohut drew on the work of his supervisees or colleagues for clinical examples. From such cases where he was one step removed (which aided the process of disguise), Kohut included often detailed discussions of eight men and only two women (Mr. E., Mr. I., Mr. K., Miss L., Mr. M., Mr. R., Mr. U., Mr. W., Mr. X., and Mrs. Y.). That changes the numbers to twenty-one men versus six women. Females were hardly negligible in Kohut's world of the self, but at the same time, it has to be noted, he was mostly drawn to the stories of men as paradigmatic of the culture, even though self psychology was almost immediately recognized by feminists as the first important psychoanalytic theory that validated the experience of women.[7]

Kohut's cases, furthermore, fit a gendered schema in which men and women act roles from his own private script. As far as men are concerned, the remote, unavailable father, the Felix of Kohut's own past, enters into his son's experience as a difficult source of idealization. Mr. A.'s father, for example, who repeatedly tried to start new enterprises in a new land, would kindle his own and his son's enthusiasm but then be forced to sell out in a panic because of his lack of familiarity with the American business scene. The father would then get deeply depressed and develop various hypochondriacal complaints, for which he would often take to his bed.[8] The scientist in *Cure* is denigrated by the overpowering mother and works out a secret "basement game" which he plays with his son.[9] Mr. B.'s father virtually abandons the family in the wake of dealing with his crypto-psychotic wife. Even in his teaching, Kohut seemed able to hear only what he wanted regarding fathers. Once in a seminar at the Institute a case was presented of a man whose father died or left home when he was about thirteen years old. The mother had been depressed and was described as a "wet-blanket" type of person. What was evolving in the analysis was an idealizing transference that seemed to be father-related.

Meanwhile, however, the patient was complaining about his wife, who was depressed and angry. A candidate asked Kohut when there would be a time in the analysis to pursue the rather obvious issue of how the patient was dealing with the wife issues that related to his mother. Kohut said dismissively: "We don't need to get into that. One idealizing transference is enough."[10]

The variation on the father theme, however, that gripped Kohut's imagination and also related directly to his experience of Felix was the idea of the "enclave" of idealization that often helps save boys (and girls, too, as far as Kohut was concerned) from the psychological tyranny of the mother. There are intimations of this idea in many cases, but the one that Kohut was most fond of (besides himself as Mr. Z) was Mr. X. In a 1973 workshop that happened to be taped, Kohut described the case in less disguise than when he later wrote it up in *The Restoration of the Self*. In the case Kohut notes that X. was a theology student in a German university who came into analysis because of work inhibitions, problems with love, and because he could not make friends. X. had gone to theology school because he identified with Jesus at twelve, who went to the temple and bested the rabbis in argument—that is, was greater and better than the father. But in fact X. felt empty and disconnected from his father and performed poorly in school. The mother, on the other hand, built him up all his life but to excess, beyond what was phase-appropriate. The patient, as a result, entered treatment brimming with overt grandiosity but was in fact extremely fragile. The father, a doctor who was never there, had always been degraded by the mother. To survive himself the father had to escape. At one point in analysis X. reported a fantasy/dream he often had. He was driving his small car on the autobahn and ran out of gas. He managed to get to the side of road. The gauge was on empty. He was stranded, at the end of the road. No one stopped to help. Then he thought, "Don't I have a reserve tank in the trunk?" Sure enough, there, under much stuff, was a canister of gasoline. He put it in the tank and drove off. After reporting it, the patient had no immediate associations to his dream/fantasy. He went off in other directions that were seemingly unrelated. But then he started talking about how there were rare moments in his life when his downtrodden father would take him out into the woods to walk. It turned out the father was really quite a huntsman, and could find the tracks of deer and identify the trees. In these fleeting moments as a young boy he could experience his father as strong and knowledgeable. When the two returned home, however, there would be an understanding between them that they would never mention these experiences. But somewhere deep in X.'s psyche was stashed away the knowledge that there was a reserve canister of a strong father whom he could look up to and on which his work in analysis could proceed.[11]

Kohut's mothers, on the other hand, have the quality of an evil archetype. In most of the analytic cases with which he was familiar, he once acknowledged directly, the "major pathogenic selfobject" was the mother.[12] In his discussion of Mr. A., Kohut notes that his patient was extremely sensitive to slights, indeed to any setback. This seems, Kohut says, to be generally related to the mother and the "unpredictability and unreliability of her empathic responses during his infancy."[13] He continues in a general vein. The child needs to experience very early on "an undisturbed primary narcissistic equilibrium," which she regulates for him. A.'s mother, Kohut surmises, must have "prepared the soil" early on for his later pathology arising from his father's radical mood swings. In making this point Kohut extrapolates backward from what he knows indirectly about her present-day personality. That, he says, was "deeply disturbed." She seemed calm and quiet on the surface (in contrast to the father's bubbling presence) but could easily "disintegrate" with "terrible anxiety" and "unintelligible (schizoid) excitement" when under stress. Some years later, in another book, Kohut used even stronger language, calling A.'s mother "severely abnormal" and possibly "latently schizophrenic." "It may thus be assumed," says Kohut, that her early mothering lacked empathy, was shallow and unpredictable, and "must have led to" A.'s narcissistic vulnerabilities, even though Kohut felt that the "hub of the patient's psychological defect" lay in his traumatic disappointment in his father.[14]

Miss F., who insisted from the couch that Kohut stop interpreting and just listen, had a mother who slipped easily into depressive self-preoccupation. Mr. C.'s mother was "chronically depressed," and, like Mr. D., had a mother whom Kohut felt had a "covert psychosis." The mother of Mr. J. "developed in her old age an open persecutory delusional system about her possessions." Mr. E.'s mother was apparently depressed to begin with and then progressively withdrew into herself as a result of her malignant hypertension. Mr. M.'s mother was incapable of providing adequate empathy for him and then died when he was twelve. Miss V.'s mother was

> subject to periodic depressions, was emotionally shallow and
> unpredictable; in addition to the periodic affective disorder

from which she suffered increasingly throughout her life, schizoid features—already present during the patient's childhood—were unmistakable. . . . The patient's mother was still living during Miss V.'s analysis; there was a good deal of interaction between the two . . . and an assessment of the mother's personality, suggesting borderline schizophrenia, could therefore be made.[15]

There is, of course, a long tradition in psychiatry that blames the mother for all the ills of her children.[16] Most of the mothers in Freud's case histories are actually silent and in the background. The fathers are far more three-dimensional. Freud does signal out for abuse Dora's mother, who is presented as a foolish woman preoccupied with household chores and whom he diagnoses as having a "housewife psychosis."[17] Psychoanalysts after Freud became obsessed with the bad mother. Bruno Bettelheim's animosity toward mothers was so extreme that he literally took troubled children away from their mothers, who were not even allowed to visit them in the Orthogenic School for prolonged periods.[18] Erik Erikson was one of the first psychoanalysts to comment critically on such attitudes, but few followed in his wake.[19] The idea of the bad mother, of course, has deep cultural grounding that puts the psychoanalytic and psychiatric stereotypes in some perspective. Kohut's portrayal of mothers is very much in the worst of this tradition. Else was always present. For all the suppleness of his theory, he seemed unable to escape the toxic influences of his own "bad mother," who became emblematic for him.

One important consequence of what Kohut considered the typical family drama, as he said once in a seminar, is the actual or fantasized homosexuality of the boys raised in it, that "yearning to get something from an idealized figure, or to get something into oneself that will fill one up and give one wholeness and completeness." Fellatio or anal penetration are thus compensatory sexualizations whose aim is to "gain self-esteem, to gain the fuel, the cement, that holds one together and makes one feel whole in this particular sexualized way." Kohut, one can say, makes homosexual family dynamics paradigmatic of the culture. He also spoke clearly and decisively for the creative potential represented by homosexuality. "People are not all cut according to the same plan," he says. Homosexuality is simply one expression of narcissism, which is not at all to be regarded as unhealthy. Homosexuality may, in fact, even represent something higher in human organization. At times in history and with some "highly developed" cultures (he was undoubtedly thinking here of the ancient Greeks) sexualized relationships between men were regarded as "proper and beautiful." Certain creative people, furthermore, simply do not develop heterosexual investments. "Who is to say," Kohut concluded passionately, "that this is less good than the capacity of some nincompoop to fall in love with women?"[20] Why should heterosexuality define our values? "The moron's capacity to copulate—this may be heterosexual—does not outweigh Socrates' homosexual propensities and the flowering of his mind and his contribution to Western culture."[21]

Kohut moved slowly, even somewhat reluctantly, from his theory of narcissism toward a psychology of the self. He was a man of caution who considered himself—and was, to a considerable degree—a conservative thinker. He seemed genuinely perplexed and was often troubled that his ideas proved so controversial. Once he had them he thought they were obvious corrections to the theory and fully expected fair-minded people to accept them readily. Kohut never thought he had the last word in the history of ideas. He was convinced that each generation has to find its own conceptual voice.[22] He did, however, believe he was the new voice of psychoanalysis for this generation, that he was the new Freud in a new land. Still, it was a revolution wrought by often painful stages. If anything, Kohut tended to stay with old models and ideas past the point of utility and into the realm of contradiction before moving forward. In this period between his two major books, Kohut struggled with clarification of the familiar as he moved toward original formulations. He redefined the landscape of aggression and rage. He pondered Freud and charisma. And he continued to reflect on what it all meant in terms of clinical treatment and healing. In his published seminars at the Institute in these years, one can see with unusual clarity his mind searching for coherence and not quite finding it, yearning for some overarching schema that would make his contributions less disparate and isolated and more whole, complete, viable. For some, of course, he remains more interesting at this point of creative confusion than later when things came together more clearly for him. Final thoughts are not necessarily best thoughts.

Until sometime in late 1974 or early 1975, Kohut retained the phenomenological approach to the idea of self that he had worked with in his first book. In this view the many selves of experience compete for position within the structures of the mind. His new emphasis in the early

1970s, however, was on the "sense of cohesion" in what he usually called the "nuclear self."[23] Such cohesion occurred in a field of psychological forces that could lead to fragmentation, but the very idea of cohesion moved Kohut away from the fractured model of ego, id, and superego into that of the self, which is by definition holistic. The courage of the humble resisters to Nazism, for example—Franz Jaegerstaetter and Hans and Sophie Scholl—intrigued him with their enduring values and quiet heroism despite the literal craziness of their world. In treating George Klumpner in this period Kohut was fascinated by what the early delay of payment meant in terms of his patient's nuclear self. Such questions of self were an important variation on a familiar theme. Kohut returned often to this notion that basic values and ambitions reside in some core place in the self. It is what gives us our vital sense of continuity in psychological experience.

> There is some kind of cohesion in the course of our lives along the time axis that makes us feel that the youngster who did this, that, or the other thing at the age of 15 is in some way still connected with the present me. That was me, and I have developed out of it. Now, I would not say that the inability to recognize that continuity is necessarily pathological. But I think that, in most instances, the capacity to recognize or to feel this essential cohesion of the self along the time axis, or to have a sense of cohesion about oneself even though one has contradictory attitudes at the same time, is part of mental health.[24]

Kohut then contrasted that sense of cohesion with schizophrenia, especially in the beginning phases, when one feels a terrifying fragmentation of the self. Is that arm mine? Am I alive? Is that image in the mirror really my face?[25]

Reflections on nuclear self experience also led Kohut in these years to consider the question of beginnings. What is this nuclear self all about? Are we born with it? How does it relate to early selfobject experience? His answer to these interrelated questions about development—an answer that was to profoundly influence other theorists[26]—was what he first called in a lecture the "virtual point of the beginning of the self."[27] It is a startling insight, partly because of its simplicity and elegance. As we have since learned about the world of the Internet, the virtual, or that dimension of being which we experience in effect but not in fact, can powerfully shape the self. The idea that the psychological reality of a baby exists as if real in the mind of the beholder in ways that fundamentally shape the baby's experience is implicit in the notion of selfobject and thus latent in Kohut's first book. But the specific idea of the baby's "virtual self" is by no means articulated in *The Analysis of the Self.* That came, apparently for the first time, almost as an aside in a 1975 seminar at the Institute that happened to be taped. At birth, Kohut said in the seminar, the baby has not one "iota of self-awareness" but is already an "anticipatory expectation in the empathic self-object mother's mind about what this child should feel as an independent self. " The baby is a complete psychological being if seen within the selfobject world of the mother and other caretakers. The baby's self, in other words, is more than an imagined future, beyond mere potential. It is a virtual reality.

Twenty-three

THE GROUP REDUX

The intensification of Kohut's self-centeredness after he was stricken with cancer in 1971 and his growing fame led to his abandonment by most of his peers and colleagues his own age. There was never a single moment when things changed. For one thing, Kohut's fame came slowly. *The Analysis of the Self* took several years to take hold and was never actually read very widely (over the years it probably sold in the tens of thousands).[1] The book, however, was talked about by everyone in psychoanalysis; in Chicago, where in addition the magnetism of Kohut's personality held sway, it clearly sparked excitement in the field not seen since the days of Freud. Much of the rejection was petty and even incidental, but Kohut experienced almost any criticism in totalistic terms.[2] He was especially vulnerable to rejection by the senior figures in psychoanalysis. Lionized for years as the logical successor to Heinz Hartmann and as one of four or five people at the epicenter of the world psychoanalytic movement, Kohut, for example, found himself often in conflict with Anna Freud and Kurt Eissler as they realized the implications of *The Analysis of the Self* and the directions in which he was moving. Anna Freud, at least, remained personally respectful. She was unfailingly polite. She sent her regards after the sixtieth birthday celebration in 1973. She continued to send stamps to Thomas and to stay in touch with the family in other ways. But not once after 1971 did Anna Freud mention his work, nor was Kohut again to write her about his ideas.[3] In private, perhaps to vent his frustration at what he considered her rejection of him, he scorned her as being "childish" and became dismissive of her work. There was, however, never an open break with Anna Freud, just a slow drift apart. Their correspondence ends with a letter from Kohut to her in German, handwritten, charming and full of fond feeling for her.[4]

The break with Kurt Eissler, on the other hand, was more explicit. Eissler's initial reaction to *The Analysis of the Self* was positive, though he probably did not fully grasp where Kohut was going with his ideas. But in December 1971, after listening to Kohut's paper on rage and aggression, Eissler told his old friend at dinner that he had not understood a thing he had said. Kohut was devastated.[5] Even then, there was never a formal break as such between Kohut and Eissler, nor was their mutual fondness called into question; Eissler sent him a telegram of congratulation on his birthday (May 3) in 1974, which became a ritual after that.[6] Yet Kohut sensed a definite pulling away on the part of Eissler as Kohut's ideas became bolder and less strictly Freudian. On April 18, 1974, for the first time, Kohut expressed annoyance and "despair" at Eissler's criticism of his paper "The Psychoanalyst in the Community of Scholars" for being superficial and having a touch of the Pollyanna. Kohut was even somewhat sarcastic in his reply, noting that one could pull out strands from his talk and infer that he had given an exhortation like advocating Christian love as the cure for all the ills of the world. "But I would not have believed that a conscientious and fair-minded reader like you could overlook the central points which I am making," he concluded.[7]

Eissler continued to write Kohut friendly handwritten letters during the next year or so (Eissler normally used German when writing Kohut by hand and English when he typed). In the fall of 1975, however, there was another rupture between them when Eissler commented critically on Kohut's long paper on Freud with wording similar to that which he used about the rage paper: "I did not understand the Freud article you had written, but will read it once more."[8] Things seemed to heal somewhat for a couple of years, or at least go below the surface, as Kohut and Eissler drifted further apart. The final straw came when Eissler weighed in on a controversy between Kohut and the literary critic Eric Heller about Heller's attack on a self-psychological interpretation of Kleist's *Michael Kohlhaas* by a student of Kohut. Eissler felt that Kohut was much too soft on Heller; he wrote that the problem was that Kohut was "shackled with self psychological theory." Eissler even added, gratuitously but tellingly, that he had "doubts that an analysis of self will initiate a new phase in the relation of psychoanalysis to other fields of research."[9] Kohut wrote

Eissler a note of deep regret: "I think I will have to let time pass in order to see how I can deal with this blow."[10] On the same day Kohut also wrote Margret Schaefer, who was the author of the paper attacked by Heller, describing Eissler as "really just one of the great number of my colleagues who attack me & my work in the most violent way."[11]

Sometimes, it should be noted, older colleagues were impressed with Kohut's emerging ideas. René Spitz, for example, after hearing a presentation by Kohut, said that he had waited all his life for such a theory.[12] Closer to home, Jerome Kavka of the Chicago Institute expressed his appreciation of Kohut's work, which prompted a note: "Nothing gives me greater pleasure and nothing provides me with greater emotional support as I continue in my work than the evidence that my findings are reverberating in sensitive, searching, and gifted minds like yours."[13] Kohut himself also never gave up yearning for acceptance by his peers and his dreams of remaining at the center of psychoanalysis. He was concerned in 1973 when he was not nominated to serve on the Executive Council of the International Psycho-Analytic Association and wondered out loud to the newly elected president of the organization whether to "take the risk" of having his name proposed from the floor in two years.[14]

But for the most part Kohut had to adjust to what can best be called a kind of psychoanalytic shunning by his orthodox older friends. Psychoanalysts often operate like a clique in high school, and once it was clear the leading figures in the field, especially in the East, felt Kohut had gone much too far, the rest fell quickly in line. Sometimes, people who had known Kohut for decades literally turned their back on him. At meetings outside of Chicago no one asked Kohut any longer to have a coffee or a glass of wine. He was passed in the halls and ignored. People looked the other way.[15] At a workshop in Paris in 1973, a group of senior analysts pointedly left at the break.[16] Kohut's old friend, Martin Stein, had led the attack on behalf of the New York Freudians by lambasting *The Restoration of the Self* in the pages of the *Journal of the American Psychoanalytic Association.*[17] The ostracism even extended to the old guard in the Chicago Institute, which, amazingly enough, voted him off the Council in 1977. The Council is the legislative body of the Institute and its members are elected by the faculty.[18] By 1977 Kohut no longer had much to do with the Council and its committees. As a result, he was outside the political loop, and the vote took him entirely by surprise. Ostensibly, the Council vote came because of a comment Kohut made at an Institute seminar that Josef Breuer, rather than Freud, really invented psychoanalysis in his work with

Anna O. The majority of otherwise mature analysts on the Council actually argued with straight faces that as a result of such ideas Kohut was no longer a psychoanalyst. In fact, the politics of the movement that led to the vote were incomprehensibly byzantine and remain murky two decades later.[19] But there is no question Kohut felt as though he had been kicked out of his own family, which surely evoked for him the trauma of being forced out of his beloved Vienna by the Nazis.[20]

Kohut's adaptive solution to the rejection by old psychoanalytic friends and colleagues took several forms. One response was to reconnect with some important people from his childhood. He had never lost contact with Siegmund Levarie, of course, but their contact seemed to grow more intense and nostalgic in the 1970s.[21] Kohut also took advantage of his trip to Vienna in 1971 to get in touch with an old friend from medical school, Wilhelm Solms-Rodelheim, and Adam Wandruszka from the Döblinger Gymnasium.[22] Jacques Palaci, as well, reentered Kohut's life in the 1970s. Palaci, who lived in Paris, wrote Kohut after the publication of *The Analysis of the Self* and they got together whenever possible. In 1973, for example, Kohut arranged to meet Palaci in Zurich for the day (Palaci flew in from Paris). They went to Le Bistro restaurant for lunch and stayed for several hours, talking and enjoying each other's company. Kohut ate slowly as they talked about everything imaginable. Afterward they walked the streets and looked at the old buildings, arm in arm, European style. Another time the same year they met in Paris in honor of the publication of the French translation of *The Analysis of the Self*. Palaci got some tickets to a performance one afternoon. Palaci was nervous because the musicians were amateurs and he was afraid they would not be up to Kohut's standards. But Kohut was delighted with the young players' spirited performance. He noted none of their weaknesses and exclaimed only on the positive aspects of the performance.[23]

Kohut, in other words, was hardly isolated, but he began to feel sometime after his sixtieth birthday celebration that he needed his group back to participate in his project, if his dreams were ever to be fulfilled. And so, fitfully as it turned out, he made an effort to reinvent the group that he had let languish after 1969. At some point in the summer or fall of 1973, either Kohut himself, or more likely John Gedo, knowing it was something Kohut would want to happen, decided to reconvene the group in order to produce a book of cases closely linked to *The Analysis of the Self*.[24] Gedo and Arnold Goldberg were now done with their book, *Models of the Mind*, and thus the two key figures were available for other tasks that related again more directly to Kohut's needs. Besides Gedo, Kohut invited Goldberg (and made him general editor of the project), as well as Michael Franz Basch, Paul and Anna Ornstein, Paul and Marian Tolpin, Ernest Wolf, David Marcus, and Meyer Gunther.[25] The idea was that these colleagues would write up their cases, most of which had been supervised by Kohut, and he would then provide some of the commentary on them. Kohut's first meeting with this group was Saturday morning, February 9, 1974, at the Institute. The *Casebook* meetings would always be held at the Institute and never in the Kohut apartment, which lent them a note of formality *and* separateness from Kohut himself. In the tape recording of that meeting, Kohut outlined his idea of what the book would be about and how he hoped the cases the group would write would effectively illustrate his theory of narcissism and stand as a companion volume to *The Analysis of the Self.* Kohut stressed that he wanted to be sure the cases were authentic, rather than dressed up to illustrate his theories neatly. He was, he said, an empirical scientist, and he wanted that truth to be honored (though it can be reasonably claimed he himself wandered far from a strict conception of both empiricism and science).[26]

The unacknowledged mission of the *Casebook* group, however—to consolidate his charisma—created problems for it almost from the outset. At first Kohut tried to keep to his word about staying with a book project that was only tangentially focused on him. As long as he was present the group's collective idealization of him buried the latent tensions. Such in general is an important part of the psychology of leadership. The group met that winter and spring of 1974 on Saturdays on a monthly basis. Kohut felt it would be good to begin the discussions with issues of termination. Gedo made the first presentation, which both Ornstein and Goldberg independently remember was a disaster until Kohut himself clarified the material.[27] Gedo, in turn, felt that the next case presentation, by Anna Ornstein, was so bad as to be embarrassing, as the patient had come nowhere near working through his "sadistic propensities." Kohut, Gedo says, agreed with him in private conversation, though one wonders, as it was this case of Anna Ornstein's that Kohut thought about all summer and that became the major case of Mr. M. in his second book, *The Restoration of the Self.* The very issues that bothered Gedo increasingly intrigued Kohut.[28]

In mid-September, with Kohut still in Carmel, the group held its own first meeting of the new academic year. Things began harmoniously, as described by Goldberg in a long, chatty letter to Kohut.[29] That peace was not to last. At the first meeting after Kohut's return, on November 16, 1974,[30] which Kohut was scheduled to attend but in the end missed, Gedo presented a case. An issue of contention arose during discussion. At one point, Marian Tolpin quizzed him pointedly on the issue.[31] Gedo was enraged that she would criticize him in her "loud and grating voice," and implied she was being impudent. Gedo felt Tolpin was a "lightweight" and, more ominously, as a current analysand of Kohut, perhaps a surrogate of the absent master (or his "Charlie McCarthy").[32] Over the course of the next few days there was a flurry of calls. Gedo demanded of Goldberg that Tolpin be kicked out of the group. Goldberg felt that was an absurd demand, besides being impossible, since she was in treatment with Kohut. Goldberg did urge Kohut to contact Gedo and try to keep him from leaving.[33] Kohut in fact talked with Gedo but was unable to appease him.[34] For several weeks there was much discussion back and forth, though never, interestingly, involving Tolpin herself, who says she did not know of the commotion she had unwittingly caused.[35] In the end Gedo angrily left the group, broke formally from Goldberg, with whom he never talked again, and considered himself from then on no longer associated with Kohut.

Things had been simmering with Gedo for some time. Not one to be accused of modesty, Gedo says of himself: "By 1974, it was clear that I would be one of the few significant theoreticians of the next generation."[36] That potential was readily recognized by Kohut, who also appreciated the fact that Gedo was the most widely read and the most cultured of the group. There is no question Gedo was Kohut's closest colleague in the early 1970s.[37] Gedo, however, was beginning to resent bitterly the late-night calls, the neediness, the deep connection.[38] As he put it, he refused to play Wilhelm Fliess to Kohut's Freud. At least such is Gedo's retrospective rendering of his feelings. Contemporary evidence would suggest much more complicated feelings on the part of Gedo. At the sixtieth birthday dinner speech, the actual text of Gedo's comments (as opposed to what was later published)[39] brimmed over with affection and praise. He spoke of his idealization of Kohut when he was a student in the two-year theory course. Gedo also made some interesting observations on Kohut's writing style and praised his work as easily equal in quality, if not in quantity, to that of Freud. Toward the conclusion of his talk Gedo said the only writer to whom he could compare Kohut was Euripides. Gedo's praise of Kohut was in fact so extreme, especially the comparison to Euripides, that many found it unseemly.[40]

Gedo, however, now says the parts of his speech that matter far more than the Euripides comparison are those in which he said Kohut's analysis of *Death in Venice* would "save him from the fate of Aschenbach" and the final quotation from a poem of Holderlin's ("A single summer grant me, great powers, and a single autumn for fully ripened song"). Both passages, Gedo says, were inserted deliberately to suggest to knowing listeners his belief that Kohut was ever in danger of reverting to homosexuality or falling into madness.[41] Gedo says he always thought Kohut's attachment to him was perverse and he has never known a more "effete person." As early as 1969, Gedo's wife, Mary, told him, "That man loves you." For the most part, however, Gedo felt that things remained well below the surface with Kohut before 1971. But after the cancer diagnosis, Gedo says, there was a profound change in Kohut's character, and Kohut began to make verbal "passes" at him.

One wonders what these "passes" were all about. "Where?—all the time, everywhere," he says. And how? When Gedo visited Kohut in the hospital in the fall of 1971, Kohut said, "I *knew* you would come!" In the summer of 1974 after a dinner, Kohut said "like a lover"[42] that "it seems forever since I have seen you." Gedo, however, does not claim that what he experienced as passes were gross and overt. They were, on the contrary, subtle and implied. "He [Kohut] knew how to *behave*; it was clear that he understood that I am no homosexual and that his wishes could not be realized."[43] In another context Gedo adds: "The 'passes' Heinz made were purely verbal, quite subtle, and cognizant of the impossibility that I would have any physical contact with him. . . . *He made me feel* I had been propositioned. That is very different."[44]

There is no question Kohut admired and was fond of John Gedo. His letters to Gedo exude respect and affection. Once he thanked Gedo for a note: "It makes life ever so much more meaningful to get a message of the kind that you sent to me. Thank you so much!" Another time Kohut called Gedo "decent" and "exceptional." Kohut was later touched by Gedo's "extravagant evaluation" of *The Analysis of the Self.* In 1972 he recommended that Gedo take his place at an event honoring Margaret Mahler that he could not himself attend:

> Among my friends there is one who is deeply and thoroughly familiar with my work, who knows Margaret's contribution well, and who would do an outstanding job at your symposium. Dr. John E. Gedo, the person of whom I

am thinking, has one of the finest minds of the younger
generation in psychoanalysis and he is, in particular, an outstanding synthesizer.[45]

In a letter in early 1973 Kohut wrote Gedo: "It's good to have you as a
friend." Even after the break Kohut wrote to his "cherished friend," hop-
ing that the "tensions" of the past would give way to a renewal of the
"precious, ineradicable moments" they once enjoyed. A few months later
Kohut wrote Gedo that he was "never out of my mind for long" and that
Kohut's free associations took him to those who were important, "and
you have often been among them."[46] It seemed never to be Kohut who
was pulling away. On the contrary, it was Gedo who withdrew, because
he felt it was Kohut's unconscious intention to annihilate his individuality in the relationship. Kohut only appeared to give up on Gedo after
Gedo's irritating comments on *The Restoration of the Self*, in which Gedo
obliquely suggested he was the one who first thought of the idea of the
self in broad terms.[47] In Ina Wolf's earthy image, Kohut in general was
like a huge arm connected at his fingertips to others with no sense of where
his arm ended and the other's began. Gedo could not tolerate such an
absence of boundaries.[48]

November 16, 1974, proved to be as much a beginning as an ending.
Kohut missed the morning presentation by John Gedo, who felt Kohut
had given free rein to Marian Tolpin to attack him. That appears not to
have been the case. Kohut's absence reflected his desire to pull back
quietly from a group that was no longer meeting his needs. But indirectly it sparked the explosion between Gedo and Marian Tolpin, as it
was only Kohut's commanding presence that had kept the simmering
tensions in the group under control. The way Kohut talked with his
colleagues at their first meeting, on February 9, 1974 (as tape-recorded
by Ernest Wolf), suggests his genuinely scientific goals in the writing of
the *Casebook*. He should be believed when he said he hoped that the
cases would reflect the authentic struggles of the analysts' work with their
patients. What was left unsaid because it was not yet fully acknowledged
to himself was that Kohut also sought to mold the group into a cohesive
set of followers who might become the basis for what was just emerging
in his own mind as a self psychology movement. It was that more grandiose
ambition that by the late fall of 1974 was clearly not going to be realized

in the group associated with the *Casebook*. Indeed, the bitter rivalries and disruptive presence of Gedo threatened Kohut's still-fragile but wildly ambitious goals. In Chicago at the time (and ever since), all anyone noticed was that Gedo broke from Kohut and the group that October of 1974. Kohut despaired over that loss and would have kept Gedo in the fold had he been able to.[49] Far more important, however, than anything John Gedo did or said was that Kohut himself withdrew from the *Casebook* project. With one exception, he never attended another meeting, never read the final manuscript, and, as Goldberg is convinced from discussions he had later with Kohut, never even read the book itself (which has on the title page "Written with the collaboration of Heinz Kohut").[50] Kohut, it would seem, turned decisively away from those he could no longer control.

In the wake of the fight, however, he asked a more select group, now notably excluding John Gedo and several others, to begin meeting in his apartment to go over the draft of his new book.[51] It was difficult for everyone to focus, given the swirl of passions, and it would be weeks before the dust would settle. But what was taking shape was quite a different enterprise from the *Casebook*. This new enterprise soon rapidly expanded in one sense, while retaining its core identity in another. In 1976 Kohut and the "sacred seven" created a Saturday workshop on self psychology at the Institute for invited guests. Kohut himself made a point of always attending the meetings of this seminar if at all possible. At the same time, smaller, more selective gatherings of the core group, with others from around the country (especially Bernard Brandchaft, Arthur Malin, Robert Stolorow, Morton and Estelle Shane, and, for a time, Evelyn Schwaber), began to assemble twice a year in private homes, first at the Wolfs' and from the fall of 1977 at the Goldbergs'; by 1979 or so the events were catered and guests shared in the expenses. Finally, a series of annual conferences, beginning in the fall of 1978, required separate planning committees that further consolidated the significance of the core group as the outreach became international.[52]

What was taking shape was truly a movement that would symbolically immortalize the memory of Heinz Kohut.

Twenty-four

THE RESTORATION OF THE SELF

Kohut committed himself to writing a new book during his summer vacation of 1974 while he was in Carmel. He was sixty-one years old. He drafted the first chapter (after finishing the German translation of his paper on charisma) before his return to Chicago in late September.[1] In contrast to his routine of previous years, however, when the pressures of clinical work had forced a slowdown of actual writing once he was no longer in California, Kohut kept up the pace that fall and into the winter. By February 1975 his new book was about "three-quarters finished",[2] by June it was "nearing completion," though it had the awful working title of *The Rehabilitation of the Self: Thoughts About the Termination of Analyses and the Concept of Cure*.[3] In Carmel a few months later, Kohut was beginning to speak about his book as a completed project. "It is a strange manuscript," he wrote in September 1975. "And although everybody tells me that it will cause a storm of attacks, I don't worry about that. I think that people will have an easier time seeing my position in the open, rather than having to guess it through a veil of allusions."[4] Less than a month later, in October 1975, he described the book as "more or less" finished; by then he had found the final title (*The Restoration of the Self*), though he still retained the awkward subtitle.[5] But in fact he worked on it for another full year, during which he refined the narrative and dropped the subtitle. As late as December 1976 he was frantically tracking down a few final references before actual publication, which came in early spring, 1977. The book was an instant success and by July had sold 11,500 copies.[6]

The Restoration of the Self is Kohut's best-written and most accessible book. He tried earnestly to avoid the language of drive theory and psycho-analytic metapsychology that weighs down *The Analysis of the Self*. He made a decision early on in the conception of *Restoration* that he was writing for a general audience as opposed to the small psychoanalytic elite. As part of this process of reaching out, Kohut enlisted the help of (and turned himself over to) a master editor, Natalie Altman, at International Universities Press.[7] An awkward and finicky writer, Kohut seldom let others influence his prose. As a result, there were severe limits to how readable he could ever really be, no matter how much he revised and re-wrote (which was a lot). But with *Restoration* Kohut bowed to an extraordinary extent to someone who minced no words in her assumed role of friendly taskmaster.

In early November 1975, Kohut sent his completed manuscript to Altman for her to begin editing. She read it carefully in preparation for an initial phone conversation later that month, in which she conveyed her general impressions. She told him she liked the book a great deal but felt there were many places where he could avoid repetitions, stop being defensive about his ideas, and consolidate various sections. She had firm views about his excessive use of "therefore" and "however," how he confused "which" and "that," and his overuse of "on the one hand . . . and on the other hand"; she also asked, tentatively, whether he had a particular reason for using dashes so often.[8] Then began the hard work of editing. In various letters she worked to get Kohut thinking about cutting out much excess. She asked him to make Mr. M. more likable ("the poor chap simply does not emerge as a creature of flesh and blood").[9] Much of their work was also on the phone, with him in his study, fetching reference books as they talked.[10] Drafts went back and forth. After each of his revisions, she would respond with further detailed notes. About the second chapter, for example, she felt large sections lacked "focus and continuity." She advised him:

> If you make Alexander an example, instead of starting out with him, you won't need your apologia on p. 156B. You can do this by transposing him to within the section. As for pp. 120–142, you could extract what pertains to termination and attach it to Chapter 1; you can move mental health to Chapter 1 or save it for value-hierarchies and save the combination of both for the end, make them a separate section

here, or, perhaps move them to pp. 201–205, which is the
only other time they come up.[11]

No one had ever worked over Kohut's prose in such a fashion.

Altman's editing continued throughout 1976. Until about March she
worked with Kohut section by section and line by line. In phone conversations and in letters, she often summarized her changes, even minor ones
like taking the parentheses out of a given line on a page 42.[12] He always
answered her promptly and with equal attention to detail, sometimes
pointing out to her words he had deleted from the text.[13] By March the
manuscript had reached the stage of actual copyediting; her questions and
suggestions for changes were communicated to him on query slips that
an editor attaches to the edges of the relevant page of the text. She did
not mince words. "I know you are fond of your neologisms 'absolutarian'
'absolutistically,' " she wrote on one slip, "but they *are* neologisms." She
wanted him to "rise to the challenge" of finding "real words to express
the meaning," and she proceeded to suggest a few ("unreserved," "unequivocal," "total," "unconditional," "stark," "unmitigated," "thorough," "complete," "pure"). He admitted, "I think you are right." She
was always very respectful, partly because she was herself sufficiently informed about psychoanalytic theory and politics to realize the risks he
was taking in the book. "I admit to gasping at your audacity in this section," she wrote of one passage, "but I'm keeping a cool head on the
barricades, I *hope*." She applauded his use of "I think" and "I believe" at
times. "This entire Chapter [there is no way of knowing which chapter
she was talking about] must have *just* the right tone. My task is to help
you achieve it." Kohut's replies on the query slips—which are 1½ inches
by 4 inches—were often small essays in a tiny scrawl. In response to a
question about his use of the word "playfulness," he wrote:

> I am using the word playfulness advisedly to contrast the
> harsh attitude of creative science [toward] that of dogmatic
> religion. The world of dogmatic religion, i.e., the world
> of absolute values, is serious; and those who live in it are
> serious because their joyful search has ended—they have
> become defenders of the truth. The world of creative science,
> however, is inhabited by playful people who approach the
> in essence unknowable reality which surrounds them and
> try to describe and explain it in various ways, knowing that

they can never get at the truth, only at analogizing approximations of it.

By the fall of 1976 the cover design was being discussed. Kohut was dissatisfied with the proposed designs from International Universities Press. He had actually asked Norma Levarie (Siegmund's wife) in July if she had any suggestions for graphic designers, as that was her business. In the end Norma Levarie herself did the cover.[14] Kohut also asked his friend Ernest Wolf to compile the index to the book, for which he gave him a whole case of fine wine (Château Margaux), which was at least five times more expensive than the cost of hiring a professional indexer would have been.[15] Kohut's work with Altman continued that fall, though they were now dealing with small final problems in the manuscript. Up to the end there was always the warmest possible trust between writer and editor. He seldom ignored her criticisms. She once told him to delete a footnote, as it was "faintly patronizing." He not only agreed but admitted in his red ink (she used blue) that the note was "*very* patronizing." He was also often light in his responses on the queries: "You are a good mother-hen," he wrote once, "and the chick will do your bidding."

Natalie Altman played an important role in shaping Kohut's murky prose into a real book. But even she could do only so much with his determined obscurity. He was adamant, for example, that the book have seven chapters (including the "Epilogue"). That preference seemed partly based on his arbitrary wish to have his book parallel the seven chapters of Freud's *The Interpretation of Dreams*. Once, however, he also said the structure was intended to copy God and the seven days of creation. She was not sure if he was joking.[16] There are also some basic narrative problems with *The Restoration of the Self*, and there remain some long Germanic strings of words hung between dashes within dashes that constitute no English sentence.[17]

Restoration nevertheless was a breakthrough book for Kohut. In it he comes out from behind the veil, as he told John Gedo. There could be no return to the mainstream world of Anna Freud and Kurt Eissler after a book like this. Kohut's old friend, Martin Stein of the New York Psychoanalytic Institute, reviewed *Restoration* in the leading organ of psychoanalytic respectability, the *Journal of the American Psychoanalytic Association*: "Sooner or later," Stein moaned audibly, "all that we know as psychoanalysis comes under fire [in this book]," including drive theory, the central role of infantile sexuality, the Oedipus complex, the tight relationship between conflict, defense, and resistance, working things through, and almost all the principles of technique handed down by Freud.[18] Stein was absolutely right. For all its qualifications and sometimes even its equivocations—and in retrospect *Restoration* reads like an exceedingly cautious book in many places—Kohut at last sharply and clearly differentiates his work from that of Freud. But even as *Restoration* closes options, it opens other opportunities. The book is Kohut's blueprint for a new psychology, the realization of his fondest dreams, toward which the pressure of illness was forcing him with mounting urgency. *Restoration* is a book to spawn a movement. It is, in one sense, a narrow clinical and psychoanalytic book written for professionals. But it is in equal parts historical, reflective, and conceptual, linking past and present in the move toward his imagined and yearned-for future.

Kohut was aware of the charge that he ignored the significance of other thinkers. In *Analysis* he had tried, not without some ambivalence, to be more imbedded in the tradition. Now that he was explicitly breaking free he knew that he had to offer a better explanation for why he had written as if no one other than he had ever had an idea. In his Preface to *Restoration* he therefore takes note of the extent to which—as others had noted—he worked in the intellectual shadows of Heinz Hartmann, Donald W. Winnicott, August Aichhorn, Jean-Paul Sartre, Alfred Adler, Carl Rogers, Otto Rank and even Indian philosophy. Kohut himself adds to the list of those whose work reverberates with his own: Michael Balint, Erik Erikson, Edith Jacobson, Otto Kernberg, Jacques Lacan, Jeanne Lampl-de-Groot, Heinz Lichtenstein, Margaret Mahler, Joseph Sandler, and Roy Schafer, "among others." Kohut claims that he has "great admiration" for these thinkers, at least "most of them," but he states it cannot be his task to note the specific connections between his project and their work. *The Restoration of the Self*, he says, is not a "technical or theoretical monograph" written from a detached point of view by an author "who has achieved mastery in a stable and established field of knowledge." On the contrary, the book is the product of someone struggling toward "greater clarity" in an area that, "despite years of conscientious effort, he was unable to understand within the available psychoanalytic framework." Indeed, Kohut says he had found himself "floundering in a morass of conflicting, poorly based, and often vague theoretical speculation." He had come to feel that the only path toward understanding would be a return to the "direct observation of clinical phenomena" and the construction of "new formulations that would accommodate my observations." Had he tried to commingle his ideas with those of others, the result, he says, would have been a tangled "thicket of similar, overlapping, or identical terms and concepts" that in no way carried the same meaning or was part of the "same conceptual context." And, so he concludes, he decided to "shed the ballast" of what others had written. He leaves it to future scholars to decide whether he was justified in his unilateral exploration of new territory.[19]

Kohut's relation to Freud in *The Restoration of the Self*, however, is another matter. All of *Restoration* takes off from Freud, and Kohut remains in constant dialogue—and disagreement—with the master. *Restoration* is in this sense a meditation on Freud, even though, Kohut argues, Freud is no longer historically, conceptually, therapeutically, or philosophically relevant. But Freud defines the standard. Freud's theory is the point of comparison against which a new depth-psychological approach worth its mettle must be tested. At times Kohut's engagement with Freud is tedious and perversely dialectic. Criteria for terminating analysis, for example, compete too simply with those of a supposedly outworn drive psychology. The idea of defensive and compensatory self structures too neatly replaces the old notions of ego defense against impulses. The new model of the self seems brittle as it struggles to silence echoes of what Freud called his structural model. And Tragic Man (whom Kohut calls "him," just prior to the healthy language change initiated by feminism) rather simplistically opposes Guilty Man. Freud almost suffocates Kohut. The only salvation is that the struggle to breathe forces Kohut to clarify his ideas in ways that changed the field forever.

It is, Kohut strongly believed, to Freud's eternal credit that he created depth psychology. At the same time, the constraints under which the theory operated were in no small measure the result of Freud's peculiar personality, which he stamped on psychoanalysis. Freud was the complete rationalist and the courageous figure who firmly believed in facing the truth whatever the consequences. The goal was to make the unconscious conscious, to cast off repressions, to shine the light of awareness on the seething cauldron of desire. That bold (and, one might add, very phallic) purpose generated its own imperatives. The point of therapy was to turn neurotic misery into ordinary unhappiness. The ideal psychoanalytic self suffered the whips and arrows with stoic resolve but keen insight. Health, as we would think of it, was an accidental result of the process, and in the

world of Freud Kohut's notion of transformation is completely alien and
exceedingly naive. In Freud's early work with hysteria, Kohut argues, he
probably cured mostly through suggestion and the mighty force of his
belief in the rightness of his views. Later, Freudian psychoanalysis became
more nuanced, but it never developed a viable theory of how it cured,
because cure was not the point. "Freud's values," Kohut says, "were not
primarily health values."[20]

Freud treasured the values of the Enlightenment. He approached his
data, which he collected through observation, with a clear-eyed empiricism. There was no doubt in his mind about the difference between the
observed and the observer. He embodied the ideal of scientific objectivity, even as he "gazed at man's inner life." It was a therapeutic stance,
says Kohut, that was particularly well suited for the emotional issues that
happened to be the leading problems of the day, namely female hysteria
and male obsessive-compulsiveness. For the former, early sexual traumas
that Freud came to feel (probably wrongly) were more fantasized than
real left repressed memories to be uncovered. With obsessive-compulsives,
early sexual conflict imbedded characterological traits like penuriousness;
the point of therapy was to cut through to first impulses. Freud's theory
of instinct and drive, especially the notion of libidinal development that
left traces in "erotogenic zones," made sense of what he saw in his office
and in the culture. It is not surprising, in the end, that Freud came to
believe that psychological "bedrock" lay in "castration anxiety" and that
there is some kind of primary aggressive drive linked mysteriously to the
idea of a death instinct.

The limits of Freud's vision, however, are immediately apparent when
one moves from easily identifiable neurotic problems to the much more
complicated and diffuse disorders of the self. Freud's theory made good
sense of patients like Anna O. and the Rat Man but is of little help with a
peeping perversion like that of Mr. E. or the chronic depression and
neediness of someone like Miss F. Kohut illustrates his point about Freud
in this connection with a brief look at pathological overeating and obesity.[21]
What obesity suggests psychologically is its origins in the child's deep
need for an empathic and modulated "food-giving selfobject." If that is
traumatically missing, if the child is sustained physically but without the
tenderness of an all-encompassing empathy, the "joyful experience of
being a whole, appropriately responded-to self" disintegrates. The child
retreats to a symbolized fragment of the whole, that is, to depressive
overeating. It is a dynamic, not a static, process. "It is this fragment of

psychological experience," Kohut says, "that becomes the crystallization point for the later addiction to food." Freud's theory of an "oral fixation" behind addiction is of little help in understanding obesity, just as a therapeutic approach that seeks to have the patient gain a "mastery of the drive" will not provide much in the way of cure.[22]

Several specific aspects of Freud's character intrigued Kohut as relevant for understanding psychoanalytic theory—just as Kohut's personality informs an understanding of self psychology. Freud, for example, hated to be looked at ("I cannot put up with being stared at by people for eight hours a day")[23] and in general shunned public praise, which Kohut feels suggests unresolved narcissistic issues dealing with exhibitionism. Freud also had a tin ear for music and disdained contemporary art with the certainty of a philistine. Neither aspect of his personality was a "defect" in the way such a concept is generally used. But both are highly revealing of the extreme rationalism Freud cultivated in himself and imposed on psychoanalysis as its ideal. Music and art in the twentieth century became often confusing, troubling, atonal, and formless, celebrations of the irrational, intentionally decadent and challenging, meaningless by old-fashioned standards. Freud the good bourgeois studiously kept both contemporary music and art out of his consciousness and went out of his way to mock examples of either one he accidentally came across. But Pablo Picasso and Anton Berg, for example, speak to the deepest levels of the primitive and fragmented self, levels to which Freud simply could not allow himself to descend. Freud was unable to immerse himself in primal states. He gained important access to the meaning of unconscious mental processes in human life, the workings of dreams, the central significance of childhood, and the reach of sexuality in the self. But his own rigidities made it impossible for him to experience what Kohut calls "archaic narcissistic states." Freud's achievements were great, Kohut concludes, but "the intensity and profundity of insight in one area had to be paid for by a comparative flatness in another."[24]

From his early work on narcissism until the mid-1970s, Kohut repeatedly stressed his strong conviction that there are many selves within the agencies of the mind. In those years, from roughly 1965 to 1975 and especially after 1972, despite the writings of people like Roy Schafer and the entreaties of John Gedo and Arnold Goldberg closer to home, Kohut actively resisted the "elegant and simple theory of mind" that put the self at the "center of our being from which all initiative springs and where all experiences end." He refused to depart from Freud's structural model for two reasons that he enumerated as late as 1972: the larger definition of self both abrogates the "importance of the unconscious" and comes from the outside, from conscious experience, "in order to create a rounded-out, cohesive theory of thought, perception, and action."[25] One could not make a more coherent argument for the old view of self within the structural model than Kohut himself made for it. It seemed to be an impregnable theoretical position from which he would never depart.

Then suddenly Kohut changed his mind and altered his whole system. He could be a curious blend of conservative and radical. He said once of himself: "Over and over in life I have started afresh."[26] It seems on this crucial issue of definition, he finally tired of being "pitchforked" from one kind of discourse to another.[27] The self now became that center of our being, from which all initiative springs. There were antecedents to Kohut's shift, of course, in the more general approach to self within philosophy for a good two thousand years and especially in the last few centuries.[28] But it was also the case that Kohut needed to emphasize the reasons for the more conventional definition of self within psychoanalysis at the very point in his theoretical development when the logic of his ideas was driving him to quite a different stance. It was too radical a switch to make unless he came completely to convince himself of its necessity, and he did that all on his own. The old formulation had to be long past being useful before Kohut could jettison it. Such was his creativity and his cognitive style.

And even then Kohut took the most conservative approach possible to what was probably the single most important theoretical change in positions he ever made. He kept both definitions of self. In *The Restoration of the Self* Kohut suggests that psychoanalysts need to begin thinking alternatively, "or even simultaneously," according to the principle of complementarity, to the idea of self at the center of one's psychological universe and *at the same time* self as a "content of a mental apparatus" (that is, within the structural model).[29] Kohut's position, one can reasonably argue, was on the cusp of theoretical confusion. Perhaps he was being political and trying to keep as many Freudians as possible on his side. But it is also true that he sought to remain honest about the complexities of any theory of self. As he wrote in some notes a few years later, he had been drawn in adolescence to the writings of Kant, Schopenhauer, and Nietzsche on the self, and had been especially influenced by Kant's notion in

The Critique of Pure Reason that the essence of reality is not knowable.[30] In *Restoration* Kohut underlines the obvious, namely that in a book of hundreds of pages on the self he never "assigns an inflexible definition to it." He is not contrite about this omission. The self is nothing more than "a generalization derived from empirical data." One cannot meaningfully differentiate self and self representations, he says. We can collect data on how inner experiences that result in a sense of "I" are established. We can describe the forms in which the self appears. And we can distinguish self types and expressions. "We can do all that," Kohut concludes, "but we will still not know the essence of the self as differentiated from its manifestations."[31]

Who "I" am *is* the self. But self, in turn, makes no sense except in the context of selfobjects, or those others in whose experience "I" becomes self. The selfobjects provide the oxygen of psychological life. There can be no self outside of an "empathic-responsive human milieu." In this regard Kohut integrates into his analysis two ideas that had begun to preoccupy him in the early 1970s: the baby's *virtual self*, which he now believed spawns the *nuclear self*. As he had first described in early 1975 and now elaborated, the fact of self experience is that parents endow a baby with a virtual self. A newborn lacks reflective self-awareness. But the baby is part of an environment into which it is "fused by mutual empathy" and is experienced as having a self. That self, which in one sense is entirely in the minds of the beholders, gradually becomes more real, though there is no clear beginning (or end) of this process, never a moment of "real" self defined in its essence as differentiated from others. There are only tracks of experience from the countless interactions nourishing a child's "innate potentialities" that create self forms in the child. Those new tracks of experience, in turn, create a nuclear self out of the "deeply anchored responsiveness of the self-objects," though, as Kohut notes, the emergent nuclear self of the child incorporates the deepest forms of the parents' own nuclear selves.[32] This "nuclear self" is the "basis for our sense of being an independent center of initiative and perception, integrated with our most central ambitions and ideals and with our experience that our body and mind form a unit in space and a continuum in time." The nuclear self is not, of course, a place in some kind of spatial relationship to our ambitions and ideals but a core dimension of self process that defines experience.[33]

Such discussion always raises the question of beginnings. If there is such a thing as a nuclear self, indeed of a self at all, where does it come from? Kohut is reluctant to "dramatize the establishment of the self by specifying a definite point at which it is said to be born."[34] It is always in process, in its beginnings *and* throughout the life cycle. What he specifically abandons in *Restoration* is his old idea of a sequence in which "self develops through the coalescence of fragments or nuclei." On the contrary, the self is there from the beginning in rudimentary form as a psychological whole.[35] Furthermore, though the end of self is, in a sense, death, he is more interested in terms of self experience in that "point in the life curve of the self" in late middle age, that pivotal moment which he (more than accidentally) happened to occupy as he wrote *Restoration*, when a "final crucial test determines whether the previous development had failed or had succeeded." In this phase, one approaches "ultimate decline" but is not quite in it. It is, he says, when we reflect on whether we have been true to "our innermost design." To face failure in that context is the most tragic experience we can have, for there is neither time nor energy to try again. There can be no second chances. The suicides of that phase of life tell the story, not of guilt, but of "the wish to wipe out the unbearable sense of mortification and nameless shame imposed by the ultimate recognition of a failure of all-encompassing magnitude."[36]

This view of self is naturally bound up in an understanding of the criteria for termination. Such criteria began to intrigue Kohut from the time of his earliest work on narcissism in the 1960s. The markers for the end of therapy are of obvious clinical importance, but they also signify what we mean in the culture psychologically, philosophically, and even spiritually by mental health and normality. Kohut understood that to challenge drive theory in a fundamental way was to question the cherished goals of psychoanalytic therapy as devised by Freud and the ego psychologists who followed him, which are the basis for defining specific termination criteria. In ways few understood or questioned, those goals—of mastering the infantile drives through more adaptive sublimations, making unconscious material conscious, and expanding and liberating the realm of the ego— derived from an instinctually based theory. The specific criteria for termination of an analysis that were based on these goals included new forms of adaptive sublimations and aim-inhibited gratifications, but they centered primarily, if implicitly more than explicitly, on finding a mate of the opposite sex with whom one had orgasms.[37] To assault this paradigm was to take on the heart and soul of clinical psychoanalysis. Proceeding cautiously, in the mid-1960s Kohut merely described "transformations" of narcissism as a kind of adjunct to the body of theory that governed termination. In *The Analysis of the Self* he typically moved well beyond that position without explicitly saying he was aware of the implications of some of his ideas. The cases, however, speak for themselves. Mr. E. becomes well when he is able to abandon his paralyzing peeping perversion and begin to look creatively at the world through a camera, which then becomes his profession and his calling. No other case in the book as dramatically illustrates the transformation of self issues in relation to termination. The suggestion with Miss F. is that she is cured when she can begin to grasp her own motivations and be empathic with herself. One sign of the end for Mr. I. is the humor in his dream of having an X-ray reveal the analyst inside his bowels and another dream of swallowing a clarinet (the analyst's voice) that keeps playing in his stomach.[38]

In 1973 Kohut wrote that he was once clear that the end of an analysis should bring about a state of mourning, the final relinquishment of one's childhood objects reactivated in the transference. The termination phase, he had firmly believed, was itself a period during which one finally separated oneself from the analyst and the "great figures" of one's childhood. Such are the criteria that derive from classical psychoanalytic theory. But Kohut felt differently now. The judgment that a patient must be in a state of mourning at the end of a completed analysis is wrong "in principle" if the issues of concern are those that deal with "disturbed self-esteem." On the contrary, what happens in a good analysis of such a patient is the "gradual transformation of the archaic grandiose self, and of the archaic omnipotent imagoes of childhood into which the self was merged." One sees not sadness but joy, an "increase of creative initiative," the emergence of the "urge to create," and the general "liberation of creative energy."[39]

Even as he wrote these lines Kohut was thinking beyond them in relation to the case of a man eventually named Mr. M. Kohut's understanding of M. was to prove decisive in his new views of what constitute appropriate criteria for termination in psychoanalysis. M. was actually a patient of Anna Ornstein, who began to discuss him in supervision with Kohut in 1969.[40] Ornstein, a practicing child psychiatrist herself, had recently finished her analytic work at the Institute, including all her necessary control cases, though she was not to graduate until 1972 because she had not yet written her research paper. She knew in 1969, however, that she wanted to become much more familiar with Kohut's work. At that point[41] she knew of his work mostly from her husband, Paul Ornstein, who talked about Kohut all the time. He urged her to have a case supervised by Kohut. As a candidate at the Institute, Anna Ornstein had found the training program in child analysis appalling. No child she had ever treated worried, as they were said to worry, about cutting off their father's penis or having sex with their mother, or any of the other adultomorphic fantasies that floated about in the minds of child analysts at the time. She sensed from what little she knew that Kohut offered a whole new approach to what was by then her life's work.

Anna Ornstein knew enough about Kohut's work (and person) not to take a garden-variety neurotic to him for supervision.[42] Ornstein was perfectly willing to bring someone into analysis on a low-fee basis, even though she no longer needed a control case, as long as the patient fit her own needs in terms of supervision and was willing to come to therapy the requisite four times a week. In retrospect, it is interesting that Ornstein assumed Kohut would not consider supervising anything but a full-scale analysis. One day in early 1969 a thirty-year-old journalist with some crippling conflicts was referred to her for therapy. This journalist, destined to be Mr. M., had several presenting complaints. His writing was increasingly blocked by infantile fantasies of large audiences, he was in despair over his wife's having left him after six years of marriage, and he was dissatisfied with his job. He aspired to be a creative writer and hoped to cure what a college professor had once told him was a flaw in his logic (and which Kohut believed was a mild thought disorder). M. felt a lack of energy when he worked and had trouble getting up in the morning. He felt only "half alive."[43]

It was the perfect case for Ornstein to bring for supervision to Kohut. Mr. M. was clearly wrestling with some profound self issues and underlying depression. He was also creative and yearned to find a way to release his talents. The key facts of his history included his adoption at three months of age after a stay in an orphanage following his birth. M.'s older brother and younger sister had also been adopted. His adoptive mother, to whom M. was quite attached, was a sickly woman who died when he was eleven years old. Two years later his "soft-skinned" and "effeminate" father remarried "for the kids" but allowed no discussion of his first wife. The brother, M. had recently learned, was a homosexual, something that disturbed him. M. himself often had sexual dreams of young boys and felt older men, including his adopted father, were attracted to him. One specific reason his wife left him was her distaste for what she saw as his sadism but which he felt was merely "playful torture" in wanting to tie down his sexual partners when he was aroused. He had fantasies of maintaining dependent women whom he could completely control.

In the first couch hour Mr. M. remarked on Anna Ornstein's Auschwitz tattoo.[44] It was her experience that her patients almost always remarked on her tattoo, though mostly along the lines of "How can I complain about my problems when you have been through Auschwitz?" M., however, responded more narcissistically in a way that reflected his self-absorption. He felt her tattoo was an imposition on him. He would now have to "watch out for her" and would not be able to be angry. The tattoo was a sign of weakness, like his adoptive mother's chronic illness. He feared not being taken care of, which centered on his dread of deep regression and a kind of pervasive "psychoeconomic imbalance" that threatened him with a "loss of self boundaries." These fears undermined his writing. He thought he might spin off into orbit. "I am afraid of . . . floating away," he said. "In so much of the writing, I am not in control." M., however, came to experience Ornstein's interventions with great pleasure. "When you talk, I rise in ecstasy," he reported. "I don't take it in; the ecstasy is that you are talking about *me* and when you are right, such elation!"

In Kohut's version of the salient facts of the case, Mr. M. experienced his adoptive mother's responsiveness to him as "insufficient and faulty." As a child he recalled looking at her quickly so that she would be unable to cover her face with a falsely friendly smile. The absence of her "primary mirroring responses" left him fixated on some "archaic forms of exhibitionism," namely the sexual sadism. The adoptive father, on the other hand, a man with intellectual interests who collected dictionaries and loved words and language and might well have become M.'s role model, seemed unable to allow himself to be fully idealized by his son. That, says Kohut, was the real tragedy of M.'s early life. The opportunity existed for his father to provide a compensatory idealized alternative to the depressed and dying mother, yet the father, for whatever reason, was unable to play that role. But however important were the adoptive parents in M.'s psychological universe, behind them lay the underlying trauma of abandonment by his biological mother. Nothing M.'s adoptive mother did to him, for example, or any failure in her empathic response to him, makes sense unless we also consider the "vulnerability of the child's psyche due to analogous earlier traumatization." Behind the layers of frustration that M. felt toward his parents "hovered always a nameless preverbal depression, apathy, sense of deadness, and diffuse rage that related to the primordial trauma of his life."[45]

The nuances of Mr. M.'s sexuality are particularly important in understanding his self pathology. Besides his heterosexual sadism, M. recalled a scene once at twelve years of age of being made to stand naked in an empty room while his father took pictures of him. The emptiness of the room symbolized for him the "lack of warmth and the unprotected exposure of his childhood." He remembered feeling humiliated but assuming an arrogant posture in response to being on display, and associated to the fact that he was the favored child, the smartest, and the one later sent to a good Eastern college. His fantasy as he thought about the picture-taking scene was that his father had adopted him for the purposes of sexual exploitation (though, except for taking the pictures, his father never did anything in reality to confirm that fantasy). Neither Ornstein nor Kohut could exclude the possibility that M. was in the throes of a "negative Oedipus complex" and "resisting" his latent homosexuality in the transference. But several details argued against such an interpretation. There was, for one thing, an almost complete absence of homosexual themes in M.'s associations. Second, the primary affect he experienced as he thought about the picture-taking scene was a deep humiliation. The suggestion, in other words, was that M. longed to be close to his idealized father. That longing then got sexualized to "stem the tide of regression" at moments of crisis and frustration. The reversal of the humiliation also entered into M.'s sadistic fantasies in the transference, which became a central theme in his thoughts about Ornstein (images of knocking her down, for example, as he walked into the office behind her).[46]

Toward the beginning of the third year of analytic work—short by the standards of the day—Mr. M. seemed to have improved significantly and announced he was ready to terminate. In fact, M. was to continue for most of that year in his "termination phase," but both Ornstein and Kohut felt an end was appropriate on many grounds. In general, Kohut says it is important to trust a patient's wish to terminate, especially after good work over many years and if there is no sign of an "immediate urgency" suggesting a flight from disturbing material. But much more specifically, Kohut felt M. had strengthened "[self] structures whose rehabilitation contributed decisively to the establishment of M.'s psychological well-being." Kohut mentions in this regard three decisive acts in M.'s life during the final phase of his analysis that are the evidence for its successful completion.

First (in thematic, not in the less important chronological order), Mr. M. bought an expensive violin near the conclusion of his analysis and almost simultaneously abandoned the idea of ever playing it. This counter-intuitive indication of "progress" Kohut sees as a result of M.'s reaching beyond the archaic levels of stimulation to which he had earlier responded and moving toward the (for him) higher levels of cognition and creativity that his writing represented. M. had taken up playing the violin during treatment. But he lacked real talent. He would never truly experience self expression in playing the violin. It was, in fact, a digression, even a retreat, from the more psychologically organized work of writing, where his skills, talents, and commitments lay.

Second, Mr. M. had had a transformative experience with a fourteen-year-old boy. M. had intentionally befriended the boy's parents in order to get to know their youngest son. M. was deeply impressed with the mature, loving way the father treated the boy with respect as an independent being while remaining very close and nurturing. Once M. took the boy to a base-ball game. At the park M. spotted an old girlfriend and worried whether he should greet her. His fear was the boy would feel he was not paying full attention to him. After some deliberation, M. did in fact greet the woman. To his immense relief, the boy was not at all disturbed. It was an uplifting experience that was "unaccountably joyful." That joy—which as a concept Kohut relates to the "total self"—came from M.'s vicarious experience (a kind of twinship with the boy) of feeling the "internalization of the functions of the idealized father." In the scene at the ballpark, in other words, M. identified with the boy but was also psychologically the supporting actor and the audience. He was both himself and his idealized father, able now to consolidate lost images in a rebuilt self.

Finally, Mr. M. founded a writing school during the termination phase of his analysis. The idea had occurred to him earlier, but he had assumed he would never be able to follow through on all the details and actually make the school happen. Then one night it came as a kind of inspiration; he awoke with "an effective motivating force impelling him toward action." Now he felt able to make the school a reality. M.'s enthusiasm was unbounded. He reported with great excitement in treatment everything to do with the school, and Ornstein was able to understand that he was a great inspiration for his students. M. felt deep empathy for his students' clumsiness with words, which came out of his own thought (or learning) disorder, yet at the same time could offer them and himself the hope for creative alternatives in writing clearly and effectively. M. now felt a "constant flow of energy" rather than his previous "bursts which were always disorganizing."[47]

The "classical position" about the Oedipus complex, says Kohut, is that a child, after some preliminary steps, is drawn inexorably in late infancy into a psychological quandary of feeling sexual desire for the parent of the opposite sex and murderous wishes toward the other parent as a rival. The inability either to satisfy one's wishes or to resolve them forces radical structural change in the psyche, which includes repression of desire in the "id" and the creation of "superego" functions built around identification with the parent of the same sex. If these new barriers are firmly drawn and yet sufficiently permeable to allow for flexibility and change, the ego can move into the next developmental stage. The child goes to school.[48]

Kohut lays out this theory in *Restoration* as an established body of fact that is basically beyond dispute. His purpose, he says, trying to convince himself as much as his reader, is not to question the Oedipus complex per se but to show that a self perspective on development opens new avenues of thinking about problems relating to psychosexual stresses and structure formation. Such perspectives take several forms. For one thing, Kohut says, Freud failed to emphasize that, at the very least, the "presence of a firm self is a precondition for the experience of the Oedipus complex." How can it be otherwise? Only a child who "sees himself as a delimited, abiding, independent center of initiative" will be able to experience the kind of desires and hatreds that so occupied Freud's imagination.[49] Kohut also asks, tellingly, what happens when the cohesive self of a normal child, experiencing a range of feelings for the first time in an assertive (and healthy) way in late infancy, encounters not borderline or psychotic parents but loving and normal enough ones with their own cohesive selves? Kohut's unequivocal answer is that such parents respond with pride and joy to this new phase of their growing child. These normal parents are "people who, despite their stimulation by and competition with the rising generation, are also sufficiently in touch with the pulse of life, accept themselves sufficiently as transient participants in the ongoing stream of life, to be able to experience the growth of the next generation with unforced nondefensive joy."[50]

In fact, nearly everything Kohut says about the Oedipus complex in *The Restoration of the Self*,[51] as well as other publications around the same time, undermines the theory as Freud articulated it. For example, Kohut says clearly (if imbedded in a sentence of ninety-seven words with one semicolon and an obscuring set of dashes) that the oedipal phase is "not the pivotal point regarding the fate of the self. " His suspicion is that such a shift in consciousness regarding psychosexual development occurs much earlier than late infancy, though he refuses to be pinned down about an exact time. Anything more precise at this point, he says, risks confining self psychology to an overly concrete characterization. Furthermore, what Freud describes as normal desires and anxieties for a child caught in oedipal dilemmas may be instead "the child's reactions to empathy failures" during this phase of life. For a child of four years of age to wish for sexual union with one parent and harbor murderous impulses toward the other suggests to Kohut a child in trouble, not one close to the true depths of experience that lurk in the human soul.[52]

Kohut also strongly disagrees with Freud that a woman's wish for a baby can be in the last analysis reduced to a wish for a penis. That, says Kohut, was one of Freud's "badly skewed opinions." On the contrary, "a healthy woman's wish for a child is, in psychological terms, grasped much more adequately as a manifestation of her nuclear self, as a manifestation of her most central ambitions and ideals—in short, as the high point of a development that has its beginning in the archaic self's urge toward self-expression."[53] In general, most of what Freud understood as primary drive expressions are in fact merely secondary phenomena. Sadism and masochism, for example, are not expressions of primary instinctual impulses that can only be tenuously held in check by the structures of defense and control in the psychic apparatus. Where one sees such drive behavior—and one sees its derivatives often in clinical practice—what has happened is that the cohesive self and its deep empathic connection with caretaking others has broken apart, releasing the drive as a "disintegration product." The drive is then enlisted in an attempt to bring about the "lost merger (and thus the repair of the self) by pathological means." This process is what Kohut meant by "sexualization." Mr. A. (the lead case from *The Analysis of the Self*, to whom he now returned), for example, had normal needs to merge with his ideal father and draw strength and greatness from him that were traumatically unmet. To find some fleeting sense of wholeness, A. sexualized his relationship to the fragments of his needs. In fantasy he enslaved a strong male whose power he sucked in through his semen.[54]

The very concept of the self, Kohut said at a meeting with his colleagues during the period in which he was writing *Restoration*, the idea of an ebullient self, of a functional unit in space and time, is altogether different from a drive bound to a zone of the body (mouth, sphincter, genitals). Such a Freudian notion of the self is possible only if you insist on starting with the unlikely idea that the drives and nothing else are the biological precondition of psychological experience.[55] In fact, Kohut, much as he tried, had trouble finding anything good to say for Freud's idea of the drives and their complicated relationship to the Oedipus complex. In *Restoration* Kohut tries to show through the case vignette of Miss V. that she struggled with some oedipal issues, but he ends up proving the opposite.[56] In seminars at the Institute he often asserted the necessity for oedipal theory, but all his illustrations were counterexamples. Once in June 1974, for example, he tried to talk about hysteria in relation to oedipal theory, but in fact could only muster examples of pseudo-hysteria in which apparently oedipal issues actually covered disturbances in the self.[57] It is as though Kohut was ahead of himself in his formulations. He could not entirely let go of an article of faith, the Oedipus complex, that had for so long served as the bulwark of his theoretical system. He knew at some level that Freud was wrong. He just could not say it in so many words.

The most important contribution to clinical theory in *Restoration* is Kohut's ideas on the "self-state dream." Freud's dream book, including its many elaborations over the years, sharply distinguishes what he calls in an intentionally derogatory way the *manifest* content of the dream from its underlying repressed, latent thoughts. What comes into our minds as a series of images during sleep is, for Freud, interesting but confused and largely superficial psychologically. What matters are the repressed thoughts stirred by the events of the dream day but linked symbolically to one's deepest childhood conflicts, which create the images in the mind we experience as a dream. Much of *The Interpretation of Dreams* deals with this tension between the phenomenological dream itself and its unconscious meanings. Freud is particularly concerned with how these two seemingly antithetical phases of the dream process get expressed. Chapter 6, for example, a chapter that Freud vastly expanded in length over the years, details the psychological mechanisms by which the dream is constructed (condensation, displacement, symbolization, and secondary revision). For Freud what the dreamer sees in his or her mind's eye is not what really matters. There is a much deeper reality behind that experience.[58]

Kohut came to question this distinction as artificial. Typically, Kohut *says* that what Freud identified as the meaning of dreams remains valid for a circumscribed realm of experience. But a "second" type of dream interests Kohut much more. These "self-state dreams" portray a person's "uncontrollable tension-increase or his dread of the dissolution of the self." In these dreams, free association, which was Freud's treasured method of reaching beyond the manifest content and into the unconscious depths, is of little help. Instead, the approach is that of "scrutiny of the manifest content and of the associative elaborations of the manifest content" to get at how the healthy sectors of the psyche are "reacting with anxiety to a disturbing change in the condition of the self." Such dreams bear some resemblance to those of children, or dreams of what Freud called "traumatic neuroses," which we might be more likely to consider dream reactions related to posttraumatic stress disorder (PTSD), or the kind of hallucinatory dreams of drugged states or when we have a high fever. Associations to such dreams lead only toward a greater focus on the anxiety itself. Correct interpretations of self-state dreams, furthermore, have little to do with unconscious thoughts and much more with the particular situation that led to the intrusion into the psyche of archaic material[59] that generated anxiety in the form of a nameless dread of disintegration.

This fear of disintegration is bedrock. Dreams that tell of fragmentation anxiety, Kohut says with examples from his practice, might include the frightening infestation of "spreading vermin" in one's home, or the "ominous discovery of algae in the swimming pool."[60] In an Institute seminar around the same time he wrote *Restoration*, Kohut gives some other examples. Fragmenting and disturbed people, he says, have dreams of things falling apart. Self-state dreams are disorganized, chaotic, exploded and exploding. Pieces from mechanical contrivances that one has to put together at home scatter about, or body parts are strewn all over, or there are rapid content shifts from one part to another of an otherwise innocuous dream. Color in dreams can also be significant in this regard, expressing the overburdened quality of the psyche, especially in those who do not usually remark on color in their dreams. Patients, for example, might report unusual greens, pinks, or phosphorescent "Day-Glo" colors. In trying to understand such dreams, what one should address is not the content as much as the tension state behind it.[61] What is at stake is the self, Kohut says in *Restoration*, and "the fragmentation of and the estrangement from [one's] body and mind in space, the breakup of the sense of [one's] continuity in time."[62]

Kohut's ideas on the self-state dream were not entirely outside of an important tradition in psychoanalysis that stressed the significance of the dream's manifest content. Thomas French at the Chicago Institute in the 1940s had been one of the key researchers in this new approach to the dream, as were many ego psychologists after the war, especially Erik Erikson.[63] It is impossible to say how much Kohut was influenced by such writers—he disdained French as mechanical and Erikson as superficial— but he could not have been unaware of the general move on the part of many thinkers in psychoanalysis away from Freud's rigid, schematic views and toward the idea that within the complex and evocative images that fill our minds each night lies the real meaning of the dream.[64] It is also true that Kohut seemed to gravitate naturally toward the interpretation of the dream itself, as one might to a work of literature or art. As early as 1960 in a seminar with some colleagues at the Institute, for example, he free-associated to someone's use of the word "crossroads" in the report of a patient's dream. Kohut said he had noticed how patients often dream of crossroads at crucial times in their treatment. "One road is clear and short, another one dangerous, with warning signs, and leading into an uncertain distance. At such moments the analyst takes heed and must ask himself whether the patient's warning is justified, whether the road is too dangerous."[65] Kohut once even suggested to an expert on projective tests the idea of doing Rorschachs on the manifest content of the dreams of people with self disorders to see how they correlated with other measures of their pathology.[66] In the course of the 1960s Kohut basically arrived at the concept of the self-state dream but not the term itself. In *Analysis* he talks of narcissistic dreams like flying or falling, of machines with spin-ning wheels, of circling the earth in a rocket outside of the gravitational pull.[67] The dream examples in *Analysis* are all clinical and serve to illus-trate the nature of narcissism as he then understood it. What is missing and only implicit in that discussion, and what is developed in *Restor-ation*, is the actual theory of the self-state dream that places it as a cornerstone in the overall psychology of the self.

The most interesting and subtle self-state dream in *Restoration* is that of Mr. W. (the psychiatrist Peter Barglow), disguised as a journalist. Barglow struggled with issues of separation dating from his childhood. In the transference he became unusually sensitive and restless when con-fronted with any kind of separation from Kohut. The clue to the signifi-cance of his feelings came in a dream toward the end of that first year, when Kohut announced he would be gone for a week in New York. In the dream Barglow is on a plane flying from Chicago to New York. He is sitting on the left side of the plane looking out the window at the south-ern horizon. Kohut commented with surprise on the inconsistency of this detail. If one were flying east, the left side of the plane would face north, not south. Barglow became "utterly confused and spatially disoriented" as he thought about Kohut's comment and the dream. For a while he could not even tell left from right, a disorientation that repeated itself often throughout the analysis. Barglow's plane dream is a particularly interesting illustration of a self-state dream of disorientation reflecting his panic and fear of fragmentation at the impending separation from Kohut. The truest and "deepest" meaning of the dream lies in his fear of disintegration, which finds expression in the tiny detail of facing the wrong way when looking out the window of the plane.[68]

The reflection of the fragmenting self in dreams is often varied and nuanced. Kohut told candidates in an Institute seminar around this time of a narcissistically disturbed patient who dreamed of taking apart a broken watch and finding it was not working because inside there was a "sensitive little flower" growing. Despite the patient's rages and confusions, in other words, he felt sensitive and scared but afraid to show or assert his needs.[69]

For all of Freud's brooding pessimism, his death instinct, which makes violence biological, his cautious ideals for therapeutic change, and his constitutional aversion to naive enthusiasms, his psychology offers qualified hope for sufferers of childhood trauma. The past as it lives in the self can be reworked, changed, transformed. But there was a correlate to the theory that history had not yet revealed to be as limited as it was. Adult experience, for Freud, is the distillate of childhood conflicts centered around the Oedipus complex. Only those events that symbolically touched the unmastered and repressed feelings of infancy had psychological salience. Life for Freud has a derivative quality. We feed off the past. There is little that is new and authentic for the adult. The Holocaust changed that. It showed that real events could stir anxieties.[70]

Kohut understood this dimension of history as not outside of but within and very much a part of his ambivalent relationship to his own Jewishness. Kohut's whole meaning structure took shape in the shadow of the Holocaust. It imposed itself on him, unwillingly and tragically. He escaped Vienna and death but not the event. His mature theory reflects that experience. In Kohut's world of the self we have no choice but to grapple with the tragic in our unrealized dreams from childhood but also in the here and now, in the world, in history. It is ever in us. Sexual conflict, however important, recedes before the despair of unmirrored ambitions and a world devoid of ideals. For Kohut the pervasive guilt Freud put at the center of psychological experience is ultimately epiphenomenal. The struggle of the self against fragmentation defines the contours of meaning in postmodern life. New patterns of family life refract this psycho-historical change for the therapist. In the late nineteenth century, large middle-class and upper middle-class families with servants furnished the patients for Freud's practice. Their sexual conflicts made sense in terms of their overstimulation in their families of origin, which were seething with explosive intimacy. A century later, as Kohut argued at some length in *Restoration*, depression stalks the clinic, based in atomistic families without a center, with everyone working and a lonely television blaring.[71]

Kohut believed in the essential goodness of people. He thought empathy was the normal experience between selfobjects. He felt the frustrations of development were, for the most part, "optimal," which is to say within the range of the correctable. He always approached mental illness as an aberration. Even the tragic, he felt, could be the wellspring of the best and most inspiring expressions of human creativity. Tolstoy, for example, wrote his best books early when he could give voice to those reverberations of great sorrow in himself and in Russia. But when the "guilt-laden moralist" took over, his "creative core" disintegrated.[72] Death itself, to take another example, can be triumphant, as with the inspiring courage of Franz Jaegerstaetter and the Scholls opposing the Nazi behemoth, or certainly awesome and moving, as in great literature when the tragic figure realizes, through his actions, the "blueprint for his life that had been laid down in his nuclear self."[73] Kohut's favorite dramatic lines that summarize the sense of *The Restoration of the Self* were from Eugene O'Neill's *The Great God Brown*: "Man is born broken. He lives by mending. The grace of God is glue."[74]

Part Five

THE BIRTH
OF THE HERO
1977–1981

Twenty-five

HEROES AND GURUS

There is a long tradition of heroes in psychoanalysis.[1] Each makes a claim to psychological truth and to an understanding of the nature of cure. Most are charismatic and exercise a powerful influence on those whose lives they touch. Key followers become disciples who carry forward the work of the master often with a certainty that has an ideological, if not religious, quality to it. Movements of varying size and endurance are spawned. Significant institutional realignment takes place. Psychoanalytic training centers are thrown into upheaval and splits often occur. Patients move toward the new approach, as do candidates, eager to ride the crest of the latest development. Books are written and journals created. A new orientation—Jungian, Rankian, Kleinian, Ferenczian, and, of course, Kohutian—is born, named, and baptized. Nor is this process of psycho-analytic death and rebirth a quiet one. Dissidents provoke huge fights. People who have been colleagues for years with complex emotional and professional ties suddenly develop permanent animosities. It is an amaz-ing process that has happened so often in the last century as to become almost ritualistic. It occurs in the name of science but clearly touches deeper human needs.

Perhaps we should not be surprised. Michael Polanyi has described with great sensitivity (and psychological astuteness) the way scientific controversies generate movements, heroes, and disciples. As Polanyi makes clear, such controversies from physics to psychoanalysis are never entirely within science, even if truth, or Truth, is the common goal. What emerges in such struggles is the central effort to discover whether "a new system of thought concerning a whole class of alleged facts" should be accepted or rejected in principle. Individual facts and certainly isolated experiences or experiments prove nothing, because a "logical gap" separates the two conflicting systems of thought. Formulations of any proposition within one framework cannot convince someone thinking within the conflicting framework. The two frameworks constitute different worlds of discourse. To listen sympathetically one accepts the doctrine, which is a "heuristic process, a self-modifying act, and to this extent a conversion." A "school" or movement emerges, further separating its members by a logical gap from those outside of it.[2]

Movements, however, also have heroes, though one should remember the modern concept of hero exists within a historical and textual tradition. The Greek priestess Hero cast herself into the sea when her lover, Leander, died. Death and suffering have always been associated with the Western concept of the hero. Otto Rank, in his study of the mythology of heroes, stresses the pattern of the birth of the hero outside the mainstream, his abandonment, followed by his miraculous recovery.[3] In the ancient Hindu tradition, on the other hand, the guru is closer to what we might call a revered teacher. Gurus usually lived within an aristocratic family, in which they had a special relationship to ceremony and caste, and served as teachers of the children. The guru became a kind of cross between an adopted father and a resident holy man (and for families of modest means the father, in his role as teacher, was regarded as the guru). The culture defined elaborate restrictions for those who related to the guru—the worst sin of all was to sleep with the guru's wife—but offered no limitations on the behavior of the guru himself. In time a more specifically religious role for the guru emerged in the culture. The Buddha was the first such charismatic guru.[4]

Richard Noll, in his work on Carl Jung, has described the way in which preening nineteenth-century figures directed these varied currents of thought and tradition into a specific notion of genius that is highly relevant for understanding contemporary psychoanalytic heroes. From the pages of romantic poetry penned by Byronic figures stalking the heath with flowing hair before their tragic early deaths came a series of figures in art and science later in the century who set themselves up as creative geniuses changing the course of history. Disciples were a mandatory part of this process, for without a following a genius remained inconsequential, empty, without echo or a symbolically immortalized future. In music the first such figure was Wagner, around whom a cult quickly gathered. The tradition generated the imperative for rebellion. The script required submission to the genius as essential for learning. That experience of discipleship sparked in turn the recognition of one's own genius. The result, inevitably, was a break with the original, revered figure and the establishment of one's own movement. No one fitted this story line better than Carl Jung, whose apprenticeship with Freud was followed by probably the noisiest of all psychoanalytic splits.[5]

In recent years history has forced these varied traditions into a narrow channel. The contemporary judgment on gurus has not been kind. Most people quickly associate the great charismatic figures of the age with genocide, from Hitler and Stalin to Pol Pot and on a smaller scale Milosevic, Karadzic, and Tudjman of the former Yugoslavia. It is only on second thought, for the most part, that figures such as Winston Churchill, Mahatma Gandhi, Martin Luther King, Jr., Nelson Mandela, and Václav Havel come to mind as counterexamples, and then it is often unclear how we figure them in our genealogy of genius. Even on a small scale, we have become painfully familiar with cult figures such as Jim Jones initiating mass suicide as an extension of their paranoid certainty and crumbling worlds. It is practically an article of faith in the popular media that charismatic figures "malign rationalism" and "exhort us to abandon critical thinking in order to realize spiritual growth."[6] Recent psychoanalytic thinking has tended to reinforce such views. Anthony Storr, for example, calling on examples that range from Jim Jones to Jesus, suggests that most gurus are "false prophets, madmen, confidence tricksters, or unscrupulous psychopaths who exploit their disciples emotionally, financially, and sexually." The guru claims special insight as a result of his unique relationship to a higher power, who confers on him the right, even the obligation, to generalize from his own experience about the nature of the human condition. Storr argues, with people such as Jim Jones in mind, that gurus as children tend to be isolated, introverted, and narcissistic. They are intolerant of criticism and tend to feel that anything less than wholehearted agreement is the same as hostility. Unpredictable and unbound by tradition, gurus must possess charisma and attract disciples without acquiring friends. They hold intense convictions, for which they claim superior wisdom, and they often invent a background of mystery. The nature of their leadership contains within it the dynamics to propel it forward. As Storr concludes: "It is intoxicating to be adored, and it becomes increasingly difficult for the guru not to concur with the beliefs of his disciples about him."[7]

Nearly everything Storr says about gurus has echoes in Kohut's life. One can tick off the categories: the special insight; the symbolic tie to the founder; the generalization from personal experience to the human condition; the childhood loneliness and the narcissism; the hypersensitivity to criticism; the acquisition of disciples and the loss of friends; the intensity of the convictions; the unpredictable behavior and freedom from the bounds of traditions; the invention of a background of mystery; and certainly the intoxication of adoration that propelled the movement forward. *Die Jünger* kept Kohut alive to continue his work of psychoanalytic rebirth as self psychology, something that began clearly to happen in the late 1970s. Several important figures joined the Chicago group in those years, including Bernard Brandchaft, Morton and Estelle Shane, Evelyn Schwaber (for a time), Robert Stolorow, and Arthur Malin. That process, in turn, kept cloning itself after Kohut's death. A National Council of Self Psychology was formed; it later became international in scope and name. Several self psychology training institutes were established in New York City and elsewhere, and even most traditional institutes came to include a self "track" in their curriculums. Splits and splintering have been perhaps the inevitable result of such growth, with the result that some in self psychology barely speak to each other, but there is also no question it all started with Heinz Kohut.[8]

Kohut once reflected with candor and humanity about this issue of his own charisma. It bothered him a lot that he seemed to have a powerful influence on his followers, for his beloved field, psychoanalysis, was supposed to be a science. He fully appreciated the negative connotations of the idea of self psychology as a "movement." Yet he felt, for example, that no one could possibly write a history of psychoanalysis or self psychology unless he was inside it. And that is the paradox. Freud's charismatic personality imposed itself on psychoanalysis, Kohut felt, and probably accounted for all the splintering of the field, as well as the tendency toward orthodoxy. Kohut as well attracted a huge following, and in an implicit comparison with Freud he once allowed himself to engage in some boasting: how 960 people came to the conference in Boston and 1,200 would have if there had been space; how people all over the world were interested in self psychology; how people from all over the country traveled to Chicago to attend the monthly meetings of the self psychology workshop in Chicago; how eight analysts at that time regularly commuted from

Canada every other week just to be supervised by Kohut; and so on. Was all that merely transference? he asked. Was it all merely a cult?[9]

Kohut, though born in Vienna, remains probably the most important American psychoanalyst and self psychology the first and most significant American-based psychoanalytic movement. Kohut self-consciously shaped that movement as the culmination of his life's work. He was undoubtedly a flawed hero. His contradictions may even have overwhelmed the project he so treasured. But maybe what he created has the potential to transcend its own peculiar origins. Certainly, Kohut himself would fully recognize the ironies of his required presence—absolute and heroic—at the birth of a movement that eventually must emerge from under his huge shadow and create its own destiny.

Twenty-six

THE AUTOBIOGRAPHY OF MR. Z

Perhaps the most remarkable thing Kohut ever did was to write an entire case history that was pure autobiography, his own story in disguised form. He did so in the summer of 1977 at sixty-four years of age. Nothing he ever did more clearly marked his heroic sense of himself. "The Two Analyses of Mr. Z," presented by Kohut as somber psychoanalytic case material and published in the profession's most respected journal, reveals his deepest psychological experience.[1]

The background to the story began when Kohut first heard a young analyst in training, Anita Eckstaedt, present her control case in Germany when he was there in December 1970.[2] The case captured Kohut's imagination, though he felt Eckstaedt "consistently misunderstood" the patient's personality.[3] Kohut seems to have asked Eckstaedt, when he first heard her presentation, for permission to write up the case on his own. She wrote him on July 8, 1971, asking tentatively for further clarification about how he wanted to use the case. He sent her his recently published book, *The Analysis of the Self*, though the copy of his actual letter in reply has not survived. In any event, her follow-up letter to him on August 9 was friendly, and she was pleased with his explanation. He now had general permission to use the case but was uncertain exactly how and when he intended to make use of it. Things were left vague with Eckstaedt. In the next few years Kohut often referred to the case in seminars and meetings. In the summer of 1975, however, while on vacation in Carmel, he decided to write it up for his new book, *The Restoration of the Self* (1977). It was in that connection that he wrote Eckstaedt on August 8, 1975, formally asking for her permission to use the case. In that letter he told her his disguise was foolproof (he made the aspiring theologian an idealistic American who was rejected by the Peace Corps and sought treatment with a younger colleague) and urged her to tell no one so that the identity of the theologian would remain hidden.[4]

In the spring of 1977, however, just after the publication of *Restoration* and as the issue of its German translation came up, Anita Eckstaedt raised two contradictory concerns. On the one hand, she wanted more recognition for her role as the analyst in treating the young man than Kohut had provided in his heavily disguised published version of the case, while on the other she was worried that in German the young man might detect himself in the case and that it was not sufficiently disguised.[5] Kohut was increasingly fed up with the dilemma. He saw no way to satisfy her mutually exclusive demands. His son, Thomas A. Kohut, remembers well the discussion back and forth about the case during the family vacation that summer in Carmel. Kohut was also recovering from the blow of being voted off the Institute Council the previous spring. Perhaps that event—to which he reacted far out of proportion to its real significance—jolted him into a new determination to identify his truer self. In any event, one day in late September Kohut suddenly disappeared into his study and came out a few days later with "The Two Analyses of Mr. Z." That case, duly translated, was substituted for the case of "X" in the German version of *Restoration, Die Heilung des Selbst*, which appeared in 1979. Kohut published the English version in the *International Journal of Psychoanalysis* the same year, after some careful editing by Natalie Altman, whom he hired on a freelance basis to go over this paper.[6] The actual format for the case may have drawn on the recently published paper "My Experience of Analysis with Fairbairn and Winnicott" (1975), in which Harry Guntrip describes his two analyses and how different and yet overlapping they were.[7]

After Kohut returned to Chicago from Carmel, he began what became an elaborate process in the fall of 1977 to throw everyone off the trail of the true identity of Mr. Z. To avoid confrontation with the obviously autobiographical details, he did not read his draft of the case out loud to his wife and son, unlike *everything* else he wrote. As a result, neither Thomas nor Elizabeth Kohut really read the case until after Kohut's death. They knew about Z in general but not in particular. Kohut in turn dealt with it glancingly in the family. He never told his wife or son that the material in

"Mr. Z" was autobiographical. It was left to Thomas to infer it after Kohut's death, but once he made his argument to his mother she was completely convinced (though we have to take his word on that, as she talked to no one and left no written record of her feelings on the subject before her death in 1992). In retrospect, Thomas is also aware how differently Kohut dealt with the response to the case compared to his other writings. Normally, he was devastated by criticism and would talk for days and weeks about this or that unfair attack. When people attacked his paper on Z, however, he always chuckled and shrugged it off. Once Thomas was with Kohut when they met a man on the street to whom Thomas was introduced. Afterward, Thomas asked if that was Z. Kohut laughed uproariously and said, "No, don't worry about it, that is not Mr. Z"; at the time, Thomas did not get the joke.[8]

With colleagues as well, beginning that fall of 1977, Kohut began to construct an elaborate ruse about Mr. Z's course of treatment.[9] The more he talked, it seems, the more real the case became. Thomas feels his father must have loved this giant prank, and that it was an extension of the many adolescent jokes he and his peers played on their teachers in school. "This was part of him being a trickster," Thomas says. "He was very much like that."[10] Kohut, for example, once took a phone call while in a conversation with Michael Franz Basch and said afterward it was Mr. Z.[11] He often talked with his colleague, Arnold Goldberg, about the case.[12] He discussed Z with some patients who had special status as therapists themselves.[13] With supervisees he often referred to the case for teaching purposes.[14] In his last, posthumously published book—*How Does Analysis Cure?*—Kohut goes on at length about the criticisms of his case of Mr. Z (especially that of Mortimer Ostow in the *International Journal of Psycho-Analysis*) and how off base everyone had been.[15] He eagerly sought out the views of colleagues on the case.[16] Before publication, he even solemnly presented "Mr. Z" in seminars at the Chicago Institute for Psychoanalysis. The paper would be distributed ahead of time with all the hush-hush that normally surrounds the presentation of a case. At the conclusion of the seminar all participants then had to return their numbered copies to protect the confidentiality of the "patient." In all ways, Kohut created the illusion that this preeminent case in his professional life was a real person he had treated.[17]

The fit between Kohut's life and that of Mr. Z is exact in all important respects. Both were only children. The mother in the case is hauntingly like what Thomas Kohut remembers about his grandmother, including her bearing and her interest in painting and poetry. And the stories from Z's childhood fit exactly with the few accounts Kohut gave of his own childhood to his son. Like Z's, Kohut's father was absent during the few years before he was five, just as the scene in the ski lodge with Z's father fits exactly the story Kohut used to tell about his own father. Certain telling details carry over from the life directly into the case history (and such small things may be the most revealing evidence of all). Thus Kohut, like Z, had an early and significant encounter with *Uncle Tom's Cabin*, a book he talked to his son about all his life. The camp counselor in the case is clearly Kohut's childhood tutor, Ernst Morawetz. Kohut's parents, like Z's, were distant with each other. Sometimes there are discrepancies. Thus Z's father once joins a small band and sings on an impromptu basis, whereas Felix Kohut was an expert piano player. Finally, the first analyst who got it all wrong was Ruth Eissler, Kohut's training analyst in the 1940s,[18] while in the case it is the Freudian Kohut himself. But such disguises tend to prove the identity of the case and the life more than dispute it.

It is also highly unlikely that if Kohut had been treating a patient as relevant for his theory as Mr. Z, he would have only thought of mentioning him, let alone writing him up, as late as the summer of 1977. The case describes two analyses that each lasted four years with a break of five and a half years between them. That means the treatment of Z stretched over thirteen and a half years. In the first analysis, before Kohut had come to his new ideas on narcissism and the self, he reports making some progress with Z but fails to reach the depths of his problems. Over five years elapse, and the patient returns. There is then another four years of a second analysis. Dreams are reconsidered, and the whole construct of the patient's self emerges with much greater clarity. He is healed. Furthermore, from one detail in the case this whole sequence can be calculated as having begun in 1954 or 1955 and ended in 1967 or 1968 (Z sends Kohut a postcard of congratulations on what can only have been his election as president of the American in 1964 just prior to his second analysis). And yet in all that time—and for the next ten years—through numerous papers and talks and through two entire books that include his most creative writings on narcissism and the self, we are to believe that the otherwise loquacious Kohut never once referred to what is clearly the archetypal case in self psychology nor mentioned its course of treatment to a single colleague. Most unlikely.

Geoffrey Cocks has made an argument for why, in part, Kohut may

have chosen the letter Z to designate the case. Kohut had long since established the principle of using in sequence the letters of the alphabet for
his cases. His first book thus begins with Mr. A. and his second opens
with Mr. M. By 1977 he had the letters S and T still free, but he jumped
to Z. Cocks thinks that the choice of the letter Z had to do with his fondness for the Triestine author Italo Svevo, whose real name was Ettore
Schmitz. Svevo was of German-Austrian-Italian-Jewish ancestry. His most
famous novel is *Confessions of Zeno,* first published in 1923 in Italian. Kohut
definitely read some version of it in German in the late 1920s, or one of
its post–Second World War English translations. One chapter that Kohut
told Thomas he particularly liked was "Psychoanalysis of the First Cigarette," which describes the hero's attempt to stop smoking, about which
Kohut was himself concerned. Zeno goes to an analyst but gives up on
him on May 3, 1915 (Kohut's birthday), and tries self-analysis.[19] My own
theory is simpler: there is something evocative and dramatic about culminating one's work with one's own story, designated by the last letter
of the alphabet.

Of course, it cannot be absolutely proven that Mr. Z never existed as
such and that the case is pure autobiography. Perhaps some day a man
will come forward with adequate documentation to prove his existence
as the real Z. The rumors about the true identity of Z that proliferated
for years were neither confirmed nor dispelled entirely by Geoffrey Cocks
(quoting Thomas Kohut) in his introduction to the selection of Kohut's
letters that was published in 1994. Cocks did not elaborate on the evidence or carry out further research on the issue himself.[20] And there are
some strong arguments against the idea of Kohut as Z. It is a surprisingly
brash thing to have done. It is also troubling to believe that someone
of Kohut's stature would falsely present case material as confirmation
of his theory. It may be difficult to retain a hold on any illusions about
the "science" of psychoanalysis, though one hopes for a remnant of faith
in the integrity of the enterprise. Such concerns, however, may be ill-
considered. Robert Stolorow, in what is perhaps an extreme view, believes that "in the current climate of litigiousness, you're in trouble if
you *don't* make up a case. It is now considered good practice in the field
to give case presentations that are actually amalgamations of several
patients. It is considered legally problematic if you use an actual patient
for a case."[21]

In addition, Kohut faced special circumstances regarding exposure as
he moved toward writing his autobiography. Self-disclosure is always

risky and could well have seemed positively dangerous for a mainstream psychoanalyst in the late 1970s. He was freer then intellectually and emotionally and not surprisingly sought a means of telling his own story in a way that integrated it into his work. But there was no easy way to do that. To be honest about his own experience would have required that he write about some decidedly personal matters. Probably no one in the world of psychoanalysis was more controversial than Heinz Kohut at the time. A frank autobiographical account would have been used against him mercilessly and might well have damaged his reputation; in this regard, besides considering his own feelings, he had to calculate the impact on his patients. Not to write up his experience, however, would have left him a mysterious figure for future generations, leaving unrealized a corner of his own dreams of greatness, or what Robert Jay Lifton would call his "symbolic immortality." The compromise between these competing inclinations Kohut found was to write an autobiographical case but in heavy disguise. The case of Mr. Z, as vicarious autobiography, was written to explicate his theory and to make available the key facts of his childhood and self-discovery in analysis for biographers, whom he undoubtedly hoped would keep his name alive.

What Kohut did was actually not as much a departure from psychoanalytic discourse as it might seem. In fact, he wrote within a tradition, if a disavowed one. Many psychoanalysts and psychologists have used disguised parts of their own experience as case material. William James wrote about an anonymous Frenchman in *The Varieties of Religious Experience*, whom he later revealed was himself.[22] Sigmund Freud, without disguise, drew heavily on his own nightly reveries for *The Interpretation of Dreams*, and it may be that his self-analysis is the hidden model for all autobiography in psychoanalysis. At the very least, Freud seldom followed his own rules of clinical decorum. In writings over three decades Freud established three basic principles for the practice of psychoanalysis: anonymity, neutrality, and confidentiality. In 100 percent of the forty-three cases that can be studied from historical sources, he was not the opaque mirror he recommended others to be; in 86 percent of these cases he deviated from his rule of neutrality; and in nearly half of his cases (twenty) he gossiped shamelessly with patients about other patients.[23] Furthermore, Freud created false covers for himself. His "Screen Memories" paper of 1899 uses himself in disguise, as even his editor James Strachey acknowledges.[24] Elizabeth Young-Bruehl also argues cogently that one of the six cases Freud mentioned in his 1919 essay "A Child Is Being

Beaten" was his own daughter, Anna, whose analysis itself, while not kept from close associates, was a closely guarded secret in the psychoanalytic world at large for many decades.[25] Secrets, one might say, abound in psychoanalysis. Anna Freud's first paper, "Beating Fantasies and Daydreams," was entirely autobiographical. The case describes a patient in loving detail but was written six months before she saw her first client.[26] In 1921 James Jackson Putnam published the case of a man, a disguised version of himself, who was being nursed by his daughter, whose rustling dress stirred masturbatory fantasies.[27] Marie Bonaparte once wrote a paper, under the pseudonym A. E. Narjani, that described what she considered the anatomical cause of female sexual frigidity—too great a distance between the clitoris and vagina. Besides hiding behind a pseudonym, Bonaparte failed to mention the three operations on her own clitoris to "correct" her own frigidity.[28] Helene Deutsch begins her autobiography, *Confrontations with Myself*, by noting that only after writing the book did she realize "it forms a supplement to the autobiography hidden in my general work *The Psychology of Women*." One can be more specific. Deutsch had several deeply troubling miscarriages. In *The Psychology of Women*[29] she uses a disguised version of herself, a Mrs. Smith, to describe what she feels are the psychological factors in miscarriage and how an identification with another pregnant friend helped her compensate for and repair her own deficiencies in this area.[30] Deutsch may also have imbedded herself in her "Hysterical Fate-Neurosis," which describes a hysterical young woman, "beautiful, cultured, and of wealthy family," who in all ways refracts the experience of Deutsch herself.[31] Karen Horney, in turn, created her famous case of Clare out of the whole cloth of her own life.[32] Melanie Klein slyly describes herself and her children in several of her papers from the 1930s and early 1940s, papers that Kohut incidentally knew in some detail.[33] Eduardo Weiss, one of Kohut's teachers at the Chicago Institute for Psychoanalysis in the 1940s, used himself in disguise in several of his papers on agoraphobia from the 1930s.[34] One can only guess how many other somber cases in psychoanalysis from Sigmund Freud to Heinz Kohut (and beyond) are in fact autobiographies of the analyst and have little to do with their supposed patients. It is a slippery slope from science to solipsism.

When all is said and done, questions inevitably linger about "Mr. Z." The proof that Kohut is Z is all circumstantial. There is no smoking gun. It is telling that Kohut did not reveal his intentions to his wife or son and left nothing in writing to be discovered later. He made Thomas swear he would destroy his patient records, which Thomas apparently did.[35] But the rules of evidence in a biography are not those that govern a criminal court of law, where things must be proven beyond a reasonable doubt. One has to take the evidence as it comes and make the best, most intelligent, and most responsible use of it possible. "Proof" of most things that matter in history is seldom entirely satisfactory, though most contemporary philosophers would seriously question the quaint nineteenth-century positivist notion of absolute, ascertainable facts. We are always searching for truth in history, though it has to be said at the same time that some things are truer than others. It seems as true as one can ever hope to know that Kohut is the subject of "Mr. Z."[36]

One wonders, of course: Why write an autobiography at all and then go to such elaborate lengths to disguise it? There is something compelling about self-disclosure for anyone deeply committed to introspection. The deepest truth may be self-knowledge. Kohut connected his life with his theory and had to believe his life was in his work—indeed, that the life was inseparable from the theory. One can say Kohut sacrificed his life to his creativity. He was also sick and essentially dying from cancer when he wrote "Mr. Z." Perhaps writing his autobiography helped him look into the abyss to ponder the facts of his own making. And yet that was not an easy task for Heinz Kohut in the late 1970s. It would have been almost impossible to write about his own experience in any other way except in disguised form. Fame, ironically, boxed him in at just the point in his life when he was freest emotionally to talk honestly about himself. Disguising himself as a case was a clever way of getting around the dilemma of his own notoriety.

One cannot overestimate the significance of the lie he had to tell to create the disguise. Faking the case was not a trivial episode in his own life or in the history of psychoanalysis. Nor is Kohut's ruse about Mr. Z isolated from other aspects of his experience. It connects with the many areas of his life shrouded in mystery—identity, sexuality, illness—where the line between truth and falsehood blurred. Yet it would be facile to dismiss him simply as a liar. He was far too complicated to fit such an easy characterization. For one thing, he intentionally misled everyone about the identity of Z as far as the case was concerned, but the life he told in the case (as best one can tell) was as true to his real story as he could make it. It was truth wrapped in an enigma. Such contradictions defined Kohut's creative struggles. Deception curiously protected the integrity of his work. Authenticity and falsehood, in this sense, are not necessarily incompatible. Kohut lied, as in "Mr. Z," because it made possible the writing of an autobiographical case that he saw, among other things, as the truest evidence for his theories. He was not incorrect.

At the same time, Kohut's urgent need to complete the task of his calling lent his project a transcendent purpose. He felt touched by fate, history, or God. Kohut had always been grandiose, something his critics had long criticized him for, as though those who were close to him were not aware of his narcissism. He had to be endured and sometimes suffered to get the gift of what he had to offer. But in his waning years all of what he was got concentrated and exaggerated as he took on the task of openly and coherently challenging Freud, of completing the outlines of a new psychology, and most of all building a movement to carry forward what he had begun. Telling his own story, secretly but surely knowing it would come out at some point, fed this process of heroic self-fashioning in the context of dreaded incompleteness.

Twenty-seven

THE WANING YEARS

Kohut's physical suffering in his waning years served as the catalyst of his heroic project. He was now truly dying. Illness created the urgency and lent his charisma new energy, intensity, focus, and meaning. There was no mistaking the change. Until the late 1970s the lymphoma was really only a darkening shadow in Kohut's life: the disease brought on an increasingly systemic decline, but its symptoms were for the most part relatively minor. But by the Christmas holidays of 1978—he was sixty-five years old—it was clear to Kohut that something else was now wrong, probably with his heart. For years Kohut had had what even then was regarded as a high normal cholesterol count. It was 265 in 1962, which he got down the next year to 200 after losing forty pounds but which was back up to 241 by 1968. In the mid-1960s he also had a "bad" EKG that prompted a life insurance company to turn him down for health reasons.[1] At first he attributed his exhaustion to overwork. But after the holidays, on January 9, 1979, Kohut entered the University of Chicago Billings Hospital for tests. He was immediately scheduled for double bypass surgery, which he underwent on January 12. Initially, he seemed to recover well. He wrote a patient, Herb Murrie, in early February: "All in all my progress toward health is steady and gratifying. Every day my endurance increases—now I can walk up 2½ flights of stairs—but there are still problems left. The sleeping is only so-so (it's hard to find a comfortable position) and I get tired toward the end of the day. I don't know when I will be allowed to return to work."[2] He even asked his doctor when he could resume normal sexual relations. Dr. Leon Resnekov replied on February 13 that it was normal to resume sex after about four weeks but advised Kohut not to try and break any "world records!"[3]

But in fact Kohut was not recovering as rapidly as he should have, and by early March he was back in the hospital. It seems that during the surgery he had contracted a virus infection, perhaps from an air bubble in the heart-lung machine employed during the operation.[4] Things went from bad to worse. Some blood drawn with a dirty needle by a careless technician gave him "purulent phlebitis with staphylococcus septicemia," which sent him into shock and nearly killed him. He required surgical removal of seriously infected veins from his wrist through his shoulder in both arms and a six-week round of aggressive antibiotic treatment. He was left exhausted and went down from his normal 128 pounds to 107 pounds.[5] He returned home and began a slow recovery that at first was complicated by a toxic rash from all the penicillin.[6] But in mid-June Kohut suddenly developed "severe vertigo" that forced him back to bed. He assumed at first it was a lesion or tumor in his brain, and told his wife, "I really have had enough now." That depression passed, and by the fall Kohut was joking about how his inner ear problem made him feel "seasick without the compensation of ocean breezes."[7]

Kohut steadily deteriorated over the next two years. He was now dealing with lymphoma, heart disease, vertigo, and the chronic allergies that had always bothered him. In the spring of 1980 problems arose with his teeth and he had "complete dentures inserted."[8] He never lost his careful, even somewhat obsessive, attention to his weight. In his medical file are a stack of 3 × 5 slips of paper stapled together that record in pencil his daily weight throughout 1978, 1979, and 1980. During that period he varied from a low of 107 pounds on May 1, 1979, to a high of 133 pounds on February 23, 1980. Most of the fluctuation, however, was around 128 pounds, which seemed to be his desired weight. What is remarkable is that he never missed a day recording his weight and noted the slightest move in either direction—down to the quarter pound. In 1979, when he was so sick, he also got in the habit of taking his temperature at least twice and often three times a day, and of course dutifully recorded each reading and the time he took it to the minute. By the fall of 1980 things began to worsen with his cancer, and the results of blood tests raised mounting concern in the doctors. In November, within days of returning from the Boston self psychology conference, he again almost died from type three pneumonia in both lobes, which required two full months of convalescence.[9]

Over that winter he began having problems with swelling in his ankles. Dr. Resnekov told him that the swelling was caused by a combination of "venous insufficiency and relatively poor contractility of the myocardium." His heart simply was not working hard enough to flush out his system. Since Kohut planned to be in Carmel later that summer, Resnekov recommended that a doctor there give him injections of gamma globulin.[10] From July through his death in early October Kohut struggled on a daily basis to stay alive.

However distressing, manifest physical illness in addition to cancer after 1978 had something of a liberating effect on Kohut. He felt no need to lie about problems with his heart or inner ear. He was able to struggle free from the tyranny of secretiveness as shame diminished. He let friends and patients into the knowledge of his physical suffering, and they in turn did things like give him gifts, especially food delicacies. Jerome Beigler at different times gave him his first mango, which he liked; the Jewish sweet halvah, which he pretended not to know about and made a show of looking up in the dictionary; and canned lychee nuts, which he apologized for not liking (Beigler told him that the intense lychee flavor was not subtle enough for his sensitive nature, which went along with his talent, an explanation Kohut accepted graciously).[11] Kohut talked easily to his old friend from medical school, Jacques Palaci, about death.[12] In the summer of 1979 he fussed to his childhood friend Siegmund Levarie about how he tired easily and felt seasick from his inner ear problems, but "when I consider where I was about three or four months ago, I have good reason to be pleased with the progress I have made."[13] The next year Levarie wrote Kohut of his astonishment at reading a description of Kohut in the *New York Times* as a "diminutive" man with "pure white hair": "My recurring vision of you since yesterday [when he read the article] is your flying through the air to your right to ward off a football shot at a goal you were tending."[14] Such images stirred hope that was otherwise fragile. When Levarie's grandchild was born in February 1981, Kohut called to congratulate him and was enthusiastic, warm, and friendly. "I will never see my own grandchild," Kohut lamented to Levarie.[15]

In this same period Kohut wrote detailed descriptions of his ailments (though nothing about the cancer) to Douglas Levin, Martha Louis Little, and Nathaniel London.[16] In late 1980 Kohut commiserated with Robert Merrill, whose wife, one of Kohut's supervisees, had recently died. "[I] felt after reading your letter and looking at the leaflets that she [Barbara Merrill] led a full and fulfilling life—and that makes death, if not really acceptable, somewhat less harsh and more bearable for those who live on."[17] Kohut reported to Levarie that he was feeling better but still "woozy," "unsteady," "lightheaded," and "feeble," but "the brain is working in the important tasks I am putting it to."[18] In the summer of 1981 Kohut was unsteady during a visit with his friend Bernard Brandchaft, and had to leave early from a restaurant in Carmel.[19] That same summer he wrote to his son: "My mind is ok, my courage unbroken, my work proceeds."[20] It was Kohut's mind that really mattered. He told Paul Ornstein: "How much time do I have? I want to live as long as I have ideas. When I no longer have ideas, I don't care. I am not afraid to die, but I am afraid I will run dry and not have ideas and not be able to think straight."[21]

Ideas sustained Kohut. He told a former patient: "We make our work. Our work makes us."[22] He remained absolutely focused. He wrote a colleague who beseeched him to read her work: "True, my time and energy are limited; but I could surely use one of my weekends to study your work and to comment on it and still meet my schedule by doing overwork during the next weekend." But that was not the issue. It was more a matter of "faithfulness to the focus of my attention that is involved for me here." And he concluded: "Whether due to my age or to the lifelong nature of my work habits, I cannot take my attention from a major task without facing a great loss in the inner continuity of my commitment. . . ."[23] And to John A. Lindon, who wrote imploring him to take him on in supervision, Kohut said no with a "melancholy smile." He would love to. But he already has a long waiting list for supervision, dozens of unread manuscripts on his desk, and uncounted unanswered letters. He simply cannot.[24] His vision of what he could accomplish remained at the center of his existence. He was sure that "in the long run" his ideas would be accepted, though not necessarily in psychoanalysis.[25] Kohut once said:

> People have a hard time playing with ideas, being relativistic the way I believe I can be. I am not saying that I am particularly brighter or anything like that, but I have a sort of knack. I can play with ideas and they can't. Everything becomes so concrete. It isn't the way they see it; that's the way it is. What we are talking about here are *vantage points*. One can, and I do (it is perfectly true) apply the vantage point of self psychology, that is, the self in the center of the psychology, the experience of the self and its maintenance as central, which I believe is an appropriate conclusion to reach.[26]

Kohut was besieged in these years with requests to give talks and read this and write that. He almost always tried to reply politely to requests, which he would then usually pass onto a colleague.[27] What is most surprising in retrospect, however, is the colossal amount of time Kohut devoted to his correspondence. Even the trivial and offensive gained his attention. Once out of the blue in 1979 Curt Mead, a young college dropout who aspired to be a writer and intellectual, wrote Kohut of the inspiration he had drawn from his work. Mead followed that up with two more long letters about his interests and commitments and sent a draft of a short story. Mead got frustrated that Kohut did not reply immediately and impetuously wrote: "Kohut, you unresponsive son-of-a-bitch," a lead that was followed by several angry paragraphs and a concluding question: "Am I going to have to pay to see you?" Amazingly enough, Kohut responded gently, thanking Mead for his letters. He said he had enjoyed them. He thought Mead had real talent as a writer. He urged Mead to forgive him for not replying and not being able to "think his way into his situation." He had been ill and had much work to do. "You have a good mind," Kohut wrote, "and you express yourself in a lively, straightforward way." He wished Mead well and hoped he would have a "good and productive life." Mead, to his credit, rose to the stature Kohut granted him and replied with an appreciation of how gracious Kohut had been toward him. "I fervently hope that the world gives you the acclaim I am convinced you deserve."

Perhaps Mead's effrontery amused him by reminding him of his own youthful self. Certainly, Kohut pondered in these twilight years what he called the "curve" of his life. He retained a remarkable sense of continuity within his own narrative, even as his body deteriorated. He said in an interview on February 26, 1981:

> I'm an old man. My hair is grey. My muscles are feeble. Yet I know I am the same person I was when I was 18, and 22, and six, when I was running and jumping. It's still in me and a part of me. There is no discontinuity. I have totally changed and yet my conviction that I have remained the same is absolute. I never feel myself chopped up in that way, however otherwise my self might be endangered. There is that sense of continuity along the time axis from the little boy in the Austrian Alps to Vienna to the well-known investigator of the self at the age of 68 in a place whose name I hardly knew when I was that young. I have no question that I am the same.[28]

His link to his Viennese origins, always important to him, now became intensely special and nostalgic. He reconnected with someone he had known from his gymnasium days, Adam Wandruszka, a professor of history at the University of Vienna who had been a Nazi in the 1930s and during the war.[29] Kohut had some misgivings about the renewed friendship ("Some rifts cannot be quite healed; but so be it!"), yet was very moved when Wandruszka nominated him for the Austrian Academy of Sciences; during his last trip to Europe in June 1980 he spent a day in Salzburg with his friend.[30] Anything Austrian touched him, as when the government awarded him the Austrian Cross of Honour for Science and Art.[31] The trauma of his forced emigration seemed to heal as Kohut slowly died a continent away.

For all his physical problems, Kohut's interests remained as wide-ranging as ever. At Gretchen Meyer's house in Wisconsin on weekends, when not too ill, he still loved to ski cross-country, chop wood, and watch birds (at which he was quite expert).[32] He also kept up his cultural involvements. He read widely in the humanities; in fact, since he had basically stopped reading psychoanalytic literature, he had more time for the reading he most enjoyed. Music as well continued to bring him great pleasure. He went to concerts whenever possible. In the late 1970s his immediate followers gave him as a birthday present a set of the Bach cantatas. He proceeded to listen to one cantata each night and expressed great joy at the gift.[33] He remained as intense as ever about his musical appreciation. He once wrote Deutsche Grammophon that he had been listening to a gift someone gave him of the Mozart string quartets as played by the Amadeus Quartet. He had discovered, however, that side seven and side nine contained the same quartet, that, in other words, side nine did not present the "B-dur KV 589" as the label said but repeated the "B-dur 499."[34] Constance Goldberg tells of the time she and her husband, Arnold, invited the Kohuts to dinner at their apartment. As she finished the preparations, she put on a classical music record before the Kohuts arrived. The setting seemed perfect. From the moment he walked in, however, Kohut was visibly nervous. She could not imagine what was wrong and hoped she had not done something awful that would ruin the evening. Kohut tried to contain himself, but after about half an hour he took Constance aside and firmly told her she really should not play such a recording as mere background music. She instantly removed the record and he became peaceful.[35]

There was a dark side of Kohut's self that emerged in these final years.

His bragging and self-centeredness in social situations was nearly out of control, driving his son at times to distraction.[36] Many evenings he imposed on his secretary, who lived near him, to type up something late in the evening without apparent awareness that his requests were completely out of order.[37] He also kept up some unusual lies, even with his most intimate of friends. At his birthday party on May 3, 1981, Kohut pretended to Robert Wadsworth not to know what a bris was and asked his friend to look into the matter. Wadsworth wrote the next day, based on *Vogue's Book of Etiquette*, published in 1948, that Jewish boys typically receive their names eight days after birth, while girls receive their names on the Friday evening or Saturday morning after their birth. Wadsworth further quoted from Charlotte Ford's *Book of Modern Manners* (1980) about the bris— the ritual circumcision—that boys must undergo on the eighth day after their birth, when they are also named. The circumcision, Wadsworth added helpfully, is done by a mohel.[38]

Kohut was also becoming increasingly obnoxious in certain situations. Once at a party of a very wealthy analyst he asked his friend, Miriam Elson, to tell him something to make him happy. She sensed he was terribly envious of the display of elegance in the house. Elson proceeded to tell a story about her grandchildren, but it did not please him at all. She realized what he wanted to hear was something great about himself.[39] Another time at a dinner party in Elson's house, Kohut suddenly told everyone to put their little fingers under the table. "Now, everybody take a deep breath," he said, "and lift the table on the count of three." To Elson's horror, he counted slowly and everyone lifted. A table set for ten with glasses, plates, and silverware was raised miraculously and evenly, as if by magic. Sometime later in Kohut's own house, at another party with assembled guests and an elegantly set table, Elson suggested enthusiastically that they do the same thing. Kohut, however, waved her off with irritation. "Oh, no," he said, "we can't do that. It might break the china."[40]

At times Kohut also became deeply regressed. In the fall of 1980, Dr. Resnekov hospitalized Kohut in Billings for his life-threatening pneumonia from November 9 to the 25th.[41] Resnekov put him in the cardiology unit because he knew it had an outstanding nursing staff. One nurse in particular, Eileen O'Shea, assumed a special relationship to the famous patient on the floor, in part because she liked him but also because the other nurses would not go near him. They thought he was "a pervert and an exhibitionist." For O'Shea he was merely a sick man who was regressed. But even she had to admit he was extreme. Each morning he would prop himself up in bed "stark naked, exposing himself." He loved the bath she gave him and would remain "fluffed up, prissy, oiled and powdered for several hours, happy like a baby." He never complained about anything. He loved those mornings, and reveled in every moment. Around noon he would slowly begin to dress and by about 2:00 p.m. when his wife showed up he would be lying in bed looking like a normal patient. Elizabeth Kohut never saw him in the mornings naked and exposed and never gave him a bath.[42] What is perhaps most remarkable about the image of a regressed Kohut in Billings is that he was days away from the most impressive performance of his life at the huge self psychology conference in Boston. One has to marvel at the contradictions of this complicated man.

As he aged, Kohut shaped himself in the context of an evolving set of his own idealized heroes. The great figures of his youth and formative professional years—Goethe and Freud—receded in significance. He still looked up to them and admired them greatly. But his "need for them lessened," he told an old friend in 1977. "I did not feel that I had to lean on them, to listen to them via their writings when I felt in need of self-confirmation or support." He felt as though he lived now in a different world and glanced back at Goethe and Freud as "something beautiful but past." His new heroes included Proust, Joyce, and the aged Eugene O'Neill, along with a rediscovered Thomas Mann and Dostoevsky. With their aid and "witnessing their suffering," he allowed himself to ask, as never before, about the nature of life in the twentieth century, with all its great violence and genocide. Was it worse, he wondered, or just different? And especially, was it different "in a decisive way that demands new values, new yardsticks, new view-points, by which to evaluate, measure, and understand it?"[43]

The most important of Kohut's "new heroes," however, was Franz Kafka, whom he quoted more than any single writer in the 1970s in books, lectures, letters, and conversations, but had never once mentioned in print before then and seems not to have used in his seminars either. Kafka, he felt, had his finger on the pulse of the age. His protagonist— whether "K." or another character—is the Everyman "exposed to the unempathic indifference of his family and who has therefore remained grotesquely grandiose and thus estranged from the world," which is the extension of his family in its coldness and emptiness. He wanders through life, "empty, flat, yearning for something he can no longer understand because the part of himself that once was eager to demand welcoming empathy and empathic response has long been buried and has ceased to be available to him." He lies in his room and listens to his family talk about him in cold voices as a cockroach. Unreachable judges try him but he can never figure out the charges. Distant rulers in a castle make him a number and reject him without explanation. He is helpless, alone, anonymous, alienated. It is very much, says Kohut, like the "big impersonal hospital" he himself came to know in hauntingly new ways after his cancer was diagnosed. The hospital embodies Kafka's world and serves as the despairing metaphor for modern life.[44]

Kohut's new heroes also brought him to a deeper understanding of the relationship between great art and historical process. In his view, for the most part, art entertains by taking us out of ourselves for fleeting moments of pleasure. That has always been partly its function. Great art, however, plays a much more significant role in shaping values and attitudes by anticipating future developments. Great art focuses on the "nuclear psychological problems" of the era. "The artist stands, as it were, in proxy for his generation." Before Freud one could see in the novels of the nineteenth century, for example, a kind of presaging of the issues of guilt that became the conceptual cornerstone of psychoanalytic theory as it took shape in the crucial decade of the 1890s. But the emotional problems of the age had shifted. Now the artist gave voice to the "crumbling, decomposing, fragmenting, enfeebled self of the child" and later the "fragile, vulnerable, empty self of the adult." But the task of the artist is more than one of giving form to our thinking. In "tone and word, on canvas and in stone" the artist also heals.

> The musician of disordered sound, the poet of decomposed language, the painter and sculptor of the fragmented visual and tactile world: they all portray the breakup of the self and, through the reassemblage and rearrangement of the fragments, try to create new structures that possess wholeness, perfection, new meaning.[45]

Kohut also came to admire greatly Marcel Proust, whom he felt foreshadowed his own new sense of time within the contemporary self. In Proustian time, the past is imbedded in the present. It is not over. It may not even be past, as Faulkner said in another context. Time in this way of thinking is neither chromatic nor kairotic.[46] It curves in on itself. The past lives in us and we are of it. To remember is not to go backward but inward.

> The Proustian recovery of childhood memories constitutes a psychological achievement significantly different from the filling in of infantile amnesia, which as Freud taught us, is the precondition for the solution of structural conflicts and thus for the cure of a psychoneurosis. The Proustian recovery of the past is in the service of healing the discontinuity of the self.[47]

Proust's huge novel, *A la recherche du temps perdu*, contains a long disquisition on the fantastic image of the narrator's life's experience evoked by the act of eating a madeleine and sipping tea, though Kohut was even more interested in the scene toward the end of the book that explains how Proust came to write it in the first place. The narrator has just returned to an unfamiliar Paris. Everything is the same and yet subtly different. He trips on a curbstone and stumbles. He feels estranged, disconnected. It is then he decides to write his novel, "not to figure out the past and its meanings in the unconscious but to reestablish a continuity within himself."[48] The psychological quest in this process that interested Kohut was "the searcher's need to establish a developmental continuity." A prolonged disruption (or a trauma, one might say) has occurred. The self is "fragmented along a time axis." In the Proustian world the "search is to heal this break and cure the self by feeling whole and historically continuous."[49] That is the challenge of art (and, of course, of psychoanalysis). The depression that lives in the mind of the adult, as Kohut put it, can be cured.[50] Its ubiquity sets the tone for the tragic. And yet it can be banished, overcome, transcended.

Twenty-eight

GOD AND RELIGION

God came to occupy Kohut's imagination in the last stage of his life and creativity. Kohut had always been interested in religion and issues of spirituality, though he never wrote a book or even a paper specifically on the subject. At a personal level, Kohut regularly attended the Unitarian Church in Hyde Park, near his home. He became friends with its minister, John (Jack) Hayward, and even at times gave sermons to the congregation. He read *Christian Century* for years and seemed particularly concerned with the application of his ideas to what is generally called pastoral counseling. Certainly, many theologians and practitioners sensed in Kohut a kindred spirit striving to define a meaningful relation to God.[1] In his clinical work, as well, Kohut paid close attention to issues of religion and spirituality. He considered "cosmic narcissism" as early as 1965 specifically in relation to wisdom and death.[2] In *The Analysis of the Self* he writes of Miss L., whose analyst subtly demeans the idealized figure of an inspiring Catholic priest in an early dream. Somewhat later, Kohut was drawn immediately to Anita Eckstaedt's case of the young theologian, whose quest for spiritual meaning was a kind of metaphor for Kohut's emerging psychology. And in lectures and conversations about clinical matters, he often made points that self-consciously dealt as much with ethics as with psychology. He once told candidates at the Institute that morality deals with those issues that have not yet been integrated into the self, and in another seminar that with an exploding population it is wrong to force everyone into the mold of feeling it is normative to have children. It is right—and just—to develop one's creative potential.[3]

Kohut's abiding interest in matters of religion was most clear in his extended comments during two interviews he gave in 1981 to a young theologian, Robert L. Randall.[4] In those interviews Kohut was in no way attempting a kind of self-psychological *Future of an Illusion*. As he told Randall, he was only providing a framework for such a task, the barest outline that needed completion and fleshing out to be really meaningful. It was not a falsely modest position. For one thing, he often took such a stance on the relation of self-psychological ideas to other realms of human experience.[5] But more importantly, Kohut outlined for Randall just that: a framework and not a completely developed set of ideas. It does not make his thoughts less interesting, but it does require us to take them in with some caution and to grant them a tentativeness Kohut himself intended. In talking with Randall, Kohut certainly never meant to hand down self-psychological dicta that would become dogma.

In his work on religion, Kohut drew his base line with Freud, especially *The Future of an Illusion*. Freud's error in this work, Kohut felt, was to apply the "yardstick of scientific values to religion." By such criteria religion seems foolish indeed. The story of the "humanoid god" who creates the world in a week is ridiculous as physics. It is pure fairy tale, "abominably poor science." Such tales of origins cannot hope to compete with scientific explorations of the world and its beginnings and the workings of the natural world. To consider another example, take the "gimmick" of the afterlife, a place where the virtuous go. That fits beautifully with all the superficial needs of what Kohut derisively called "Guilty Man," or the self Freud imagines. Freud's whole purpose was to unmask the completely irrational, fantastical, illusionary nature of religious beliefs, which in their deeper understanding are merely projections from our own early experience of infantile helplessness.

In that very rationalism lies Freud's profound misperception of the true purpose of religion, which is simply in another realm from science. There are three great cultural enterprises for Kohut: science, art, and religion. Science deals with explanations. Art deals with beauty. Religion's unique function is to "shore up, to hold together, sustain, to make harmonious, to strengthen, man's self." For many in the twentieth century psychoanalysis robbed religion of those functions and became a substitute religion. This has profoundly influenced religion, but it has also placed a terrific burden on psychoanalysis itself, corrupting its true mission to search for psychological truth. The key to the religiosity of psychoanalysis lies in the adoration of and excessive loyalty toward the founder by its followers. No physicist in his right mind would ever place Newton on such a level. We have discovered all kinds of new laws since Newton and yet no one would claim that that represents a rebellion against him. Things move forward, and new giants appear who enhance our understanding of the world and our capacity to explain it.

But there is more to Kohut on religion than a critique of Freud. He also seeks to outline more precisely the "human needs" religion meets. Such needs begin in matters of idealization, which lie at the heart of any effort to understand religion from a self-psychological point of view. Kohut would never fall prey to simple reductionism. "I would have no doubt that anything as encompassing and broad and basic as religion is to man . . . could not possibly relate to just one dimension of the self." That said, he recognizes the centrality of idealization in his reflections about religion and returns to them often. And for good reason. Idealizing needs[6] is perhaps the most conspicuous aspect of religion. We can hardly dispense with a concept of God, "because there must be something idealizeable, something that nears perfection or that is perfect, something that one wants to live up to, something that lifts one up." The fragmenting self, he notes, is weak, chaotic, and disharmonious. In religion one searches for and often finds a sense of uplift and healing from that fragmentation. This may come from a particularly inspiring sermon, which lifts one out of the humdrum of everyday existence and gives meaning where there had been emptiness. The service itself, with its familiar rituals and words and song, may inspire and soothe. Even the rhythms of the church year can be significant in this regard. "The mere unrolling of specific holidays in the course of a twelve month period . . . the gradual decline with winter, and the rebirth with Easter spring, appeals to something deep in all of us."

Such experiences touch the psychological core of our first encounters with the majestic mother who uplifted us as babies and held us close to her. That baby alone is "frightened, disheveled, fragmented." The mother, on the other hand, is "calm, big, powerful." Uplifted, we merged into the mother's greatness and calmness. Later, Kohut says, we all suffer various narcissistic blows, which can be powerfully disorienting. Some find it soothing to go into a church and sit there. Others might experience a similar kind of healing in a more abstracted spiritual form, as by climbing to the top of a mountain, looking down into the Grand Canyon, or walking in the woods. Still others find uplift in listening to beautiful music. But whatever the form, such spiritual uplift is a central part of how we understand the role of religion in our lives. And this sense we have of God's purpose evokes our earliest encounter with the maternal selfobject matrix. Kohut here offers no simplistic causal relation between God and our earliest selfobject experiences. We do not merely seek uplift from God because our mothers once picked us up to hold and feed and soothe us. Religion is not, as it was basically for Freud, a rather mundane human institution but rather a complex interplay of human psychological needs and the deeper workings of the divine. Unlike Freud, Kohut grants a God and then tries to understand our psychological relation to him (or her).

Did Kohut himself believe in God? He often talked as though he did and was at ease in the world of human strivings toward some kind of God concept. Like his parents, especially his mother, Kohut was open to religious experience, especially in its Christian form (though he despised dogmatic forms of any religion). Kohut, his son firmly believes, considered himself a Christian by faith.[7] His friend Jack Hayward once referred jokingly, but tellingly, to Kohut's "Christian restraint."[8] His whole discourse is Christian.[9] Such attitudes, on the other hand, competed with the scientist in him who believed in a rational ordering of the world one can perceive by good empirical methods. He once told a colleague of a dream. In it a large airplane was dropping out of the sky. He was clinging to it like a bird. Kohut commented, "I was afraid but yet I remain a strong atheist."[10] Did he mean it? Kohut was surely aware that his spiritual inclusiveness might turn off his more agnostic colleagues, who, it is fair to say, dominate psychoanalysis. "The science of the self will not therefore become a religion," he once asserted rather too defiantly, just because it directs attention to subjects often treated by "mystics, vitalists, and theologians."[11] Perhaps, one can only conclude, Kohut was of at least two minds about God. Maybe he was not at all sure himself what he believed. As with so many things, it would seem he lived creatively within the contradiction of believing and not believing.

Nevertheless, Kohut found solace at the end in connecting his psychological ideas with theological reflections on death, which he came to see as the absence of empathy, a negation, a kind of black hole in psychological life. After he got cancer, Kohut came to understand (if not quite say) that empathy is a life force, the self equivalent of libido. To be cut off from others, to be unconnected with human or symbolic others, to be utterly unto oneself or locked within the self as in psychosis, is to be dead. As he put it in 1973: "From the moment when man is born it is empathy, the wordless psychological extension of the human environment to the baby which separates him from the inorganic world: from death, from the meaninglessness of racing solar systems, from incomprehensible spaces, and from the ever more incomprehensible vastness of endless time. . . . It is this expansion of the self beyond the limits of the individual which is the barrier to meaninglessness, to pessimistic despair."[12]

Dying, in turn, came to have a special meaning for him. His point on this subject is that in the actual process of dying, the way others relate to us and how we use them is vital. People tend to withdraw from the dying person. If someone can connect at that stage and convey genuine feelings such as "You're dying. I will also cross that threshold one of these days. The way you handle this is an inspiration to me. I will get a great deal of strength from watching how you do this," that dying person will feel confirmed. He also generalized that idea in other contexts. "Tragic Man does not fear death as a symbolic punishment (castration) for forbidden pleasure aims (as does Guilty Man); he fears premature death, a death which prevents the realization of the aims of his nuclear self. And, unlike Guilty Man, he accepts death as part of the curve of his fulfilled and fulfilling life."[13] It's the same with a rose.

> There is a seed, there is a flowering, there is a wilting, there is a death and the next generation of roses takes over. I think that one isn't really fully alive if one doesn't somehow down deep in one's bones feel this eternal rhythm of life, this coming and going of which one is only a link in a chain. To me this is an uplifting thought, not a discouraging thought. It goes beyond my individuality to something broader and more enduring than this little me that is common, hasn't been here during Plato's time and will not be here in a thousand years when there's another Plato or maybe nothing. Who knows? Why do I have to be around and have been around? I wasn't and I won't. That doesn't disturb me.

Religion also supports the dying person in a myriad of "idealizing selfobject" ways quite aside from the hope for an afterlife. There are enduring issues in the world, like the great mystery of creation, both of the world and of the complexity and beauty of human culture. None of that is accidental but it will in some way endure, whether or not we observe it. That is more accurately what we mean by eternal life than the fairy tale of heaven with winged angels singing hallelujah. That "doesn't particularly

send me," Kohut says. It sounds rather "boring." In fact, "the greatness
of experience is timeless." It has intrinsic value, even should the human
race become extinct some day. That's what the God concept is all about
at its most idealized and philosophical level. "There is something about
this world in our experience that does lift us up beyond the simplicity of
an individual existence, that lifts us into something higher, enduring, or,
as I would rather say, timeless."[14] This uplift had long interested Kohut.
At the end of life it is possible to revive the earliest psychological union
with the mother in a new and creative form. The illusion of the eternal
life of the self must be given up in the face of the certainty of death. In its
place one invests (at least the potential for such investment exists) the ideals
one cherishes. This shift is not a mystical one but a "sad and realistic
goodbye to oneself." The "most perfect" artistic representation of this
process, Kohut says, is the end of Beethoven's Piano Sonata opus 111.[15]

Religion as well meets important mirroring needs through what is
usually called grace, or the idea that "there is something given to you,
some innate perception of your right to be here and to assert yourself,
and that somebody will smile at you and will respond to you and will be
in tune with your worthwhileness." In the Old Testament, a crucial text
that defines the idea of grace is Psalm 84:11: "For the Lord God is a sun
and shield; the Lord will give grace and glory. No good thing will he
withhold from them that walk uprightly." That basic idea runs through
the Christian sacred texts, though it is added, of course, that Jesus becomes the medium through which the grace of God flows. The psychological point is that God's grace is available for us to heal our wounds
and to mirror our needs simply for the asking, in the same way the protective, secure mother, especially the gleam in her eye, provided cohesion for ourselves through all the vagaries of development. But if that
mother, as in *Long Day's Journey into Night*, is a drug addict, there is no
grace and the family degenerates into drunken brawling.

Life and creativity in general, Kohut felt, emerge out of this fall from
grace, which is a kind of self-psychological version of original sin. At best
we have a glimmer of the mother's gleam. But we are spurred on by the
very "shortcomings of that early grace," which in religious terms is the
perfect mirroring and calmness of God. To elaborate his point Kohut
considers music and observes that the perfect chord is not what makes
music appealing. It is rather the "deviation into dissonance" and the complex ways the music returns to consonance. The melodies and harmonies
reach out through structures of movements, creating tensions that express

the unease, until there is at last a return to balance, or at least an illusion of harmony and peace. That process is what Kohut meant by the "curve of life." He even ironically thanks God for the scars and trauma of life. They spur us on to new ways of solving problems. "If life were perfect, man would never have created religion or art or science."

The third specific selfobject need Kohut identifies as being met in religion is what he called alter ego or twinship, which he felt religion satisfies in the locale of the church or sacred environment and especially in one's participation in the congregation. Religion, of course, is both a solitary and a communal experience. Much of what religion does in meeting idealizing and mirroring needs is solitary. Something goes on in private between you and your concept of God. But religion is also communal. Church surrounds you with worshipers like yourself who have made common faith commitments. However different your lives might be in other respects, in church you and they are joined in a common spiritual quest before a God you jointly recognize and conceive and to whom you direct your prayers in a shared and utterly familiar liturgy. Week after week, year after year, you return to the same pews and sing the same songs and listen together to the sermons. Such intensely experienced rituals tend to flatten out what might be otherwise felt as significant differences between people in terms of personality, background, wealth, profession, or even appearance. Within the sacred space of the church you become more like your neighbor. You abandon the extraneous and emphasize the essential. The human bonds deepen in this circle of reflected sameness. And that is enormously reassuring. You become one of God's children in a powerfully shared experience.

Twenty-nine

THE HEALING
OF PSYCHOANALYSIS

Until the bitter end, Kohut remained interested in the general issues of healing in psychoanalysis. Inevitably, given his illness, he never managed to complete a final statement that coherently presented all his ideas. Many important thoughts lie scattered in transcribed lectures and letters, though the central text remains his ambiguous and posthumously published book, *How Does Analysis Cure?*, which he committed himself to writing sometime in early 1980. He was getting weaker by the month. He began work intensely that summer in Carmel. He kept light novels by his desk for relief and when stuck for ideas sometimes leafed through a thesaurus. He said it stirred his creativity, the way Leonardo da Vinci would crumple up pieces of paper and throw them on the floor as the beginning of a sketch he would then elaborate.[1] On his return to Chicago that fall, Kohut wrote to one colleague that he planned to call his new book "How Does Analysis Cure? (Contributions to the Psychology of the Self)." A few months later he wrote his German friend, Tilmann Moser, that he hoped his new manuscript would "instruct semi-courageous analysts, like those of yours in Freiburg, that . . . 'classic' feelings of guilt on behalf of a necessary abstinence standing in the way of free and generous emotional response can be cleared away." By June Kohut was "90% finished" with his book, but his rapid physical decline in the summer and fall of 1981 prevented him from completing the writing, let alone the editing.[2] After his death Elizabeth Kohut—presumably carrying out her husband's own wishes—asked Arnold Goldberg to finish the book. He in turn enlisted the assistance of Paul Stepansky, then a young historian of psychoanalysis doing freelance writing. Goldberg and Stepansky completed and revised the manuscript but discovered that Mrs. Kohut, surprisingly, would not allow major changes to what was, after all, a very rough text. Harsh words were exchanged. Some fees were withheld and the completed bibliography was not submitted, which led Mrs. Kohut to request that Robert Wadsworth put together what is undoubtedly Kohut's least impressive bibliography of all his books. In the end, there were compromises on both sides. In 1984 the University of Chicago Press brought out *How Does Analysis Cure?* nearly three years after Kohut's death.[3]

Full of wonderful asides, as well as many interesting ideas and formulations, and a book of great subtlety, *Cure* remains the most obscure of Kohut's major writings. Students, advanced ones as well as the general public, wander glassy-eyed through its pages. The text has the feel of someone without full control of his narrative. Kohut often writes of things he has already elaborated in earlier books and papers. *Cure* may be the most annoying book to read in all of psychoanalysis.[4] But it is also an appealing, open, humane attempt to define the therapeutic nature of self psychology, which Kohut by then was convinced was the future of psychoanalysis. One might think of *Cure* (along with Kohut's other writings on clinical psychoanalysis toward the end) as the last will and testament of a man straining from his deathbed to share his final thoughts before himself passing on.

In *Cure* Kohut for the most part moves beyond his ideas of a two-pronged theory of self that took shape after *Analysis* and lingered past *Restoration*. The self, he now argues, is purely and simply our center of initiative, the "I" of experience, and nothing more or less. One cannot think about psychological life except in this context. He thus argues that "all forms of psychopathology" result from the defects, distortions, or weaknesses in the self. "All these flaws in the self are due to disturbances of self-selfobject relationships in childhood," he says categorically.

The clarification of terms led Kohut as well to take the hyphen out of "self-object." He had been considering such a move since 1977.[5] The hyphen had always been stylistically awkward, especially when talking about the self-object and the self. Was it to be a self-self-object relationship? But more decisively, the removal of the hyphen represented a "significant firming of this concept" and marked Kohut's feeling that this central concept in self psychology was not an "ad-hoc construct" but a viable notion that he hoped would "find an enduring place in analytic thought."[6] The absence of a hyphen makes selfobject the property of the self. It is, in this sense, a decisive step away from Freud (though he remained deeply connected to traditional discourse by continuing to use the drive concept of object). Typically, Kohut milked the symbolism of removing the hyphen for all it was worth. In *The Restoration of the Self*, which appeared in the early spring of 1977, it was still "self-object." By that May, however, he had decided it had to be "selfobject," and celebrated the decision at a meal at the Wolfs' home with the Goldbergs and Tolpins. There was a big toast and general agreement that this was the propitious moment. Constance Goldberg found herself laughing at the bombast of it all, though she had to marvel at how much it meant to Kohut himself, who turned the event into a rite of passage with overtones of a religious ritual.[7]

By the time of *Cure*, Kohut also came to understand his classification of basic self needs in new ways. For most of the 1970s, Kohut argued that the two poles of self expression were mirroring and idealization. What he called aspirations toward twinship, or the sense of one's reflected self in others, was a dependent state of mirroring. In *Restoration* this essentially dualistic schema hardened in Kohut's mechanistic formulation of what he called the "bipolar self," which constitutes the structural basis of self experience. He even argued (unfortunately, one might say) that there was a kind of "tension arc" between the two poles of mirroring and idealization that reifies these clinical concepts.[8] After the publication of *Restoration* in 1977, some talked loosely of Kohut's model of the bipolar self as a new paradigm in psychology, which even Kohut disagreed with and tried to discourage.[9] Criticism of the bipolar self and its tension arc developed quickly after Kohut's death.[10] The idea of a bipolar self is, at best, of dubious significance. It has not been sufficiently noted, however, that Kohut himself all but abandoned the formulation as soon as he had published it. After *Restoration* came out in 1977, he avoided using the concept in his scientific writings and barely mentions it in his correspondence. In *Cure* there is only one reference to it, and then by allusion.[11] One suspects Kohut recognized that the idea of a bipolar self with its tension arc was too dualistic and much too neat, too simple, and too abstract. He also changed his mind about the significance of twinship in the period between his last two books. In *Cure* he grants twinship equal status with mirroring and idealization.[12] A three-way "tension arc" is not a very elegant formulation. The developmental origins of twinship, he now feels, lie in such experiences as kneading dough next to Mother or "shaving" alongside Father. Such formative events, he says, lack the drama of the Freudian "primal scene," but may be truer in terms of self cohesion.[13]

While Kohut firmly believed by the time of *Cure* that the self *is* experience and the essence of our relationship to the world, he never lost his conviction that self is necessarily an idea about subjectivity in cultural context. And that context changes over time. Freud wrote of the great narcissistic injuries to human pride with Copernicus, Darwin, and himself. Kohut questions the neatness of such a characterization, noting furthermore that with sufficient historical perspective one can see a sequence from injury to liberation. In the pre-Copernican cosmos we were low in the heavenly order, without a lot of agency in the hierarchy of the divine. Copernicus put us back into the maelstrom and asserted human primacy, in part by wiping out all the gods. Nor is Darwin really the threat Freud imagined. Rather than being an affront to our pride, a truly workable theory of evolution joyfully integrates us into nature, grounds us, and deepens our sense of self. Finally, Freud's very notion of a dichotomous self, especially its radical split between what is conscious and unconscious and its deeply repressed knowledge of sex, was rooted in the cultural life of Vienna before the deluge. There were splits everywhere. Science and art progressed while dark, subterranean forces stirred unseen below the surface. Freud's model of self perfectly expresses that split. Now, however, the contemporary self, reflecting and embodying the political and cultural world, is "enfeebled, multifragmented (vertically split), and disharmonious." If the experience of Copernicus, Darwin, and Freud is any indication, however, such is often the response to radically new perspectives that can give way to liberating visions.[14]

Toward the end of his last decade, culminating in *Cure*, Kohut increasingly emphasized that the heart of psychoanalysis (which he once defined as "the science of the human soul") is the "introspective-empathic method."[15] Kohut's initial insight in the 1950s had been that introspection and empathy are the way of knowing in psychoanalysis. As he constructed a general theory in his last decade, he returned often to that principle, deepened now by his increasingly expansive understanding of the role of empathy in cure. The more he found himself thinking about unifying concepts like that of the self at the center of initiative, however, the more he asserted the foundational significance of empirical clinical evidence.

He was, in fact, straying into "metapsychology" in these years. That was the point. At the same time, he struggled not to get lost in clouds of speculation. "I am above all a relativist," he wrote in 1980. "Theories are mainly means to an end for me. They don't become 'hallowed.' . . . Any theory is a replaceable metaphor for me. I use it as long as it does its job. I use another when the other helps me to see more, to understand more, to increase my operational leverage."[16] There is no observation without theory, he believed, but specific concepts themselves are always changeable. One must be particularly cautious about elegant interpretations, for there is always the possibility that what appears to be so true is really "no more than a testimony to the cleverness of a theoretical mind . . . able to arrange a variety of selected data into a cohesive whole." If that happens, then the so-called therapeutic efficacy of the new approach is nothing more than the "self-righteous conviction of the therapist." And to further complicate matters, these same results may be achieved by others who are bound to the innovator by transferences and identifications. Still, Kohut felt he had found a new way of listening to patients and understanding the deepest meanings of their communications. Other approaches, especially the Freudian, pollute the clinical environment. He dismissed out of hand supposed facts generated by what he considered such outworn perspectives. What is needed is an openness to self issues via the introspective-empathic method: "Only the protracted unbiased attempt to understand analytic material with the aid of the guidance of self-psychological insights will allow analysts to arrive at a meaningful evaluation of the relevance of the self-psychological point of view."[17]

Kohut's ideas on these interrelated issues converged in *Cure* on his distinction between "experience-near" and "experience-distant" theory in psychoanalysis. At one level, the distinction he is making is the philosophical one between degrees of abstraction in any theorizing. Initially, Kohut, as has always been conventional in psychoanalysis, privileged the "experience-near." In *Analysis*, for example, the main argument he advances in favor of seeing the self as a "content of the mental apparatus" as opposed to "one of the agencies of the mind" is that it keeps it "low-level" and "comparatively experience-near." In *Restoration*, as he brings into focus a sense of the self at the center of initiative, it nevertheless remains yoked—according to what he calls the principle of complementarity—to the old idea of self as a content of the mental apparatus. By the time of *Cure*, however, when by any criteria his understanding of the self is more abstract, he purposely refuses to describe it as "experience-distant." In fact, he changes the meaning of the distinction itself to keep his theories "experience-near." His example is of a little girl who for the first time walks away from her mother and turns to keep a bond through visual contact. The little girl's normal experience is one of reassurance in the "confirming reverberation of her mother's proud smile." He asks how we know that is "normal." His answer—though murky—is that "experience-near" theory allows us to grasp the true dynamics of the girl's self at that transformative moment. The more distant formulation would put it in terms extremely remote from her experience and probably in the context of obscure oedipal strivings. What is "near" in this case for Kohut is present, observable, palpable—and self-psychological. What would be "distant" would be an explanation from the outside, and in Freudian, drive terms.[18] A theory of self, one might say, inevitably keeps one experience-near.

Kohut's views on normality—and therefore the fundamental assumptions that determine the goals of psychotherapy—became increasingly relativistic at the end. One could say he thought through the full implications of his work on the "transformations of narcissism" from the mid-1960s. As early as his paper "On Courage" from the early 1970s (published posthumously), Kohut noted that "normality is often a (almost unfathomably) complex state—more complex at any rate than those forms of pathology which rest on regression and primitivization."[19] In a taped seminar in 1974 he elaborated this view by noting that it is being normal that allows us to react to things in all kinds of ways. It is pathology that is single-minded, concrete, directed, and limited.[20] In another seminar around the same time, however, Kohut made a different point that is closer to the older psychoanalytic view: "Again, the difference between normal and abnormal is only quantitative"; in other words, the regressive pull of infantile desires is powerful and general.[21] The conceptual tension between these statements suggests the struggle within Kohut himself at the time. As with any new idea he ever came to, he only pushed beyond traditional views cautiously and after going through a period in which he clung to the old alongside the new. By the time of *Cure*, however, he had moved to the more radical position that was the logical extension of his earlier, informal comments in seminar and in his paper "On Courage." He stresses in *Cure* that judgments about normality cannot be based on prevalence or percentages. His favorite aphorism in this period was that dental caries is ubiquitous but it is not normal.[22] As a more general formulation, he found most appealing the C. Daly King definition of normality as *"that which functions in accordance with its design."*[23] Such a definition makes normality relative to purpose. "We need to grasp each person's mental health individually," Kohut wrote in a late letter. Struggle, even intense and "persistent" battles in the self, may be part of "some highly significant lives." It is extremely difficult and can be dangerous to define the normative, especially in clinical work. He even began to wonder whether we really know what psychopathology is (except, perhaps, for extreme psychotic conditions). "I am increasingly disinclined to accept as useful the dichotomy between health and disease."[24]

Kohut's new position on normality in general brought into focus what he had been slowly moving toward in the last half decade regarding the Oedipus complex, namely that it is merely one possible developmental form of self disorder and that the only thing worth discussing is an oedipal phase in self development as opposed to a universal complex that is the defining moment in psychological experience. He had no doubt that one can identify and observe children in the throes of what is classically called an Oedipus complex, and that such an experience in childhood has repercussions for the adult self. But to call the complex universal and essential misses the forest for the trees. Where one sees a young child locked into a hothouse of sexual and aggressive feelings with his or her parents, the whole family is in a crisis in which empathy has been "distorted in a specific way." The parents, for whatever reason, are unable to respond to the "child's total oedipal self (the child's affection and assertiveness)" and instead respond to "fragments of the child's oedipal self, " that is, only to the child's sexual and aggressive drives.[25] Kohut remained cautious at times about completely discarding oedipal language, but basically never retreated from the position, once he got there, that what has always been called the Oedipus complex is already a self disorder. "What we call the complex," he says, "is really only *secondary disintegration of a primary healthy state.*"[26]

Kohut was once asked in an interview what he thought about the charge that he was simply uncomfortable with infantile sexuality. He strongly disagreed and said he has no such discomfort but just views it all differently from classical analysts. Homosexual wishes expressed by a patient, for example, hardly mean that in treatment "bedrock" has been reached by unveiling the drive. On the contrary, he is interested in what the wish means for the self. Someone who wants to be penetrated by a strong man, for example, is sexualizing the original wish to have a strong father whose substances one can take into oneself in order to feel whole and alive.[27] What matters, Kohut makes clear in *Cure*, is whether the cohesive self has been formed and can endure. That may—or may not—be correlated with a specific sexual orientation. In a footnote to the text at this point, Kohut acknowledges his view is a "value judgment," though he emphasizes that it is equally a value judgment to say heterosexuality is normative and the essence of the healed self.[28]

Kohut became increasingly easy in the 1970s about commenting on therapeutic process, or what is usually called in psychoanalysis the "theory of technique." As a younger teacher and supervisor, he shied away from making observations on technique, fearing that candidates too easily latched onto prescriptions. By his last decade, however, he seemed to feel more at ease in talking about the clinical implications of his theories of self. He felt in general that the self-psychological approach brings out the best in analysts and focuses attention on relevant issues in the patient. The Freudian and ego-psychological tradition against which he argued, one should note, was still dominant and could be tyrannical, which Kohut felt was the result of the insecurities of a historically new approach to healing. But it made no sense any longer to continue to idealize Freud's analogy of the therapist as a kind of psychological surgeon.[29] In general in his writings Kohut tried to be gentle with his classical colleagues and not attack their clinical approach too directly. He had plenty of enemies without making more gratuitously. But what he really believed was another matter. That came out in seminars and meetings and in other informal settings when he talked more freely. In such contexts he made clear that he felt most classical analysts, while decent people who were smart and well trained, were in fact for the most part cold and unempathic in the way they treated patients. Given the theory, he said, how could they be otherwise? And if for whatever personal reasons they did act differently and not according to script, if they betrayed what he called the "zero point of normal behavior" for therapists, they had to feel guilty. All the trappings of analytic reserve and distance built into the three-quarters of a century of writings on the theory of technique had created a horrible analytic bind. Rules of caution about "parameters," the whole idea of a "defense transference" in which virtually anything the patient said meant the opposite, and the iconic use of the couch, had created a discourse that displaced a more natural and human search for understanding between two people. The analyst had no "leverage" in the classical theory of technique, as Kohut put it once. All you could do as a therapist was to issue edicts and prohibitions: Be strong, don't be anxious, be like me. It is not surprising, he says in *Cure*, that self psychologists are "more relaxed," "more easygoing," have "fewer misgivings about making themselves emotionally available," and generally act in a "less reserved manner" than most analysts. The theory of self makes that possible, indeed requires it.[30]

Kohut brimmed with therapeutic optimism. Freud in this regard had been exceedingly cautious. At best he felt psychoanalysis could open some new choices for people and turn neurotic misery into ordinary unhappiness.[31] Kohut, on the other hand, felt the task at hand was not in theory simply to relieve neurotic symptoms but to "firm the self" so that it can "avail itself of the talents and skills at an individual's disposal." He remained concerned whether in his enthusiasm for his new approach, and in the enthusiasms of his followers, self-psychological cure was simply healing by suggestion (something he felt was true for Freud himself in the early days of treating hysterics). But unlike other flashy cures that come and go just as quickly, Kohut said, he came to his new approach painstakingly and with perseverence. Cure in self psychology, as he put it, as is true generally in psychoanalysis, is also always healthfully incomplete. A false and totalistic change in the self is the currency of cults.[32] Still, the ambitious goal Kohut defines for analysis informed by his ideas is for the patient at the end to be able "to experience the joy of existence more keenly."[33]

The mature Kohut was not interested in writing a cookbook for psychoanalysis. The process, he felt, was far too complicated for such an approach.[34] But he had worked out in his mind a set of coherent therapeutic principles that grounded clinical self psychology. Most of all, he was concerned that analysts be themselves and act in the clinic in ways that are true to their own authentic values and aspirations. Since people are different, it is a logical corollary that good treatments can be conducted in very different settings.[35] Second, he felt it was important to recognize the self needs of patients that so often lie buried beneath disguised or muted depression. Freud used to say that every new insight cost him a patient, and Kohut himself frankly acknowledged, "I spoiled many analyses earlier in my career by not seeing the tendrils of . . . healthfully grandiose desires."[36] Third, he had a definite opinion that elaborate screening of patients through interviews often conducted by someone else, as well as preliminary face-to-face psychotherapy before the real thing got under way, was a huge hindrance to treatment. Someone who is psychotic—or schizoid or paranoid—and therefore probably unable to benefit from the experience of prolonged empathic immersion required for analytic cure will be quickly apparent and weeded out. For the rest, he felt, it was better to get started without all the preliminaries that robbed the analyst of crucial and highly relevant information that tends to emerge early in the process.[37]

Kohut also had much to say about "countertransference," or the feelings in the analyst about the patient that can hinder treatment. The whole issue—about which there is an exceedingly large literature—he believed had gotten off track by the failure to distinguish between neutrality and minimal response. A therapist can and should be neutral in the sense of maintaining an evenly hovering attention and not forcing oneself on the patient's experience, but that hardly means remaining mostly quiet, distant, reserved, unavailable.[38] Sometimes, of course, patients act out in relation to the therapist. Things can get very testy. The goal, however, is always to understand and try not to take it personally, not to rush judgment, humor someone, or be Olympian ("this is the way everyone feels"). Any countertransference reaction, Kohut says he learned from painful experience, is actually the result of one's own narcissistic vulnerabilities. One part of that process is not understanding what the patient is going through at that moment in the treatment. If you can get that, he told some candidates once, you will feel secure with all kinds of passing problems that arise. You can admit your mistakes to yourself, take a deep breath, change your behavior, and move on. You will also be able to welcome objectively accurate if sometimes critical comments about yourself by patients, especially when well into treatment, as the result of progress in self cohesion and therefore a less clouded view of the world, rather than as signs of acting out. The main thing, however, is not to let fears of countertransference block your own creative response to patient needs. Kohut once described giving a tightly wound male patient a joking kick in the butt as he left the office, and of course in his last lecture described letting a seriously depressed woman hold two of his fingers at one point in the therapy.[39]

Kohut's notions about cure in psychoanalysis departed sharply from the prevailing paradigm. As with so much else, the objective correlative was Freud, whose key ideas carry over from his early work with hysterics. Metaphor, one might say, is everything.

I have often in my own mind, compared cathartic psychotherapy with surgical intervention. I have described my treatments as psychotherapeutic operations; and I have brought
out their analogy with the opening up a cavity filled with
pus, the scraping out of a carious region, etc. An analogy of
this kind finds its justification not so much in the removal
of what is pathological as in the establishment of conditions
that are more likely to lead the course of the process in the
direction of recovery."[40]

The task of therapy is to remove the pus. Health and recovery emerge
out of that process. Real change in the self, in the logic of the metaphor,
is postanalytic. Freud modified these early views somewhat over the years.
For one thing, treatment soon lasted much longer than the six months
typical of the 1890s. With his failure in the analysis of Dora, he understood transference and recognized the need for more prolonged analysis
of the dynamics of the relation between patient and therapist. His new
understanding of transference, as much as anything, prompted him to
write his papers on technique just before the first war.[41] But the metaphor of pus removal as the task of therapy carries over into his most mature thoughts on the "seething cauldron" of the id in his formulation of
the structural model in 1923.[42] It is even implicit in his grim and pessimistic late paper "Analysis Terminable and Interminable" (1937). The ego
is weak and dependent and the instincts perpetually erupt from an ever-
replenishing source. Infection returns.[43]

Kohut, on the contrary, sees cure in psychoanalysis in the most complete sense of what he once called "transformed narcissism" as eminently
possible. Not to realize the implicit goals of one's nuclear self, of course,
is truly tragic and is the basis for the widespread depression in the culture. But we are not condemned to the tragic. That is the hope of psychoanalysis. Kohut's views on healing the self grow out of his Edenic image
of the possibilities of healthy development. A person who feels himself as
"a cohesive harmonious firm unit in time and space" connected with his
past and moving toward a "creative-productive future,"

at each stage in his life . . . experiences certain representatives of his human surroundings as joyfully responding to
him, as available to him as sources of idealized strength and
calmness, as being silently present but in essence like him,

and, at any rate, able to grasp his inner life more or less accurately so that their responses are attuned to his needs and allow him to grasp their inner life when his is in need of such sustenance.[44]

Trauma results from the profound and continued disruption of this union between self and selfobjects. Nor is trauma the outcome of a single act or event, however painful or disruptive. Such "gross events of childhood," as he put it in *Restoration*, are usually little more than "crystallization points for intermediate memory systems, which, if pursued further, lead to truly basic insights about the genesis of the disturbance." The real problem is almost always the underlying vulnerability in self structures that emerges out of chronic failures on the part of the selfobjects.[45]

The earliest and therefore most profound traumatic disruptions in the self-selfobject tie cannot be retrieved in the transference. It is in the nature of such trauma that it remains preverbal and inarticulate. To evoke it is to stir fears of disintegration. What is at stake is psychological death. "Clearly, the attempt to describe disintegration anxiety is the attempt to describe the indescribable."[46] One can only analyze the indirect effects of the way the self deals with the trauma in what Kohut calls "compensatory structures." The self creates new forms. The clinical conclusion Kohut draws is that "there is no single analytic road toward cure." His broader, more philosophical point, however, is the human capacity for growth, change, rebirth, even re-creation of the self. "It is my impression that the most productive and creative lives are lived by those who, despite high degrees of traumatization in childhood, are able to acquire new structures by finding new routes toward inner completeness."[47] These structures are not isolated (that is, repressed) or split off. Continuities must be felt in the healthy self. All that is genuine, Kohut says, is in depth. In what he calls the "segmental," as opposed to the "sectorial," one example he gives is that when we feel uplifted by a "great cultural ideal," the ancient feeling of uplift at the experience of being picked up by our "strong and admired mother and having been allowed to merge with her greatness, calmness, and security may be said to form the unconscious undertones of the joy we are experiencing as adults."[48]

What intrigues Kohut in *Cure* for the first time is the actual sequence that results in healing the self. Here cure begins (though it does not end) with empathy, which at various times he named the "recognition of the self in the other"; "the expansion of the self to include the other"; "the accepting, confirming and understanding human echo"; and the "word-less psychological extension of the human environment" that separates us from death, the "incomprehensible vastness of endless time," and the "barrier to meaninglessness, to pessimistic despair."[49] Kohut's "best" definition of empathy, analogous to his "terse scientific definition" in the 1950s as "vicarious introspection," was "the capacity to think and feel oneself into the inner life of another person." Also in *Cure*, Kohut suggests for the first time the idea of empathy with oneself, or entering into an empathic relationship with those former, split-off, and perhaps discarded fragments of one's own self. To keep his boundaries clear, Kohut always emphasized (certainly excessively) that empathy is not the same as sympathy. In fact, sympathy, like empathy, means participation in the suffering of others and putting onself in another's place. "It [sympathy] became a key concept in the Enlightenment's concern with the foundations of a secular humanist ethics," says Peter Brooks, "both the cornerstone of ethics (for Rousseau, for instance) and something more problematic and worrisome because of the potential for theatrical enactment and deception implicated in the concept."[50] Empathy in this sense is the psychoanalytic version of sympathy, Kohut's actualization of Rousseau. But whatever the overlap with sympathy, empathy in this broad sense is not something magical or mystical. It is not "God's gift bestowed only on an elect few." Empathy can be trained, developed, nurtured. Indeed, it must be for psychoanalysis to realize its potential.[51]

Given its significance, what is remarkable is that empathy should have been underground for so long. Freud had noted in passing that empathy was central to clinical understanding but never elaborated the significance of his idea. It was left entirely undeveloped in psychoanalysis, never located at the heart of the enterprise. In fact, it got all but lost conceptually, People talked about it, but it had no place in theory. Kohut's role, as he saw it, was to reawaken analysis to the obvious. The analogy he came to as a way of understanding his contribution was with the discovery of perspective in the fifteenth century based on the architectural drawings of Brunelleschi. Surely, people knew at some level that a person looked smaller if far off and larger if up close. How, then, could the geniuses of art never paint it that way? They had to have known what the eye sees, and yet they did not know. Brunelleschi hardly improved human vision during the Renaissance. But what he did was give people a new theory that allowed the world to be perceived "more correctly." The old unquestioned, time-honored, culturally imbedded theory of perception controlled how humans saw the world. A perceptual change at that level of the self is both all-encompassing and, in a sense, obvious. It also occurs only by unlearning theories that no longer work. Artists in the latter part of the fifteenth century at first had to struggle to stop seeing in the old way as they painted images on the canvas. In the same way, Kohut felt, his theory of empathy allows therapists to become newly aware of "formerly un-recognized configurations" if they can stop seeing patients through a glass darkly.[52]

Empathy for Kohut came to have a remarkable range. He had long emphasized four crucial points. First, empathy is the oxygen of psycho-logical life. We cannot breathe without it. To talk about it as somehow outside the self is absurd.[53] Second, therapists who seriously employ empathy not only see things differently but change the world they en-counter. Even psychosis, for example, within certain limits, "is in the mind of the beholder."[54] Third, the capacity for empathy is not gender-related. Both sexes have an equal capacity for (or blockage against) empathy.[55] Fourth, since empathy is such a powerful bond between people—and is a much more important uniting force than sex—it serves to counteract "man's destructiveness against his fellows." Empathy is the hope of peace.[56] The new insight in *Cure*—though the idea is still implicit in the book and is only made really clear in his final lecture at Berkeley— is that empathy in and of itself cures. Without anything else happening, without a single interpretation or explanation occurring, empathy in a therapeutic setting has a healing effect on a patient. The experience of prolonged empathic immersion, even for those traditionally dismissed as "unanalyzable," is curative.

At the same time, Kohut never questioned the importance of expla-nation as an essential element in what he considered cure in psychoanaly-sis. He did, however, come to appreciate new meanings of what he regarded as the essential work of interpretation, especially in relation to empathy. Some patients, he notes, require prolonged periods of "only" empathy, which eventually must be followed by interpretation as well.[57] And yet the two blend together. Kohut's key point is that there is a much more complex and synergistic relationship between empathy and explana-tion than has been appreciated in psychoanalysis, and this relationship makes the healing process a seamless web of experience. Mirroring, he once said, means giving the right interpretation, just as any kind of explanation "should be regarded as an extension and deepening of the understanding phase."[58] But the process is not static. Healing in psychoanalysis is phased, sequential, and increasingly profound. Good explanations do much more than expand the realm of cognition (which is basically the Freudian and ego-psychological idea of what interpretation is all about). The goal is rather an "accretion of psychic structure." The empathic bond between the patient and analyst in turn deepens and matures along with good explanations. Interpretation, in this sense, is a "higher form of empathy."[59]

For all its new ideas, in one very important sense Kohut's notion of healing in *Cure*, which is to say his most mature thoughts on the subject, remain deeply imbedded in its Freudian past. As early as *Analysis* he had developed a theory of "optimal frustration" and "transmuting internalization" that explained cure in drive terms growing directly out of Freud's 1917 essay "Mourning and Melancholia."[60] Kohut's theory grew out of Freud's developmental explanation for the emergence of psychic structure, especially during the oedipal period. The precondition for the formation of such structure in that model, as Kohut put in in 1971, is that the psychic apparatus must be ready for "specific introjects." Frustration then occurs in the object of attachment, or the selfobject, which leads to a "breaking up" of the "aspects of the object imago that are being internalized." The "psychoeconomic" dimension of the process is crucial. If the frustration is too great, the psyche is overwhelmed. But if "optimal," there is a process of "effective internalization" in large part because it can proceed in a "fractionated," or dosed, way.[61] Healing in therapy is directly analogous. The empathic ground must be prepared. Then there will be disappointment. Explanation makes sense of what has happened. Structure is what results. In a homey example he once used, Kohut recalled being empathic with a patient. Then one day just before a session, he opened a letter from a colleague accusing him of ruining psychoanalysis. During the hour the criticism in the letter entered his head and he drifted. Suddenly, the patient started bellyaching and said something was wrong with the office, it was cold, and so forth. Kohut told the patient that, on the contrary, he had perceived something important. He then explained his distance in the previous half hour, openly and honestly. It was accepted in large part because the explanation came in the context of the patient's generally feeling understood. The relationship deepened and the patient acquired a tiny bit of psychological organization for dealing with future frustrations. Such is cure in psychoanalysis, as Kohut saw it.[62]

It matters that Kohut in time took his ideas about healing out of the drive language of their initial formulation. The notion of what is optimal, for example, came to include much more than what its oedipal model allowed in 1971. Thus he told candidates in 1975 that "the delimitation of the self out of its more primitive stages, out of its merger stages is enhanced by optimal frustration. Optimal breaches of empathy, optimal failures of the empathic response by optimal shortcomings are found to be organized into aspects of the self."[63] In *Restoration* Kohut explained transmuting internalization in terms of our ingestion of protein. We might eat beef but do not in the process become cows. The protein is, instead, transmuted into a form that we can use in our digestion.[64] But Kohut never relinquished the notion that frustration is an essential element in healing. In *Cure* at one point he stresses that no analyst can possibly meet all the demands of a patient. Nor is that even desirable. What matters is that the patient must feel basically understood, which makes it possible to interpret the retreats that follow the disappointments. New structures that enhance self-esteem are the result.[65] At another point, he argues that the analyst is always there, week after week, month after month, year after year. One day he is sick or away. The patient relapses and indulges in acting out. If it is later explained empathically and really understood by the patient in depth, that moment can become transformative.[66]

Psychoanalytic healing, in the end, is an imaginable prospect for Kohut. One can confront despair and find avenues of hope. Trauma can be reworked and even transformed. It is not easy. Cure is a long, slow process for Kohut. There are no weekend miracles in his clinical world. But he specifically embraces the prospect of feeling joy at the end of treatment, of firming the self, and of realizing creative potentials and fulfilling ambitions deeply imbedded and otherwise perhaps lost. The cure, however, extends beyond the individual. Psychoanalysis had drifted into formalism by the 1970s and risked irrelevance. Kohut invigorated the humanism long dormant in the enterprise. He had no doubt that self psychology, in turn, contributed to a healing of history. Only by extending empathy in all areas of human endeavor, he felt, can we stave off our own annihilation. Self psychology moves toward that kind of life-enhancing understanding. In taking such a position, Kohut was not offering himself as a redeeming guru for all humanity. He meant much less than that, and more.

Thirty

NEW CLINICAL DIRECTIONS

Kohut's expansive ideas on the nature of healing in psychoanalysis during his last years connected synergistically with his actual work.[1] Things changed. There were, of course, continuities. He treasured his identity as a psychoanalyst, kept the iconic couch as his primary therapeutic instrument, never experimented with the fifty-minute hour, and never wavered in his commitment to prolonged treatment as the ideal toward which one should strive. But if Kohut's therapeutic right hand lay firmly on the analytic Bible, his left wandered off with age, experience, fame, cancer, and most of all a new theory to explain to himself what he was doing.

He had always been relatively easy about what are called "parameters" in psychoanalysis (basically breaking the rules).* In his last decade such experiments entered a qualitatively new realm of therapeutic action. One of his favorite patients was Gail Elden. In the fall of 1971 he called her to say he had received some "rather disturbing news" about his health. He suggested they take a walk, for he was concerned about her reaction to his cancer and wanted to try and help her deal with it. The analysis of Herb Murrie, who was a patient of Kohurt's for the last four years of the analyst's

---

*Kurt Eissler (no less), "The Effect of the Structure of the Ego on Psychoanalytic Technique," *JAPA* 1 (1953): 110, first defined a parameter as "the deviation, both quantitative and qualitative, from the basic model of technique which requires interpretation as the exclusive tool." A parameter, he said, should be introduced into treatment only when nothing else works; should never be used except minimally; should lead to self-elimination; and its effect on the transference must never be such that it cannot be abolished by interpretation.

life, was interrupted when Kohut had heart surgery followed by complications during the first part of 1979. Kohut stayed in touch with Murrie via three very charming, handwritten letters as he was recovering. The following year, after treatment had resumed but during his vacation in Carmel, Kohut also wrote Murrie, who was an artist, about his very positive impressions of a television documentary on Picasso. Kohut sent his regards to Murrie's wife, Lisa, whom he had clearly met.[2]

Kohut increasingly had no qualms about close contact with patients after therapy was concluded, and sometimes long before that. With those in the field, he readily enlisted as followers talented former analysands (such as Michael Franz Basch), gave clear messages to others that he expected them to join the group after the completion of their analysis (Peter Barglow), and included some in his group of followers while they were still in treatment (Marian Tolpin). The boundaries blurred. With "regular" patients, Kohut was equally at ease with postanalytic contact. Kohut always took the time, even if he did not have it, to relate to former patients. Just two weeks before his death and in a very bad state, Kohut wrote a chatty letter to Leah Averick, a former patient, about her work. She had written him, and his policy was to reply to such letters if at all possible. Kohut congratulated Averick on her work (she was a social worker) and responded to her question about parental reactions to children leaving home in a very thoughtful way. "My outlook on the emotional response of the parental generation when the child permanently moves away is that, while it confronts the parent with a considerable change, it is the parent who experiences this change joyfully who should be considered normal—however infrequent such normality may be." Kohut then elaborates at some length on this question of what often blocks a parent from relinquishing a specific selfobject function that a child meets and wonders if those needs become pervasive. Kohut's reply was surely more than Averick expected or, in a certain sense, deserved. Yet he knew her longings for contact and respected them without any condescension.[3]

Kohut was equally at ease with Jerome Beigler, a psychiatrist who entered therapy with Kohut in 1975. Kohut saw Beigler twice a week for the next six years. At the first session, Beigler, who was concerned with his own relationship to his Jewish identity, wanted to know whether Kohut was Jewish. Kohut talked about this and that and muttered something about who was Jewish, anyway? In the end Beigler was not sure what he had said, though Kohut ended with the comment that Beigler could teach him some Yiddish expressions and they could manage that way. Beigler found therapy with Kohut revitalizing and rejuvenating. He began to see all kinds of new things in his patients and found his whole life changed. Before therapy, Beigler could hardly drag himself home at the end of the day. Now he began to feel elated and felt a license to be much less rigid. He found Kohut "open, experimental, and charming," quite modest and always considerate. But it was his remarkable empathy that most impressed Beigler. Kohut could always sense Beigler's inner feelings. Sometimes in therapy Beigler would get so upset that he could say nothing more. Kohut would sense that and fill the space with gentle talk that was not the harsh and demeaning interpretations of the old school but a kind of empathic bath.

Beigler was also impressed with the elegance Kohut imparted to things. Once, when Kohut was sick, Beigler had his session in Kohut's apartment. The analyst specially ground some fresh coffee for him. He also gave Beigler occasional presents. Some four months before his death, Kohut gave Beigler a present for Father's Day, *A Dictionary of Foreign Terms*, inscribed "Happy Father's Day (plus 4), *sit venia verbis* [May the words be graceful], to Jerry, Heinz, 6-25-81." The "plus 4" was because it was four days past Father's Day. It was a significant present to give just before his own end, a parting gift.[4]

Beigler was left with two sustaining images of his former analyst, both, interestingly, outside of the formal clinic. Once, crossing Michigan Avenue in a terrific wind, the kind that can only blow off the lake in a Chicago winter, Beigler saw Kohut struggling to get across the street. Beigler came to help him. He took his arm, surprised that Kohut would let him help, and was taken aback at how thin he was. Another time Beigler got off a bus near the Institute and was feeling awful. He was absorbed in his own misery when suddenly he felt a gentle arm around his shoulder. It was Kohut.

Kohut's work with Marian Tolpin was probably more therapeutically radical than anything he did with anyone else.[5] Tolpin is a psychiatrist who has been a leader in self psychology for the last two decades.[6] She was in treatment with Kohut from 1971 until late 1979 or early 1980; she was vague about the exact dates, recalling only that she began around the time he got lymphoma in 1971 and ended after he had heart surgery in January 1979 but well before his death in October 1981. In retrospect she thinks she may have stopped therapy because she was avoiding him as he died, though she acknowledged she was in complete denial at the time about such connections, as she was about his lymphoma. Kohut was Tolpin's third therapist, and the analysis was decidedly for herself. She had been out of medical school for a number of years but only more recently, in the 1960s, had completed her psychoanalytic training; she had interrupted her career to raise her children.

Tolpin saw Kohut three times a week. He was completely flexible about meeting her special needs. "Whatever was on my agenda was part of the treatment," she said. She was then in her fifties, with a lot of psychiatric and psychoanalytic experience behind her. What she wanted was more treatment but also active supervision so that she could more effectively apply Kohut's ideas with her own patients. So together Kohut and Tolpin evolved an innovative (and by classical standards strictly verboten) format for her sessions. Whenever she wanted to talk about herself she lay down on the couch. When she felt like talking about her patients in supervision, she sat in the chair face-to-face.[7]

Once in a supervisory mode, Tolpin talked with Kohut of her frustration with a patient who simply would not terminate her analysis unless Tolpin agreed to see her occasionally in a quasi-social way. Tolpin was uncomfortable with such an arrangement. She and Kohut talked the issue through at great length and examined it from all points of view. Finally, Kohut said to her, "You have to do what you have to do." He meant that she could not exceed the limits of what she as a psychoanalyst and a person could tolerate in the way of postanalytic contact. The other side of Kohut's approach to treatment is that a responsible and trained psychoanalyst can, indeed must, evolve a style that suits her or his own capacities and commitments. Technique, Kohut felt according to Tolpin, is "simply what you do based on your understanding of the patient." The worst sin is faithfully to follow rules that block the expression of one's humanity and therapeutic creativity. Kohut, for example, in general liked to write or especially phone people after a seminar, meeting, talk, or almost any kind of encounter, to explore further some aspect of what had transpired earlier. That habit carried over to his therapy with Tolpin, and he would fairly regularly call her after a session that was emotionally stormy, or if he felt he had a further insight into what had come up during the session.

One of the curiosities of Tolpin's therapeutic/supervisory relationship with Kohut is that she was also simultaneously in an important professional relationship with him, meeting with him in seminars and other settings and herself beginning to write about self psychology. As if their relationship were not complicated enough, there was also social contact (dinners and such things). She says that for her it was easy to move between these worlds. She says she had "an extremely open relationship with him" that carried over to "our intellectual discussions in the group." She says she felt no compunction about telling him she disagreed with him. "It's not like I would avoid saying something because he turned up his nose or didn't like it."

At other times, Kohut could be decidedly more conventional. In 1971 a second-year candidate at the Institute, David Solomon, went into therapy with him.[8] Solomon had begun his training analysis with Anne Benjamin, but she got sick and he needed a new analyst. His good friend Arnold Goldberg recommended that he have an interview with Kohut. Solomon had no real sense of who Kohut was, just that he was on the staff and fairly noted. For Solomon it was mostly important that Goldberg recommended him. Solomon and Kohut talked, and Solomon could feel something unusual about this man. Kohut wanted to know the familiar things about Solomon, his past and his concerns. But he ended by asking, "What are you interested in when you're not doing this stuff?" Solomon said he liked to cook and knew about food and wines. "We start Monday," Kohut said.

For the next four years Solomon saw Kohut four times a week. He fell quickly into the routines, like the way Kohut left the bill on the corner of the desk at the end of each month. You were to pick it up without comment and either place payment on the same corner of the desk at the next session or mail it in. In general, Solomon was impressed with how hard Kohut worked. He took some general notes in a spiral notebook during the first two sessions but otherwise only wrote down dreams. Solomon could always hear him writing when he reported a dream. Solomon was most impressed with how intent and entirely focused Kohut was. "It gave you the feeling that you mattered, that you were getting the absolute best from this extraordinary man."[9] Solomon found that Kohut seldom said anything for the first twenty minutes and would then start commenting and interpreting more actively. Solomon's sense of the pattern was that Kohut wanted first to find where you were for that day before he began to interpret.

Solomon had come from a working-class immigrant background. His father ran a junk business. Solomon worked at the business on the side while he was in medical school, and even later would help his family if necessary by driving the truck. Once during analysis and Solomon's residency in psychiatry, his father got sick. So Solomon would get up early, make the rounds in the truck and pay off people, return home, change clothes, and resume his life as a psychiatrist in the hospital. As a child Solomon had often visited the Art Institute. He had a facility with drawing. But his parents not only failed to develop his talent, they actively discouraged it. They thought that the only kind of "paint man" who could support himself was one who did living rooms. Kohut was impressed with how far Solomon had come from this working-class life and particularly how sophisticated his tastes had become; he saw it as a form of narcissistic transformation. Along these lines, Kohut also assumed something of a father-substitute role in nourishing Solomon's continuing education. Once Solomon complained that he was giving up on his subscription tickets to the opera. He was getting fed up with Wagner. Kohut said to stick with it. The first time go to only one act, then leave. The next year when it returns, go to another. Eventually, you will stay through the whole thing.[10]

In everything Solomon felt understood, mirrored, valued. It was quite an experience. Solomon himself has what he says is a quick temper, and he certainly knows what it means not to be understood. But he *never* felt Kohut made any mistakes or disappointed him. "I don't remember ever getting angry at him," Solomon said. "I never felt that he screwed up, and I never felt that he was not there and not working hard and making an effort and that we were working at this. We were sort of comrades in arms." There was only one impasse. Anne Benjamin had not been Jewish, and Solomon had come to wonder, even before she got sick, whether their ethnic difference might be a factor in what he felt was her inability to really understand him. At some point early in his treatment with Kohut, Solomon was meditating on this issue and asked Kohut directly whether he was Jewish. There was complete silence from behind the couch.

Kohut himself wrote a contemporary letter about Solomon that has since been published. The letter provides an interesting window on his treatment that complements Solomon's view of things. In the letter Kohut is commenting generally on how long it takes to gain real progress in understanding someone else. As an example, he reports a dream Solomon had. Three men were engaged in a remarkable ritual. "On the roof of a tall building, blindfolded, they marched along a beam—slavishly following a religious rule. They had to count their steps, but they all miscounted and fell one after another to their deaths." Solomon had no associations that clarified the meaning of the dream. Solomon only noted his anxiety about premature heart disease and how he wanted to take a vacation. Otherwise, both he and Kohut remained baffled about what the dream meant. During the next day's session, however, they came to understand that the dream portrayed Solomon's "ritualizing attitude toward work and toward life as a whole." The three men were acquaintances in the National Guard who always went to church to avoid service rather than out of any sense of religious duty. Solomon's wish for a vacation had also aroused great guilt in him. He had hardly taken any time off in his life in the fear that he would lose all his values and fall into delinquency. Solomon worked like a machine and could not allow himself any breaks or freedom. He could not be spontaneous or joyful. As Kohut reports— and as Solomon remembers—it was an important moment of insight in his analysis.[11]

After termination Solomon moved at the edges of the self psychology group. He began to attend the monthly meetings but otherwise was not an integral member of the group until after Kohut's death. He felt, in fact, that Kohut kept an almost classical postanalytic distance from him, though he added that something in himself might have contributed to the distance. Certainly, as one contrasts Solomon's postanalytic experience with that of someone like Marian Tolpin, one has to be impressed with the different approaches to different individuals Kohut seemed to take. And he could be unpredictable. In 1979 (four years after the analysis), out of the blue, Kohut called Solomon and asked him to help him buy a car. He said he was simply not good at driving a bargain and hated all the double-dealing you get from car salesmen, who assure you of one price and then change their line when you are hooked. He would much rather avoid the hassle and lose a few hundred dollars. Solomon agreed to buy the car for Kohut, though he was a little puzzled at the request. Kohut's call was followed by a letter from Elizabeth detailing *exactly* what kind of car they wanted.[12]

Kohut was never predictable. Herb Murrie knew nothing about psychoanalysis.[13] He was an artist and graphic design firm executive who stumbled into therapy with Kohut in 1977. Murrie was in his early forties and in the midst of a marital crisis. He and his wife went to see a couples therapist who told him in no uncertain terms that if he wanted to save his marriage he needed to have some therapy of his own. She suggested he consult with Kohut, who she said would certainly not see him himself, as he was no longer taking patients, but would be in a position to evaluate him and make a good recommendation.

Murrie's first impression of Kohut was that of the perfect European professor—frail in physical stature but quite impressive nevertheless. He seemed to exert immense authority with a gentle hand, and Murrie felt as though he was meeting with Freud himself. He knew immediately that in the best of worlds this was a man he would like to be seen by. Murrie's experiences with the consultations fed this fantasy. At the end of the first interview Kohut asked Murrie if he would come back for a second session. Murrie thought that was odd but agreed. At the end of the second consultation, Kohut said that he knew it was strange but he would like to see him a third time. Murrie thought that either Kohut was going to take him on or he must be "one hell of a case" and "completely screwed up" to require all this consultation just to get a referral. But at the end of the third interview, Kohut said, "Herb, with your permission, I have someone who is finishing up in August [this was June], and if you can wait until August I would like to be your analyst."

Murrie saw Kohut four times a week for the next four years, though there were interruptions due to Murrie's business travels and in the last year due to Kohut's illness. Murrie never did fully understand why Kohut had taken him on. A part of him felt unusually interesting, though as soon as he allowed that idea to surface he had to question it. How could someone like himself, of such small stature, be of real interest to a great man like Heinz Kohut? "For a long time I really did not understand the magnitude and respect Heinz had throughout the world." Maybe, Murrie mused, he just happened to be the perfect case for some crucial paper that would wind up Kohut's life's work on narcissism. Murrie worked out a serviceable theory. He was the guinea pig. Kohut did not really need his case but it fit some larger whole. He was "the frosting on top of the cake." For Murrie's part of the bargain he got treated by someone who was "as good as they come in the psychoanalysis business." Murrie did not feel used. Kohut let him know he cared for him. Kohut might tell a poignant story, or refer to something important that Murrie had accomplished, or even "use some example of when he was a younger person, and his insecurity about something." It was a clear demonstration to Murrie that there was more than research to the analysis.

Besides, Murrie probably was interesting to Kohut. He is a good artist, a talent that he has more recently been able to develop after all the years of making a living off its applied, commercial forms. Murrie is also deeply spiritual and in his youth crossed religious boundaries in ways that refract Kohut's own experience. Murrie was born a Jew in a family that celebrated Passover but rarely attended temple. His parents had fled the revolution in Russia. Murrie's first job after college was with a very Christian man who worked on him subtly for a year and a half to get him to go to church with him. Then, during his first service, Murrie had a conversion experience. Murrie was soon going to church three times a week. He became a prize for the evangelicals as a born-again Jew and testified throughout the city. "My mother," Murrie said, "was going out of her mind." Before long, however, Murrie met and married a Danish Lutheran who was a very moderate Christian. Murrie's minister once tried to force her into a born-again experience, which Murrie found very distasteful. Slowly but surely he left the church and "never looked back." He remained a Christian by faith, however, which is where he was spiritually when he met Kohut.

The analysis in general proceeded smoothly at first. "I had so much to talk about," said Murrie. "So many problems. Dreams. Problems. Enormous conversations to cover these things." But then he began to get a little better and things got tougher. He had trouble thinking of things to say. And it went on and on. There was no end in sight. Murrie began to get suspicious of the enterprise. He also got into some conflict with Kohut over all the travel necessary to develop his business. He designed packages, and he often had to travel to make bids and get contracts. It led to a running battle. Kohut stressed how important it was for him to be there, not to take his therapy lightly, and to recognize how much more work was needed. The message was that Murrie was resisting treatment. That made Murrie angry, though he also acknowledges there were times when he might have rescheduled a meeting to return to Chicago in time for a session. But Murrie had stopped hurting as much and felt the pull of his business and the need to make his own money. The struggle over travel raised the issue again of whether he really mattered to Kohut or was just a case for his work on narcissism. "Was I just a corpse," he asked, "a body, and he was doing the autopsy? Did he really care about me as a human being?"

There was also a running battle over the expense of the analysis. Murrie did not seem to object to the hourly fee of $100. The issue was that

Kohut charged Murrie for all missed sessions. Once Murrie accidentally wrote out and mailed a check to Kohut for $400 instead of the $1,400 he actually owed him. When he next saw him, Kohut insisted on looking at the deeper meanings of the mistake. It made Murrie very angry and skeptical. It seemed petty and revealing of an unnecessarily hard-nosed aspect of psychoanalysis. Another issue was that it was hard for Murrie to get angry at Kohut to his face. "He came across to me as someone who you would just not get angry with." He carried "too much stature in that frail little body" and had "such an aura of great power or great intellect and great something." In fact, Murrie was so upset about his confused feelings that he felt Kohut himself was sorry he had made an issue of the check.

Murrie was deeply impressed with Kohut's humanity. He loved some of the stories he told, like seeing Freud off at the train station. Kohut also had good timing. By his third year, Murrie was in a much better place with his wife and children but now started complaining about his work, especially the way all his employees brought their troubles to him and the irrational needs of the designers he had to work with. He was always in the middle, incredibly busy, pulled in a million different ways. Kohut listened; then at a crucial moment he said, "My God, you are so lucky." Murrie, right in the middle of a tirade, was caught short by the comment. "How could you say that?" he asked. Kohut replied: "You have so many people depending on what you do. Do you know how many people are out there dreading to go to work and watching the clock as each minute goes by during the eight hours of their work day? Have you ever looked at the clock, Herb?" Murrie had to admit he had not had time to look at the clock. "That's what I mean," said Kohut. "How wonderful it is." Murrie's fondest memory of this event is the sound of Kohut's voice, soothing and calming. There may have been a slight laugh to it. It left a huge impact.

Murrie remarked on how seriously Kohut took everything. In 1981, shortly before Kohut's death, Murrie started a greeting card company called California Dreams. Kohut got very enthusiastic about the concept because of the rich social aspect of what such forms of communication represented, especially after Murrie explained how a variety of cards had evolved, from the simple birthday greeting to expressions of much deeper emotions. Murrie explained to Kohut in detail how the cards were being produced, who the principal artist was, the nature of the inking, and so on. Kohut got into every detail of the process. He said that when the cards were done he wanted to see them. When the first batch of eighty were completed, Murrie brought them into session (which was by then, in the spring of 1981, in Kohut's apartment). Kohut took them and asked if he could keep them so that he could examine them more carefully. A week later he laid out the cards carefully for Murrie, sorted into stacks ranging from what he thought were the very best to the least effective. Murrie said Kohut showed exquisite taste—except that in the end his favorite cards never sold, and the only ones the company made any money on were the ones like that showing a woman with big breasts and a candle in her cleavage with the legend "Bust Out—it's your birthday!"

It was very hard for Murrie when Kohut died. In the fourth year of treatment Kohut had said he thought Murrie had made some important progress, though there were still some issues to work on. He thought the time was not far off when he could cut down to two sessions a week rather than four.[14] He gave Murrie lots of hints about how he would not last forever and "that kind of thing," though he was very subtle about it. Still, "no matter how sick he was, or how weak he was, there was a spirit as if there is nothing wrong." Murrie never left a session thinking Kohut was about to die. When Kohut did die, however, Murrie was left with awful feelings of abandonment and incompleteness. "He didn't get to close the wound," Murrie put it. "He cut me open. He operated. He replaced everything. But he didn't get the chance to finish the job." But Murrie was also left with a feeling of freedom "from obligation." And he added: "Only years later did I understand the luck and good fortune of having Heinz Kohut as my psychoanalyst."

Kohut's death also brought back all of Murrie's confused feelings about his father's death when he was eleven. Murrie loved his father. He was outgoing, talented, and charismatic. He had been in vaudeville and played semipro baseball. He was always laughing and joking, though he was also decidedly authoritarian. In the house where he lived during the summers, Murrie's father would get up at 3:00 a.m. to go fish off a pier. Often Murrie would join him in a kind of communion as they hauled in the perch. One fateful morning Murrie did not join his father, who had a massive heart attack on the pier but managed to walk back to the house and lie on the couch, where he died. Murrie lay in his room listening to his mother cry, pretending it was all a bad dream. But he also came to feel relief, a sense of freedom from the pressure of his father's authority. Murrie experienced much of the same mix of feelings when Kohut died. He was in anguish at the shock of losing someone who had mattered so much to him. But he also felt the freedom. He was no longer responsible for having to turn his life over to somebody and keep that appointment and feel guilty if he missed it. Relief and anguish were equally mixed.

In his last decade, as more people sought to understand his evolving theories, Kohut filled an increasing portion of his practice with supervision of other therapists. He had always liked the format. He once noted in a seminar with some pride that he hardly ever had a supervisee lose a patient—though he then proceeded to describe three such losses. "I hope I'm not falsifying something in my memory," he noted. In general, however, he felt he had a better overall success rate in supervision than in his own practice, in which he often lost patients "because of my own extreme sensitivities." But in supervision he felt he had more objectivity since he was one step removed from the patient's attacks and idealizations. Ironically, he added, it was dealing with patients' idealizations that were the most difficult for most therapists. It is "nothing to get the psychoanalytic Nobel Prize for," he said, but he found "people become uncomfortable when they're being idealized, and they reject the patient's idealizing transference."[15]

The actual stories of people's supervisory work with Kohut are rich and varied. Ernest Wolf, for example, was in supervision with Kohut from 1966 to 1968.[16] He saw Kohut once a week and discussed one case over the two years. Kohut would listen without interrupting for a relatively long time, then pick something up from the case material that interested him and launch into a discussion of that. Wolf experienced the process as pretty much the way Kohut taught a class. Wolf would begin his supervisory sessions by reading from his process notes. He was too intimidated by Kohut at that point in his life to add much in the way of gloss or interpretation. In fact, Wolf felt on the spot. He never felt free. As long as he was in supervision he could not do analysis. Wolf recognizes this reticence was his issue, but it also suggests something structurally difficult about supervision as it is often experienced by the candidate. Furthermore, Wolf felt Kohut was wrong in his diagnosis of the case, which was that of a man with an anxiety disorder. Because of his general exposure to Kohut's ideas, Wolf was already thinking in self terms, and he kept trying to understand the case along those lines. Wolf, who still has occasional contact with the patient, feels certain now that Kohut was wrong. But for the entire two years of therapy Kohut never changed his view.

Paul Ornstein had a different experience with Kohut in supervision.[17]

He first sought out Kohut in 1966 to help him with a case that Ornstein thought was surely a classic Oedipus complex. But after hearing the first three sessions summarized, Kohut said no, the man's problem was not oedipal at all. The problem, Kohut said, is that the oedipal issues were too blatantly on the surface. "This man has a different problem. He has a problem with his tension regulation. It is a basic, fundamental narcissistic issue." Ornstein went home quite confused and somewhat discouraged. He thought he was a pretty good analyst, yet he had not even made the right diagnosis. Ornstein discussed the conflicting diagnoses with the colleague who had referred the patient to him. "Your job in the next four years," the colleague said, "will be to convince the patient that the oedipal issues are his problem." Ornstein had enough sense to recognize the absurdity of such a position but remained confused as he continued with the case and the supervision. Nothing he had learned during his four years of course work at the Institute was making any sense. Kohut led Ornstein gently toward new insights. At critical moments, by way of summarizing or for further clarification, Kohut sometimes would pull out a relevant page from the draft of what he was writing and read it to Ornstein. That led Ornstein to ask if he could just borrow the manuscript itself and not have to get it page by page. "Forget about what I wrote," Kohut replied. "Your patient will teach you how to analyze him." This approach had a great impact on Ornstein. Kohut only turned to written theory after complete immersion in the clinical data. He would not let Ornstein read the theory and impose it on the data.

Ornstein found his supervisory conversations with Kohut enormously rewarding. In fact, he stayed in supervision with Kohut for the rest of Kohut's life, though they met only once a month after the Cincinnati institute, where he was on the faculty, became independent in 1973. He also determined to make his struggles a joint marital venture, and so convinced his wife, Anna Ornstein, to take a case to Kohut for supervision. They could then travel together to Chicago for their supervision and share the experience of learning. Ornstein says that Kohut's style in supervision was never to take notes while in session; he would later make a record of the meeting, which Ornstein found amazingly accurate, often more detailed and accurate than Ornstein's own notes about the patient. Ornstein had no doubt about Kohut's phenomenal memory. Kohut later gave these records to Ornstein with the comment that there were some pretty good thoughts about the patient in them and hoped Ornstein would be able to make use of them.

People came from all over. Angela Sheppard was a Canadian analyst who got interested in Kohut's work in the late 1970s. She wrote him and asked if she could consult with him for a session about a case while she was in Chicago.[18] He wrote back right away that one hour would hardly be sufficient, since he insisted that the case material itself be presented during the session. "I do not read case material ahead of consultative session," he said. He therefore suggested that, despite the fee of $100 per hour, it would be much better to meet twice while she was in Chicago. He was less helpful with those who came hoping to impress. Pietro Castelnuovo-Tedesco, for example, Blakemore Professor of Psychiatry at Vanderbilt University, wrote asking for supervision—and sent his twelve-page vita with his letter. Kohut did not bother to reply.

Sheldon Meyers was different.[19] After Meyers graduated from the Institute in 1975, he joined the self psychology workshop, which met monthly. As the newcomer to the group, he was made coordinator of the workshop. He found the meetings enormously stimulating and Kohut fascinating. He had not had much direct contact with Kohut during his training but found the discussions exciting. Meyers noted how many people in the group came from out of town and had supervision with Kohut around the time of the meetings. He thought, "If they meet with him, why shouldn't I"? Supervision would be a good way to get to know Kohut and his ideas better. His only concern was that it was not all that politically astute for a recent graduate to be too closely identified with Kohut. But he decided the value of what he might learn overrode such political considerations.

For three years, between November 1978 and the spring of 1981, Meyers had weekly supervision with Kohut, who sat in his hard-backed wooden chair dispensing advice. Kohut seemed "stiff and austere" to Meyers, though "informal and loose in his body language." Kohut did not take notes during his supervisory sessions, but at the beginning of the next meeting he would summarize what had happened the last time. It gave the supervision continuity. Kohut also worked at broadening Meyers's classical training. One patient they talked about, for example, a woman who traveled from Evanston for her sessions in downtown Chicago, often had trouble with traffic and was late. She would then ask for fifteen extra minutes at the end to make it up. She was Meyers's last patient of the day, so it was possible for him to grant the request. But such "gratification" countered his classical training and instincts. Kohut encouraged Meyers to give in to the request. It would be good for the transference. It was clearly the kind of indulgence she had never gotten from her parents. Only good could come from meeting the patient's needs in this case. In retrospect, Meyers agrees that Kohut was absolutely right.

There was one funny moment in Meyers's work with Kohut. Meyers arrived for his session soaking wet from having just come out of a storm. Kohut saw him dripping and asked spontaneously if he wanted to borrow his suit, as he kept an extra one in the closet. Meyers was taken aback, for he was at least forty pounds heavier than Kohut and would have looked ridiculous in his suit and probably would have ripped it apart at the seams. Kohut was at first surprised at the hesitation, but when he noticed Meyers comparing their body sizes he laughed. So Meyers sat down wet and they went to work. On reflection years later, Meyers came to think of this story as illustrating that Kohut's empathy was sometimes "forced and automatic," which seems an odd way to configure it. More to the point, it seems, is the further observation Meyers makes that Kohut's offer of the suit made him "more human, less ideal, and it enhanced our working alliance."

For most of his work with Kohut, Meyers presented the case of an angry middle-aged man who was out of touch with his feelings and resistant to treatment. Meyers's inclination, based on his previous training, was to interpret these resistances to the patient and try to get him to gain insight into them. Kohut encouraged Meyers to avoid such interpretations, which a patient almost always experiences as a criticism. The patient, Kohut said, was engaging in treatment the only way he could and the way he needed to. The anger was the transference. Kohut said just to accept it and see later what it means.

Kohut was equally at odds with the classical approach to dream interpretation. He was mostly interested in dreams as broad reconstructions of what the patient had felt as a child that were being revived in therapy, rather than in the specific meanings of dream elements or their drive equivalents. Early in treatment, for example, the patient dreamed of a pig that was being born. It needed resuscitation. He cut off the pig's head and then resuscitated it. He felt he was doing something crazy. In the hour Meyers had told the patient that "the pig represented something very disturbing inside of you that you feel you can't handle appropriately once it pops out." Kohut said there was nothing essentially wrong with that view of the dream, but encouraged him to be more general, to stress, for example, that the patient sees himself as a pig and that his birth in the dream suggests the sordid, horrible way he experienced the world he grew up in. At the same time, Kohut encouraged Meyers to convey to the patient how hard it was for the patient to get close to Meyers; the patient should try to acknowledge that and to understand it was because he had missed closeness from his parents. Meyers followed Kohut's advice and found the treatment made much more rapid progress.

There was one point of disagreement between Kohut and Meyers that was never resolved. The patient's father was extremely harsh and authoritarian. Kohut jumped on evidence of that, saying it was just like Daniel Paul Schreber's father (Freud wrote about Schreber in 1910), and wanted Meyers to write up the case along those lines. He was excited because he said it showed it does not always have to be the mother who is the essential figure in the psychopathology of the patient. The only problem was that Meyers never saw it that way and from the further treatment of the case after Kohut died is quite certain he was right. The mother was much more important in the psychological life of his patient than the father ever was. But Kohut was never ideological about his idea in supervision with Meyers, never forced it on his junior colleague. He accepted that Meyers had to follow his own instincts with his own patient. He said time would tell, in any event.

During almost exactly the same period of time that Meyers was working with Kohut, Jule Miller traveled to Chicago from St. Louis for supervision.[20] Because of the distance, Kohut usually met Miller in double-length sessions on a monthly basis. Miller was an experienced analyst who wanted to explore Kohut's approach more deeply in his work. During their twenty-three meetings between 1978 and 1981, Miller presented the termination phase of one long analysis, the beginning of another case, and various "spot" presentations. In form Kohut's meetings with Miller were much like those with Meyers. As usual, Kohut never took notes but would begin each new session by reading a summary of their previous meeting. Miller was always impressed with the completeness of Kohut's account.

Because Miller was so experienced at the time he worked with Kohut, he was more aware than most of the real differences in approach to patients that Kohut was suggesting in his work. He was also in a good position to test the efficacy of Kohut's ideas clinically. Miller, for example, felt Kohut was deeply committed to the idea of interpreting material "as if it means what it seems to mean." Analysts, Kohut seemed to feel, too often look first for deep hidden meanings. Once a patient of Miller's arrived for his session an hour early. Miller told the patient he had "set up a situation of disappointment." It got nowhere. Kohut suggested he say instead that, like a young child eager to see his father, the patient had come early. He wanted to be there with him. Interestingly, sometime later the patient again came an hour early. Miller tried Kohut's approach and could see visible relaxation in the patient. Along the same lines, the patient once told Miller some inside information about a celebrity whom he knew Miller was interested in. Miller interpreted the remark along oedipal lines and pointed out its competitive aspects. The patient, visibly deflated, remarked, "What you said punctured my balloon." Kohut said the way to read the comment was to see it as a positive enactment in the transference. The patient was excited and pleased, as a little boy is to tell something important to his father. He wanted to bring Miller pleasure. That was of far greater psychological significance than whatever elements of competition might be lurking at some level of the patient's consciousness.

Kohut told Miller it was important to tell his patient when he was making progress and to do it not in a neutral tone of voice but with enthusiasm. If the patient feels deflated, Kohut also said, the analyst is probably doing something wrong. Avoid the interpretation of issues that are tangential to the transference, such as slips of the tongue. That only humiliates the patient and repeats his experience with fragmentation. Furthermore, Miller should readily accept gross forms of identification as a sign of progress. In time such identifications will become more refined and in most cases give way to an internalization of the appropriate aspects of the analyst's functioning. Identification, in other words, was a fragile sequence that should not be disturbed but recognized for its important role in the healing process. Miller's patient once dreamed of his building and Miller's merging. Kohut's central advice was not to overinterpret the dream. In a related vein, Kohut helped Miller recognize how he had always cut short patients' idealization of him because he found it so uncomfortable. Miller came to recognize in his work with Kohut that ironically it is much easier to deal with a patient's rage than his or her idealization.

Kohut emphasized that the analyst should focus on the patient's healthy tendencies rather than his regressive ones. For example, Miller's patient had two dreams. In the first he was uncertain whether to sit with some women or some homosexual men. The meaning here was rather patent in terms of the patient's struggles with his homosexuality and wish to transcend it. But a couple of weeks later the patient dreamed of sitting at a bar with some women. Behind him were some heterosexual men playing cards and laughing. He felt embarrassed. Miller's question to the patient was why he felt embarrassed. Kohut felt what Miller did was wrong in two respects. First, Kohut felt it was wrong in general to ask questions of patients. He felt the burden for understanding the patient rests with the analyst. Questions abrogate that responsibility. It is better to listen and then interpret when things begin to make sense. Second, Kohut felt that Miller was focusing on the wrong branch of the interpretive tree. He should instead have pointed out to the patient that there had been a move in the two dreams from the stark choice in the first dream to one of being with women and happy or joining the heterosexual men. He said Miller's question focused on the patient's regressive tendencies and was bound to make him feel embarrassed. The correctness of Kohut's approach was immediately apparent in the following session, when the patient said he had felt Miller was trying to push him back into homosexuality with his question.

Frederic Arensberg was in supervision with Kohut from 1977 until 1980.[21] Arensberg was then in full-time private practice in New York City. He was a widely eclectic practitioner. In 1972 Dr. Arensberg had started an analysis with a patient named Carl. Over a period of time, Arensberg and Carl got into a difficult transference-countertransference bind. On the one hand, Carl was struggling to find a parental figure who would embody idealizable qualities and capacities that he was longing to connect with. On the other hand, he needed to gain access to his own true feelings and wishes, which seemed tenuous at best. These were easily driven into hiding by Arensberg's failures in empathy. When Carl's longings were shattered and his state of disruption was not understood, he would react by either withdrawal or rage, which at times became relentless and practically unbearable to Arensberg. Since Arensberg really cared intensely about Carl, the stalemate began to feel quite desperate.

Arensberg had some acquaintance with the work of Heinz Kohut and had inadvertently mentioned this to Carl as having some importance to him, although he had not incorporated Kohut's views into his clinical approach. The patient became an avid reader of Kohut's work. One day Carl brought in a copy of *The Analysis of the Self*, which he had heavily marked

and underlined with a yellow marker. He spoke of it with great enthusiasm and told Arensberg he had to read it. That would be the only way to
understand him, he reported. At first Arensberg was cautious, indeed
suspicious, and for some three months interpreted Carl's praise of Kohut
as a resistance. But finally he got the book and read it for himself and
became half-convinced it might be relevant. But since the ideas in *Analysis* were so far outside of his experience, Arensberg felt the need to have
his work supervised by a seasoned clinician who used self psychology
theory. He decided to call Kohut himself directly and ask for advice.

On the phone Kohut was friendly. He said he knew people in New
York but none he felt comfortable recommending for supervision. He
suggested instead that Arensberg consider coming out to Chicago for
supervision with him. With some trepidation Arensberg agreed and they
set a date.

At that first meeting Arensberg was so terrified he found his knees
shaking. He assumed this famous man would drag him on the carpet and
brand him as a complete incompetent. Instead, Kohut greeted Arensberg
in his comfortable Institute office and was very warm and calming. Even
as he related his story nearly twenty years later, Arensberg choked on some
tears. Kohut, sensing the younger man's anxiety, spent most of the first
session putting him at ease and assuring him he was a good therapist and
destined to carry out his analysis with Carl. Arensberg could feel the tension draining from him. He felt an immediate bond and knew he was in
the hands of a true master. In fact, Arensberg's attachment to Kohut from
the outset was so strong that he seriously considered quitting his job in
New York and moving his entire family to Chicago so that he could enter
analysis with him. In supervision Arensberg found himself almost unwittingly trying to move into his own therapeutic issues. Kohut understood
the motives behind these maneuvers and without any put-downs kept the
supervision focused and gently steered Arensberg back into the problems
of his analysis of Carl. But Kohut did allow Arensberg to idealize him and
gave him, for example, signed copies of various offprints.

The most general insight Kohut helped Arensberg gain about the
impasse that had developed between him and his patient was Arensberg's
inability to understand Carl's intense need to idealize him. Arensberg had
tried to break through the idealization in good Freudian fashion and had
instead stirred a cauldron of rage. Kohut got Arensberg to see that as a
result of his childhood experience, Carl desperately sought to use him as
an idealized selfobject who would bring some cohesion to his personality.

Kohut also helped Arensberg see that the way he brought himself into the therapy by talking about his own feelings was experienced by Carl as intrusive.

Back in New York Arensberg shared Kohut's insight with Carl. From then on the two became allies in the therapy rather than antagonists. Soon a pattern was established. Carl began talking much more (and with more feeling) and Arensberg took more complete notes to bring to his supervision with Kohut. About every other month Arensberg would take an early Thursday morning plane to Chicago, rush by cab to the near North Side, and have one or two sequential sessions in the late morning. During the noon break he often visited the Art Institute (Arensberg's wife is an artist) and then returned for a third session in the middle of the afternoon. He would then take an evening flight back to New York. It was exhilarating for Arensberg but also done at some expense. He had to give up an entire day of his practice, pay the plane fares, and pay Kohut's fee. Each trip cost Arensberg several thousand dollars in direct and indirect costs. After 1979, when Kohut had his heart attack, they had their sessions by phone.

One of Kohut's recommendations that Arensberg never followed was to take Carl out of the group he had long had him in. Kohut felt a vulnerable patient like Carl was much too sensitive to handle the failures in empathy common in groups. Group therapy was calculated to foster narcissistic injuries and thus a dangerous form of treatment for many classes of patients. But more generally, groups were inherently risky. The leader could much too easily use his charisma to control its members for all kinds of insidious purposes. The example Kohut quoted was Hitler and Nazi Germany.

The supervisory setting was a face-to-face encounter. Arensberg would discuss his recent work with Carl from his notes, and Kohut would respond. Sometimes Kohut would expound on an issue of theory as it related to something concrete in the material. Such theorizing never amounted to more than about 10 percent of the supervision, but it provided Arensberg with what he says now is the bulk of his real knowledge of self psychology.

In the end, Arensberg and Carl made significant progress, though after the period of the supervision Carl decided he would make further progress if he got a different analyst. They both felt they had come a long way and parted with good feelings. Arensberg's own parting with Kohut came when he attended the memorial service in Chicago after his death.

Arensberg introduced himself to Mrs. Kohut, expressed his condolences and the nature of his contact with her husband, and requested a picture. She was kind enough to send him a photograph a few months later, which he had enlarged and still has hanging in his office. He has often gazed at it over the years in his struggles to heal. He knows now he will never again turn away the idealization of a desperately vulnerable patient.

Thirty-one

GENTLE INTO

THAT GOOD NIGHT

Do not go gentle into that good night,
Old age should burn and rave at close of day;
Rage, rage against the dying of the light.
                                    —Dylan Thomas

The Berkeley campus lecture hall was filled to capacity that Sunday morning in early October 1981.[1] Some 400 people were seated, another 100 wandering in the aisles or outside on the plaza. It was a typically beautiful California day. The sun was warm, the grass still mostly green, the trees lush.

Excitement tinged with dread filled the air. It was the final day of the fourth annual conference on self psychology. There had been a pre-conference on Thursday for the uninitiated, then a full round of lectures and workshops on aspects of self psychology for participants on Friday and Saturday. And yet, unaccountably, Heinz Kohut himself had not yet appeared at the conference. At the three previous self meetings—in Chicago, Boston, and New York—Kohut had been everywhere. He had greeted old friends and new acquaintances personally. He had attended plenary sessions in his trademark faded grey V-necked sweater, sitting in the front row, and had joined actively in the questioning and discussion. Whenever possible, he had attended workshops, where he was animated and lively, always at the center of the dialogue. In the evenings special banquets with celebratory speeches, as in Chicago in 1978 and Boston the following year, had featured him and his work. And at the very end of the self conferences, Kohut had commented on the conference as a whole, its themes and issues, and identified questions for the future.

This weekend Kohut was a very sick man, holed up in a hotel room. His decade-long struggle with lymphoma had reached a crisis. His retreaded heart was increasingly fragile. Nagging inner ear problems continued to torment him. For months he had hardly been eating, and his once-robust frame now barely tipped the scales at 100 pounds. He was so skinny his bones protruded. He could only sit in a straight chair with a pillow underneath him.

But almost no one knew the extent of his decline. No colleague from Chicago had seen Kohut since July, when he left for his vacation in Carmel. He was then weak but active, writing his last book, even seeing a few patients. Calls over the summer from friends yielded little concrete information. He had a way of brushing off personal inquiries and talking at length about himself without revealing anything of significance. The ruse was carried through at the conference by Elizabeth Kohut, who attended many sessions herself and tried to look untroubled. When asked about Kohut's health, she indicated only that he was weak and resting at the hotel but definitely planned to speak to the conference participants on Sunday morning. Friends anxiously consulted each other and tried to pry more information out of her. But no amount of whispered huddling at the margins of a busy conference brought forth any more concrete information about Kohut's physical state.

Kohut had, however, invited Jacques Palaci to visit him Saturday at the hotel.[2] Palaci had made it a point to travel from Paris for the meetings since they first began in 1978. Kohut always tried to do something special with Palaci, and they had established a tradition of visiting for a day or so after each conference. It is not surprising Kohut chose Palaci to visit him that Saturday. Palaci was Kohut's link to the past, to his youth, to Vienna. Nothing would be compromised by revealing to Palaci how sick he really was.

Elizabeth Kohut's look when she greeted Palaci at the door was his first indication of just how serious things were with his old friend. But nothing could have prepared him for what he saw when he came to Kohut's bedside. Palaci instantly recognized the imminence of death in the pallor of Kohut's skin, the edema that caused his belly to swell, the major loss of weight that left him an empty shell, and the odors of the sickroom. The mere fact that Kohut stayed in bed when Palaci walked in suggested to him the seriousness of the situation. Kohut hated to appear helpless or sick.

Motioning Palaci to his side, Kohut greeted him warmly. He did not deny to this friend how sick he really was. He brought him up to date quickly on his various ailments and the status of his lymphoma. He also shared how awful the night before had been. He was taking three times the prescribed doses of all his drugs but nothing could touch his pain. "Living like that is not worth it," he said. "I'm not afraid of dying, and it's coming soon. But I do have concerns for who will continue my work." And with that Kohut gossiped about the three men—Arnold Goldberg, Paul Ornstein, and Michael Franz Basch—who he felt could conceivably emerge as leaders of self psychology after his death. Conversation then turned to personal issues. Palaci told his friend he was separated from his wife, about which Kohut was deeply empathic. He had known Diana, who was an artist, for years and had always loved to talk with her about her work. In fact, it had always surprised Palaci the way Kohut could so totally immerse himself in the interests of someone who neither knew nor cared about psychoanalysis. But now it was time to console his friend. Kohut reminded Palaci that creative people are not as stable as others, and his separation was probably the price of marrying an artist. It put the issue in perspective for Palaci and both made him feel understood and gave him some hope for the future.

Kohut then confided in Palaci how difficult he knew it was going to be to give his talk the next day. Still, he was determined. Palaci asked whether Kohut was really up to making such a presentation. Indeed he was, asserted Kohut. All these people had gathered to honor him, to examine his ideas, and to see him. He could not disappoint them. Besides, he had a plan. He would remain in bed until the last minute, then get hooked up with a vial of adrenaline dripping directly into a vein near his heart. He had arranged for an ambulance to transport him to the lecture hall just before he was supposed to speak. Palaci could only shake his head in amazement. He knew when set on such a course Kohut was not to be dissuaded.

Palaci left Kohut to rest, though a few hours later he called to make sure he was okay. In that phone conversation Palaci mentioned that while sitting on the bed talking he had dropped his comb out of his pocket. "I'm so glad," Kohut said. "Now I can think of you every time I comb my hair."

The night went badly. Bernard Brandchaft happened to be staying in a room just down the hall from Kohut. After a busy day at the conference, Brandchaft and his wife had returned to their room to watch a TV presentation of *Jacques Brel Is Alive and Well and Living in Paris*. Brandchaft loves music and was very moved by the production, as he always is when he hears it. In the midst of it, however, around 10:30, he heard some noise in the hallway. Brandchaft opened his door a crack and to his astonishment there was Kohut, in his pajamas and bathrobe, shuffling about. He was obviously distressed. Brandchaft walked out and asked him what was wrong and could he help. Kohut waved him off, not unfriendly but decisive. Brandchaft felt Kohut was embarrassed to be seen in that condition and that he wanted to preserve a favorable image of himself in his friend's mind, even in this extreme situation. Brandchaft returned to his room, but he was frightened. Peeking through his door, he watched Kohut to be sure he had not fallen or somehow hurt himself. After a while and in obvious pain, Kohut returned to his room. Brandchaft closed his door and immediately called Arnold Goldberg, who he knew would be the most likely person to be in close touch with the situation. Goldberg said there was no way to help and that, in any event, Elizabeth was with Heinz and would take care of him.[3]

Somehow, Kohut made it through the night. The next morning, after dressing slowly and painfully, he set off for the conference hall. On the way, he stopped with his wife for a brief lunch at McDonald's, which he boasted of later to his son. He loved such symbols of America, his adopted country.[4] At half past ten, just as the four other panelists wound up their comments, the ambulance arrived at the plaza outside the Berkeley campus lecture hall. A curious crowd instantly gathered near the ambulance. The driver removed a wheelchair, and Kohut got out of the front seat to sit in it. He had a grim, set look on his face that baffled many who knew him. He seemed to look through them. He was completely focused. A silent parting of those gathered near the ambulance made room for Kohut to pass, with his wife at his side, and approach the entrance to the lecture hall. At the doorway Kohut deliberately rose from the wheelchair and began the long walk to the podium.

Kohut had sent out advance word that he would definitely make it for a few brief comments at the end of the morning session. The panelists on stage and most of the conference participants in the hall thus knew that the stir at the back of the room signaled his arrival. Arnold Goldberg, the last speaker at the long table covered with a white cloth, instantly ended his comments. All eyes turned to the door. Some stood at their seats to get a better view. Kohut walked alone and firmly down the long aisle, up the three steps to the proscenium, and took his place stage right at the far end of the table.

For most people in the hall, his appearance, while suggestive of the seriousness of his medical condition, did not really give it away. He was pale, to be sure, even ashen, and it was clear he had lost weight, for his neck looked scrawny and his high cheek bones were sharply accentuated. But everything else disguised his state, and the anxiety about his absence that had hung in the air during the conference now completely dissipated with him actually in the room, seated at the long table on the stage. He was alive, and without too much denial one could be convinced he even looked well. Had he not walked down the long aisle and up to the stage on his own? And when he started talking he was clearly the familiar Kohut of everyone's memory and imagination: the high-pitched voice that ranged from a comforting sing-song to a sharp whine or cackle; the soft and appealing lilt of his Viennese accent, which had entered into the transferences of a thousand patients in three decades of psychoanalytic practice; the hand gestures to emphasize certain points; the self-deprecating jokes; the warmth and human energy that he radiated; and, surely, the charisma, whatever it is, that filled the room and suddenly changed the entire atmosphere of the conference. Everyone felt the air changing.

The topic of Kohut's lecture was empathy.[5] He apologized for taking up the subject again, both in the lecture and in his recently completed draft of *How Does Analysis Cure?* In both contexts he was returning to the subject, despite the fact that he had decided a couple of years ago that he was "sick of that topic." He had written himself out about it. Yet people kept criticizing him "over and over again" with the same arguments and profound misunderstandings. It wore him out. "I was wasting my time, my emotions, my energy," he said. He felt he should get on with some new ideas. But "idiot that I am," he said with a slight smile, he eventually came to feel that "when people keep asking you the same damn question, something must be wrong!"

Kohut's lecture ranged over many old and new aspects of his topic, reminding himself and his listeners how central empathy had been to his life's work on narcissism and what he was now calling self psychology. Empathy is the way of knowing in psychoanalysis, he argued. It is also the precondition for cure in psychotherapy; indeed, even without anything else happening in the treatment, an authentically empathic therapist can effect significant healing in the patient. Empathy alone is not the goal. Psychoanalytic psychotherapy consists of empathy *and* explanation, and it is that unique combination that distinguishes the enterprise and insures lasting change in the self. At the same time, there is no question Kohut privileges empathy. He even suggests that what is generally called "interpretation" in psychoanalysis could be considered a "higher form of empathy." Kohut's final lecture, in other words, reframed the problem of cure in psychoanalysis, going beyond even the discussion in his last book, *How Does Analysis Cure?*

After half an hour, however, and clearly tiring, Kohut announced he wanted to close. His head was beginning to tilt slightly forward, as though its weight was difficult to support. He looked, if that was possible, even paler than he had at the beginning of the lecture. His hand gestures had become subdued, and the scrunching of his nose and adjustment of his glasses less pronounced. The eyes seemed sadder. Everything spoke of a profound exhaustion.

But in fact he had trouble stopping. He knew it was his last lecture. And so, first, he reiterated that empathy must not be abused for vaguely supportive measures and that it must be appreciated on its various levels of development. He uttered that pronouncement even though he knew immediately it had the tone of a hard-and-fast rule. Hardly wanting to go out on a fussy note, he added quickly, by way of qualification, "Certainly, I'm not stodgy." The more you know the freer you can be to experiment and find your own truth and avoid "some ritual that one sticks to anxiously." We don't really know yet how to treat people with serious self disturbances, he went on. But with time and care and patience we will discover the best approaches and the most effective ways to blend empathy and explanation.

That thought brought to mind a clinical example. Many years ago Kohut had been involved in a long analysis treating a severely disturbed woman. After abruptly leaving another analysis, she lay down on the couch her first day and said it felt as if she was in a coffin and that the top was about to close with a click. Here Kohut mimicked the sound by opening his mouth widely and twice loudly clicking with his tongue. He had always been good at such imitations. He was a natural actor, which early on he had learned to turn to professional advantage. As a resident in neurology at the University of Chicago School of Medicine in the 1940s, for example, he was famous for being able to act out perfectly the odd neurological tics that are described in the textbooks and must be memorized

for boards.[6] That double click was one of his great moments of performance. Watching it made you feel the coffin closing.

Over the years of treatment with the woman, Kohut noted that she
was so deeply depressed there were many times he thought he would
lose her to suicide. Once he was even spontaneously moved to ask if she
would like to hold onto his fingers while she talked. "Maybe that would
help you," he said to her. It was a "doubtful maneuver," he added, and
he was not recommending it in general. But he was desperate. So he
pulled his chair closer and reached out and gave her two of his fingers
to hold. The patient clasped Kohut's fingers tightly. It made him think
of the "toothless gums of a very young child clamping down on an empty
nipple." That was his thought, indeed his interpretation. He did not
say it. That would come later. But he thought it. It was fully formulated in his mind.

Then Kohut really did end. "I'm quite sure this will be the last self
psychology meeting that I will attend," he said gravely, as many in the
audience of five hundred began to cry, aware now more than ever that he
was announcing his own end. "I wanted to do my utmost to be able to
go through with my promise [to attend]. So, let's all hope for a good
future for the ideas embodied in self psychology." And he said good-bye.

The applause was tumultuous now, the tears abundant. Kohut raised
his hands: "Enough, enough. I know your feelings. I want to take a rest
now."

For several minutes Kohut acknowledged the standing ovation. His
exhaustion, however, was palpable, and soon he signaled to Arnold
Goldberg, sitting to his right, that it was time to leave. They walked together to the stairs at the right of the stage. Kohut moved slowly and
carefully. He made it down the stairs, but once he got close to the audience, with the hall electric with all the emotion of the event, a crowd surged
forward. People wanted to talk with him, be near him, touch him. Kohut,
frail and completely exhausted, got scared. In desperation he turned to
Goldberg: "Keep them off me. Please keep them off me." Goldberg therefore positioned himself in front of Kohut and literally pushed people away
from him, like a blocker in football, as they walked down the aisle to the
exit of the auditorium.[7]

Outside in the beautiful sunny day, Elizabeth Kohut waited with a car
to take her husband back to the hotel.[8] People huddled on the esplanade
as they watched Kohut climb gingerly into the back seat and drive off. He
spent that night resting and trying to recover enough from the conference

to take the flight back to Chicago. He called his son and said in German, "I was broken but somehow I got through this."[9] He also called friends who he feared might have been hurt by his failure to acknowledge their presence in the audience as he walked to the stage. Ernest Wolf, for example, found such a message on his machine in Chicago when he returned later that evening.[10] Kohut also asked the Goldbergs, who were staying in the same hotel, to change their tickets so that they could fly back with him. This proved to be complicated and in the end Arnold was able to fly on Kohut's plane but Constance had to take another flight. At the airport the next morning he was met with a wheelchair and taken directly to the plane. During the flight he realized that his patient, Jerome Beigler, was not far off and sent a message by an attendant for him to come visit. Beigler found Kohut sitting with his belt undone and his trousers open due to his hugely swollen abdomen. He was jaundiced and generally edematous, puffy from the accumulation of fluid that his weakened heart could not properly circulate throughout his body.[11]

In Chicago Kohut was taken off the plane in another wheelchair for transport to a car. As they reached the limousine, he signaled to Elizabeth to give the man pushing him a big tip.[12] To the end he was a man of etiquette, formality, and generosity. Kohut at first returned to his apartment, where he spent Monday night. He had two half-read books at his bedside: Victor Hugo's *Les Misérables* (in French) and Moses Haddad's *History of Roman and Greek Literature*. For his son it was one of the "most painful" things in his life to retrieve those books after his father's death.[13] By Tuesday morning it was clear Kohut needed to be hospitalized. And so early on October 6 he entered Billings. Kohut was initially admitted for lymphoma but fainted during the intake proceedings and was moved immediately to a "step-down" room in the cardiac unit where he could be closely monitored.[14]

The next twenty-four hours were a blur of preparations for death. Kohut's condition steadily worsened and he was often in pain. Yet he struggled to reach closure on a number of fronts. He wrote notes to both Ernest Wolf and Paul Ornstein, again apologizing for his remoteness in Berkeley but more importantly making a final connection.[15] He had a phone conversation with Arnold Goldberg. He reviewed and signed the contract for a collection of essays and interviews (*Self Psychology and the Humanities*) and had it put in the mail.[16] He worked out with his wife and son the details of having his manuscript, *How Does Analysis Cure?*, edited and published. He reiterated his insistence that his clinical records be destroyed but that his other papers be made available within five or ten years.[17] He even made sure a photograph would be sent to a colleague.[18] He might as well have been at his desk.

By the afternoon of Wednesday, October 7, Kohut felt comforted that he had done everything he could concerning the details of his death. Remarkably, as people sometimes do before death, he rallied and began to feel better in the early evening. He played a game of Scrabble with his wife.[19] He talked of the past and his life with her and both noted that their thirty-third anniversary was in two days.[20] It was a touching moment of intimacy.

It was not to last. Around 9:00 p.m. Kohut took a turn for the worse and knew it was almost over. An eager and very nervous intern happened to be on call and was summoned to deal with his needs. She bustled in and said something about all the pretty flowers. He cut her off and said, "Let's get down to business." She adjusted the machines and did what she could to make him comfortable. Other doctors attended. Within a few hours he began to drift in and out of consciousness and soon became comatose.[21]

Kohut died at 3:00 a.m. in the morning on Thursday, October 8, 1981.

He was cremated and buried four days later in the Meyer family plot in the Forest Home Cemetery in Milwaukee. His grave is marked by a simple plaque in the ground in lot 7, block 8, section 6, with the words "Dr. Heinz Kohut, M.D." On the day the family gathered in the cemetery, October 12, the University of Chicago lowered its flags to half-mast to mark the passing of its distinguished faculty member.[22]

The memorial service later that month went according to the script Kohut had worked out in detail with his son. The service was held at 3:00 p.m. on Saturday, October 31, 1981, in the First Unitarian Church on Woodlawn Avenue at 57th Street, where Kohut had long been a member and had even spoken from the pulpit over the years.[23] Rev. John F. Hayward, the minister of the church and Kohut's longtime friend, presided. Robert W. Wadsworth was the guest organist, though he was so upset it was almost embarrassing how badly he played.[24] On the inside back cover of the program was an appeal for the Kohut Memorial Fund requesting donations, first, to insure posthumous publication of his works "in the manner he had stipulated before his death," and, second, to meet the needs of young scholars in the humanities to train at the Institute. The service began with the Prelude and Fugue in E minor by J. S. Bach. Then there were readings from Genesis 1:26–28 and 31 and from the

Talmud; and of "Pied Beauty" by Gerard Manley Hopkins, *Gitanjali* 92 by Rabindranath Tagore, and "O World" by Mark Van Doren. Michael Franz Basch and Charles Kligerman spoke in memory of Kohut. The ushers were Sheldon Meyers, David Terman, Robert J. Leider, and Kenneth M. Newman. The Interlude was a recording of Bach's chorale prelude "Wer nur den lieben Gott lasst walten" as performed by Helmut Walcha, followed by praise and prayer by Mr. Hayward. The service ended with everyone singing "A Mighty Fortress Is Our God" by Martin Luther, the words and music to which were included in the program. Kohut had been insistent with his son that the service end with this moving and classic Christian hymn.

An open reception followed at the Kohut apartment. People milled about eating and drinking, conversing casually as one does at such events. Some of Kohut's Jewish colleagues expressed surprise to Thomas, tinged with irritation, that the service had concluded with the Luther hymn. In fact, they were upset there had been a church service at all. These were the same people who had asked Thomas after his father's death if the family would be sitting shiva. At the time, Thomas had no idea what it meant to sit shiva, and is convinced to this day his father also would not have known.[25] Most people, especially those from out of town, conveyed their condolences to the family. There was a general sense of being richer for having had one's life touched by Heinz Kohut. One person, however, was inconsolable. Robert Wadsworth asked Arnold Goldberg, "Now what do I do with the rest of my life?"[26]

In the waning moments, many recalled the poignancy of Kligerman's words at the service: "Heinz was ready for death. He always had a firm conviction that each person had almost an inborn agenda, a destiny to fulfill, that compared to eternity it mattered little how long one lived, provided one lived up to one's potentialities in pursuing his ideal."[27]

APPENDIX:
ON SOURCES

NOTES

ACKNOWLEDGMENTS

INDEX

APPENDIX: ON SOURCES

There are essentially two kinds of sources on which this book is based. The first consists of the oral testimony I gathered between 1982 and 1999 from those who knew Kohut, including his family, his patients, his colleagues, and his childhood friends. The more formal interviews I tried to tape-record, though this was not always possible. Other conversations, sometimes after seminars, on the phone, or at social functions, I wrote up immediately and dated. If the material was sensitive in any way, I later confirmed it in a follow-up conversation, call, or e-mail. As a further check, I asked certain key individuals to read all or parts of the draft manuscript of the book and then modified the text to be sure the way I stated things reflected the full sense of what I had been told more informally. Some people disparage oral history as a valid source. It is dependent on the vagaries of memory, they say, and can border on gossip. But it seems to me it would have been a profound failing on my part not to tap the collective memory of Heinz Kohut for this biography. The trick is to evaluate the oral record with the same critical method one otherwise applies to more familiar sources. Historians have too long idealized the written word. I have learned all kinds of important things about Kohut from what people told me. Oral testimony has added texture, completeness, nuance, and lots of details to the story.

The second source for this book is the written record, which in turn takes two forms. The most obvious is Kohut's own scientific books and papers, as well as the relevant published scholarship in psychoanalysis. I have read, taught, and written about Kohut so often and repeatedly that whole sections of his books are virtually committed to memory. My notes brim with references. Kohut once (*Lectures*, 50) tells of receiving a letter from a man who reported that his analysis had helped somewhat but left him with his fear of heights, from which he was only cured when he read a footnote in *The Analysis of the Self*. Kohut concluded with a smile, "Sometimes footnotes cure." Such is the dream of any scholar.

The other and more complicated part of the written record, however, is the Kohut correspondence. Kohut kept his personal files in alphabetical order by correspondent and for each person in chronological sequence. If he replied to a letter, he attached a copy to the incoming original. He had a secretary at the Institute who typed up many business letters, but he kept his own files in his study in his apartment (I saw the metal file cabinet myself when I interviewed him for *Humanities* in early 1981). He was also quite thorough about replying to letters, so in most cases the letters in both directions, incoming and outgoing, are available. One can trace his relationship with Anna Freud, for example, under *F*, or with Kurt Eissler under *E*. He knew his correspondence would be of historical interest.

While Kohut was still alive, Paul Ornstein began to select from Kohut's letters those that were of the greatest scientific interest to be included in his project of publishing the Kohut papers. The first two volumes of the *Search for the Self* sequence appeared in 1978; included in the second volume were nearly 100 pages of excerpts of letters (2: 851–938). Two years later, Kohut published two letters (with footnotes!) in the volume from the first self psychology conference, *Advances in Self Psychology* (449–469). In both *Search* and *Advances*, the name of the recipient was omitted and only the date included. In some cases, parts of the letters were also deleted. The point of publication was not biographical but scientific. Long after Kohut's death, Ornstein published (1991) another set of letters in the fourth volume of the *Search* series (4: 569–729).

In the meanwhile, plans were under way to publish a more complete selection of the Kohut correspondence as a separate book. Thomas Kohut, presumably with the support of his mother, selected Geoffrey Cocks to edit that volume. Thomas went through all the letters and culled from them anything having to do with patients. A remaining question is what else he might have chosen to remove. He then had copies made of the letters and sent them to Cocks, who teaches at Albion College. Thomas also made copies of some letters of his own from his father that were not in the files (as Cocks makes clear in his response to a review of *Curve* by Helen Kross Golden in *Psychoanalytic Books* 6 [1995]: 7), though at some point Thomas also seems to have sent Cocks the originals of letters from Kohut to him and his mother, which is, of course, a small but important part of the total correspondence (Cocks e-mail to me, August 31, 1999). Cocks worked from that set of copies of the correspondence (and the handful of originals) to select perhaps 10 percent of the total for publication in *Curve*, consulting with Thomas Kohut along the way. Once the book was published in 1994, Cocks shipped the complete set of copies to the Chicago Institute to be stored in the Kohut Archives, though what he sent did not include the copies of the Kohut letters to Elizabeth and Thomas (at least they never ended up in the Kohut Archives).

Arnold Goldberg had long since set up these archives as a place to store materials relating to Heinz Kohut. The Kohut Archives include his early lecture notes from the school of social work in 1952–1953 and the transcript from the late 1950s of his famous Freud course at the Institute. There are also transcripts of several other lectures. There are his early vitae, which provide the details of his professional career and how it developed and include listings of the many committees on which he served at the Institute and for the American Psychoanalytic Association. There are many tapes of his talks. Memorabilia include his five framed diplomas, from his 1941 Illinois medical license to his certificate of graduation from the Institute in 1950, the set of cups received from five younger colleagues upon the publication of *The Analysis of the Self* in 1971, and various plaques and awards. In fourteen archival boxes are stored other material: his copy of his graduation paper from the Döblinger Gymnasium; his medical records; and many letters from Kohut given to the Institute by various recipients. The heart of the collection, however, is the letters that have remained in place as they arrived from Geoffrey Cocks, in twelve archive boxes, with the last two consisting of the ones included in the *Curve* volume.

There are always problems with the availability of source material in history. In psychoanalysis, especially, secretiveness has been the mainstay of archival records. Much of Freud's work still lies under "lock and key," as Peter Gay puts it (*Freud: A Life for Our Time,* 743). With Kohut, things are much more open at this point, though it is telling that Cocks, presumably with Thomas Kohut's approval, describes the copies of letters that were turned over to the Chicago Institute archives as the "professional correspondence" (*Curve,* 33). The opposite of professional is either "personal" or "clinical" or both. What exactly was left out? Cocks says with certainty he read *all* of Kohut's letters (his emphasis; *Psychoanalytic Books,* 7), which suggests that the correspondence as deposited in the Kohut Archives is complete. But since he worked for the most part from copies sent to him by Thomas Kohut, how can he be sure? Why does Thomas Kohut insist on holding onto the original letters? I know from my work that quite a few letters that appear in *Curve* do not have copies of the original in the Kohut Archives. Perhaps they simply got lost in the confusion of two shipments. The more distressing possibility is that other important letters were withheld somewhere along the line. In the collection of Robert Wadsworth correspondence, for example, there are no letters from before 1977. In reply to my inquiry about this matter, Thomas Kohut (e-mail, August 26, 1997) basically had no explanation and seemed as puzzled as I am. He thinks it must be the result of some vagary on the part of his father ("His correspondence wasn't an archive, after all," Thomas adds).

I want to be clear that I have no particular reason to suspect Thomas Kohut is withholding material. But since he alone has read the original letters, arranged for the hand-picked editor of the selected correspondence to work basically from copies, and very definitely did not make the complete and original correspondence available to me, one has to wonder about what is technically called the venue of the correspondence that has ended up in the Kohut Archives.

All of the materials I gathered in my research for this book will be turned over to the Kohut Archives after publication. That includes hard copies of all my handwritten notes and the electronic files of other material. I will also donate the tapes of my interviews, original photographs, copies of articles and other papers I gathered over the years, and whatever miscellaneous items I find lying about my study.

To be complete I would have to say there is a third source of data for this book: the storehouse of my own impressions of a man I knew and with whom I even compiled a book. The details of that subjective encounter are described in the Preface to this book and in a few stray notes where I draw on something I directly experienced. I can only add that the man I thought I knew reasonably well became infinitely more remote and at the same time intrusively familiar in my psyche as my work proceeded.

NOTES

ABBREVIATIONS FOR
FREQUENTLY CITED SOURCES

Works by Heinz Kohut

Analysis   *The Analysis of the Self: A Systematic Approach to the Psychoanalytic Treatment of Narcissistic Personality Disorders* (New York: International Universities Press, 1971).

Cure   *How Does Analysis Cure?*, ed. Arnold Goldberg with the collaboration of Paul E. Stepansky (Chicago: University of Chicago Press, 1984).

Curve   *The Curve of Life: Correspondence of Heinz Kohut: 1923–1981*, ed. Geoffrey Cocks (Chicago: University of Chicago Press, 1994).

Humanities   *Self Psychology and the Humanities. Reflections on a New Psychoanalytic Approach*, ed. Charles B. Strozier (New York: Norton, 1985).

Lectures   *Heinz Kohut: The Chicago Institute Lectures*, ed. Paul and Marian Tolpin (Hillsdale, NJ: Analytic Press, 1996).

Restoration   *The Restoration of the Self* (New York: International Universities Press, 1977).

Search   *The Search for the Self: Selected Writings of Heinz Kohut: 1950–1978*, ed. Paul H. Ornstein, vols. 1 and 2 (New York: International Universities Press, 1978) and vols. 3 and 4 (Madison, CT: International Universities Press, 1991).

Other Sources

Inventory   "Inventory of Jewish Wealth" for Heinz Kohut and Else Kohut, forms from the Viennese State Archives: Oesterreichisches Staatsarchiv, Archiv der Republik (HF-Abg. F 679; HF-NHF 1; VA 17.666; VA 37.820).

SE   *The Standard Edition of the Complete Psychological Works of Sigmund Freud*, tr. James Strachey, in collaboration with Anna Freud, assisted by Alix Strachey and Alan Tyson, 24 vols. (London: Hogarth Press, 1953–1974).

Seminars   *The Kohut Seminars on Self Psychology and Psychotherapy with Adolescents and Young Adults*, ed. Miriam Elson (New York: Norton, 1987).

Journals

AJP	*American Journal of Psychiatry*
AJPT	*American Journal of Psychotherapy*
IJP	*International Journal of Psycho-Analysis*
JAPA	*Journal of the American Psychoanalytic Association*
PQ	*Psychoanalytic Quarterly*
Progress	*Progress in Self Psychology*

Frequently Cited Interviews

AG 1	Arnold Goldberg, July 20, 1983.
AG 2	Arnold Goldberg, April 2, 1996.
AG 3	Arnold Goldberg, January 14, 1997.
AG 4	Arnold Goldberg, March 8, 1999.
BB	Bernard Brandchaft, October 21, 1995.
BBT	Barbara Bryant Tweedle, January 2, 1983.
CK	Charles Kligerman, September 22, 1983.
EK 1	Elizabeth Kohut, May 20, 1982.
EK 2	Elizabeth Kohut, July 20, 1983.
EW 1	Ernest Wolf, December 20, 1990.
EW 2	Ernest Wolf, March 31, 1996.
EW 3	Ernest Wolf, August 30, 1996.
GM	Gretchen Meyer, April 1, 1996.
JB	Jerome Beigler. July 10, 1987.
JG 1	John Gedo, July 11, 1987.
JG 2	John Gedo, August 29, 1996.
JM	Jay McCormick, November 9, 1983.
JP 1	Jacques Palaci, October 8, 1985.
JP 2	Jacques Palaci, October 17, 1987.
JP 3	Jacques Palaci, October 19, 1990.
LS	Louis Shapiro, April 3, 1996.
ME	Miriam Elson, December 5, 1997.
MT	Marian Tolpin, August 25, 1998.
PO	Paul Ornstein, May 20, 1996.
PT	Paul Tolpin, August 15, 1996.
SL 1	Siegmund Levarie, October 7, 1985.
SL 2	Siegmund Levarie, January 28, 1997.
SL 3	Siegmund Levarie, March 2, 1997.
SQ	Susan Quinn, transcript of her interview with Kohut, March 29, 1980.
TAK	Thomas A. Kohut, November 1 and 2, 1996.
WL	Walter Lampl, May 25, 1997.

PREFACE

1. This term means different things to different people. I speak of "relational psycho-analysis" in a broad, inclusive way. The best recent book on the subject, especially in relation to Kohut, is Judith Guss Teicholz, *Kohut, Loewald, and the Postmoderns: A Comparative Study of Self and Relationship* (Hillsdale, NJ: Analytic Press, 1999). See also Lewis Aron, *A Meeting of Minds: Mutuality in Psychoanalysis* (Hillsdale, NJ: Analytic Press, 1996); and see the review essay based on this book by Robert D. Stolorow, "Principles of Dynamic Systems, Intersubjectivity, and the Obsolete Distinction Between One-Person and Two-Person Psychologies," *Psychoanalytic Dialogues* 8 (1998): 859–868; Stephen A. Mithell, *Relational Concepts in Psychoanalysis: An Integration* (Cambridge, MA: Harvard University Press, 1988); Stephen A. Mitchell, *Influence and Autonomy in Psychoanalysis* (Hillsdale, NJ: Analytic Press, 1997); and Stephen A. Mitchell with Margaret J. Black, *Freud and Beyond: A History of Modern Psychoanalytic Thought* (New York: Basic Books, 1995). Emanuel Berman has written a good review essay on the subject, "Relational Psychoanaly-sis: A Historical Background," *AJPT* 51 (1997): 185–203. Compare Robert Galatzer-Levy and Bertram J. Cohler, *The Essential Other: A Developmental Psychology of the Self* (New York: Basic Books, 1993); and Howard A. Bacal and Kenneth M. Newman, *Theories of Object Relations: Bridges to Self Psychology* (New York: Columbia University Press, 1990). The broader history of subjectivity has been most recently and ex-pertly traced by Charles Taylor, *Sources of the Self: The Making of the Modern Identity* (Cambridge, MA: Harvard University Press, 1989). The self psychology movement currently includes its own divisions, especially those interested in "intersubjectivity." See Donna Orange, George E. Atwood, and Robert D. Stolorow, *Working Intersubjectively: Contextualism in Psychoanalytic Practice* (Hillsdale, NJ: Analytic Press, 1997); Robert D. Stolorow and George Atwood, *Contexts of Being: The Intersubjective Foundations of Psychological Life* (Hillsdale, NJ: Analytic Press, 1992); Robert D. Stolorow, George E. Atwood, and Bernard Brandchaft, eds., *The Intersubjective Perspective* (Northvale, NJ: Jason Aronson, 1994); Robert D. Stolorow, Bernard Brandchaft, and George Atwood, *Psychoanalytic Treatment: An Intersubjective Approach* (Hillsdale, NJ: Analytic Press, 1987); and George Atwood and Robert Stolorow, *Structures of Subjectivity: Explorations in Psychoanalytic Phenomenology* (Hillsdale, NJ: Analytic Press, 1984). For yet another contending current voice in self psychology, see Joseph D. Lichtenberg, Frank M. Lachman, and James L. Fosshage, *Self and Motivational Systems: Toward a Theory of Psycho-analytic Technique* (Hillsdale, NJ: Analytic Press, 1992). In all these developments, the pivotal figure historically in the transition from one model to another within psychoanalysis, from drive theory as embodied in ego psychology to the variety of relational approaches today, is Heinz Kohut.

2. Heinz Kohut, *Self Psychology and the Humanities: Reflections on a New Psycho-analytic Approach,* ed. Charles B. Strozier (New York: Norton, 1985).

3. *Lincoln's Quest for Union: Public and Private Meanings* (New York: Basic Books, 1982).

4. Steven Marcus, "Psychoanalytic Biography and Its Problems: The Case of Wilhelm Reich," *Psychoanalysis: Toward the Second Century,* ed. Arnold M. Cooper, Otto F. Kernberg, and Ethel Spector Person (New Haven: Yale University Press, 1980), 35–36. Erik Erikson's two studies that have so profoundly influenced the way biography is written are *Young Man Luther: A Study in Psychoanalysis and History* (New York: Norton, 1958) and *Gandhi's Truth: On The Origins of Militant Nonviolence* (New York: Norton, 1969). Lytton Strachey, *Eminent Victorians* (New York: Penguin, 1986 [1918]), 9.

1 PREHISTORY

1. On the status of the parents in Vienna's Jewish elite, SL 1 and 2; on where they lived, letter to me from Mrs. H. Weirs of the Israelitische Kultusgemeinde Wien, February 21, 1991; on Felix as "dashing," EK 1; the ages of Felix and Else at the birth of Heinz Kohut are inferred from their wedding certificate, which lists the date of birth for both of them (Else: November 24, 1890; Felix: May 12, 1888); for the story of Else, see EK 1 and TAK. Kohut talked often of his father's unusual musical talents and how the first war interrupted his progress toward a concert career (besides EK 1 and TAK, see SQ; his interview with *People Magazine,* February 20, 1979; and what he told friends such as Arnold Goldberg [AG 1]). Curiously, however, neither his first cousin, Walter Lampl, nor his best friend from his Vienna school days, Siegmund Levarie, recalls Felix playing the piano much in the home, or any discussion of a bygone concert career (specific follow-up phone interviews with both men, April 29, 1999). On the other hand, Thomas A. Kohut recalls many stories from his father *and* grandmother of Felix playing four-hand with Else while she sang Schubert lieder. At least it is certain Felix was not in business before the war. He established his company, Bellak & Kohut, only in 1920 (the *Wiener Adressbuch* [*Lehmanns Wohnungs-Anzeiger für Wien 1921/22, Jg 63*] lists the company [the 1920 volume is missing from the archives], but the *Eintragung im Wiener Handelsregister* A 46.134 indicates the company was established on February 17, 1920). Music mattered a great deal to Kohut and he was otherwise consistent in his stories about his father, especially to his wife (see EK 1 in this regard). The best conclusion one can draw is therefore that Felix was a highly skilled pianist with aspirations to a career in music. When the war interrupted those dreams, he seemed to abandon his gift and only return to it fitfully. That is basically the line of argument in this book. I want to thank Geoffrey Cocks, who, after reading the draft of my manuscript, first raised the issue with me of whether Felix was in fact *that* good of a pianist before the war. He also shared all of his research findings on the question from his correspondence with Elizabeth Kohut in an e-mail to me of May 7, 1999.

2. See PO. Actually, in the interview Ornstein refers to Rabbi Kohut of Poland, not Hungary, but he must mean Alexander Kohut, who in 1868 was elected secretary of the Congress of Jewish Notables. After he came to America in 1885, Alexander

Kohut was a key figure in the Jewish Theological Seminary in New York City. His son, George Alexander Kohut, was also a famous rabbi and teacher in America, and his widow, Rebekah, became well known for her two autobiographies, *My Portion: An Autobiography* (New York: Albert & Charles Boni, 1927) and *More Yesterdays: An Autobiography (1925–1949)* (New York: Black, 1950), as well as a book about her son, *His Father's House: The Story of George Alexander Kohut* (New Haven: Yale University Press, 1938). George Alexander also edited a festschrift in honor of his father, *Semitic Studies in Memory of Rev. Dr. Alexander Kohut* (Berlin: S. Calvary, 1897). Adolf Kohut wrote a massive dictionary of famous Jews, *Berühmte Israelitische Maenner und Frauen in der Kultur-geschichte der Menschen,* 2 vols. (Leipzig-Reudnitz: A. H. Payne, n.d.).

3. "1860s": SQ; "adult life": WL (*lampl* is the diminutive of the word for lamb); "were Christian": TAK.

4. Marsha L. Rozenblitt, *The Jews of Vienna: 1867–1914, Assimilation and Identify* (Albany: State University of New York Press), 13–17. See also Michael Ignatieff, "The Rise and Fall of Vienna's Jews," *New York Review of Books,* June 29, 1989, 21–25.

5. Bruno Bettelheim, *Freud's Vienna and Other Essays* (New York: Knopf, 1990), 60. Bettelheim, perhaps revealing his own ambivalence about his Jewishness, talks generally about "immigrés" in this passage, rather than the obvious and important point that it was Jews who constituted most of the emigrés and virtually the only ones who mattered in terms of transforming the culture of Vienna. See also Bruce F. Pauley, *From Prejudice to Prosecution: History of Austrian Anti-Semitism* (Chapel Hill: University of North Carolina Press, 1992).

6. In the *Geburts-und Heiratsmatrikeln sowie Sterbeurkunden des Martikelamtes der Israelitscher Kultusgemeinde Wien,* Bernhard is listed as *Lehrer aus Holics* when he married in 1878 and as a *Volksschullehrer* at the birth of his first child, Anna, in 1879. Heinz Kohut referred to him (though not definitively) as a *Bürgerschullehrer* in a letter to Siegmund Levarie, February 24, 1979; see *Curve,* 386. Thomas A. Kohut, in my interview (TAK), says Bernhard was a gymnasium teacher, as did Elizabeth Kohut (EK 1).

7. Kohut to Siegmund Levarie, February 24, 1979, *Curve,* 386–387.

8. TAK; Kohut to August Aichhorn, June 2, 1946, *Curve,* 48.

9. The information about Mitzi is from WL. The story of Willy is from TAK; see also Kohut to Siegmund Levarie, June 2, 1939, *Curve,* 48.

10. Rozenblitt, *The Jews of Vienna;* Stern, *The Politics of Cultural Despair.*

11. "of the way": Walter Lampl to Geoffrey Cocks, March 10, 1993, reported in the Introduction to *Curve,* 8 n. 25, and repeated to me, WL; "looked Jewish": TAK (see also my interviews with two members of the Chicago Institute for Psychoanalysis staff who knew Else, Cecile Block, January 24, 1997, and Eva Sandburg, January 18, 1997); "her vote": SL 2 and further elaborated in an interview on May 9, 1999; "noted Rabbis": SL 3 and PO.

12. TAK.

13. WL.

14. SL 2.

15. WL.

16. Rozenblitt, *The Jews of Vienna*, 128. Rozenblitt (133) also points out that there were more converts in Vienna than elsewhere in Europe, most being young working-class women seeking to marry Catholic men they met in the factories or workshops. Hans Lampl divorced his Jewish wife early on and before he changed his official affiliation, which is why his son, Walter, grew up Jewish but had a converted father. See WL.

17. Sander L. Gilman, *Freud, Race, and Gender* (Princeton: Princeton University Press, 1993).

18. Freud, "The Future of an Illusion," *SE* 21: 3–56, which concludes famously: "No, our science is no illusion. But an illusion it would be to suppose that what science cannot give us we can get elsewhere." Cp. Peter Gay, *Freud: A Life for Our Time* (New York: Norton, 1988), 523–537.

19. Gay, *Freud*, 140; Freud, *Jokes and Their Relation to the Unconscious* (1905), *SE* 8: 3–258; *The Freud/Jung Letters: The Correspondence Between Sigmund Freud and Carl G. Jung*, ed. William McGuire, tr. Ralph Mannheim and R. F. C. Hull (Princeton: Princeton University Press, 1974).

20. Beller, *Vienna and the Jews*, 189–190.

21. Ibid., 13.

22. Ignatieff, *The Rise and Fall*, 21.

23. Stern, *The Politics of Cultural Despair*. See also William J. McGrath, *Dionysian Art and Populist Politics in Austria* (New Haven: Yale University Press, 1974), who discusses the curious example of the Pernerstorfer circle in Austria in the 1870s and 1880s. In this group lay the beginnings of the *völkisch* movement, which preceded the rise of virulent anti-Semitism at the end of the century. The Pernerstorfer circle, however, were mostly Jewish and came from liberal families. Their initial turn against their assimilationist parents' liberalism led them to embrace *völkisch* ideas with fervor. What seems plausible, though McGrath is cautious on this point, is that they were trying to prove the authenticity of their Germanness in their attack on the old liberalism and their overidentification with *völkisch* ideas of nationalism. Cp. the German case: Marion A. Kaplan, *Between Dignity and Despair: Jewish Life in Nazi Germany* (New York: Oxford University Press, 1998).

2 BEGINNINGS

1. TAK.

2. Stefan Zweig, *The World of Yesterday*, an autobiography (New York: Viking Press, 1943, 22.

3. Letter from H. Weirs of the Department of Records of the Israelitische Kultusgemeinde Wien, June 18, 1997. Walter Lampl helped clarify what was customary in Vienna at the time, as did my colleague at City University, Professor Samuel Heilman, in a conversation on September 3, 1997, as well as the helpful archivist at the Leo Baeck Institute in New York.

4. *Search* 4: 395–446. For a complete discussion of the case, see below, Chapter 26. Throughout this book I always indicate when I am using "Mr. Z" as my source of information about the life of Kohut himself.

5. Kohut, "The Two Analyses of Mr. Z," *Search* 4: 398–399.

6. Charles Kligerman, "Eulogy" delivered at Kohut's memorial service in the First Unitarian Church of Chicago, October 31, 1981, typescript in the collection of Ernest Wolf. Hardly anyone I interviewed over the years failed to make this same point in some form, from old friends like Siegmund Levarie to Jacques Palaci; or younger ones like Arnold Goldberg, Paul Ornstein, or Enest Wolf; or patients (see Chapters 11 and 30). I should add it was also my experience.

7. The best recent history of the war is John Keegan, *The First World War* (New York: Knopf, 1999).

8. Peter Loewenberg, "The Psychohistorical Origins of the Nazi Youth Cohort," *Decoding the Past: The Psychohistorical Approach* (New York: Knopf, 1982), an article that builds on an earlier study by Martin Wangh, "National Socialism and the Genocide of the Jews—A Psycho-Analytic Study of a Historical Event," *IJP* 45 (1964): 386–395, describes the psychological experience of those Germans born in 1913 whose fathers rushed off to war either to die or to return in the shame of defeat. Loewenberg argues that that experience shaped the coming of Nazism. It also had an impact, it seems, in the making of a psychoanalyst.

9. TAK: See also the war records for Felix, Österreichisches Staatsarchiv (Kriegsarchiv), Vienna.

10. SQ.

11. TAK.

12. Most of the information in this paragraph is from SQ. The farina story is a personal communication from Eva Sandburg, June 21, 1997, who was herself from Vienna and was for many years on the staff of the Chicago Institute for Psychoanalysis, where she would occasionally trade stories of the past with Kohut.

13. *Search* 4: 398–399, 402, and 420.

14. *Search* 4: 398–399 and 405–406. The name of the lover is from TAK.

15. *Search* 4: 437–439.

16. Freud, "Thoughts for the Time on War and Death," *SE* 14: 275, 278–279.

17. SQ and TAK; e-mail to me from Thomas A. Kohut, May 10, 1999; and *People Magazine*, February 20, 1979, 61.

18. The firm of Bellak & Kohut was established on February 17, 1920, with its offices on Lercherfelder Strasse 54–56. The firm sold finished products like stationery, as well as industrial papers, wholesale. See *Eintragung im Wiener Handelsregister* (A 46.134) and the Bellak & Kohut advertisement in *Wiener Adressbuch, Lehmanns Wohnungs-Anzeiger für Wien* 1921/22, Jg. 63, Erster Band (Verlag: Österreichische Anzeigen Gesellschaft.

19. SL 1 and 2; TAK; personal communication, Ernest Wolf, June 21, 1997.

20. Kohut to Felix Kohut, July 15, 1923, *Curve*, 37.

21. "his father": *Search* 4: 433–444 (the disguise is thin, as Thomas Kohut, in TAK, recalls his father talking of this actual ski trip in some detail); "extremely pleased": Kohut, "Concluding Remarks," October 13, 1978, *Curve*, 373.

22. "for hours": interview with Charles Kligerman, September 23, 1983; cp. his "Eulogy"; see also SL 1; "to try" (and about Duke Ellington): SL 3.

23. I am indebted to John Gedo, in his dinner address at the celebration of Kohut's sixtieth birthday, June 2, 1973, available in the Kohut Archives in its unedited form, for suggesting this idea, which I have elaborated in my own terms.

24. *Search* 4: 402–403 and 420–422.

25. *Search* 4: 403. Note that Thomas Kohut (TAK) also reported that his father referred often to *Uncle Tom's Cabin* as an important book from his childhood.

26. *Search* 4: 431–432.

3 THE TUTOR

1. "Fräuleins and Mademoiselles": SQ; "art museums": GM.

2. Kohut was quite specific in his interview with Susan Quinn (SQ) about having spent the first four years of elementary school at home with tutors. "In grammar school for the first four years I was taught at home by my future grammar school teacher, you know. But then I went into his class and did very well. . . ." Note also this was confirmed by his childhood friend, Siegmund Levarie (SL 2), and by his widow, Mrs. Elizabeth Kohut (EK 2), though she said, somewhat vaguely and without conviction (and certainly incorrectly) that he stayed home for two years.

3. "another man": *Search*, 4: 406; "in Vienna": WL and SL 2.

4. SL 2.

5. TAK; Ernest Wolf, *Psychoanalysts Talk,* ed. Virginia Hunter (New York: Guilford Press, 1994), 168–169; Kohut to Arnold Goldberg, May 5, 1980, *Curve*, 399; Kohut to Siegmund Levarie, May 22, 1939, *Curve*, 46; EK 1 and 2; SQ.

6. In "Mr. Z" the tutor is disguised as a thirty-year-old camp counselor who is in the boy's life for two years, from the time he is eleven until thirteen, which is the same time period he gives for his actual tutor in his interview with Susan Quinn (SQ). That interview was the only time he was so specific on the record. Kohut himself as an adult talked to many colleagues about Morawetz but was always vague about the details of the relationship (as he was about so many things). He seems to have been vague even with his family. Kohut's widow (EK 1) thought Morawetz entered Kohut's life at eight, while his son (TAK) told me he thought it was more like fourteen. But neither family member was at all sure about these dates, which were offered merely as their own approximations. The best conclusion one can draw from the available evidence is that Else hired the tutor in the spring or summer of 1924 in preparation for what she knew would be the educational and emotional challenges of Heinz's work in the gymnasium.

7. *Search* 4: 404.

8. Ibid., 404–405. Geoffrey Cocks, in his "Introduction" to *Curve*, 7, says Kohut had "one or two homosexual encounters" with Morawetz, an assertion that he repeats in a later essay, "The Curve of Heinz Kohut's Life," *Treating Mind and Body: Essays in the History of Science, Professions, and Society under Extreme Conditions* (New

Brunswick, NJ: Transactions Publishers, 1998), 128. What is astonishing about this assertion is that it comes from reading "Mr. Z." There is no other source for information about the details of the sexual aspects of the relationship.

9. EW 1.

10. Kenneth Dover, *Greek Homosexuality* (Cambridge, MA: Harvard University Press, 1978).

11. In my taped interview with Kohut on February 12, 1981, he said this, but Elizabeth Kohut later insisted it be cut from the published version of the interview in *Humanities*, 224–231.

12. *Search* 4: 404.

4 YOUNG MAN KOHUT

1. The actual address of Else's store is possible to tie down because it is in the Inventory. The address of the Kohut postwar apartment in the Ninth District, however, is not known. By the time the Nazis started the Inventory, the Kohuts were living in their house at Paradiesgasse 47. Siegmund Levarie, on May 9, 1999, described a few details of the unremarkable apartment. The other details in this paragraph are from WL and SL 2.

2. WL.

3. SL 2, WL, and TAK. On Jews in the Nineteenth District, see Rozenblitt, *The Jews of Vienna*, 76–77. Else's car is listed in the Inventory.

4. "reserved seats": SL 2, with more details from a conversation on May 9, 1999; "me deeply": Kohut to the Metropolitan Opera, August 3, 1968, *Curve*, 211–212; "next room": TAK.

5. Siegmund Levarie, personal communication, May 9, 1999. Rozenblitt, *The Jews of Vienna*, 99–122, says students generally had such knowledge at seventeen or eighteen. Levarie was sure, however, that it was several years earlier for him and Heinz at the Döblinger Gymnasium.

6. Religion was required of all students several times a week. Catholics and Jews, however, were separated for these classes. In the first five to six years at the gymnasium, the Jewish religion instructor was a Rabbi Simmels. In the last few years, Murmelstein took over. Personal communication, Siegmund Levarie, May 9, 1999.

7. SL 1.

8. SL 1. See also Weidinger's letters to Kohut, January 7 and February 25, 1957, after Kohut got in touch with him in connection with his upcoming visit to Vienna. On January 7 Weidlinger reported that he had been called up for military duty in 1941 and had led an anti-aircraft battery in East Prussia, Lithuania (Riga), and in many other cities of the old Reich, until he "became part of the marine" in Drontheim, Norway. In 1945 he was taken prisoner by the English but managed an "adventurous escape" in 1946. He then returned to teaching for a while, retiring in 1951.

9. SL 2 says that of the 30 students who began in their class, only 12 or 14 had sur-

vived by the last two years. Oskar Weidlinger, however, when he wrote Kohut in 1957, named the 33 students who were in Heinz's *Matura* class, including those he knew nothing about and those whose addresses he had; Weidinger to Kohut, January 7, 1957. The discrepancy between Levarie's memory and Weidinger's listing may be due to Weidinger's having counted those who *began* in Heinz's class, while Levarie was recalling the number who *ended*.

10. SL 2.
11. SL 1 and 2. See also Rozenblitt, *The Jews of Vienna*, 99, for a good discussion of the curriculum in general for gymnasiums in Vienna at the time.
12. TAK. The Levarie quote is from SL 2. The name of the math teacher is from Kohut to Siegmund Levarie, April 29, 1939, *Curve*, 46.
13. TAK, SL 2, EK 2.
14. Haupt-Katalog from the Döblinger Gymnasium, 1924–1932.
15. SL 2, WL, and JM (for guitar story).
16. SQ on his reading; note also SL 1.
17. *Humanities*, 242.
18. SL 1. Levarie added on May 6, 1999, that Heinz was disappointed in Musil.
19. SQ. On his tutoring in French, see SL 2 and Kohut to Jacques Palaci, October 4, 1976. See also Levarie to Elizabeth Kohut, February 10, 1982, where he describes visiting the house he and Heinz had stayed in that summer. In the interview, Levarie noted that Madame Vénacourt had come to Vienna the previous winter to sign up students and had somehow connected with both the Kohuts and the Löwenherzes. Levarie also said he and Heinz arrived by train and grabbed a cab to the Vénacourt address. An hour later they arrived, having been cheated by the cab driver, for the house was practically around the corner from the station.
20. SL 2.
21. The discussion that follows is from the typescript of the thesis—clearly Kohut's own—in the archives.
22. SL 2 and the Haupt-Catalog of the Döblinger Gymnasium.
23. Walter Z. Laqueur, *Young Germany: A History of the German Youth Movement* (London: Routledge & Kegan Paul, 1962), xi–xii, 6–7, 25–29, 62–63; and George Mosse, "The Influence of the Völkisch Idea on German Jewry," *Studies of the Leo Baeck Institute* (New York, 1967), 84–86. On Erikson, see Lawrence Friedman, *Identity's Architect* (New York: Scribner, 1999), 47–57.
24. TAK. Walter Lampl (WL) told me he retains a mental picture of Kohut's Boy Scout lodge in the Nineteenth District. For a history of the Pfadfinder, see Michael Rosenthal, *The Character Factory: Baden-Powell and the Origins of the Boy Scout Movement* (New York: Pantheon, 1984).
25. Laqueur, *Young Germany*, 70.
26. *Search* 2: 661.
27. Philippe Ariès, *Centuries of Childhood: A Social History of Family Life*, tr. Robert Baldick (New York: Vintage, 1962); and John Demos, *Past, Present, and Personal: The Family and the Life Course in American History* (New York: Oxford University Press, 1986).

28. Anna Freud, *The Ego and the Mechanisms of Defense,* tr. Cecil Baines, rev. ed. (London: Hogarth Press, 1969 [1936]). Kohut himself thought the last chapter of Anna Freud's book to be "the greatest contribution she ever made." See Kohut to Thomas A. Kohut, February 4, 1969, *Curve,* 226. She later extended these ideas in Anna Freud, *The Writings of Anna Freud* (New York: International Universities Press, 1958), 5: 136–166; see also Elizabeth Young-Bruehl, *Anna Freud: A Biography* (New York: Summit, 1988). The concept of totalism was very important for Erikson, especially his *Young Man Luther: A Study in History and Psychoanalysis* (New York: Norton, 1958), and Robert Jay Lifton, *Thought Reform and the Psychology of Totalism: A Study of "Brainwashing" in China* (New York: Norton, 1961).

29. Erikson's major conceptual work was his first: *Childhood and Society* (New York: Norton, 1950), though identity and the life cycle figure in almost everything he wrote; see Lawrence Friedman, *Identity's Architect.*

30. Friedman, *Identity's Architect,* is good on the reviews of Erikson's major writings. The feminist critique of Erikson was made most tellingly by Carol Gilligan, *In a Different Voice: Psychological Theory and Women's Development* (Cambridge, MA: Harvard University Press, 1982). The most articulate challenge to the very idea of storm and stress in adolescence is Dan Offer et al., *The Teenage World: Adolescents' Self-Image in Ten Countries* (New York: Plenum Medical, 1988). See also Dan Offer and Melvin Sabshin, eds., *Normality and the Life Cycle: A Critical Integration* (New York: Basic Books, 1984).

31. Letter from John Gedo to me, February 18, 1996.

32. SL 1 and 2, WL, and JP 1 and 2. The interview is SQ.

33. Letter from H. Weirs of the Department of Records of the Israelitische Kultusgemeinde Wien, June 18, 1997. Weirs guessed that the date for the bar mitzvah would have been April 20, 1926, based on customary practice.

34. I had separate conversations with Walter Lampl and Siegmund Levarie about this issue on October 7, 1997. Levarie (SL 3) recalled that on the way to the funeral he bought an expensive necktie. Professor Samuel Heilman, in a conversation on September 3, 1997, clarified for me that a son would only be allowed to recite kaddish if he had been bar mitzvahed.

35. Ernest Wolf, "Introduction," in Allen Siegel, *Heinz Kohut and the Psychology of the Self* (London: Routledge, 1996), 8. Wolf made the same point after I presented in the home of Arnold Goldberg, December 1, 1990, and in EW 2, when he further used himself as an example of a German Jew unidentified with Judaism at the core of his being, as though that somehow spoke to the experience of Heinz Kohut. I would say it simply reflects Wolf's projection. More interestingly, Thomas Kohut (TAK) made a similar argument about his father's identity. Neither Wolf nor Thomas Kohut, however, knew about the bris or the bar mitzvah. The son inevitably shaped his image of his father's identity in the context of the father's contradictory self presentation.

5 IN THE UNIVERSITY

1. Carl E. Schorske, *Fin-de-Siècle Vienna: Politics and Culture* (New York: Knopf, 1980), 38–39, 126. See also Gordon Brooks-Shepherd, *The Austrians: A Thousand-Year Odyssey* (New York: Carroll and Graf, 1996), 9. Schorske argues that the university for the most part in the 1930s resisted the populist, anti-Semitic right. Siegmund Levarie, in a personal communication on May 9, 1999, strenuously disagrees. He was also there.

2. SL 2.

3. *Search* 4: 397. My suspicion is that the friend was probably Siegmund Levarie, who was in Chicago during 1932–1933 (see below), though it might have been Franz Krämer, who is Geoffrey Cocks's guess; see *Curve*, 208, n. 1. Cocks's guess here almost certainly reflects as well the view of Thomas Kohut, since Cocks worked closely with Thomas Kohut in putting together *Curve*; on tonsils, see Kohut to John Van Prohaska, May 27, 1965; "athletic appearance": *Search*, 4: 396–397; "at the university": He was working hard. In his second year in medical school, Kohut published an article with one of his professors: Kapeller-Adler and Kohut, "Ueber Imidazolkoerperausscheidung im Saeugetierharn," *Giochem Zeitschrift* 272 (1934): 341–347; "dinner table": TAK.

4. *Search* 4: 406.

5. SL 2 and personal communication May 9, 1999.

6. Kohut to Siegmund Levarie, March 24, 1936, *Curve*, 37–38. See also Kohut to Siegmund Levarie, May 22, 1939, in which he expresses concern whether Levarie had unpacked his *Letzter Hand* edition of Goethe that he had shipped to Chicago; his letter to a former patient on his upcoming Fulbright award to study in West Germany ("They may be Germans, but, after all, there is also Goethe, don't forget"), Kohut to Rolf Meyersohn, July 22, 1960; and the discussion below, p. 48, about Kohut's giving a complete set of Goethe to Jacques Palaci when he visited him in Turkey.

7. Kohut to Peter Roth, June 20, 1980, *Curve*, 404; Zweig, *The World of Yesterday*, 39–41; SQ; and EW 2. Kohut's favorite coffee house was Sluka, near the university. See Kohut to Anna Freud, August 14, 1971, *Curve* 257.

8. SQ; SL 2; JP 1. On the libretto, see Kohut to Tilmann Moser, December 4, 1973, *Curve*, 295.

9. TAK. Levarie, on May 6, 1999, explained to me that the Vienna Symphony practiced in the hall of the music conservatory, to which he had a key. He and Kohut often slipped in to listen to the rehearsals.

10. WL. See Michael H. Kater, *Different Drummers: Jazz in the Culture of Nazi Germany* (New York: Oxford University Press, 1992).

11. Magistrat und Landesarchiv der Stadt Wien, the legal records of residence in Vienna, gives the exact dates of Kohut's stay in Paris (letter to me from Herbert Koch, Melderarchiv, Vienna, July 10, 1997). Siegmund Levarie (SL 2), furthermore, recalled Kohut's half year in Paris. Jacques Palaci (who was in Paris with Kohut), in his first interview with me, remembered it as the whole year. Palaci,

however, must have been wrong; the records of legal residence in Vienna clearly take precedence as a source.

12. SL 2. Levarie himself took off his first year when he was in Chicago, and then between 1933 and 1935 he attended the music conservatory and barely attended university classes. But after that he caught up and got his Ph.D. in 1938. Elizabeth Kohut, in my first interview with her in 1983, as well as Arnold Goldberg (AG 1), said that they believed from what Kohut had communicated to them it was rather remarkable to leave university for a semester and yet not miss a beat in one's studies. Siegmund Levarie, in a second conversation on this subject on April 27, 1999, confirmed that what Kohut did was a "big deal."

13. Kohut to Siegmund Levarie, March 24, 1936, *Curve*, 38. See TAK for comments on the enduring impact of his experiences with the syphilitic patients.

14. *Search* 4: 397. Jerome Beigler reports that he specifically asked Jacques Palaci twice before Polaci's death whether Kohut had girlfriends in Paris, and Palaci said no. See Beigler to me, July 5, 1998.

15. Kohut was born on May 3, 1913, and Palaci on February 14, 1915.

16. JP 2. The anecdote in the next paragraph is from the same interview.

17. JP 2.

18. JP 1 and 2.

19. WL and SL 2 and 3.

20. Interview with Esther Menaker, November 8, 1995. See also her memoirs of Vienna, *Appointment in Vienna: An American Psychoanalyst Recalls Her Student Days in Pre-War Austria* (New York: St. Vincent's Press, 1989).

21. Interview with Esther Menaker, November 8, 1995; Kohut to Peter Roth, June 20, 1980, *Curve*, 404; and personal communication, Arnold Goldberg, March 8, 1999.

22. Siegmund Levarie (SL 2) said he thought that Marseilles was a Jew. Levarie, however, did not know Marseilles personally. Esther Menaker (interview, November 8, 1995), besides knowing Marseilles in Vienna, also had the experience with her husband, William, of being in the New York discussion group founded by Theodore Reik during the war, which led in time, to the creation of the first nonmedical psychoanalytic institute in America, NPAP, or National Psychological Association for Psychoanalysis. Menaker said that Reik, to her and her husband's great annoyance, was always pushing Marseilles forward in the group because he was a non-Jew, just as Freud had earlier pushed forward Carl Jung for the same reason.

23. Elke Muhleittner and Johannes Reichmayr, "The Exodus of Psychoanalysts from Vienna," *The Cultural Exodus from Austria,* ed. Friedrich Stadler and Peter Weibel (New York: Springer-Verlag, 1995), 103. Cp. the less satisfactory Reuben Fine, *The History of Psychoanalysis* (New York: Jason Aronson, 1990), 73–90.

24. Esther Menaker, interview on November 8, 1995. Cp. Muhleittner and Reichmayr, "The Exodus of Psychoanalysts from Vienna," p. 104, who note how firmly rooted anti-Semitism was in Austrian politics and culture. Since the end of the nineteenth century, the German nationalist and Christian Socialist forces had

been actively preaching anti-Semitism, playing on the Catholic and religiously informed hatred of Jews. "When it came to the organized excesses against the Viennese Jews," they write, "the consent or non-committal attitude of the population provided a fertile ground for the terror and the abuses of National Socialist functionaries and hangers-on, for profiteers and perpetrators. 'Jew hunts' were greeted with lively approval."

25. TAK. Thomas Kohut clearly understood from his father that Kohut left Marseilles because he felt Marseilles was inadequate as a therapist.

26. Kohut to Peter Roth, June 20, 1980, *Curve*, 404.

27. Various students have collaborated in collecting Aichhorn's papers since his death. See August Aichhorn, *Erziehungsberatung und Erziehungshilfe: Zwölf Vorträge über psychoanalytische Pädagogik,* ed. Heinrich Meng (München: Rowohlt, 1959); and Otto Fleischmann, Paul Kramer, and Helen Ross, eds., *August Aichhorn, Delinquency, and Child Guidance: Selected Papers* (New York: International Universities Press, 1964).

28. My biographical information on Aichhorn is from George J. Mohr, "August Aichhorn, 1878–1949: Friend of the Wayward Youth," *Psychoanalytic Pioneers,* ed. Franz Alexander, Samuel Eisenstein, and Martin Grotjahn (New York: Basic Books, 1966), 348–359. Aichhorn took a special interest in another young Viennese, Erik Erikson, to whom he wrote on September 17, 1933, a solicitous letter on Erikson's departure from Vienna. Original in the Freud Society in Vienna and a copy provided me by Lawrence Friedman; see as well Friedman, *Identity's Architect,* 97–101. See also Elizabeth Kohut interview with Richard C. Marohn, April 9, 1984, in a half-hour videotaped program, "August Aichhorn and Heinz Kohut," for the American Society for Adolescent Psychiatry. The tape is in the Kohut Archives. Compare Kohut's touching comments after Aichhorn's death, *Search* 1: 131.

29. SQ.

30. SQ.

31. EW 2; "identification with him": Kohut to Aichhorn, September 2, 1946, *Curve,* 51–52, which is in reply to a letter from Aichhorn, July 21, 1946, *Curve,* 49.

32. GM and TAK. See also Kohut's memorial to Ross on her eightieth birthday, March 1970, *Curve,* 243–244. As Gretchen Meyer told me, there was among the Meyer ancestors a half-Jewish grandfather, which meant the family by Nazi criteria as defined in the 1935 Nuremberg Laws was Jewish. As an American Protestant, Elizabeth might not have remarked on or even noticed this fact of her background, except for her experience in Vienna in the 1930s.

33. Elizabeth Kohut to Richard C. Marohn, April 9, 1984; "August Aichhorn and Heinz Kohut," videotaped interview; TAK; and Arnold Goldberg, personal communication March 3, 1999.

34. JB and letter to me July 5, 1998.

6 A CRUMBLING UNIVERSE

1. Brooks-Shepherd, *The Austrians*, 274–318; Gertrude Schneider, *Exile and Destruction: The Fate of Austrian Jews, 1938–1945* (Westport, CT: Praeger, 1995), 12. See also Norman Bentwich, "The Destruction of the Jewish Community in Austria, 1938–1942," and Herbert Rosenkranz, "The Anschluss and the Tragedy of Austrian Jewry, 1938–1945," in *The Jews of Austria: Essays on their Life, History, and Destruction*, ed. Joseph Fraenkel (London: Vallentine, Mitchell, 1967); and Raul Hilberg, *The Destruction of the European Jews* (Chicago: University of Chicago Press, 1961).

2. SQ. See also Charles Kligerman, "Eulogy," in which he mentions the specific effect of the Nazi takeover on Kohut's self-esteem. Compare Kohut's discussion of the "anticipatory function" of art in relation to the Nazis, *Humanities*, 88–90.

3. SL 2; "their beards": Schneider, *Exile and Destruction*, 15.

4. JP 1 and 2. In JP 1, Palaci asked *me* whether Kohut was Jewish before telling me the story of meeting Kohut on the street after the Anschluss; he then added more details to the story when I interviewed him again five years later. It was Palaci's question to me in that 1985 interview that alerted me to the significance of this theme in Kohut's life. If he did not know Kohut was Jewish, who did? And why would he not know? When I mentioned Palaci's uncertainty to Paul Ornstein when I interviewed him in 1996, Ornstein said Palaci had always indicated to him that he knew Kohut was Jewish. I cannot explain this contradiction, except that Palaci may have gotten the issue cleared up from what I told him during our 1985 interview and thereafter conveyed his new understanding in conversation with Ornstein.

5. Schneider, *Exile and Destruction*, 15.

6. SL 2 and Sigmund Levarie to me, May 9, 1999.

7. Kohut to Siegmund Levarie, August 23, 1938, *Curve*, 39–40, and November 8, 1938, *Curve*, 43.

8. Muhleittner and Reichmayr, "The Exodus of Psychoanalysts from Vienna," 105–121, note that the effects of the Anschluss on psychoanalysis in Vienna were catastrophic. Some 95 of the original 150 members of the Viennese Psychoanalytic Society, counting from its beginnings in Freud's Wednesday Circle in 1902 to its dissolution in 1938, emigrated. By 1938 another 26 had died. The rest emigrated, except for a few, most notably Aichhorn.

9. Kohut to Kurt Eissler, October 12, 1952, *Curve*, 64–65. Kohut added more details to the story in a letter to Alexandre Szombati, July 12, 1968, *Curve*, 207–208. Cp. Gay, *Freud*, 629, and Ronald W. Clark, *Freud: The Man and the Cause* (New York: Random House, 1980), 512 (though note that Clark has Freud leaving June 2 and Gay on June 3).

10. Kohut in his after-dinner talk at his birthday celebration, June 2, 1973, in the private tape collection of Ernest Wolf; the edited version was published as "The Future of Psychoanalysis," *Search* 2: 663–684.

11. Kohut to Levarie, November 29, 1938. For a larger discussion of this "contradic-

tion," see Geoffrey Cocks, *Psychotherapy in the Third Reich: The Göring Institute*, 2d ed. (New Brunswick, NJ: Transaction Publishers, 1997).

12. Kohut to Levarie, August 23, 1938, *Curve*, 39–40.

13. Kohut to August Aichhorn, March 7, 1947, *Curve*, 56.

14. Inventory.

15. Kohut to Levarie, August 23, 1938, *Curve*, 39.

16. Kohut to Siegmund Levarie, October 5, 1938; Elke Muhleittner to me, June 22, 1997, on the nature of medical school exams; and Siegmund Levarie, personal communication, November 30, 1999, on the Nazi buttons.

17. Cocks, "Introduction," *Curve*, 9 (the information is from Siegmund Levarie). In talking with me on May 5, 1999, Levarie stressed how close Kohut was to Levarie's mother. "Was spared": Schneider, *Exile and Destruction*, 25; Rosenkranz, "The Anschluss," 481–482; "bureaucratic style": Inventory; "eclipse in Vienna": Kohut to Siegmund Levarie, November 8, 1938, *Curve*, 42.

18. Kohut to Siegmund Levarie, November 8, 1938, *Curve*, 42–43, and the unpublished letter of November 29, 1938. For the joking reference, see the addendum to the November 29 letter, dated November 30. For the name of the hospital where Kohut was working, see also Cocks, Introduction, *Curve*, 9.

19. Elizabeth Kohut, videotape interview with Richard Marohn. See also Kohut to Peter B. Neubauer, July 12, 1968, *Curve*, 208–209. This photograph was used as the frontispiece—placed vertically rather than horizontally—for the festschrift that was published for Aichhorn shortly after his death. See Otto Fleischmann, Paul Kramer, and Helen Ross, eds., *Delinquency and Child Guidance* (New York, 1965).

20. Inventory; Kohut to Siegmund Levarie, March 1, 1939, *Curve*, 43; Kohut to August Aichhorn, August 26, 1947, *Curve*, 57, and December 28, 1948.

21. Kohut to Siegmund Levarie, March 18, 1939, *Curve*, 45.

7 A NEW AMERICAN SELF

1. Kohut to Siegmund Levarie, June 2, 1946, *Curve*, 46–47.

2. SQ about the intellectuals in the camp and EK 1 about the chess.

3. On the accounts, Kohut to Levarie, April 29, 1939, *Curve*, 46; on being medical assistant, Kohut to Levarie, May 22, 1939, *Curve*, 47.

4. Kohut to Siegmund Levarie, May 22, 1939, *Curve*, 47.

5. Kohut to Siegmund Levarie, April 29, 1939, *Curve*, 45.

6. Ibid.

7. Thomas A. Kohut (TAK) wondered if Else believed her Christianity would save her. It must be remembered, however, that Thomas Kohut thinks of his grandmother as Catholic.

8. Inventory.

9. Thomas A. Kohut (TAK) testified to the surprising number of possessions Else brought with her to America. Kohut, in a letter to Aichhorn, June 2, 1946, *Curve*, 48, notes his mother had hidden away money when she left Vienna. Eva Sandburg, personal communication, January 18, 1997, who left Vienna at the same time,

noted that the Nazis often allowed Jews to take some possessions with them but never any money. Sandburg's own family arrived in Brazil with many trunks of goods but absolutely broke.

10. The date of Else's departure from Vienna is noted on a form dated March 21, 1962 (in the Kohut Archives), which she filed in an attempt to recover some of what had been stolen from her.

11. Kohut to Siegmund Levarie, October 27, 1939.

12. On October 27, 1939, Kohut wrote Levarie from his uncle's London apartment about his pneumonia. Since Kohut left at the end of February for America, that meant he spent four months in London. Seven years later, however, Kohut wrote to Aichhorn, June 2, 1946 (*Curve*, 47) that he had only spent six weeks in London. The contemporary letter obviously supersedes the later memory. It is otherwise a minor issue, except for determining the timing of his illness in relation to the outbreak of the war.

13. Kohut to August Aichhorn, February 2, 1947.

14. For information about this stay, TAK; EK 1 and 2; and Kohut to Siegmund Levarie, October 27, 1939.

15. Kohut to Siegmund Levarie, March 27, 1940, on the day Kohut arrived in Chicago and about the performance of Bach's *Passion*; *Humanities*, interview with me, 237, on the $25; SQ regarding the twelve-day passage (from which I inferred the day he left England).

16. SL 2.

17. Personal communication, Siegmund Levarie, May 5, 1999.

18. Most of the information in this paragraph is from my second interview with Siegmund Levarie. During that session Levarie let me read his correspondence with Wadsworth during the 1940s, from which I drew my own impressions recorded here. These are particularly valuable letters, since there are mysteriously no Wadsworth letters from before 1977 in what has been deposited by the family in the Kohut Archives.

19. Robert Wadsworth to Siegmund Levarie, December 17, 1941.

20. TAK. Gretchen Meyer had the same general understanding of Wadsworth. Others with direct acquaintance with him, like Arnold Goldberg (AG 2), Constance Goldberg (April 4, 1996), Ernest Wolf (EW 2), and John Gedo, *Spleen and Nostalgia: A Life and Work in Psychoanalysis* (Northvale, NJ: Jason Aronson, 1997) (and in several more informal conversations), were more certain Wadsworth was homosexual, though of course it was only their impression. Ernest Wolf (EW 2) said Wadsworth presented as a "queen." Siegmund Levarie, in a conversation on May 5, 1999, after he had read a draft of this book, strenuously objected to calling Wadsworth a homosexual. He said Wadsworth was much too "puritan" ever to have been a homosexual, by which he meant actively engaged in homosexual activity, though he agreed with the descriptors "tall and exceedingly thin, effeminate, shy, neurotic, full of strange movements and mannerisms, odd and yet captivating."

21. John Gedo, *Spleen and Nostalgia*, 323 (and in several informal conversations). I know firsthand of the rumors from my own many years of involvement in the world of the Institute and Chicago psychoanalysis.

22. PO. Ornstein's point about old friends is not really supported by the evidence. In the 1940s Kohut's closest friend was Jay McCormick, whom he only saw intermittently after 1948; he never saw Barbara Bryant after 1946 (though as she was an ex-girlfriend that is perhaps less surprising); and he completely lost touch with the world of the third floor of the "Home for Crippled and Destitute Children," which included Thomas Szasz, Richard Landau, Charles Spurr, William Early, and others. In fact, Onstein's point is valid only as far as Charles Kligerman and Wadsworth himself are concerned.

23. SL 2. Kohut wrote to Aichhorn, June 2, 1946, *Curve*, 48: "About five years ago she [Else] opened a shop with some money she had managed to hide away and has had great success with it." Aichhorn wrote back that he was "amazed" at the success of his mother's adjustment to America; see Aichhorn to Kohut, July 21, 1946, *Curve*, 50. The name of the store is from SL 2; what she sold is from GM and TAK; the address is from the Inventory (in the 1960s Else sued the Austrian government for recovery of some assets, and those records are included in her old Nazi file).

24. JM. SQ for the myth; cp. Kohut to Siegmund Levarie, April 2, 1981, *Curve*, 427–428.

25. Arnold Goldberg, personal communication, March 3, 1999.

26. Kohut vita from the 1940s, in the archives. See also his application to the Institute, 1944, Candidate File, Chicago Institute for Psychoanalysis. Kohut's friends and lovers all remembered different hospitals: Barbara Tweedle said he interned at Woodlawn Hospital, as did Jay McCormick; Levarie said it was Roseland Hospital; and Elizabeth Kohut said it was Jackson Park Hospital. One wonders how there could have been such confusion.

27. He was awarded his medical license on August 11, 1941, number 24,536 of the state of Illinois. See Kohut's vita from 1955.

28. Kohut was one of the twenty-four residents who served under Richter between 1936 and his retirement in 1966. In 1962 Richter was elected president of the American Neurological Association; see Kohut to Richter, November 8, 1962, and Richter's reply on November 20, 1962. Howell Wright, chair of pediatrics at the time (and my stepfather), told me October 29, 1990, that Richter was brilliant but "arrogant, pushy, and difficult." On the date Kohut began his residency, see his "Specialty Record" in the hospital.

29. On his salary, see Kohut to August Aichhorn, June 2, 1946, and September 2, 1946, *Curve*, 48 and 52; the article is Kohut, Richter et al., "Neuro-optic Myelitis," *Journal of Nervous and Mental Disease* 101 (1945): 99–114; Richter's intention to make Kohut head of the neurology section is from Richter's then colleague in pediatrics, Howell Wright, October 23, 1990.

30. Charles Kligerman, "Eulogy."

31. JM.

32. SL 1. The Wadsworth quote is from his letter to Siegmund Levarie, December 17, 1941.

33. Kohut to August Aichhorn, June 2, 1946, *Curve*, 48.

34. SL 2.
35. BBT.
36. JM.
37. TAK. For Kohut's nostalgia about neurology, see Kohut to Brunlik, November 14, 1969; on imitating tics, JM; on empathy, Douglas Detrick, personal communication in a letter, October 11, 1983; on hospital staff shortages, interview with Howell Wright, October 23, 1990. Kohut's 1940s publications: Kohut, Richter et al., "Neuro-optic Myelitis"; Kohut, "Unusual Involvement of the Nervous System in Generalized Lymphoblastoma," *Journal of Nervous and Mental Disease* 103(1946): 9–20; Kohut, "Encephalitis," *Medical Clinics of North America* (January 1947), Chicago Number; Kohut, "Emotional Maturity," book review, *Journal of Clinical Psychopathology* 9(1948): 601–605.
38. PO.
39. Peter Barglow (interview, December 18, 1995) noted the self-effacing way Kohut spoke of how an Institute exhibit on his career made him seem like "St. Heinz," and Paul Ornstein (PO) described the way Kohut reacted with revulsion at the images broadcast on television of Jews wailing at the Western Wall after the 1967 war. One has to suspect such attitudes grew out of his ambivalence about his mother's religious commitments.
40. Charles Kligerman, in my interview with him (CK), which was otherwise reserved, distant, and mostly uninformative, let slip his attitude about Kohut's involvement in the Unitarian Church.
41. *Medical Tribune*, December 21, 1964.
42. In Kohut's vitae through the late 1950s he continued to list proudly his American citizenship.
43. TAK; EK 1; GM; and CK.

8 PSYCHOANALYSIS, AT LAST

1. Nathan G. Hale, *The Rise and Crisis of Psychoanalysis in the United States: Freud and the Americans, 1917–1985* (New York: Oxford University Press, 1995), 167. In 1911 Ernest Jones had presented a paper before the Chicago Neurological Society. In the late 1920s N. Lionel Blitzsten founded the Chicago Psychoanalytic Society. He was given permission by his former analyst in Berlin, Franz Alexander, to take on patients, because Alexander thought the Chicago population consisted mostly of Indians! See Douglas Kirsner, *Unfree Associations: Inside Psychoanalytic Institutes* (London: Process Press, 2000), Ch. 3.
2. George H. Pollock, "The Presence of the Past," *Annual of Psychoanalysis* II (1983): 3–27; and Kirsner, *Unfree Associations*. The Chicago Institute in the 1930s may well have been the only first-class center of higher learning anywhere in the country then or later to have such an equality of gender balance.
3. Pollock, "The Presence of the Past." See also interview with Louis Shapiro, April 3, 1996. John Gedo, *Spleen and Nostalgia*, 52 of his manuscript but deleted

from the final book (and quoted with permission of the author), discusses the way the Institute was closely connected to the local departments of psychiatry in Chicago through what was then called the "Associated Psychiatric Faculties of Chicago." When he applied for his residency he was first interviewed at the Institute!

4. The nature of the training also turned psychoanalysis into a de facto subspecialty of psychiatry, something Freud feared; see Sigmund Freud, "The Question of Lay Analysis" (1926), SE 20: 179–258. On this Kohut completely agreed. See Kohut to Anna Freud, August 4, 1964, Curve, 99–103. Kohut's candidate file was made available to me through the good offices of Jerome Kavka and Thomas Pappadis.

5. Interview with Bertram J. Cohler, October 19, 1996. Kohut said this to Cohler when he was a candidate in the 1970s. In the 1990s, Cohler, now a distinguished professor at the University of Chicago, came out himself as a homosexual. "Be rejected": PO; "turned down": Kohut to August Aichhorn, September 2, 1946, Curve, 52; "been rejected": Kohut to August Aichhorn, September 2, 1946, Curve, 52 (for some reason, Kohut reported to Aichhorn that Helen McLean wrote the letter, though that was clearly wrong); "Period of analysis": Thomas M. French to Kohut, February 2, 1943, in Kohut's Candidate File, Chicago Institute for Psychoanalysis.

6. See Kohut's September 29, 1946, reapplication to the Institute, Candidate File, Chicago Institute. In the same file, in his "Student Record," someone has typed in that he began his analysis with Eissler in April 1942, which is impossible since he did not even first apply to the Institute for admission until November 1942. I can only assume it is a clerical error, especially since it is typed and not in Kohut's handwriting, though I cannot rule out the possibility that Kohut lied at the time of his reapplication to extend the number of hours that he had spent in his training analysis.

7. Kohut reported to Ross that Dr. Van der Heide had told him to get an analysis with a training analyst. He complained, however, that he couldn't afford that, so Heide suggested that he apply to Ross "for an analysis through the 'Institute,' " by which he must mean through the clinic. It is not clear how Ross, who was probably in an administrative capacity, responded, but within a few weeks Kohut had decided to seek analysis with Ruth Eissler and pay the fee (probably with his mother's help). Kohut to Helen Ross, undated, but from the context shortly after the letter of rejection from French on February 2, 1943. In the Candidate File, Chicago Institute.

8. Kohut to August Aichhorn, September 2, 1946.

9. I interviewed Barbara Bryant Tweedle on January 2, 1983, when she was sixty. She was one of the most beautiful women of her age I have ever met.

10. Levarie (SL 2) told me Bryant's mother was at first "horrified that her daughter might team up with a poor refugee," though he said it with some irony and Bryant herself said nothing about her mother's opposition to her relationship with Kohut.

11. BBT.

12. Kohut was an instructor in neurology from July 1, 1943, to July 1, 1944, an instructor in neurology and psychiatry from July 1, 1944, to July 1, 1947; and an assistant professor of psychiatry from July 1, 1947, to July 1, 1949; see his "Specialty Record." On Richter's reaction, Howell Wright, October 23, 1990; JM; and Ernest Wolf, in a draft labeled "Yasskey paper" from his files that I consulted October 27, 1991.

13. JM.

14. Peter Giovacchini in Virginia Hunter, *Psychoanalysts Talk* (New York: Guilford Press, 1994), 197.

15. Charles Kligerman, in his "Eulogy," said he used to walk with Kohut on the Midway, the long expanse of grass that stretches past the hospital and the university, and talk about art, music, and Vienna, but that the "talk inevitably turned to Freud and psychoanalysis, a subject which poured out of Heinz with irresistible enthusiasm." Kligerman, however, almost certainly telescoped his memories in this passage. After graduating from medical school in 1941, Kligerman began a residency in internal medicine and lived briefly on the same floor as Kohut before being called into military service. It was only when he returned from the war that he himself went into psychiatry and moved back onto the floor with Kohut in the hospital. By then Kohut had very different interests and undoubtedly did talk "with irresistible enthusiasm" about Freud. This sequence is apparent from a close read of Kligerman's text, as well as my interview with Jay McCormick (JM).

16. BBT.

17. JM.

18. BBT.

19. Peggy McCormick sat in on my interview with Jay and often added her own stories, like this one.

20. Interview with Cecile Block, January 24, 1997. Block, who was on the staff of the Institute for many years, was a friend of Else's from the 1940s. Kohut, who saw Block every day for several decades, *never* took the opportunity to have a conversation with her about his mother. "Modest exhibitions": Siegmund Levarie possesses several of her paintings and showed me one when I interviewed him on March 27, 1997. Thomas A. Kohut also talked of his grandmother's paintings; "some suitors": TAK.

9 CANDIDATE AT THE CHICAGO INSTITUTE

1. Kohut to August Aichhorn, June 2, 1946, *Curve*, 47–48. The records of the Kultusgemeinde indicate that Willy died in Auschwitz on August 25, 1942, at 12:05 p.m.

2. Kohut to August Aichhorn, March 7, 1947, *Curve*, 55–56. The two Aichhorn letters to Kohut are dated November 19, 1946, and February 19, 1947.

3. August Aichhorn to Kohut, September 13, 1946; "in his cases": August Aichhorn

to Kohut, November 19, 1946; September 13, 1946; February 19, 1947; August 1, 1947; October 27, 1947; December 20, 1947; January 3, 1948; February 7, 1948; May 14, 1948; February 1949; June 15, 1949; and July 7, 1949. "rebuild their lives": August Aichhorn to Kohut, July 21, 1946, *Curve*, 49–50. Somewhat later, on January 3, 1948, Aichhorn went out of his way to send his greetings to Else.

4. Kohut to August Aichhorn, January 14, 1948, *Curve*, 58; "would be a luxury": August Aichhorn to Kohut, July 21, 1946, *Curve*, 50; "could send him": Kohut to August Aichhorn, June 2, 1946, *Curve*, 48.

5. Kohut to August Aichhorn, February 2, 1947. The detail about the man covering Kohut with a coat while he lay unconscious and Kohut's later unsuccessful efforts to locate him is from JM. "at the Institute": Kohut to August Aichhorn, September 2, 1946; "loving detail": Kohut to August Aichhorn, February 2, 1947, and December 28, 1948; "with his income": Kohut to August Aichhorn, June 2, 1946, and September 2, 1946, *Curve*, 48, 51–52.

6. Kohut to August Aichhorn, June 21, 1948; "hotter than Vienna": Kohut to August Aichhorn, August 26, 1947, *Curve*, 57.

7. Kohut to August Aichhorn, October 12, 1946, *Curve*, 53. In Kohut's letter to George J. Mohr, September 19, 1946, he confirms his interviews with the members of the training committee, though there is nothing in his file to indicate their decision (or reasons for it). See Kohut's Candidate File, Chicago Institute.

8. The specific courses Kohut took are available from his "Student Record" in his Candidate File; Kohut to August Aichhorn, August 26, 1947, *Curve*, 57, and December 28, 1948. Cp. Gedo, *Spleen and Nostalgia*, 25–38, which describes in detail his course work at the Institute in the 1950s.

9. Charles Kligerman, "Eulogy."

10. Besides Weiss and Benedek, he studied with Maxwell Gitelson, Catherine Bacon, Franz Alexander, Ruth Eissler, Thomas French, Helen McLean, Adelaide Johnson, Margaret Gerard, Lucia Tower, Gerhard Piers, Harry B. Lee, George Mohr, Emmy Sylvester, and Fritz Moellenhoff. From his Candidate File, Chicago Institute (which also lists the individual courses).

11. Kohut to August Aichhorn, October 12, 1946, *Curve*, 54–55.

12. Peter Giovacchini in Virginia Hunter, *Psychoanalysts Talk* (New York: Guilford Press, 1994), 199.

13. All the information about Kohut's control cases is from his Candidate File at the Chicago Institute.

14. Sigmund Freud, "Mourning and Melancholia," *SE* 14: 237–260. Kohut's comments on the case are in Kohut to August Aichhorn, January 14, 1948, *Curve*, 58, and Kohut to August Aichhorn, August 26, 1947, *Curve*, 57.

15. August Aichhorn to Kohut, May 14, 1948; "facade of neutrality": Kohut to August Aichhorn, May 4, 1948; "from the others": Kohut to August Aichhorn, December 28, 1948; "learning from him": August Aichhorn to Kohut, February 7, 1948; on Kramer as a Viennese Jew, see JB.

16. Kohut to August Aichhorn, January 14, 1948 (*Curve*, 58), states that he is about to get his third control case, but some delay occurred, probably something clini-

cal to do with the case itself, for he reports the same thing at the end of the year; see Kohut to August Aichhorn, December 28, 1948.

17. Kohut to August Aichhorn, May 4, 1948; on the significance of the third control, interview with Louis Shapiro, April 3, 1996.

18. August Aichhorn to Kohut, May 14, 1948; Kohut to August Aichhorn, December 28, 1948.

19. Kohut to Helen Ross, June 9, 1950, and Kohut to George J. Mohr, November 8, 1950, Candidate File, Chicago Institute.

20. The article first appeared as Heinz Kohut and Siegmund Levarie, "On the Enjoyment of Listening to Music," *PQ* 19 (1950): 64–87, and is reprinted in *Search* 1: 135–158. On Kohut's primary responsibility for the paper, see Kohut to August Aichhorn, January 14, 1948, *Curve*, 58, and interview with Siegmund Levarie, October 17, 1997. On the music paper as his first, see Kohut to Aichhorn, January 14, 1948 (*Curve*, 58): "Recently I have also been writing on a work that I will perhaps finish in not too long a time." Cp. as well the following note.

21. Geoffrey Cocks's footnote to Kohut letter to John Gedo, August 25, 1965, *Curve*, 125, n. 2, notes Kohut's participation in the McLean seminar but has the date for it wrong (it was in the fall of 1947; see the "Student Record" or transcript of courses in Kohut's Candidate File, Chicago Institute). Paul Ornstein, in his Introduction to *Search* 1: 10, says that this essay on *Death in Venice* was Kohut's first psychoanalytic paper. Ornstein worked with Kohut himself in preparing these essays for publication, so the assertion carries a good deal of weight, though in a personal communication on November 9, 1997, Ornstein pointed out to me that Kohut did not have much to do with arranging the papers in the *Search* volume. But to the extent that Kohut claimed primacy for the Mann essay his own memory was probably faulty, or, more likely, he revised his memory to make the impressive essay on Mann the leadoff paper of the collection. Since there was overlap in the writing of the papers, there may also have been some simple confusion. Siegmund Levarie specifically remembers that his paper with his friend was Kohut's first paper in psychoanalysis. Levarie was also always introduced to Kohut's analyst colleagues as "the man I wrote my first music paper with." Siegmund Levarie, personal communication, May 8, 1999. Even more convincingly, Kohut in his letter to Aichhorn on January 14, 1948 (*Curve*, 58), says he was then almost done with the music paper that was clearly begun in 1947 and conceived sometime that year after the Bart—k concert. The Mann essay was conceived in the same general period as the music paper but appeared to have a much longer germination stage; it was only put together in anything approaching a final state as his graduation paper in 1950 (Kohut told this to Ornstein, who related it to me November 9, 1997).

22. Kohut, "*Death in Venice* by Thomas Mann: A Story About the Disintegration of Artistic Sublimation," *PQ* 26 (1957): 206–228. *Search* 1: 107–130. On when he prepared the paper for publication, see Kohut to Bruno Walter, November 26, 1956, *Curve* 69–70; and Kohut to Harry Slochower, December 31, 1968. The Baedaker's Guide reference is to Anthony Heilbut, *Thomas Mann: Eros and Literature*,

quoted in Gordon A. Craig, "The Man Nobody Knew," *New York Review of Books* 3 (February 29, 1996): 34–37. See also Si Fullinwider, "The Freud Revolution," *History Today* (April 1992): 23–29. Paul Ornstein (PO) is my source for why Kohut withheld publication.

23. Freud says of Leonardo da Vinci, for example: "Because his love for his mother had been repressed, this portion was driven to take up a homosexual attitude and manifested itself in ideal love for boys." And later: "We must be content to emphasize the fact . . . that what an artist creates provides at the same time an outlet for his sexual desire. . . ." Sigmund Freud, "Leonardo da Vinci and a Memory of his Childhood," *SE* 11: 59–137, quotes on 132.

24. Kohut revisited *Death in Venice* in an aside in his 1976 paper, "Creativeness, Charisma, Group Psychology: Reflections on the Self-Analysis of Freud," *Humanities*, 171–211; note pp. 193–194, casting his interpretation of the story into his new language of narcissism. This later formulation, however, is much less elegant than the original, partly because it just precedes his much freer language of the self. Compare, however, the brief discussion of Kohut's later view of *Death in Venice* by Paul Ornstein, "Introduction," *Search* 1: 10–13.

25. GM. See also Charles Kligerman, "Eulogy."

26. SQ. See August Aichhorn to Kohut, November 19, 1947; Kohut to August Aichhorn, February 2, 1947; Kohut to August Aichhorn, postscript dated September 12, 1948, to letter dated June 21, 1948. On the forgettable Doris, see SL 3.

27. Kohut to August Aichhorn, postscript dated September 12, 1948, to letter dated June 21, 1948, and December 28, 1948.

28. Kohut to Elizabeth Meyer, August 16, 1948, *Curve*, 59–60.

10 DOMESTICITY

1. Charles Kligerman, "Eulogy."

2. GM and ME; "Aichhorn connection": TAK.

3. TAK.

4. Gretchen Meyer to Kohut, September 4, 1958, and Kohut to Gretchen Meyer, September 8, 1958; "extensive nursing": TAK and GM.

5. A copy of the memorial is not in his papers in the archives and neither Thomas nor Gretchen Meyer produced it, despite three years of requests.

6. Siegmund Levarie to Kohut, November 30, 1966, and Kohut in reply, December 6, 1966; "of New York": SL 3 and personal communication, May 9, 1999.

7. Kohut to Siegmund Levarie, October 30, 1956.

8. Kohut to George H. Carter, May 12, 1974. See also Peter Vander Veer to Kohut, January 15 and April 29, 1974, as well as Kohut to Vander Veer, January 21, 1974.

9. TAK. Kohut kept a separate file for his own medical records (which is in the archives), including a detailed noting of his weight. On smoking, see Kohut to Sydney J. Harris, July 5, 1969, *Curve*, 72. Compare Kohut's letter to the Depart-

ment of Health, Education, and Welfare, March 19, 1977, *Curve*, 341–342. On running, see Kohut to Ignacio Matta-Blanco, August 21, 1969, where he says his best time since they had run together in Rome was six minutes and fifty seconds, which implies he hoped for better. Both Thomas A. Kohut and Charles Kligerman mention Jackman Field. Kligerman adds that Kohut was quite a sight and well known in the neighborhood for his running with his stopwatch around his neck. He started running, it should be noted, a decade or so before it became trendy in America.

10. JM about staying up late; TAK on the books and the studies of literature; GM on Pasternak.

11. Ernest Wolf, "Interview," Virginia Hunter, *Psychoanalysts Talk* (New York: Guilford Press, 1994), 166, and EW 3; "shoes custom-made": Marian Tolpin, personal communication, June 21, 1997.

12. JM, JB, CK.

13. Kohut to Jacques Palaci, October 20, 1974; on Bach, GM; "developments in jazz": Kohut to Miles D. Miller, December 9, 1957; on the coat, JB and Siegmund Levarie, personal communication, May 9, 1999.

14. TAK. Note Kohut's toast to Moellenhof at a dinner, "The Life of Fritz," November 1960, *Curve*, 72–74; "in Switzerland": Charles Kligerman, "Eulogy," and personal communication, Siegmund Levarie, May 9, 1999; "on Halsted Street": interview with Ina Wolf, August 8, 1996.

15. Kohut to Siegmund Levarie, September 10, 1951, *Curve*, 63–64. On Siena, TAK.

16. SQ.

17. Note, for example, Kohut to "P," August 24, 1979, *Search* 4: 635.

18. I am indebted to Margret Barglow, who researched the issue of the shorthand with her mother, a woman from Germany who also learned shorthand as a young woman and then, like Kohut, adapted it to English as an adult. Margret Barglow sent her mother a copy of the shorthand in which she was able to recognize many German characters but also many English words spelled out. She also clarified for me why when one changes languages one's shorthand necessarily becomes unique. Margret Barglow to me, September 23, 1998. Kurt Gödel, the mathematician, also wrote in an obscure shorthand; see John W. Dawson, "Kurt Goedel and the Limits of Logic," *Scientific American* (June 1999), 81.

19. TAK and GM; "in the winter": August Aichhorn to Kohut, November 19, 1946; October 27, 1947; December 20, 1947; and July 7, 1949.

20. Kohut to Siegmund Levarie, September 10, 1951, *Curve* 63–64; "yet longed for it": Kohut to Margaret Mahler, May 23, 1970.

21. Kohut's manuscript text of his after-dinner speech at his birthday symposium, June 2, 1973, which was published in edited form in *Search* 2: 663–664. See also Kohut to Stephan Stewart, October 16, 1957. TAK described the other details of the trip; "led to chaos": Kohut to John Gedo, *Curve*, 325.

22. See pp. 239–240.

23. Kohut to The Honorable Richard J. Daley, August 21, 1964, *Curve*, 105; "were destroyed": Comments by Maynard Hutchins to the faculty of the University of

Chicago regarding charges in the Illinois State Legislature of Communism on campus, May 6, 1949.

24. Kohut to The Honorable Richard J. Daley, August 21, 1964, *Curve*, 105.

25. TAK and GM. See also Kohut to John F. Hayward, January 17, 1963; September 28, 1966; and February 6, 1968, *Curve*, 78, 145–146, and 189–190.

26. See the interesting recent study by Rael Meyerowitz, *Transferring to America: Jewish Interpretations of American Dreams* (Albany: State University of New York Press, 1995), and compare the experience of Erik Erikson, in Friedman, *Identity's Architect*.

11 THE COUCH

1. M. Barrie Richmond to Kohut, September 3, 1974, which includes a transcript of Kohut's comments at an Institute workshop.

2. Jay McCormick (JM) describes a scientific meeting at the Institute in the late 1950s when Kohut "viciously" attacked someone who dared to support a psychotherapeutic approach to a clinical problem.

3. Kohut to Arnold Goldberg, June 18, 1975. At the same time, Kohut had little real interest in technique per se. Paul Ornstein had a scheme to interview Kohut on videotape about technique in the late 1970s, but it never came to fruition. Kohut was simply not that interested in the subject. See PO.

4. See George Pollock's handwritten notes for his comments at an Institute reception, July 27, 1984, to raise money for the Kohut Memorial Fund; PT; LS.

5. *Lectures*, 20. On being stumped, Kohut to Edward Teller, May 16, 1974, printed without the attribution in *Search* 2: 889–890; "can't even listen": Arnold Goldberg, personal communication, March 8, 1999; "Kohut's clinical skills": Ernest Wolf, "Interview," *Psychoanalysts Talk*, 179; "by the paper": AG 1.

6. AG 1; "in the transference": *Search* 2: 623–624.

7. All Klumpner references are from my interview with him on April 2, 1996. I sent him the draft of this segment, which he approved along with some corrections in a letter of February 26, 1998. Sometime after the conclusion of the treatment, Kohut wrote up the case and included it as part of his long essay "On Courage." He never published his essay, but he talked about the case at times with students and mentioned it in his last book, *Cure*. When I edited "On Courage" for posthumous publication in *Humanities*, I deleted the case, as it seemed unintegrated into the narrative. Paul Ornstein, however, subsequently published it as "From the Analysis of Mr. R." in *Search* 3: 183–222.

8. Kohut to Douglas Levin, January 5, 1975. Note also *Cure*, 73.

9. Kohut to Douglas Levin, January 5, 1975.

10. *Analysis*, 283–286. There is some question whether the exchanges between them were in fact quite as dramatic as Kohut wrote them up in 1971, or most of all whether she was the first patient about whom he came to understand these issues. He acknowledged to Susan Quinn (SQ) a decade later that he was not actually

sure his work with Miss F. was the turning point. "Whether it really was or not I cannot tell," he said.

11. Arnold Rachman, personal communication, June 4, 1996. Rachman went on to say that Kohut's response to Miss F. seemed modeled on that of Carl Rogers, though that seems a much more unlikely idea.

12. *Restoration*, 151–170, and an additional comment, 190–191. My interview with Barglow was conducted on December 18, 1995. I sent the first draft of this segment to him for review. He called on March 2, 1998, to add further details and correct some minor errors, but otherwise approved the presentation. Initially Barglow wanted to remain anonymous, but after we served together on a panel at the American Psychological Association meetings on August 14, 1998, he was comfortable revealing his identity. On December 17, 1998, in a personal communication, I confirmed once again that he was comfortable with my using his actual name.

13. JM, CK, and JG 2.

14. See in this regard Kohut's discussion in *Restoration*, 160–161.

15. *Restoration*, 154.

16. PT.

17. Basch died of brain cancer in 1996 before I could conduct an interview, though I did know him for two decades. He was one of my teachers when I was a candidate at the Institute, and for several years in the early 1980s we both taught at Rush Medical School. I often talked with him at self psychology conferences and once, very early, he heard me give a presentation on Kohut. Unless otherwise noted, the facts of Basch's life and his experiences with Kohut are from my interview with his widow, Carol Basch, October 28, 1998. On his disappointment at not having been analyzed later by Kohut, Basch also talked openly with his friend, Robert Jag Lifton; Lifton, personal communication. Paul Ornstein (PO) told me the same thing, and added that Basch always remained so grateful to Kohut for unlocking his creativity that he allowed no one to say anything critical of Kohut in his presence.

12 MR. PSYCHOANALYSIS

1. Kohut to Anna Freud, August 4, 1964, *Curve*, 98–103. See also Kohut to Gardner Lindzey, June 3, 1979.

2. The committee of the American Psychoanalytic Association that approved his application, however, was displeased with the infrequency of supervision on two of his control cases. See Karl Menninger to George Mohr, February 3, 1953. See Kohut's Candidate File at the Chicago Institute. Kohut moved slowly into clinical psychoanalysis. See *Medical Tribune*, December 21, 1964, 8. On his indecision, see Kohut's application to enroll in the Institute, September 29, 1946, Candidate File, Chicago Institute.

3. Kohut left his professorship at the University of Chicago in 1949 but remained a

NOTES

lecturer until he died and regularly taught a seminar for residents. See Robert M. Galatzter-Levy, "Heinz Kohut as Teacher and Supervisor: A View from the Second Generation," *Progress in Self Psychology*, vol. 4: *Learning from Kohut*, ed. Arnold Goldberg (Hillsdale, NJ: Analytic Press, 1988), 3–42, esp. 12–17. See Kohut's letter to Robert J. Thurnblad, December 17, 1962, *Curve*, 78, in which Kohut expresses his gratitude for a present the residents in his seminar had given him. He extends his fondest hopes that Thurnblad and all his colleagues will be "good psychiatrists who will obtain continued gratification from the intellectual and emotional pleasure that comes with the deepening understanding of people and their problems."

4. At a scientific meeting in May 1965, for example, Kohut commented on the theoretical inadequacy of French's work on psychosomatic diseases and how his ideas corrupted those of Freud. He then wrote up his thoughts in a letter (which has been lost) to Samuel D. Lipton. Lipton wrote back on May 27, 1965, asking if he could circulate the letter. Kohut replied the next day that he appreciated his consideration in asking and said it was okay, though he asked him to be discreet. "dislike Kohut": Arnold Goldberg, personal communication, April 2, 1996.

5. Kohut to Merton M. Gill, December 15, 1964, *Curve*, 108. In the letter Kohut makes reference to his letter to the members of the American (to which Gill is responding), *President's Newsletter* 5 (November 1964), as described by Geoffrey Cocks in footnote 1 to the Gill letter. Compare as well the Minutes of the curriculum committee of the Institute, January 13, 1976, in the Kohut Archives.

6. LS for all the details about the workings of the committee in this and the next paragraph. Philip D. Rubovitz-Seitz, in an e-mail to me of April 5, 1999, disputes the centrality of Kohut on the committee. It was his "impression" that Fleming was more important. Rubovitz-Seitz, however, was not at the Institute when the curriculum was revised. Louis Shapiro was a staff member during the entire period. "stirred opposition": Franz Alexander, an analysand and student of Sándor Ferenczi, was interested in shortening psychoanalysis but also in what we would now call psychosomatic medicine. Of his many papers, see "Analysis of the Therapeutic Factors in Psychoanalytic Treatment," *PQ* 19 (1950): 482; "Psychoanalysis Revised," *PQ* 9 (1940)1; "Psychoanalysis Comes of Age," *PQ* 7 (1938): 299; and "The Problem of Psychoanalytic Technique," *PQ* 4 (1935): 588.

7. Nathan G. Hale, *The Rise and Crisis of Psychoanalysis in the United States: Freud and the Americans, 1917–1985* (New York: Oxford University Press, 1995); Kirsner, *Unfree Associations*.

8. Heinz Kohut, "Remarks on the Curriculum of the Chicago Institute for Psychoanalysis," April 1960. This draft of what was clearly a talk has no indication of its purpose. Compare Kohut's published discussion of curriculum issues, including a comparison of the differences in the approach of the Chicago and New York institutes, "The Psychoanalytic Curriculum," *Search* 1: 319–336. "highly 'cathected' ": Kohut's comments as recorded in the minutes of the curriculum committee of the Institute, January 13, 1976.

9. Notes of Peter Barglow from the course in 1965, as typed up in 1968, eighty-one

pages. Compare the notes of Philip D. Seitz from 1958–1960, which he has recently published with annotation and commentary as Philip D. Rubovitz-Seitz, *Kohut's Freudian Vision* (Hillsdale, NJ: Analytic Press, 1999). There is a story that Kohut reviewed the Barglow notes and found them inadequate, preferring the Seitz version. Conversation with Allen Siegel, June 21, 1997. Siegel discusses this course in some detail in his *Heinz Kohut and the Psychology of the Self* (London: Routledge, 1996).

10. See his 1949 "Lecture on the Death Instinct," written out on twenty-four 3 × 5 slips of paper. Another example is more personal. At the first self psychology conference in 1978 I was on a panel with Kohut on the applications of self psychology to the "Sciences of Man." At the panel, he was very good and spoke completely off the cuff, without a note in front of him. Later, when I began to work with him on what became *Self Psychology and the Humanities*, I found among the papers he gave me to edit an eighty-page triple-spaced manuscript of what he planned to say on that panel.

11. EW 3.

12. Paul Tolpin to Anders Richter, November 28, 1979. For some evaluations, see Institute for Psychoanalysis Teaching Evaluation, which has no date, and two letters, one from Janice Norton, May 31, 1961, and one from Ana Marquinez-Castellanos, April 9, 1979.

13. See the transcript of Gedo's after-dinner address at the symposium honoring Kohut's sixtieth birthday, June 3, 1973; cp. Gedo, *Spleen and Nostalgia*, 26. Marian Tolpin, in an interview on December 28, 1997, vehemently disagreed that Kohut required candidates to take notes. She says that many did but only because the lectures were so brilliant.

14. Morris I. Stein to James W. Anderson, July 3, 1997. Quoted with permission of Stein (in conversation January 19, 1998), though Anderson provided me with the letter August 20, 1997, in which Stein wrote up his experience. Stein elaborated on many additional details to this story in a letter to me February 4, 1998. As Stein told me, there is some question in Anderson's mind whether Freud actually said what Kohut attributes to him.

15. *Humanities*, 237. The reference to his mother as "crazy" is on tape in the original interview that I conducted, but Mrs. Kohut insisted it be taken out for publication. The tape is available in the Kohut Archives. "far and wide": Kohut to Kurt and Ruth Eissler, June 22, 1962, *Curve*, 76.

16. Kohut to Kurt Eissler, October 22, 1963, *Curve*, 84–87.

17. Kohut to Rudolph M. Loewenstein, January 24, 1963.

18. Kohut to Victor Rosen, November 7, 1965, *Curve*, 128–130. Within the year, Rosen in fact married the woman and then, in the swirl of the ensuing controversy, resigned his post as president of the American. Later, in 1973, Rosen seems to have committed suicide, though there is some question about the cause of his death, and if it was a suicide whether it had anything to do with the controversy surrounding his marriage. See Geoffrey Cocks's illuminating footnote, *Curve*, 129 n. 1.

19. On Goldwater, besides TAK, note Kohut's letter to *Christian Century* 81 (1964):1306–1307. During the presidential campaign of 1964 a poll was taken of psychiatrists on the psychological "unfitness" of Barry Goldwater; see Warren Boroson, "What Psychiatrists Say About Goldwater," *Fact* 1, no. 5 (September–October 1964): 24–27. The poll was also condemned by the American Psychiatric Association and the American Medical Association. See *New York Times*, May 5, 1966, and Geoffrey Cocks, *Curve*, 139 n. 1. For the statement, see Heinz Kohut, A. Russell Anderson, and Burness E. Moore, "A Statement on the Use of Psychiatric Opinions in the Political Realm by the American Psychoanalytic Association," October 5, 1964, *JAPA* 13 (1965): 450–451.

20. Anna Freud to Kohut, June 8, 1964, and Kohut to Anna Freud, May 21, 1964. See SQ on the handshaking.

21. Kohut to Anna Freud, August 4, 1964, *Curve*, 98–103; cp. JM.

22. The fund-raising was initiated by Kurt Eissler. Their letters, all in 1965, were May 6 from Eissler to Kohut; May 11 from Kohut to Eissler; May 13 from Eissler to Kohut; May 16 from Eissler to Kohut; May 20 from Eissler to Kohut; May 25 from Kohut to Eissler; June 5 from Kohut to Eissler; and June 23 from Eissler to Kohut. Kohut also worked later that year to raise some money at the meetings of the International Psycho-Analytic Association in Amsterdam; see Kohut to Eissler, September 25, 1965. Kohut also sent out a series of letters in the summer; see Kohut to Saul K. Pollack, Othilda Drug, Alex Kaplan, and Gaston E. Bloom, all on August 11, 1965.

23. See, for example, Kohut to Eissler, October 12, 1952, and December 8, 1955, though by March 28, 1956, it was "Dear Kurt." *Curve*, 64–66.

24. Kohut to Kurt Eissler, July 7, 1961, and January 4, 1963; "she to him": once, curiously, he asked her to return to him the copy of a letter (March 17, 1961) and, later, on May 10, 1963, he returned to her a Freud medal that she sent as a gift because he already had one.

25. Kohut to Kurt Eissler, January 21, 1970, July 1, 1970, and November 19, 1970.

26. Ruth Eissler to Kohut, February 1, 1961, and Kurt Eissler to Kohut, September 23, 1966.

27. Ruth Eissler to Heinz and Elizabeth Kohut, December 29, 1966.

28. JM. See also Kohut to Aichhorn, December 28, 1948, which describes his work with Kramer. Kohut told Marian Tolpin of Kramer's significance in the 1970s; from the discussion that followed my presentation to the Self Psychology Workshop at the Chicago Institute for Psychoanalysis, June 21, 1997; "arrogant and peculiar": JB; "old friends": CK; "they were published": Kohut to Hartmann, May 27, 1964, May 20, 1965, and October 16, 1969. Cp. Kohut letters on March 13, 1964, and May 16, 1966, *Curve*, 96 and 141; "in the 1950s": see, for example, Heinz Hartmann to Kohut, March 19, 1952.

29. Kohut to Charles Brenner, May 10, 1962. The original notes are in the archives.

30. Kohut to Martin Stein, May 10, 1965; "colleagues were thinking": TAK.

31. Quotes in order: Kohut to Burness E. Moore, June 14, 1973; to Siegmund Levarie, June 15, 1964; to Magistra Stefi Pedersen, April 11, 1972. Virtually every

colleague he worked with later repeated this last line to me in some context, and I heard it myself once.

13 ON EMPATHY

1. Sigmund Freud, "Group Psychology and the Analysis of the Ego," *SE* 18: 110 n. 2 and 110.

2. Michael Franz Basch, "Further Thoughts on Empathic Understanding," *Progress in Self Psychology*, vol. 6: *The Realities of Transference*, ed. Arnold Goldberg (Hillsdale, NJ: Analytic Press, 1991), 3–4.

3. In the beginning of psychoanalysis, Freud says, he and Breuer had relied on "abreaction" and hypnosis to heal, approaches that gave way in time to a reliance on free association to uncover unconscious material. Now (he says in 1914 in what was his most complete statement on the subject) the analyst "employs the art of interpretation mainly for the purpose of recognizing the resistances which appear . . ., making them conscious to the patient." Sigmund Freud, "Remembering, Repeating, and Working-Through," *SE* 12: 147. Compare his more pessimistic thoughts about therapeutic efficacy, "Analysis Terminable and Interminable," *SE* 23: 211–253.

4. Sándor Ferenczi, *The Clinical Diaries of Sándor Ferenczi*, ed. Judith Dupont, tr. Michael Balint and Nicola Zarday Jackson (Cambridge, MA: Harvard University Press, 1985). See also *Ferenczi's Turn in Psychoanalysis*, ed. Peter L. Rudnytsky, Antal Bokay, and Patrizia Giampieri-Deutsch (New York: New York University Press, 1996); Arnold William Rachman, *Sándor Ferenczi: The Psychotherapist of Tenderness and Passion* (Northvale, NJ: Jason Aronson, 1997); and Rachman, "Death by Silence (*Todschweigen*): The Traditional Method of Silencing the Dissident in Psychoanalysis," *The Death of Psychoanalysis: Murder? Suicide? Or Rumor Greatly Exaggerated?*, ed. Robert M. Prince (Northvale, NJ: Jason Aronson, 1999), 153–164.

5. The phrase is that of Esther Menaker in my interview with her, February 9, 1996. She was a candidate at the institute in Vienna when Ferenczi died. Ferenczi's most famous paper and the one that apparently got him into trouble with Freud is "The Confusion of Tongues." Note, however, Peter Gay's argument that Freud's principal objection was to Ferenczi's clinical practice and not his final paper, *Freud*, 585–586. On Freud chastising Ferenczi, see Gay, *Freud*, 578–579.

6. Arnold Goldberg, personal communication, April 3, 1996.

7. The recent rediscovery of Ferenczi and understanding of his great significance in the early history of psychoanalysis are therefore results of the work of Kohut. Until the paradigm shifted, Ferenczi inevitably was left on the margins. Intellectual history often moves in contradictory ways that defy chronology. See Howard A. Bacal, "British Object-Relations Theorists and Self Psychology: Some Critical Reflections," *IJP* 68 (1987): 81–98.

8. Kurt Eissler to Kohut, October 6, 1966, with a copy of his manuscript on psychic

energy attached; Kohut's reply, September 28, 1966; "his own terms": Erik Erikson, Ch. 2, "The Theory of Infantile Sexuality," *Childhood and Society* (New York: Norton, 1950), 48–108.

9. For others as well. It is fair to say Kohut opened the floodgates to a large and mostly derivative literature. Some recent work (in chronological order): Dan H. Buie, "Empathy: Its Nature and Limitations," *JAPA* 29 (1981): 281–307; Michael Franz Basch, "Empathic Understanding: A Review of the Concept and Some Theoretical Considerations," *JAPA* 31 (1983): 101–127; two volumes, *Empathy I* and *Empathy II*, ed. Joseph Lichtenberg, Melvin Bornstein, and Donald Silver (Hillsdale, NJ: Analytic Press, 1984); Steven T. Levy, "Empathy and Psychoanalytic Technique," *JAPA* 33 (1985): 353–379; Alfred Margolis, "Toward Empathy: The Uses of Wonder," *AJP* 141 (1984): 1025–1035; David M. Berger, "On the Way to Empathic Understanding," *AJPT* 38 (1984): 111–121; Howard E. Book, "Empathy: Misconceptions and Misuses in Psychotherapy," *AJP* 145 (1988): 420–425; Leslie Brothers, "A Biological Perspective on Empathy," *AJP* 146 (1989): 10–19; Ivan J. Miller, "The Therapeutic Empathic Communication (TEC) Process," *AJPT* 43 (1989): 531–545; a special "Symposium on Empathy" in *Psychoanalytic Dialogues* 4 (1994); and Stefano Bolognini, "Empathy and 'Empathism,' " *IJP* 78 (1997): 279–292.

10. On Gitelson, see John Gedo, *Spleen and Nostalgia*, 91. Kohut later asked to read these comments; see Kohut to John Frosch, November 22, 1959, *Curve*, 71–72. The empathy paper itself appeared in *JAPA* 7 (1959): 459–483, and is reprinted in *Search* 1: 205–232. "future of psychoanalysis": Louis Shapiro (LS), who was there, talked with Alexander; "Paris in 1957": Kohut to John Frosch, November 22, 1959, *Curve*, 71–72; "probably in Carmel": SQ.

11. *Search* 1: 205–206.

12. Ibid., 208–209.

13. Ibid., 212–214.

14. Ibid., 214–217.

15. Kohut to August Aichhorn, March 7, 1947, *Curve*, 56.

16. *Search* 1: 223–224.

17. Ibid., 228.

18. Ibid., 231–232.

19. See, for example, "Childhood Experience and Creative Imagination: Contribution to Panel on The Psychology of Imagination" (1959), *JAPA* 8 (1960): 159–166, *Search* 1: 271–274. Kohut told Bernard Brandchaft (BB), who asked him when he first felt frustrated with classical psychoanalysis: "Bernie, I think I always knew it right from the beginning. But I didn't have the courage to believe what I knew." And in another conversation: It's "all there [in the early papers]," he said, just not formulated "as clearly and not as courageously."

20. Kohut, "Observations on the Psychological Functions of Music," *JAPA* 5 (1957): 389–407, *Search* 1: 233–253.

21. Kohut was concerned in these years with "applied analysis," or what Freud had called "angewandte Psychoanalyse." His most extended essay was "Beyond the

Bounds of the Basic Rule: Some Recent Contributions to Applied Psychoanaly-sis," *Search* 1: 275–304. See also Kohut to Leo Nedelsky, January 23, 1963, *Curve*, 80, and Kohut to Robert H. Koff, January 21, 1965, *Search* 2: 861–862. His inter-est in Goethe was expressed mostly in dialogue with Kurt Eissler. See Kohut to Eissler, March 28, 1956, and Eissler's reply, April 2, 1956, as well as Kohut's later letters October 22, 1963, *Curve*, 84–86, and November 7, 1963, *Curve*, 87–88.

22. Peggy McCormick read widely in history and was fascinated with the whole story of Hitler and prewar Germany. She tried several times to get Kohut, who knew of these things firsthand, to talk with her about his experiences. After being com-pletely rebuffed several times, she got the message that he would say nothing on the subject. JM.

23. Kohut to Dr. and Mrs. Alexander Mitscherlich, August 18, 1964, *Curve*, 103–104. See Alexander and Margarete Mitscherlich, *The Inability to Mourn (Der Kampf um die Erinnerung)* (New York: Grove Press, 1975); and his book, *Society With-out the Father (Auf dem Weg zur vaterlosen Gesellschaft)* (New York: Harcourt, Brace & World, 1969).

24. *Search* 1: 307; compare the *Bulletin of the Philadelphia Association of Psychoanalysis* 10 (1960): 156; and Kohut to Martin Wangh, November 20, 1962, *Curve*, 77.

14 NEW FORMS

1. Kohut to Siegmund Levarie, June 6, 1965, *Curve*, 122.

2. SQ.

3. AG 2. Terman's story is from an interview on May 18, 1983. Kohut's last two-year sequence was 1961–1963, after which he stopped for two years while he was president of the American; see *Lectures*, 126–127.

4. Heinz Kohut, "Forms and Transformations of Narcissism," *JAPA* 14 (1966): 243–272; *Search* 1: 427–430. Kohut was somewhat overeager about getting the paper published as soon after it was delivered as possible. In January 1965 Kohut called John Frosch, the editor of the *Journal*, to pressure him to get the paper out soon. Frosch wrote back on January 23, 1966, explaining that he had sensed some edgi-ness in Kohut's voice and wanted to assure him he would do what he could. Frosch also said he had published in the *Bulletin* both of Kohut's talks to the business meetings when he was president, which was unusual. If anything, he could be accused of "over-Kohuting" the journal. Kohut replied on February 7 (*Curve*, 138–139) in an effort to defuse things but again stressed strongly that he hoped the paper would come out soon.

5. Kohut to Alexander Mitscherlich, February 22, 1965, *Curve*, 111.

6. Freud's "On Transience" (1915) is in *SE* 14, esp. 305 and 306, and his "On Hu-mor" (1928) is in *SE* 21. Kohut had first written on transience in his eulogy to Maxwell Gitelson, February 14, 1965. He sent a copy to Anna Freud. What Kohut said in his eulogy was that "Freud once pondered why it should be that the *pass-ing* of the people and of the things which we love should be taken by us as an

imperfection; it seemed incomprehensible to him that the transience of people, of things, and of values should somehow diminish our joy in them. On the contrary, he said, if we are brave enough to face the limits which are inexorably imposed on us [that] should heighten our enjoyment and should increase our love even as it attaches itself slowly and painfully to the *memory* of what we have lost."

7. Kohut to Anna Freud, March 2, 1965, *Curve*, 113.

8. "Although in certain areas I arrived at conclusions that go beyond the outlines indicated by Freud, the general pattern of my own thought has also been determined by them." *Search* 1: 429.

9. *Search* 1: 427. Note Hartmann, "Contributions to the Metapsychology of Schizophrenia" and "The Development of the Ego Concept in Freud's Work," *Essays on Ego Psychology* (New York: International Universities Press, 1962), 192, 287–288.

10. Charles Kligerman, "Eulogy." Kligerman says early in his career Kohut tried to buy into the party line.

11. Cp. Kohut's discussion of this in *Seminars*, 9.

12. Kohut called the two forms the "idealized parent imago" and the "narcissistic self," a term he later came to consider tautological and therefore changed to the "grandiose self."

13. Kohut relates his ideas about the narcissistic self to Freud, "Instincts and Their Vicissitudes" (1915), *SE* 14:109–140, esp. 136, on the "purified pleasure ego," in which everything pleasant is regarded as inside and all bad outside it. *Search* 1: 430. Kohut connects his ideas about the idealized parent imago to loss and internalization and with what Freud thought about superego formation. Kohut emphasizes that the ego ideal "corresponds" developmentally to the idealized parent imago, that is, becomes its carrier. The idealized parent was originally experienced as perfect and omnipotent. The values and standards of the superego in turn become absolute. In that sense the original narcissism "passes through" the cherished object before it is reinternalized. *Search* 1: 434. Kohut returns to this idea in greater detail in *Analysis*, Ch. 2, 37–56.

14. Kohut's argument with Erikson over identity was deep and abiding. He felt the term was confusing, more appropriately a part of sociology, superficial, and based on "extrospective" observations. See *Search* 1: 443, n. 11. Cp. Kohut to Henry D. von Witzleben, January 11, 1969, *Curve*, 222; *Analysis*, xiii–xiv; and *Seminars*, 6, 65, and 222–224.

15. Kohut, "Creativeness, Charisma, Group Psychology," *Search* 2: 801 and 801, n. 5.

16. *Search* 1: 444.

17. Anna Freud, *Normality and Pathology in Childhood*, in *The Writings of Anna Freud*, 8 vols. (New York: International Universities Press, 1966–1980), vol. 6, introduced the concept of "lines" of development, a term she seems to have taken from her father in *Inhibitions, Symptoms, and Anxiety*, *SE* 20: 107 and 151; see Young-Bruehl, *Anna Freud*, 487–488, n. 28.

18. Kohut's attempt to force his ideas into the conceptual schema of Anna Freud led at times to exceedingly complex—and contradictory—formulations, as in *Seminars*, 78. At other times, he was comfortable thinking about narcissism as a "line

of development," as in "Narcissism as Resistance and Driving Force in Psychoanalysis," *Search* 1: 556.

19. Kohut to Fritz Morgenthaler, March 7, 1969, *Curve*, 232–234, esp. 234.

20. *Search* 1: 451, n. 16.

21. Ibid., 454–455. Cp. Kohut's touching letter to Dr. Myriam G. dos Santos, February 15, 1968, *Curve*, 190–191.

22. Kohut here quotes Freud, "Humour" (1927), *SE* 21: 161, who begins his paper
on humor by linking it to the human capacity to overcome fear of death. In Freud's
case he tells the joke of the criminal who is led out to the gallows on Monday
and remarks, "Well, the week's beginning nicely." Cp. Charles B. Strozier, "The
Soul of Wit: Kohut and the Psychology of Humor," *Psychohistory Review* 16(1987):
47–68.

23. *Search* 1: 458.

15 THE DEATH OF ELSE

1. Else came to believe that one of her best friends, a man who lived in her building, was stealing from her. She wanted Kohut to help her get a lawyer; TAK. A
letter from Kohut to James M. Goldinger, October 3, 1970, suggests that sometime that spring or summer she had been committed to the Monticello Nursing
Home. The records of her stay there are, unfortunately, no longer available. From
TAK it is clear that for an extended period before her commitment her paranoia
was becoming apparent to the family.

2. TAK.

3. It may be that Kohut also got free of some of these personal struggles through a
systematic experience of self-analysis. The evidence for such a "self-analysis,"
however, is highly tangential, even slippery. One might conclude from "Mr. Z"
that sometime in the 1960s he went through just such an extended period of self-
analysis, which undid the stupefying work of Ruth Eissler some twenty years
earlier. The self-analysis in this interpretation of the case would be Z's second
analysis. Geoffrey Cocks takes for granted that Kohut conducted just such an
analysis and then describes its consequences for Kohut as a fait accompli, see
Geoffrey Cocks, "Introduction," *Curve*, 20, and the more extended argument in
his unpublished "From K to Z: European Roots of Heinz Kohut's Psychology,"
Southern California Psychoanalytic Society, Los Angeles, March 18, 1995. Somewhat more caution, however, is in order. Kohut never talked to a single person (as
far as I can tell from quite extensive interviewing) about having conducted a self-
analysis in the 1960s. His widow did not mention it when I interviewed her twice
in the 1980s (though I also did not ask her about it directly), and Kohut's son,
Thomas, whom I did ask directly, was equally unaware of a specific period of self-
analysis that his father conducted in the 1960s. The most that Thomas Kohut or
people such as Paul Ornstein and Arnold Goldberg could note or recall is that
Kohut, like most analysts, frequently engaged in periods of self-analytic scrutiny;

TAK, PO, and AG 3. Was that introspective stance formalized and focused at a certain moment in time for Kohut in the mid-1960s? It seems unlikely. Hardly a modest man, Kohut would probably have talked about such an experience in terms of the parallel with Freud's own self-analysis in the 1890s. That would have been in character. Besides, Kohut was hardly shy about drawing other parallels between himself and Freud. He told Anna Freud that like her father he was an "incorrigible optimist" because he also was the first-born son of a young mother; Kohut to Anna Freud, April 6, 1969, *Curve*, 235 (Kohut returned to this story in Freud's life in *Seminars*, 64, where he stressed that the belief that one is a conqueror often leads to success). The "second analysis" of Z would therefore seem to be merely part of the disguise in constructing the case.

4. *Search* 4: 417.
5. Ibid., 430–432.
6. Kohut to James M. Goldinger, October 3, 1970; "angry afterward": personal communication, David Marcus, June 20, 1998; "dream last night": personal communication, Paul Tolpin, June 20, 1998; "put on him": TAK.
7. Personal communication, Jerome Beigler, June 21, 1997; on the call, personal communication, Jorge Schneider, June 22, 1998; on the brothers, TAK; and on the conversion, TAK and SL 1. Else left stocks valued at $22,040 and personal property of approximately $2,000. See Alex Elson of Elson, Lassers and Wolf, to Kohut, November 1, 1972, regarding the transfer of Else's stock.

16 FAMILY AND OTHER STRUGGLES

1. ME.
2. Kohut to Robert G. Page, June 18, 1968, *Curve*, 201–203. The point of the letter was Kohut's long complaint about not being allowed to play billiards with Tom. The club had imposed a new rule that no one under eighteen could enter the billiards room. "at the Met": Kohut to Metropolitan Opera, August 3, 1968, *Curve*, 211–212; Kohut to Anna Freud, January 4, 1969, *Curve*, 221. "fulfilling experiences": *Search* 4: 444.
3. Kohut to Thomas A. Kohut, July 4, 1963, *Curve*, 83–84.
4. JM.
5. Kohut to Thomas A. Kohut, November 17, 1968, *Curve*, 216–217. On Woodstock, see TAK.
6. Kohut to Everett M. Dirksen, June 18, 1968, *Curve*, 199–200.
7. Quoted by Geoffrey Cocks in *Curve*, 217–218 n. 1. These two items—as is true of many of the more personal letters in the collection of Thomas A. Kohut—do not have copies in the Kohut Archives in Chicago; see Appendix.
8. Kohut to Thomas A. Kohut, April 10, 1969, *Curve*, 236–237.
9. Kohut to Alexander Mitscherlich, May 11, 1970, *Curve*, 245–246.
10. SL3; "perhaps almost daily": Thomas Kohut (TAK) stressed how important Wadsworth remained for Kohut as far back as he could remember. See also GM.

Levarie made the same point in many conversations and interviews, though he was, of course, removed from the scene after 1953.

11. JG 1. "des Geistes": Kohut to Mitscherlich, May 18, 1970. What Kohut really felt about Hartmann's ideas is revealed in "Introspection and Empathy," *Search* 3: 97 n. 3, which argues that Hartmann's idea of adaptation is as superficial as Erikson's of identity. Kohut drafted this paper in 1968 but never published it. It is only due to Paul Ornstein's editorial efforts that it is available. "sending flowers": Kohut to Hartmann, October 16, 1969. "gave his approval": the quote is from Kohut's concluding comments at the first self psychology conference in 1978, published as "Reflections on Advances in Self Psychology," *Search* 4: 285. Ornstein (PO) says Kohut told him Hartmann returned an edited copy of the manuscript. Both Ornstein and I have looked for the copy that Hartmann read but it does not appear to have survived. "Hartmann deepened": Kohut to Hartmann, December 17, 1963; May 27, 1964; May 20, 1965; May 16, 1966 (*Curve*, 141); and October 16, 1969.

12. Anna Freud to Kohut, January 4, 1966, *Curve*, 133; Kohut to Anna Freud, December 28, 1965; regarding the honorary degree, Kohut had worked with Eissler on her seventieth birthday celebration and he did, of course, have access to the corridors of power in the university.

13. Kohut, "Notes Concerning Anna Freud in Chicago: December, 1966," draft in Kohut Archives. "of the planning": Kohut to Anna Freud, October 28, 1966, *Curve*, 151–152; Kohut to Anna Freud, December 2, 1966, *Curve*, 155–156; and Kohut to Anna Freud, December 6, 1966, *Curve*, 156. "was no problem": Anna Freud to Kohut, August 27, 1966; Kohut to Anna Freud, September 6, 1966. "obligations she had agreed to": the letter appears to be lost. She may have sent a telegram, or even phoned. "university that fall": the letter appears to be lost. He may also have sent a telegram or phoned.

14. Ernest Wolf in Siegel, *Heinz Kohut and the Psychology of the Self*, 6; "Jewish in me": "Notes Concerning Anna Freud in Chicago: December, 1966."

15. Tovey to Coco, July 5, 1967, *Curve*, 169–170; "loathsome": Anna Freud to Kohut, February 19, 1967, *Curve*, 159–160; Kohut to Freud, March 5, 1967, *Curve*, 160–162.

16. Kohut to Anna Freud, July 12, 1968, *Curve*, 206–207; see also Kohut to Freud, July 28, 1968; Anna Freud to Kohut, June 4, 1969; Kohut to Anna Freud, June 7, 1969; Kohut to Anna Freud, July 4, 1969.

17. Kohut to Kurt Eissler, May 10, 1965; Kohut to the Chairmen of the Training Committees of the Component Societies and study groups of the IPA, Chairmen of the Education Committees of the approved training institutes of the American, and representatives of the regional membership groups, October 1, 1966. "Eissler in 1964": Kohut to Kurt Eissler, July 27, 1964, *Curve*, 97–98.

18. Kohut to Anna Freud, October 11, 1966, *Curve*, 146–150.

19. Kohut to Anna Freud, July 5, 1968, *Curve*, 204–206.

20. Kohut to Anna Freud, December 3, 1968, *Curve*, 219–220; Kohut to Anna Freud, January 4, 1969, *Curve*, 220–222. "this is leading to": Anna Freud to Kohut, November 24, 1968, *Curve*, 218–219. "of the International": the actual letter seems

to have been lost, but Anna Freud begins her letter of November 24, 1968: "It is high time for me to answer your letter from Carmel." *Curve*, 218.

21. *Seminars*, 31–32. "explaining in writing": Kohut to Anna Freud, September 9, 1969, *Curve*, 240–241. A further mark of Kohut's disorientation was that he seriously considered an offer in March from Roy Menninger to be head of the Menninger Clinic. See Kohut to Roy Menninger, March 3, 1969, *Curve*, 231–232. "period of work": Kohut to Anna Freud, February 16, 1969, *Curve*, 230–231. Kohut expressed many of the same sentiments to Ruth Eissler on the same day, following her note of condolence about the election on February 14, 1969. Kohut never bore grudges in this kind of battle. Rangell was, in fact, elected president of the International. Over the years Kohut kept in touch with him and called to express his deep sympathy (and perhaps commiserate) when Rangell had bypass surgery many years later. See Leo Rangell to Kohut, May 19, 1980. "candidacy in Rome": Anna Freud to Kohut, February 10, 1969, *Curve*, 228–230; Kohut to Anna Freud, April 6, 1969, *Curve*, 235–236.

22. Personal communication, Elizabeth Kohut, May 23, 1986. "if you will": Charles Kligerman, "The Search for the Self of the Future Analyst," *Progress in Self Psychology: Dimensions of Self Experience*, ed. Arnold Goldberg (Hillsdale, NJ: Analytic Press, 1989), 5:264–265. "of a disappointment": Gedo, *Spleen and Nostalgia*, 17.

17 ON COURAGE

1. Kohut to John Gedo, September 10, 1968.

2. "Psychoanalysis in a Troubled World," *Search* 2: 511–546.

3. "Peace Prize 1969: Laudation," *Search* 2: 563–576; first published in *JAPA* 19 (1971): 806–818. John Gedo had the idea of giving Kohut a translation of his talk upon his return from Europe, and enlisted his friend, Ernest Wolf, in the project. Ernest Wolf, whose language was German, did the first draft of the talk, then Gedo "polished the phraseology." See Wolf in *Psychoanalysts Talk*, 171.

4. Kohut to Jacques M. Quen, December 3, 1974.

5. See Alexander Mitscherlich, *Auf dem Weg zur vaterlosen Gesellschaft (Society Without the Father)*, tr. Eric Mosbacher (New York: Harcourt, Brace, and World, 1969); Alexander and Margarete Mitscherlich, *The Inability to Mourn: Principles of Collective Behavior*, tr. Beverley R. Placzek (New York: Grove Press, 1975); and Alexander Mitscherlich, *Die Idee des Friedens und die menschliche Aggressivität, Vier Versuche* (Frankfurt: Suhrkamp, 1984 [1969]).

6. What Kohut really thought about Mitscherlich's work was more mundane. In a confidential report for the *Annual of Psychoanalysis* on March 6, 1972, he wrote that a paper submitted to the journal by Mitscherlich was typical of all his writings—"polemic, a bit sermonizing, with forcefully expressed opinions, broadly—but not deeply—informed, vigorous and stimulating but not profound in its reflections and often—all too often!—fuzzy in its logic and reasoning." He

recommended publication but only because of Mitscherlich's renown and contributions to the revival of psychoanalysis in Germany. He also suggested putting the essay in "an inconspicuous position in the volume," as if apologizing for its low quality. See Kohut, Confidential Report to the *Annual*, March 6, 1972.

7. Kohut seems to have made notes for the paper in the late 1960s and wrote a first draft in the early 1970s (I finished it after his death; see *Humanities*, xii); Kohut to Basch, April 17, 1974, refers to the courage paper—which he was then doing further work on—that "I read to you and the rest of the group some time ago." The "group" here is a confusing reference. It is unlikely that it was his 1969 group, for Paul Ornstein's detailed notes from those meetings show no discussion of the paper, and there was no formal reconstitution of the group until after this letter to Basch.

8. *Humanities*, 9–11, 42.

9. Ignatieff, *The Rise and Fall*, 22, and an interview with Siegmund Levarie, May 9, 1999.

10. *Humanities*, 50.

18 THE GROUP TAKES SHAPE

1. Kohut to Anna Freud, April 6, 1969, *Curve*, 236.

2. Charles B. Strozier and Daniel Offer, eds., *The Leader* (New York: Plenum, 1985), 22–39. On the rings, see Phyllis Grosskurth, *The Secret Ring: Freud's Inner Circle and the Politics of Psychoanalysis* (New York: Addison-Wesley, 1991), and cp. Paul Roazen, *Freud and His Followers* (New York: New York University Press, 1984), 176. On the group and for the Stekel quote, Peter Gay, *Freud: A Life for Our Times* (New York: Norton, 1988), 173–174.

3. TAK.

4. Kohut to Ernest Wolf, August 10, 1977, *Curve*, 351–352.

5. Kohut brought up the rings at dinner with the Wolfs on January 30, 1976, as noted in Ina Wolf's date book and in her "Chronology," prepared at my request in October 1998.

6. Personal communication from a conversation with Michael Franz Basch after a presentation I made at Rush Medical School, November 13, 1984. Note also Ernest Wolf, "Introduction," in Allen Siegel, *Heinz Kohut and the Psychology of the Self* (London: Routledge, 1996), 10–11.

7. Marian Tolpin, panel discussion on Kohut that I chaired at the annual self psychology conference in Chicago, November 15, 1997, said: "My life was touched . . . by a genius, unexpectedly, and it gave a dimension to our lives as analysts that we hadn't dreamed of."

8. Arnold Goldberg, Chicago panel, November 15, 1997, said: "[I was used by Kohut] all the time. He was clearly, clearly, unabashedly exploiting all of us, but it was so reciprocally valuable that you didn't mind it, and I guess at times you could become blind or deaf to it but he would have me do so many things that I

ordinarily would never think of doing or want to do or would rebel at doing, but it was for me. It really was. But it was for him. And I would say absolutely, one hundred percent of my relationship with him was, I guess, the only mutual exploitation, something like that. We were part of his mission. And he clearly . . . had a goal and a mission and a task and he felt it was transcendent. It was more than all of us. And I think we all felt that."

9. *Humanities*, 202. Charles Lindholm, *Charisma* (Cambridge, MA: Basil Blackwell, 1980), 64, picks up on this point as crucial for understanding the theory of charismatic leadership in general.

10. Kohut to Michael Franz Basch, April 17, 1974.

11. Such at least is the way Arnold Goldberg remembers it; interview May 12, 2000.

12. See, for example, Kohut to Gedo, August 25, 1965, *Curve*, 123–125.

13. Gedo, *Spleen and Nostalgia*, 59. Compare Kohut to Dr. A. Kagan of International Universities Press, January 28, 1969, *Curve*, 224–225.

14. Gedo, *Spleen and Nostalgia*, 61.

15. John Gedo and Arnold Goldberg, *Models of the Mind: A Psychoanalytic Theory* (Chicago: University of Chicago Press, 1973).

16. Heinz Kohut, "Recommendation" for Arnold Goldberg, presumably to the relevant committee of the Chicago Institute for Psychoanalysis, January 15, 1972.

17. Personal communication, Arnold and Constance Goldberg, January 8, 1997.

18. Kohut to Goldberg, November 3, 1972, *Curve*, 272–273.

19. On the review, AG 1. The directions to restaurants in Italy are on a sheet of paper in the possession of Ina Wolf, who shared it with me.

20. Testimony of Gail Basch, November 19, 1996, at the annual conference on the psychology of the self in Washington, D.C.; on addressing Kohut, Basch to Kohut September 4, 1973, or May 13, 1974, even though Kohut addressed Basch as "Mike," as in March 7, 1975; the breakthrough to "Heinz" for Basch occurred on May 7, 1975; AG 2 emphasized Basch's tenuous but creative position on the margin of the group; Basch was to publish three well-received books on psychotherapy that made Kohut's insights widely available: *Doing Psychotherapy* (New York: Basic Books, 1980), *Understanding Psychotherapy* (New York: Basic Books, 1988), and *Doing Brief Psychotherapy* (New York: Basic Books, 1995).

21. Basch to Kohut, May 11, 1978; Kohut to Michael Franz Basch, April 17, 1974; Basch to Kohut the same day, 1974; Basch to Kohut, August 8, 1975; Basch to Kohut, March 26, 1976; Basch to Kohut, December 8, 1976.

22. Eulogy by Michael Franz Basch at the memorial service for Kohut, October 31, 1981, copy in the Wolf collection.

23. My interview with Paul Ornstein was on May 20, 1996, and with Anna Ornstein on October 3, 1998. Both were also on the panel at the self psychology conference in Chicago, November 15, 1997. Over the years I have had a number of more informal conversations with both the Ornsteins.

24. Kohut to Stanley M. Kaplan, January 7, 1976, recommending Anna Ornstein for appointment to full professor at the University of Cincinnati Medical Center.

25. Anna Ornstein, comments at the panel, Chicago self psychology conference, November 15, 1997.

26. Ibid.

27. Comment by Paul Ornstein on a paper I gave at the New York Institute for Psychoanalytic Self Psychology, March 29, 1996.

28. PO. I heard this story at least ten times over the years, though mostly second-hand, before I asked Ornstein about it directly in my interview with him. The story has assumed apocryphal significance. Curiously, when I asked Thomas Kohut (who was the other person there with Paul Ornstein) about it he could not remember the scene. He had no doubt it occurred and that Ornstein was reporting it accurately. He just said his father did such things so frequently he had no recollection of this particular event.

29. Ernest Wolf, "Introduction," Siegel, *Heinz Kohut*, 15.

30. See, for example, Kohut to Mel Albin, July 9, 1977; EW 2; on Kohut's fondness for Wolf, see Ina Wolf's date book and "Chronology," October 1998.

31. Wolf adds, mysteriously, that there is as yet no biography, "nor is the time ripe to reopen old wounds and rekindle the barely banked fires of controversy." Ernest Wolf, "Introduction," Siegel, *Heinz Kohut*, 7.

32. EW 2 and 3.

33. Ina Wolf, "Chronology," October 1998.

34. Ernest Wolf in manuscript in his personal collection, dated October 27, 1991; see also EW 2.

35. PT and MT. Both of the Tolpins also had much to say on the Chicago self psychology panel, November 15, 1997.

36. The meetings were held April 12 and 18, May 10, 17, and 24, June 7, 21, and 28, and July 12. Paul Ornstein kept detailed notes on the meetings, a copy of which is in the archives and is the basis for the account that follows.

37. The details in this paragraph about the meetings come from a short interview with Arnold Goldberg on May 12, 2000, though I was myself in the apartment a number of times and worked with Kohut in his study. I also know the building well. My mother lived there.

38. Kohut to Anna Freud, April 6, 1969, *Curve*, 236.

39. JG 1.

19 THE ANALYSIS OF THE SELF

1. SQ.

2. "Self Psychology and the Psychoanalytic Movement: An Interview with Dr. Heinz Kohut," *Psychoanalytic and Contemporary Thought* 5(1981): 492–493.

3. PO.

4. The first quote is from Kohut to Anna Freud, April 6, 1969, *Curve*, 235–236; the second from Kohut to René Spitz, June 6, 1969. "new thoughts to be added": Kohut's notes on his holiday card to a former patient, Wilda Daley, December 1969, a copy of which she gave me on October 22, 1987.

5. The two major reviews of *Analysis* were Hans Loewald, in *PQ* 42 (1973): 441–451, and Martin James, in *IJP* 44 (1973): 363–368. Loewald puts more emphasis on its

ideas as defining a separate line of development for narcissism and is critical of Kohut for his "forced dichotomies." A few years later, C. Hanley and G. Masson, "A Critical Examination of the New Narcissism," *IJP* 57 (1976): 49–66, return to the contrast between narcissism and object relatedness but with a sharper note of criticism of Kohut. Stephen Mitchell, "Twilight of the Idols: Change and Preservation in the Writings of Heinz Kohut," *Contemporary Psychoanalysis* 15 (1979): 170–171, adds the unhelpful point that Kohut leaves unanswered the relation of his new ideas to classical theory. More recently, writers—even those close to self psychology—continue to read *Analysis* as basically concerned with narcissism and defining a separate line of development. See Leon Batter, "Observation and Theory in Psychoanalysis: The Self Psychology of Heinz Kohut," *PQ* 60 (1991): 361–389, and Lynne Layton, "A Deconstruction of Kohut's Concept of the Self," *Contemporary Psychoanalysis* 26 (1990): 420–429.

6. The ideas in this paragraph have been developed during many discussions with Robert Jay Lifton over the years. The specific idea that Freud's model imagines the self as the victim of drives is from a conversation on November 30, 1999.

7. Freud's only real attempt to think about the psychoses was in his important essay on Daniel Paul Schreber, "Psycho-Analytic Notes on an Autobiographical Account of a Case of Paranoia (Dementia Paranoides)" (1911), *SE* 12: 3–82.

8. *Analysis*, 26.

9. Note, among her other works, Melanie Klein, *Envy and Gratitude, and Other Works, 1946–1963* (London: Hogarth Press and the Institute of Psycho-Analysis, 1975); *Love, Guilt, and Reparation, and Other Works, 1921–1945* (London: Hogarth Press, 1975); and *The Psychoanalysis of Children*, tr. Alix Strachey, rev. with H. A. Thorner (New York: Delacorte Press, 1975). A biography that includes a good summary of her work is Phyllis Grosskurth, *Melanie Klein: Her Life and Work* (Cambridge, MA: Harvard University Press, 1986).

10. *Analysis*, 3.

11. Kohut to Joseph Lifschutz, June 4, 1971, *Curve*, 255.

12. *Analysis*, 16–17, 23. Compare Jonathan Lear, *Love and Its Place in Nature: A Philosophic Interpretation of Freudian Psychoanalysis* (New York: Farrar, Straus & Giroux, 1990), 37: "Archaic mental functioning knows no firm boundary between mind and body, and so archaic mind is incarnate in the body."

13. Compare *Lectures*, 243–257; "and depression": *Analysis*, 20.

14. See also Freud, "The Dynamics of Transference," *SE* 12: 97–108, and Lecture 27 of the *New Introductory Lectures, SE* 16: 431–447, esp. 443–447; "of the physician": Freud, "Fragment of an Analysis of a Case of Hysteria" (1905), *SE* 7: 116; "stalking-horse for him": Freud, *The Interpretation of Dreams* (1900), *SE* 5: 562–563.

15. *Analysis*, 25, 27, 32. Kohut actually writes of the "grandiose or exhibitionistic image of the self" (25), but the context reasonably allows one to extend that to the idea of "self images" as representing his understanding of one way of talking about the grandiose self and the idealized parent imago. His discussion of the "cohesive self" is on 32.

16. Ibid., 26–32. See esp. 28: "If the child, however, suffers severe narcissistic traumas, then the grandiose self does not merge into the relevant ego content but is retained in its unaltered form and strives for the fulfillment of its archaic aims. And if the child experiences traumatic disappointments in the admired adult, then the idealized parent imago, too, is retained in its unaltered form, is not transformed into tension-regulating psychic structure, does not attain the status of an accessible introject, but remains an archaic, transitional self-object that is required for the maintenance of narcissistic homeostasis." Kohut elaborates further at some length on the conceptual difference between transference in drive theory and his understanding of transference; see 203–220. Note 210–211 on the analogy of transference in analysis with the theater (which is borrowed without credit from Freud, *SE* 12: 154); on his ideas versus those of Melanie Klein, 212–218; Margaret Mahler, 218–220; and Michael Balint, 220.

17. *Analysis*, xiv–xv.

18. William James, *Psychology: Briefer Course* (London: Macmillan, 1892), 176. I was led to this quote by Russell Meares, *The Metaphor of Play: Disruption and Restoration in the Borderline Experience* (New York: Jason Aronson, 1993), 22. Note Erik Erikson's interesting elaboration on the "I" experience in "The Galilean Sayings and the Sense of 'I'," *Yale Review* 70 (1981): 34–56.

19. Kohut calls this process *"passage* [of the narcissistic cathexes] *through the idealized self-object* [Kohut's italics]," *Analysis*, 42; cp. 39.

20. Ibid., 46–47 and 51–52. One example Kohut provides of such needing is that of addicts, a group of patients that had always interested him; see Kohut, Discussion at the meeting of the American Psychiatric Association in 1956 of Thomas Szasz's paper, "The Role of the Counterphobic Mechanism in Addiction," *Search* 1: 201–203. Addicts, Kohut says, are usually traumatically disappointed in the mother, who failed to provide the necessary empathy for the child's needs. As a result of that early failure, the child is deprived of the experience of being optimally soothed, and is especially vulnerable around issues of sleep. The drug the addict turns to replaces the "defect in the psychological structure," which can at least temporarily create sufficient self-soothing to insure sleep and a modicum of chemically induced self-esteem. In analysis such patients often become quickly addicted to the therapeutic process itself. "The transference-like condition which establishes itself in such analyses is indeed the reinstatement of an archaic condition." The patient turns to the analyst to perform crucial functions to maintain a "narcissistic homeostasis which his own psyche is unable to perform." The profound depletion of the addict's self is best illustrated in the craving he experiences when separated from the soothing therapist, who is in turn intensely idealized.

21. *Analysis*, 47–49.

22. Ibid., 53–56.

23. Ibid., 98. This passage is actually a reference to a detail in the case of Mr. E. The use of Mr. E. seems out of place in this context, as he is the classic example of the therapeutic mobilization of the grandiose self in a mirror transference, while here Kohut uses him to illustrate something about the idealizing transference.

24. Ibid., 57–73. All quotes about Mr. A. in this and the next few paragraphs are from this section of *Analysis*.

25. Martin Bergmann and Milton E. Jucovy, eds., *Generations of the Holocaust* (New York: Basic Books, 1982).

26. Judith Kestenberg to Kohut, December 7, 1977, and Kohut to Kestenberg, December 14, 1977; my interview with Judith Kestenberg, September 30, 1990.

27. PO. Ornstein talked with Kohut at length at the time about attending the workshop and Ornstein agreed it would be a waste of Kohut's time.

28. This detail Kohut added in a seminar with Candidates at the Chicago Institute for Psychoanalysis; see *Lectures*, 9.

29. *Analysis*, 74–101, esp. 80ff. For a more detailed discussion of this case, see "A Case of Chronic Narcissistic Vulnerability," *The Psychology of the Self: A Casebook*, ed. Arnold Goldberg with the collaboration of Heinz Kohut (New York: International Universities Press, 1978), 363–437.

30. Freud, *The Ego and the Id, SE* 19: 50n.

31. Freud wrote in "Recommendations to Physicians Practising Psycho-Analysis," *SE* 12: 118: "The doctor should be opaque to his patients and, like a mirror, should show them nothing but what is shown to him." The heart of Kohut's clinical and theoretical work was to oppose the conventions of coldness that had become almost mandatory within psychoanalysis.

32. *Analysis*, 89. The question of the analyst's relation to a patient's idealization is a topic of great concern to contemporary "relational" or "postmodern" psychoanalysis. See Judith Guss Teicholz, *Kohut, Loewald, and the Postmoderns: A Comparative Study of Self and Relationship* (Hillsdale, NJ: Analytic Press, 1999), 112–113.

33. *Analysis*, 260–262.

34. Ibid., 264, 267.

35. The following discussion of Miss F. is taken from *Analysis*, 283–293.

36. Sheldon J. Meyers, "On Supervision with Heinz Kohut," *Progress in Self Psychology: Learning From Kohut*, ed. Arnold Goldberg (Hillsdale, NJ: Analytic Press, 1988). I also interviewed Meyers on April 1, 1996.

37. *SE* 14: 100–102.

38. *Analysis*, 105–108.

39. Ibid., 114–15.

40. Ibid., 115.

41. The "mirror" in this transference can be confusing, especially given the work of Jacques Lacan and his idea of the "mirror stage." Kohut's and Lacan's ideas were converging but not entirely overlapping. See Elizabeth Roudinesco, *Jacques Lacan*, tr. Barbara Bray (New York: Columbia University Press, 1997); Mikkel Borch-Jacobsen, *Lacan: The Absolute Master*, tr. Douglas Brick (Stanford: Stanford University Press, 1991); and Paul Hamburg, "Interpretation and Empathy: Reading Lacan with Kohut," *IJP* 72 (1991): 347–361. Kohut himself refers to the work of P. Elkisch, "The Psychological Significance of the Mirror," *JAPA* 5 (1957): 235–234.

42. The full case history of Mr. E. appears in *The Psychology of the Self: A Casebook*,

263–296. Except for Kohut's own case of Mr. Z, the case of Mr. E. is the most interesting and elegant in self psychology and certainly one of the best cases written up by anyone in psychoanalysis in the last half century. This discussion of Mr. E. draws on Kohut's vignettes from *Analysis*, 10, 15, 117–118, 130–132, 136, 158–159, 173, 313–315; on one of my published interviews with Kohut (March 12, 1981) in *Humanities*, 251 (the goldfish eyes and looking like his mother); and on an unpublished part of the same interview (the detail that Mr. E. had become a noted and talented photographer). Kohut makes very interesting use of this case in his long paper "Creativeness, Charisma, Group Psychology: Reflections on the Self-Analysis of Freud," *Search* 2: 793–843, esp. 800–813. Cp. *Lectures*, 45–46 and 80–83. Mr. E.'s actual analyst also provided useful details, but for reasons of confidentiality his name cannot be revealed.

43. Kohut provides two further brief case illustrations of this conceptual point with Mr. G. and Mr. O., *Analysis*, 93 and 95n.

44. *Analysis*, 126–128. On pp. 80–82 of *Analysis* Kohut uses Mr. B. as an example of a patient in an idealizing transference. In this section, on the other hand, Kohut mentions Mr. B. as a good example of someone in a mirroring transference. It seems to me there are two possible explanations for this sloppiness. One is that Kohut simply confused case material from another patient and substituted it for that of Mr. B. Kohut would not be the first psychoanalyst to get confused by his own disguises. The other, more intriguing, possibility for the double use of Mr. B. is that for all of Kohut's elaborate distinctions between the idealizing and mirroring transferences, in the end both merge in the earliest psychological experience of the self. Whatever is the case, I use vignettes from the analysis of Mr. B. in two sections of this chapter because they are so relevant for explaining Kohut's ideas.

45. Kohut confusingly calls this form of the mirroring transference "secondary," because it follows a period of stable idealization. It also happens that a mirror transference can be replaced by a stable idealizing transference, either as the "third phase in instances of secondary mirror transference or at the end of a primary mirror transference." *Analysis*, 174.

46. Ibid., 137–140.

47. Ibid., 176 ("demands for attention"), 271 ("as an independent"), 272 (gratify analyst's needs), 273 (reflects analyst's impatience).

48. Ibid., 148–150. I have made my own translation of the Horace quote.

49. Ibid., 159–160.

50. *SE* 5: 339–508.

51. *Analysis*, 168; "off the ground," 169; "bodily tensions," 243.

52. Ibid., 170–172. Kohut's full quote (172) is that "They [dreams in color] often appear to signify the intrusion of unmodified material into the ego in the guise of realism, and the ego's inability to integrate it completely. One might say that the technicolor expresses the ego's subliminally experienced anxious hypomanic excitement over certain intrusions of the grandiosity and the exhibitionism of the grandiose self." Needless to say, in using the example of Mr. A. at this point

Kohut is once again collapsing his otherwise sharp distinction between the idealizing and mirroring transferences. He covers himself in the text by talking about "narcissistic transferences" in relation to color in dreams, but the section of the book is that dealing with the mirroring transferences.

53. Ibid., 229–232.

54. Ibid., 232–234. The subtext of Kohut's point here is his disagreement with classical psychoanalytic theory, which would interpret reactions like that of Mr. B. as expressions of his unconscious guilt. As Kohut says, in narcissism it is always shame that matters, that is, "they [NPDs] react to the breakthrough of the archaic aspects of the grandiose self, especially to its unneutralized exhibitionism." See ibid., 232.

55. Anna Freud to Heinz Kohut, December 10, 1967, *Curve*, 182–184, esp. 183.

56. *Analysis*, 19, 67. One of the most relentless and most interesting criticisms of the language of ego psychology is Nathan Leites, *The New Ego: Pitfalls in Current Thinking About Patients in Psychoanalysis* (New York: Science House, 1971).

57. Freud, "Three Essays on the Theory of Sexuality," *SE* 7: 123–245.

58. *SE* 14: 246, 256–258.

59. Freud, *The Ego and the Id* (1923), *SE* 19: 3–66.

60. *SE* 21: 57–145; "charge into anxiety": *SE* 20: 75–175, esp. 109; "moral masochism": *SE* 19: 157–170, esp. 165–166.

61. Anna Freud, *The Ego and the Mechanisms of Defense*, trans. Cevil Baines, rev. ed. (London: Hogarth Press, 1968 [1936]).

62. Heinz Hartmann, *Ego Psychology and the Problem of Adaptation*, trans. David Rapaport (New York: International Universities Press, 1958 [1939]); Erik H. Erikson, *Childhood and Society* (New York: Norton, 1950).

63. Erikson, "The Theory of Infantile Sexuality," *Childhood and Society*, 48–108.

64. Erik Erikson, *Insight and Responsibility* (New York: Norton, 1964), 29.

65. Ibid. Erikson makes something of the same argument about what he calls Martin Luther's moratorium; *Young Man Luther: A Study in History and Psychoanalysis* (New York: Norton, 1958); "have it destroyed": James Strachey, Introduction to "Project for a Scientific Psychology," *SE* 1: 290; "inner consistency": Erikson, *Insight and Responsibility*, 31; "external stimuli": *SE* 1: 281–397; "of the mind": Erikson, *Insight and Responsibility*, 30.

66. Erikson, *Childhood and Society*, 64.

67. *Analysis*, xiii–xiv. The influence of some, like Sullivan, remained on the margins; see *Search* 1: 218–219, and Kohut to Arnold Goldberg, November 3, 1972, *Curve*, 273.

68. Kohut himself had some reluctance to talk about his work as representing a paradigm shift—though he certainly believed it—and left it to the group to make such claims, which he could then modestly disavow. Marian Tolpin, personal communication, August 25, 1998, clarified that the members of the group talked all the time about a paradigm shift in self psychology, but Kohut himself seldom did. Cp. *Search* 4: 514–515.

69. There is a good deal of interest in connecting Kohut with other thinkers, espe-

cially in object relations. The best recent work is Judith Guss Teicholz, *Kohut, Loewald* (1999). The standard collection of essays comparing Kohut to other thinkers is Douglas W. Detrick and Susan P. Detrick, eds., *Self Psychology: Comparisons and Contrasts* (Hillsdale, NJ: Analytic Press, 1989). Among the British in particular, Kohut got to know Michael Balint personally through his junior colleague, Paul Ornstein. They met at a conference in 1969 and had dinner together with their wives. Later they exchanged friendly letters (Michael Balint to Kohut, September 16, 1969, and Kohut to Balint, September 23, 1969), though Kohut told Ornstein he could not read *The Basic Fault* (or anything else for that matter right then) before he finished *Analysis*; PO. Kohut's great idol among English analysts was Edward Glover, whom he once described to Ornstein as his "analytic ideal"; "he learned more from Glover than from anybody else" (PO). Glover is granted an astonishing three references in the text of *Analysis* (29, 206, and 215) besides mention in the bibliography. Kohut repeated the phrase that he "learned more from Glover than from anyone else" in "Greetings," *Reflections*, 17. As Ornstein notes, it is hard to figure out why he would say such things about Glover. Note also Howard A. Bacal and Kenneth M. Newman, *Theories of Object Relations: Bridges to Self Psychology* (New York: Columbia University Press, 1990); Robert M. Galatzer-Levy and Bertram J. Cohler, *The Essential Other: A Developmental Psychology of the Self* (New York: Basic Books, 1993); Michael Robbins, "Current Controversies in Object Relations Theory as Outgrowth of a Schism Between Kohut and Fairbairn," *IJP* 62 (1980): 477–492; and Robert J. Marshall, "Hyman Spotnitz and Heinz Kohut: Contrasts and Convergences," *Modern Psychoanalysis* 23 (1998): 183–196.

70. Martin James, *IJP* 54 (1973): 363–368. James did, however, praise Kohut, who he said has done for narcissism what Dickens did for poverty in the nineteenth century. Everybody knew each existed and was a problem. All suffered pangs of conscience that more was not done to study it, and existing sources were rich for understanding it. But the "undoubted originality" of Dickens and Kohut was to put together what everybody knew "in a form which carries appeal to action."

71. Kohut to Martin James, June 18, 1973, *Curve*, 278–280; Kohut to William H. Gillespie, June 20, 1973, *Curve*, 280–284. That Kohut copied his letters to Freud is inferred from her letter to him July 2, 1973, *Curve*, 285, which begins, "Even though you told me to keep the information in your first letter to myself. . . ." Kohut may have written her a separate letter that has been lost.

72. Kohut to Joseph Sandler, June 23, 1973, *Curve*, 284–285, and Anna Freud to Kohut, July 2, 1973, *Curve*, 285.

73. PO.

74. Kohut told John Gedo, who did some early work on Ferenczi in the 1960s, of his respect for several of Ferenczi's papers, but distanced himself from Ferenczi's "flights of fancy" and "later restlessness." He also told Gedo how unfortunate it was that candidates no longer studied Ferenczi in detail. See Kohut's after-dinner speech at his sixtieth birthday celebration, June 2, 1973, tape in collection of Ernest Wolf; Kohut to John Gedo, October 26, 1966; Arnold Rachman, "Sándor

Ferenczi and the Evolution of a Self Psychology Framework in Psychoanalysis," *Progress* 13 (1997): 341–366; and John Gedo to me, March 15, 1996.

75. BB; Kohut to Samuel D. Lipton, June 5, 1964; on the baby as evil, see *Seminars*, 103–104; Kohut to Anna Freud, October 11, 1966, *Curve*, 147; Kohut to Anna Freud, October 28, 1966, *Curve*, 151–152. At a meeting of the American in Paris in 1973, for example, Kohut goes into the Kleinian perspective to disagree with it at some length. See the tape collection of Ernest Wolf.

76. TAK.

77. PO.

78. *Seminars*, 53–59, esp. 56 and 57. See Donald W. Winnicott, "Transitional Objects and Transitional Phenomena," *IJP* 34 (1953): 89–97.

79. SQ.

80. See Edwin Kahn and Arnold Rachman, "Carl Rogers and Heinz Kohut: A Historical Perspective," *Psycho. Psychology* (in press). Arnold Rachman, personal communication, pointed out to me the geographical/institutional proximity between the two men. It is a long and arduous journey, however, from the University of Chicago Department of Psychology to the Department of Psychiatry and an even longer trek across rough terrain to the downtown Institute for Psychoanalysis.

81. Mario Jacoby, *Individuation and Narcissism: The Psychology of the Self in Jung and Kohut* (New York: Routledge 1990 [1985]). Cp. Lionel Corbett and Paul K. Kugler, "The Self in Jung and Kohut," *Progress* 5 (1989): 189–208.

82. The issue of Jung's complicated relationship to the Nazi regime in Germany between 1933 and 1939 has deeply divided those who have written about him. The sharpest criticism has come from Richard Noll, *The Jung Cult* (Princeton: Princeton University Press, 1994) and *The Aryan Christ* (New York: Random House, 1997); see also the earlier work of Paul Roazen, *Freud and His Followers* (New York: Knopf, 1975). For the other side of the argument, see Jay Sherry, "Jung, the Jews, and Hitler," *Spring* (1986): 163–175; and Aniela Jaffe, "C. G. Jung and National Socialism," *From the Life and Work of C. G. Jung* (Einsiedeln, Switzerland: Daimon Verlag, 1989), 78–102. Thomas Szasz (Kohut's old friend) has also weighed in with some interesting observations: "Freud and the Freudians have deprived Jung of many of his best ideas and, to boot, have defamed him as an anti-Semite. Actually Jung was far more candid and correct than Freud in identifying psychotherapy as an ethical rather than technical enterprise; and Freud was far more anti-Christian than Jung was anti-Semitic." See *Heresies* (Garden City, NY: Anchor Press, 1976), 136. One might note, regarding Szasz's last point, that the Jews in Europe lacked hegemonic power, which makes Jung's anti-Semitism quite different politically and ethically from Freud's reserve regarding the Christian world. Jung also positioned himself to benefit from the Nazis after 1933—at the expense of his disdained Jewish colleagues.

83. For Kohut's awareness of Jung's ideas, see *Search* 3:225. For his interest in the Freud-Jung relationship, see *Search* 2: 823n, 881, and 893.

84. William James, Lecture VI of *Pragmatism's Conception of Truth* (1907), *The Works of William James*, ed. Frederick H. Burkhardt, Fredson Bowers, and Ignas K. Skrupskelis, 16 vols. (Cambridge, MA: Harvard University Press, 1975), 2: 95.

20 DEATH AND THE SELF

1. TAK. The preferred technical term is "lymphoma," but the more colloquial usage is "lymphatic cancer." Lymphoma, one of the four major types of cancer, affects the lymphatic system and can assume different forms (including Hodgkin's disease) with varying prognoses. Felix Kohut, Heinz's father, died at forty-nine years of age in 1937 of leukemia. The reference to the trip to Vienna is in Kohut to Anna Freud, August 14, 1971, *Curve*, 257. See also Heinz Kohut to John Van Prohaska, May 27, 1965, which suggests Kohut had long worried whether he was a bleeder and had something wrong with his blood.

2. John E. Ultmann to Kohut, June 6, 1977.

3. Kohut's notes to himself in his medical record, and in a letter from Dr. Donald Sweet to Kohut, July 3, 1977. Sweet was standing in for Dr. John E. Ultmann, who was away on vacation until October 4.

4. Dr. Donald Sweet to Kohut, July 23, 1977, and Kohut's notes to himself in his medical records.

5. TAK. In the interview, Thomas Kohut first said the autopsy revealed 40 percent of his body weight consisted of tumors. When I expressed surprise, he said that maybe it was 20 percent, but in any event an astonishing amount.

6. John Gedo, *Spleen and Nostalgia*, 145–146. In a personal communication September 9, 1998, Gedo emphasized that Kohut did not assert his cancer was caused by the radiation leak but "unmistakably" implied it. In the same letter, Gedo added that he was under the impression that Charles Kligerman visited him in the hospital. Paul Ornstein (PO) also visited, as did Arnold Goldberg (personal communication, March 16, 1999).

7. Susan Sontag, *Illness as Metaphor* (New York: Farrar, Straus & Giroux, 1978).

8. See Susan Sontag, *AIDS and Its Metaphors* (New York: Farrar, Straus & Giroux, 1988).

9. ME.

10. TAK.

11. Kohut to Anna Freud, June 11, 1968, *Curve*, 198. The one very important exception to Kohut's practice of reading his papers to his wife and son was his "The Two Analyses of Mr. Z," TAK.

12. Kohut to Tilmann Moser, October 23, 1973, *Curve*, 292; Kohut to Morris A. Sklansky, September 2, 1973, *Curve*, 286, for reference to the vacation; and Kohut to Michael Franz Basch, September 9, 1973, on where the Kohuts went in Europe (besides Paris, they traveled to Rome, Vienna, and Salzburg).

13. Kohut to Thomas A. Kohut, September 12, 1971, *Curve*, 259.

14. Kohut to Clemens de Boor, May 19, 1974, *Curve*, 310.

15. Kohut to Jacques Palaci, June 24, 1975.

16. TAK.

17. Robert Jay Lifton, personal communication, September 9, 1999.

18. Constance Goldberg, January 20, 1997. John Gedo (JG 1) once told me that all the wives of Kohut's male friends hated him. "Talk to the wives," Gedo advised. However, in a letter to me, September 9, 1998, Gedo said he felt that Elizabeth

did try quietly and tactfully to restrain Kohut when he became an embarrassment in social situations but that there was no way to do it without humiliating
him.

19. JG 1.

20. TAK.

21. Gedo, *Spleen and Nostalgia*, 147 (he was there). Goldberg told me pretty much
the same story in his first interview (AG 1). Gedo elaborated in a personal communication of September 9, 1998, that Thomas began the argument at dinner, which
Gedo felt was mere adolescent provocation, and Kohut responded seriously.

22. SL 2.

23. Robert W. Wadsworth to Kohut, September 4, 11, 18, and 19, 1977; April 21,
August 10 and 28, September 6, 1979; July 21, September 1 and 27, November 2,
December 3, 1980; and June 16, 1981.

24. JG 1. The phrasing in the latter part of the sentence is an elaboration in a personal communication, September 9, 1998.

25. JG 1.

26. Interview with Gail Elden, November 3, 1995.

27. AG 3.

28. *Lectures*, 158, 305.

29. Personal communication, Arnold Goldberg, June 21, 1998.

30. The term "middle knowledge" was first used in connection with people who
were actually dying. See Avery Weisman and Thomas Hackett, "Predilection
to Death: Death and Dying as a Psychiatric Problem," *Psychosomatic Medicine*
33 (1961). Needless to say, it has broader meanings. See Robert Jay Lifton, *The
Broken Connection: On Death and the Continuity of Life* (New York: Basic
Books, 1979), 17.

31. Arnold Goldberg, "Obituary," *IJP* 63 (1982): 257.

32. AG 3, EW 2, and Paul Tolpin in panel discussion, Chicago self psychology conference, November 15, 1997.

33. Personal communication, Robert J. Leider, M.D., October 19, 1996.

34. Kohut to Alexander Mitscherlich, July 6, 1974. Compare his informal comments
at a presentation on November 15, 1975, at the University of Cincinnati School
of Medicine, tape in the collection of Ernest Wolf.

35. AG 3.

36. Janet Malcolm, *Psychoanalysis: The Impossible Profession* (New York: Knopf, 1981),
119.

37. PO; Kohut wrote Warren Bennis, April 10, 1977, a warm note in which he thanks
Bennis again (who was then leaving the presidency of the University of Cincinnati) for giving him an honorary degree in 1973 and hosting various seminars in
his honor. Kohut adds: "The value of a man's life is hard to measure—but one
approach to estimating it would be by focusing on the significance of his activities." He notes that there must have been thousands of other things he did as
president that were of greater significance, but he hopes in the long run he will
look back on giving Kohut the degree and recognizing him as worthwhile and will

"contemplate it with pride as the sign of an early recognition of an important new development in modern psychology." See Kohut to Michael Franz Basch, September 14, 1973, *Curve*, 290; Kohut to Anna Freud, December 25, 1971, *Curve*, 260; and on the Harvard invitations, Gerald L. Klerman and Gerald L. Borofsky to Kohut, September 24, 1975; Miles Shore to Kohut, January 16, 1978; John Michael Murphy, Gil Noam, and Dennis Norman to Kohut, October 19, 1979.

38. Robert Kohrman to Kohut, October 23, 1972, and Kohut to Kohrman, October 25, 1972. Note EW 2 and Wolf's account of the birthday events in Hunter, *Psychoanalysts Talk*, 171–173. It is possible Wolf's idea was related to Kohut's "Laudation" in honor of Alexander Mitscherlich's sixtieth birthday in Germany, a piece Wolf and Gedo translated as a gift for Kohut when he returned. See *Search* 2: 563 for the reference to Mitscherlich's sixtieth birthday.

39. Kohut to Rudolph M. Loewenstein, March 3, 1973, *Curve*, 274.

40. Program for the "Symposium on History and Psychoanalysis," June 3, 1973. Jacques Palaci (JP 3) recalled a dinner party at the Kohut house that weekend for the distinguished guests but which not a single colleague from Chicago attended.

41. "The Future of Psychoanalysis," *Search* 2: 663–684. The highly worked-over draft of his talk is in the archives. It is clear he spent many months preparing his comments, which he then memorized and delivered extemporaneously. See also Kohut to Jeanne A. Lampl-de-Groot, June 10, 1973, *Curve*, 277, in which he explains that his delay in replying to her letter was due to his absorption in his paper for the banquet. Cp. John Gedo to me, February 28, 1999.

42. EW 3.

43. John Gedo helped clarify for me that these ideas are essentially clinical in nature in an interview I conducted with him on August 29, 1980.

44. Michael Franz Basch, comments at the memorial service for Heinz Kohut, First Unitarian Church of Chicago, October 31, 1981.

45. TAK.

46. Robert Jay Lifton, personal communication, January 14, 1997.

47. *Analysis*, 109–112. David Terman, personal communication, August 30, 1996, first alerted me to the significance of this passage. Compare *Cure*, 72, where Kohut also briefly discusses lying.

48. Personal communication, Arnold Goldberg, June 21, 1998.

49. Kohut to Levarie, August 11, 1979, *Search* 4: 631; cp. his first use of the Beethoven story, "Notes from the Training Analysts' Seminar" at the meeting of May 29, 1956, and another time, Kohut to Paula Heimann, July 7, 1967. Carla DeFraine, "Motivation and Belief in Personal Lying," Ph.D. dissertation, Vanderbilt University, 1997, uses Kohut's self theory to study lying, though ironically without consideration of the man himself. The paying of taxes is from TAK.

50. In Kohut's medical file, which he put together himself, the stapled papers on which he recorded his weight every day for three complete years, from 1977 to 1979, have survived.

51. Kohut to the manager of the North Underground Garage, April 10, 1977, and to Louis V. Surico, assistant director for "Auto Parking" in the Parks Department,

April 20, 1977, with a copy to the manager, when the problem was solved; Kohut to Kate Rosenthal, December 26, 1976, *Curve*, 331, regarding the radiator.

52. Meeting of the group, February 22, 1975—typescript in Wolf collection.

53. Kohut to Jeanne Lampl-de-Groot, June 10, 1973, *Curve*, 277.

54. JP 1. Kohut himself told me basically the same thing once in conversation during our collaboration on *Humanities*; both Arnold Goldberg and Marian Tolpin refer to Kohut's not reading after 1971 in the panel after the self psychology conference in Chicago, November 15, 1997; and Kohut told Susan Quinn (SQ) the same thing.

55. Kohut's list of his favorite recordings, which he typed up and on which he made some corrections by hand (crossing out Mendelsohn's Piano Trios Nos. 1 and 2, for example) is attached to the letter of thanks he received from an International Repertory editor, George Dadisman, January 20, 1978.

56. EW 2. Note also SQ and Kohut to Susan Donnelly, February 2, 1981.

57. Kohut, "Reflections on Advances in Self Psychology," *Search* 4, 300–309 (originally comments at the end of the first self psychology conference in October 1978).

58. L. Bryce Boyer, for example, complained about Kohut's supposed plagiarism of ideas from Peter Giovacchini and himself in a letter that was passed on to me by Avner Falk on December 26, 1990. When I interviewed Boyer myself on July 16, 1996, however, he backed off considerably from his charges and talked only vaguely (and wrongly) of his "impression" that much in *The Analysis of the Self* had been plagiarized from his book with Giovacchini, *Psychoanalytic Treatment of Characterological and Schizophrenic Disorders* (New York: Jason Aronson, 1967), which uses the term "self-object" and is not in the bibliography of Kohut's book, though there is a mention of a much earlier article of Boyer's, "On Maternal Overstimulation and Ego Defects, *Psychoanalytic Study of the Child* 11 (1956): 236–256.

Closer to home, Robert Stolorow, in an interview with me, October 21, 1995, spoke grandly of how Kohut "came to agree with us [himself and Bernard Brandchaft]" on the idea that if you establish empathic contact with a borderline patient he or she stops looking like a borderline and becomes more normal, more narcissistic. This was an important idea of Kohut's that he had talked about for several years, the first documented instance being in 1974 (within certain limits, he said to candidates at the Institute in a seminar, "psychosis is in the mind of the beholder," and if you establish empathy with someone who is psychotic, he is no longer psychotic; see *Lectures*, 148; cp., however, his somewhat contradictory statement, 36). Kohut elaborated the same idea to Stolorow in a letter on February 16, 1981, *Curve*, 424: "Insofar, in other words, as the therapist is able to build an empathic bridge to the patient, the patient has in a way ceased to be a borderline case (a crypto-psychotic) or a psychotic and has become a case of (severe) narcissistic personality disorders." The next month (March 4) Stolorow wrote Kohut asking for permission to quote the sentence in an article he was writing with Brandchaft. Kohut gave him permission on March 9. The article appeared three years later: Bernard Brandchaft and Robert D. Stolorow, "The Borderline Concept: Pathological Character or Iatrogenic Myth?" *Empathy II*, ed. Joseph Lichtenberg, Melvin Bornstein, and Donald Silver (Hillsdale, NJ: Analytic Press, 1984), 333–366, which fully recognizes Kohut's work as early as 1972 leading up to the crucial idea (see 342 and 343; the Kohut quote is on 344). There is no question, in other words, that at the time Stolorow had the sequence of discovery correct (and he and Brandchaft even affectionately dedicate their article to the memory of Kohut). It would seem that it has become something different in memory. Note also in this regard Stolorow's surprising claims for himself in "Subjectivity and Self Psychology: A Personal Odyssey," *Progress in Self Psychology: New Therapeutic Visions*, vol. 8, ed. Arnold Goldberg (Hillsdale, NJ: Analytic Press, 1992).

59. John Gedo to me, June 28 and September 18, 1996. Gedo claims two of Kohut's contemporary letters support his claims, but I read them differently. I think they suggest the generosity of Kohut toward the work of him and Arnold Goldberg. On September 19, 1968, Kohut wrote a long letter to Gedo and Goldberg, praising and trying to provide a helpful critique of their manuscript-in-progress. On January 20, 1969, Kohut again wrote the two, reasonably asking after reflection for more recognition of his precedence for the ideas of the self they discuss. Goldberg has no doubt Kohut's request was entirely fair (see Goldberg to me, November 4, 1998), which is also how I read Kohut's letter. Gedo strenuously disagrees.

60. John Gedo to me, July 6, 1966. Gedo felt he had suggested the title to Kohut on a trip they took together to a meeting in Princeton. In the acknowledgments to *The Analysis of the Self*, Kohut thanks Charles Kligerman for helping him "decisively in formulating the title of this book."

61. The substance of my comments on Terman are from an interview on August 30, 1996. Other notes are to specific aspects of his experiences with Kohut.

62. David Terman to Kohut, January 30, 1974.

63. In the academic year 1976–1977, which was my first year as a candidate at the Institute, I was a student in the year-long psychoanalytic theory course that Terman co-taught and for which he led the weekly discussion group.

64. John Gedo, personal communication, August 29, 1996.

65. Ernest S. Wolf, John E. Gedo, and David M. Terman, "On the Adolescent Process as a Transformation of the Self," presented at a meeting of the Chicago Psychoanalytic Society, May 1972. The presentation of this paper stimulated Kohut to make some interesting comments on his own adolescence, *Search* 2: 659–662.

66. Kohut to David Terman, February 19, 1975. On February 25 Kohut wrote Terman again, asking for permission for Paul Ornstein to include an edited version of the letter in his papers; see *Search* 2:896–899. Ornstein presents Kohut's letters in these volumes without the name of the recipient, so the fact that Kohut was writing Terman is obscured rather than clarified by the publication. Furthermore, the point of publishing the letter at all seems mostly to have been political, that is,

Kohut sought to prove to the traditionalists—and perhaps to himself—that he firmly believed in the Oedipus complex.

67. It was customary at the time for the *Bulletin* of the Philadelphia Psychoanalytic Society to report the discussions in the Chicago Psychoanalytic Society, but the library of the Philadelphia Society has since lost these early records, and the Chicago Institute library seems never to have owned a copy.

68. John Gedo, who remembers the meeting, says Kohut was there and "stabbed him [Terman] in the back." John Gedo to me, September 18, 1998.

69. David Terman, personal communication, August 3, 1996.

70. Terman's read of the politics of the movement is that Basch seemed to identify with Kohut's rejection of Terman and spent several years as the point man in blackballing Terman from being let into the group until relatively late in the 1970s. Terman was only then admitted because Arnold Goldberg insisted. Personal communication, August 3, 1996.

71. "Varieties of Oedipal Distortions in Severe Character Pathologies," reported by William S. Robbins, *JAPA* 25 (1977): 201–218, esp. 202–205.

72. David Terman, "The Self and the Oedipus Complex," *Chicago Annual of Psychoanalysis* 13/14 (1984/1985):87–104.

73. *Restoration*, 9, 114, and esp. 220–248; *Cure*, 10, 22, 71, 91, 97, 213 n. 2, 214 nn. 13 and 15, 219 n. 8.

74. David Terman to me, August 3, 1996, which he wrote as part of our extended dialogue on his experiences with Kohut, is explicit about not wanting to call Kohut's appropriation of his ideas plagiarism. Terman once in public cautiously and obliquely expressed his feelings, in a eulogy to Kohut that he delivered to the Chicago Psychoanalytic Society, January 26, 1982 (typescript in Wolf collection): "Heinz's presence among us was not always easy. Such a commanding figure inspires many difficulties, intellectual and personal, in those around him—from envious competition on the one hand to idolatrous worship on the other. Heinz's personality sometimes did not make these difficulties easier. Though he was unfailingly personally courteous, his, I think, inevitable, absorption with his own ideas may have closed him off to the input of others and hence exaggerated the distance that many already felt."

21 ON RAGE

1. Douglas Kirsner, "Self Psychology and the Psychoanalytic Movement: An Interview with Dr. Heinz Kohut," *Psychoanalytic and Contemporary Thought* 5(1981): 483–495.

2. In *Restoration* Kohut treats rage as part of a general discussion of the drives (69–83) and only focuses on rage itself on 77–78, though even then it is considered with shame and he moves quickly into a broader, philosophical discussion of method. There is nothing in *Restoration* that equals the clarity and elegance of the 1972 paper.

3. *Psychoanalytic Study of the Child* 27 (1972): 360–400, reprinted in *Search* 2: 615–658. Cp. Kohut's summary of his ideas in an interview with Lewis Z. Koch, n.d., though copyrighted 1999 and clearly conducted about 1978. I am grateful to Arnold Goldberg for sending me a copy of the interview (with Koch's permission).

4. SQ.

5. On August 14, 1971, Kohut wrote Anna Freud that "I hope [a month in Carmel] will give me the necessary leisure to prepare the Brill lecture for November," and on December 25, 1971, he wrote her that the lecture in fact did go well (*Curve*, 257–258 and 259–260). Kohut also inexplicably told his old friend, Philip Seitz, a year or so later that his understanding of rage grew out of his experience with cancer. Seitz was surprised at the time, for he did not know Kohut had cancer. Interview with Philip Seitz, March 26, 1999.

6. For Freud's comment, see "New Introductory Lectures," *SE* 22: 66; the book of Emil Ludwig's that Freud criticized so sharply was *Kaiser Wilhelm II*, tr. M. Colburn (London: Putnam, 1926). The Ludwig biography of Freud was *Dr. Freud: An Analysis and a Warning* (New York: Helmans, Williams, 1947). Lionel Trilling's review of the Ludwig biography appeared in the *New York Times*, December 14, 1947.

7. Cp. *Lectures*, 63–77 and 195–209 (esp. 197).

8. Reactions, however, can be delayed and in substitutive form. Mr. P., for example, who was raised a fundamentalist Christian, took pleasure in cruelly exposing the often-denied ethnicity of others in social situations. It turned out in therapy that Mr. P. had been himself humiliated by his mother, who made him expose his genitals to her for many years so that he would be forced to reveal to her any evidence of masturbation.

9. The example of divorce is in *Cure*, 220 n. 11.

10. In a personal communication, September 12, 1999, Robert Jay Lifton, after reading this passage in the manuscript, pointed out that Albert Speer was in fact wildly romantic and shared Hitler's dreams. Speer related to Hitler as a son to a father. Speer even asked Lifton if he would treat him in psychotherapy to help him understand why he got so attracted to such an evil and unattractive man.

11. John Demos, "Introduction of Dr. Heinz Kohut," *Reflections on Self Psychology*, ed. Joseph D. Lichtenberg and Samuel Kaplan (Hillsdale, NJ: Analytic Press, 1983), 9–10. Kohut wrote his paper in 1973 but only first published it in *Freud: The Fusion of Science and Humanism*, ed. John E. Gedo and George H. Pollock, *Psychological Issues*, Monograph 34/35 (New York: International Universities Press, 1976): 379–425. It was reprinted in *Search* 2: 793–843, which it should be noted puts the paper in sequence according to publication date, rather than when actually written. He called it a "somewhat rambling" paper; see Kohut to Carl E. Schorske, March 3, 1973. See also Kohut to Fritz Morgenthaler, March 23, 1973 (*Curve*, 274–275), and to Peter Kutter, March 13, 1973, both of which refer to his just-completed paper. The next year, in a seminar at the Institute on February 15, 1974, Kohut mentioned his "long paper" dealing with Freud's self-analysis "that

sort of rambles about many different things." *Lectures*, 80. Kohut had actually made a first stab at the ideas in his charisma paper when he was writing *Analysis*. The concluding chapter was to be a discussion of just these issues. He decided, however, that the material did not work and he put the draft away until I edited and published it as "On Leadership" in *Humanities*. For the most part, his discussion in the charisma paper vastly improves on the leadership essay. This discussion of the charisma paper is based on Kohut's text but draws as well on the tape of Kohut's presentation to the Center for Psychosocial Studies, January 19, 1974, from the personal collection of Ernest Wolf.

12. In *Search* 2:820, Kohut at this point refers to Mary Gedo's Northwestern University Ph.D. dissertation (1977), *Picasso's Self-Image*.

13. For further thoughts on the group self, see Kohut to Graham Little, July 1, 1980.

14. *Search* 2:634–636; *Analysis*, 106 n. 1; Kohut to me, March 17, 1981. Cp. *Lectures*, 223–224. Note Rafael Moses, "The Group Self and the Arab-Israeli Conflict," *International Review of Psycho-Analysis* 9 (1982): 55–65; Ruthellen Josselson, "Tolstoy, Narcissism, and the Psychology of the Self: A Self-Psychology Approach to Prince Andrei in *War and Peace*," *Psychoanalytic Review* 73 (1986): 77–95; and at least twenty Ph.D. dissertations that have been written on literary topics using Kohut's work since 1981 (readily available in any database search).

15. Kohut to Erich Heller, December 1, 1976, *Search* 2: 909.

22 SELF AND THEORY

1. As David Terman, personal communication, August 30, 1997, put it: "To know Heinz Kohut is to know self psychology."

2. *Lectures*, 51–53. Cp. Arnold Goldberg, *Being of Two Minds: The Vertical Split in Psychoanalysis and Psychotherapy* (Hillsdale, NJ: Analytic Press, 1999).

3. Compare, for example, his comments at a 1973 Paris workshop, tape in the Wolf collection.

4. For reasons of confidentiality, I am unable to reveal any names in this context.

5. Kohut to May Weber, October 28, 1973, *Curve*, 293–294; see also SQ.

6. SQ.

7. The first—and still the most important—paper to make this point is Judith Kegan Gardiner, "Self Psychology as Feminist Theory," *Signs: The Journal of Women in Culture and Society* 12 (1997): 761–780.

8. *Analysis*, 59–62.

9. *Cure*, 218 n. 3.

10. Interview with Thomas Pappadis, June 23, 1997.

11. From the tape of the workshop at the meetings of the International Psycho-Analytic Association in Paris in 1973; personal collection of Ernest Wolf. See also *Restoration*, discussion of Mr. X., 199–219.

12. "Reflections on Advances in Self Psychology," *Search* 4: 298 (originally Kohut's comments at the end of the first self psychology conference in October 1978). Note that these comments follow a discussion of the "ugly breast" imagery de-

scribed by Melanie Klein, which, he says, need not be defensive but a more direct reflection, as in a self-state dream, of the "genetic constellation."

13. *Analysis*, 63.

14. Ibid., 61, 63–64; *Restoration*, 190.

15. *Analysis*, 59, 196, 257, 293, 313–315; *Restoration*, 7–8.

16. Robert Kramer, "The 'Bad Mother' Freud Has Never Seen: Otto Rank and the Birth of the Object-Relations Theory," *Journal of the American Academy of Psychoanalysis* 23 (1995): 293–321. See also Karen Horney, "The Dread of Women," *IJP* 13 (1932): 348–360; and Molly Ladd-Taylor and Lauri Umansky, eds., *"Bad" Mothers: The Politics of Blame in Twentieth-Century America* (New York: New York University Press, 1998).

17. *SE* 7: 20.

18. Richard Pollak, *The Creation of Dr. B* (New York: Simon and Schuster, 1997), 10, 21–22, 151, 158–62, 250–251, 254, 280, 283–285.

19. Erik Erikson, *Childhood and Society*, 288–297, for his discussion of "Mom-ism." John Demos argues in Joel Pfister and Nancy Schnog, eds., *Inventing the Psychological: Toward a Cultural History of Emotional Life in America* (New Haven: Yale University Press, 1997), 71, that the turning point in this process was the Civil War, which spawned a vast corpus of folk songs and ballads about mothers. Within psychoanalysis, it is worth noting that Melanie Klein reverses the "bad mother" archetype by blaming the children and making them evil, a point for which I am indebted to Tessa Philips, personal communication, August 8, 1998.

20. Arnold and Constance Goldberg, January 20, 1997.

21. *Lectures*, 40–41, to which I have added some important words and phrases the editors, Paul and Marian Tolpin, deleted from the text. The original of Kohut's lecture to candidates at the Institute, June 11, 1976, is in the Wolf tape collection.

22. "Conversations with Heinz Kohut," *Humanities*, 215–269.

23. Paul Ornstein, the editor of Kohut's papers, argues by implication in his index to *Search* 4 that in the 1950s Kohut had the idea of the nuclear self but not the language (*Search* 1: 443n) and again used the idea in *Seminars*. Kohut may have used the term for the first time in 1970 (*Search* 2: 579); it became central in his vocabulary from the time of his paper on rage (*Search* 2: 624n).

24. *Lectures*, 58.

25. Ibid., 58–69.

26. Marian Tolpin, "On the Beginning of a Cohesive Self," *Psychoanalytic Study of the Child* 26 (1971): 316–352.

27. Sherry Turkle, *Life on the Screen: Identity in the Age of the Internet* (New York: Simon and Schuster, 1995).

23 THE GROUP REDUX

1. The publisher, International Universities Press, declined to provide sales figures.

2. Kohut to Tilmann Moser, October 23, 1973, *Curve*, 291–292, and Kohut to Robert Gardner, November 2, 1973, *Curve*, 294–295.

3. Kurt Eissler to Kohut, September 22, 1971.

4. Kohut to Anna Freud, July 9, 1980, *Curve*, 409–410. Once in conversation with me in the winter of 1980–1981, Kohut expressed his disdainful feelings about Anna Freud with what seemed to me surprising vehemence.

5. AG 2.

6. Copies of telegrams exist in the archives for 1978 and 1979.

7. Kohut to Eissler, April 18, 1974, *Curve*, 306–307.

8. Kurt Eissler to Kohut, October 13, 1975. The paper Eissler was referring to was "Creativeness, Charisma, Group Psychology: Reflections on the Self Analysis of Freud," *Search* 2: 793–843.

9. Eissler actually wrote his comments in a seven-page, single-spaced letter to Margret Schaefer, December 4, 1978, a copy of which he sent to Kohut, which begins with the assertion that Kohut is "one of the very few friends I have."

10. Kohut to Kurt Eissler, December 11, 1978, *Curve*, 379.

11. Kohut to Margret Schaefer, December 11, 1978, *Curve*, 378–379. In the year before the controversy erupted, there were quite a few letters back and forth between Kohut and Heller (these are now in the archives). Kohut's initial letter to Margret Schaefer is April 15, 1975.

12. PO.

13. Kohut to Jerome Kavka, December 4, 1975.

14. Kohut to Serge Lebovici, September 13, 1973, *Curve*, 288. Note also Kohut to Anna Freud, August 23, 1971, *Curve*, 258–259.

15. CK.

16. William Gillespie to Kohut, September 8, 1973.

17. Martin Stein, review of *Restoration*, *JAPA* 27 (1979): 665–680. Kohut had strong feelings that there was an active suppression of self psychology at institutes in America and around the world. It was very disappointing for him. It seemed to him a kind of censorship that ran counter to the expression of new ideas so essential to the search for truth. See Kohut to Daniel Offer, December 15, 1978.

18. This structure had been instituted by George Pollock when he was elected director in the 1960s.

19. AG 2 and EW 2, who gave me as good an account as I have heard of the events leading up to the vote (though I have talked with many other people about it). Everyone is clear, however, that the real motivation behind the vote was raw envy and dislike of Heinz Kohut. The baffling figure is George Pollock, the director of the Institute. Goldberg (who was also voted off the Council with Kohut) feels Pollock maneuvered the vote to punish Goldberg for trying to establish a self psychology track in the curriculum, something Pollock himself vehemently denies; see interview with George Pollock, May 27, 1998. Jerome Kavka, personal communication, April 2, 1996, agrees with Goldberg that the real issue was that the self psychologists were pushing for a separate track ("too hard," in the view of Kavka). Wolf feels, and in this he is surely correct, that if there had been a split between the Freudians and the self psychologists in the Institute it would have occurred at this point (he is now sorry the split did not occur). That it did not

was due to Kohut's refusal to let such a split develop. See Kohut to Arnold Goldberg, May 1, 1978, *Curve*, 366–367. As a candidate at the time, I also recall the turmoil and Arnold Goldberg saying that Kohut himself, while terribly upset, vetoed any talk of creating a new institute. Goldberg, noted for his wry humor, suggested that self psychologists wear T-shirts with "Kohutian" printed across the front.

20. On the image of being "kicked out of his own family," see AG 3; on his lingering hurt, see SQ; cp., as well, Kohut to Lotte Kohler, June [sic] 1978, in *Curve*, 368–371. Nothing, however, is simple. Miriam Elson (ME) saw Kohut on the street the day after the Council vote. As far as she could tell, what he was most upset about was that he would no longer be able to eat the catered lunches at the Institute served by Mrs. Stucky. Kohut was voted back on the Council two years later; see George Pollock to Kohut, May 29, 1980. Kohut never let the Council fight deter him from continued involvement in the affairs of the Institute. He served on committees before and after the vote; see Kohut to Pollock, January 5 and June 27, 1979, for example. He even wrote some exam questions for candidates during the last year of his life; see Kohut to David Dean Brockman, March 9, 1981.

21. See, for example, Kohut to Levarie, February 24, 1979, *Curve*, 386–387, and April 2, 1981, *Curve*, 427–429. Kohut, it seems, also regularly called Levarie to chat.

22. Kohut wrote a silly letter to Wilhelm Solms-Rodelheim's dachshund from his own Mops, March 3, 1973, *Curve*, 273–274. He describes his meeting with Wandruszka in a letter to Michael Franz Basch, September 14, 1973, *Curve*, 289–290 (note Cocks's footnote on the other letters between Wandruszka and Kohut, 290n).

23. JP 1; for another meeting, see Kohut to Jacques Palaci, October 20, 1974, in "Letters to Jacques: Selected Letters of Heinz Kohut to Jacques Palaci," edited by Joseph Reppen and Francesca Reppen, *Psychoanalytic Review*, 84 (1997): 820–821; cp. Kohut to Jacques Palaci, March 6, 1974, *Curve*, 302–303.

24. Ernest Wolf, *Psychoanalysts Talk*, 173, says Kohut, "beginning to think of himself, a little bit, as a great man," announced, "We need a casebook," and got it off the ground. Wolf repeated that story to me in an interview on March 3, 1996. He turned to John Gedo as the leader. Gedo, however, while he is certain he never had a conversation with Kohut about forming the group, may have been a more central player than Wolf remembers, as best one can tell from some later correspondence. As the *Casebook* moved toward actual publication, Wolf wrote to Gedo on November 11, 1976, asking him how he (Gedo) wanted to be acknowledged. "We esteem the important role you took in getting this project off the ground," Wolf wrote. Gedo replied on November 15: "I [was] instrumental in collecting the people who carried out [the] work into a group. [The] task I had in mind was quite different from what you eventually decided to do." And he added: "A friendly acknowledgment of my role in forming the group would amount to being thanked for being so cooperative about the kidnaping and murder of one of my children. I have neither forgotten nor for-

given the perpetrators. . . ." Letters and copies in the personal collection of John Gedo. Gedo further clarified in a letter to me, September 19, 1998, his real surprise when he learned Kohut planned to participate in the meetings of the *Casebook*. That is what he meant in his November 15, 1976, letter to Wolf about the "kidnaping" of the project. Gedo imagined a group he would lead that would consist of Goldberg, Wolf, Paul and Marian Tolpin, Meyer Gunther, and Basch, and would not promote Kohut's views but develop its own. On this last point, see also Gedo to me, September 18, 1998. It is worth noting as well that Goldberg, in a personal communication to me on October 5, 1998, recalls the *Casebook* as having begun as Gedo's idea.

25. It was Gedo who suggested the inclusion of Gunther and Marian Tolpin. See Gedo to me, September 18, 1998. Arnold Goldberg, May 12, 2000, was certain the idea of the *Casebook* was Gedo's. In that same conversation, Goldberg also noted more personally that he was through his divorce and ready for something new.

26. Meeting of Kohut with the group, February 2, 1974, tape in the Ernest Wolf collection.

27. PO and AG 3. Needless to say, this sentence (and the next two) are judgments rendered retrospectively and in light of the fight that ensued.

28. John Gedo, *Spleen and Nostalgia*, 339.

29. Arnold Goldberg to Kohut, September 15, 1974. In the letter, Goldberg describes the content of the discussions and the personalities of those in the group. He notes the group worked out the procedural issues of writing the book and then turned to talking about the first case. Goldberg becomes a lively reporter, David Marcus was "remarkable." He was vigorously defending the "pure Kohut" position in ways that were quite extreme. Michael Basch, in turn, was less tight and both relaxed and verbal. He even switched from "Dr. Kohut" to "Kohut," though never to "Heinz." Basch talked a lot about how he actually behaved as an analyst and thankfully not about Piaget. Even Marian was relaxed enough to let Goldberg talk with her afterward about her case without any sign of her customary tension or irritability. John Gedo, Goldberg notes without any sense of future distress, was his "usual self" and talked a lot. Ernest Wolf was mostly quiet and "taciturn." Paul Ornstein was "delightful as always" with his infectious enthusiasm. Goldberg also notes that earlier in the day he, Gedo, and Wolf had had lunch to discuss the edited book they had begun, "Psychoanalysis: An Intellectual System." He hopes Kohut will contribute.

30. "November 16, 1974": John Gedo, in a letter of resignation to the group, November 24, 1974, refers to "last Saturday's meeting." Personal file, John Gedo. November 24 in that year fell on Sunday. Since the events to which Gedo refers unfolded over the course of a week, his presentation must have been on November 16. Gedo also deals with this dating issue in his letter to me, September 9, 1998.

31. Arnold Goldberg in a personal communication to me October 5, 1998, and Marian Tolpin, in MT and on the panel at the self psychology conference in Chicago,

November 15, 1997, remember the issue under discussion was whether Gedo should turn off a light after the patient requested him to do so. Gedo, however, says the light issue arose in his presentation from the previous spring and that it was Kohut himself who raised the issue. See Gedo to me, September 9, 1998; note Gedo's write-up of this case, "Discussion of the Case of Kate," *Beyond Interpretation: Toward a Revised Theory for Psychoanalysis*, rev. ed. (Hillsdale, NJ: Analytic Press, 1993 [1979]), 86–98, esp. 97–98. Gedo says the issue on which Marian Tolpin quizzed him in the November meeting had to do with a patient financing his analysis. Given the discrepancies in memory, I have left the issue purposely vague in the text.

32. John Gedo to me, June 28, 1996; the "loud and grating voice" is from John Gedo, *Spleen and Nostalgia*, 341; the "being impudent" is from John Gedo to me, September 9 and 18, 1998. Marian Tolpin, needless to say, strenuously objects to Gedo's account of these events and regards as "paranoid" his idea that in criticizing him she was not speaking for herself but was giving voice to Kohut's views of Gedo's work. See MT. In Gedo's letter to me of September 9, 1998, he grants that he may have been wrong about Tolpin's acting on behalf of Kohut, but it is what he believed at the time.

33. Personal communication, Arnold Goldberg, December 29, 1997. Goldberg added that he felt Kohut would have done whatever he suggested to keep the group going, as it was in his interest. "Kohut would have sold them all [that is, all members of the group] down the river, if it served his purposes. He used them all." Goldberg made this same point in the panel discussion at the self psychology conference in Chicago, November 15, 1997.

34. John Gedo to me, September 18, 1998.

35. MT.

36. John Gedo to me, July 6, 1996.

37. AG 1 and PO both agreed on this point.

38. Gedo, alone among my informants, feels that Kohut stayed up late drinking wine and may have been an alcoholic. See John Gedo, *Spleen and Nostalgia*, 312–313; JG 1; and Gedo to me, June 28, 1996. It is worth noting that Gedo's "evidence" for his claim is circular. Kohut, he says, stayed up late and must have been drinking, which is why he stayed up late.

39. The original text is in the archives. The heavily edited paper later appeared as "To Heinz Kohut on his 60th Birthday," *Annual of Psychoanalysis* 3 (1975): 313–322. Cp. as well Gedo's loving review of Kohut's notions about idealization in "Forms of Idealization and the Analytic Transference," *JAPA* 23 (1975): 485–505, which he submitted for publication in July 1974.

40. At the banquet itself (which I attended), displeasure was not apparent on anyone's face as far as I could tell. Later, however, Kohut apparently raised objections to the speech (especially the Euripides comparison), and his observation that Gedo's comments were inappropriate has colored how everyone I have talked with remembers now how they felt then.

41. John Gedo to me, July 30, 1996, and September 9 and 18, 1998. In *Death in Venice*,

Aschenbach falls in love with the boy Tadzio. Holderlin, who spent many decades in an institution, was slipping into the madness when he wrote the poem from which Gedo quoted.

42. "like a lover" is a detail Gedo mentioned the first time he told me this story in JG 1.

43. John Gedo to me, February 18, 1996.

44. John Gedo to me, June 28, 1996.

45. Kohut to Selma Kramer, June 13, 1972.

46. Kohut to John Gedo, November 11, 1969; May 12, 1971; November 13, 1971; February 22, 1973; May 3, 1977 (*Curve*, 323); and September 15, 1975 (*Curve*, 324–325). Compare May 15, 1976.

47. John Gedo to Kohut, June 22, 1977.

48. Personal communication, Ina Wolf, August 29, 1996.

49. Thomas A. Kohut made this point with absolute certainty in his interview with me (TAK).

50. Personal communication, Arnold Goldberg, June 21, 1998. See *The Psychology of the Self: A Casebook*, ed. Arnold Goldberg (New York: International Universities Press, 1978).

51. Arnold Goldberg's date book from 1974 indicates several meetings with Kohut in the apartment in late November. It is not clear which formally launched the new group. On Friday, November 22, the Kohuts went out to dinner with the Goldbergs and the Wolfs. See the "Chronology" by Ina Wolf.

52. It took me countless conversations, phone calls, and letters with members of the group, especially with Arnold and Constance Goldberg and Ernest and Ina Wolf, to sort out this sequence and its approximate dates. I am grateful for their help. No one from the time, needless to say, kept written records. The last and most consequential set of conversations took place on February 7, 1999. Note also Arthur Malin to me, April 20, 1999. Self psychology has become a diverse and often contentious field since Kohut's death. Note Morton and Estelle Shane, "Self Psychology After Kohut: One Theory or Many?" *JAPA* 41 (1993): 777–797, and the special issue of *Psychoanalytic Dialogues* on "Self Psychology After Kohut: A Polylogue," 5 (1995): 351–543.

24 *THE RESTORATION OF THE SELF*

1. Kohut to Jacques Palaci, September 18, 1974.

2. Kohut to Natalie Altman, February 27, 1975. A week or so later Kohut wrote to George Klumpner, March 3, 1975, *Curve*, 320–322, about his manuscript.

3. Kohut to Peter Loewenberg, June 17, 1975, *Curve*, 323–324.

4. Kohut to John Gedo, September 15, 1975, *Curve*, 324–325.

5. Kohut to James P. Gustafson, October 14, 1975, *Curve*, 327–328.

6. Kohut wrote urgently to Jacques Palaci, June 13, 1976, *Curve*, 329–330; and December 11, 1976, Reppen, *Psychoanalytic Review*, 822–823; and July 19, 1977,

Reppen, *Psychoanalytic Review*, 824. The references he wanted from Palaci were to works by Jacques Lacan ("Le stade de miroir"); Franz Pasche ("L'antinarcissisme"); Jacques Pontalis ("Naissance et reconnaissance du 'self' "); and one of Palaci's own articles ("Réflexions sur le transfert et la théorie du narcissisme de Heinz Kohut"). Kohut mentions the number of copies of his book that had been sold up to that point in his July 19, 1977, letter to Palaci. International Universities Press refused to provide me with sales figures for either *Analysis* or *Restoration*.

7. In November 1998, Natalie Altman let me read her entire file from her work with Kohut. We also talked several times and she elaborated on many details. She even edited this chapter, which nicely closes the historical circle.

8. Natalie Altman to Kohut, November 18, 1975; Kohut to Altman, November 25, 1975; and Altman to Kohut, November 25, 1975 (clearly after their phone conversation).

9. Natalie Altman to Kohut, December 30, 1975. Kohut replies to Altman, January 7, 1976, explaining that much of the "flesh and blood" of the case appears in the *Casebook*, though he says some of that can be imported into his narrative.

10. Personal communication, Natalie Altman, November 19, 1998.

11. Altman to Kohut, undated copy with some handwritten marginalia by Altman.

12. See, for example, Altman to Kohut, March 2, 1976.

13. Kohut to Altman, March 7, 1976.

14. Kohut to Norma Levarie, July 25, 1976, *Curve*, 330 (and editor's note 1); Natalie Altman to Kohut, September 16, 1976.

15. Ernest Wolf, October 4, 1998, told me of doing the index and Kohut's gift. The current price of a case of Ch‰teau Margaux, which I checked, is well over $2,000.

16. Personal communication, Natalie Altman, November 21, 1998.

17. "Empathy is not just a useful way by which we have access to the inner life of man—the idea itself of an inner life of man, and thus of a psychology of complex mental states, is unthinkable without our ability to know via vicarious introspection—my definition of empathy . . .—what the inner life of man is, what we ourselves and what others think and feel." *Restoration*, 306.

18. Martin Stein, review of *Restoration*, *JAPA* 27 (1979): 665–680; quote is on 673.

19. *Restoration*, xix–xxii.

20. Ibid., 64.

21. Addictions had always interested Kohut. See *Search* 1: 201–203.

22. *Restoration*, 80–81.

23. Ibid., 293; *SE* 12 (1913), 134: "I cannot put up with being stared at by other people for eight hours a day (or more)."

24. *Restoration*, 290–297.

25. *Search* 2: 659–660.

26. Kohut to Philip C. Gradolph, February 13, 1977, *Curve*, 337.

27. *Advances in Self Psychology*, ed. Arnold Goldberg (New York: International Universities Press, 1980), final "Reflections" by Heinz Kohut, 488.

28. Charles Taylor, *Sources of the Self: The Making of the Modern Identity* (Cambridge,

MA: Harvard University Press, 1989); Arnold Goldberg, *The Prisonhouse of Psychoanalysis* (Hillsdale, NJ: Analytic Press, 1990) and *A Fresh Look at Psychoanalysis: The View from Self Psychology* (Hillsdale, NJ: Analytic Press, 1988); Jerome Bruner, *On Knowing: Essays for the Left Hand* (Cambridge, MA: Harvard University Press, 1979) and *Acts of Meaning* (Cambridge, MA: Harvard University Press, 1990); Meares, *The Metaphor of Play* (Northvale, NJ: Jason Aronson, 1993); Paul Ricoeur, *Oneself as Another*, tr. Kathleen Blamey (Chicago: University of Chicago Press, 1992); Douglas Kirsner, *Unfree Associations: Inside Psychoanalytic Institutes* (self-published on the Internet); Teicholz, *Kohut, Loewald*; and Philip Cushman, *Constructing the Self, Constructing America: A Cultural History of Psychotherapy* (New York: Addison-Wesley, 1995).

29. *Restoration*, xv.

30. Kohut, "Notes in preparation for the examination, due June 2, 1979," for the "Workshop on Self Psychology" that met monthly at the Institute, published as "Four Basic Concepts in Self Psychology," *Search* 4: 447–448. See 450–454, where Kohut lists his various definitions of self and sharply differentiates it from identity. Compare the paper Kohut and Ernest Wolf published in 1978, "The Disorders of the Self and Their Treatment: An Outline," *IJP* 59 (1978): 413–425, reprinted in *Search* 3: 359–385; note the highly schematic definitions on 363–386, which are out of character for Kohut and almost certainly reflect Wolf's approach more than Kohut's.

31. *Restoration*, 310–311.

32. Ibid., 85, 99–100. Kohut says (100): "The *nuclear* self, in particular, is not formed via conscious encouragement and praise and via conscious discouragement and rebuke, but by the deeply anchored responsiveness of the self-objects, which, in the last analysis, is a function of the self-objects' own nuclear selves."

33. Ibid., 177. For Kohut's thought on the spatial element in his new sense of the self, see Kohut to Lloyd Etheredge, April 12, 1977, and *Lectures*, 210–213.

34. *Restoration*, 241.

35. *Search* 2: 753.

36. *Restoration*, 241. Cp. Elliot Jacques, "Death and the Mid-Life Crisis," *IJP* 46 (1965): 502–514.

37. Erik Erikson (of all people), *Childhood and Society*, probably stated what psychoanalysis meant by "genitality" better than anyone: "A system must have its utopia," he says (92). "For psychoanalysis the utopia is 'genitality.' " And genitality in turn (265) "consists in the unobstructed capacity to develop an orgastic potency so free of pregenital interferences that genital libido (not just the sex products discharged in Kinsey's 'outlets') is expressed in heterosexual mutuality, with full sensitivity of both penis and vagina, and with a convulsion-like discharge of tension from the whole body."

38. *Analysis*, 167–168, 117–118, 131–132, 136, 158–159, 173, and 313–315.

39. *Search* 2: 724–728.

40. The personal information about Anna Ornstein is from an interview I conducted with her on September 15, 1998, and in two follow-up phone calls October 4 and

19, 1998, after she had gone over the draft of this chapter. She is the unidentified author of the case history of Mr. M., "Transformation of Archaic Narcissism," in Arnold Goldberg, ed. *The Psychology of the Self: A Casebook* (New York: International Universities Press, 1978), 121–164 (I secured permission from both Anna Ornstein and Goldberg to reveal this information). I will indicate separately in the discussion that follows when I take data from her write-up of Mr. M. in the *Casebook* and when from Kohut's chapter in *Restoration*.

41. John Gedo to me, March 9, 1996; Gedo, *Spleen and Nostalgia*, 61; John Gedo to me, July 17, 1996.

42. Jule P. Miller, "How Kohut Actually Worked," *Progress in Self Psychology*, ed. Arnold Goldberg, vol. 1 (New York: Guilford Press, 1985), 13–30. All references are to this text.

43. *Casebook*, 121–124.

44. In the *Casebook*, the tattoo is disguised as a "small physical defect" (128).

45. *Restoration*, Ch. 1, esp. 25–29. There are details in what Kohut writes about the case that do not appear in Ornstein's version in the *Casebook* (and vice versa). It is pretty clear that Kohut wrote his chapter based in part on her presentation of the case at the seminar in the spring of 1974 but probably mainly on his own notes from the three years of supervision of the case. As everyone told me who was in supervision with Kohut, he took advantage of his remarkable memory and made elaborate notes on cases after he met with supervisees.

46. The essential details of this paragraph are from Ornstein in the *Casebook*, though some elements of the interpretation are from Kohut, *Restoration*.

47. The three "acts" are in *Restoration*, 41–48. Lynne Layton, "A Deconstruction of Kohut's Concept of the Self," *Contemporary Psychoanalysis* 26 (1990): 420–429, esp. 425–428, notes critically that Kohut fails to mention the fact that Mr. M. also began a new relationship with a young woman during his termination phase (see Ornstein in the *Casebook*, 162). Layton argues that Kohut fails to understand that empathy requires boundaries so that one can be separate from the other, "and thus it is absurd to assign empathy to a realm of selfobject relations that is sharply differentiated from the realm of object love" (426). From that already far-fetched position, she goes further: "Kohut, rather than being a theorist of 'the self,' has legitimized in his theory the distortions in development that a patriarchal, Western culture, dominated still by the Protestant Ethic, has brought forth and called normal" (428). Undoubtedly, Kohut saw Mr. M.'s relationship at the end of his therapy as important but secondary to his self healing, as he argued one often sees in such cases; see *Analysis*, 296–298.

48. *Restoration*, 225–227.

49. Ibid., 227. Howard B. Levine argues that self psychology is essentially a psychology of homeostasis. The narrative story of self-psychological analysis tells of the individual's "adaptive struggles" for "organization, modulation, and stimulation," which are expressed and played out in the "vicissitudes of the analyst-patient relationship." Such needs are analogous to, if not identical with, similar needs that existed in childhood in relation to primary objects and were in general unmet

or surrounded with trauma. The very fact that the needs extend into adulthood is evidence that they were not met in childhood. Thus the term "deficit" becomes important for Kohut in *Restoration* (though Levine does not appreciate the extent to which the same idea, if not the term, is there in *Analysis*). See Howard B. Levine, "Mahler and Kohut: A Comparative View," Selma Kramer and Salman Akhtar, eds., *Mahler and Kohut: Perspectives on Development, Psychopathology, and Technique* (Northvale, NJ: Jason Aronson, 1994), 127. See also Lawrence Friedman, "Kohut: A Book Review Essay," *PQ* 49 (1980): 393–422; and Howard B. Levine, "Some Implications of Self Psychology," *Contemporary Psychoanalysis* 19 (1983): 153–171.

50. *Restoration*, 237.

51. Ibid., 240.

52. Ibid., 247.

53. *Search* 2: 786–787.

54. Ibid., 127–128.

55. Unpublished typescript of a meeting on February 22, 1975, in the personal collection of Ernest Wolf.

56. *Restoration*, 220–222.

57. *Lectures*, 109–124, esp. 115–118; cp. 355–356.

58. *SE* 5: 339–508.

59. *Restoration*, 109–110.

60. Ibid., 105.

61. *Lectures*, 149 and 163. Cp. Mr. A. in *Analysis*, 169–172.

62. *Restoration*, 105.

63. Thomas M. French, "Reality Testing in Dreams," *PQ* 6 (1937): 62–77, and "Insight and Distortion in Dreams," *IJP* 20 (1939): 287–298; Erik Erikson, "The Dream Specimen in Psychoanalysis," *JAPA* 2 (1954): 5–56. See also Calvin S. Hall, *The Meaning of Dreams* (New York: Harper and Row, 1953), on a vast sample of normal dreams, an approach that Franz Alexander (of the Chicago Institute), in his review in *PQ* 22 (1953): 438–440, found superficial because of Hall's "ignorance" of Freud's distinction between the latent and manifest content.

64. Martin Stein, review of *Restoration*, *JAPA* 27(1979):675, labels Kohut's self-state dreams as merely "anagogic" and says Kohut not only ignores what Freud says in this regard (though Stein quotes Freud's "Remarks on the Theory and Practice of Dream Interpretation," *SE* 19: 108–121, which in fact has nothing to say about what Kohut is describing) but basically revives an "old view of dreaming" that interprets the dream as "abstract, inspirational, and without relation to unconscious conflict, in essence ego-syntonic." Stein fails to observe that the Jungian interpretation of dreams is probably the closest to what Kohut is getting at, however different self-state dream theory is from Jung's belief in the grounding of the dream in the collective unconscious.

65. "Notes from Training Analysts' Seminar," November 15, 1960, p. 7, in Kohut Archives.

66. "Would the study of manifest dreams give you leads concerning the crucial im-

ages and stories which you might expect to find in the projective tests of people with narcissistic disorders? People and their twins; people seeing themselves in a mirror; people flying; people admiring some symbol of greatness or strength—these might be such possible images and contents. Then I would be on the lookout for the cohesion of fragmentation of these figures." Kohut to Jeffrey Urist, March 13, 1972, *Curve*, 266–267.

67. *Analysis*, 4–5, 243–245, 87, 145.

68. *Restoration*, 153 and 154. In *Lectures*, 86–87, Kohut says Barglow asked him directly where he was going and Kohut told him. See also Tolpin's "Preface" to *Lectures*, xvi–xviii. For more on Barglow, see Chapter 11 above.

69. *Lectures*, 108.

70. One of the clearest discussions of this essence of Freud in relation to adult experience is Philip Rieff, *Freud: The Mind of the Moralist* (New York: Viking, 1959), though Erik Erikson was hardly unaware of the same point; see esp. *Young Man Luther* and *Gandhi's Truth: On the Origins of Militant Nonviolence* (New York: Norton, 1968). The specific point about the Holocaust and psychoanalysis is from Alec Wilkinson's brilliant short essay on women psychosomatically blinded by witnessing the Cambodian genocide, "A Changed Vision of God," *New Yorker*, January 24, 1994, p. 6.

71. *Restoration*, 267–280. For other discussions of Guilty and Tragic Man, see 132–133, 207, 239–243. Compare *Lectures*, 138, and *Search* 2: 752–757.

72. *Search* 2: 761–762.

73. *Restoration*, 133 n. 15.

74. Ibid., 287.

25 HEROES AND GURUS

1. The topic of heroes has also interested psychoanalysts themselves. See Otto Rank, *The Myth of the Birth of the Hero: A Psychological Interpretation of Mythology* (New York: Brunner, 1952). Compare Joseph Campbell, *The Hero with a Thousand Faces* (New York: Pantheon, 1949). See the interesting recent study, Anthony Storr, *Feet of Clay* (New York: Free Press, 1996). I have had many discussions on this general topic with my colleague Robert Jay Lifton in the last decade at our Center on Violence and Human Survival at John Jay College. See his recent book, *Destroying the World to Save It: Aum Shinrikyoo, Apocalyptic Violence, and the New Global Terrorism* (New York: Metropolitan Books, 1999), with its discussion of "guruism."

2. Michael Polanyi, *Personal Knowledge: Towards a Post-Critical Philosophy* (New York: Harper & Row, 1964), 151–152. The better-known work of Thomas S. Kuhn, *The Structure of Scientific Revolutions* (Chicago: University of Chicago Press, 1970), on paradigm shifts is less psychologically astute and misses the way competing schools of thought, especially in a field such as psychoanalysis, have within the dynamics of the struggle itself the impulse toward conversion, discipleship,

and gurus. Kohut himself notes in his paper on charisma that a leader needs to have followers who serve "as a regulator of his self-esteem." See *Humanities*, 202.

3. Rank, *The Myth of the Birth of the Hero*.

4. Wendy Doniger, presentation at Wellfleet meetings of Robert Jay Lifton, October 1997. Cp. Daniel Gold, *The Lord as Guru: Hindi Saints in Northern Indian Tradition* (New York: Oxford University Press, 1987).

5. Noll, *The Jung Cult*.

6. Wendy Kaminer, "Why We Love Gurus," *Newsweek*, October 20, 1997.

7. Storr, *Feet of Clay*, xi–xvii. In this "Introduction" Storr gives an outline of his theory. The book itself then consists of a series of chapters, each on a different figure.

8. *Cure*, xii; Arthur Malin to me, April 20, 1999; I am also on the faculties of two self psychology institutes in New York, know personally about the others, and take part in the annual meetings sponsored by the International Council of Self Psychology.

9. Kirsner, "Self Psychology and the Psychoanalytic Movement: An Interview with Dr. Heinz Kohut," 484–486.

26 THE AUTOBIOGRAPHY OF MR. Z

1. "The Two Analyses of Mr. Z," *IJP* 60 (1979): 3–27; reprinted in *Search* 4: 395–446.

2. Heinz Kohut to George D. Goldman, March 7, 1981.

3. *Lectures*, 308–318, esp. 311. See also Kohut's discussion of the case, 55–57.

4. Anita Eckstaedt to Kohut, July 8, 1971; Eckstaedt to Kohut, August 9, 1971; Kohut to Eckstaedt, August 8, 1975. The case appears in *Restoration* as that of "X.," 199–219. Besides the 1973 Paris workshop at the meetings of the International, I have talked with several of Kohut's colleagues (Arnold Goldberg, Marian Tolpin, and Ernest Wolf, among others) who recall Kohut's fondness for the case and especially the dream of the young man on the autobahn (see *Restoration*, 203–204).

5. Anita Eckstaedt to Kohut, March 3, 1977, and Kohut to Eckstaedt, March 29, 1973. See also TAK. After much delay, Eckstaedt responded to some of my questions in a letter of February 17, 1999, but added nothing new to the contemporary archival record, and in fact contradicted it in one important sense by stressing that her *only* concern at the time was protecting the identity of the patient in the German translation.

6. Heinz Kohut, *Die Heilung des Selbst*, tr. Elke vom Scheidt (Frankfurt am Main, 1979); *Search* 4: 395–446 has the English version. The dating of when he wrote the paper can be determined from a letter to Lars B. Lofgren, September 21, 1977, *Curve*, 352; Donna Orange, in a personal communication, August 1999, suggested the connection with the Council vote; interview with Natalie Altman, August 11, 1998, on the editing.

7. Harry Guntrip, "My Experience of Analysis with Fairbairn and Winnicott," *International Review of Psychoanalysis* 2 (1975): 145–156.

8. TAK. The issue of what Mrs. Kohut believed about Mr. Z is complex. Marian Tolpin, who knew all the players, feels strongly that one must be skeptical of Thomas Kohut's motivations, given his ambivalence toward his father, when he reports his mother accepted his own inferences about the case. Tolpin (who otherwise is quite convinced "Mr. Z" is pure autobiography) refuses to believe that Mrs. Kohut ever agreed the case was autobiographical, given how protective she was of Kohut's memory. Tolpin has insistently made this point to me twice in seminars when I presented at the Chicago Institute for Psychoanalysis on June 18, 1997, and June 20, 1998; cp. Helen Golden's review of *Curve* and the reply by Geoffrey Cocks, *Psychoanalytic Books* 6 (1995): 1–11. I am less certain that one can be so sure about anyone's motivations, especially those of a widow pushed offstage all her adult life by a force of nature like Heinz Kohut. Thomas A. Kohut is also a distinguished historian who understands that his responsibility to his father's memory extends beyond his personal feelings. He also sees the case as a good example of his father's creativity and cleverness, not a blot on his name. Besides being out of character, why would Thomas Kohut lie about what his mother told him?

9. The closer the colleague the more trouble Kohut took to cover his tracks. Arnold Goldberg, for example, can date exactly when he first talked with Kohut about the case—the fall of 1977—and recalls the many discussions they had after that about the case (AG 3). Everybody in the group can recall conversations with Kohut about the case, which suggests the extent of his cover-up. The only significant figure who continues to dispute Kohut as Z is Paul Ornstein. He recounted to me the Eckstaedt story, though he confused the dates, and his discussion with Kohut about the substitution of "Mr. Z" for the case of the theology student (X.) in the German translation of *Restoration*. But he had that talk after the fall of 1977, so it proves nothing. He also feels that since Kohut read all his papers to Elizabeth and Thomas he would not have been able to disguise an autobiography, but Ornstein does not realize this is the one paper Kohut never read to his family. Finally, Ornstein committed himself to do a book on "Mr. Z" in 1987. Elizabeth, as literary executor of the estate, had to cosign the contract so he could republish the case. Neither at the time nor later did she say anything to him about Z as Kohut. This, I must say, is baffling, though not about Kohut but about his widow, since she and Thomas came to the conclusion in 1983 that Z was Kohut. See PO.

10. TAK.

11. Interviews with Carol Basch, October 28, 1998, and AG 2. Basch himself, unfortunately, died before I could conduct a formal interview with him about his experiences with Kohut.

12. AG 3.

13. Gail Elden to me, March 23, 1995.

14. Interview with Sheldon Meyers, June 19, 1997.

15. *Cure*, 84–91. Mortimer Ostow's criticism of the case—that Kohut had simply conducted a bad analysis the first time and got it right the second time around—was published as "Letter to the Editor," *IJP* 60 (1979): 531–532.

16. Kohut to Leon L. Altman, April 18, 1978.

17. As a candidate myself at the time, I was in one such seminar, taught by Paul Tolpin in the spring of 1978, at which Kohut was a guest.

18. TAK. Thomas Kohut says that he delayed making his conclusions about the case known until after the death of Ruth Eissler to avoid harming her reputation unnecessarily.

19. Geoffrey Cocks, " 'Playing with Psychological Fire': The Austrian Years of Heinz Kohut," Kohut Memorial Lecture, Self Psychology Conference, October 22, 1994 (draft manuscript from author). The fact that Kohut "definitely" read *Confessions of Zeno* is from Siegmund Levarie, personal communication, May 14, 1999. The "first cigarette" reference is to Kohut to Sydney J. Harris, July 5, 1960. *Curve*, 72. Cocks actually says Kohut had the letter *K* available as well, but he is mistaken; see *Analysis*, 137–140. Cocks also misses that Kohut had available the letters *T* and *U*. Donna Orange, who read this book in manuscript, wondered at this point in the text whether Kohut was influenced in selecting the letter *Z* by Stefan Zweig.

20. Cocks, "Introduction," *Curve*, 4–5. For many years, there was something of an unofficial taboo placed on even breathing the idea of "Mr. Z" as autobiography by those colleagues closest to him who continued his work and kept the flame alive. Some of the stories in this regard border on gossip, but I know from personal experience that I presented once to a seminar in New York in 1989 and mentioned that I thought Kohut was Z. There followed many frantic long-distance phone calls and so much general angst (about Z and other issues) that Arnold Goldberg asked me to present to a small group in his home, December 1, 1990.

21. Interview with Robert Stolorow, October 21, 1995.

22. William James, *The Variety of Religious Experience* (New York: Modern Library, 1936), 156–158. Compare Louis Menand, "William James and the Case of the Epileptic Patient," *New York Review of Books* 45 (1998): 81–83, 86–93; and Howard Feinstein, "The 'Crisis' of William James: A Revisionist View," *Psychohistory Review* 10 (1981). On July 7, 1978, a Ph.D. student, James W. Anderson, wrote Kohut about this story of William James and asked for his help in his research. Kohut sent Anderson to Ernest Wolf for consultation on the dissertation and wrote Anderson to congratulate him on finishing the work on June 11, 1980. Anderson brought this sequence to my attention in a personal communication, June 21, 1997, and I later located the relevant materials in the Kohut Archives. I am also indebted to Anderson for raising this general question of the tradition of autobiographical disguise in psychoanalysis and psychology, which put me on the track of other examples. In time, I was helped with leads to other examples of disguised autobiography by friends and colleagues who got interested in my project, including Tessa Philips, Douglas Kirsner, John Forrester, Peter Barglow, and Franco Paparo.

23. David J. Lynn and George E. Vaillant, "Anonymity, Neutrality, and Confidentiality in the Actual Methods of Sigmund Freud: A Review of 43 Cases, 1907–1939," *AJP* 155 (1998): 163–171.

24. *SE* 3:301–322, esp. 309, where Strachey gives the details.

25. Sigmund Freud, " 'A Child Is Being Beaten,' A Contribution to the Origin of Infantile Sexual Perversions," *SE* 17: 175–204; Elisabeth Young-Bruehl, *Anna Freud: A Biography* (New York: Summit Books, 1988), 104; Esther Menaker, *Appointment in Vienna* (New York: St. Martin's Press, 1989), as well as a number of private conversations I had with her between 1996 and 1998. Menaker was in analysis with Anna Freud in the early 1930s (and her husband with Helene Deutsch) and attended courses at the Vienna institute. Menaker, astonishingly, only learned much later about Anna Freud's analysis with her father. Peter Gay, *Freud: A Life for Our Time* (New York: Norton, 1988), 439, confirms that Freud "never alluded to this analysis [of Anna] in public and only rarely in private," and he adds that Anna Freud herself was "no less discreet," which is a protective way, if there ever was one, of not calling it a secret. Paul Roazen says he was the first to let out the "secret" of Anna Freud's analysis with Pappa in *Brother Animal: The Story of Freud and Tausk* (New York: Knopf, 1990 [1969]), 100, for which he was to suffer personal and professional attacks; see Paul Roazen, "Freud's Analysis of Anna," *The Death of Psychoanalysis: Murder? Suicide? Or Rumor Greatly Exaggerated?*, ed. Robert Prince (Northvale, NJ: Jason Aronson, 1998), 141–151. Even Kohut was appalled by Freud's analysis of his own daughter, which, he said, "appears to me to have gone too far." Kohut to Helmut Thoma, July 20, 1974, *Curve*, 312.

26. Young-Bruehl, *Anna Freud*, 103–109.

27. James Jackson Putnam, Ch. 10, "Remarks on a Case with Griselda Phantasies," *Addresses on Psycho-Analysis*, with a preface by Sigmund Freud (London: Hogarth Press, 1951 [1921]). Ernest Jones wrote Freud on September 13, 1913, that "[Putnam] sends me a dream of his own relating to incest with his daughter, thus confirming your surmise about the Griselda paper." Freud replied: "We are glad to let every man decide delicate questions to his own conscience and on his personal responsibility." See *The Complete Correspondence of Sigmund Freud and Ernest Jones, 1908–1939*, ed. R. Andrew Paskauskas (Cambridge, MA: Harvard University Press, 1993), 225 and 226.

28. See Lisa Apignanesi and John Forrester, *Freud's Women* (New York: Basic Books, 1992), 337–338. Bonaparte was obsessively interested in surgery on the female genitals. See, for example, Marie Bonaparte, "Notes on Excision," *Psychoanalysis and the Social Sciences* (New York: International Universities Press, 1950), 2: 67–83.

29. Helene Deutsch, *Confrontations with Myself* (New York: Norton, 1973).

30. Apignanesi and Forrester, *Freud's Women*, 315–317. Forrester kindly e-mailed me about the relevant passage in his book on September 18, 1998, and in the same communication brought to my attention the passage in *Confrontations With Myself.*

31. Helene Deutsch, "Hysterical Fate-Neurosis," Lecture II, *Psycho-Analysis of the Neuroses*, tr. W. D. Robson-Scott (London: Hogarth Press, 1951), 29–49. It is worth noting that Deutsch's biographer, Paul Roazen, treats these autobiographical themes in her writing. See Paul Roazen, *Helene Deutsch: A Psychoanalyst's Life* (Garden City, NY: Anchor/Doubleday, 1985).

32. Bernard J. Paris, *Karen Horney: A Psychoanalyst's Search for Self-Understanding* (New Haven: Yale University Press, 1994), 10–21 and 127–134.

33. Phyllis Grosskurth, *Melanie Klein: Her World and Her Work* (Cambridge, MA: Harvard University Press, 1986).

34. Franco Paparo to me, December 12, 1997. See Eduardo Weiss, "Agoraphobia and Its Relation to Hysterical Attacks and to Trauma," *IJP* 16 (1935): 59–83.

35. TAK.

36. It should be noted that Thomas Kohut first allowed the idea of his father as Mr. Z to surface in 1994 through the medium of Geoffrey Cocks's introduction to *Curve*, but without the supporting evidence as detailed in this chapter it was not entirely convincing. No one has ever doubted Kohut's "Mr. Z" is self-referential: see Doris Brothers, "Dr. Kohut and Mr. Z: Is This a Case of Alter Ego Counter-transference?" *Progress* 10, or from a different point of view, Francis Baudry, "Kohut and Glover: The Role of Subjectivity in Psychoanalytic Theory and Controversy," *Psychoanalytic Study of the Child* 53 (1998): 3–24.

27 THE WANING YEARS

1. John B. Arnold wrote Kohut on November 13, 1962, of his cholesterol test results, assuring him that his 265 was nothing to worry about. A year later, Arnold's secretary wrote Kohut on September 6, 1963, of his new count of 200. Kohut wrote James R. Forsythe, medical director of the Minnesota Mutual Life Insurance Company, on March 22, 1966, explaining that his bad EKG came shortly after he had stopped smoking and gone on a diet. Forsythe replied on April 1, 1966. Kohut wrote his regular doctor, Oglesby Paul, July 22, 1968, of his concern over his cholesterol count of 241, especially after an ophthalmologist found in a routine eye exam "arcus senilis" in his left cornea and a trace of it in the right and "mumbled something" about cholesterol deposits. Paul replied on July 29, 1968, that he never worried about cholesterol unless it was over 255, and that to lower it would require a diet that would be "most unhealthy." Still, Kohut worried and was retested a month later. His count, as Kohut wrote on a piece of paper dated August 16, 1968, had dropped to 232.

2. Kohut to Herbert Lee Murrie, February 24, 1979.

3. Leon Resnekov to Kohut, February 13, 1979.

4. EW 1.

5. Kohut to Melvin Sabshin, June 10, 1979; see also Kohut to Martha Louis Little, May 8, 1979. The fault of the hospital is from EW 1. Kohut, noting this conversation in his file, talked of the dirty needle to Pierce Gardner, who in turn wrote an angry letter to the director of the labs, James E. Bowman. Bowman wrote back May 25, 1979, with a copy to Kohut.

6. Kohut to Melvin Sabshin, June 10, 1979.

7. Kohut to Douglas Levin, June 23, 1979 (about the vertigo as a tumor); to Nathaniel London, July 1979 (about what he told his wife); and to Ursula Mahlendorf, October 26, 1979 (about the sea breezes).

8. As Kohut wrote in hand on a piece of paper he inserted in the medical file he kept.

9. Heinz Kohut to Jacques Palaci, December 11, 1980, in Reppen, *Psychoanalytic Review*. Kohut also wrote Douglas Detrick on December 6, 1980, *Curve*, 414: "I came down with a serious, life-threatening pneumonia shortly after returning to Chicago from Boston."

10. Leon Resnekov to Kohut, June 10 and June 25, 1981.

11. Jerome Beigler to me, July 5, 1998.

12. JP 3.

13. Kohut to Siegmund Levarie, August 11, 1979.

14. Siegmund Levarie to Kohut, November 10, 1980.

15. SL 1. As Levarie told me this he fought back a tear and broke into the present tense, as though Kohut were still alive.

16. Kohut to Douglas Levin, June 23, 1979; to Martha Louis Little, May 8, 1979; and to Nathaniel London, July 17, 1979.

17. Kohut to Robert Merrill, November 1, 1980.

18. Kohut to Siegmund Levarie, February 21, 1980.

19. BB.

20. Kohut to Thomas A. Kohut, August 17, 1981, *Curve*, 433.

21. PO.

22. Comment reported by Hyman Muslin, in Eduardo R. Val, *The Psychotherapy of the Self* (New York: Brunner/Mazel, 1987), xiii.

23. Kohut to Helen Block Lewis, January 10, 1977.

24. Kohut to John A. Lindon, May 27, 1980.

25. Handwritten, undated note to Robert Stolorow, probably late in 1979 as it refers to a recent self conference in Los Angeles.

26. Kirsner, "Self Psychology and the Psychoanalytic Movement: An Interview with Dr. Heinz Kohut," 488.

27. Joanna Helen Fanos to Kohut, September 15, 1980; Wolf to Kohut, October 8, 1980; Kohut to Fanos, undated but clearly in early October 1980; Shirley Braverman to Kohut, February 2, 1979; Arnold Goldberg to Kohut, February 23, 1979; Constance Goldberg to Braverman, March 2, 1979; Kohut to Braverman, March 2, 1979; and Braverman to Kohut, March 11, 1979; Robert Galatzker-Levy, "Kohut as Teacher and Supervisor: A View from the Second Generation," *Progress* 4 (1988): 47.

28. *Humanities*, 236. In this interview with me I was impressed with Kohut's intensity as we sat alone in his study. It was a matter of great urgency for him that I understand his sense of continuity in his life.

29. Jacques Palaci (JP 1) recalled that Wandruszka stood well to the right of Kohut in the 1930s.

30. Kohut to Michael Franz Basch, October 6, 1977, *Curve*, 361; Kohut to George Kalmar, June 24, 1980. Kohut joined the Academy on May 16, 1979. See *Almanach für das Jahr 1979*, Österreichische Akademie der Wissenschaften, Wien, 1980. I am grateful to Panu Hallamaa for sending me a copy of this document.

31. Kohut to Edward A. Adler, March 2, 1977.

32. Gerald Adler to Kohut, May 24, 1978. Adler sent Kohut information, clearly in reply to a letter of Kohut's that is lost, about two recordings of bird songs that accompanied a popular guide to bird watching.

33. Ernest Wolf, "Introduction," in Siegel, *Heinz Kohut and the Psychology of the Self.*

34. Kohut to Deutsche Grammophon, June 13, 1979.

35. Constance Goldberg, January 16, 1997. Once in the winter of 1980 I had an appointment with Kohut to conduct an interview. I lived out of town but in Chicago stayed with my mother, whom he knew. He needed to change the time of the interview. He left messages for me at the Institute, at Rush Medical School, where I taught a seminar in those days, and with my mother, asking me to call him back early in the evening. His concern was that I might call and disturb him during his evening ritual of listening to recorded music. He spent at least half an hour making all these calls to reach me. Since it was Kohut and seemed so urgent, secretaries and various analysts all over Chicago were making frantic efforts all afternoon trying to find me. I got the message in time.

36. SQ about relations with Anna Freud; TAK.

37. Eva Sandburg, personal communication, January 11, 1997. I have this story secondhand, for the secretary refused to grant me an interview. Sandburg, however, always heard of Kohut's behavior the next day.

38. Robert Wadsworth to Kohut, May 4, 1981.

39. ME.

40. Ibid.

41. Ina Wolf's detailed "Chronology," which she constructed from her date book at my request in October 1998. See also Kohut to Jacques Palaci, December 11, 1980. He told Palaci he would require two months of convalescence and might still need a bronchoscopy.

42. Interview with Eileen O'Shea, December 10, 1997. I accidentally found O'Shea through Arnold Goldberg's neighbor and friend, Harvey Fried, who remembered her from 1980 and vaguely recalled that she had had some relevant experiences with Kohut in her capacity as a nurse at the University of Chicago Hospital. When I phoned her, O'Shea was very friendly and cooperative during our interview, stressing how much she liked Kohut as a person and how he never complained about his illness. She let drop, however, a reference to the way the other nurses regarded him, which I asked her directly about. She then reluctantly but as honestly as she could got into the details of what she had experienced with him. She realized the importance of what she had to tell me. She was also very eager for me to corroborate her story, and gave me the name and phone number of a co-worker, Julie Schneider, who she thought might remember Kohut, as well as of the woman, Yoshie Tanabe, who was then the head nurse of the unit. Neither woman, unfortunately, once I located them, could remember Kohut after nearly two decades. I called Schneider on December 11, 1997. The same day I called Tanabe in Hawaii and left a message; she wrote me on December 23, 1997. Resnekov is no longer alive. I am left with an apparently reliable witness but an unsettling story that cannot be independently verified. While I found O'Shea quite

by accident, once I had learned of her experience with Kohut, to omit it entirely from my book would seem irresponsible. But I do tell it with some misgivings.

43. Kohut to Henry D. V. Witzleben, April 7, 1977, *Curve*, 344–346, esp. 345.

44. *Search* 2: 680–681. See also Kohut to Daniel X. Freedman, February 26, 1971, *Curve*, 253–254, which, amazingly, as though his unconscious intuited his disease, was written shortly before the diagnosis of his cancer. Cp. Kohut to Morris A. Sklansky, September 2, 1973, *Curve*, 286–288.

45. *Restoration*, 285–286. Cp. *Search* 4: 557; *Humanities* "Conversations" with me; and "On Empathy," *Search* 4: 525–535. That mission can come unwittingly. Kohut was fascinated with the way Verdi was the unchallenged master of opera in the Western world, until suddenly Wagner burst on the scene. It was a huge narcissistic injury for Verdi, who responded by writing his greatest operas in his seventh and eighth decades, including *Otello* and *Falstaff*. See *Lectures*, 70–71.

46. Philip Rieff, *Freud: The Mind of the Moralist*, distinguishes kairotic from chromatic time; see also Frank Kermode, *The Sense of an Ending: Studies in the Theory of Fiction* (New York: Oxford University Press, 1967).

47. *Restoration*, 181–182; see also the notes on 181 and 288, which elaborate other aspects of Proust's novel useful for understanding Kohut's sense of the self.

48. *Humanities*, 235.

49. Ibid., 217. See Ernest Wolf, "Self Psychology and the Humanities: Conversations with Heinz Kohut," unpublished paper for presentation at the pre-congress of the eleventh annual self psychology conference, October 15, 1988.

50. *Humanities*, 215.

28 GOD AND RELIGION

1. On the Unitarian Church, see Chapter 10 above; on giving sermons, TAK; on the *Christian Century*, AG 1. On pastoral counseling, see Randall C. Mason, "The Psychology of the Self—Religion and Psychotherapy," *Advances in Self Psychology*, 407–425; interviews with Kohut by Robert L. Randall, March 22 and April 12, 1981; and David Moss, "Narcissism, Empathy and the Fragmentation of Self: An Interview with Heinz Kohut," *Pilgrimage* 4 (1976): unnumbered pages. Since 1981, more than ten Ph.D. dissertations from departments of religion have been written using Kohut's work (and can be easily accessed in any database).

2. *Seach* 2: 457–460. Cp. Kohut to Anna Freud, March 2, 1965, *Curve*, 113.

3. *Lectures*, 26, 267, 289.

4. Interviews with Kohut by Robert L. Randall, March 22 and April 12, 1981, which Randall graciously shared with me. The ideas and quotes in what follows, unless otherwise specified, are from the Randall interviews. In his earlier interview on religion with David Moss for *Pilgrimage* in 1976, Kohut was much more guarded, distant, and less interesting. I am also grateful to Constance Goldberg, who sent me a copy of Moss's manuscript, "Imago and Introject: A Profile of Carroll Wise," which includes material on Kohut.

5. In my "Conversations" with Kohut, I once asked him about the impact of economic considerations on the self, i.e., about class differences. He prefaced his
   response in this way: "I have the impression that what I can be most helpful with
   is not to provide answers to such questions but to give conceptual tools and psychological attitudes with which others can answer such questions." *Humanities*,
   224.
6. *Analysis*, 260–262.
7. TAK.
8. John F. Hayward to Kohut, December 31, 1963.
9. The only qualification in this regard is that in the Randall interviews Kohut was
   perhaps more decisively Christian because he was sitting in his study with a Christian theologian. His stance may have reflected his empathy, in other words, as
   much as anything to do with faith or identity.
10. Peter Barglow, interview, December 18, 1995.
11. *Search* 2: 752.
12. *Search* 2: 663–684.
13. *Search* 2: 757.
14. Mario Jacoby, *Individuation and Narcissism*, 75–76, points out that with such
    ideas on death Kohut moves into realms in depth psychology that had been until
    then largely occupied by Jung. "But he seems to refuse to take notice of Jung's
    findings," probably for political reasons.
15. Kohut to Raymond Prince, May 4, 1967, *Curve*, 168.

29 THE HEALING OF PSYCHOANALYSIS

1. Douglas Detrick to me, November 11, 1983. Detrick actually visited Kohut in
   Carmel the following summer, but his work habits during the writing of his last
   book were surely the same the previous year.
2. Kohut to Evelyne Schwaber, October 2, 1980, *Curve*, 412; Kohut to Tilmann
   Moser, January 26, 1981, *Curve*, 419; and Kohut to George Pollock, June 7, 1981,
   Curve, 429.
3. Personal communication, Arnold Goldberg, April 3, 1996. Note the allusions to
   the struggles in Mrs. Kohut's Preface to *How Does Analysis Cure?*, ix. She also
   refers in that preface to Thomas Kohut's help in preparing the manuscript. One
   can only guess his actual role.
4. Morton and Estelle Shane, two disciples, described the writing in *Cure* as "crisp"
   and the logic "clear" in their review, though they got some distance a few years
   later; see *International Review of Psychoanalysis* 15 (1988): 394–398, and "Self
   Psychology After Kohut," *JAPA* 41 (1993): 777–797. A more interesting view is
   that of Robert Wallerstein, "How Does Self Psychology Differ in Practice?" *IJP*
   (1985): 391–404, whose main regret about *Cure* is that Kohut felt the need by
   the end to define his project as separate from mainstream psychoanalysis.
5. Kohut to Ninon Leader, September 9, 1978, in which he says that "about a year

ago," after consulting with colleagues and friends, he decided to dispense with the hyphen. In the personal collection of Ernest Wolf.

6. Ibid.

7. Constance Goldberg, personal communication, January 6, 1997; the idea of the event as a religious ritual is from Robert Jay Lifton, personal communication, September 9, 1999. Arnold Goldberg, in an interview October 19, 1996, also re-called and mocked the "hyphen removal dinner," though he added, as an ironic comment on his own sarcasm, that of course the removal of the hyphen mat-tered a great deal. A year later, on the eve of the first printed appearance of the unhyphenated term—in a paper written with Ernest Wolf and published in Ger-many—the Kohuts stopped by the Wolfs on their way home from Gretchen Meyer's house in Wisconsin. Ina Wolf made a Flemish pot-au-feu for which she put a whole chicken and a smoked pork butt into a large pot with white wine and spices and vegetables and cooked it up. The two couples sat around the kitchen table. They toasted the removal of the hyphen, and Kohut made much of the event as having been consecrated right there over the Flemish meal. See Ina Wolf, "Chronology." See also Ina Wolf to me, August 2, 1996, and our several discus-sions later that month when I stayed with the Wolfs and listened to Ernest Wolf's Kohut tape collection.

8. *Restoration*, 3, 49, 133, 171–173, 177–191, 194–199, 200, 205–209, 243, 311.

9. Kohut to Tilmann Moser, March 7, 1981, *Curve*, 425. Note, however, that as late as 1979 at the fall meeting of the American Psychoanalytic Association, Kohut served on a panel at which Paul Ornstein, Sheldon Meyers, Ernest Wolf, and Michael Franz Basch extolled the wonders of the "bipolar self."

10. Robert Stolorow, Bernard Brandchaft, and George Atwood, *Psychoanalytic Treat-ment: An Intersubjective Approach* (Hillsdale, NJ: Analytic Press, 1987), 20. See also Siegel, *Heinz Kohut and the Psychology of the Self.* John Riker, "The Philo-sophical Importance of Kohut's Bipolar Theory of the Self," *Progress* 12: 67–83, is more respectful of Kohut's idea, though his purpose is philosophical rather than clinical.

11. *Cure*, 99; Kohut to Douglas Detrick, December 6, 1980, *Curve*, 414; and Kohut to Tilmann Moser, March 7, 1981, *Curve*, 425. The concept of the bipolar self is mentioned in an article Kohut published with Ernest Wolf, "The Disorders of the Self," *IJP* 59 (1978): 413–425, *Search* 3: 363, but that paper was written by Wolf and only reviewed by Kohut.

12. In this connection, see David A. S. Garfield and Marion [sic] Tolpin, "Selfobjects in Psychosis—The Twinship Compensation," *AJPT* 50 (1996): 178–193.

13. *Cure*, 192–204 (note 202–204, where he argues that classification schemes must never harden and we should always treat them as our "helpmate," not our "mas-ter"). Cp. his discussion of twinship in *Lectures*, 34–36. Michael Franz Basch, *Practicing Psychotherapy* (New York: Basic Books, 1992), 19, argues that twin-ship is essential to psychotherapy. Doris Brothers, "Dr. Kohut and Mr. Z: Is This a Case of Alter Ego Countertransference?" *Progress* 10, has muddied the conceptual waters by further distinguishing an alter ego transference from that of twinship.

Tessa Philips, much more usefully, in an unpublished paper, "To Tell the Truth in Healing, To Hear the Truth in Healing," argues that the disavowed parts of Kohut's own experience made it difficult for him to arrive at the concept of twinship until late in his life.

14. This paragraph is essentially based on *Cure*, 54–63; the quote is on 61. For more on splitting, see *Lectures*, 50–54; for Freud on fetishism, *SE* 21: 149–157. Cp. Kohut's thoughts on autonomy with *Restoration*, 82–83. The Freud reference is *SE* 22: 173. Cp. Judith Guss Teicholz, *Kohut, Loewald*, 115–118.

15. *Restoration*, 298, on the introspective-empathic method; *Search* 2: 686 n. 1 on psychoanalysis as "the science of the human soul" (compare *Search* 2: 696, where he calls psychoanalysis "the science of complex mental states"). See Leon Balter and James H. Spencer, "Observation and Theory in Psychoanalysis: The Self Psychology of Heinz Kohut," *PQ* 60 (1991): 361–395.

16. Kohut to J. Gordon Maguire, June 20, 1980. Compare in this regard his comments to Susan Quinn (SQ) about how there is nothing uniform in psychoanalysis and never has been, and his remark to Robert Stolorow, February 16, 1981, that he was a "relativist with regard to both the concept of borderline pathology and the concept of psychosis."

17. Kohut, "Reflections," *Search* 3: 299. Cp. Remarks on Receiving the William A. Schonfeld Distinguished Service Award from the American Society for Adolescent Psychiatry (1980), in Wolf collection.

18. *Cure*, 186–187 (cp. *Analysis*, xv, and *Restoration*, xv). See also the very important editorial note, 226 n. 8. Arnold Goldberg, in a personal communication January 22, 1999, said Kohut had told him in conversation more than once that this example of the little girl was intended specifically as a refutation of the developmental model of Margaret Mahler.

19. *Humanities*, 22.

20. Seminar, January 19, 1974, at Center for Psychosocial Studies, Wolf collection.

21. *Lectures*, 95.

22. *Cure*, 14.

23. Ibid., 187 (King's italics). See C. Daly King, "The Meaning of Normal," *Yale Journal of Biology and Medicine* 17 (1945): 493.

24. Kohut to Leo Sadow, April 11, 1980 (see *Search* 4: 661–662). There is no reason to believe Kohut in this letter was including schizophrenia, clinical depression, or any clearly demarcated psychotic condition in this blurring of distinction between health and normality. He was definitely including, however, what he had once called NPDs and what in psychiatry are loosely called "borderlines."

25. *Cure*, 11–12.

26. Kirsner, "Self Psychology and the Psychoanalytic Movement: An Interview with Dr. Heinz Kohut," 490–491. Kohut wrote Robert Stolorow on February 16, 1981, that the structural model can be serviceable in identifying and naming visible clinical conflicts. Keeping the theory in this sense, he says, follows the important principle that you move from the surface to the depths. And there you should not be mistaken: "Conflict leads to psychopathology only when it arises in

consequence of a disorder of the self." Oedipal conflicts produce familiar symptoms of hysteria, anxiety, phobias, and compulsions but disturb the cohesion of the self only during a specific period in development. One of the beauties of this way of thinking about things, which he adds he is willing to discard if clinical evidence appears to discount it, is that such a view of the self can be accommodated with all kinds of "transitional forms of psychopathology."

27. SQ.

28. *Cure*, 7, 211 n. 1. Compare *Lectures*, 216–217.

29. After-dinner speech at the birthday celebration, June 2, 1973, from tape in Wolf collection ("The Future of Psychoanalysis," *Search* 2: 663–684). Freud says (*SE* 12: 115): "I cannot advise my colleagues too urgently to model themselves during psycho-analytic treatment on the surgeon, who puts aside all his feelings, even his human sympathy, and concentrates his mental forces on the single aim of performing the operation as skilfully as possible." Compare *SE* 12: 171, which Kohut alludes to in *Cure*, 112–113. See Paul Stepansky, *Freud, Surgery, and the Surgeons* (Hillsdale, NJ: Analytic Press, 1999).

30. *Cure*, 81–82; *Lectures*, 10; meeting of Kohut with the group, February 22, 1975, typescript in Wolf collection.

31. *SE* 19: 50n and *SE* 2: 305.

32. In his interview with Susan Quinn (SQ) Kohut discusses at some length contemporary fad therapies and what they are doing in self terms.

33. *Restoration*, 282–285. Kohut walked a fine line here. It has been argued that self psychology is an adjustment or conformist psychology that fosters positive thinking in ways that are in complete contrast with the dialectical thought of psychoanalysis. See B. Rothschild, "Der Neue Narzissmus—Theorie oder Ideologie?" *Psychoanalytisches Seminar Zürich, Die neuen Narzissmustheorien* (Frankfurt am Main: Syndikat, 1981), 25–62. Jacoby, *Individuation and Narcissism*, 109–110, however, who reviews Rothschild's work from a Jungian perspective, believes it is quite unfair to Kohut's views.

34. *Lectures*, 23.

35. Ibid., 96–97. Arnold Goldberg, personal communication, June 20, 1998, said Kohut's lesson here was that you have to know your limits and recognize that these will vary from person to person.

36. Ibid., 20, 75.

37. Ibid., 38. See Kohut to Peter A. Martin, March 19, 1977, *Curve*, 340–341, for the reference to the untreatability of schizoid or paranoid personalities. Kohut in general, of course, vastly expanded the kind of psychological issues brought into psychoanalysis. But there were limits. For an exception to his own rule about eliminating the preliminaries, see the discussion of his interviews with Herb Murrie in Chapter 30 below.

38. *Restoration*, 250ff. The Tolpins in their Preface to *Lectures*, xix–xx, have arranged a number of good quotes from the lectures to illustrate Kohut's views on this issue.

39. *Lectures*, 13–14, 21, 98–99, 106, and 112–115.

40. *SE* 2: 305.

41. *SE* 12: 83–173.

42. *SE* 19: 3–68.

43. *SE* 23: 211–253.

44. *Cure*, 52. Compare his discussion of Bismarck, 19–20, and of Van Gogh, 212 n. 2.

45. *Restoration*, 187–188 and n. 8 on same pages. This view of trauma is consistent with his discussion in *Analysis* (see, for example, 65–66 regarding Mr. A.), and his many statements in *Cure*, including 42–43, 81, 83, 101–102, 107, 178, 181, 204, 216 n. 4, 219, n. 7, 220 n. 11.

46. *Cure*, 16, which he then illustrates with his own disguised experience from a dream of Mr. Z, 16–17.

47. *Restoration*, 43–44.

48. *Cure*, 49–50. Such experiences are "telescoped." See *Cure*, 6. The "telescoping of analogous experiences" was first formulated in *Analysis*, 39, 53, 56, 58, 85, 147, 248, 292–294. Cp. Kohut's comments on the genetic as opposed to the etiological points of view, *Lectures*, 19.

49. Quotes assembled in *Pilgrimage* by David Moss, in *Search* 2: 705.

50. See Peter Brooks, "Illicit Stories," *Trauma and Self*, ed. Charles B. Strozier and Michael Flynn (New York: Rowman and Littlefield, 1996), 241. See also SQ for Kohut's lengthy discussion of empathy as not sympathy or intuition. Compare Freud (*SE* 18: 108 and 110n) with Michael Franz Basch, "Further Thoughts on Empathic Understanding," *Progress* 6 (1990): 4. It is worth noting that Kohut's attempt to distinguish empathy so sharply and artificially from sympathy got him into some confused terrain in his Berkeley lecture; see *Search* 4: 530.

51. *Cure*, 82–83. See 220 n. 9 for a discussion of empathy with oneself.

52. *Cure*, 172–191, esp. 175–176. Cp. Chris Jaenicke, "Kohut's Concept of Cure," *Psychoanalytic Review* 74 (1987): 537–548.

53. Besides *Cure*, 82–83, see *Search* 2: 705ff and "On Empathy," *Search* 4: 525–535.

54. *Lectures*, 148 (cp. 285); *Search* 4: 545; SQ, in which he discusses this issue at length; and Chapter 20, note 58, above.

55. Kohut's after-dinner speech at the symposium honoring his sixtieth birthday, June 2, 1973, tape in the Wolf collection. Kohut appears to have edited out these comments from the published version of the speech, "The Future of Psychoanalysis," *Search* 2: 663–684.

56. *Search* 2: 705.

57. *Cure*, 94–95 and 105; cp. *Restoration*, 88.

58. The point about mirroring is in SQ; interpretation as deepening empathy is in *Cure*, 184–185.

59. *Search* 4:534. Some valuable discussions of empathy inspired by Kohut include Dan H. Buie, "Empathy: Its Nature and Limitations," *JAPA* 29 (1981): 281–307; Michael Franz Basch, "Empathic Understanding: A Review of the Concept and Some Theoretical Considerations," *JAPA* 31 (1983): 101–126; Steven T. Levy, "Empathy and Psychoanalytic Technique," *JAPA* 33 (1985): 353–378; Alfred Margulies, "Toward Empathy: The Uses of Wonder," *AJP* 141 (1984): 1025–1035; David M. Berger, "On the Way to Empathic Understanding," *AJPT* 38 (1984):

111–120; Howard E. Book, "Empathy: Misconceptions and Misuses in Psycho-therapy," *AJP* 145 (1988): 420–424; Leslie Brothers, "A Biological Perspective on Empathy," *AJP* 146 (1989): 10–19; Ivan J. Miller, "The Therapeutic Empathic Communication (TEC) Process," *AJPT* 43 (1989): 531–545; and Stefano Bolognini, "Empathy and 'Empathism,' " *IJP* 78 (1997): 279–293.

60. *SE* 14: 239–258.
61. *Analysis*, 49–50. Note also 28, 62, 65, 74, 79–83, 100–101, 105–108, 165–168, 267.
62. SQ.
63. *Lectures*, 223.
64. *Restoration*, 3–32; Kohut to Lloyd S. Etheredge, September 26, 1977, *Curve*, 353–355; and *Cure*, 52.
65. *Cure*, 69ff. He adds (78): "If that is the 'corrective emotional experience,' then so be it."
66. *Cure*, 103. "this issue": Many have argued, in an ever-expanding number of papers, that structure develops out of the continuity of empathic and interpretive experience in therapy, rather than as a result of frustration. Howard Bacal, "Optimal Respon-siveness and the Therapeutic Process," *Progress* 1 (1985): 202–227; David Terman, "Optimum Frustration: Structuralization and the Therapeutic Process," *Progress* 4 (1988): 113–126; and the most recent article in the series, David S. MacIsaac, "Op-timal Frustration: An Endangered Concept," *Progress* 12 (1996): 3–16.

30 NEW CLINICAL DIRECTIONS

1. It can well be asked why Kohut kept working at all when he was so sick. The answer may be, in part, that he needed the money. His fees had always been low. In the early 1960s he charged about $25 per hour. George Klumpner, who was in analysis from the fall of 1963 until the spring of 1970, made annual payments for his therapy that increased from $4,260 to $6,265, a rise that reflected a gradual increase in the fee as well as an increase in the number of sessions per week (from four to five); Klumpner to me, April 2, 1999. As late as 1974 Kohut was still charging $50 per hour, though he planned that year to begin charging new patients $55 per hour. Heinz Kohut was not a rich doctor. In 1970 he grossed $48,115, which after expenses of $8,865 left him with a net income of $39,250. For 1974 his projected gross income was $62,811 and his net $51,317; see Coopers and Lybrand (CPA) to Kohut, January 10, 1974. By the middle of the decade his con-sultation fees had risen, along with his fame, to $100; by the end of it they had reached $125, though he was also seeing far fewer people by then; David Solomon, interview, July 29, 1997; cp. Fred Arensberg, interview, March 16, 1996, and Sheldon Meyers, personal communication, April 18, 1999. His income may have exceeded $100,000 for the first time in his life just before he died; JB. There was even some (very quiet) grumbling that his modesty was keeping fees low for others, especially younger psychoanalysts, who felt they were in no position to charge more than Kohut; David Solomon, interview, July 29, 1997.

2. Kohut to Herb Murrie, February 4 and 24, and March 1, 1979, and September 3, 1980.

3. Kohut to Leah Averick, September 23, 1981. My interview with her was on July 10, 1987.

4. Jerome Beigler to me, November 18, 1997.

5. MT; interview.

6. I have known Marian Tolpin myself for twenty-five years, first when I was a candidate at the Institute where she was my teacher and later when we were colleagues in self psychology. On many occasions we have talked about Kohut, though the material for this section on her therapeutic experiences with Kohut comes from an interview on December 28, 1997.

7. Tolpin did not seem to feel this mix of therapy and supervision was that unusual for Kohut by the 1970s, but I have talked with no one else who reported anything like Tolpin's experience. Furthermore, one person I interviewed who was in supervision with Kohut in fact longed for therapy with him but never found a way to make it happen. See below on Fred Arensberg.

8. Interview with David Solomon, July 29, 1997.

9. Solomon repeated this idea in the interview, but the quote itself is from a conversation on June 21, 1997.

10. Kohut apparently felt comfortable giving such advice to some patients. Solomon told me he had heard from another analysand (whose name he could not divulge) that Kohut had advised him how to shave. Go against the grain, he said. You get closer that way.

11. Kohut to Tilmann Moser, February 15, 1972 (original in German), *Curve*, 263–264. In the letter Solomon is not identified by name. He identified himself to me in his interview.

12. Elizabeth Kohut to David Solomon, April 21, 1979. In the personal collection of David Solomon.

13. Interview with Herb Murrie, July 28, 1997. In early 1998 I sent Murrie a draft of what I had written from my interview. He made a number of corrections in the text and returned it to me on March 16, 1998.

14. The national norm for analysis in the United States had become four times a week by the 1950s (Freud initially saw patients six times a week). See Nathan G. Hale, *The Rise and Crisis of Psychoanalysis in the United States: Freud and the Americans, 1917–1985* (New York: Oxford University Press, 1985).

15. *Lectures*, 24–25.

16. EW 2.

17. PO. Note also Ornstein's comments on a presentation I gave at the New York Institute for Psychoanalytic Self Psychology, March 3, 1996.

18. Kohut to Angela Sheppard, February 10, 1979.

19. Sheldon J. Meyers, "On Supervision with Heinz Kohut," *Progress in Self Psychology: Learning From Kohut*, ed. Arnold Goldberg (Hillsdale, NJ: Analytic Press, 1988). I also interviewed Meyers on April 1, 1996.

20. Jule P. Miller, "How Kohut Actually Worked," *Progress in Self Psychology*, ed. Arnold Goldberg, vol. 1 (New York: Guilford Press, 1985), 13–30. All references are to this text.

21. Interview with Frederic Arensberg, March 16, 1996. Arensberg and I talked several times after that and exchanged notes. At first the patient, here named Carl, was reluctant to grant permission to publish this segment. I rewrote it twice, radically altering the disguise. In the end, he wanted it close to the original but with some of his editing. It is this version I am publishing and for which he gave his formal, written permission on January 2, 1998.

31 GENTLE INTO THAT GOOD NIGHT

1. I am able to evoke the concrete details of the conference because I was there.

2. Most of what follows is from JP 1, with some additional comments about Kohut's friendship with Palaci's wife, Diana, from JP 2. It is worth noting that Palaci was more emotional about his old friend in my 1985 interview than either of my subsequent two interviews, partly, no doubt, because it was closer in time to Kohut's death in 1981 but also, perhaps, because I happened to interview him on the fourth anniversary of Kohut's death.

3. BB.

4. TAK.

5. For the most part the text of Kohut's extemporaneous lecture that I use here is the transcribed and edited version, later titled "On Empathy," published in *Search* 4: 525–535. Ornstein notes he in turn relied in part on an earlier transcript provided by Robert J. Leider. I have, however, watched the videotape of the lecture more times than I can count and made many further corrections to the published transcripts, as well as noting Kohut's appearance, gestures, tics, mannerisms, and in general the physical surround of the room.

6. CK.

7. Arnold Goldberg, personal communication, June 24, 1997.

8. See Ina Wolf, "Chronology." For most respondents the sequence of events from Sunday through Thursday had gotten blurred; their reports to me were confused and contradictory—which is why Ina Wolf's contemporary diary record, noting so many details, is so important.

9. TAK.

10. Ina Wolf, "Chronology."

11. JB. Beigler also wrote me separately of this incident, November 18, 1997.

12. Arnold Goldberg, personal communication, January 12, 1999.

13. TAK.

14. Interview with Carla Rosenthal, October 14, 1998.

15. EW 2; PO.

16. I had received the copy of our joint contract from Norton for what became

Humanities just before the Berkeley conference and gave it to Mrs. Kohut during the meetings. It arrived, signed, in the mail for me (I was then living in Springfield, Illinois) on Friday, the day after he died.

17. Thomas A. Kohut, personal communication, 1982.
18. Not long before Kohut died, Robert Stolorow visited Kohut in Carmel. Kohut welcomed him into his study and showed him the view and the manuscript of *Cure*. Kohut then said he wanted to take a photograph of the two of them together. He set up the camera on a tripod and intended to use the automatic device to take a picture of both of them. It was all ready to go when Kohut discovered something was wrong with the film in the camera. Rather than give up on the project, he insisted that Stolorow go to the local drugstore to get more film. Stolorow did, returned half an hour later, they loaded the camera, and the picture was taken. Within days there was the Berkeley conference, Kohut's return to Chicago, and his death on Thursday, October 8. Early the next week, Stolorow received his print of the photo at his university office. Interview with Robert Stolorow, October 21, 1995.
19. AG 4; Charles Kligerman, "Eulogy."
20. GM.
21. EW 3; interview with Carla Rosenthal, October 14, 1998.
22. Ina Wolf, "Chronology."
23. The details of the service are mostly from the program prepared for the service. I was also there myself.
24. Constance Goldberg, personal communication, April 4, 1996.
25. "I bet he didn't know what that was, either," Thomas said to me (TAK).
26. AG 1 and personal communication, May 10, 1991.
27. Charles Kligerman "Eulogy."

ACKNOWLEDGMENTS

Any book accumulates debts to friends and colleagues, but the scope of this project and the problems I encountered along the way make me unusually grateful to certain key figures. Front and center are Arnold and Constance Goldberg. They had faith in my work from the outset and never wavered during the dark years. The Goldbergs often gave me hospitality when I stayed in Chicago and granted many valuable formal interviews, not to mention scores of more informal ones over coffee at their kitchen table at the beginning of the day and over wine at the end. Arnold also fought many battles on my behalf and helped at critical points. He once arranged (December 1, 1990) for me to give a presentation in his living room for seven hours to some colleagues disturbed about some of my early findings; he helped raise money for my research; he created the Kohut Archives and then did everything humanly possible to ease my work in them; and he critically read my manuscript in its penultimate and then final versions.

David Terman also entered my world of Kohut at the outset. He played a crucial role reading chapters as they emerged and made invaluable comments on the final text in two versions. I am indebted to Dave as well for his help in securing funding for me to get the calendar year 1998 off from teaching to finish writing; and to Mari for her hospitality when I stayed with them during research trips.

My colleague at CUNY and good friend, Robert Jay Lifton, probably heard more of my Kohut over the years than anyone and had much of great value to contribute to my understanding of the self. Robert and I talked of Kohut and related issues in more seminars than I can remember and in innumerable conversations. We even once made a joint presentation at his Wellfleet meetings on Erikson (whom he knows better than anyone) and Kohut. The stamp of Lifton's insights is everywhere on my work and my debt to him can only be partially acknowledged in the specific notes in which I mention his name. His reading of the manuscript was unusually thorough and was accompanied by many hours of conversation on various problems. He once gave me twenty-six pages of notes on what I had written—and that was only on the first twelve chapters!

My brother, Robert Strozier, himself a writer and editor, went over the manuscript with a fine-toothed comb and improved it immensely, forcing me to clean up jargon and speak to a larger audience than my psychoanalytic peers. I thought I knew what a comma was until Bob read my book.

A geographically distant friend, Tessa Philips, heard about my developing ideas in rough form via e-mail late in 1997, sometimes even before they made any sense to me. She read drafts before they were really presentable, of course read the final versions, and was always supportive, intelligent, and helpful in her comments.

I benefited from a number of other critical (and critically helpful) readings of my manuscript, by Michael Flynn, Betty Jean Lifton, John Gedo, Phyllis Grosskurth, Donna Orange, Fay Sawyier, and Geoffrey Cocks. Larry Friedman read the first few chapters. Even where I failed to take their advice, I appreciate the care they devoted to the book.

Jerome Kavka, psychoanalyst and archivist at the Chicago Institute for Psychoanalysis, helped me in the delicate negotiations that led to my being permitted to read Kohut's candidate file and later reviewed several chapters touching on the history of the Chicago Institute. Jerry was also a genial host when I was working in the Kohut Archives and pushed aside his papers so I could use his desk.

My notes record the many people who have granted me interviews over the years. I can only thank them collectively. I must, however, single out for special mention Siegmund Levarie, who also read the manuscript carefully and spent hours poring over it with me, making sure every umlaut was in place and all the details of Kohut's childhood were accurate, and then opening up his photograph albums for me to scour through; Walter Lampl, who granted me two long telephone interviews and several shorter ones later dealing with specific issues *and* took some photographs of Vienna sites during one of his trips there; John Gedo, who, besides his interviews, wrote me many long letters on various details of his relationship with Kohut; and all the Kohut patients who shared with me the details of their treatment.

Ernest and Ina Wolf have been keenly interested in my work and have done much to facilitate it. They granted useful interviews, formal and informal, and Ina prepared an extremely valuable chronology of social events and other happenings with the Kohuts in the 1970s. They also graciously put me up in their house for a week in August 1996 while I listened to Ernest's extensive tape collection and read materials from his files.

Elke Muhleittner helped me with some translations of documents and was generally informative about Vienna and psychoanalytic history. Her friend and co-author, Johannes Reichmayr, proved invaluable in tracking down documents in the Vienna archives and from the Dšblinger Gymnasium when it proved impossible for me to travel to Vienna. Etty Cohen lent her insight and investigative skills by researching the Hebrew background of the name Kohut. Yoram Hazan of Jerusalem helped me think through some issues in conversation and e-mail. Norm Hellmers, superintendent of the Lincoln Home in Springfield, Illinois, helped me find the brother of Robert Wadsworth.

My dear friends Dan and Marge Offer, from the early days in particular, and Mary Ann Dillon and John Crayton, from later on, often put me up and put up with me during my research trips to Chicago.

Mel Laucella, who got his Ph.D. from the Union Institute partly under my direction, did prodigious research for me over several years, locating difficult references, obscure articles, and stray writings by Kohut not in his collected papers; obtaining a complete list of dissertations related to Kohut's work; and in many other ways helping me in my work. Emily Fisher transcribed my interviews accurately and well.

The Chicago Institute for Psychoanalysis trained me in psychoanalysis, which I found more interesting than graduate school. In my work for this book, the Institute's former director, the late Thomas Pappadis, and his staff were *always* helpful in making their resources available. Kris Susman opened many doors, as did Eva Sandburg, who regaled me as well with stories from her own Vienna days and with useful gossip about the Institute during the Kohut years.

A number of institutions provided forums for presentation of my ideas

over the years, including my institute, TRISP, or the Training and Research Institute in Self Psychology, where I serve as a training and supervising analyst and where I have talked so much and so often for so many
years about Kohut I could not possibly list all the occasions; the TRISP
Saturday seminars at which I presented on Kohut for some five years in a
row; the annual self psychology conference at which I gave the "Kohut
Memorial Lecture" in 1997, one of the pivotal experiences of my life for
many reasons; the New York Institute for Psychoanalytic Self Psychology,
where I am on the faculty and at which I presented in 1997 and 1999; and
NPAP, where I presented in 1998. In the spring of four years—1997, 1998,
1999, and 2000—I also presented my unfolding chapters to the Self Psychology Workshop of the Chicago Institute for Psychoanalysis, experiences that were both informative and moving.

I am grateful to Gail Elden, who supported several of my trips to the
Kohut Archives in 1995 and 1996, and to the National Endowment for
the Humanities for a Summer Research Award in 1988 that allowed for
some early interviewing. The book would never have been written, however, without a most generous grant from Irving Harris, along with a
match from the Kohut Memorial Fund (headed by an old friend, Allen
Siegal), which freed me from teaching for the calendar year 1998.

I am grateful to the staffs of several libraries, especially the New York
Public Library, YIVO, and the Leo Baeck Institute. But no place can match
the significance for me of the Kohut Archives. I will always treasure the
many hours I spent crawling over boxes and pushing letters and documents aside for just enough space on a desk for my laptop.

I give special thanks to my patients, past and present, for helping me
understand things more than they could ever realize.

My agent, Charlotte Sheedy, tolerated my delays and never stopped
believing I had something to say about Heinz Kohut. It was only through
her initiative that I ended up with the best publishing house in the world.

My editor, Jonathan Galassi, played a key role when he took me on as
his project. He warmly encouraged me and read everything carefully. It
is fair to say this book would be half what it is, which is to say very little,
without him. At the end, Paul Elie, also of FSG, gave the manuscript a
superb reading that led to yet another major revision. Paul's comments
led me to alter the narrative structure in some basic ways that clarified
the argument. I am also eternally grateful to the copy editor, Walter
Havinghurst, who caught more errors than I would have thought possible and in his careful editing immeasurably improved the text.

Heinz Kohut is dedicated to Cathy, whom I have known now just about as long as it has taken me to write it. She has lived through the highs and lows of my writing more than anyone, helped me work through the angst of this white-haired man marching across the landscape of my dreams, and tolerated on a daily basis the way this distant figure became an ex-officio companion of our lives for eighteen years.

INDEX